RUFUS JONES (1863–1948) was a philosopher by training, a religious mystic, a preacher, an editor, and a Professor of Philosophy at Haverford College at the time *The Quakers in the American Colonies* was published. ISAAC SHARPLESS was the President of Haverf̶o̶r̶d̶... M. GUMMERE, h̶... *... Study in Costume* before she...

Date Due

FREDERICK B. TOLLES is Howard M. and̶... Professor of Quaker History and Research at Swarthmore College, and also director of the Friends Historical Library there. He is the author of *George Logan of Philadelphia; James Logan and the Culture of Provincial America; Quakers and the Atlantic Culture;* and *Meeting House and Counting House* (available in a Norton Library paperback edition).

W9-ADJ-440

AMERICAN HISTORY TITLES
IN THE NORTON LIBRARY

THE QUAKERS

IN THE

AMERICAN COLONIES

BY

RUFUS M. JONES

ASSISTED BY

ISAAC SHARPLESS

AND

AMELIA M. GUMMERE

New introduction by FREDERICK B. TOLLES

The Norton Library

W · W · NORTON & COMPANY · INC ·

NEW YORK

289.673 JON 1966

Jones, Rufus Matthew, 1863-
The Quakers in the
American colonies, by

Books That Live
The Norton imprint on a book means that in the publisher's
estimation it is a book not for a single season but for the years.
W. W. Norton & Company, Inc.

28066
289.673
Jon

INTRODUCTION TO 1966 EDITION

THE BOOK you have just opened was first published many years ago in 1911. It was originally written as part of a great historical scheme conceived by an English Friend, John Wilhelm Rowntree, and carried into effect after his death chiefly by an American Friend, Rufus M. Jones of Haverford College. The purpose of the scheme was to recount in scholarly detail, yet in readable fashion, the history of Quakerism as a form of spiritual or mystical religion and to set it in its long historical context. Over a period of twelve years from 1909 to 1921, there appeared six large books, which immediately took their place as the standard modern history of the Religious Society of Friends and its mystical forebears. Rufus Jones published the first volume, *Studies in Mystical Religion,* in 1909. The volume now in your hands followed in 1911. In 1912 and 1919 William Charles Braithwaite, an English Friend, published *The Beginnings of Quakerism* and *The Second Period of Quakerism.* In 1914 Jones brought out *Spiritual Reformers in the 16th and 17th Centuries* and in 1921 he completed the "Rowntree Series" with *The Later Periods of Quakerism.* Taken as a whole, this massive series was a notable achievement in historical writing, notable not only for its scholarship but for its readability. Each one of the books, though integrally related to the others, could and can stand alone as a superb independent treatment of its subject.

There is a curious and revealing fact about this great series, which this volume on colonial Quakerism illustrates: not one of its authors was a professional historian. Rufus Matthew Jones (1863–1948), its principal author, was by training and inclination a philosopher. (This, however, by no means exhausted the fields of his competence: he was also a religious mystic, a preacher, a college teacher, a writer, an editor, and a humanitarian.) Amelia Mott Gummere (1859–1937), one of his collaborators, was a housewife. Isaac Sharpless (1848–1920), his other collaborator, was an astronomer and a college president. Together these three non-historians produced what must be called a classic of Quaker history.

In the light of Quaker tradition, it is not surprising that this book should have been written by amateurs in history. Until recent times, almost all Quaker history has been written by non-professionals. Just as the ministers in quiet Quaker meetings have always been on weekdays farmers, schoolteachers, craftsmen, or businessmen, so in the writing of history Friends have tradition-ally thought that any concerned Friend, if properly moved to the task, could write the history of his religious society. After all, a landed gentleman and colonial proprietor named William Penn had been the first historian of Quakerism when he wrote *The Rise and Progress of the People Called Quakers* in 1694. And the fourth contributor to the "Rowntree Series," William Charles Braithwaite, was by profession a lawyer and a banker. In the preaching of the Gospel, Friends have often been said to have abolished the clergy; actually, what they did was to abolish the laity by insisting that any man or woman rightly moved by the Lord could perform any religious task—and what task, they in-quired, had not its religious aspects? You too, they implied, can write history.

That the non-professional historians who fashioned this book should have succeeded so well should surprise no one. Laymen they were, without professional training in history, but they were all well educated, well read in history, able to write clear and eloquent English. All of them had previously written works of history—Rufus Jones a long and sensitive account of a millennium and a half of mystical religion, Amelia Mott Gummere a com-prehensive study of the development of Quaker costume, Isaac Sharpless a scholarly narrative of Quaker government in Penn-sylvania. Above all, these three were deeply concerned Friends, convinced that they were performing something more than a merely intellectual exercise in recording the history of Quakerism. They were expressing themselves religiously in trying to explain why the earliest Friends came to the colonies to preach and "convince" in the teeth of certain persecution, how John Woolman schooled himself to live consistently as a saint, how the Pennsylvania

Quakers were able to govern the colony for nearly seventy-five years without once fighting the Indians.

There are, to be sure, a few points at which interpretations other than theirs have come to be expressed. Quakerism and Puritanism, for instance, are here treated as diametrically opposed to each other in many respects, whereas recent scholars have found the two theologies quite close together in that both were based on the operation of the Holy Spirit. There were devious but important intricacies in colonial New Jersey history which Amelia Mott Gummere hastened over in order to reach the inspiring career of John Woolman. And the story of Pennsylvania Quaker politics is told here in a manner which is considerably more favorable to the Friends than has been the case in certain more recent accounts. But the basic facts are all here, and interpretation can always vary with the reader.

This book is still the standard work on early Quakers on the North American continent. There is no other book in existence which covers the story of the Friends in the colonies with anything like the authority of this work or in anywhere near so great detail.

Frederick B. Tolles

SWARTHMORE, PENNSYLANIA
May, 1966

PREFACE

THE story of the Quaker invasion of the Colonies in the New World has often been told in fragmentary fashion, but no adequate study of the entire Quaker movement in colonial times has yet been made from original sources, free from partisan or sectarian prejudice and in historical perspective. By far the most important history of American Quakerism covering our period is Bowden's *History of Friends in America* (London, vol. i. 1850, vol. ii. 1854), but it is plainly written from the Quaker point of view and does not furnish a critical investigation of Quakerism and its work in the New World. Thomas's *History of the Society of Friends in America* (written originally for the American Church History Series, and published separately in 1895) is an excellent piece of work, done in an impartial and historical spirit, though too brief to allow of much detail. Weeks's *Southern Quakers and Slavery* (Baltimore, 1896) is scholarly and judicial, and is the best work in existence for the section covered.

There have been many accounts written from the anti-Quaker point of view, but they are for the most part one-sided and coloured by prejudice, and they are obviously lacking in penetration into the inner meaning of the type of religion which they undertake to present. Bancroft has given considerable space to the Quakers in his *History of the United States*. His account is sympathetic, but it is largely an abstract treatment of their religious principles rather than a truly historical picture.

This volume is an attempt to study historically and critically the religious movement inaugurated in the New World by the Quakers, a movement important both for the history of the development of religion and for the history of the American Colonies, and to present it not only in its external setting but also in the light of its inner meaning. It has been written as a contribution toward the completion of a plan to write a full history of the Quaker movement on the two continents, conceived by my beloved friend, John Wilhelm Rowntree, and interrupted by his death. No one can now accomplish precisely what he was conceiving—

> Ah ! who shall lift the wand of magic-power
> And the lost clew regain ?

But a group of his friends have resolved that, as far as possible, his work shall go forward, and we hope that eventually the projected series may be brought to completion.

I have been assisted in the present volume by Isaac Sharpless, who has written the section on Pennsylvania, and by Amelia M. Gummere, who has written the section on New Jersey. I have received valuable suggestions and help from William Charles Braithwaite, of Banbury, England ; Norman Penney, of London ; Augustine Jones, of Newton Highlands, Massachusetts ; Professor Allen C. Thomas, of Haverford, Pennsylvania ; and John Cox, jun., of New York City. I have, with permission, made use of the map in Weeks's *Southern Quakers and Slavery* in locating some of the places on my map of the southern colonies. My wife has read the proofs and prepared the Index, and has in many other ways assisted in my work on this volume.

HAVERFORD, PENNSYLVANIA,
March 1911.

CONTENTS

BOOK IV

THE EARLY QUAKERS IN NEW JERSEY

BOOK V

THE QUAKERS IN PENNSYLVANIA

MAPS

(At end of Volume)

INTRODUCTION

AMERICAN Quakerism is closely bound up in origin and history with the wider religious movement which had its rise in the English Commonwealth, under the leadership of George Fox.[1] This type of religion, which took root in the American Colonies in 1657, and which grew to be a significant and far-reaching influence in at least ten Colonies, had already for ten years been powerfully stirring the middle classes, and had rapidly gathered numbers in the English counties. When the volunteers went forth for "the mighty work in the nations beyond the seas," as they expressed their mission, they were the representatives of an expanding body of believers at home, the executives of a matured policy of spiritual conquest, and they went forth to their "hardships and hazards" with an organised financial support behind them.[2] They felt, as their own testimony plainly shows, that they were not solitary adventurers, but that God was pushing them out to be the bearers of a new and mighty word of Life which was to remake the world, and that the whole group behind

[1] The history of the rise of Quakerism has been written for this series by William Charles Braithwaite in the volume *The Beginnings of Quakerism*.

[2] At a great General Meeting held at Scalehouse, near Skipton, in England, in 1658, an Epistle was issued which called for funds to push the work in the Western world. The following extract indicates the spirit of the document : " Having heard of the great things done by the mighty power of God in many nations beyond the seas, whither He hath called forth many of our dear brethren and sisters to preach the everlasting gospel . . . our bowels yearn for them and our hearts are filled with tender love to those precious ones of God who so freely have given up for the Seed's sake their friends, their near relations, their country and worldly estates, yea and their lives also. We, therefore, with one consent freely and liberally offer up our earthly substance, according as God hath blessed every one—to be speedily sent up to London as a freewill offering for the Seed's sake." (The MS. of this Epistle is in the Library at Devonshire House, London, in Portfolio, 16-1.)

them was in some sense embodied in them. Throughout all the years during which the campaign of spiritual conquest was being pushed forward, the entire Society in England was pledged to the task of carrying its " truth " into the life of the New World, and even as early as 1660 George Fox was planning for the founding of a Colony in America, where Quakers could try their faith and work out their ideals unmolested.[1] A study of Fox's printed *Epistles* will convince any one that the " Seed in America " was always prominent in his thought and in his plans.[2] In fact no other religious body in the Old World more completely identified itself with the fortunes of its apostles in the New World than did the Quakers, then in the youth and vigour of their career.

Throughout the entire period covered by this history —1656 to 1780—Quakerism was an expanding force in the Colonies, and there were times within this period when it seemed destined to become one of the foremost religious factors in the life and development of America. It is clearly evident from their own writings that at the opening of the eighteenth century the Quaker leaders *expected* to make their type of religion prevail on the Western continent. They believed, in fact, that their " Principle " was universally true and would make its way through the race, and that their experiment was only the beginning of a world-religion of the Spirit. The New World seemed to them a providential field to be won for their truth. It was in the New World alone that favourable opportunities offered in the seventeenth and eighteenth centuries for the application of Quaker ideals to public life, and the opportunities were quickly seized. In Great Britain there were insuperable bars which kept Quakers out of public service to the state and forced them to adopt a life apart from the main currents. One famous Quaker, John Archdale, who took a prominent part in the making of three American Colonies—Maine, North Carolina and South Carolina—was elected to the English

---

[1] Letter of Josiah Coale to George Fox from Maryland, January 1661. A. R. Barclay Col. of MSS. in Devonshire House, No. 53.

[2] Fox's *Epistles* (first ed. 1698 ; American ed. 1831, 2 vols.).

Parliament in 1698, but his refusal to take an oath cost him his seat, and ended all attempts on the part of Quakers to enter the field of politics. In America the situation was quite different. In the Puritan Colonies of New England, Quakers were, of course, without the privileges of franchise or office-holding, and in Episcopalian Colonies like Virginia, where uniformity was insisted upon, the way to influence in the government was tightly closed to them; but in Rhode Island the only obstacle to position in Government affairs which the Quakers met was the difficulty of bearing responsibility for war-preparation. In that Colony for more than a hundred years Quakers were continually in office, and for thirty-six terms the Governorship of the colony was occupied by members of the Society. In Pennsylvania they had one of the largest and most influential Colonies of the New World in their own hands. They came into possession of West Jersey in 1674, and five years later East Jersey also passed into their hands, so that they had the governmental control of New Jersey until it became a royal Colony.

Until 1701 they were the only organised religious denomination in North Carolina, and the administration of the Quaker, John Archdale, profoundly shaped the history of both Carolinas. Naturally Quakers in the Old World looked to the New as a land of promise, and no pains were spared to spread the "Seed" in the favourable regions along the Atlantic coast, so that by the middle of the eighteenth century there were more Quakers in the Western hemisphere than in Great Britain. They formed half the population of Newport in 1700 and for many years after, and down to the middle of the eighteenth century they were a majority of the population of the South Narragansett shore of Rhode Island, now Washington County. There were at this period three thousand Quakers in the southern section of Massachusetts, once the territory of the Pilgrim Fathers. About one-third of the inhabitants in the Piscataqua region of Maine and New Hampshire were Quakers.

Lynn, Salem, Newbury, and Hampton had large Meetings, and many of the inland rural districts of Massachusetts and Rhode Island were predominantly Quaker. They formed a large proportion of the Long Island towns and the towns of Westchester County on the mainland, and by the middle of the century they constituted an influential body in New York City. There were not less than twenty-five thousand Quakers in Pennsylvania before the end of our period, and probably not far from six thousand in New Jersey. There were by official figures three thousand in Maryland, probably four or five thousand in Virginia, and about the same number in the Carolinas. They were thrifty, prosperous, and quiet in their modes of life, but contributing their share of the hard labour which turned the dense forests into flourishing fields, and their share also of those subtler formative forces which prepared the way in the wilderness for a great national life, then hardly dreamed of. It is no doubt a home-spun narrative, but history is no longer aristocratic. It does not confine its purview to selected heroes and purple-tinted events. It has become interested in the common man and in plain every-day happenings, and this story, though modest, is a contribution to the real life of America.

The extent of the Quaker influence in the political life of the Colonies has not been generally realised. The " holy experiment " of Penn had striking and dramatic features which have always impressed the imagination, but the quieter work of New England and Carolina Quakers has received much less notice and has waited long for a historian. But while emphasising this neglected field of Quaker activity, we must not lose our perspective and balance. The Quakers' supreme passion was the cultivation of inward religion and an outward life consistent with the vision of their souls. " Experiments in government " whether successful or unsuccessful, whether wise or unwise, were never their primary aim. Beneath these ventures, there always existed a deeper purpose—to make a fresh *experiment in spiritual religion*—as the living pulse of all Quaker aspiration, and by this central aim the movement must be finally estimated and judged. These American Quakers of the period here studied believed, with a white-hot intensity, that they had discovered, or rediscovered, a new spiritual Principle which they thought was destined to revolutionise life, society, civil government, and religion. The Principle (and they always spelled it with a capital P) which they claimed to have discovered was the presence of a Divine Light in man, a radiance from the central Light of the spiritual universe, penetrating the deeps of every soul, which if responded to, obeyed, and accepted as a guiding star, would lead into all truth and into all kinds of truth. They thought that they had found a way to the direct discovery of the Will of God and that they could thereby put the Kingdom of God into actual operation here in the world. The whole momentous issue of life, they insisted, is settled by personal obedience or disobedience to the inward Divine revelation. The wisdom of the infinite God is within reach of the feeblest human spirit ; the will of the Eternal is voiced in the soul of every man ; it is life to hear and obey ; it is death to follow other voices. This underlying conception forms the spring and motive of all the distinctive activities of the colonial Quakers. They risked everything they had on the truth of this Principle, and they must be judged by the way in which they worked out their experiment in religion. They were champions of causes which seemed new and dangerous to those who heard them, but behind all their propaganda there was one live central faith from which everything radiated——the faith that God speaks directly to the human spirit, and that religion, to be true and genuine, must be a reality of first-hand experience.

There have been many individuals in the Christian Church who have been exponents of this mystical idea that God manifests Himself inwardly to the soul of man and that His real presence can be directly, immediately, *experienced*. The testimony of such mystics has profoundly interested our generation and their experiences have received searching psychological examination at the hands of experts.[1]   The novel and interesting thing about this Quaker experiment is that it furnishes an opportunity to study inward mystical religion embodied in a group and worked out through a long span of historical development.   We shall here see the intense personal faith of one or a few fusing an entire group and creating an atmosphere, a climate, into which children were born and through which they formed their lives ; we shall be able to study the effect of the cooling processes of time on this faith so intense at its origin ; we shall discover how this startlingly bold Principle met the slow siftings and testings of history ; and we shall find out how any merely inward and mystical facts must be supplemented and corrected by the wider concrete and objective experience of the race.

It is true, no doubt, that religion is in the last analysis a personal matter, but it is also true that nobody cut apart from social interests and isolated from the purposes and strivings of a group of fellows could become a *person* at all, or could exhibit what we mean by religion. And, therefore, while we go to biography for our most definite accounts of religious experience, it is through the unfolding of history that we can trace out the full significance of a first-hand faith like the one here in question, and only in the vast laboratory of history, where every hypothesis must submit to a stern test, can it be fairly verified or transcended.   The following chapters as they unfold will present the Quaker Principle in sufficient detail, will exhibit it in sharp collision with other views, and will show its points of strength and weakness ; but a few clues indicated here in the Introduction will perhaps help the reader to find his way more easily and more intelligently.

[1] James, *Varieties of Religious Experience* ; Coe, *Spiritual Life* ; Granger, *The Soul of a Christian* ; Pratt, *The Psychology of Religious Belief* ; Ames, *The Psychology of Religious Experience* ; Delacroix, *Les Grands Mystiques chrétiens* ; Inge, *Christian Mysticism* ; Von Hügel, *The Mystical Element in Religion* ; Evelyn Underhill, *Mysticism* ; Jones, *Studies in Mystical Religion.*

1. One point which this volume will clearly settle is the fact that there existed in the Colonies, before the arrival of the Quaker missionaries, a large number of persons, in some instances more or less defined groups of persons, who were seeking after a freer and more inward type of religion than that which prevailed in any of the established Churches.

The period of the English Commonwealth witnessed an extraordinary revival of faith in man's power to discover the inward way to God, and mystical sects, some of them wise and sane, some of them foolish and fanatical, swarmed almost faster than they could be named. These mystical sectaries had one idea in common : they believed that God was in man and that revelation was not closed. They were waiting for the dawn of a fresh Light from heaven.[1] Wherever English Colonists of this period went these sectaries went too. They were a constant annoyance to New England Puritans, to Dutch Calvinists, and to Virginia Churchmen. They generally gathered kindred spirits around them and quietly—or sometimes noisily—propagated their mystical faith. They exalted personal experience, direct intercourse with God, and so put much less stress than their neighbours did upon the forms and doctrines which had come to be regarded as essential elements of a sound and stable faith. This was the prepared soil in which Quakerism spread at its first appearing, and without which the efforts of the propagators, however valiant, would almost certainly have been futile. The Quaker missionaries simply gave positive direction to tendencies already powerfully underway. They brought to clear focus ideas which were before vague and indefinite, and they fused into white heat spirits that were feeling after and dimly seeking what they now heard in their own tongue. The first " Quaker Churches " in America were formed out of this sort of material ; and so too were many of the Meetings which came into being at later periods of expansion.

---

[1] See chapters xiv.-xx. of my *Studies in Mystical Religion.*

2. One of the first tasks which confronts the historian who proposes to deal with the religious life of the Colonies—especially of the New England Colonies—is to understand and fairly estimate the collision between the Puritans and the Quakers. In many respects they were both the product of a common movement, the spiritual offspring of the same epoch. They both possessed a passion for righteousness—a moral earnestness —that hardly has a historical parallel except in the great Hebrew prophets. They both took a very pronounced stand against " natural pleasures," enjoyments of " the world " and of " the flesh," in fact against actions of any kind along the line of least resistance. They were both opposed to fashions and customs which fostered, in any way, looseness of life, or which ministered, in any degree, to personal pride and selfishness. In short, they were both " puritan," in the ancient sense of the word, in their moral basis and in their conception of social proprieties. They both hated tyranny with an intense hatred, though they took very different ways of destroying it ; and they both abhorred sacerdotalism in religion, though they drew the line where sacerdotalism began at very different points.

But if they were allied in spirit in some common elemental aspects ; they were nevertheless exponents of very antagonistic types of religion which, seen from the different angles of vision and perspective, were absolutely irreconcilable, and it was still the fashion then to count it sin to be weak in infallibility. Our generation is so open-minded and hospitable ; so weaned of the taste of finality-doctrines, that we look almost with amazement at these exponents of the fiery positive ; these tournaments to settle which " infallible truth" really *was* infallible. We must, however, always bear in mind that religious indifference is a distinctly modern trait. The testimony of the Rev. Mr. Ward of Ipswich, Massachusetts, in 1645, might be paralleled in almost any ecclesiastical writing of that period : " It is said that men ought to have liberty of conscience and that it is *persecution* to

debar them of it.   I can rather stand amazed than reply
to this.   It is an astonishment that the brains of a man
should be parboiled in such impious ignorance." John
Callender, writing of the freedom established in the little
Colony on the island of Rhode Island says with much
truth : " In reality the true Grounds of Liberty of
Conscience were not then [1637] known, or embraced
by any Sect or Party of Christians ; all parties seemed
to think that as they only were in possession of the
Truth, so they alone had a right to restrain and crush
all other opinions, which they respectively called Error
and Heresy, where *they* were the most numerous and
powerful." [1]

Here in the same field were two exponents of the
" fiery positive," both profoundly, sincerely conscious of
the infallible truth of their convictions, and with their
lives staked upon divergent and irreconcilable conceptions
of Divine revelation.   For the Puritan, revelation was a
miraculous projection of God's Word and Will from the
supernatural world into this world.   This " miraculous
projection " had been made only in a distinct " dispensation," through a limited number of Divinely chosen,
specially prepared " instruments," who received and
transmitted the pure Word of God.   When the " dispensation " ended, revelation came to a definite close.
No word more could be added, as also none could be
subtracted.   All spiritual truth for the race for all ages
was now unveiled ; the only legitimate function which
the man of God could henceforth exercise was that of
interpretation.   He could declare what the Word of God
meant and how it was to be applied to the complicated
affairs of human society.   Only a specialist in theology
could, from the nature of the case, be a minister under
this system.   The minister thus became invested with an
extraordinary dignity and possessed of an influence quite
sui generis.

For the Quaker, revelation was confined to no " dispensation "—it had never been closed.   If any period

[1] John Callender's *Historical Discourse* (Boston, 1739).

was peculiarly "the dispensation of the Holy Spirit," the Quaker believed that it was the present in which he was living. Instead of limiting the revelation of the Word of God to a few miraculous "instruments," who had lived in a remote "dispensation," he insisted that God enlightens every soul that comes into the world, communes by His Holy Spirit with all men everywhere, illuminates the conscience with a clear sense of the right and the wrong course in moral issues, and reveals His Will in definite and concrete matters to those who are sensitive recipients of it. The true minister, for the Quaker of that period, was a *prophet* who spoke under a moving and by a power beyond his human powers, and so was, in fresh and living ways, a *revealer* of present truth, and not a mere interpreter of a past revelation. The Quaker "meeting" was, in theory at least, a continuation of Pentecost—an occasion for the free blowing of the Spirit of God on men. It was plainly impossible in the seventeenth century for those two types of Christianity to live peaceably side by side. A tragic collision was inevitable.

3. There is another problem in Quaker history no less urgent than the problem of collision with divergent conceptions of truth, and that is the strange fact that a movement so full of vitality and power at its origin ceased to expand with the expanding life of America. So long as the "tragic collisions" lasted, the Quakers flourished and seemed sure of a significant future in the unfolding spiritual life of America ; as soon as they were free and unopposed there occurred a slowing-down and a loss of dynamic impact on the world. No treatment of colonial Quakerism can be adequate which fails to face this somewhat depressing fact, for the historian who presents the assets and achievements of a movement is under obligation to deal squarely as well with its liabilities, weaknesses, and failures.

The thing which above everything else doomed the movement to a limited and subordinate rôle was the early adoption of the ideal that Quakers were to form a "peculiar people." In the creative stage of the movement the leaders were profoundly conscious that they had discovered a universal truth which was to permeate humanity, and form, by its inherent demonstration and power, a World-Church—the Church of the living God. It was in that faith and in the inspiration of that great idea that the pioneer missionaries went forth. Then gradually, at first unconsciously, in the face of a very stubborn world that not only was not persuaded, but further went positively to work to suppress the alleged "fresh revelation," the movement underwent a radical change of ideal. The aim slowly narrowed down to the formation of a "spiritual remnant," set apart to guard and preserve "the truth" in the midst of a crooked and perverse generation that would not see and believe. The world-vision faded out, and the attention focused on "Quakerism" as an end-in-itself. The transformation which occurred in this case has many striking parallels in the history of other spiritual experiments. The living *idea* organises a definite Society for the propagation of it, and lo, the Society unconsciously smothers the original idea and becomes absorbed in itself! It is a very ancient tragedy, and that tragedy happened again here in this movement. The transformation is written large on the Records of the meetings and in the Journals of the leaders. "Truth" soon came to be a definite, static thing. No creed was made and no declaration of faith was adopted, but a well-defined body of Quaker conceptions soon came into shape, and came also into habitual use. Not only did the ideas of the Society crystallise into static concepts of truth, the form of worship too became fixed and well-nigh unalterable. There was no "programme" of service and no positive prearrangement, but it was soon settled that silence was the essential "form" for true worship, and that spiritual ministry must be spontaneous, unpremeditated, and of the "prophetic" type.

The primitive aim at simplicity and the desire to escape from slavery to fashion underwent a corresponding change and dropped to the easy substitute of a fixed form of dress and speech, which soon became itself a kind of slavery. A definite attitude toward music and art and "diversions" in general was adopted so that individuals might be relieved of the difficulty, and incidentally of the danger, of personal decision. Marriage with "the world's people" was made as difficult as it possibly could be made. In short, a Quaker became a well-marked and definitely-labelled individual—quite as rigidly *set* as any of the "religious orders" of Church history and quite as bent on preserving the peculiar type. Men spent their precious lives, not in propagating the living principles of spiritual religion in the great life of the world, but in perfecting and transmitting a "system" within the circle of the Society, and the heart-burnings and tragedies which mark the lives of the consecrated men and women who, in these days, bore the ark, were too often concerned with the secondary rather than with the primary things of spiritual warfare. The martyrdoms for the world-cause were heroic, dramatic, and of universal interest ; these later travails and tragedies often seem petty, trivial, and unnecessary, and they make a very limited appeal to human interest.

The movement was hampered from the start, and in every stage of its history during the period of this volume by the imperfect conception of the inward Light, and of the whole relation between the Divine and the human, which was consciously or unconsciously adopted. This was perhaps inevitable, as every movement is necessarily more or less bound up with the prevailing ideas, the intellectual climate, of the age in which it takes its rise. In the seventeenth and early eighteenth centuries a dualistic universe was taken for granted. There was a sharp distinction, a wide chasm, between the "natural" and the "supernatural." The urgent question with every-body was—not how *the entire universe from material husk to spiritual core could be unified and comprehended as an organic whole*, but how the chasm which sundered the two worlds could be miraculously bridged. It is not our problem to-day, but it was the one the Quaker was facing. His opponents said that the chasm was bridged by a miraculous communication of the Word of God in a definite and finished Revelation. *He* said that it was bridged by the communication of a supernatural Light given to each soul. The trouble was that he never could succeed in bringing into unity the two things assumed to be sundered. On the one hand there was the "mere man," whom he assumed, as everybody else did, to be, in his natural condition, non-spiritual and incapable of doing anything toward his own salvation; and on the other a Divine Light, or Seed of God, projected into this "natural man" as the illuminating, saving, and revealing Principle in him. The Light was distinctly conceived as something supernatural and foreign to man as man—something added to him as a gift.

With this basal conception for his working theory, the Quaker naturally and logically looked upon the true minister as a passive and oracular "instrument" of the Holy Spirit. His message, in so far as it was "spiritual," was believed to come "through him and from beyond him." He was not a teacher or an interpreter, he was a "revealer" through whom Divine truth was "opened." The direct result of such a view, of course, was that human powers were lightly esteemed and quite distrusted. Instead of having a principle which brought the finite being, with all his potential powers, into organic union with the self-revealing, co-operating God, thus producing a spiritual, developing, autonomous personality, with an incentive to expand all its capacities; he had a fundamental conception which tended toward a distrust and suppression of the native powers. Spiritual messages, instead of being thought of as the contribution which a person himself makes when he is raised to his highest and best by co-operation with the Divine Spirit in whom his finite life is rooted, were thought of as messages oracularly "given" to him—his part being simply that of a transmitter.

The human element in man's spiritual activities was

discounted and almost eliminated in order to heighten the Divine aspect, as in an earlier theology the human element in Christ had been suppressed to exalt His divinity. That this unpsychological theory worked out badly in practice there can be no question in the mind of anybody who studies the movement historically ; but it only means that they were unsuccessful and unhappy in their way of *formulating* their theory of Divine and human intercourse. What they wanted to say was that God and men were in direct correspondence, and that man at his best could lay hold of life and light and wisdom and truth which ordinarily transcends his narrow finite self. Of such heightened correspondence there is plenty of evidence. The only pity is that their wrongly-formulated theory so often stood in their way and hampered them and prevented them from a normal use of all their capacities.

Their failure to appreciate the importance of the fullest expansion of human personality by education is the primary cause of their larger failure to win the commanding place in American civilisation of which their early history gave promise. Their central Principle, properly understood, called for a fearless education, for there is no safety in individualism, in personal responsibility, or in democracy, whether in civil or religious matters, unless every individual is given a chance to correct his narrow individualism in the light of the experience of larger groups of men. If a man is to be called upon to follow "his Light," he must be helped to correct his *subjective seemings* by the gathered objective wisdom of the race, as expressed in scientific truth, in historical knowledge, in established institutions, and in the sifted literature of the world. The Quaker ideal of ministry, too, calls for a broad and expansive education even more than does that of any other religious body. If the particular sermon is not to be definitely prepared, then the person who is to minister must *himself* be prepared. If he is to avoid the repetition of his own petty notions and commonplace thoughts he must form a richer and more comprehensive experience from which to draw,

For every fiery prophet in old times,
And all the sacred madness of the bard,
When God made music thro' him, could but speak
His music by the framework and the chord.[1]

George Fox had moments of insight into the importance of this objective element, and in a great sentence he urged the founding of educational institutions for teaching " everything civil and useful in creation " ; but institutions of such scope unfortunately did not get founded. If there could have been established, in the northern, central, and southern sections of the Atlantic coast line, institutions adapted to the right education of Quaker youth, as Harvard and Yale were to the education of the Puritan youth, there would be quite another story to tell. As the problem *was* worked out, no adequate education for Quaker youth was available. They soon found themselves largely cut off from the great currents of culture, and they thus missed the personal enlargement which comes when one is forced to make his own ideals fit into larger systems of thought, and is compelled to reshape them in the light of facts. The absence of constructive leaders, the later tendency to withdraw from civic tasks, the relaxing of the idea of reshaping the world, which this history reveals, were due, in the main, to the lack of expansive education. The beautiful old-fashioned home passed on to the child who came into it the stock of truth and the definite ideals which were alive in it ; it fed the growing mind with the literature which its people had produced, and the Meetings furnished a spiritual climate that was sweet and wholesome to breathe, but there was nothing to lift the youth up to a sight of new horizons. He was more or less *doomed* to the level of the past. The denominations that were training the fittest of their sons to become thinkers and leaders were sure sooner or later to win the birthright and to take away the blessing from the Quakers.

With the Revolutionary War there came a great awakening, which showed itself most definitely in a determination to provide larger opportunities for Quaker

[1] Tennyson's " Holy Grail."

education. Steps were taken in each section of the country to provide for the education of the new generation. It was a fortunate awakening and it has led to great results, but it came too late to enable the Quakers to achieve the place in the civilisation of the Western world which their early history prognosticated. They were already being left behind, and were already accepting the view that they were to be a small and isolated sect—" a remnant" of God's people. The fateful years which were selecting the dominating religious forces of America were the years of colonial development, and during those eventful years the Quakers were not awake to the chance that was going by. Then, too, when the awakening did come, there was still a long period during which contracted ideals of education prevailed. Nobody seemed able to get beyond the narrow plan of "guarded education," which is not, in the true sense of the word, *education* at all. It is still only the transmission of certain well-defined and "safe" ideas and tends to produce uncreative and unconstructive minds. It is a well-meant plan for the propagation of an existing body of ideas, but it does not and cannot make large and forceful leaders and creators of fresh ideals.[1] The whole trend of the century before had been toward the preservation of a definite type and had fostered the timid attitude. It was not to be expected, when the awakening came, that there would be men ready for the bold experiment of a broad and fearless education which set the youth free, with open mind, to study "everything civil and useful in creation," and which left him to make his own selection of what was to be truth for him. The Quaker has slowly found the road to that genuine type of education, but he has come to it late. Whether he now has recovering power enough to repair the damages of the past and can still realise the destiny which seemed his in the last half of the seventeenth century, is not a question to be answered here, but it is a fact that his

---

[1] "Guarded" is often used in another sense, namely, that young and tender children, while being educated, are to be shielded from immoral influences, which is, of course, highly commendable.

failure to provide for an adequate education during the formative years lies at the base of his larger failure to *arrive*.[1]

4. In one particular respect the colonial Quakers made a very important contribution to religion—they produced saints, and these saints were and remain the finest and most fragrant bloom of American Quakerism.

Sainte-Beuve has given, in his *Port Royal*, a penetrating account of persons who have been transformed into saintly life through the reception of Divine grace. " Such souls," he says, " arrive at a certain fixed and invincible state, a state which is genuinely heroic, and from out of which the greatest deeds are performed. . . . They have an inner state which before all things is one of love and humility, of infinite confidence in God, and of severity to themselves, accompanied with tenderness for others." This is an accurate account of the colonial Quaker saint—invincibly fixed in purpose, genuinely heroic, ready for great deeds, possessed of infinite confidence in God, and withal tender in love and humility. I am not sure that our busy and commercial age would call these saints " efficient "—they were not trained and equipped as modern social workers are—but they were triumphantly beautiful spirits, and the world still needs beautiful lives as much as it needs " efficient " ones, and the beautiful life in the long run is dynamic and does inherit the earth.[2]

These rare and beautiful souls, like great artistic creations of beauty, are not capable of explanation in utilitarian terms, nor can their origin be traced in terms of cause and effect, but it can safely be said that they never come except among people consecrated to the Invisible Church. It requires a pure and fervid devotion to the Pattern in the mount, a loyalty to the holy Jerusalem—the Urbs Sion mystica—to fashion a Christian

---

[1] It must not be concluded because Quakerism did not flourish under these conditions and limitations that therefore its *spiritual ideal* has broken down. On the contrary, it has hardly yet been given an adequate trial.

[2] John Woolman is the consummate flower of the type I have in mind. It was a saying of his that " some glances of real beauty may be seen in their faces who dwell in true meekness."

saint, whether Catholic or Quaker. No one can be wholly absorbed in the affairs of an actual earthly church without being marred by the politics of it, and without becoming small and narrow and provincial by reason of the limitations of locality and temporal climate. The saint belongs to an actual church, to be sure, loves it and serves it, but he keeps his soul set on the vision of the Church Invisible in which the saints of all ages are members with him, and in that vision he lives.

There must also be a loosening of the hold on "the world" to prepare a saint of this type. There must at least be no rivalry to disturb the concentration of soul on eternal Realities. The very rigour of renunciation, the stern demands of a religion which cuts its adherents off from primrose paths of life, seem almost essential to the creation of this kind of saintliness. It is only by strict parallelism with celestial currents, only by drawing on invisible and inexhaustible resources of Grace, only by the cultivation of a finer spiritual perception than most possess that inward grace and central calm are achieved ; only by stillness and communion that spiritual poise and power are won. There were, in the days of which I am writing, many Friends who had found the secret inner way into a real Holy of Holies. They had learned how to live from within outward, how to be refreshed with inward bubblings, how to walk their hard straight path with shining faces, though they wist not their faces did shine. The Quakers have no "calendar," no bead roll, and they have always been shy and cautious even of the word "saint," but almost every Meeting from Maine to South Carolina had during the period under review some persons who through help from Above refined and sublimated their nature and all unconsciously grew sweet and fragrant with the odour of saintly life.

5. One other positive contribution which they made to genuine spiritual religion remains to be catalogued—their contribution to the spread of lay-religion, by which I mean a form of religion dissociated from ecclesiasticism, and penetrating the life and activities of ordinary men.

The real power of Quakerism lay in the quality of life produced in the rank and file of the membership. This history is weak, no doubt, in biographies of luminous leaders who rose far above the group and stood out as distinct peaks. Colonial Quakerism would have proved a barren field for a Carlyle, who assumed that history is the biography of heroes, raised by their genius head and shoulders above the level of their contemporaries. The real glory of this movement was the "levelling up" of an entire people. Farmers, with hands made rough by the plough-handle, in hundreds of rural localities not only preached messages of spiritual power on meeting-days, but, what is more to the point, lived daily lives of radiant goodness in simple neighbourhood service. Women who had slight chances for culture, and who had to do the hard work of pioneer housewifery, by some subtle spiritual alchemy, were transformed into a virile saint-hood which made its power felt both in the Sunday gathering and in the unordained care of souls throughout the community. It was a real experiment in the "priesthood of believers," and it was an incipient stage of what has become one of the most powerful spiritualising forces in our country—the unordained lay ministry of a vast multitude of men and women who have attacked every form of entrenched evil, and who, in city and country, are taking up the "cure of souls" with insight and efficiency.

It will be obvious to the reader that this book is not written from the point of view of the antiquarian. The historical facts have been carefully gathered, sifted, and verified, and they are as accurate as research could make them, but the central interest from first to last has been to discover how a group of men and women wrought out their souls' faith in an earlier century. They were persons who believed that within the deeps of themselves they touched the Infinite, that within their own spirits they could hear the living word of the Eternal. They believed this mighty thing, and they tried to make their belief real in life and word and deed. It is worth while perhaps even in this busy age to stop amid the din of commercial activity to see how plain people, raised to a kind of grandeur by their faith, tried to bring to the world once again a religion of life, and endeavoured to show that God is, as of old, an Immanuel God—with us and in us, the Life of our lives.

BOOK I

THE QUAKERS IN NEW ENGLAND

CHAPTER I

A PRE-QUAKER MOVEMENT

THE beginnings of our American colonies are, for the most part, inextricably bound up with the history of the differentiation and development of great religious movements in England and on the continent of Europe. The tiny commonwealths, brought hither in sailing vessels of the seventeenth century, were begotten in religious faith, and were formed and shaped by zealous men to whom some peculiar type of religion was dearer than country, more precious even than life itself. The story of colonial America can no more be told with religion left out than it could be told with the economic aspects of soil and forests and food-stuffs omitted, or with the fact of Indian neighbours neglected. As it was religion that was in most cases the creative spring which pushed these colonists to sea in their venturous ships, so too it was for many years religion which shaped the policies, supplied the controlling ideas, and furnished the fundamental interests of these forefathers of our national life.

I am not here undertaking the large task of studying the religious development of colonial America, but I shall be quite satisfied if I can well perform the simpler task of telling the story—surely complex and intricate enough—of one single religious movement which profoundly influenced the course of American history, and powerfully affected the personal lives of the citizens in nearly all the original colonies,—I mean the coming of the Quakers.

The first Quakers to land on American soil were two

women, named Mary Fisher and Ann Austin,[1] who came from England by way of Barbadoes, and who landed in the city of Boston on the 11th of July 1656, to the consternation of the magistrates of this Puritan town, then twenty-six years old. George Bishop's statement, addressed to the magistrates in 1660, is hardly an exaggeration: " Two poor women arriving in your harbour, so shook ye, to the everlasting shame of you, and of your established peace and order, as if a formidable army had invaded your borders." [2]

To understand why the arrival of these " two poor women " of the Quaker faith produced such consternation in the peaceful town, we must go back and pass in review a very famous and important religious movement in Massachusetts history. It is important here for two reasons : first because it illustrates admirably the way in which the Puritan colonists dealt with persons who laid claim to a *present* revelation, an immediate experience of Divine communications ; and secondly, because it was a direct preparation for the spread and propagation of Quakerism. I refer to the story of Anne Hutchinson and her " party "—often called, though unfairly, the " Antinomian controversy." This controversy, as all our primary authorities admit, came near disrupting the colony even while it was in its swaddling clothes, and it seriously threatened to frustrate the plans of the founders. It was the most dangerous storm the nascent Puritan commonwealth weathered, for Pequots and Narragansetts never brought the Colony to such a close strait as did this woman's tongue and wit.

The whole controversy arose over the nature and extent of the Divine influence on the human soul. Anne Hutchinson, the chief actor in this somewhat tragic drama, was born about 1590, being the daughter of Francis Marbury, a well-known London preacher. She was married to William Hutchinson about 1612, and

[1] Elizabeth Harris came to Maryland the same year, but apparently slightly later. See chapter on "The Planting of Quakerism in the Southern Colonies."
[2] Bishop's *New England Judged* (edition of 1703), p. 7. The first edition was published in 1661, but this is extremely rare.

passed the next twenty years of her married life quietly at Alford in Lincolnshire, where she listened, as occasion offered, with great satisfaction and admiration to the preaching of John Cotton, minister of St. Botolph's church in English Boston. He migrated to Boston in New England in 1633, and William Hutchinson and his wife followed him to the New World in the autumn of the next year, their oldest son, Edward, having already accompanied John Cotton.

John Winthrop tells us that Mrs. Hutchinson was "a woman of a ready wit and bold spirit."[1] John Wheelwright, her brother-in-law and fellow-sufferer, says: "As for Mrs. Hutchinson, she was a woman of good wit, and not only so, but naturally of good judgment too, as appeared in her civil occasions. In spirituals, indeed, she gave her understanding over into the power of [inward] suggestion and immediate dictates."[2] Cotton Mather, imitating an earlier account, sets her down as possessing "an haughty carriage, busie spirit, competent wit, and a voluble tongue"—"a *non-such* among the people."[3] Thomas Welde, her most unrelenting and ingenious foe, informs us that she had "a haughty and fierce carriage, a nimble wit and active spirit, and was more bold than a man, the breeder and nourisher of all distempers," and he does not neglect to mention her "voluble tongue" and he thinks that her "understanding and judgment" were "inferior to those of many women."[4] Johnson declares that she was "the masterpiece of women's wit!"[5]

There is also a like consensus of opinion upon her social helpfulness and sympathetic spirit. She was a gifted nurse and peculiarly skilful in dealing with "ailments peculiar to her sex." She was the person

---

[1] Winthrop's *History of New England from 1630 to 1649*, edited by James Savage (Boston, 1853), vol. i. p. 239.

[2] *Mercurius Americanus*, printed in Bell's *John Wheelwright*, Prince Soc. Pub. (Boston, 1876), p. 197.

[3] Mather's *Magnalia* (Hartford, 1853), vol. ii. pp. 516 and 517. Mather is here following Welde.

[4] Welde's *Rise, Reign, and Ruin of Antinomians, etc.*, 1st ed. 1644, p. 31.

[5] Johnson's *Wonder-working Providence*, lib. i. c. 42.

instinctively sent for at times of childbirth, and she knew how to penetrate into the mysteries of morbid states and mental and spiritual troubles which abounded under the new and hard conditions of frontier life. Even Welde, for whom she is " the American Jezebel," admits that she was " a woman very helpful in time of child-birth and other occasions of bodily disease, and well furnished with means for those purposes." [1] She had thus a natural entrée to women's hearts, and possessed as she was of sympathy, kindliness, manifold interests, and withal of that indescribable trait which we name " magnetism," she was destined to play an important rôle in the new settlement.[2]

This gentlewoman, admitted by all authorities to have possessed a brilliant mind and kindly nature, and as certainly possessed of a genuine passion for a religion of vital reality and inward power, hit upon the plan of holding a "women's meeting" at her house each week, for the primary purpose of presenting the substance of the previous Sunday sermon to the women of the community who had been prevented from attending the original service. This meeting opened to her exactly the career for which her talents and gifts fitted her, and she very quickly became " a burning and a shining light " in this little circle of women. We can hardly imagine, with our crowded, complex lives, how monotonous and limited were the lives of the women in those primitive days. The absorbing interests for them were the neighbourhood " news," and the affairs of the Church, even down to the details of the " headings " of the last Sunday sermon, or the last Thursday " lecture " !

There is little ground for assuming, as so many writers have done, that Anne Hutchinson was insatiably "ambitious" and "light-headed." She simply had the wit to start a movement which struck a line of native interest in the community and which peculiarly suited her own gifts and genius, and the natural results followed.

[1] Welde, *op. cit.* p. 31.
[2] See, for a sketch of her character, G. E. Ellis's *Puritan Age in Massachusetts,* pp. 307 seq.

The "women's meeting" proved to be as popular as the modern fads which sweep like a contagion through our present-day social circles, and, almost before she knew it, she found herself a person to be reckoned with throughout the little commonwealth, and the leading influence in the town of Boston.[1] The Hutchinson "meeting," by an almost unconscious propulsion, soon passed beyond its original scope, which was to review and comment upon the sermon of the preceding Sunday. The leader began to compare sermons, and to mark off one type of religious teaching which they heard from the Rev. John Cotton as higher than another type which they heard from the Rev. John Wilson ; and little by little she herself became the prophet and expounder of the "higher type," with the imminent danger of brewing ecclesiastical jealousies.

The important point now is to get before us a clear conception of these *two types of religion* upon which the community was cleaving into two parties. Most modern writers give up the distinction as hopeless, and tell us that the whole controversy was a notorious instance of "confused theological jargon," out of which nobody, either then or now, could, or can, make any clear sense. It is true that Winthrop's account is full of confusion, and that he himself says : "No man could tell (except some few, who knew the bottom of the matter) where any difference was."[2] And yet as soon as we go for light to the actual words of the main actors themselves, we find that those of the Hutchinson party were champions of a type of religion sharply differentiated from that expounded and exhibited by the clergymen of the Colony, excepting only John Cotton, with whom Anne Hutchinson was well pleased, and John Wheelwright, her brother-in-law.

The two types were named respectively " a covenant of Grace," and "a covenant of Works." The foremost exponents of the former type were Anne Hutchinson herself ; her brother-in-law the Rev. John Wheelwright,

---

[1] Winthrop says : "All the congregation of Boston, except four or five, closed with [her] opinions." *Op. cit.* vol. i. p. 252.

[2] *Op. cit.* vol. i. p. 255.

pastor of the little congregation at Mount Wollaston (now Braintree) ; Sir Harry Vane, then Governor of the Colony ; and the Rev. John Cotton, the most shining intellectual light at that time on the American continent.   He, how-ever, drew back when the movement reached the perilous edge, and took his place, whether honourably or dishonour-ably, among the opposers of the " new opinions."   There were many prominent persons, besides the "exponents," who were warm sympathisers with the " new opinions," and who shared the opprobrium and penalties which were meted out to those who dared to think for themselves and to diverge from the beaten track of the prevailing theology.   The most noted of these sympathisers were William Coddington, John Coggeshall, William Aspinwall, Nicholas Easton, Mary Dyer, and Captain John Underhill (a somewhat serio-comic actor in the drama), some of whom, with many more here unnamed, will reappear in the Quaker ranks.   The leaders of the opposition forces were John Winthrop, the loftiest figure in that colonial commonwealth, though for the moment superseded in the governorship ; Rev. John Wilson, pastor of Boston ; Rev. Hugh Peters, pastor of Salem, and later prominent in the greater drama of the Civil War in England ; John Endicott, and Thomas Dudley, both of large fame in the governorship ; Rev. Thomas Welde, the ungentle historian of the controversy, and all the other ministers of the Colony.

The real issue, as I see it in the fragments that are preserved, was an issue between what we nowadays call "religion of the first-hand type," and "religion of the second-hand type," that is to say, a religion on the one hand which insists on "knowledge of acquaintance" through immediate experience, and a religion on the other hand which magnifies the importance and sufficiency of "knowledge about."   Anne Hutchinson precipitated the controversy by an assertion—under the existing circumstances as certain to produce a furious controversy as a flaming firebrand in dry prairie grass is sure to produce a conflagration—that John Cotton preached a covenant of Grace, and that the other ministers of the Colony preached a covenant of Works.[1]

This latter phrase, which was a coinage of the Reformation, had come to mean *a legal system of religion*, or what St. Paul branded as "a religion of the letter"— a thing of "beggarly elements." Those who used the phrase intended it to characterise a form of religion which consisted essentially in a system of correct views, in the acceptance of a set of Divine commandments and sacred ceremonies, and the aim to live a life of strict obedience to this elaborate, divinely communicated system. Worship under this system is based on the commands of the covenant; it is not something springing out of the inward disposition of the worshipper. It was one of the central features of this "system" that the relation between God and man was a relation of covenant. By the "fall," the direct *fellowship-relation* with God had been broken and annulled. God was no longer Friend but just Judge. This Judge, instead of destroying the sinful race, made a *covenant*, in which He showed His mercy and opened the way of escape for man. This covenant, set forth in the Holy Scriptures, contains a full, complete, and final expression of God's will and requirements — all that pertains to life and salvation. Man's part is, not to question why, not to pry into the inscrutable will, but to *comply strictly with the terms of the covenant*. Under this covenant the "minister," by whatever name he may be called, is an exalted personage, quite in a class apart. He is the official interpreter of the terms and the meaning of the covenant. He is the mouthpiece of the covenant-maker, the highest spokesman of the will revealed in the covenant. The simple point for us is this, that Anne Hutchinson did not like that type of religion—it was to her mind only "legalism," mere "letter," and it left the inward life unchanged and untransformed, however

[1] The proceedings of the "Examination of Mrs. Hutchinson" are given in an Appendix to Hutchinson's *Massachusetts Bay*, ii. 482-520. My statement is founded on Hugh Peters's testimony (p. 491). Mrs. Hutchinson claimed that Peters did not report her fairly. But the evidence is clear that she did make these two classes: those in the covenant of Grace and those in the covenant of Works.

correct the outward conformity might be ; and she boldly announced this type of religion to be actually existing in the Colony, and to be supported by all the ministers except John Wheelwright, her brother-in-law, and John Cotton, " teacher " in the Boston church.

Against this legalistic religion of rules and commandments, with its remote, absentee God, she set what she called the " covenant of Grace." By this she meant, and so did her contemporaries, a religion grounded in a direct experience of God's grace and redeeming love, a religion not of pious performances, of solemn fasts and sombre faces, of painful search after the exact requirements of the law, but a religion which began and ended in triumphant certainty of Divine forgiveness, Divine fellowship, and present Divine illumination.

Winthrop tells us that " Mrs. Hutchinson brought over with her two dangerous errors : (1) That the Person of the Holy Ghost dwells in a justified person. (2) That no sanctification can help to evidence our justification."[1] I admit that this second " error " sounds like " theological jargon," but it is only a seventeenth - century way of saying that no deeds however holy, no acts however saintly, are in themselves a sufficient evidence of a restored and vital relation with God ; or as John Wheelwright put it in his famous fast - day sermon : " There is nothing under heaven may justify any *but the revelation of the Lord Jesus Christ* [in him]."

Out of these " errors," Winthrop says, there sprang the view that the Christian—the true Christian—is *united with* the Holy Ghost, and of himself becomes dead and " hath no gifts and graces, nor other sanctification, but the Holy Ghost Himself."[2]

These " errors " sound at this distance remarkably like some of St. Paul's " truths " ; for example : " I am crucified with Christ, nevertheless I live ; yet not I, Christ liveth in me." " Christ is made unto us sanctification." " Ye are builded together for a *habitation of God through the*

---

[1] Winthrop, *op. cit.* vol. i. p. 239.
[2] *Op. cit.* vol. i. p. 239.

Spirit."[1]   John Cotton had, even before his coming to
America, been a fervent expounder of this inward
religion, and he undoubtedly held the essential principles
of Mrs. Hutchinson's teaching.   William Coddington,
writing to the magistrates of the Colony in 1672 to
protest against the persecution of the Quakers, calls upon
those in authority to "turn to the Light within you, even
Christ in you," and then he (having himself been one of
the Boston founders who sailed on the *Arbella*) adds:
"This [teaching of inward Light] was declared unto you
by the servant of the Lord, John Cotton, on his lecture
day, when the ships were ready to depart for England.
He stated the difference; it was about Grace.   *He
magnified the Grace in us*; the priests [*i.e.* the other
ministers] the Grace without or upon them.   All the
difference in the country was about Grace, but the
difference was as great, he said, as between light and
darkness, heaven and hell, life and death."[2]   Cotton did
not, however, go as far as the other expounders of "the
covenant of Grace" did.   He held for the "indwelling of
the Holy Ghost" but not for a personal *union* of the
believer with the Holy Ghost.[3]   Governor Vane went to
the far extreme, and held the view that there is a personal
union between the believer and the Holy Ghost, so that
a divine life is actually begotten in the soul.[4]

But the most important document in the controversy
for an understanding of the "covenant of Grace" is,
beyond question, Wheelwright's "Fast-day sermon."
John Wheelwright was born in the Fen country of
Lincolnshire, probably in 1592.   He matriculated at
Cambridge University at about the age of eighteen,
receiving his B.A. degree in 1614 and his M.A. in 1618.
He was intimately associated with Oliver Cromwell, and
the Protector once made the remark: "I remember the
time when I was more afraid of meeting Wheelwright

---

[1] Gal. ii. 20 ; 1 Cor. i. 30 ; Eph. ii. 22.
[2] William Coddington's *A Demonstration of True Love* (1674), p. 17.   Compare Winthrop's account of this sermon, vol. i. p. 254.
[3] Winthrop, *op. cit.* vol. i. p. 240.
[4] Winthrop, *op. cit.* vol. i. p. 246.

at football, than I have been since of meeting an army in the field, for I was infallibly sure of being tripped up." [1]

He had a successful career as vicar of Bilsby, where "he was instrumental in the conversion of many souls, and was highly esteemed among serious Christians." [2] He was, however, "silenced" for nonconformity, and his vicarage was treated "as though vacant" and his successor appointed in 1633, ten years from the time of his installation.[3]   He landed in Boston in May 1636, being now married to his second wife, Mary, the daughter of Edward Hutchinson, a sister of William Hutchinson, husband of Anne.   There was a strong movement made to appoint Wheelwright a "teacher" in the church of Boston, but this plan was blocked by the vigorous opposition of Winthrop, who questioned his "soundness," asserting that he [Wheelwright] held the views that: (1) "a believer was more than a creature," *i.e.* partook of God in such a way as to be more than "a mere creature," and (2) "that the Person of the Holy Ghost and a believer were united." [4]   He was, therefore, settled at Mount Wollaston. On the 29th of January 1636, Wheelwright was invited to preach the fast-day sermon in the Boston church, which sermon led to his banishment from the colony.[5] His text was taken from Matt. ix. 15, "Can the children of the bridechamber mourn as long as the bridegroom is with them?"   He first points out that the reason for fasting is always the *absence* of Christ, since the real ground for joy and rejoicing is the presence of Christ. It is, he claims, not enough to have the gifts of the Spirit, we must have the Lord Himself; not enough to seek from the Lord "fruits and effects," but we must "see Him with a direct eye of faith and seek His Face."   "If we part with Christ we part with our life, for Christ is

---

[1] Bell's *John Wheelwright*, p. 2.

[2] Brooks's *Lives of the Puritans*, p. 472.

[3] Winthrop calls him "a silenced minister," vol. i. p. 239.

[4] Winthrop, vol. i. p. 241.   Wheelwright himself denied holding the views as attributed to him by Winthrop, *op. cit.* vol. i. p. 242.

[5] Winthrop, vol. i. pp. 256-257.   The sermon is printed in full in Bell's *John Wheelwright*.

our life "—not merely "the author of our lives," but the very root of our being, the very Life of our life.[1]

It is not enough to be under a covenant of Works, we must have Christ Himself—His very presence. The true Gospel is the revelation of Jesus Christ as our wisdom, our righteousness, our sanctification and redemption. We can attain to nothing truly spiritual until He comes into us with His righteousness, and becomes Himself our redemption. He is the Well of life of which the wells in the Old Testament were types. If the Philistines fill the Well with earth—the earth of their own inventions—the servants of the Lord must open the Well again![2]

He is the Light that lighteth every one that cometh into the world, and if we expect to keep Christ, we must hold forth this Light. There is nothing under heaven can justify any one but the revelation of the Lord Jesus Christ within him, and when He converts any soul to Himself He reveals, not some *Work*, but Himself. To look for salvation by anything short of Christ Himself is a covenant of Works, for under the covenant of Grace nothing is revealed for our righteousness but Christ Himself. This experience enables the soul to *know* that it is justified, for the faith of assurance hath Christ for its object. He gives a new heart through His working in us. This is the covenant of Grace.[3]

He admits that those under the covenant of Grace, *i.e.* those who have the inward, mystical experience, are few in number, "a little flock," while those under the covenant of Works are strong in numbers, but one *in the life* shall chase a thousand.[4] He admits also that those under a covenant of Works—the legalists, or letter Christians—are in appearance "a wondrous holy people," but the more "holy" they appear the more dangerous

---

[1] Bell, *John Wheelwright*, pp. 158-159.
[2] *Ibid.* pp. 161-163.
[3] *Ibid.* pp. 164-167.
[4] It is interesting to find that Wm. Dewsbury, who came to see the *Woodhouse* sail for America in 1657 with its load of Quaker apostles, said : "Before one of you that is in the Resurrection and Life in Christ, shall a thousand flee . . . for you in the life are the host of Heaven."—Dewsbury's *Works*, p. 171.

they are, for when Christ, who is our real sanctification, comes to the soul He makes "the creature nothing."

He admits further that this spiritual doctrine will "cause combustion in the Church," but did not Christ come to cast fire upon the earth! Peace and quietness are not the things to be most sought—but the truth of God. "To fight courageously for the Lord and to be meek are not opposites, but stand very well together." If the call for it comes, we must be willing to lay down our lives to make the truth prevail.[1]

Those who wish to enjoy the *presence of Christ* must (1) be faithful in life and word; (2) be full of love; and (3) "live pure and blameless lives and *give no occasion for others to say that we are libertines or Antinomians*!"[2] The greatest "friends" of the Church and of the commonwealth are those who hold forth Christ Himself, and who labour and endeavour to bring Him to the hearts of the people. The supreme sin is opposition to the Light and persecution of those who bring the Light. Those who have the *real presence* are in happy estate. If they lose their houses, and lands, and wives, and friends, or even lose religious ordinances, yet they cannot lose the Lord Jesus Christ—this is their great comfort. Though they should lose *all* they have, yet being made one with Christ and He dwelling in their hearts, they cannot be separated from Him.[3]

This sermon should leave no doubt in anybody's mind as to what the issue was. It was the old yet ever new issue between a religion of the past and a religion of the present, a religion based on historical facts and promises and a religion based on inward personal experience.

At the General Court, which convened on the 19th of March, attended by all the ministers in the Colony, Wheelwright was summoned, proceeded against, and

---

[1] Bell, *John Wheelwright*, pp. 167-171.

[2] No occasion *did* appear, except possibly in the case of Captain Underhill, and yet the slanderous epithet of "Antinomianism" was fixed upon the movement. Cotton Mather admits that the "opinionists," as he calls them, "appeared wondrous holy, humble, self-denying, and spiritual."—*Magnalia* (Hartford, 1853), vol. ii. p. 509.

[3] Bell, *John Wheelwright*, pp. 175-179.

condemned for having incited sedition and having shown contempt in his fast-day sermon. The action against Wheelwright aroused the citizens of Boston, and they presented a remonstrance signed by "above three score" leading persons in the town, in which petition they respectfully declared that the doctrine by "our brother Wheelwright is no other but the expressions of the Holy Ghost Himself," and they claim that the effect of his sermon has not been to incite sedition, "for wee have not drawn the sword as sometime Peter did rashly, neither have wee rescued our innocent brother as sometime the Israelites did Jonathan, and yet they did not seditiously. The covenant of Grace held forth by our brother hath taught us rather to become humble suppliants to your worships, and if wee should not prevaile, wee should rather with patience give our cheeks to the smiter." [1]

Sentence against Wheelwright was deferred to the next General Court. The case, however, hung on for months, was thoroughly canvassed in a Synod, and finally in November 1637 the Court pronounced sentence of banishment, giving the victim fourteen days "to settle his affairs" and "depart the Patent." [2] Alone and hardly knowing whither he went, the exile made his difficult way to Exeter, New Hampshire, in a weather so intense that, as he humorously writes, "the very extract-spirits of sedition and contempt," had they been in him, "would have been frozen up and indisposed for action." [3]

We must go back now to the case of Anne Hutchinson, for her views come more clearly to light through the proceedings against her, which accompanied and followed those against her brother-in-law. A Synod of all the ministers in the Colony—the first ever held in America— met at Cambridge, beginning the 9th of September 1637, and lasting twenty-four days, to thresh out the theological differences. All the "opinions" at issue were gone over in minute detail. The result was that "eighty-two opinions" were discovered and declared to be "some blasphemous, others erroneous, and all unsafe," besides

---

[1] Bell, p. 21.   [2] *Mercurius Americanus*, Bell, p. 228.   [3] *Ibid.* p. 228.

"nine unwholesome expressions," and "the Scriptures abused." Mrs. Hutchinson's "meetings," being of a "prophetical way," were voted to be a nuisance and "without rule."

The further definite results were the sentence against Wheelwright at the following General Court, as we have seen, and the trial at the same Court of Anne Hutchinson. This Court met, also at Cambridge, on the 12th of November 1637. Before it, with John Winthrop presiding, and with only three sympathisers in the company of men composing it—John Coggeshall, Thomas Leverett, and William Coddington—Anne Hutchinson appeared to defend herself. The charges brought against her were: (1) "Of having troubled the peace of the commonwealth and churches." (2) "Of having divulged and promoted opinions that cause trouble." (3) "Of having joined in affinity and affection to those upon whom the Court has passed censure" [Wheelwright and others]. (4) "Of having spoken divers things prejudicial to the honour of the Churches and the ministers." (5) "Of having maintained a meeting in your house, not comely in the sight of God, nor fitting your sex."

She was further charged, absurdly, with having "broken the law against dishonouring parents"; the "parents" in this case being the "fathers of the commonwealth." She was also charged with "seducing many honest persons"—"simple souls"—by "opinions known to be different from the Word of God," and with leading such persons to "neglect their families" and to "*spend* [*i.e.* waste] much time." To these points, marshalled by Governor Winthrop, the Deputy-Governor Thomas Dudley added other charges which are really "echoes" of Winthrop's. That "all was peace until you came"; that "by venting strange opinions you have made parties, and now have a potent party in the country"; and "that you have disparaged our ministers," which was really the sore spot.

On all these points Mrs. Hutchinson, calm, clear-headed, and straightforward, was more than a match for her accusers, and soon forced the issue deeper. The Court next took up the real matter at issue—the question of the two types of religion—the covenant of Works and the covenant of Grace. Deputy-governor Dudley raised this point and declared that he could *prove* that Mrs. Hutchinson had said that "the Gospel in the letter and in words is only a covenant of Works," and that she had claimed that those not holding as she herself did—to inward experience—were in this lower stage or covenant.[1] Whereupon Hugh Peters, the main *witness* to prove this point, came forward with the testimony, based on a private conference which the ministers had held with Anne Hutchinson, that she had said that Mr. Cotton alone preached the covenant of Grace, and that all the other ministers preached the covenant of Works, "knowing no more than the apostles did before the resurrection" [*i.e.* before enduement with the Holy Spirit] and that they did not have "the seal of Christ." Other ministers corroborated this testimony, and Deputy-governor Dudley pushed the charge a little further by insisting that she affirmed that "the Scriptures *in the letter* held forth only a covenant of Works," or as we should say to-day, are a part of externals, and not the primary matter of religion. She admitted having said so, and supported her point by quoting 2 Cor. iii. 6 : "The letter killeth, but the Spirit giveth life." [2]

It came out, in a speech of Hugh Peters, at the opening of the Court on the second day of the proceedings, that "the main thing against her is that she charged us with not being able ministers of the Gospel, and of being preachers of a covenant of Works." [3] A little later he insists again, that she said that "we ministers are not sealed with the spirit of Grace, that we preach in judgment, *but not in experience*." "She spoke out plump that we were not sealed." [4]

John Cotton, who was naturally in a most delicate and trying position, bore his testimony with much dignity,

---

[1] Hutchinson, *Massachusetts Bay*, ii. 489. [2] *Ibid*. vol. ii. pp. 495-496.
[3] *Ibid*. vol. ii. p. 501. [4] *Ibid*. vol. ii. pp. 505-506.

insight, and boldness. He said that Mrs. Hutchinson had not made such *positive* statements as were now being charged against her, that the brethren at the time of the conference had not taken her words "so ill as now," and that there *was* an actual difference between a religion of works, or letter, and one of the Spirit, pointing out that even the Apostles were for a time in the lower stage, without the witness of the Spirit, and in that stage they had been unable to preach the covenant of Grace—a religion of experience. He called to mind that Mrs. Hutchinson had said, "*You can preach no more than you know.*" And he declared that by "the seal of the Spirit" she meant "the full assurance of Divine favour, witnessed by the presence of the Holy Spirit."[1]

Anne Hutchinson herself, in a moment of rashness, now gave her enemies the key to her inner sanctuary, and lost her case by what Hugh Peters would call a "plump confession" that she sometimes received "revelations," had "openings," and "was given to see spiritual situations." "I bless the Lord," she exclaimed, "that He has let me see which was clear ministry and which was wrong. He hath let me distinguish between the voice of my Beloved and the voice of Moses." "Now," she continued solemnly, "if you do condemn me for speaking what *in my conscience I know to be the truth*, I must commit myself unto the Lord." This confession led to the following conversation :

Mr. Nowel.—How do you know that that (which was revealed to you) was of the Spirit?

Mrs. H.—How did Abraham know that it was God that bid him offer his son?

Dep.-Gov.—By an immediate voice.

Mrs. H.—*So to me by an immediate revelation.*

Dep.-Gov.—How! an immediate revelation?

Mrs. H.—By the voice of His own Spirit in my soul.[2]

Here in this discussion we find the real nerve of the issue. Here was "a mere woman" who claimed direct connection with the fount of Life and Light, who insisted

[1] Hutchinson, *Massachusetts Bay*, vol. ii. pp. 504, 505, 509.
[2] *Ibid.* vol. ii. p. 508.

that revelation is not closed, but that she herself has immediate openings like those given to Abraham. To those listening to her the claim sounded, as the wisest of them, Governor Winthrop, said, like the "most desperate enthusiasm in the world." To him, to them all, her "confession" seemed "a marvellous providence of God," a clear "mercy of God" vouchsafed to them. On her own testimony she had showed herself to be "under a devilish delusion," near kin to the worst enthusiasts of history — the Anabaptists.[1] It was now a plain and easy matter to move straight toward her condemnation and sentence.

Before sentence was pronounced, however, one valiant voice was raised in her behalf. William Coddington, seeing that judgment was about to be pronounced, defended her with what, under the circumstances, was rare boldness. He pointed out that the Court was acting unfairly in the double capacity of judge and accuser, and that the original charges against her had not been proven. He then took up the "special providence" of her own confession: "And now for that other thing which hath fallen from her occasionally by the Spirit of God; you know that the Spirit of God witnesseth with spirits, and there is no truth in Scripture but God bears witness to it by His Spirit, therefore I would intreat you to consider whether those things alleged against her deserve censure."[2]

"But," insisted Peters, conscious all the time of the real sore spot, "I was much grieved that she should say that our ministry was legal."

"What wrong was there," asked Coddington, "to say that you were not able ministers of the New Testament or that you were like the apostles—methinks the comparison was very good."[3]

But Coddington was risking himself in vain; her fate was already sealed, and Governor Winthrop proceeded to pronounce sentence. "If it be the mind of the Court that Mrs. Hutchinson is unfit for our society, and if it

---

[1] Hutchinson, *Massachusetts Bay*, vol. ii. p. 514.
[2] *Ibid.* vol. ii. p. 516.　　　[3] *Ibid.* vol. ii. p. 519.

be the mind of the Court that she shall be banished out of our liberties and imprisoned until she shall be sent forth, let them hold up their hands." [1]   All but three voted in the affirmative.

The victim was now separated from her family and condemned to a semi-imprisonment in the house of the Rev. Thomas Welde at Roxbury, where she was hard beset with clerical inquisition, and where she underwent a good deal of mental depression.[2]   It is a matter of no importance that under this unbearable strain her clerical inquisitors drew from her certain " errors and heresies." In the spring of 1637—25th March—the Church of Boston proceeded to "excommunicate" her.   All her powerful friends were silenced now.   Governor Vane had gone back to England, glad to be out of the theological tempest.   Wheelwright was eating the hard bread of exile in New Hampshire.   Coddington and his sympathisers had been forced out of the government and out of the colony.   John Cotton must have passed many silent hours of inward anguish as he halted between the two issues, but he finally deserted his friend, who had singled him out as the one minister in the colony who clearly preached the covenant of Grace, and he swung over, clear over, to the safe side, with the other ministers, and bitterly lamented that he had been " abused and made a stalking-horse of." [3]   He was selected to pronounce "admonition" against her, which he did, "with much detestation of her errors," though the awful sentence of excommunication was read by the pastor, Mr. Wilson: " In the name of the Lord Jesus Christ, and in the name of the Church, I do not only pronounce you worthy to be cast out, but I do cast you out ; and in the name of Christ I do deliver you up to Satan. I do account you from this time forth to be a heathen and a publican. I command you in the name of Jesus Christ and of this Church as a leper to withdraw yourself out of this congregation."   As the outcast slowly found her way

[1] Hutchinson, *Massachusetts Bay*, vol. ii. p. 520.

[2] It is important to note her physical condition—she was soon to give birth to a child.   [3] Winthrop, vol. i. p. 304.

down the aisle, to go out for ever into exile, Mary Dyer stepped forth from her seat, took her place by Anne Hutchinson's side and went out with her—one day to come back again !

Mrs. Hutchinson now found her way to the new colony which her friends had gone on ahead to found in the island of " Aquiday "—Aquidneck—now called the island of Rhode Island. This island was destined to be the shelter and safe nursery of Quakerism in the days of its early stress in the New World, and we must now briefly study the new, strange colony which owed its birth to the " Antinomian" turmoil in Massachusetts Bay.[1] The new colony was founded by persons who were either banished for taking a sympathetic part in the Hutchinson controversy, or who revolted against the heavy hand of authority in Massachusetts Bay.[2] Winthrop says: " At this time the good providence of God so disposed that divers of the congregation, being the chief men of the Antinomian party, were gone to Narragansett to seek out a new place for plantation."[3] The fact was that the Court which banished Wheelwright and condemned Anne Hutchinson, also dealt vigorously with the citizens of Boston who had signed the petition in

[1] There were doubtless many things involved in this famous controversy. The subtle political issues between the party of Winthrop and the party of Vane I have not touched upon. The lukewarmness of the citizens of Boston, when the colony was girding itself for the Pequot war, was supposed by Winthrop and others to be due to the prevalence of the "new opinions" in religion. But it is clear, nevertheless, that the central trouble lay in these two points : The leaders of the new party had boldly criticised the ministers of the colony for being legal and not spiritual ; and secondly, they had insisted on the fact of present revelation as against the view that God's Word is found only in a Book. It was for these heresies that Wheelwright was forced to wander through the snow to Exeter, and it was for these heresies that Anne Hutchinson was flung out of the colony as a leper. These exiles had thus already struck the central issues which the Quakers forced to the front a score of years later.

[2] The Rhode Island Colony must be carefully distinguished from the Providence Colony, founded by Roger Williams, also an exile from the Massachusetts Colony. Roger Williams has the honour of being one of the brave path-breakers toward the light, and he was undoubtedly the first in the New World to annunciate clearly the doctrine of soul-liberty. I have no desire to detract from the fame which properly belongs to him, but it is a plain fact that the island colony in the southern end of Narragansett quickly outstripped in importance the one founded at Providence, and it was here on this island of Aquidneck that the principle of spiritual freedom got its most impressive exhibition in the primitive stage of American history.

[3] Winthrop, vol. i. p. 311.

favour of Wheelwright. Twenty of the signers in fear "acknowledged their fault" and were forgiven; the rest were "disarmed," in which list were a number of the founders of the little colony on Aquidneck—the persons "disposed by the providence of God to seek out a new place for plantation."[1] The little party sent John Clarke, with two companions, on ahead to locate the place of settlement and, with the advice and assistance of Roger Williams, with whom they took counsel, they decided upon Pocasset (now Portsmouth), on the island then called "Aquiday," now called "Rhode Island."[2] On the 7th of March 1638, nineteen members of the new colony signed in Providence a civil compact for the incorporation of their new "Body Politick," and they proceeded to elect William Coddington, clearly the leader and foremost person in the little group, their Judge. The simple form of government, which was here initiated, was slightly modified in January 1639, when a plan was drafted which provided for "three elders" to assist the Judge, and they were to report their acts every quarter to the assembled freemen with this curious arrangement for veto : " If by the Body [of freemen] or any of them, the Lord shall be pleased to dispense light to the contrary of what by the Judge and Elders hath been determined formerly, that then and there it shall be repealed as the act of the Body."[3]

In April 1639 the little colonial hive at Pocasset "swarmed" and formed a new town, which was named Newport, on the other edge of the island.[4] At first it was an independent settlement under a separate government, with Coddington for "Judge," Nicholas Easton, John Coggeshall, and William Brenton as "Elders," while the settlement at Pocasset chose William Hutchin-

[1] Of the "founders" William Aspinwall was banished, John Coggeshall was disarmed and disfranchised, William Coddington and nine others were given leave to depart within three months, and were afterwards hurried off.

[2] See John Clarke's "Ill Newes from New England," printed in 4 *Mass. Hist. Soc. Col.* ii. The name was changed from Aquidneck to Rhode Island 13th March 1644.

[3] *Rhode Island Colony Records*, i. p. 63.

[4] Nicholas Easton built the first house in Newport. (See *Narr. Hist. Reg.* vol. viii. p. 240.)

son, husband of Anne, for Judge. The two settlements
were united under one government in March 1640 with
William Coddington of Newport as Governor, and
William Brenton of Pocasset (at this time changed to
Portsmouth) as Deputy-governor. A year later, namely
in May 1641, the assembled citizens unanimously declared
that "this Body Politick is a Democracie ; that is to say,
it is in the Power of the Body of Freemen, orderly
assembled, or the major part of them, to make Just
Lawes by which they will be regulated." [1] Under the
same date this memorable act was passed : "*It is ordered
that none bee accounted a delinquent for doctrine.*" [2] In
November of the same year it was decreed that the
"Law of the last Court, made concerning Libertie of
Conscience in Point of Doctrine be perpetuated." [3] And
this colony, in the face of severe tests and difficulties,
maintained this principle in practice. [4]

In 1641 the persons who composed the Newport
settlement seem to have arranged themselves into two
religious groups. One party, with Coddington, Coggeshall, and Nicholas Easton as leaders, formulated views
which seem extraordinarily akin to those later held by
the Society of Friends ; while the other group, led by
John Clarke, formed a Baptist Church.

It is extremely difficult now to get the facts on these
important points. Winthrop says, under date of 1641 :

"Mrs. Hutchinson and those of Aquiday Island broached new
heresies every year. Divers of them turned professed Anabaptist, [5] and would not wear any arms, [6] and denied all

---

[1] *Rhode Island Colony Records*, i. 112.

[2] *Ibid.* p. 113.   [3] *Ibid.* p. 118.

[4] Cotton Mather gives this account of freedom of faith in the Rhode Island
Colony : "I believe there never was held such a variety of religions together on
as small a spot of ground as have been in that colony." "If a man had lost
his religion he might find it at the general muster of the opinionists." "Rhode
Island hath usually been the Gerizzim of New England."—*Magnalia*, ii.
520-521.

[5] The term "Anabaptist," used in such an account, hardly means more than
that the person was a dissenter from the established faith and held strongly for
inward experience in religion. See my *Studies in Mystical Religion*, chapter on
"The Anabaptists" (London, 1909).

[6] Nicholas Easton was fined five shillings in 1639, for coming to meeting
without his weapons.—*Rhode Island Colony Records*, i. 95.

magistracy among Christians, and maintained that there were no churches since those founded by the apostles and evangelists, nor could any be, nor any pastors ordained, nor seals administered, but by such, and that the church was to want these all the time she continued in the wilderness, as yet she was." [1]

It is not probable from what we know that any of the persons prominent in this "spiritual circle" denied magistracy or were opposed to settled social order. It is probable that they did insist that religion must be an affair of experience and that a true church could not be established or maintained by persons who were "out of the life" and only externally religious. The real situation comes out somewhat clearer in another passage in Winthrop:

"Other troubles arose in the island of Aquiday by reason of one Nicholas Easton, a tanner, a man very bold, though ignorant.[2] He using to teach [i.e. taking upon himself to teach] where Mr. Coddington their Governor lived, maintained that man hath no power or will in himself, but as he is acted [upon] by God, and that a Christian is united to the essence of God." [3]

Winthrop undertakes to show, by inference, that this view of Easton's makes God the author of sin, and has blasphemous consequences. But Easton did not push his view to dangerous lengths and apparently held, exactly what Friends later held, that there is something of God in man, and that man becomes a truly "spiritual being" by reason of this Divine connection. Winthrop further says that Mr. Coddington, Mr. Coggeshall, and some others joined with Nicholas Easton, "while Mr. Clark [John Clarke], Mr. Lenthall and some others dissented, and publicly opposed, whereby it grew to such heat of contention that it made a schism." [4]   There was, it plainly appears, thus differentiated here in Newport, fifteen years

---

[1] Winthrop, ii. 46.   Winthrop is here giving a description of what is known as the "Seeker" attitude (see *Studies in Mystical Religion*).   It is likely that some of the group in Newport insisted that only spiritual persons can perform spiritual exercises.   There is no evidence that they went further than this.

[2] This is an instance of Winthrop's unfairness through prejudice.   Easton was a man of high standing and excellent mental parts.   He was three times President of the Colony, six times Deputy-Governor, and three times Governor.

[3] Winthrop, ii. 48.   [4] Winthrop, ii. 49.

before the coming of the Quakers, a group of persons who were Quakers in everything but name.[1]

Even more striking, if anything, was the situation in Portsmouth. Letchford, who resided in New England "almost the space of four years" prior to 1641, and who spent some time in the Colony on Rhode Island, says, after commenting on the state of religion at Newport:

> "At the other end of the Island there is another town called Portsmouth, but no church [*i.e.* no established church]; there is a meeting of some men who there teach one another and call it prophesie."[2]

This looks as though a meeting was being held in Portsmouth at this date in which the members spoke as they felt "moved" (for that is what "in the way of prophesie" means), exactly as the Quaker meeting was held a little later.[3]

---

[1] It should be remembered that this was at least six years before George Fox began his religious activity in England.

[2] Letchford's *Plaine Dealing* (Boston reprint, 1868), p. 94.

[3] We shall see in later chapters that there were other pre-Quaker circles in the colonies all ready to be merged into the wider Quaker movement as soon as it made itself felt on these shores. The "circles" at Salem and at Sandwich, Mass., were the most important ones. Mrs. Hutchinson did not live long enough to hear of the Quaker movement, for the spread of which she did much to prepare the way. Her husband, William Hutchinson, died in 1642, and soon after she moved with her family into the territory of the Dutch, settling near Hell Gate in West Chester Co., New York. Here in the autumn of 1643 she was murdered by Indians, who "slew her, and her family, her daughter and her daughter's husband, and all their children," except a little girl who was carried into captivity. This calamity was hailed in the Puritan Colony as a "Divine Judgment." (See Welde's *Rise, Reign, and Ruin*, and Mather's *Magnalia*.) Anne Hutchinson's sister, Catharine Scott, and her family, formed the nucleus of the original group of Friends in Providence.

CHAPTER II

THE QUAKERS AT THE GATES

THE Quaker message had first been heralded in London by women, and the first attempt to win over the Universities of England to the "truth," as the early Quakers persistently called their Gospel, was made by women. So too, the first Quakers to reach the American hemisphere were women, who in deep seriousness regarded themselves as apostolic messengers under divine call and direction. They were Mary Fisher and Ann Austin. Their first place of landing and of missionary activity was the island of Barbadoes, where they arrived near the end of the year 1655. The island of Barbadoes was, during the seventeenth century, the great port of entry to the colonies in the western world, and it was during the last half of that century, a veritable "hive" of Quakerism. Friends wishing to reach any part of the American coast, sailed most frequently for Barbadoes and then reshipped for their definite locality. They generally spent some weeks, or months even, propagating their doctrines in "the island" and ordinarily paying visits to Jamaica and often to Antigua, Nevis, and Bermuda. Large Friends' meetings rapidly sprang up on all these islands. Barbadoes had been first occupied by the English in 1605, and had submitted to the authority of the commonwealth in 1652. Sugar-making had, as early as 1640, become its great industry, being carried on by negro slaves who had been brought from Africa, and the island enjoyed unrestricted trade. It was just now at the height of its prosperity and large fortunes were being made there. It is estimated that there were 25,000 inhabitants, and not less than 10,000 slaves. Of the inhabitants Clarendon said they were principally men "who had retired thither only to be quiet and to be free from noise and oppressions in England." Among these quiet, comfortable, prosperous people, the two "publishers of the truth" as we have seen, came in 1655, and they spent about six months here publishing their message.

Mary Fisher was, at the time of her visit, a young, unmarried woman of about twenty-two years of age, adorned with somewhat uncommon "intellectual faculties" and marked by "gravity of deportment."

She had been a servant in the home of the Tomlinsons of Selby in Yorkshire, and had been "convinced" of the truth of the Quaker message in the early years of Fox's ministry, and went forth as a minister herself in 1652. The first two years of her ministry were mostly spent in York Castle, where she endured two terms of imprisonment, one of sixteen months and one of six. Between these two imprisonments, Mary Fisher, with a woman companion, undertook the hazardous mission of carrying the Quaker message to the students of Cambridge University. The students jeered and derided, "with froth and levity." The mayor of the city ordered the women to be stripped to the waist and "whipped at the market cross till the blood ran down their bodies," a sentence which was cruelly executed, while the women prayed the Lord to forgive their persecutors.[1] Little is known of the life of Ann Austin, previous to her American visit, except that she was already "stricken in years," the mother of five children, apparently a resident of London, and plainly enough valiant and ready for the perils of her dangerous calling. Their work in Barbadoes seems to have been successful. As they were leaving the island for their hazardous venture in New England, Mary Fisher wrote to her friends in England: "Here is many convinced and many desire to know the way." On their return, after they had been flung out of Boston,

[1] Besse, *Sufferings of the Quakers* (London 1753), vol. i. p. 85.

they continued the work in Barbadoes, and had their faith and zeal well rewarded. Lieutenant-Colonel Rous, a wealthy sugar-planter, and his son John were the first to identify themselves with Friends and to join the movement. They were in fact the first persons in the West Indies to become Quakers. The son, John Rous, came forward almost immediately in the ministry, and before the year was out had issued a characteristic Quaker tract: "A Warning to the inhabitants who live in pride, drunkenness, etc., also something to the Rulers, that they rule rightly and do justice on the wicked." [1]

In the month of July 1656, Master Simon Kempthorn, in his ship *Swallow*, sailing from Barbadoes, brought those two women into Boston harbour. Governor Endicott was at that moment absent from the city, and Deputy-governor Richard Bellingham found himself confronted with an "extraordinary occasion." He seems to have been equal to it. He ordered the women to be kept on the ship while their boxes were searched for books containing "corrupt, heretical, and blasphemous doctrines." One hundred such books were found in their possession. These were seized and burned in the market-place by the common hangman.[2] This being done the women were brought to land and committed to prison on the sole charge of being "Quakers," deprived of light, and of all writing materials, though as yet no law had made it a punishable offence to be a Quaker. A fine of five pounds was laid upon any one who should speak with them, and, to make assurance doubly sure, their prison window was closely boarded up. They were furthermore "stripped stark naked," and searched for "tokens" of witchcraft upon their bodies.[3] There was one bright spot in the dark experience. One man (who was evidently Nicholas Upsall) came to the prison and offered gladly to pay

---

[1] Letter to Margaret Fell.—Swarthmore Collection, in Devonshire House, London, i. 66.

[2] Snow, in his *History of Boston* (1825), says that Nicholas Upsall, a citizen of Boston, endeavoured to buy these Quaker books.—Snow, *op. cit.* p. 196.

[3] See Bishop's *New England Judged* (London, 1703), p. 12. Henry Fell, in a letter to M. Fell, gives an account of the searching of these women as suspected witches.—Swarthmore Collection, i. 66.

the fine of five pounds if he might be allowed to have conversation with the Quaker prisoners.[1]

After they had been kept five weeks in confinement under these extraordinary conditions, the master of the vessel which brought them was put under a bond of one hundred pounds, to see that they were transported to Barbadoes, and he apparently was compelled to pay the costs of their transportation.[2]   The Boston jailer had to content himself with their bedding and their Bibles for his prison fees.   Governor Endicott, on his return, remarked that if *he* had been at home they would not have got away without a whipping.

George Bishop, whose book is the main source of our information on the details of the New England " invasion " asks of the magistrates the pertinent question :   " Why was it that the coming of two women so shook ye, as if a formidable army had invaded your borders." [3]   The answer, given at the time, was a string of vague charges and hysterical epithets.   A clearer answer can perhaps be given at this distance and from the perspective of historical review.

It must be said in the first place that the judgment of the officials, and particularly of the ministers, in the Massachusetts Colony had been seriously prejudiced by rumours and accounts that had preceded the arrival of the two women.   Anti-Quaker pamphlets had already come from the press in great numbers, and they were unsparing in their accounts of the new " heresy."   Some of these pamphlets were written by ministers who, either before or after the publication of their attack, were settled in New England and were in high repute there. Francis Higginson, the author of *A Brief Relation of the Irreligion of the Northern Quakers*, published in 1653, and one of the earliest polemics against Friends, was a New Englander.   Thomas Welde, who had been a

---

[1] See Henry Fell's letter to M. Fell.—Swarthmore Collection, i. 66.

[2] The master of the vessel which took them to Barbadoes was put under a bond of one hundred pounds to land them there and not to suffer any persons in the Colony to speak with them in the harbour before they sailed.

[3] *New England Judged*, p. 7.

minister in high favour in Massachusetts, and who had taken a very prominent part in the heresy trials and expulsion of Anne Hutchinson and her friends, was the principal author of two violent anti-Quaker Tracts, *The Perfect Pharisee under Monkish Holinesse*, and *A further Discovery of that Generation of Men called Quakers*, issued in 1653 and 1654. Samuel Eaton, author of *The Quakers confuted*, published in 1654, was brother of Theophilus Eaton, a governor of New Haven, and had been a preacher in New England. Christopher Marshall of Woodkirk, who had been James Nayler's pastor, and who poured forth a torrent of abuse upon George Fox and the Quakers, had intimate associations with Boston, where he had been a member of John Cotton's Church, and had been trained in the ministry by that famous teacher.[1] The writings of trusted leaders such as these had made Quakerism an accursed thing before any Quaker crossed the Atlantic. The Quakers were already catalogued as a new type of religious *Enthusiasts*, like the sect which for a hundred years had made the name of Münster a word of terror.[2] In fact one of the Massachusetts "Declarations" against the Quakers traces their pedigree directly to these fanatics of the century before :

"The prudence of this Court was exercised in making provision to secure Peace and Order against their Attempts, whose design (we were well-assured by our own experience *as well as by the example of their Predecessors in Münster*) was to undermine and ruin the same."[3]

The allusion to Münster comes out also in a Petition sent in 1658 to the General Court for severe laws against the Quakers. The petitioners say :

"Their [the Quakers] incorrigibleness, after so much means used both for their conviction and for preserving this place

---

[1] See *Transactions of the Cong. Hist. Soc.*, March 1903, p. 224. For Marshall's attacks on Fox, see *Journal*, i. 107.

[2] A fanatical band of Anabaptists captured the city of Münster in 1534, and disturbed the world with their strange "Kingdom."

[3] *New England Judged*, p. 3.

from *contagion*, being such, as by reason of their malignant obduratices [*sic*], daily increaseth rather than abateth our fear of the spirit of Muncer [Münster], or John of Leyden revived." [1]

Nearly all the Massachusetts enactments against the Quakers refer not only to their "horrid opinions" and "diabolical doctrines," but also to their dangerous leaven of "mutiny, sedition and rebellion," their subtle designs to "overthrow the order established in Church and commonwealth." This was, as we in this calm generation know, a pure figment of the imagination, but it was, nevertheless, a live and propulsive idea then in the minds of the ministers and magistrates, and must be reckoned with in judging their treatment of the Quakers. [2]

There was always hanging over the Puritan colonists, another terror, to us very pale and remote, to them very real and imminent—the terror of witchcraft ; the awful power of Satan to transform a human person into a tool of malice and mischief. Bellingham's own sister-in-law had been executed as a witch only a few months before the arrival of these two Quaker women, and the eager search of their naked bodies for "tokens" was very significant ; and if a mark or blemish had been found on their bodies, something besides *books* might have burned in the market-place.

There can be no doubt that these "phobias," these unreasoned and morbid delusions, were potent factors in predisposing the authorities to a sternly hostile attitude toward these harmless women missionaries. But there was a deeper and solider ground for their hostile attitude than these "obsessing ideas" furnish. These women were the bearers of a type of religion sharply at variance, and in fact irreconcilable with that already established in Massachusetts. Feeble as they were, they were the

---

[1] *Massachusetts Archives*, vol. x. p. 246.
[2] This hysterical fear of " designs to overthrow the established order " was a prominent element in the treatment of the Hutchinson party, though there was not the slightest ground for it. Cotton Mather, even after overwhelming evidence that the Quakers had no designs against established order, still in his day called them " dangerous villains."—*Magnalia*, vol. ii. p. 256.

vanguard of an army, and they represented a new spiritual empire in array against the spiritual empire which the Puritan in stern consecration was building. There was no delusion in the statement of the Court that "the tenetts and practices of the Quakers are opposite to the orthodoxe received opinions and practices of the *godly*," *i.e.* of the Massachusetts ministers.[1] We must try to see fairly and honestly what these "tenetts and practices" were.

The central truth on which the Quaker of that period staked his faith and to which he pledged his life, was the presence of a Divine Light in the soul. It is an important historical fact that every Quaker in 1656 held this inward Light in the Soul to be the essential truth of religion.[2] God, they said, has placed a Divine principle— something of Himself—in every man. This Light within condemns every step toward sin and evil, it approves every act of rectitude and every movement in the direction of righteousness. It is, in fact, a continuation now in many lives of that Christ, that Word of God and Light of the World and incorruptible Seed of God that was incarnate in One Life in Galilee and Judea.[3] As fast and as far, they said, as any one obeys this Light it leads him into all truth and into perfection of life, "sets him atop of the devil and all his works." "In this Eternal Life and Power," they said, "you continually grow up in the Life of God—the life that never dies."[4] Salvation was, thus, for them not a transaction but a transformation : not a forensic escape from the penalty due for their sins, but an actual deliverance from *sin*

---

[1] Proceedings of the General Court held in Boston 19th of October 1658.

[2] Cotton Mather says with much revulsion : "They call men to attend to the mystical dispensation of a Light within, as having the whole of religion contained therein."—*Magnalia*, vol. ii, p. 523.

Neal in similar vein says : "The Light within they affirmed to be sufficient to salvation without anything else."—*Hist. of New England*, vol. i. p. 322.

[3] "This Seed and Birth of God in us is a living Principle ; yea, it is a measure of the same Life and Spirit of Jesus Christ."—From George Keith's *Immediate Revelation*, p. 248.

"The Quakers believe both in a Christ without and a Christ within, but not as two Christs, but one and the same without as within."—John Whiting, *The Sword of the Lord Drawn*, p. 5.

[4] Edward Burrough, *Works* (1672) p. 75.

itself. "To witness [*i.e.* experience] God within you, the Immanuel, the Saviour, God-with-you, is the whole salvation, there is no other to be expected than this. To witness that God dwells in us and walks in us is to be begotten by the Word of God, to be born of the Immortal Seed and to be a New Creature." [1] Not only did they insist that they possessed within themselves a Principle of moral illumination, a Power at war with sin in them, an Immanuel-God working· in them to free them from all sin and to raise them to immortal life, but they claimed still further that they were the recipients of direct revelations.

"I have had," said Fox, "a word from the Lord as the prophets and apostles had." They were simple, humble men and women, quite devoid of cheap ambitions, and singularly free from vain desire to gain mastery over their fellows by bold assumptions ; but they believed, with a conviction which no torture could shake, that the infinite God revealed His will in their souls. They held it for certain that they moved under orders from above, and that even in matters of seemingly slight importance they were *guided* as by a heavenly vision. One of the men who was called to pass through the martyr-baptism on Boston Common has left this simple, straightforward account of his " call " :

"In the beginning of the year 1655, I was at the plough in the east part of Yorkshire in Old England, near the place where my outward being began, and as I walked after the plough, I was filled with the Love and the presence of the Living God which did ravish my heart when I felt it ; for it did increase and abound in me like a living stream, and the Love and Life of God ran through me like precious ointment giving a pleasant smell, which made me stand still ; and as I stood a little still, with my heart and mind stayed on the Lord, th ҆ Word of the Lord came to me in a still small voice, which I did hear perfectly, saying to me, in the secret of my heart and conscience, 'I have ordained thee a prophet unto the Nations.' " [2]

---

[1] Burrough, *A General Epistle to the Saints.*
[2] From a letter of Marmaduke Stephenson written from Boston Prison.—*New England Judged*, pp. 131-133.

Similar accounts of experiences, believed to be " openings " of call and guidance, could be given from almost every Quaker pamphlet of that period, and there can be no question that the leading Friends of that date felt themselves to belong to the order of prophets and apostles.[1]   This faith and expectation created the peculiar type of meeting, known as " the meeting for worship," which was one of the most unique features of the Quakerism that was now knocking for admission at the port of Boston.   The members sat down in silence, with no ordained minister, with no prearrangements, no preparation for vocal service of any sort.   They believed that sensitive souls could become aware of celestial currents, and that no words should be spoken in prayer or ministry until the lips were divinely *moved*.   It was a bold experiment, an attempt to realise the prophetic ideal of Jeremiah that there should be a new Israel, with God's law in their inward parts, and with His will written in their hearts.[2]   It meant nothing less than the claim that revelation is continuous, and that by the work of the Divine Spirit there is a true *apostolic succession*.

Another bold feature of this new religion was the absence of all sacraments.   The sacraments are " shadows," they said ; Christ came to bring men to realities, and they were satisfied that they had found the realities.   " The Spirit of God changes the ground [*i.e.* nature] of the soul, and transmutes it into His own nature, while all those things which men strive so much about are but shadows." [3]   " There is," says another of their leaders, " a spiritual communion which reaches beyond all

---

[1] The inference which their opponents drew was that they denied, or even discarded the Holy Scriptures, and they were almost invariably "examined" on this point.   As a matter of fact, they never denied or discarded the Scriptures ; they simply denied that they were the *only* Rule of faith and practice ; since, they insisted, the Light of Christ in the heart in conjunction with the Scriptures is most certainly a guide and rule.   They were also supposed to be very unsound on the doctrine of the Trinity, and they were frequently "tested" on this article of faith.   They generally gave this discreet if somewhat inconclusive answer : "The Father, Son, and Holy Spirit we own [*i.e.* believe in], but a Trinity of Persons the Scriptures speak not of !"   See Humphrey Norton's *Ensign*, p. 8.

[2] Jer. xxxi. 33-34.

[3] Francis Howgil, *Works* (1676), p. 53.

visibles and is above all mortal and fading things."
"The Lord," is the mighty claim of still another, "hath
brought me into a life which I live by the springing up
of life within me."

It was, thus, a religion of first-hand experience, based
primarily not on historical happenings but on inward
events. Its messengers declared that they had found the
perennial springs of Life, and they claimed that these
springs were bubbling within their own souls. In the
power and joy of this "inward bubbling," the Quaker felt
a *certainty* of his election which the Puritan did not have.
"As I was walking in the fields," says Fox, "the Lord
said unto me, 'Thy name is written in the Lamb's book
of life,' and as the Lord spoke it I believed."[1] "The
Lord said unto me," writes William Robinson just before
his execution in Boston, "'thy soul shall rest in everlasting peace and thy life shall enter into rest.'"[2] This
note of certainty rings through all the writings of the
first Friends. "We are raised from the dead, we are
born of the Immortal Seed, and we have entered into
God's Eternal Life—the Life that never dies," is the
constantly recurring testimony. John Fiske, who more
than any other historian of Colonial America has
succeeded in understanding the Quaker position, very
truly says:

"The ideal of the Quakers was flatly antagonistic to that
of the settlers of Massachusetts. The Christianity of the
former was freed from Judaism as far as was possible; the
Christianity of the latter was heavily encumbered with Judaism.
The Quaker aimed at complete separation between Church and
State; the government of Massachusetts was patterned after
the ancient Jewish theocracy in which church and state were
identified. The Quaker was tolerant of differences in doctrine;
the Calvinist regarded such tolerance as a deadly sin. For
these reasons the arrival of a few Quakers in Boston in 1656
was considered an act of invasion and treated as such."[3]

Even more obnoxious to the Puritan, certainly to the

---

[1] *Journal*, vol. i. p. 35.
[2] Letter from Wm. Robinson written in Boston Prison 19th of 8th month 1659.
[3] Fiske, *Dutch and Quaker Colonies*, vol. ii. p. 112.

Puritan divines, than their ideals or than their theology was the Quakers' estimate of official ministers. They could be as tender as a woman toward any types of men who were low down, hard pressed and sore bestead, but they were relentless against what they called "hireling ministry." They used very vivid phrases to describe it, and they were as intolerant of it as the writer of Deuteronomy had been of the idolatry of his day. They hewed at it as fiercely as Samuel had hewed Agag.

Quakerism was, one sees, a type of religion at every point in sharp contrast with that which the Puritans had established in the Massachusetts Bay Colony. They were, as has been said, two different spiritual empires. The leaders were incapable of understanding each other, and there was foredoomed to be a clash with tragic consequences. We shall dwell as little as possible on the tragedy, and we shall endeavour to understand the attitude of the persecutors as well as undertake to bring to clear light in these pages the mission of the Quakers in the New World and the type of their religion.

Two days after Ann Austin and Mary Fisher, without bedding and without Bibles, sailed out of Boston harbour, that is, August 7th, 1656, a ship carrying eight Quakers—"pretty hearts, the blessing of the Lord with them and His dread going before them" [1]—sailed in. They were Christopher Holder, a valiant apostle of New England Quakerism, John Copeland, Thomas Thurston, William Brend, Mary Prince, Sarah Gibbons, Mary Wetherhead, and Dorothy Waugh. With them also came from Long Island a man by the name of Richard Smith, of whom we shall hear later. Officers of the Commonwealth were sent on board the ship to search their boxes for "erroneous books and hellish pamphlets," [2]

---

[1] Letter of Francis Howgil in Caton Collection of MSS.

[2] Humphrey Norton's *New England's Ensign*, p. 8. The title-page of *New England's Ensign* reads : It being the account of Cruelty, the professor's pride and the articles of their faith signified in characters written in blood, etc. This being an account of the sufferings sustained by us in New England (with the Dutch) the most part of it in these two last years 1657, 1658. Written at sea by us whom the wicked in scorn call Quakers in the second month of the year 1659. London, 1659.

and the Friends, after the examination of their views on the Divine Nature and the Scriptures, were lodged in the prison vacated two days before—a prison which, Bishop says, addressing the magistrates in 1660, "ye have supplied with the bodies of the saints and servants of Jesus, for the most part ever since: scarce one taken out, but some one or other put into his room." [1]

The examination above referred to gave the prisoners their one chance of delivering the message for which they had come, though the soil on which the seed fell was not likely to be of a very receptive sort. One of the Boston ministers (Humphrey Norton says it was John Norton) during the examination quoted the passage from 2 Peter, "we have a more sure word of prophecy," [2] to prove that the Scriptures are the only rule of faith and sole guide of life. This was the Quaker's master-text and the prisoners at once accepted the challenge. They forced the minister to admit that the passage referred to the Word of God manifested within the soul when the spiritual day dawn has come and the Day Star has risen in the heart. "Where is the 'dark place' of which the text speaks?" John Norton asked William Brend. "It is under my hand," answered the old Friend, with his hand on his breast. The Friends then turned questioners and asked John Norton whether the Eternal Word was a sufficient rule and guide or not. He said "Yea." He was then asked whether it was *his* rule and guide. He replied that it was when he was rightly guided. The magistrates then cried out to know what was the difference between him and the Quakers! As the examination came to an end Governor Endicott, now home from his journey, made the significant remark: "Take care that you do not break our ecclesiastical laws, for then you are sure to stretch by a halter." [3]

They were kept for eleven weeks in close confinement, deprived of all material comforts, and frequently examined by the ministers of the Colony. At the end of this period

---

[1] *New England Judged*, p. 41.   [2] 2 Peter i. 19.
[3] *Ensign*, p. 9; *New England Judged*, p. 10.

the master of their vessel, though somewhat recalcitrant, and citing his rights as a citizen to convey freeborn Englishmen whithersoever he would, was compelled under a bond of £500 to transport the eight Quakers back to the mother country.   One of the most interesting episodes of their imprisonment was the correspondence carried on between them and Samuel Gorton of Warwick, Rhode Island.   He himself had endeavoured to expound a mystical religion, and had suffered much for his doctrines.   He had been banished from Massachusetts and had founded a tiny colony at Warwick, under the patronage of the Earl of Warwick, where he and his followers found peace, and he seems to have conceived the idea of opening his colony as a base of activity for the Quakers.   His first letter is dated 16th September 1656, and is addressed "To the Strangers and out-casts, with respect to carnall Israel, now in prison at Boston, for the name of Christ."   He writes:

"The report of your demeanour . . . . as also the errand you come upon hath much taken my heart, so that I cannot withhold my hand from expressing its desires after you.   That present habitation of yours ourselves have had a proof of from like grounds and reasons that have possessed you thereof, unto which in some measure we still remain in point of banishment under pain of death, out of these parts. . . . No doubt but the bolts will fly back in the best season, both in regard of your-selves and us."

Then after some odd and peculiar advice to them, and comments upon his own buried condition " in a corner of the earth grudged even as burying-place," he adds:

"But our God may please to send some of his Saints unto us to speak words which the dead hearing them shall live.   I may not trouble you further at this time, onely if we knew that you have a mind to stay in these parts after your enlargement (for we hear that you are to be sent back to England) and what time the ship would saile, or could have hope the Master would deliver you, we would endeavour to have a Vessell in readinesse, when the Ship goeth out of harbour, to take you in, and set you where you may enjoy your liberty." . . . "In Spirit cleave unto

Him (as being in you) who is ever the same all sufficient: In whom I am yours, Samuel Gorton." [1]

The Friends wrote a long and appreciative answer to this friendly letter, beginning with the salutation : " In that Measure [of Light] which we have received, which is eternall, we see thee and behold thee and have onenesse with thee." They then declare that their minds are set to stay in Massachusetts—" we are unwilling to go out of these parts, if here we could be suffered to stay, but we are willing to mind the Lord, and," they add, " if He in His wisdome shall raise thee up, and others for that end, we shall be willing to accept it." [2] They were, however, prevented from accepting his offer because the captain was under bond to take them to England, and to land them nowhere else. Richard Smith, a little later, was sent home to Long Island by sea, lest by any chance he might spread the contagion of his heresy, if he were allowed to go by land.

But in spite of all these precautions to keep the commonwealth immune, there were positive signs of infection. There was living at this time in Boston an honest, independent-minded man, already well advanced in years, named Nicholas Upsall. He was, in the language of the time, " sober, and of unblameable conversation," and, though diligent, his inward longings for the refreshment of his soul were unsatisfied. He heard, with the rest, of the arrival of the two Quaker women, and he tried to save the hundred books which were doomed to go up in smoke, but the report of their doctrines interested and impressed him rather than disturbed him. He heard that the women were being starved in the prison, and he resolved that they should be fed. By the payment of five shillings a week, he induced the jailer to let him feed them and throughout their imprisonment they ate his provisions. As events pro-

---

[1] Gorton's *Antidote Against the Common Plague of the World*. Printed in *Rhode Island Historical Collection*, vol. ii.

[2] Their letter is also printed in the *Antidote*. Gorton also wrote a second letter in which he notes that " God hath frustrated our desired design we doubt not but for the best."

gressed he was carried on with them farther than he had expected. While the eight Quakers were in prison, the General Court of Massachusetts, with the sanction of the "Commissioners of the United Provinces," passed their first law against the Quakers—"a cursed sect of heretics who take upon themselves to be immediately sent of God, and infallibly assisted by the Spirit."[1] The law enacted a fine of £100 upon any master of a sailing craft who should bring a Quaker to the Colony, and a fine of £5 upon any one who should bring into the jurisdiction any Quaker book, or conceal one in his house.[2] It was further enacted that if by any means a Quaker should make his way into the Colony, he should be arrested, whipped, committed to the house of correction, kept constantly at work, and prevented from having conversation with any one until he was once more out of the jurisdiction.

While this law was being proclaimed through the streets of Boston, preceded by beat of drum, the old man Nicholas Upsall, standing in front of his own door, raised his voice in protest. He was brought before the court, and here, "in tenderness and love," he solemnly warned the magistrates against the course they were pursuing. He was fined £20 and banished from the Colony, spending the winter of 1656 in Sandwich in the Plymouth Colony, and making his way in the spring to that haven of rest for persecuted Christians, the island of Rhode Island, where he received a kindly welcome from the citizens of the Aquidneck Colony.[3] His tale of hardship won the hearts of the Indians, who were unsophisticated in theology. One of the chiefs called him "friend," and offered to build him a comfortable house, if he could accept his hospitality, commenting with instinctive insight on the old man's persecutors : "What a God have the English who deal so with one another over the worship of their God."[4]

---

[1] *Colony Records of Massachusetts*, vol. iv. part i. p. 277.

[2] *Ibid.* p. 308.

[3] The Order fining Nicholas Upsall "for reproaching the honoured magistrates, and speaking against the law made and published against the Quakers," is in *Colony Records of Massachusetts*, vol. iv. part i. p. 279.

[4] *The Ensign*, p. 14.

Nicholas Upsall became fully convinced, and accepted the truth which the Quakers taught. He is thus the first fruit of the planting in New England, the first citizen of Massachusetts to join his lot with the Quakers.

The knocking at the gates had thus begun ; the next year, 1657, was to witness something like an incipient " invasion."

We must now return for a brief examination of the progress of the work in the West Indies ; for the development of Quakerism there is bound up essentially with the spread of the new faith on the American continent. George Rofe, an important Quaker traveller, writing from Barbadoes as early as 1661 calls this island " the nursery of the truth."[1] So in fact it was, for it sent a small army of missionaries, strange as it sounds to-day, to Massachusetts, and one of the Boston martyrs, William Leddra, came from this "nursery of truth." Besse gives a list of two hundred and sixty Friends who suffered persecution in Barbadoes.[2]

Henry Fell, of Furness, reached Barbadoes in October 1656, and he gives a graphic account of the situation as he found it. "Truly Mary Fisher is a precious heart, and hath been very serviceable here, so likewise hath John Rous and Peter Head, and the Lord hath given a blessing to their labours, for the fruits thereof appear, for here is a pretty many people convinced of the truth, among whom the Lord is placing His name.   They meet together in silence in three several places in the island." Fell at once threw himself into the *service*, and crossed controversial swords with Joseph Salmon,[3] a leading Ranter, already known to George Fox. Fell says that he had never met any one who had the *form of truth in words* so well as Salmon : he got away with the great people who protected him whenever the Quaker began questioning him, and many were so bewitched with him that they would hear nothing against him.   The

---

[1] Letter in the Stephen Crisp Collection, Devonshire House, No. 102.
[2] Besse's *Sufferings*, vol. ii. pp. 278-351.
[3] For Salmon, see my *Studies in Mystical Religion*, pp. 472, 475-477.

Governor, a great friend of Lieutenant-Colonel Rous, was moderate towards Friends. He took no offence at John Rous's "warning," or at Henry Fell's hat or "thouing" of him ; as for Friends' lives, he said they were inoffensive and unblameable, but their judging of others he could not bear. William Dewsbury, one of the foremost of the builders of Quakerism in England, wrote letters both to the Governor and to the Lieutenant-Colonel, a circumstance which shows the close interest with which the growth of a Quaker community in Barbadoes was followed in the mother-country. Fell found the morals of the island poor, the people often "filthy," and some of the ministers notorious drunkards. He tried again and again to speak in the churches, but they were so guarded by the "rude multitude," that he always found himself ejected from the building before he had uttered more than a few words. Many were convinced and came to meetings, but it was hard to persuade them to take up the cross and avow themselves Friends. Four or five meetings a week were attended by Fell and Rous, and convincement followed.[1]

Henry Fell, after trying in vain to get passage to New England, for the master of the ship refused to carry him, returned to England in the autumn of 1657, reaching London after capture by the Spaniards, and a journey through France to Rochelle, but only to return a little later to promote the work in Barbadoes. John Rous was the only ministering Friend left in Barbadoes, and he was eager to get passage for New England. He writes, however, "here are some precious Friends, which, I know, if there were none in the ministry with them, will stand witnesses for God against the world here." [2] But a few months later, Peter Evans of Barbadoes reported that, in the absence of ministers, coldness had got in and there was need for some who could declare the testimony of truth with authority.[3] A number of Friends, including Henry

---

[1] These particulars are taken from an important series of Henry Fell's letters in the Swarthmore Collection.

[2] To Margaret Fell, 2nd July 1657, Swarthmore Collection, i. 80.

[3] To George Fox, 28th April 1658, Swarthmore Collection, iii. 110.

Fell, were in the island the following year, and we hear of growing meetings and many convincements.

Work was begun in several other of the West Indian plantations though we have few details. Early in the year 1656 Mary Fisher, John Rous, and Peter Head had paid a visit to the island of Nevis and planted the seed there. John Bowron, of Cotherstone in Durham, after carrying the Quaker message to the Orkneys, embarked there for the West Indies, and in the years 1657 and 1658 visited Surinam, then an English plantation under Lord Willoughby. There he travelled for several hundreds of miles among the natives, who were mostly naked, and he was listened to with respect as "a good man come from far to preach the white man's God."

"He went to their sort of worship, which was performed by beating upon holly-trees, and making a great noise with skins, like a sort of drums, and he declared the word of the Lord among them by an interpreter . . . and spake to their kings, who were arrayed with fish-shells hung about their necks and arms, and they spake to him in their language and confessed he was a good man come from far to preach the white man's God." [1]

This was the earliest piece of what we should now call Foreign Missionary work. Two Friends visited Jamaica, which had been captured from the Spaniards in May 1655 by Admiral Penn, the father of William Penn. As an English plantation it was just making headway against disease and the Spaniards when its capable Acting-Governor, Colonel Edward D'Oyley, asked advice of Secretary Thurloe as to the correct treatment of Quakers. The letter is a charming revelation of the fair-minded but perplexed official who finds the real Quaker very different from the portrait drawn in malicious public prints.

"There are some people," he writes,[2] "lately come hither called Quakers, who have brought letters of credit and do disperse books amongst us. Now my education and judgment

---

[1] *Piety Promoted*, vol. i. p. 234.
[2] 28th Feb. 1657/8, *Thurloe State Papers*, vol. vi. p. 834.

prompting me to an owning of all that pretend any way to godliness and righteousness—whereof these people have a very great appearance—and the prints telling me that the heads of the people are contriving against the Government, and accounted conspirators against His Highness (so the book calls them), hath put me to some stand how to carry myself towards them, and humbly to seek your honour's directions, that my carriage in being tender to them, who are people of an unblameable life, and to whose acting I am a stranger, may not procure blame from him in whose service I am—being desirous to steer my course to the interest I serve and to appear very heartily and clearly His Highness's faithful subject."

In 1660 Richard Pinder, of Ravenstonedale near Sedbergh, and George Rofe, of Halstead, carried the Quaker message to the Bermudas. They were received by many whose expectation was towards God,[1] and were soon holding three or four meetings a week to the great torment of the priests. A public dispute with the ministers of the main island was arranged by the Governor, after which they were freely tolerated and meetings increased greatly in several places. Several settled meetings were begun, "at which many knew where to wait to receive the Lord's secret strength."

The growth of Quaker communities in the West Indian plantations, especially in Barbadoes, was followed with keen interest by English Friends. It shows the moral alertness of Fox's mind that as early as the year 1657 he addressed an epistle " to Friends beyond sea that have Blacks and Indian Slaves." In this he points out that God hath made all nations of one blood and that the gospel is preached to every creature under heaven, " which is the power that giveth liberty and freedom and is glad tidings to every captivated creature under the whole heavens." And so, he says, "ye are to have the mind of Christ and to be merciful, as your heavenly Father is merciful."[2] In such language as this we find the germs of the testimony which in after years the Society of Friends bore on the subject of slavery.

[1] See Swarthmore Collection, iv. 39, containing documents from Pinder, 17th August 1660, and from George Rofe somewhat earlier.
[2] Fox, Epistle No. 153.

CHAPTER III

THE FOUNDERS OF NEW ENGLAND QUAKERISM

MANY famous ships have had their names imperishably woven into the story of the American colonies, and the coming of the precious human freight on the *Mayflower*, the *Arbella*, and the *Welcome* has profoundly shaped the current of western civilisation. But of all the ships which brought pioneer founders to these shores none ever brought passengers more bravely consecrated to the ideals for which they sailed, and none has left a stranger narrative of Divine guidance, than the ship *Woodhouse*, which brought the original " apostles " of Quakerism to New England. The captain's " log " is declared to be—

" A true relation of the voyage undertaken by me Robert Fowler, with my small vessel called the *Woodhouse, but performed by the Lord*, like as He did Noah's Ark, wherein He shut up a few righteous persons and landed them safe, even at the hill Ararat." [1]

The action of the Massachusetts authorities against Quakers had made shipmasters wary of that kind of passengers.[2] They were very unprofitable cargo. It was evident that they must have a ship of their own if they were to carry out their designs in the New World.

[1] There is a manuscript of this extraordinary ship's log, endorsed by George Fox, in the Devonshire House Library in London, A.R.B. MSS. i.
[2] Soon after the banishment of the eight ministers, recorded in the last chapter, a ship brought Mary Dyer and Ann Burden to Boston, both of whom had become convinced of Quakerism in England. Mary Dyer's story will be told later. Ann Burden had come over to settle up the estate of her deceased husband, who had been a citizen of Boston. She, however, was not allowed to remain to collect her debts, and the master of the ship was compelled to carry her back. He was given the privilege of seizing a sufficient quantity of her goods to cover his charges, but he nobly declined to accept such an offer.

Go they must; for, as one of them wrote, " the Lord's word was as a fire and a hammer in me, though in the outward appearance there was no likelihood of getting passage." [1] At this juncture of affairs, Robert Fowler of Bridlington, a Quaker convert of four years' standing, who had been " one of the first fruits unto God in the east parts of Yorkshire," felt it *laid upon him* to build a ship " in the cause of truth," and as he was building it, " New England was presented " before him. He was a member of Holderness Monthly Meeting, and the ancient minute book of that meeting quaintly says that " the power of the Lord wrought mightily in Robert Fowler, and others who gladly received the word of life," and it continues " the Lord anointed them with his Spirit, and that led them into truth and righteousness, and some were fitted to labour in his vineyard." The boat which he felt himself called to build was only a small craft, far too small for ocean service, but the builder was deeply impressed that the God of the waters could guide it, as He did Noah's Ark, and he brought it up to London and offered it for the hazardous voyage.[2] Eleven Friends, " firmly persuaded of the Lord's call " to New England, were eagerly waiting for a means of passage, and they thankfully accepted what seemed to them a " providential ship." Six of them were of the former party, already expelled from Boston.[3] These were Christopher Holder, John Copeland, William Brend, Sarah Gibbons, Mary Wetherhead, and Dorothy Waugh. Christopher Holder at the time was a resident of Winterbourne in Gloucester-

[1] Letter of Henry Fell to Margaret Fell, 19th of February 1657, in the Swarthmore Collection i. 68.

[2] There is a manuscript in the Swarthmore Collection (i. 397) which contains the following items of " Monies Disbursed for the Service of Truth."

" To New England "—

For Provisions for voyage	.	.	.	.	. £29 10 0
Paid to the Master for part of his freight		.	.	30 0 0
For bedding and other things		.	.	12 8 0
In money	.	.	.	.	35 4 4
To Wm. Brend	.	.	.	.	1 10 8
,, M. Wetherhead	.	.	.		2 0 0
,, Sarah Gibbons	.	.	.		4 10 0

[3] Thomas Thurston, who was of the former party, took another way of reaching Boston, as we shall see; Mary Prince found another field of service, no less romantic and no less hazardous, in the East.

shire, "a well-educated man of good estate," who had already been well tested in suffering for his faith, having passed a term of imprisonment in "ye gayle in Ilchester." John Copeland was also well educated, and, like Holder, in the early prime of life. He was a native of Holderness in Yorkshire. William Brend was, in the language of the time, "an ancient and venerable man," "known to many as one who feared God in his generation." He had come to manhood in the days of Queen Elizabeth, but was still of an iron constitution and an indomitable spirit. Sarah Gibbons was a young woman whose early history is obscure, and whose years of service were cut short by the untimely sinking of a canoe in which she was making a landing at Providence in 1659—"but," writes one of her friends, "she was kept faithful to the end." Mary Wetherhead was a young woman from Bristol, who, after her short period of dangerous service in New England, was shipwrecked and drowned with two of her companions, Richard Doudney and Mary Clark. Dorothy Waugh had been a serving-maid in the family of John Camm of Preston Patrick, where she was "convinced and called to the work of ministry."[1] During the intervening period before her voyage in the *Woodhouse*, she had been in many jails in various parts of England. She was not as well equipped intellectually as her companions were, and she was apparently not over judicious,[2] but she had an intensity of zeal and considerable power in ministry.

The new volunteers were William Robinson, Humphrey Norton, Richard Doudney, Robert Hodgson, and Mary Clark. William Robinson was a London merchant, a young man of education, successful in his affairs, and possessed of a fine and lofty spirit, ready to endure to the death for his soul's vision of truth. Humphrey Norton first comes into notice in 1655. He had, before sailing in the *Woodhouse*, performed an extensive service in Ireland, where he had learned how to suffer severe persecution. He had, too, shown his fearless spirit in

[1] See *First Publishers of Truth*, p. 255.
[2] Mary Prince writes to George Fox, "I was ensnared by D. Waugh, but I am out through the love of God."—Swarthmore Collection, iv. 58.

the proffer of himself as a substitute prisoner to take the place of George Fox who was lying in Launceston. In April 1656 he wrote to Fox: "The want of thy showing forth unto Israel lies now upon me," and he declares that he is ready to lay down his life for his imprisoned friend, and that he is going to Cromwell to offer himself body for body.[1] He wrote, with the help of two other Friends, the earliest account we have of the first publishing of Quakerism in New England.[2]

Richard Doudney's life is unknown previous to his American visit, and there are no biographical details available. His friends describe him as "an innocent man who served the Lord in sincerity." Robert Hodgson is likewise an obscure character. The most impressive event of his life known to us is told in the chapter on the Planting of Quakerism in New York. There are hints in existing letters that he was not always wise in propagating the truth, and there are rumours that he "headed a rent in Rhode Island," but these mutterings of criticism and jealousy in the little band must not be taken too seriously, for they are too commonly the sins of the saints to create surprise here.

Mary Clark was the wife of John Clark, a London tradesman, and had come into fellowship with Friends about the time of their rise in London. She had already endured much for her faith, and much was still reserved for her in America.

William Dewsbury boarded the *Woodhouse* off the Downs, 3rd June 1657, and gave the band a word of encouragement. He wrote two days later to Margaret Fell:

"They were bold in the power of the Lord and the life did arise in them . . . . many dear children shall come forth in the power of God in those countries where they desire to go."[3]

On the way to London from Holderness two of the sailors of the *Woodhouse* had been "impressed" for naval

---

[1] *Journal*, i. 318.   The letter is given in full in the Cambridge *Journal*.
[2] H. Norton's *New England's Ensign*, 1659.
[3] Letter in the Caton Collection of MSS. in Bowden, vol. i. p. 68.

service, and Robert Fowler was left with only two men and three boys to man his ship for the voyage. At Portsmouth, however, he succeeded in completing his crew, though the old sea-captains there remarked that they would not go to sea in such a small vessel if Fowler would give it to them. Fowler's " log " tells us in curious metaphorical language that while they were waiting at Portsmouth, " some of the ministers of Christ went on shore and gathered sticks, and kindled a fire and left it burning," which means that they made converts and started a meeting there. " At South Yarmouth again we went ashore and in some measure did the like," *i.e.* left more sticks burning. An interesting letter from William Robinson to Margaret Fell sent from Portsmouth, refers to the kindling of this fire, and indicates that two more Friends were expected for the voyage. They were probably Joseph Nicholson and his wife who reached New England later.[1] The letter says :

"I thought it meet to let thee know that ye ship that carries friends to new ingland, is now riding in Portsmouth harbour : we only stay for a faire winde : ye two friends : ye man and wife, which thou tould me off when I was at Swarthmore, I heare nothing of their cominge to London as yet.

"Robert Hotchin is with me at this place for we came heather this afternoon to have a meeting at this place seinge ye wind is at present contrary, but we intend if the Lord permitt to returne back again to ye ship to-morrow." [2]

Finally, about the middle of June, " leaving all hope of help as to the outward," the little vessel struck out on its course. " The Lord caused us to meet together every day," the quaint narrative says, " and He Himself met with us, and manifested Himself largely unto us, so that by storms we were not prevented [from meeting] above three times in all our voyage," and in these meetings they believed that they had definite " openings " as to how to steer the ship.

On one occasion, as they " were taking counsel of the

[1] There is an entry in the Kendal accounts in June 1657 of expenses "for Joseph Nicholson and his wife for New England."
[2] Swarthmore Collection, iv. 126.

Lord, the word from Him was, 'Cut through and steer your straightest course and mind nothing but me.'" At another time when they believed themselves beset by men of war, Humphrey Norton, who seems to have been the "oracle" of the party, had a revelation in the morning that "*they* were nigh unto us that sought our lives" but with it came the assurance :

"'Thus saith the Lord, ye shall be carried away as in a mist.' . . . Presently we espied a great ship making toward us, but in the very interim, the Lord God fulfilled his promise wonderfully to our refreshment." "Thus it was all the voyage," the log continues. "The faithful were carried far above storms and tempests, and *we saw the Lord leading our vessel as it were a man leading a horse by the head*,[1] we regarding neither latitude nor longitude [*sic*], but kept to our Line [*i.e.* our Light] which was and is our Leader, Guide, and Rule."

Two openings of great comfort were granted to the little group which assured them that they were being guided toward the land they sought. The first inward sight came, as the narrative puts it :

"When we had been five weeks at sea, when the powers of darkness appeared in the greatest strength against us, having sailed but about three hundred leagues, Humphrey Norton, falling into communion with God, told me that he had received a comfortable answer, and that about such a day we should land in America, which was even so fulfilled."

The other opening came a little before land was sighted :

"Our drawing had been all the passage," the account says, "to keep to the southward, until the evening before we made land, and then the word was, 'Let them steer northwards until the day following,' and soon after the middle of the day there was a drawing to meet together before our usual time and it was said to us that we should look abroad in the evening ; and as we sat waiting before the Lord, they discovered land."

They found that they were "in the 'creek' which led between the Dutch Plantations and Long Island, whither the *movings* of some Friends called them."

---

[1] This was a common figure to express complete Divine guidance. William Edmundson says that he was brought to a place where he was needed, "by the good hand of God, as a horse is led by the bridle."

"The power of the Lord fell much upon us and an irresistible word came unto us, 'That the seed in America shall be as the sand of the sea.' It was published in the ears of the brethren, which caused tears to break forth with fulness of joy."

Robert Hodgson, Richard Doudney, Sarah Gibbons, Mary Wetherhead, and Dorothy Waugh, were put on shore at New Amsterdam (now New York City), "whither they had movings," and the rest of the party passed on towards Newport, meeting their closest danger in the passage through Hell-gate—a danger which, the "log" says, was revealed in a vision both to the master of the vessel and to Robert Hodgson, several days before. The little band of "apostles" finally arrived safely at Newport, the 3rd of August.

It is evident that these spiritual Argonauts took themselves very seriously. The Lord "led their ship, as a man leads a horse by the head," and He steered their vessel "as He did Noah's Ark to the hill Ararat." Every danger was "opened" to them in advance, and they were landed where they wished to be. One sees at once that we are dealing here with "enthusiasts" and not with every-day matter-of-fact voyagers. They had no question that they were "sent," that they were "guided," that they were the Lord's prophets, and in this faith we shall see them meet their dangers and carry through their *commission*. This Fowler document, like many another writing of the Friends in this earliest period, contains many occurrences of a semi-miraculous sort. They are carried away from their enemies in a mist, and they are told how to steer even when they know little or nothing of latitude and longitude. Religious literature furnishes many illustrations of the way in which a group of persons living on the verge of ecstasy, and exalted by enthusiastic faith, read the miraculous into ordinary happenings, and are unaware of actions which they themselves perform in a kind of subconscious state. There is no necessary reason to conclude that this "log" is consciously *improved* by the writer of it; it is almost certainly a naïve but honest account written by an enthusiast, who is so sure

of the Lord's leading that he unconsciously belittles his
own knowledge of nautical affairs.

Humphrey Norton's account of his own " conversion
experience " gives us a pretty good glimpse of the type of
persons we have before us.   He says, speaking of his
" convincement and call " :

" In my distress—when gross darkness covered me—I heard
a cry that Light was broken forth and that there was a measure
of it given to every man, but so dark was I and so grossly blind,
that what this Light was I knew not ; nor amongst all professors,
priests nor others, had I ever heard it spoken of, nor preached
for salvation.   Then called I to question all that ever I had read
or heard, to the last tittle of my old belief. . . . My desire to
live justly and to *enjoy God*, set me to inquire after this new Light
and what *effect* it had amongst such as did believe in it.   I heard
that it did convince of sin ; and, being believed in, obeyed and
followed, led out of all manner of uncleanness.   Then said I
in my heart, if so, it should not want following, for I was weary
of my sin, yea I loathed my life."   "And believing in this
Light . . . I have obtained mercy, peace with God, redemption
from all filthiness of flesh and spirit, have been made an heir
to His kingdom, a member of His body, a minister of His Spirit,
and an inheritor of His Eternal rest, blessed forever." [1]

Rhode Island was the most favourable and receptive
spot in North America for them to light upon.   It had
been preparing, as we have seen, through a score of years
for exactly the *seed* that was now to be sown.   Here at
last was a little corner of the earth consecrated to
freedom of belief and worship, where one could follow his
inward Light without fear of dungeon or gibbet.   A
letter from Rhode Island was sent in 1658 to John
Clarke, the Agent of the Colony, to secure a charter from
the English Government, urging him to plead " *that we
may not be compelled to exercise any civil power over men's
consciences*, so long as human orders in point of civilisation
are not corrupted and violated."   The letter continues :

" We have now a new occasion . . . because a sort of people
called by the name of Quakers have come amongst us, and *have
raised up divers who seeme at present to be of their spirit*. . . . Wee
have found noe just cause, to charge them with the breach of

---

[1] The *Ensign*, pp. 2-3.

the civill peace, only they are constantly goeinge forth amongst them about us and vex and trouble them in poynt of religion and spirituall state, though they returne with many a fowle scarr in their bodies for the same." [1]

Anne Hutchinson herself was dead, but those who had shared her views and had gone into exile with her were admirable material for a Quaker meeting. Mary Dyer, Anne Hutchinson's closest friend in her hour of hard trial, had just returned from England to her home in Rhode Island, having had her first taste of Boston jail on her landing. While in England she had become "convinced" of the truth of the Quaker message, had thrown in her lot with the new Society, and had already been recognised as a minister of that faith. She was thus a dynamic Quaker nucleus to begin with. Some of the foremost families among the founders of the Rhode Island Colony—William Coddington, Joshua Coggeshall, son of John, Nicholas Easton and his son John, and Walter Clarke, son of Jeremiah Clarke, an original founder, appear to have accepted the Quaker faith as soon as they heard it, and at once became pillars in the first Quaker meeting in the New World. With them came over to Quakerism, it would seem, a large number of the inhabitants of the island, and the pilgrims from the *Woodhouse* must have thought that their dream of a "seed like the sand of the sea-shore" was well on its way to be realised! [2] Only four years from the time of

[1] *Colony Records of Rhode Island*, vol. i. pp. 396-397.

[2] Callender in his *Historical Discourse* says: "In 1657 some of the people called Quakers came to this Colony and Island; and being persecuted and abused in the other Colonies, that together with the opinions and circumstances of the people here, gave them a large harvest; many, and some of the Baptist Church [of which Callender was a member] embraced their doctrines and particular opinions, to which many of their posterity, and others, still adhere."—p. 118.

John Rous, 7th Nov. 1657, writing from Rhode Island, challenged Governor Endicott to arrange for a meeting with the Massachusetts officials for a free discussion of the Quaker faith, and he asks Endicott to send his answer to Nicholas Easton who was thus already a convinced Friend.—*Ensign*, p. 59.

Peterson says, in his *History of Rhode Island*, under date of 1656 (it should be 1657): "This year some of the people called Quakers came to this Colony, being persecuted and abused in the other Colonies, and many of the principal inhabitants embraced their doctrines, among whom were William Coddington, Nicholas Easton and his two sons, Philip Shearman, Adam Mott, and many others (p. 36).

the landing of these "Argonauts" at Newport, an annual meeting was established on the island, to which the Friends, springing up in scattered parts of New England, largely through their labours, came year after year—a meeting which, under the name of "The Yearly Meeting for Friends in New England," has had a continuous history to the present day.[1]

The cordial reception which the settlers on Rhode Island gave the Quakers, and the formation here of a base of operations and a quiet retreat from the storms of persecution, at once aroused the Puritan colonies. They had formerly refused to admit Rhode Island as a member of the Union of New England colonies, but now they showed themselves eager for *co-operation* in the face of common danger which menaced their peace, if not their spiritual empire. On the 12th of September 1657 the Commissioners of the United Colonies, "being informed that divers Quakers are arrived this summer at Rhode Island which may prove dangerous to the Colonies," "thought meet to manifest their minds" in a letter to those in authority in Rhode Island.

"We suppose," they wrote, "you have understood that last year a companie of Quakers arrived in Boston upon noe other account than to disperse theire pernicious opinions," and then they recount how by "prudent care" they have seen to it that "all Quakers, Ranters, and such notorious heretiques might be prohibited coming among

---

[1] There seems no uncertainty about the year in which this meeting was established. George Bishop says: "About that time [*i.e.* 1661] the General Meeting at Rhode Island, about sixty miles from Boston, was set up and you [the inhabitants of Boston], made an Alarm that the Quakers were gathering together to kill the people and fire the town of Boston!"—*New England Judged*, p. 351. John Burnyeat also gives valuable testimony in his *Journal*. He writes: "I took shipping for Rhode Island, and was there at their Yearly Meeting in 1671 which begins the ninth of the Fourth month (June, new style) *every year* and continues much of a week, and is a General Meeting once a year for all Friends in New England."—Burnyeat's *Journal* (Barclay's reprint), p. 196. George Rofe appears to have been the "beginner" of this Yearly Meeting. He was in New England in the summer of 1661 and he writes from Barbadoes of that visit: "We came in [*i.e.* landed] at Rhode Island, and we appointed a General Meeting for all Friends in those parts, which was a very great meeting and very precious, and continued four days together and the Lord was with His people and blessed them. There is a good seed and the seed will arise."—George Rofe to Richard Hubberthorne, *A.R.B. Collection*, No. 62 (Devonshire House, London).

us" and that "such as arise from amongst ourselves" shall be "removed." "But," they continue, "it is by experience found that meanes will fall short without further care by reason of your admission and receiving of such, from whence they may have opportunity to creep in amongst us, or meanes to infuse and spread their accursed tenates to the great trouble of the colonies, if not to the subversion of the lawes professed in them." "To preserve us," this is their appeal, "from such a pest, the contagion of which within your colony were dangerous, we request that you take such order herein that your neighbors may be freed from that danger, that you remove those Quakers that have been receaved, and for the future prohibite their cominge amongst you." [1]

The Rhode Island answer, signed by Benedict Arnold, President of the Colony, 13th October 1657, is a dignified refusal to swerve from the settled policy of toleration.

"Our desires are," they say, "in all things possible, to pursue after and keepe fayre and loveing correspondence and entercourse with all the colonys," and they add that they will return all persons that "fly from justice in matters of crime"— "but as concerning these which are now among us, *we have no law among us whereby to punish any for only declaring by words, their mindes and understandings concerning the things and ways of God, as to salvation and an eternal condition.*" . . . "And as to the dammage that may in likelyhood accrue to the neighbor collonys by theire being here entertained, we conceive it will not prove so dangerous as the course taken by you to send them away out of the country as they come among you." [2]

This letter, above quoted, was sent by the "Court of Trials." Five months later the General Assembly of the colony sent a Letter to Governor Endicott of Massachusetts to be imparted to the Commissioners of the United Colonies in which the principle of freedom is again as stoutly asserted: "Freedom of conscience we still prize as the greatest hapines that man can posess in this world." Quakers, they say, as all other people who

---

[1] *Records of the Colony of Rhode Island,* i. 374-376.
[2] *Ibid.* i. 376-378.

come to Rhode Island, must be subject to all civil duties and preserve peace and justice, and if the aforesaid Quakers fail in these respects "to the corruptings of good manners and disturbinge the common peace and sosieties "—

"We shall present the matter unto the supream authority of England, humbly craveing their advice and order, how to carry ourselves in any further respect towards these people soe that therewithall theire may be noe damadge or infringement of that chiefe principle in our charter concerninge freedom of consciences, and we alsoe are soe much the more encouraged to make our addresses unto the Lord Protector, for that we understand there are or have beene many of the foresayed people suffered to live in England; yea even in the heart of the nation." [1]

It was thus settled from the start that the Quakers were to be absolutely safe in Rhode Island, if nothing could be urged against them except peculiarity of religious opinions, and the time was not far distant when they were to become the actual rulers of the Colony, as we shall see. But, as the Letter from the "Court of Trial" of Rhode Island says, the Quakers were not satisfied to stay where there was no opposition.[2]

This was, however, not because they liked opposition and enjoyed a fight, but because they believed that they had come over to America under a commission from the Most High to sow their seed of truth in the soil of Massachusetts. They rejoiced in the spread of truth on the safe island in the Narragansett, and they were glad to see the "seed" spring up there, but they were especially thankful for a safe base of operations for the more strenuous campaign for which they had come over; and it was just because this "campaign" was proving effective that that Letter from the Commissioners of the United Colonies was written.

A Letter of John Copeland's, written a week after the *Woodhouse* came into Newport, says:

---

[1] *Records of the Colony of Rhode Island*, i. 378-380.
[2] " We finde that in those places where these people aforesaid, in this Colony are most of all suffered to declare themselves freely, and are only opposed by arguments in discourse, there they least of all desire to come."—*Op. cit.* p. 377.

"Christopher Holder and I are going to Martha's Vineyard in obedience to the will of our God, *whose will is our joy*. Humphrey Norton is at present in Rhode Island, Mary Clark is waiting to go toward Boston; William Brend is towards Providence. The Lord God of Hosts is with us, the shout of a King is amongst us; the people fear our God!"[1]

Mary Clark had come over under a "special moving" to bear her testimony in Boston. She was, as Bishop tells us, "the mother of children, having a husband in England whom she left, being moved to come unto you."[2] She delivered her message, but it was answered by twenty stripes of a three-corded whip, "laid on with fury," then with twelve weeks of prison silence, and then she was sent out of the jurisdiction in winter season, probably back to Rhode Island.[3] A little later she went to her death by shipwreck.

Holder and Copeland were to have more visible fruit for their labour. They went, as planned, to Martha's Vineyard where they met only stern rebuff from the white settlers, though the Indians were kind to them, took them in, saying, "you are strangers and the Lord has taught us to love strangers,"[4] and finally carried them in their canoes to the mainland of Massachusetts. The travellers started now directly on foot through the woods for Sandwich, which, like Newport, was receptive soil for their truth, partly owing, perhaps, to the quiet work of Nicholas Upsall who had spent the preceding winter there in exile.[5]

---

[1] Quoted from Bowden's *History of Friends in America*, vol. i. p. 67. William Robinson was apparently labouring in Rhode Island though he is not mentioned.

[2] *New England Judged*, p. 50. See also Besse's *Sufferings*, vol. ii. p. 181.

[3] Mary Clark was the first Quaker woman in America to suffer whipping for her religious views. She had many followers, however.

[4] Norton's *Ensign*, p. 22.

[5] A magistrate of Plymouth Colony calles Nicholas Upsall "the instigator of all this [Quaker] mischief."—*History of Barnstable County*, p. 169. I am convinced that there were a number of centres in the Plymouth Colony where there were "seekers" and where there was no loyal support for the existing system. There is in existence a Letter from the Governor and Magistrates of Massachusetts which supports this view. It is dated 2nd Sept. 1656, and was written to the Commissioners of the United Colonies, telling of the arrival of Quakers who are "fitt Instruments to propogate the Kingdome of Sathan," and urging the "beloved Brethren and Naighbors of the collonie of Plymouth" to make preparation for guarding against "such pests." The Letter says that there is a great lack in Plymouth Colony of "a due acknowledgement of and encouragement to the Minnesters of the Gosspell." There has been apparently "a crying downe

"Their arrival," Bowden says, "was hailed with feelings of satisfaction by many who were sincere seekers after heavenly riches, but who had long been burdened with a lifeless ministry and dead forms of religion."[1] Sandwich was a town of Plymouth Colony and if it had its "sincere seekers," it also had its proportion of persons who stood for the *status quo*. Humphrey Norton has given us a lively account of the commotion :

"Great was the stir and noise of the tumultuous town, yea, all in an uproar, hearing that we, who were called by such a name as Quakers, were come into those parts. A great fire was kindled and the hearts of many did burn within them, so that in the heat thereof some said one thing and some said another ; but the most part knew not what was the matter."[2]

The two Quaker missionaries, after two trips to the town of Plymouth, one of them a forced trip, and after being "conveyed six miles" toward Rhode Island by a constable who hoped in vain that they would not come back—were finally arrested "as extravagant persons and vagabonds," and conveyed fifty miles in the direction of Rhode Island, with a threat of being whipped, if they ever returned, which thing they were pretty certain to do ! They had made only a short visit in the town of Sandwich, but the results of it were great. A number of the leading townspeople were convinced by this first visit and were henceforth ready to risk goods and lives for their new views of truth, a risk they were very soon called to face. One of the magistrates of the town writing the year following—December 1658—says that the Quakers "have many meetings and many adherents, almost the whole town of Sandwich is adhering towards them."[3] The records show that seventy-five persons were presented in court during that year for attending "meeting," and this in spite of the fact that there was a fine of forty shillings placed upon every person who

of minnestry and minnesters" and the Letter declares that the way to meet this "new engine of Sathan" is to "reinstate a pious orthodox minnestry"—*Plymouth Records*, vol. ii. p. 156.

[1] *Op. cit.* i. 71.   [2] *Ensign*, p. 22.
[3] Letter of Justice James Cudworth, printed in Besse, ii. p. 191, and in *New England Judged*, p. 168.

allowed a Quaker meeting in his house and a fine of ten shillings for every "hearer" who attended, "yea and if nothing be spoken at the meeting, as it sometimes falls out!"[1]

The extent of the "convincement" comes to light in a passage from Cotton Mather's *Life of Rev. Samuel Newman*: "How many straits he underwent in that dark day when he was almost the only minister whose invincible patience held out under the scandalous

[1] See Cudworth's Letter. The first law against the Quakers in the Plymouth Colony was passed in 1657 and is an interesting "relic." It is as follows : "Whereas there hath severall psons come into this Gov^{r}ment comonly called Quakers whose doctrines and practises manifestly tends to the subversion of the foundamentals of Christian Religion, Church Order and Civill peace of this Gov^{r}ment as appeers by the Testimonies given in sundry depositions and otherwise. It is therefore enacted by the Court and the Authority thereof that noe Quaker or pson comonly soe called bee entertained by any pson or psons within this Gov^{r}ment under the penaltie of five pounds for every such default or bee whipt ; It is also enacted by this Court and the Authority therof that if any Rantor or Quaker or pson comonly soe called shall come into any towne within this Gov^{r}ment, and by any pson or psons bee knowne or suspected to bee such the pson so knowing or suspecting him shall forthwith acquaint the Constable or his deputie of them on paine of Presentment and soe liable to cencure in Court whoe [*i.e.* the magistrate] forthwith on such notice of them or any other Intelligence hee shall have of them shall dilligently endeavor to apprehend him or them and bring them before some one of the majestrates whoe shall cause him or them to bee comitted to Goale, there to be kept close prisoners with such victualls onely as the Court aloweth untill he or they shall defray the charge both of theire Imprisonment and theire Transportation away ; Together with an engagement to returne into this Gov^{r}ment noe more or else to be continewed in close durance till further orders from the Court. And forasmuch as the meetings of such psons whether strangers or others proveth disturbing to the peace of this Gov^{r}ment. It is therefore enacted by the Court and the Authority thereof that henceforth noe such meetings bee assembled or kept by any pson in any place within this Gov^{r}ment under the penaltie of forty shillings a time for every speaker and ten shillings a time for every hearer that are heads of families and forty shillings a time for the owner of the place that pmits them soe to meet together ; and if they meet together att theire silent meetings soe called then every pson soe meeting together shall pay ten shillings a time and the owner of the place forty shillings a time."—*Plymouth Records*, vol. xi. pp. 100-101. In 1658, it was decreed : "Noe Quaker or Rantor or any such corrupt pson shall be admitted to be a freeman." "All such as refuse to take the oath of fidelitie as quakers shall have noe voat or shall be imployed in any place of trust" (*ibid.* p. 100). In 1659 it was declared "that many persons in Plymouth Colony are being corrupted by reading Quaker books, writings and Epislles which are widely distributed," it was therefore decreed that all such books shall be seized (*ibid.* p. 121). In 1660, it is noted that the Quakers "have bine furnished with horses and thereby they have made speedy passage from place to place poisoning the Inhabitants with their cursed tennetts," it is therefore decreed that "if any one shall furnish them with a horse or horse kind, the same shall be seized on for the use of the government" (*ibid.* p. 126). In June 1661 it was decreed that "Quakers and such like vagabonds" shall "bee whipt with rodds soe it exceed not fifteen stripes" and made to depart the government" (*ibid.* pp. 129-130).

neglect and contempt of the ministry which for a while the whole country of Plymouth was bewitched into!"

It appears from Justice Cudworth's Letter that the Court had just imposed fines amounting to *one hundred and fifty pounds* on the new Quaker disciples, and yet they steadily increased in number. A poor man, himself lame, father of seven or eight children, had his two cows taken from him for attending meeting. "What are you going to do now?" the marshall asked, as he drove away the cows. "God who has given me these will still provide for us," was the poor man's answer, and he stood by his faith.

One of the most dramatic incidents of the period was the convincement of Isaac Robinson and his influence in the formation of a Quaker centre in Falmouth. He was a son of the famous "Separatist" pastor, John Robinson. In 1659 the General Court of Plymouth sent Isaac Robinson and three others to attend Quaker meetings in order to endeavour to "reduce them from the error of their ways." [1] Instead of convincing the Quakers of error, he himself became convinced of their truth, embraced their doctrines and was dismissed from civil employment in the Colony. He was faithful to his father's advice to "expect the breaking out of more light!" Finding life now uncomfortable in his old home he, with thirteen others, sailed around the cape to the Succoneset shore, where he built the first house in Falmouth and became a leader of the Quaker group in this town.

The beginning was thus made. Almost simultaneously two Quaker meetings sprang into being, one in Newport and the other in Sandwich, and when Christopher Holder and John Copeland returned to Newport they had the satisfaction of feeling that there were at least two *live centres* in the new land. Holder and Copeland had hardly left the Plymouth Colony when another *Woodhouse* passenger, Humphrey Norton, appeared there and carried

[1] *Records of Plymouth Colony*, xi. p. 124. It is an interesting fact that one of John Winthrop's sons, Samuel, joined Friends.

forward the work the other two had begun. He, too, was
soon in the hands of the authorities, and was charged
with holding the doctrine of a Light within sufficient for
salvation. His answer was that the Scriptures say that
" the Grace of God that bringeth salvation hath appeared
unto all men," and they also say that this " Grace is
sufficient."   " This little grain," the *Ensign* says, " stopped
the lion's mouth." Norton was thereupon conveyed fifty
miles toward Rhode Island, and as he went out of the
Colony, William Brend came in, to continue the work.
The latter, together with John Copeland and Sarah
Gibbons, who joined him, soon formed a very live Quaker
circle in the town of Scituate. They won to their cause
a noble-minded magistrate named Timothy Hatherly, but
notwithstanding his friendship they were given a cruel
scourging before they got away from the Colony.[1]

After an unusually terrible experience in New Haven,
where he was flogged and branded with an H, Humphrey
Norton went once more into Plymouth Colony.[2] Before
going forth on this second expedition to the country of
the Pilgrims, Norton passed through a profound inward
experience of God's " call " to Plymouth, attended with
an overwhelming sense that sufferings were awaiting him
there.   John Rous, who had recently arrived from
Barbadoes,[3] was his companion on this perilous journey.
They reached Plymouth the first of June 1658, and were
immediately arrested and imprisoned. The examination
of their doctrines failed to show them to be " heretics,"
though Governor Prince called them " Papists and Jesuits
and inordinate fellows," but they were finally brought

[1] It is a persistent tradition that the Pilgrims of Plymouth Colony did not
persecute other Christians who differed from them in faith. If they had not been
powerfully urged to take extreme measures to guard their heritage perhaps they
would have given the freedom which they came to seek. But any one who believes
that they did not persecute would soon have that idea expelled by reading either
Norton's *Ensign* or Bishop's *New England Judged*. One is sorry to discover
that John Alden was one of the magistrates who took part in the harrying of the
Quakers in Plymouth Colony.

[2] He tells us that, during this New Haven ordeal when the spectators thought
he was being killed, he so felt the Presence of the Lord that " he was as if covered
with balm."—*Ensign*, p. 51.

[3] John Rous, William Leddra, and Thomas Harris came together to New
England from Barbadoes near the end of 1657.

under sentence for refusing to take an oath—a very common trap for catching a Quaker when no criminal charge could be established. For this fault they were scourged, though the people thronged about them to shake their hands and as usual they advanced their cause by their sufferings for it. "This persecution," writes John Rous, "did prove much for the advantage of truth; for Friends did with much boldness own us openly in it, and it did work deeply with many." It must have done so, for the whole southern part of Massachusetts was, as we shall see, honeycombed with Quakerism by the year 1660.

CHAPTER IV

THE MARTYRS

NEARLY simultaneously with the invasion of Plymouth Colony and of Newport by the Quaker missionaries, William Brend, the veteran missionary of the *Woodhouse* party, had been proclaiming his Truth in the city of Providence and the surrounding regions. Roger Williams, though heroically devoted to liberty of thought and speech, was by mental constitution and temperament impervious to the message of the Friends. He was by natural bent of mind unmystical, and he had no sympathy with the idea of inward personal revelations. He was as ready as any of the great theologians of Massachusetts to give his reasons for the hope that was in him, and he stood possessed of a very definite set of doctrines and practices, which were to his mind essential to a right conception of Christianity, but, like Gamaliel and unlike most of his contemporaries, he was willing to allow others to *try their faith* undisturbed.

There were others in the Providence community, however, who were already predisposed to the Quaker Truth. The most important person in the prepared circle at Providence was Catherine Scott, a sister of Anne Hutchinson. She was the wife of Richard Scott, a man of considerable standing and influence in the colony at the head of Narragansett Bay. The Quaker missionaries always seem guided by an unerring instinct to prepared families like this one of Richard Scott's, and here in this home the first conquests to the new faith in Providence were made. We shall hear later of the heroic mettle of the women of this household.

The next locality to be selected for missionary effort was the town of Salem.   Like Newport and Sandwich this historic town already had a little company of spiritually-minded people who were dissatisfied with a "covenant of Works," and who longed for the day-dawn and for the arising of the Day Star in their hearts.   There is a remarkable passage in a letter written in 1657 from Barbadoes by Henry Fell to Margaret Fell of Swarthmore Hall, in which he mentions Plymouth Colony and Salem as two places where a spiritual "seed" can easily be cultivated.

"In Plimouth patent," he says, "there is a people not soe ridged as the others at Boston and there are great desires among them after the Truth.   Some there are, as I hear, convinced who meet in silence at a place called Salem.   Oh truly great is the desire of my soule towards them and the love that flows out after them dayly, for I see in the Eternal Light the Lord hath a great worke to do in that nation." [1]

There is an interesting passage bearing on this Salem group, in Cotton Mather's *Magnalia* :

"I can tell the world that the first Quakers that ever were in the world were certain fanaticks here in our town of Salem, who held forth almost all the fancies and whimsies which a few years after [Mather thinks Quakerism began in England in 1652] were broached by them that were so called in England, *with whom yet none of ours had the least communication.*" [2]

There had been influences at work in Salem for a score of years which tended to form such a group as that here revealed.   Roger Williams, though only a lay-preacher, had been chosen minister of the Salem Church in 1631, and, after a period of similar service in Plymouth Colony, had been invited back to Salem as minister in 1634.   Though not a mystic and not encouraging faith in inward guidance, yet he was a powerful advocate of "independency" in religion—the absolute separation of religion from State control—and he insisted that every act of religion should be a personal matter, belonging

---

[1] Letter in Swarthmore Collection, i. 66.
[2] *Magnalia* (Hartford ed. of 1853), ii. 523.

within the private domain of the worshipper himself. He was utterly opposed to tithes or to any forced support of religion. That he had many supporters in Salem is beyond question, and there can be no doubt that his powerful personality and his vigorous exposition carried many members of the Church out of the ruts of orthodoxy. There were, too, many immigrants in Lynn and Salem who were of the " Seeker " type, others who held the position of the Anabaptists, persons who had come thither expecting to find freedom for their " seeking " and for their independent views. One of the most prominent persons of this type was Lady Deborah Moody, who was forced to migrate to Long Island, where we shall again meet her.[1] Many of her sympathisers went with her, but many also remained behind and quietly cultivated their freer and more liberal form of religion. In such ways and under such influences there had developed in this stronghold of orthodoxy a fellowship of persons who were in positive dissent from the established form of faith and practice, and who were ready to follow the lead of the Quaker messengers.

It is a mystery how the news of this " spiritual circle " in Salem got to Barbadoes in 1657, for no Friends had yet been there, but it is probable that Mary Fisher and Ann Austin heard of it while they were in Boston and carried the report back with them. In any case, it was true ; and as soon as Christopher Holder and John Copeland had accomplished their first piece of work in Plymouth Colony—" where there were desires after the truth "—they started out from Rhode Island (which Henry Fell, in the above-mentioned letter, says the Puritans called " the island of error ") for the more hazardous enterprise in Salem, where the little group of " convinced wor- shipers " were waiting for encouragement. They seem to have sought out in secret the persons who were favour- ably inclined to their message before they made their risky appeal to the Salem public. Humphrey Norton says that they told their little group of listeners " the things

[1] Book II. chap. i.

which they had seen and heard and their hands had handled of the word of life "——which means that they did what all true religious leaders do, they endeavoured to transmit an experience rather than to discourse on abstract doctrines, and he tells us further that " the Word was soon ingrafted in their hearers," so that in a short time they, too, became "possessors of the same experience and fellow-sufferers with their teachers ! " [1]

But they were not content to do their work in a corner. They hoped, somewhat vainly as the sequel showed, that they could carry conviction in a public address. Christopher Holder, " moved of the Lord," as Bishop tells us, rose on Sunday morning, in Salem Meeting (21st September 1657) " after the priest had done," to speak a few words in the line of the latter's " message." Speaking in public after the minister had finished was a common practice and a recognised privilege in Puritan times, but it was a bold proceeding for a Quaker to undertake in the home town of Endicott ! He had hardly started when he was seized by the hair and " his mouth violently stopped with a glove and handkerchief thrust thereinto with much fury by one of the church members, a commissioner." [2]

The two visitors were taken to Boston on Monday and there received thirty stripes apiece with a three-cord knotted whip, which cut their flesh so cruelly that a woman spectator (for such things were done in public) fell in a faint. They were then put in a bare cell, with no bedding, and kept three days and nights without food or drink, and in addition were imprisoned nine weeks, in New England winter weather, with no fire. And by a special order of the Governor and Deputy-Governor, though there was no existing law to give warrant for it, the prisoners were severely whipped twice each week, the first punishment consisting of fifteen lashes and each successive one being increased by three lashes.[3]   As this order was issued

---

[1] Norton's *Ensign*, p. 60.   [2] *New England Judged*, p. 50.
[3] The law of 14th October 1656 provided that Quakers coming into the jurisdiction of Massachusetts should be committed to the house of correction and *at their entrance* should be severely whipped.

when two weeks of the imprisonment had passed, the total number of lashes endured by these long-suffering men at this time would be three hundred and fifty-seven!

When the glove and handkerchief were being thrust into Holder's mouth, Samuel Shattuck, apparently one of the "dissenting circle," pulled away the hand of the commissioner to keep Holder from being choked. He was at once arrested as a "friend of Quakers," taken to Boston, and put under bond not to go to any meetings of the Quakers and to answer at the next Court. It was soon found that the Quaker visitors had been entertained in the home of Lawrence and Cassandra Southwick, who were evidently the leaders of this little "circle" in Salem. They, too, were taken to Boston. The husband was turned over to the authorities of his Church to be dealt with, but Cassandra was imprisoned seven weeks and then fined forty shillings for having in her possession a "paper on Truth and the Scriptures" which her guests had written. This "paper" was almost certainly "a Declaration of Faith and Exhortation to obedience," issued by Christopher Holder and John Copeland, and signed also by Richard Doudney, who had meantime found his way into Massachusetts and had been arrested because "his speech betrayed him" and made his hearer judge him a Quaker disciple. He was thus joined again with his fellow-travellers Holder and Copeland, and was a signer of the "Declaration on Truth and the Scriptures."

This is the earliest formal Declaration of Faith issued by any of the Quaker messengers either in the Old or the New World. It is a strikingly orthodox document, and approaches as nearly as possible to the theological views then in vogue in the Churches.

"We do believe," it declares, "in the only true and living God, the Father of our Lord Jesus Christ . . . who at sundry times and in divers manners, spake in time past to our fathers by the prophets, but in these last days hath spoken unto us by His Son . . . the which Son is that Jesus Christ that was born of the Virgin; who suffered for our offenses, is risen again for our justification, and is ascended into the highest heavens and sitteth at the right hand of God the Father: Even in Him do we believe, who is the only begotten Son of the Father, full of grace and truth.   And in Him do we trust alone for salvation ; by whose blood we are washed from sin.   [We believe in] the Holy Ghost, the Spirit of Truth that proceedeth from the Father and the Son, by which we are sealed and adopted sons and heirs of the Kingdom of heaven, by which Spirit the Scriptures of Truth were given forth. . . . The Scriptures we own to be a true declaration of the Father, Son and Spirit, in which is declared what was from the beginning, what was present and was to come."

The writers of this document were evidently endeavouring to disarm their theological opponents by showing that they were "sound" on the fundamental tenets of universal Christian belief, and they shrewdly put these points of agreement in the foreground of their Declaration, and only at the end of the paper touched upon their own peculiar doctrine of "the Light which showeth you the secrets of your hearts and the deeds that are not good."   "While you have the Light," they say in conclusion, "believe in the Light that you may be children of the Light, for, as you love it and obey it, it will lead you to repentance, bring you to know Him in Whom is remission of sins. . . . This is the desire of our souls *for all that have the least breathing after God*, that they may come to know Him in deed and truth and find His power in them and with them." [1]

If this Declaration was prepared, as appears, to be a conciliatory document and to quiet the opposition, it was a complete failure.   Another paper, written "against the persecuting spirit, with a warning against those who indulge in it"—a paper no longer extant—was issued about the same time by the three Friends, and was peculiarly resented by the ministers of the Colony.   In fact it was the discovery of that paper which brought the extra lashes, before mentioned, on the prisoners in the Boston jail.   But even the possession of the conciliatory document proved a criminal offence in the case of Cassandra Southwick, for, as we have seen, she was kept

[1] This Declaration was first brought to light by Goold Brown the grammarian, and is printed in full in Bowden i. 91-92.

seven weeks a prisoner and was fined forty shillings " for having and owning to the truth of the Paper the strangers had written."

The Southwicks, "a grave and aged couple," together with some of their friends, revolting from this spirit of persecution, now withdrew entirely from the Church services in Salem, and met on " First-days " in each others' houses for " quiet waiting on the Lord." [1] The Southwicks were apprehended, catechised on " the sufficiency of the Light within," which they admitted, and were put in the House of Correction. They were thereafter constantly harried and fined to the verge of poverty, and finally banished from the Colony. After their banishment two of their children, Daniel and Provided, having no estates to cover their fines, were ordered to be sold into slavery, though no shipmaster could be found to execute the order.[2]

The Christian spirit of these Salem Quakers comes out beautifully in a Letter which they wrote from their prison in Boston :

"For our part, we have true peace and rest in the Lord in all our sufferings, and are made willing in the Power and Strength of God, freely to offer up our lives, in this cause of God for which we suffer, yea, and we do find, through Grace, the enlargement of God in our imprisoned estate, to Whom alone we commit ourselves and families, for the disposing of us according to His infinite wisdom and pleasure, *in whose Love is our Rest and Life*." [3]

It is evident that the converts to Quakerism in the New

---

[1] Besides the Southwicks and Samuel Shattuck, Joshua Buffum and wife and son Joseph, John Small, John Burton, Edward Harnet, Nicholas Phelps (whose home was in Ipswich), Edward Wharton, Samuel Gaskin, John Daniels, Joseph Pope and wife, Anthony Needham and wife, George Gardner, Thomas Bracket, Henry Trask and wife belonged to this Salem circle (see *Annals of Salem* ii. 399 and *New England Judged*, pp. 56-64). Besse also speaks of twelve persons, unnamed, who were fined for not attending Church and presumably joining with Friends.—Besse ii. 188.

[2] The details of the attempted sale of the two Southwick children are given in Besse ii. 197 and in *New England Judged*, pp. 107-112. Whittier has told the incident in his " Cassandra Southwick." The order to sell Daniel and Provided Southwick " to any of the English nation at Virginia or Barbadoes " is in the *Records of Massachusetts Colony*, vol. iv. part i. p. 366.

[3] There is ground for a suspicion that Cassandra Southwick and some others of the Salem group were inclined to adopt extreme ascetic views regarding the marriage relation. She seems to have held the opinion that to have children after the flesh was to fall from the higher life in the Spirit. See Joseph

World immediately rose to the heroic spirit and the complete confidence in God and their Cause which characterized the Quaker "apostles" who came among them. After the arrest of Holder, Copeland, Shattuck, and the Southwicks in September 1657, a new law against Quakers was passed, 14th October 1657, defining the punishment which was to be meted out to the persons who are called "the cursed sect of Quakers."[1] It inflicted a fine of one hundred pounds on any one who should bring a Quaker into the Colony; forty shillings for every hour that any one should entertain or conceal a Quaker, and it provided that any Quaker returning after having once suffered should, if a man, have an ear cropped; for a second offence the other ear, and for a third have his tongue bored with a hot iron; if the offender was a woman she was to be severely whipped and on the third offence to have her tongue bored.

By May of 1658, the eleven who came over in the *Woodhouse*, and in addition John Rous, William Leddra, and Thomas Harris of Barbadoes, and Mary Dyer of Rhode Island, were all at work in New England.[2] Thomas Harris made his way to Boston, where he was arrested, flogged, and imprisoned. William Brend and William Leddra pushed on to Salem, where they held a meeting in the woods, but were surprised and carried off. William Brend, though the oldest of the band of missionaries, was called to pass through the most cruel sufferings that were meted out in Boston to any prisoner. The tale is too awful to tell in detail, but the inhumanity can be judged from the fact that one incident in his round of torture consisted of one hundred and seventeen blows on his bare back with a tarred rope. He was found dying—"his body having turned cold" and "his flesh having rotted"

Nicholson's Letters to Margaret Fell.—Swarthmore Collection, iv. 107-108. Major Hawthorne of Salem reported that he had heard "Consander Southieck" say that she was greater than Moses, for Moses had seen God but twice, and then only His back parts, but that she had seen Him three times face to face!— *Massachusetts Archives*, vol. x. p. 264.

[1] *Records of Massachusetts Colony*, vol. iv. part i. p. 398.

[2] In August six of the missionaries left New England for Barbadoes. They were William Leddra, Thomas Harris, William Brend, Robert Hodgson, Sarah Gibbons, and Dorothy Waugh.

—and a physician was hurried in to treat his mangled body and implored to save his life, for the magistrates were now thoroughly frightened by the impression which their brutality was making on the citizens of Boston. John Norton, however, was still stout in his remorseless attitude, saying of William Brend : " He endeavoured to beat the gospel ordinances black and blue, and it was but just to beat *him* black and blue." [1] When John Rous and Humphrey Norton heard what their aged friend was passing through they felt impelled to go to Boston. Upon their arrival they went to hear John Norton's sermon. One could hardly expect them to appreciate it. Here is John Rous' account of the visit to the Church :

" Humphrey Norton and I were moved to go into the great meeting-house at Boston upon one of their lecture days, where we found John Norton their teacher set up, who, like a babbling Pharisee, ran over a vain repetition near an hour long. When his glass was out he began his sermon, wherein, among many lifeless expressions, he spake much of the danger of those called Quakers, a flood of gall and vinegar instead of the cup of cold and refreshing water ! How often hungry souls have been deceived by him I leave to that of God in their consciences to judge." [2]

Humphrey Norton adds to the reader : " Thou mayest see the husks on which the New England priests feed their flocks ! " They were almost immediately arrested, imprisoned, and flogged. Rous has left an account of one week's tale of suffering :

" On the Second-day (Monday) they whipped six Friends [Salem colonists who had attended the meeting]; on the Third-day

---

[1] The *Ensign*, p. 78.

[2] *Ensign* p. 55. The Magistrates had enjoined Rev. Mr. John Norton to prepare a document " to manifest the evill of theire [the Quaker] tenets and the dainger of theire practices," and to answer their writings by which " divers of weak capacities are deceived."—*Records of Massachuse.ts Colony*, vol. iv. part i. p. 348. Norton's " Declaration " was published in 1659 under the title " The Heart of New England Rent at the Blasphemies of the present Generation." He tries to prove that the Quakers are offspring of the Münster fanatics, and he says : " The Wolf which ventures over the wide sea, out of a ravening desire to prey upon the sheep ; when landed, discovered, and taken hath no cause to complain, though for the security of the flock he be penned up, with that door opening into the fold fast shut, but having another door purposely left open, whereby he may depart at his pleasure, either returning from whence he came, or otherwise quitting the place."

of the week the gaoler laid William Brend . . . . neck and heels, as they call it, in irons, as he confessed, for sixteen hours; and on the Fourth-day the gaoler gave W. B. 117 strokes with a pitched rope: on the Fifth-day they imprisoned us, and on the Seventh-day we suffered.   The beating of W. B. did much work in the town, and for a time much liberty was granted, for several people came to us in the prison, but the enemy, seeing the forwardness and love in the people towards us, plotted, and a warrant was given forth that if we would not work we should be whipped once in every three days, and the first time have fifteen stripes and the second time eighteen, and the third time twenty-one.   So on the Second-day was a se'ennight after our first whipping, four of us received fifteen stripes apiece, the which did so work with the people that on the Fourth-day after we were released, so we returned to Rhode Island."

In his letter already quoted, which he dates "from the Lion's den called Boston prison," 3rd September 1658, John Rous gives a graphic review of the work which had so far been accomplished in the face of a most vigorous and relentless persecution :—

"Truth is spread here above two hundred miles, and many in the land are in fine conditions, and very sensible of the power of God, and walk honestly in their measures.   And some of the inhabitants of the land, who are Friends, have been forth in the service, and they do more grieve the enemy than we, for they have hope to be rid of us, but they have no hope to be rid of them.   We keep the burden of the service off from them at present, for no sooner is there need in a place, but straightway some or other of us step to it, but, when it is the will of the Father to clear us of this land, then will the burden fall on them. The Seed in Boston and Plymouth Patents is ripe, and the weight very much lies on this town, the which being brought into subjection to the Truth, the others will not stand out long.   The Seed in Connecticut and Newhaven Patents is not as yet ripe, but there is a hopeful appearance, the gathering of which in its time will much redound to the glory of God.   We have two strong places in this land, the one at Newport in Rhode Island, and the other at Sandwich, which the enemy will never get dominion over, and at Salem there are several pretty Friends in their measures. . . . There are Friends, few or more, almost from one end of the land to the other that is inhabited by the English." [1]

---

[1] Letter of John Rous to Margaret Fell, 3rd September 1658.—Swarthmore Collection.

Sarah Gibbons and Dorothy Waugh had, in the early spring of this same year, accomplished an almost impossible journey. They travelled on foot from Newport "in great storms and tempests of frost and snow"— what we should call March blizzards—all the way to Salem. "They lodged in the wilderness day and night— through which they cheerfully passed to accomplish the will and work of God to their appointed place, where their message was gladly received." [1] They had two weeks of undisturbed labour among those who "gladly received their message," and then they "felt moved" to try Boston, where they received the usual barbaric whipping which "tore their flesh," and they then were allowed to go away again to Rhode Island, which to the Friends of that period was the "habitation of the hunted-Christ, where we ever found a place of rest when weary we have been." [2]

A still more astonishing journey was made in the summer of 1658 by Josiah Coale and Thomas Thurston, the latter of whom had been in the party of eight that landed in Boston in 1656. They came over from England to Virginia, where they published their message, and then travelled all the way on foot from Virginia to New England "through uncouth passages, vast wildernesses, uninhabited countries, deemed impassable for any but the Indians." "For outward sustenance," writes Josiah Coale "we knew not how to supply ourselves, but without questioning or doubting, we gave up freely to the Lord, knowing assuredly that His presence was with us ; and according to our faith so it was, for His presence and love we found with us daily." [3] They touched the hearts of the wild Susquehanna Indians, who not only gave them "courteous entertainment" but also accompanied them to the Dutch Settlement in New Amsterdam and nursed Thomas Thurston through a dangerous illness. [4] Through such hardships they came, because they too felt "the fire and the hammer" in their souls. Josiah Coale was one of

---

[1] The *Ensign*, p. 15.   [2] The *Ensign*, p. 69.
[3] Josiah Coale's Letter to George Bishop.—Bowden. i. 123.
[4] *New England Judged*, p. 29 ; and Besse ii. 196.

the finest spirits among the entire band of " publishers of Truth " in the colonies. He was born about 1633, " of a highly respectable family," near Bristol, and, like so many of his generation, he passed through a deep travail of soul before he found peace. He had revolted in his youth from formal religion, and he nowhere could find anything which answered to his heart's need. " How to come into the way of life," he says, " I was still a stranger." At length, under the ministry of John Audland and John Camm in Bristol in 1654, he found " the way of life," and gave himself up into God's service, to follow whithersoever he might lead. " He baulked no danger," wrote William Penn of him, " and he counted nothing too dear for the service of his Lord." He possessed a rare and unusual gift in ministry, and at his best he powerfully carried conviction. When the occasion called for it his speech was " like an ax, a hammer, or a sharp piercing sword," and then again it became " soft and pleasant, like streams of immortal life running through him." In prayer he was favoured with surpassing grace and power, and often seemed transported as he pleaded for the Light to break upon souls who were in the dark. [1] During his brief period of lab - in New England he devoted himself especially to the Indians in Martha's Vineyard and in Plymouth Colony. He had lived much among the Indians on his long journey, and he had in a peculiar way the key to the Indians' hearts. They loved him, trusted him, and " had true breathings to know his God." As soon as he turned from the Indians " to sound the day of the Lord " among the colonists he met a different reception. He was dragged from a Friend's house in Sandwich and was committed to prison, where he appears to have remained until his departure from the Colony.

Christopher Holder, John Copeland, and John Rous were the first to suffer under the law of October 1657. After his release from the terrible imprisonment recorded above, Christopher Holder took passage for the West

[1] See William Penn's " Testimony Concerning Josiah Coale," Introduction to Coale's *Works* (1671).

Indies; where he probably spent the winter,[1] but he continually felt "the fire and the hammer" within him, and was eager to be back where his friends were risking their lives and where he knew he was needed. In February 1658, he sailed from Barbadoes by way of Bermuda for Rhode Island, and after a period of labour in this safe field he put out again with his old-time companion, John Copeland, to face the dangers of the stern Massachusetts law. They were arrested in August 1658 in the town of Dedham and brought before Governor Endicott in Boston, who said, "You can be sure that your ears will be cut off." John Rous, who meantime had been labouring in Rhode Island, and had returned to the field of danger, was seized about the same time and was brought to trial with the other two. "There was a great lamenting for me by many when I came again," he says, "but they were not minded by me. I was much tempted to say I came to the town to take shipping to go to Barbadoes, but I could not deny Him who moved me to come hither, nor His service, to avoid sufferings." After a frivolous examination in theology, they were sentenced to lose an ear apiece.

Among those who came to be spectators of the execution of this barbaric sentence was Catherine Scott of Providence—"a grave and sober ancient woman of good breeding, education and circumstances, of unblameable conversation."[2] She was, as we have seen, a sister of Anne Hutchinson,[3] and had been the first to become a Friend in Providence, and she had come to Boston to show her sympathy with the sufferers. She was the mother of many children, all of whom became Friends, for as John Rous beautifully expressed it, "the power of God took place in all her children." Her daughter Mary was later to become the wife of Christopher Holder. Because Catherine Scott made too free critical comments on the execution of the ear-cropping, she was given ten stripes and was told, in words heavy with sinister meaning,

---

[1] A letter from Peter Evans mentions service by Holder in St. Christopher and Nevis during the winter of 1658.—Swarthmore Collection, iii. 110.
[2] *New England Judged*, p. 94.   [3] See Winthrop i. 352.

that " if she came hither again there was likely to be a law to hang her." Her brave answer was : " If God calls us, woe to us if we come not. I have no question that He whom we love will make us not count our lives dear unto ourselves for His name's sake." " We shall be as ready to take away your lives as you will be to lay them down," was the ominous reply of Endicott.[1]

At the General Court of Massachusetts, held the 19th of October 1658, the final step was taken to end, if possible, the " inroads " of " this pernicious sect." Whippings, fines, ear-croppings, and imprisonment had proved utterly futile. Still the Quakers came just as though they were wanted. When John Rous and Humphrey Norton heard of William Brend's terrible sufferings, they started at once for Boston, as we have seen, because they could not eat or sleep for their desire " to bear their part with the prisoners of hope, for a testimony of Jesus."[2] What could be done with such men ? Neal was right when he said : " Such was the enthusiastic fire of the Quakers that nothing could quench it."[3]

The only thing left to be tried was the penalty of last resort—death. The clergy of the Colony, especially John Norton, must be held primarily responsible for this extreme law of 1658.[4] It was passed with much difficulty, and was carried in the House of Deputies by a majority of only one, and was from the first unpopular in general with the lay citizens.[5] The law, largely composed of railing and abuse against the Quakers, contained this clause : " And the said person, being convicted to be of the sect of the Quakers, shall be sentenced to banishment, *upon pain of death*."[6] It was now to be settled whether *anything* could " quench their enthusiastic fire."

---

[1] *New England Judged*, p. 95. [2] *Ensign*, p. 79.
[3] Neal, *History of New England*, i. 306. [4] See *New England Judged*, p. 86.
[5] A few citizens were in favour of stern measures. See Petition in *Massachusetts Archives*, x. 246.
[6] This law is to be found in full in *Records of Massachusetts Colony*, vol. iv. part i. p. 345. The first official recommendation of the death penalty was made at the meeting of the Federal Commissioners of the United Colonies, held in Boston in the autumn of 1658, with Endicott presiding. A resolution was passed denouncing the Quakers as blasphemers, and recommending the several colonies, which they represented, to pass laws making it a capital offence for banished Quakers to return.

The native leaders of the Salem group were the first to receive sentence under the capital law. After two years of almost constant persecution, the chief members of the new society were banished from the jurisdiction of Massachusetts by Order of the General Court held the 11th of May 1659.[1]

Lawrence and Cassandra Southwick found their way to Shelter Island, near the eastern end of Long Island, which was a safe refuge for persecuted Friends, for it was owned and governed by Nathaniel Sylvester, a Friend. Here they peacefully lived in their new-found faith for a brief period, and quietly finished their earthly course. Joshua Buffum, another of the group, moved to Rhode Island, while Samuel Shattuck, Nicholas Phelps, and Josiah Southwick made their way to England through Barbadoes. They appear to have landed in Bristol in February 1660, where they found themselves once more in a storm centre of persecution. William Dewsbury has given us a vivid picture of the scene. On the 7th of February a meeting was held at the house of Edward Pyott in Bristol while a great mob filled the streets around, storming to break up the meeting which, in spite of the noise and fury, was " precious in the life of the Lord who filled His tabernacle with His glory in which Friends parted with joy in the Lord." In the evening the mob attacked the house in which the banished Friends were staying, and where William Dewsbury was spending the evening with them. The news had just arrived of the martyrdom of William Robinson and Marmaduke Stephenson (soon to be recounted), and the little group of Friends were sitting bowed with grief while the mob raged outside. Dewsbury says :

"We were bowed down before our God, and prayer was made unto Him, when they knocked at the door. It came upon my spirit it were the rude people, and the Life of God did mightily arise, and they had no power to come in till we were clear before our God. Then they came in setting the house about with muskets and lighted matches, so after a season of time they

---

[1] *Records of Massachusetts Colony*, vol. iv. part i. p. 367. See also *ibid.* p. 349.

came into the room where I was, and Amor Stoddard with me :
I looked upon them when they came into the room [and] they
cried as fast as they could well speak, 'we will be civil, we will
be civil.' I spake these words, 'see that you be so.' They run
forth of the room and came no more into it but run up and
down in the house with their weapons in their hands, and the
Lord God, who is the God of His seed . . . caused their hearts
to fail and they pass[ed] away, and not any harm done to any
of us." [1]

The next day the Friends visited George Bishop,
whose home was in Bristol, making their way through the
mob who were "struck at their hearts by the majesty of
God and stood gazing upon us."   One can easily imagine
the author of *New England Judged* seizing this opportunity
to get at first hand the details of the sufferings of which
he was to be the historian.

For a brief time there was a solemn pause before the
Massachusetts law was put to a supreme test, but there were
heroic spirits quite ready for the worst the law could do.
Every Friend in the ministry in America had undoubtedly
read and had been moved by George Fox's remarkable
Epistle written from Launceston Prison, an Epistle which
shows in the writer the highest marks of spiritual leadership :

" Let all nations hear the sound by word or writing.   Spare no
place, spare no tongue nor pen, but be obedient to the Lord God ;
go through the work : be valiant for the truth upon earth ; and
tread and trample upon all that is contrary. . . . The ministers
of the Spirit must minister to the spirit that is in prison, which
hath been in captivity in every one, that with the Spirit of Christ
people may be led out of captivity up to God, the Father of
spirits, [may] do service to him, and have unity with him, with
the scriptures and one with another. . . . Be patterns, be
examples in all countries, places, islands, nations, wherever you
come, that your carriage and life may preach among all sorts of
people, and to them ; then you will come to walk cheerfully over
the world, answering that of God in every one." [2]

The unconquerable spirit of the leader had infused itself

---

[1] Letter of Dewsbury to Margaret Fell (Swarthmore Collection, iv. 134) ; and
Letter of A. Parker to Margaret Fell (Swarthmore Collection, i. 169).   The date
of Dewsbury's letter is fixed by internal evidence.
[2] *Journal*, i. 315.

into the entire band of "publishers," and they were sure in the end to defeat the law makers. In September 1659 William Robinson, Marmaduke Stephenson, Mary Dyer, and a little girl of eleven years, named Patience Scott, daughter of Richard and Catherine Scott of Providence, were apprehended as Quakers. This child of eleven had come on foot from Providence, under a definite "moving of the Lord," as she believed, "to bear her testimony against the persecuting spirit." William Robinson was a *Woodhouse* voyager. Marmaduke Stephenson was a Yorkshire farmer who was on a religious mission in Barbadoes when he heard of "the law to put the servants of the living God to death," and he heard within himself "the word of the Lord, saying 'Go to Boston.'"[1] He was one of a party of eight Friends who at this crisis formed a second apostolic expedition to the American colonies.[2] Mary Dyer was the wife of William Dyer of Newport, and a type of person whose fire was not likely to be quenched by the terror of statutes! Nicholas Davis of Plymouth Colony had come to Boston on business about the same time and, being a Quaker, was caught in the same drag-net. The little girl from Providence proved mighty in her childish wisdom, and "confounded the lawyers and doctors," but she was declared to have "an unclean spirit" and was turned over to her family as too young to come under the law. The other four were banished "on pain of death the 12th of September 1659." Nicholas Davis returned home, and so, too, for the moment did Mary Dyer. The other two started directly for Salem and went about the work to which they felt called, travelling as far as New Hampshire. The same day Christopher Holder was seized in Boston,

---

[1] Letter from Boston prison, in *New England Judged*, p. 133.

[2] See letters of Henry Fell, Peter Pearson, Robert Malins, Peter Cowsnocke, and Philip Rose in the Swarthmore Collection. Peter Cowsnocke was from the Isle of Man, and with Philip Rose and Edward Teddes, both Warwickshire Friends, seems to have been lost at sea on the passage from Barbadoes to Rhode Island. (Henry Fell to Fox, Swarthmore Collection, iv. 182; Nicholson to Margaret Fell, 3rd April 1660, Swarthmore Collection, iv. 107; and record cited in William White's *Friends in Warwickshire*, p. 23). Henry Fell, Robert Malins from Bandon, Ireland, Ann Cleaton, Marmaduke Stephenson, and Peter Pearson, another Yorkshireman, were the other five of the party.

when on his way to England, was kept in prison two months, and then banished " on pain of death." [1]

While he was still in prison, Mary Dyer came to Boston in company with Mary Scott and Hope Clifton of Providence, and five days later William Robinson and Marmaduke Stephenson, having returned from their eastern journey, were apprehended. With these men there were a number of other Friends who had been " convinced," and who came up with them to Boston, " moved of the Lord," as the old account has it, " to look your bloody laws in the face and to accompany those who should suffer by them." [2]

In this strange group of volunteers were Daniel Gould of Newport, Robert Harper of Sandwich, William King, Hannah Phelps, Mary Trask, Provided Southwick, and Margaret Smith of " the first fruits " of Salem, and Alice Cowland, who brought linen with her to wrap the dead bodies of those who were to be martyred ! [3]

It is easy for us, at this comfortable distance, in an ordered society in which one believes what he wants to believe—or peradventure believes nothing at all—to say that these Friends walked of their own accord into the lion's den, that they knew the teeth of this new law would bite, and that they should have remained in safe territory. That is undoubtedly true, but it indicates a superficial acquaintance with the spirit of these Quakers. There are persons, or at least there once were, who find all their life-values altered and all their utilitarian calculations shifted by an inner impulse which says irresistibly, " thou must ! " These Friends loved their lives and their homes as much as others did—they would have preferred

---

[1] The death sentence is to be executed ''in case he be found within this jurisdiction three daies after the next shipp now bound thence to England be departed from this harbor.''—*Records of Massachusetts Colony*, vol. iv. part i. p. 391.

[2] *New England Judged*, p. 119. William Robinson in a letter to George Fox says : '' The Lord did lay it upon me to try their law.''

[3] These Friends were confined for two months and were then sentenced to receive the following punishments : Daniel Gould thirty lashes ; Robert Harper and William King fifteen each ; Margaret Smith, Mary Trask, and Provided Southwick ten each. Alice Cowland, Hannah Phelps, Mary Scott, and Hope Clifton were '' delivered over to the Governor to be admonished.''

the life of comfort to the hard prison and the gallows rope if they could have taken the line of least resistance with inward peace, but that was impossible to them. They were as sensitive to the call of duty as the musician is to the power of harmony ; they could no more ignore what seemed to them "the movings of the Lord" than a creator of beauty can ignore the laws of his art. They were not gifted with psychological analysis, and they did not raise the question whether these·"calls" and "movings" were due to "auto-suggestion," or were actually from the mouth of God. They had learned to obey the visions which they *believed* were heavenly, and they had grown accustomed to go straight ahead where the Voice, which they believed to be Divine, called them.

They were *commissioned* to plant the truth in Massachusetts, and they "could not do otherwise" in this crisis than go up and "look the law in the face." Their course, I admit, was not "rational," in the narrow sense of rational, but the great life of loyalty and sacrifice never runs in any narrow groove of "pure" rationality. It cannot be explained and plumbed by utilitarian formulae, for life is always richer than any crystallised rules and concepts about it ; but it turns out in the sweeps of history that to die for a truth, to be loyal to vision even on the gallows, *is* as rational a course as that of the compromiser who saves his neck and puts up with half a truth !

In any case there can be no question that these banished Quakers who came back believed that they were "moved" to do so, and were convinced in their minds that the God who led them into danger would use their deaths to advance the truth more than their lives could advance it. It was plainly in this faith that they came.

Here is William Robinson's testimony :

"On the 8th day of the 8th Month, 1659, in the after part of the day, in Travelling betwixt Newport in Rhode Island and Daniel Gould's house, with my dear Brother, Christopher Holder, the Word of the Lord came expressly to me, which did fill me immediately with Life and Power, and heavenly Love, by which he constrained me, and commanded me to pass to the Town of Boston, to lay down my life, in his Will, for the Accomplishing of His Service, which He had to be performed at the Day appointed. To which heavenly voice I presently yielded Obedience, not questioning the Lord how He would bring the Thing to pass, since I was a Child, and Obedience was Demanded of me by the Lord, who filled me with living Strength and Power from His heavenly Presence, which at that time did mightily Overshadow me, and my Life at that time did say Amen to what the Lord required of me, and had Commanded me to do, and willingly was I given up from that time, to this Day, to do and perform the Will of the Lord, whatever became of my Body; for the Lord had said unto me, 'thy Soul shall rest in Everlasting Peace, and thy Life shall enter into Rest, for being Obedient to the God of thy life.' I was a Child, and durst not question the Lord in the least, but rather was willing to lay down my Life, than to bring Dishonour to the Lord; and as the Lord made me willing, dealing Gently and Kindly with me, as a Tender Father by a Faithful Child, whom he dearly Loves, so the Lord did deal with me in Ministering his Life unto me, which gave and gives me Strength to perform what the Lord required of me; and still as I did and do stand in need, he Ministered and Ministreth more Strength, and Virtue, and heavenly Power and Wisdom, whereby I was and am made strong in God, not fearing what Man shall be suffered to do unto me." [1]

Marmaduke Stephenson's testimony is of like import and is withal a beautiful account of a simple, guileless man's call to stern duty:

"In the beginning of the year 1655, I was at the Plough in the east parts of Yorkshire in Old England, near the place where my outward Being was, and as I walked after the Plough, I was filled with the Love and the Presence of the Living God which did Ravish my Heart when I felt it; for it did increase and abound in me like a Living Stream, so did the Love and Life of God run through me like precious Ointment, giving a pleasant Smell, which made me stand still; and as I stood a little still, with my Heart and Mind stayed on the Lord, the Word of the Lord came to me in a still small Voice, which I did hear perfectly, saying to me, in the Secret of my Heart and Conscience, 'I have Ordained Thee a prophet unto the Nations.' And at

---

[1] Written in Boston Gaol, 19th of 8th month, 1659, in Bishop's *New England Judged*, pp. 127-129.

the hearing of the Word of the Lord I was put to a stand, being that I was but a Child for a Weighty Matter. So at the time appointed, Barbadoes was set before me, unto which I was required of the Lord to go, and leave my dear and loving Wife and tender Children; For the Lord said unto me immediately by his Spirit, That he would be a Husband to my Wife, and as a Father to my Children, and they should not want in my Absence, for he would provide for them when I was gone. And I believed that the Lord would perform what he had spoken, because I was made willing to give up myself to his Work and Service (with my dear Brother), under the Shadow of His Wings, who hath made us willing to lay down our Lives for His own name Sake. So, in Obedience to the Living God, I made preparation to pass to Barbadoes in the 4th month, 1658. So, after some time, I had been on the said Island in the Service of God, I heard that New England had made a Law to put the Servants of the Living God to death, if they returned after they were sentenced away, which did come near to me at that time; and as I considered the Thing, and pondered it in my Heart, immediately came the Word of the Lord unto me, saying, Thou knowest not but that thou mayst go thither. But I kept this Word in my Heart, and did not declare it to any until the time Appointed. So, after that, a Vessel was made ready for Rhode Island, which I passed in. So, after a little time that I had been there, visiting the Seed which the Lord hath Blessed, the Word of the Lord came unto me, saying, Go to Boston, with thy Brother, William Robinson. And at His Command I was Obedient, and gave up myself to do His Will, that so His Work and Service may be accomplished; For, he had said to me, That he had a great Work for me to do; which is now come to pass: And for yielding Obedience to, and obeying the Voice and Command of the Everlasting God, which created Heaven and Earth, and the Fountains of Waters, Do I, with my dear Brother, suffer outward Bonds near unto Death. And this is given forth to be upon Record, that all people may know, who hear it, That *we came not in our own Wills, but in the Will of God.* Given forth by me, who am known to Men by the name of

MARMADUKE STEPHENSON,

But who have a new Name given me, which the World knows not of, written in the book of Life.[1]

Written in Boston-prison
in the 8th Month, 1659."

---

[1] *New England Judged*, pp. 131-133.

Mary Dyer wrote in a similar strain:

"I am by many charged with the guiltiness of my own blood, in my coming to Boston. But I am therein clear and justified by the Lord in whose will I came. . . . I have no self-ends, the Lord knoweth, for if my life were freely granted by you, it would not avail me, so long as I should daily hear or see the sufferings of these people, my dear brethren and seed, with whom my life is bound up, as I have done these two years. . . . It is not my own life I seek (for I choose rather to suffer with the people of God than to enjoy the pleasures of Egypt) but the Life of the seed which I know the Lord hath blessed. . . . Do you think you can restrain those whom you call 'cursed Quakers' from coming among you, by anything you can do to them! God hath a Seed here among you for whom we have suffered and yet suffer and the Lord of the harvest will send more laborers to gather this seed. In love and in the spirit of meekness,

MARY DYER." [1]

These three were brought before the General Court on the 19th of October and asked why they had come. "In obedience to the call of the Lord," was their answer. Governor Endicott was plainly embarrassed, and, hesitating to take the final step, he sent the prisoners back to the jail. The next day after the morning sermon which had called loudly for extreme measures with this "cursed sect," [2] the prisoners were called and given this sentence: "Hearken, you shall be led back to the place from whence you came and from thence to the place of execution, to be hanged on the gallows till you are dead." "The will of the Lord be done," was Mary Dyer's response. "Take her away, Marshall," called the Governor. "Yea, joyfully shall I go," answered the unmoved woman. [3]

The execution was set for the 27th. As the time approached the thoughtful people, those who loved freedom and had suffered in Old England for their own bold views, began to revolt in spirit against the violence and cruelty about to be enacted. Many were "amazed and

---

[1] *New England Judged*, pp. 288-291.   [2] *Ibid.* p. 120.

[3] The death sentence of these three Friends is given in *Records of Massachusetts Colony*, vol. iv. part i. p. 383. The court ordered "That the Rev. Mr. Zackery Simes and Mr. John Norton repair to the prison and tender their endeavours to make the prisoners sensible of their approaching danger and prepare them for their approaching end."—*Ibid.* p. 383.

wondered," in the quaint language of the day, "the thing struck among them." A multitude of citizens flocked about the prison on the morning of the execution, and "William Robinson put his head out of his window and spoke to the people concerning the things of God," and they listened with serious attention.[1] An officer endeavoured to disperse the crowd, but finding that he was unable to do it, he rushed to the prison "in a fret and heat, furiously hurling some of us down stairs, and shut us up in a low dark 'cub' where we could not see the people."[2] Then there breaks out this fine account of the last moments together, written by one who was in the company :

"Shut up in this dark and solitary place we sat waiting upon the Lord. It was a time of Love, for though the world hated us and despitefully used us, yet the Lord was pleased in a wonderful manner to manifest His supporting Love and kindness to us in our innocent suffering. And especially the two Worthies [Robinson and Stephenson] who had near finished their course bore themselves with a heavenly cheerfulness and they spake many sweet and heavenly sayings of comfort."[3]

Lest the victims might speak and stir up the people again, drums were beat as they marched to the gallows. They did *try* to speak, but the drums made such a din that the people heard only the words, "This is the day of your visitation." But their faces spoke in spite of the drums, for "glorious signs of heavenly joy and gladness were beheld in their countenances." They walked hand in hand, with Mary Dyer in the middle. "Are you not ashamed to walk thus between two young men?" asked the coarse official. "No," replied the exalted woman, "this is to me the hour of the greatest joy I ever had in this world. No ear can hear, nor tongue can utter and no heart can understand the sweet incomes and the refreshings of the Spirit of the Lord which I now feel."[4]

The doomed men, on the steps of the gallows, gave their last brief call to the people to follow the Light of Christ,

---

[1] "Daniel Gould's Narrative" in *New England Judged*, p. 476. Gould was a fellow-prisoner. [2] *Ibid*. p. 476.
[3] Gould's Narrative, *ibid*. pp. 476-477. [4] *New England Judged*, p. 134.

and the two men sealed their faith with their lives.   At the last moment Mary Dyer, her arms and legs already bound and her face covered with a handkerchief, loaned for the purpose by her old pastor of the Boston Church, the Rev. Mr. Wilson, was "reprieved." The sudden "reprieve" of Mary Dyer was in reality a piece of acting : there had been no intention of actually hanging her. John Winthrop, Jr., Governor of Connecticut, had pleaded with the magistrates of Boston, "as on his bare knees," not to hang the Quakers ; Governor Temple of Acadia and Nova Scotia had offered to take them away from Massachusetts and to provide for them at his own expense ; finally Mary Dyer's son, William Dyer, had begged for his mother's life.

Under these circumstances the Court decided not to hang the condemned woman.   The Colonial Records for 18th October 1659 contain this order :

"It is ordered that the said Mary Dyer shall have liberty for forty-eight hours to depart out of this Jurisdiction, after which time, being found therein, she is to be forthwith executed. *And it is further ordered that she shall be carried to the place of execution and there to stand upon the Gallows with a rope about her neck until the* Rest be executed ; and then to return to the prison and remain as aforesaid." [1]

She stubbornly refused to accept her life, if the law was still to remain against "the suffering seed." She was, however, set on horseback and carried away toward Rhode Island.   After a short stay at home, she went on a religious visit to Shelter Island in Long Island Sound. We get one glimpse of her from John Taylor, who was labouring in Shelter Island at the time of this visit.   He says :

"One who came to Shelter Island was Mary Dyer. She was a comly woman and a grave matron and even *shined in the Image of God.*   We had several brave meetings there together and the Lord's power and presence was with us gloriously." [2]

But "the fire and hammer" were in her soul and she

[1] *Records of Massachusetts Colony*, iv. part i. p. 384.
[2] *Memoir of John Taylor*, p. 21.

could not stay away from "the bloody town of her sad and heavy experience."

"She said," John Taylor tells us, "that she must go and desire the repeal of that wicked law against God's people and offer up her life there." She arrived in Boston the 21st of May 1660. "Are you the same Mary Dyer that was here before?" asked Endicott. "I am the same." "You will own yourself a Quaker, will you not?" "I own myself to be reproachfully so called." Then followed the expected sentence.[1] "This is no more than what thou saidst before." "But now," said the Governor, "it is to be executed." "I came," she said solemnly, "in obedience to the will of God at your last General Court, desiring you to repeal your unrighteous laws of banishment on pain of death; and that same is my word now, and earnest request, although I told you that if you refused to repeal them, the Lord would send others of His servants to witness against them."

Her husband, one of the foremost citizens of Rhode Island and a founder of the Aquidneck Colony, pleaded for his wife's life.[2] She was offered her life, as she stood on the ladder of the gallows, if she would return home. "Nay I cannot," was her firm answer. "In obedience to the will of the Lord God I came and in His will I abide faithful to death." She was asked if she would like one of the Elders to pray for her, and she answered in the simplicity of her spirit, "Nay, first a child, then a young man, then a strong man before an Elder," and then with words about her "eternal happiness" she went to meet the Saviour "in whose image she shined" even here below.[3]

The only other capital execution was that of William Leddra of Barbadoes[4]—a strange place, we should think to-day, to furnish to the city of Boston a martyr for

[1] The sentence is given in *Records of Massachusetts Colony*, vol. iv. part i. p. 419.
[2] See William Dyer's letter to Governor Endicott in Roger's *Mary Dyer*, pp. 94-97.
[3] John Taylor's testimony is: "She has gone into Eternal life and glory forever."—*Op. cit.* p. 22.
[4] He was a native of Cornwall, England, but had for some time made his home in Barbadoes, where he had been an "approved minister."

spiritual religion. He had already, like his aged friend William Brend, suffered almost unspeakable torture from whippings and hard prison experiences—" in the bloody den," as Bishop calls it—and had been banished on pain of death. He returned and was re-imprisoned in December 1660. He was chained to a log of wood and kept all winter in "the miserable cold" of an unheated prison. The charges against him were sympathy with those who had been executed, refusal to remove his hat, his use of thee and thou—in fact, the crime of being a Quaker. When he saw that he was to be sentenced under the Act of October 1658, he appealed as an English subject for a trial under the laws of England, but his appeal was refused. He was then urged to recant, and was promised his life if he would "conform." "What," he answered, "act so that every man who meets me would say, 'this is the man that has forsaken the God of his salvation!'" Remaining unshaken, he was sentenced to death, the date set for the execution being the 14th of March.[1]

He died in the same triumphant spirit which characterised his companions in martyrdom.

"I testify," he wrote shortly before his death, "in the fear of the Lord and witness with a trembling pen, that the noise of the whip on my back, all the imprisonments, and banishments on pain of death, and the loud threatenings of a halter did no more affright me, through the strength and power of God, than if they had threatened to bind a spider's web to my finger. . . . I desire, as far as the Lord draws me, to follow my forefathers and brethren in suffering and in joy. My spirit waits and worships at the feet of Immanuel."[2]

On the day before he went to death, he wrote a beautiful and tender letter to "the Little Flock of Christ," in which he said :

"The sweet influences of the Morning Star, like a flood, distilling into my habitation [a dark cold room, "little larger than a saw-pit," where he was still chained to a log] have so filled me with the joy of the Lord in the beauty of holiness that my spirit is as if it did not inhabit a tabernacle of clay, but

---

[1] *New England Judged*, p. 317.   [2] *Ibid*. pp. 296-297.

is wholly swallowed up in the bosom of eternity from whence it had its beginning. . . . As the flowing of the ocean doth fill every creek and branch and then retires again toward its own being and fulness, leaving a savour behind, so doth the Life and Power of God flow into our hearts making us partakers of His Divine Nature, therefore let *this Life* alone be your joy and consolation." [1]

He died as a martyr should, in calm faith, with noble bearing. The spectators bore witness that "the Lord did mightily appear in the man." [2]

As Mary Dyer's lifeless body hung from the gallows and swung in the wind Humphrey Atherton of Boston pointed to it and said in jest—"She hangs there as a flag!" Like many things said in jest on historic occasions, the word was literally true. She did hang as a flag—she was a sign and a symbol of a deathless loyalty—and it was a sign which the wayfaring man could read. Her death showed, as did also the deaths of the other martyrs, that, whether right or wrong in their fundamental beliefs, a people had come to these shores who were not to be turned aside by any dangers or terrors which mortal man could devise, who were pledged to loyalty to the voice of God in their souls and ready to follow it, even though it took them to the hardest suffering and death. Every martyr was, thus, in truth a flag.

[1] An "Epistle to the Society of the Little Flock of Christ," in *New England Judged*, pp. 299-302.

[2] From a letter written by Thomas Wilkie of Barbadoes.—Bowden's *History*, i. 315.

Joseph and Jane Nicholson of Cumberland, England, fell under the provisions of the capital law and they were in prison in irons when Mary Dyer was hung, but for some reason—for fear that their execution would excite the common people of Boston, Joseph Nicholson says—they were allowed to go free. Joseph Nicholson wrote *The Standard of the Lord lifted up in New England*, London, 1660.

Edward Wharton of Salem was fellow-prisoner with William Leddra through all his last imprisonment and barely escaped with his life. For saying that Robinson and Stephenson were wickedly killed and that the guilt of their blood was greater than he could bear, he was whipped with twenty lashes and fined twenty pounds. Early in the year 1660 he was arrested in his house for being a Quaker and brought before Governor Endicott. He was kept nearly a year in prison, through the winter, being in the same "cub" with William Leddra, and at the Court which sentenced Leddra to death, Wharton was banished on pain of death, and given ten days to leave the jurisdiction. He stayed in Boston and attended his friend to the gallows and caught his lifeless body as it fell from the scaffold, and with three other brave Friends he gave the body burial. He then went quietly to his home and wrote to the authorities of Boston that he was there and expected to stay there!—*New England Judged*, pp. 315-325 and p. 342. Besse, ii. 220-221.

CHAPTER V

THE KING'S MISSIVE

WHILE these Friends were thus joyously dedicating their lives to purchase freedom to worship God, and to win the privilege of holding the faith which to their souls seemed true and spiritual, their fellow-believers in England were putting forth every exertion in their power to stop "the vein of innocent blood" which was flowing in Boston.

George Fox, an extraordinarily sensitive, sympathetic, and even telepathic person, had been deeply moved by the sufferings of those who were in some measure his disciples. He says :

"When those were put to death (in New England) I was in prison at Lancaster, and I had a perfect sense of their sufferings as though it had been myself, and as though the halter had been put about my own neck, *though we had not at that time heard of it.*" [1]

Christopher Holder and his companions, John Copeland and John Rous, were now in England, visible "witnesses," with their cropped ears, of the way the bearers of the gospel of inward Light were treated in the Puritan Colony. Samuel Shattuck, Josiah Southwick, and Nicholas Phelps of Salem, banished from their home for espousing the cause of the Quakers, were also in England bearing their testimony. In 1659 Humphrey Norton told his powerful story of suffering and wrongs.[2] This was followed in 1660 by *The Standard of the Lord*

---

[1] Fox's *Journal*, i. 507. Fox is probably incorrect here in regard to the date of his *experience*. News of the martyrdom of Robinson and Stephenson reached England in February 1660 (see Dewsbury's account and A. Parker's letter to Margaret Fell, Swarthmore Collection, i. 169), while Fox was not imprisoned in Lancaster until May 1660. [2] *The New England Ensign.*

lifted up in New England, written by Joseph Nicholson, who with his wife had extensively laboured and greatly suffered in New England ; and the next year came the first edition of George Bishop's book, packed with an array of atrocious persecutions—his *New England Judged,* a copy of which King Charles II. read. It is said that the King was reading in Bishop's book the account of a Friend's appeal from the cruel course of the Colony to the privileges of the laws of England, and came upon Major-General Denison's slighting remark on authority and procedure in England. Denison, it seems, had met the Quakers' claim of a right to appeal to the English government for justice with the scoffing remark that it would do no good if they did. "This year," he said, "you will go and complain to Parliament, and the next year they will send out to see how it is, and the third year the government will be changed!"[1] *i.e.* nothing will be done. The King was deeply impressed by this passage, and noted the difference between this language and the humble tone of the address from New England on the occasion of his accession. He called his courtiers and read the passage to them, and added : "Lo, these are my good subjects of New England, but I will put a stop to them!"[2] In addition came a very concrete list of sufferings which was presented to the King in the form of a Petition signed by the men who had been banished from Massachusetts. The list contained the following items :

1. Two honest and innocent women stripped stark naked and searched in an inhuman manner.

2. Twelve strangers in that country, but freeborn of this nation, received twenty-three whippings, most of them with a whip of three cords with knots at the ends.

3. Eighteen inhabitants of the country, being freeborn English, received twenty-three whippings.

4. Sixty-four imprisonments "of the Lord's people," amounting to five hundred and nineteen weeks.

5. Two beaten with pitched ropes, the blows amounting to an hundred and thirty-nine.

---

[1] *New England Judged*, p. 82.   [2] Sewel's *History*, i. 492.

6. An innocent old man banished from his wife and children, and for returning put in prison for above a year.

7. Twenty-five banished upon penalties of being whipped, or having their ears cut, or a hand branded.

8. Fines, amounting to a thousand pounds, laid upon the inhabitants for meeting together.

9. Five kept fifteen days without food.

10. One laid neck and heels in irons for sixteen hours.

11. One very deeply burnt in the right hand with an H after he had been beaten with thirty stripes.

12. One chained to a log of wood for the most part of twenty days in winter time.

13. *Five appeals to England denied.*

14. Three had their right ears cropped off.

15. One inhabitant of Salem, since banished on pain of death, had one-half of his house and land seized.

16. Two ordered sold as bond-servants.

17. Eighteen of the people of God banished on pain of death.

18. Three of the servants of God put to death.[1]

19. Since the executions four more banished on pain of death and twenty-four heavily fined for meeting to worship God.[2]

To offset these vivid portrayals of wrongs endured, the authorities in Massachusetts presented their side of the case. They had sent a Petition to King Charles, soon after his accession, expressing their loyalty to his government and hope of his favour to their Colony. "May it please your Majesty," they wrote, "in the day you happily know that you are king over your Brittish Israel to cast a favourable eye upon your poore Mehibboseth," *i.e.* Massachusetts Colony. In this address they took occasion to defend themselves for their treatment of the Quakers, by making the latter out to be a type of persons not fit to live on the earth. "They are open blasphemers," the address says, "open seducers from the glorious Trinity, the Lord's Christ, the blessed gospel, and from the Holy Scriptures as the rule of life. They are open enemies to the government itself as established in the hand of any but men of their own principles. They are malignant promoters of doctrines

---

[1] William Leddra was executed after this was written.
[2] Besse's *Sufferings*, i. pp. xxx.-xxxi.

directly tending to subvert both our church and state." [1]
In addition to this Petition to the King the Court of
Massachusetts sent an address to Parliament and instructions to its London Agent, Leverett, to do his utmost to
prevent an action which would tie the hands of the
colonial authorities from acting in their own way with the
Quakers.[2] Richard Bellingham also wrote a pamphlet
setting forth the necessity of suppressing the Quakers.
" There is more danger," he declared, " in this People to
trouble and overcome England than in the King of the
Scotts and the Popish Princes of Germany." [3]

After serious consultation among Friends in England
it was decided to lay the Quaker sufferings before the
Privy Council, and it was arranged for Edward Burrough
to prepare an Address to the King—" Some Considerations," it is modestly called—presenting the true situation
and urging him to use his power to stop the persecution
now going on in his Colony. He refutes point by point
the charges in the " Petition and Address of the General
Court " of Massachusetts. He denies that Quakers have
ever been "impetuous or turbulent," that they have ever
" lifted up a hand or made a turbulent gesture " against
any authority either in Church or State, or that they have
ever been " found with a carnal weapon about them," or
that they had committed any crime, " saving, that they
warned sinners to repent." Those who have gone to
death in the Colony have been " martyred for the name
of Christ," solely for a " difference in judgment and
practice concerning spiritual things." He insists that these
sufferers went to New England because they were " moved
of the Holy Spirit " to go, and that those who have died
there have died " for a good conscience "—which was the
simple truth.

When the news of William Leddra's execution reached

---

[1] Printed in *Records of Massachusetts Colony*, vol. iv. part i. pp. 450-453.
Quoted also in Edward Burrough's " Some Considerations Presented unto the King
of England Being an Answer unto a Petition and Address of the General Court of
Boston in New England." *Works* of Edward Burrough (London, 1672) pp.
756-763.
[2] *Hutchinson Collection*, p. 329.
[3] Quoted in Howgil's Popish Inquisition, *Works*, p. 259.

the Friends in England, Edward Burrough sought an interview in person with the King. He said to the King, " There is a vein of innocent blood opened in thy dominions which will run over all, if it is not stopped." To which the King at once replied, " but I will stop that vein." " Then stop it speedily," said Burrough, " for we know not how many may soon be put to death." " As speedily as ye will. Call the Secretary and I will do it presently." [1] The secretary came and a mandamus was prepared on the spot. Edward Burrough pressed that it be despatched with haste. " But I have no occasion at present to send a ship thither," answered the King. " If *you* care to send one you may do it," and he gave Burrough the privilege of naming the messenger to carry the mandamus. Burrough at once named Samuel Shattuck, the Salem Quaker who had been banished from the Colony on pain of death! and the King appointed him as his royal messenger.

The Friends then chartered a ship of Ralph Goldsmith, himself a Quaker, and agreed with him for three hundred pounds to sail in ten days for Boston with the King's messenger and missive.[2]

The colonists were warned in advance by the colonial agent, Leverett, that the Quakers had brought their grievances to the notice of the King, and there was an ominous impression in the minds of many that they had much to fear from the new sovereign, who was known to have no sympathy with the theological or political ideals which were the very pillars of the New England commonwealth. It seemed wisest to bow somewhat to the threatening storm, and so an order was issued by the colonial authorities, permitting all Quakers then in prison " to depart and go for England." [3] This order released twenty-seven Quakers who were at the time in Boston prison, most of whom were " convinced " colonists, though the list included some newly arrived Quaker " publishers " : Elizabeth Hooton, Joan Brocksoppe, Mary Mallins,

---

[1] See Sewel's *History*, i. 473.
[2] This account is taken from Fox's *Journal*, i. 507-509.
[3] *Records of Massachusetts Colony*, vol. iv. part i. p. 433.

Catherine Chattam, and John Burstow and Peter Pearson, who had already done extensive missionary work in the Colonies.

Meantime another Friend was being doomed to death and was in imminent danger of execution. This was Wenlock Christison. His origin and antecedent history are unknown. He suddenly *appears* in New England leaving no clear trail behind him. He always claims to be a British subject and he once directly implies that he has come from England. Harrison, in his valuable monograph,[1] thinks that Christison was of Scottish descent and that the blood of the Covenanters flowed in his veins. At any rate he was possessed of martyr-fibre. He first comes to public notice as one among many Friends who were thrown into prison in Boston, 13th December 1660. He had just come from Salem and was evidently moving about from place to place, as the way opened for him to perform religious service. He was arrested, and banished on pain of death. After his release he visited Plymouth Colony, where he was imprisoned fourteen weeks, in cold winter weather, " tied neck and heels together," flogged " with twenty-seven cruel stripes on his naked body," and deprived of his Bible and clothes—" waistcoat, two other coats, hat and bag of linen "—to the value of four pounds for prison fees. This was for " coming into one Colony when he was banished from another."

Being at length released, he returned to Boston and suddenly appeared before the Court, precisely as they were pronouncing sentence of death on William Leddra! The magistrates were " struck with a great damp " when they saw another man " unconcerned for his life come to trample under the law of Death." " For a little space of time, there was silence in the Court, but recovering from the swoon, one of the Court cried out, ' Here is another, fetch him to the bar.' "[2]

Then followed this dialogue : " Is your name Wenlock Christison ? "

[1] Harrison's *Wenlock Christison and the Friends in Talbot County, Maryland* (Baltimore, 1878), p. 16.
[2] *New England Judged*, p. 319.

" Yes."

" Wast not thou banished on pain of death?"

" Yes, I was."

" What dost thou here then?"

" I am come to warn you, that you shed no more blood."

It was hoped that Leddra's death would awe him into submission, and on the day of that Friend's execution Christison was given an opportunity to renounce his views and so save his life. " Nay," was his reply, " I shall not change my religion, nor seek to save my life. I do not intend to deny my Master, and if I lose my life for Christ's sake I shall save it."

His brave manner and saintly bearing made a profound impression on some of the magistrates, and Governor Endicott had difficulty in securing a capital sentence. For two weeks there was a stern division in the Court, and " a spirit of confusion." A determined minority stood out against " the bloody course," and urged a change of policy. Governor Endicott was so incensed by the opposition that he struck his fist on the table and declared, " I could find it in my heart to go back home " [i.e. to England]. " Record those who will not consent—I thank God I am not afraid to give judgment." He then pronounced the sentence of death to be executed on 13th June 1661.[1] Then the calm, unmoved victim spoke these solemn words : " The will of the Lord be done. In the will of God I came amongst you, and in His counsel I stand, feeling His eternal power, that will uphold me to the last gasp. Be it known unto you all, that if you have power to take my life from me, my soul will enter into everlasting rest and peace with God ; and if you have power to take my life from me, the which I question, I believe, you will never more take Quakers' lives from them. Note my words : Do not think to

---

[1] Richard Russell was one of the magistrates who refused to give his consent to the prisoner's death, and the whole Court was much moved by the receipt at this very time of Edward Wharton's letter saying that though banished on pain of death he was at his home in Salem and intended to remain there, about his occupation. See Besse, ii. 223, and Sewel, i. 488-490.

weary out the living God by taking away the lives of His servants. What do you gain by it? *For the last man you put to death, here are five come in his room.*[1] *And if you have power to take my life from me God can raise up the same principle of life in ten of His servants and send them among you in my room.*"

He was not called upon, however, to suffer his penalty, and he lived to see his predictions fulfilled. Just before the time appointed for his hanging an order was granted for his release and for the liberation of a large number of Friends as related above. The release was due to the desire to propitiate those who were using the Quaker persecution as a ground for royal interference, for the magistrates realised that only by most delicate diplomacy could they preserve satisfactory relations with the mother-country, though they hardly suspected the humiliation which Goldsmith's ship was bringing them.[2]

Ralph Goldsmith, though buffeted in the early part of his voyage with heavy storms, brought his ship across in six weeks and anchored in the harbour on a " First-day." The people of the city flocked on board to ask for letters but were told that no letters would be delivered on " First-day "! They reported on shore that the ship was loaded with Quakers, some of them persons banished on pain of death.

Samuel Shattuck tells it in his own quaint way as follows :

"When wee came into Boston harbour many came on ship-board for Newes and Letters ; But were somewhat struck in Amaze when they saw what wee were. When wee came on shoar," Shattuck continues, "wee found all very still and a very great calme ; the moderate sort (as I met them) Rejoiced to see me and some of the violent wee met as men chained and bowed down and could not look us in the face."[3]

---

[1] The five newly arrived " publishers of truth."

[2] There is an entry in the *Massachusetts Colonial Records* which appears to be a letter from Wenlock Christison signifying his willingness to depart from that jurisdiction if he is granted his freedom, adding, " I know not yt ever I shall com into it any more." (*Massachusetts Archives*, x. 273). He did, however, continue to labour within that jurisdiction and was various times afterwards arrested and punished. (See *New England Judged*, pp. 433, 440, 457, and 467).

[3] *Aspinwall Papers*, part i. p. 160.

So they passed on to the home of the Governor and asked for admission to his presence. As they insisted that they could deliver their message only to the Governor himself, they were ushered into his presence, Samuel Shattuck wearing his hat. Endicott in anger ordered the hat taken off, which was done by a servant. Whereupon Shattuck produced his credentials as a royal messenger and showed the mandamus. The Governor at once uncovered and ordered the Quaker's hat to be given back to him, and then he read the mandamus which was as follows :

"CHARLES R.

"Trusty and well-beloved, we greet you well. Having been informed that several of our subjects among you, called Quakers, have been and are imprisoned by you, whereof some have been executed, and others (as hath been represented unto us) are in danger to undergo the like ; we have thought fit to signify our pleasure in that behalf for the future, and do hereby require, that if there be any of those people called Quakers amongst you, now already condemned to suffer death or other corporal punishment ; or that are imprisoned, and obnoxious to the like condemnation, you are to forbear to proceed any further therein ; but that you forthwith send the said persons (whether condemned or imprisoned) over into their own kingdom of England, together with their respective crimes or offences laid to their charge ; to the end such course may be taken with them here as shall be agreeable to our laws and their demerits. And for so doing, these our letters shall be your sufficient warrant and discharge.

"Given at our Court, at Whitehall, the 9th day of September 1661, in the 13th year of our reign.

"To our trusty and well-beloved John Endicott, Esq., and to all and every other governor or governors of our plantations of New England, and of all the colonies thereunto belonging, that now are, or hereafter shall be ; and to all and every the ministers and officers of our plantations and colonies whatsoever, within the continent of New England.

"By his Majesty's command,

"WILLIAM MORRIS." [1]

---

[1] This incident is happily and beautifully told by Whittier in "The King's Missive." Whittier's poem provoked severe criticism from the Rev. Dr. George E. Ellis, on the ground that the poem was historically inaccurate, and considerable discussion ensued. The substance of the discussion is given in Pickard's *John Greenleaf Whittier*, pp. 775-785.

It was an extremely trying order and a humiliating situation. To send the prisoners to England was plainly out of the question, and the order was imperative that they should "proceed no further," either with death sentences or with "other corporal punishment." "We shall obey his Majesty's commands," was the Governor's laconic decision as he turned to Samuel Shattuck, and this order was issued :

"To William Salter, keeper of the prison at Boston, you are requested, by authority and order of the General Court, to release and discharge the Quakers who at present are in your custody. See that you do not neglect this. By order of the Court.

"EDWARD RAWSON, Secretary."[1]

As a result of this order a large release of prisoners was made, among them the venerable Nicholas Upsall who had lain in the prison of his own city for two years. John Chamberlein, who had been convinced of the Quaker truth at the gallows, when Robinson and Stephenson were executed, was also among those who were liberated, and the Friends gathered at his house for their meeting of rejoicing, Chamberlein's house being at this period the regular meeting-place of the Friends in Boston. Shattuck's letter, already quoted from, gives a fresh impression of the joy and triumph which the new turn of affairs brought to the long-suffering band :

"The coming of our ship is of very wonderfull service, for the Bowells of the moderate sort are greatly refreshed throughout the Country, and many mouths are now opened, which were before shutt and some of them now say, Its the welcomest ship that ever came into this Land."

The authorities of the Colony had, as we have seen, anticipated royal interposition and had already changed their policy of dealing with the Quakers, but none the less this "missive" from the King marks an epoch in the history of colonial Puritans. They might congratulate Charles the Second and ask him to "cast favourable eyes on poore Mehibboseth," but in their hearts they knew that a dangerous turn of the tide had set in, and that the

[1] Besse, ii. 226. Sewel, i. 492-496.

enemy of their faith and of their ideals was now their sovereign. They no longer had behind them the great moral and spiritual England of the Commonwealth, and they were never again to have an entirely free hand in working out their lofty vision of a New England, which in their dreams was to be a New Jerusalem——a Republic of the saints of God. They had fought their Armageddon and it was a drawn battle. It was now unmistakably evident that the Colony must henceforth be *shared* with these unwelcome Quaker guests. The founders of it had used their extreme measures to keep the Colony immune and they had failed. Their own people were in revolt against their system of expulsion and extermination, they saw ten Quakers coming for every one who was killed, and now one of these same Quakers, banished on pain of death, had come boldly in as the inviolable messenger of an anti-Puritan king. "Give Mr. Shattuck his hat!" "The King's command shall be obeyed!" were two sentences which must have cost brave old Endicott profound pain.

There was a momentary lull in the storm of persecution, but it was only a temporary relief and no surrender, for so long as John Norton remained the guardian of orthodoxy, and so long as John Endicott was left as the representative embodiment of the Puritan ideal, there could be little peace for the Quaker, with his claim of an inward Light, even though there were a danger that King Charles might occasionally be stirred to call a halt, and to show that he meant what he said in the Declaration of Breda.[1]

On the constitutional point of transferring their prisoners to England to be tried the colonists did not yield an iota, and in the weighty deliberations which followed upon their duties to the King they showed a good measure of the spirit which swept through New England again more than a hundred years later. They declared that their "patent" was the foundation of the

[1] "We do declare liberty to tender consciences, and that no man shall be disquieted or called in question for differences of opinion in matters of religion."

rights of the Colony, and they asserted that "any imposition prejudicial to the country, contrary to any just laws of ours not repugnant to the laws of England, is *an infringment of our right*"; and they further declared that, "it may well stand with the loyalty and obedience of subjects to plead with their princes against all such as shall endeavour the violation of their privileges."[1] But from this time forward frequent interferences occurred on the part of the King. It is true that he informed the Massachusetts officials, through their agents, that Parliament had made sharp laws against the Quakers, and "we are content you should do the like,"[2] but in the same letter the King insists that all public officers in the Colony shall be chosen without reference to their religious opinions and profession, and royal commissions after this date more than once called a halt on Quaker persecution, as we shall see. It is with some humiliation that we are compelled to thank Charles II. for the first stay of persecution, since interferences by a royal prerogative later endangered the colonial charters and attempted to thwart the democratic experiment of the colonists in every way possible, but the harried Quaker took his temporary relief without much compunction! For the moment, however, the relief was slight.

The old law inflicting banishment on pain of death had already been altered, before the King's "missive" came, and a new law had been drawn up designed to be more *effective* and at the same time not so obnoxious to the Home Government, or so revolting to the people. This new law, passed the 22nd of May 1661, was the atrocious "Cart and Whip Act." It began with the statement that the Court was "desirous to try all means, with as much lenity as may consist with our safety, to prevent the intrusion of the Quakers," followed with the usual amount of vigorous description of the persons so named. It was then enacted that any person "not giving civil respect by the usual gestures, or by any other means

---

[1] *Records of Massachusetts Colony*, vol. iv. part ii. p. 25.
[2] *Colonial Papers*, 28th June 1662.

manifesting himself to be a Quaker, shall . . . be stripped naked from the middle upwards and be tied to a cart's tail and whipped through the town, and from thence immediately conveyed to the constable of the next town, towards the borders of our jurisdictions, and so from constable to constable till they be conveyed through any of the outwardmost towns of our jurisdiction." If "such vagabond Quaker" returns, he is to be whipped out again, and so on for three times. The fourth time he is to be branded on the left shoulder with the letter R and whipped out of the Colony. Then, if finally the said Quaker proves to be "an incorrigible rogue and enemy of the common peace," he is to suffer, if there is anything left of him, under the old law of 1658.[1] Some of the Friends who were liberated from prison when the change of policy was initiated, were punished under this new law. Peter Pearson and Judith Brown were selected, among the prisoners in custody when the Act was passed, to be the first examples of its cruelty. They had both been banished and had returned "to look the law in the face," and probably for this reason they were chosen to suffer at the cart-tail. They received twenty stripes on their naked backs as they went through Boston on their way out of the "jurisdiction." All the other Friends set free at this great "delivery" were ordered to be driven out of the territory by a guard of soldiers. John Chamberlein was whipped nine times at the cart's tail "because he suffered a meeting at his house,"[2] and was liberated a second time by the King's missive. George Wilson, also a native citizen, was whipped with Chamberlein through three towns, the executioner using for the purpose an ingeniously cruel whip which tore the flesh in barbarous fashion.[3] Josiah Southwick and Nicholas Phelps had returned from their banishment in the autumn of 1661. Phelps, whose constitution had been undermined by what he had undergone, died soon after his arrival. Southwick, with almost excessive Quaker frankness, appeared before

---

[1] *Records of Massachusetts Colony*, vol. iv. part ii. p. 2.
[2] *Aspinwall Papers*, part i. p. 161.   [3] Besse, ii. 224.

the authorities and announced his return to his country. He was apprehended and whipped through Boston, Roxbury, and Dedham, and then carried fifteen miles and left in the wilderness. The next morning he fearlessly returned to his home in Salem, having told his torturers that he "cared no more for what they could do to him than for a feather blown in the air."[1]

The terrible "Cart and Whip Act" was re-enacted, in slightly modified form, the 8th of October 1662, and under this law some of the most harrowing tortures were inflicted.[2] Two instances, both of which are historically too important to be omitted, will suffice, and many of the details can be spared. The first instance is the case of Alice Ambrose, Mary Tomkins, and Ann Coleman.

These three Friends, about whose earlier history little is known, had come from England, probably in the summer of 1662, with a sense of a call to pioneer service in the Colonies. Their chief interest to us lies in the fact that they were "the first publishers" of the Quaker message in what later came to be a great Quaker centre, namely, the Piscataqua region—particularly the country about Dover and Portsmouth, New Hampshire—and also in the region which they call "the Province of Mayn."[3]

Edward Wharton, of Salem, one of the foremost of the native Quaker ministers of the early period, and George Preston, also of Salem, with two of the English women, Alice Ambrose and Mary Tomkins, made their way to Dover, and took up their headquarters in an inn there, where they received many inquirers, made many convincements, and solidly established their truth in the minds of a group of the Dover people, though they came into violent collision with the ministers of the town, especially with one whom they call "priest Rayner." They found here in Dover a prepared group ready for their views, much like the groups which had existed in

---

[1] *New England Judged*, p. 356.

[2] *Records of Massachusetts Colony*, vol. iv. part ii. p. 59.

[3] These women were not actually the first Quaker missionaries to reach the Piscataqua region, as William Robinson and Marmaduke Stephenson had already been there in 1659 (see Bishop, p. 117), though we have no details of their work.

Newport, Sandwich, and Salem.   There had come to the
Piscataqua region, at an earlier time, some who were
unwelcome in Massachusetts because of their too free
religious views.   There were survivors of the great
Hutchinson controversy still living in the region, and
the ministry of the famous Hansard Knollys, the third
minister to come to the Dover church, had led many in
the direction of Anabaptist ideas.   The result was that
the little band of " publishers " left behind, as they pushed
farther eastward, a goodly number of believers in their
way of life.   From Dover they crossed over the Piscataqua
river into the Province of Maine, by invitation of Major
Shapleigh, a magistrate and leading citizen in the township of Kittery, evidently in the part since set off as the
township of Eliot.   " He was an enquiring man," Bishop
tells us,[1] a seeker, and he " kept a priest in his house " and
had a room set apart for public worship.   Under the
ministry of his new guests he and his wife were " convinced of truth," and became " obedient " to their new
light, and " truth got great dominion in the hearts of the
people there," which means that a Quaker meeting was
begun in the Province of Maine.   After a thorough
canvas of that region the four Friends returned to
Massachusetts.

Later in the year, as winter was approaching, the two
women, with Ann Coleman as companion, decided to
revisit those who had " received the truth in Piscataqua
river."   They had not been long in Dover before the
magistrates were stirred up by one of the ministers—the
" priest Rayner," who had disputed with them on the
former visit—to apply the " Cart and Whip Act " to the
visitors.   The following order was issued by a deputy-
magistrate named Walden :

" To the constables of Dover, Hampton, Salisbury, Newbury,
Rawley, Ipswich, Wenham, Lynn, Boston, Roxbury, Dedham ;
and until these vagabond Quakers are carried out of this jurisdiction.   You and every of you are required, in the King's
Majesty's name, to take these vagabond Quakers, Ann Coleman,

---

[1] *New England Judged*, p. 363.

Mary Tomkins, Alice Ambrose, and make them fast to the cart's tail, and driving the cart through your several towns, to whip them upon their backs, not exceeding ten stripes apiece on each of them, in each town, and so convey them from constable to constable till they come out of the jurisdiction." [1]

It was in the heart of a northern winter when these women were stripped to the waist and tied to the cart to trudge under the lash through these eleven towns, the snow lying "half-leg-deep," as they passed through Hampton; but we are told that "the presence of the Lord was so with them, in the extremity of their sufferings, that they sang in the midst of them to the astonishment of their enemies." [2]   Deliverance came unexpectedly in Salisbury, for Walter Barefoot asked to be made deputy-constable, and taking the matter into his own hands fearlessly set the women free.[3]

The women went straight back toward Piscataqua river, revisited Major Shapleigh on the way, and then came into Dover, where they again endured treatment too cruel and barbarous to be told in detail.[4]

The other extraordinary application of "the Cart and Whip Act" is the case of Elizabeth Hooton. She was the first woman "convinced" by Fox's preaching in England, and she was the first woman to manifest a gift for public ministry. She went through many dreadful persecutions in England, and finally laid down her life in the island of Jamaica.[5] She was at the time of her New England suffering advanced in years, and had made her

[1] This is dated at Dover, 22nd December 1662, and is signed by Richard Walden, though Bishop says that "priest Rayner" drew it up. When Alice Ambrose was asked her name she said, "My name is written in the Lamb's book of Life." "Nobody here knows that book," answered Walden.—*New England Judged*, p. 366.

[2] *New England Judged*, p. 367.

[3] Bishop says that John Wheelwright, "an old priest," advised the constable to go on with the whipping, p. 368.

[4] Besse, ii. 228. *New England Judged*, pp. 370-374.

[5] In *Devonshire House Portfolio*, No. 3, there are many papers by Elizabeth Hooton, to the priests about 1651, to Cromwell, to the Mayor of London, and a number to the King. Portfolio 3, 27 gives her sufferings in New England; 3, 35 is a lamentation for Boston in New England; 3, 36 a lamentation for Boston and Cambridge in New England; 3, 39 a threatening letter to the rulers of Boston; 3, 40 lays open cruelty in New England at Boston, Cambridge, Salem, etc.; also 3, 42 and 3, 43; 3, 45 gives passages on New England.

way to Virginia from Barbadoes, and had travelled all the way from Virginia through incredible hardships to Boston, where she was at once thrust into prison. Being released from prison she was conveyed to the limit of the Colony and left in the wilderness, making her way as best she could to Rhode Island. She went from there to Barbadoes and took ship again for Boston! Here she was taken by the constable and put on ship for Virginia, and after suffering for the faith there, she returned to England, but only for the purpose of carrying out her original plan— to preach in New England!

She now procured from the King a special license to permit her to build a house in America, and with the King's document sailed for Boston. Here she applied for liberty to build a house for herself to live in and for Friends to meet in. The privilege was stoutly refused, and this unwearied woman next started for the Piscataqua region.

At Hampton she was imprisoned. At Dover she was put in the stocks and kept four days in prison. Then she made her way back to Cambridge, where she was locked up in "a close, foul dungeon," and kept two days and nights without food or drink. A Friend, for there were by this time convinced Friends in almost all the New England towns, hearing of her sufferings, brought her some milk for which he was fined five pounds. An order was next issued for whipping this poor woman out of the jurisdiction, though she showed the King's document granting her the privilege of owning a house wherever she would in the Colony. She was tied to a post in Cambridge and given ten lashes with a three corded knotted whip. Then she was taken to Watertown, where she received ten lashes more. On a cold, frosty morning she was brought into Dedham, where, tied to a cart, the tortured body had ten lashes more. Torn and bleeding after a long day's journey she was left at night in the woods, and by what seemed to her friends a miraculous preservation she arrived next day at the town of Rehoboth (now the town of Seekonk) and made her way to Newport.

Notwithstanding this usage, to us seemingly unendurable, Elizabeth Hooton returned to Cambridge, where, after being "abused by a wicked crew of Cambridge scholars," she was whipped again, first in the town of Cambridge, and then from constable to constable through three towns toward Rhode Island. Again she went back to Boston and endeavoured to give her message. She was this time taken to the House of Correction and given ten stripes, and then whipped at a cart's tail through Roxbury, Dedham, and Medfield, and left, at the end of her whipping, in the woods. She got to a town where there were Friends who refreshed her, and, with indomitable persistence, she went back to Boston ! She was again whipped out of the town and threatened with death if she returned. We are told that " her inward consolations did so abound that she was able to bear all her afflictions in holy triumph, and in humble meekness she declared that she was willing, for the love she bore the souls of men, to suffer all and more for the seed's sake." [1]

Whether this sort of insistent importunity be judged holy boldness or fanaticism will depend largely, I suppose, upon the point of view—"the psychological climate"—of the person judging. This woman, it is plain, was " possessed " with a conviction of duty, and she believed that the way to break down the odious laws and the system of enforcing conformity was to impress the public with the inhuman character of the system, and to show the magistrates the utter futility of the laws for accomplishing their purpose, and she put the law and the system to this extreme test. The entire story of what was suffered on the tender bodies of men and women in the effort to break down the system of intolerance and to secure free worship cannot be told here in detail. I have made a complete list of all the sufferers and what they underwent, but it is too bulky to print here.

[1] Besse, ii. 228-231 : *New England Judged*, pp. 410-418. Elizabeth Hooton had still further sufferings in Boston, Salem, and Braintree, and on one occasion travelled on foot seventy miles to reach Rhode Island. She was in Boston at the time of Governor Endicott's death and attended his funeral, where she probably tried to speak (see Bowden i. 259). She died in the island of Jamaica in 1671.

The strain was in some instances too great for human nerves to bear, and a few persons—to us, with our knowledge of hysteria, suggestion, and auto-suggestion, surprisingly few—lost their mental balance and did things which belong properly to the list of fanatical acts. In 1663 Thomas Newhouse entered a church, and broke two empty bottles, crying out as he did so that thus those who persecuted Friends should be dashed in pieces. Thomas Newhouse appears to have been mentally unsettled. He became "lost to truth" and was disowned from the Society of Friends.[1]

In 1661, Catherine Chattam, another victim of harsh persecution, appeared in Boston clothed in sackcloth and ashes as a sign of troubles which the Lord would bring upon that persecuting city.[2]

There are two pitiful cases of women who were driven over the verge of sanity by the fury of the persecution which their families endured. The first of these was Lydia Wardel of Hampton. She was "a chaste and tender woman of exemplary modesty," but, harrowed by the treatment which was inflicted on her husband, and still more by the stripping and scourging of women which she had seen, she felt driven to appear unclothed in the congregation at Newbury. She yielded to the obsession and appeared as "a naked sign." The poor woman should have received wise medical treatment. Instead, both she and her husband were outrageously whipped.[3]

The other case was that of Deborah Wilson, wife of Robert Wilson of Salem and sister of Joshua Buffum and

[1] See William Edmundson's *Journal*, p. 61. Dr. Ellis in his *Massachusetts and its Early History*, p. 114, has related how two Quaker women, Sarah Gibbons and Dorothy Waugh, entered John Norton's church in Boston in 1658, and broke two bottles " as a sign of his emptiness." This incident is probably apocryphal. The two women did enter the church and "speak a few words," whereupon they were arrested and kept three days in jail without food. (*New England Judged*, p. 58.) None of the early authorities mention the bottles. See interesting note in Hallowell's *Pioneer Quakers*, p. 73.

[2] It must be remembered that both the Puritans and the Friends were diligent readers of the Hebrew prophets, and they, especially the Friends, made much of these "signs," which the prophets often felt called upon to "act" in person. Catherine Chattam was unmercifully whipped for this "acted sign," and passed through a severe illness from the strain, but she appears to have wholly recovered. She afterwards became the wife of John Chamberlein of Boston.

[3] *New England Judged*, pp. 376-377

Margaret Smith.   She, overwrought by the sufferings of her family, had a similar obsession, and felt constrained to walk through the town of Salem as "a naked sign."   As a punishment she was tied to a cart by the side of her mother and her sister Margaret Smith, and the three were whipped through the town, while her husband, "himself not altogether of her way, followed after, clapping his hat sometimes between the whip and her back." [1]

Margaret Brewster, in 1677, was, as she claimed, "raised up as one from the dead, and came from a sick bed" "to bear a testimony and be as a sign to warn the bloody town of Boston to end its cruel laws."   With her hair about her shoulders, ashes on her head, her face coloured black, and sackcloth on her upper garments, she came, attended by two other women, on Sunday morning into the Rev. Mr. Thatcher's meeting-house.

> "She came and stood in the Old South Church,
>   A wonder and a sign,
> With a look the old-time sibyls wore
>   Half-crazed and half-divine." [2]

It was a misguided act, no doubt, but no modern reader who studies the case in full can fail to conclude that her persecutors, who insisted that she "took on the shape of the devil," and who whipped her at the cart's tail from the Old South Church through the town of Boston, were at least as "misguided." [3]

Sad enough these instances of hysterical tendencies undoubtedly are, but no modern historian would think seriously of citing them as proof that the Quakers were lawless, immodest, or fanatical.   That they could stand such inhuman treatment for ten years—a veritable reign of terror—and keep calm and unmoved, and have only these few instances of hysteria and misleading impressions, speaks well for the character of their sanity and restraint. There is, so far as I know, no instance, in the list of sufferings, of any Quaker who "recanted," or who even

---

[1] *New England Judged*, pp. 383-384.

[2] Whittier's "In the Old South Church," which deals with this episode.

[3] For Margaret Brewster's trial see Besse, ii. 261-265.

gave up his practice of the unimportant Quaker "testimonies," such as wearing the hat and saying "thou," in order to win his freedom or to spare himself torture. Not only is the story unsullied by lapses of cowardice, it is further an unbroken record of noble bearing toward the instigators and inflicters of their torment. They did undoubtedly believe that the judgments of Heaven were to fall on their persecutors, and it is possible that they enjoyed the prospect—they were human ; but in any case they reviled not, they did not murmur, they raised no hand or threat. They forgave and even prayed for their torturers, and literally fulfilled the words of their Master —" Love your enemies." [1]

[1] Governor Endicott died in March 1665, and in May of that same year the royal commissioners *commanded* the General Court of Massachusetts to allow Quakers to attend to their secular business without molestation. In 1675, however, a law was passed prohibiting Quaker meetings in the Colony, and in 1677 constables were ordered to make diligent search for such meetings and to " break open any door where peaceable entrance is denied them." This second brief period of persecution marks the end of the persecution of Quakers *as such* in New England, Margaret Brewster being the last woman to suffer whipping.

CHAPTER VI

LATER EXPANSIONS IN NEW ENGLAND

IN the early 'seventies of the seventeenth century there came in New England a new period of Quaker expansion —the greatest since the first " invasion " in 1657. This expansion was due primarily to the visit of George Fox, the founder of the Society. He sailed from England in the ship *Industry* the 12th of August 1671, in company with William Edmundson, Thomas Briggs, John Rous, John Stubbs, Solomon Eccles, James Lancaster, John Cartwright, Robert Widders, George Pattison, John Hull, Elizabeth Hooton,[1] and Elizabeth Miars, and he landed in Barbadoes the 3rd of October after a perilous voyage. At the time of his arrival Fox was in broken health, too ill and weak to walk for any distance. During his three months of heavy labour in the island he steadily gained in physical power and in conquering spirit. Convincements were made, meetings were settled, and those in authority in the island were impressed with the message and the spiritual ideals of the Friends. Fox wrote at this time his famous Letter to the Governor of Barbadoes, in which he endeavoured to clear the Quakers " from scandalous lies and slanders," and to show that they held the essential doctrines of orthodox Christianity. This Letter has frequently been cited as a Declaration of Quaker faith. It is not that, however, for it deals only slightly

---

[1] Elizabeth Hooton wrote in 1670 to Margaret Fox, who was then in prison : " I have a great desire to see thee, if thou could but come to thy husband before he go : so the Lord give thee some liberty that thou may see him. . . I know nothing but I may go with him ; it hath been much on me to go a great while, and to do the best that is required for him."

and feebly with the distinctive truth of the Quaker message ; it is rather what it claims to be—a document written to clear Friends of slander and heresy on points of catholic, *i.e.* universal, Christianity.[1]

From Barbadoes the party of publishers crossed over to Jamaica, where, during seven weeks of strenuous labour, a great convincement of people was made. Here Elizabeth Hooton, who had come to care for Fox on his journey, suddenly, almost without a warning illness, passed away in peace. From Jamaica Fox sailed, in the teeth of a tempestuous storm, to the shore of Maryland, and after a period of labour there, which will be reviewed in a later chapter, he made his way overland to New England, arriving at Newport the 30th of May 1672. On arrival, he writes, " We had two very good meetings, and many justices, with the governor [Nicholas Easton], the deputy-governor and captaine, and all was satisfyed, and som of them said they did not think there had been such a man in the world." [2] Fox was entertained by the governor, Nicholas Easton, who travelled with him extensively during his stay in the Colony. The Yearly Meeting of 1672 was a memorable time. Not only was Fox there, but also John Burnyeat, John Cartwright, George Pattison, John Stubbs, James Lancaster, and Robert Widders—all eminent ministers from abroad —were in attendance. The governor and the deputy-governor sat in the sessions, and the people flocked in from all parts of the island and the country round about, and Friends were " so knit and united " that it required two days for leave-taking when the meetings were over. " And then," Fox says, " being mightily filled with the presence and power of the Lord they went away with joyful hearts to their various habitations in the several

---

[1] The Letter is printed in the *Journal*, ii. 155-158. This visit of Fox and his companions resulted in a very large increase of Quakerism in Barbadoes and in the other West Indies. Some impression of the size of the Society in Barbadoes can be gained from the fact that the Quaker fines between the years 1658 and 1695 amounted to £11,000. There were at the high water period of Quakerism in the island five meeting-houses there. See *Journal of Friends Historical Society*, v. 43.

[2] I am quoting from a MS. Journal of Fox's American travels, now in the Bodleian Library (MS. Bodleian Addition A 95, f. 16).

colonies where they lived." [1]   There are many indications, in Friends' journals and in other contemporary documents, that Ranters abounded in many parts of the Colonies during the seventeenth century. Fox found them in considerable numbers in Rhode Island, and he laboured to make them see that he had no sympathy with their moral and spiritual chaos. " I had a great travell," the MS. Journal says, " on my spirit concerning the ranters, for they had been rude at a ffriends' meeting where I was not at, and I apoynted a meeting amongst them, and I knew that the Lord would give me power over them, *and He did !* "

During his stay in Newport, Fox wrote a letter to the magistrates and officers of the Colony which shows the practical bent of his mind and the breadth of his social and civic interests. He declares that there is a law of God which voices itself in every man and reveals the principle of conduct toward others. He then recommends the Legislature to pass " a law against drunkenness and against them that sell liquors to make people drunk," [2] and " a law against fighting [probably duelling] and swearing." He urges them to " look into all your ancient liberties and privileges—your divine liberty, your national liberty, and all your outward liberties which belong to your commons, your town, and your island Colony." He recommends " that you have a market once a week in your town and a house built for that purpose ; " " that some one be selected in every town and place in all your Colony to receive and record all your births, marriages, and them that die." " Mind that which is for the good of your Colony and the commonwealth of all people—stand for the good of your people which is the good of yourselves." " Stand up for the glory of God, that it may shine over your Colony ; take off all oppression in your Colony, and set up justice over all in your Colony,"

---

[1] *Journal*, ii. 169. The Colonies represented would be Rhode Island, Massachusetts, New Hampshire, Province of Maine and New York especially Long Island.

[2] This is one of the first suggestions ever made in America to prohibit the sale of intoxicants by legal enactment.

" and stand fast in the liberty wherewith Christ hath made you free, in life, glory, and power." [1]

It was at this time that Quakerism was planted on the western shore of the bay, in Narragansett. Fox writes :—

"We went to Narragansett, about twenty miles from Rhode Island, and the Governor, Nicholas Easton, went with us. We had a meeting at a Justice's house, where Friends had never had any before. [2] It was very large, for the country generally came in ; and people came also from Connecticut and other parts round about, among whom were four Justices of the Peace.[3] Most of the people had never heard Friends before ; but they were mightily affected with the meeting, and there is a great desire amongst them after the Truth." [4]

This seed became a great tree, for this western shore of Narragansett Bay proved good soil for the message of the Inward Light, and produced many powerful ministers and intellectual leaders of the Society.

Another interesting episode of this period was the theological collision with Roger Williams, the founder of Providence. Fox and the governor with a retinue of Friends went up by water from Newport to Providence, where, according to Fox, " God's blessed seed was exalted and set above all." The account of the Providence visit, as given in the MS. Journal, is very quaint : " I had a lardge meeting and a great travell." " The people here were above the priests in high notions," but they " went away mightyly satisfyed, and said they had never heard the like before." [5] His second meeting was held in " a greate barne which was soe full of people, yt I was extremely soaked with sweat, but all was well."

These two meetings and the fame of Fox's preaching powerfully stirred Roger Williams. He was now an old

[1] This letter is in the archives of the Rhode Island Historical Society, at Providence. It is printed in *The Friend* (Phila.), vii. 55 (1833).
[2] This was almost certainly Jireh Bull's house. See Hazard's *College Tom*, p. 9.
[3] Jireh Bull, Samuel Wilson, and William Heferman were the justices of Narragansett (*ibid*. p. 9).
[4] *Journal*, ii. 171. The MS. Journal says that this meeting was the 13th of July.
[5] He mentions that there came to the meeting " a woman who was bad and skoffed, but she went away and was struck sick."

man, but the fire of his youthful days rekindled in him
when he heard how the Quakers were spreading their
doctrines among the people, and how the multitudes were
flocking after the apostle of Inward Light.[1] He had
attended the Yearly Meeting at Newport in 1671, where
he endeavoured to have some public discourse with Friends,
but he was " stopt," he tells us, " by the sudden praying of
the governor's wife," and when he stood up again he was
" stopt by John Burnett's [Burnyeat who was in Newport
in 1671] sudden falling to prayer and dismissing the
assembly."[2] He kept away from Fox, when the latter
was holding his great meetings in Providence, for " having
once tried to get public speech in the Assemblies of
Friends," he was resolved " to try another way and to offer
a fair and full Dispute."

Thereupon he drew up fourteen propositions which he
sent to the deputy-governor, John Cranston, for him to
deliver to George Fox. The Deputy Governor, however,
for some unknown reason, kept them in his possession
until the 26th of July, when it was found that George Fox
had left Newport. Roger Williams claimed that this
delay was made by a collusion with Fox : " in the Junto
of the Foxians at Newport it was concluded for Infallible
Reasons that his Holiness G. Fox should withdraw."
" He knew that I was furnished with artillery out of his
own Writings. He saw what consequences would roll
down the mountaines upon him. . . . and therefore this old
Fox thought it best to run for it and leave the work to his
Journeymen and Chaplains to perform in his absence."[3]
Any one who knows the traits and character of George
Fox knows that whatever else happened he did not " run
away " " for fear of the consequences which would roll
down upon him ! " He himself declares, in the *New
England Firebrand Quenched*—the " Firebrand " being
George Fox's name for this " apostle of soul liberty "—

---

[1] Williams says (in his *George Fox Digged Out of his Burrowes*) that he had
" long heard of the great name of George Fox" and had " already read his book
in folio" (*The Great Mystery of the Great Whore*).

[2] *George Fox Digged Out of his Burrowes*, edited by J. Lewis Diman (publications of the Narragansett Club), vol. v. p. 19.

[3] *George Fox Digged Out of his Burrowes.*

"I neither saw nor ever heard of any propositions from Roger Williams, nor did I go away in fear of him or them."

Fox, having spent two months in Rhode Island, had started on his return journey south before Roger Williams' challenge was delivered to him. His friends—"the Foxian Junto," as Roger Williams calls them—went forward to arrange for the great debate. John Stubbs, John Burnyeat, "and six or seven others," went to the home of Williams in Providence to arrange the preliminaries. "Their salutations," Roger Williams quaintly says, "were in silence when they came and when they departed—drink being offered and accepted by some."[1] The date fixed upon for the opening of the "debate" was August 9, 1672, and the place chosen was "the Meeting House of the Quakers" in Newport, though to satisfy some who objected to having the "discussion carried away from the home town," it was arranged to have seven propositions debated in Newport and seven in Providence. The champion against the Quakers, now more than three-score and ten, rowed by boat thirty miles to meet his opponents. "God graciously helped me," he says, "in rowing all day with my old bones so that I got to Newport toward the midnight before the morning appointed." Meantime, to supply the place left by the departure of Fox, William Edmundson opportunely arrived in Newport, an apostle of Quakerism from Ireland, and one of the foremost of the early Quaker missionaries who came to colonial America. There were now three Quaker debaters against the doughty old man who, however, felt himself quite equal to the battle.[2] Governor Nicholas Easton attended the debate, and "maintained the civill peace!" The fourteen propositions, as drawn up by Roger Williams, were as follows:

[1] *George Fox Digged Out*, p. 35.
[2] This is Roger Williams' characterisation of his opponents: "John Stubbs, learned in the Hebrew and Greek, I found him so"; "John Burnet [Burnyeat] of a moderate spirit and an able speaker"; and W. Edmundson, "who proved to be the chief speaker, a man not so able nor so moderate as the other two"—"a stout, portly man of a great voice, he would often vapour and preach long, and when I had patiently waited till the gust was over, and began to speak, he would stop my mouth with a very unhansome clout of a grevious interruption," "a pragmatical and insulting soul." See *George Fox Digged Out*, p. 38.

"I. The People called Quakers are not true *Quakers* according to the Holy Scriptures.

II. The Jesus Christ they profess is not the true Jesus Christ.

III. The spirit by which they are *acted* is not the Spirit of God.

IV. They doe not own the Holy Scriptures.

V. Their Principles and Professions are full of contradictions and hypocrises.

VI. Their Religion is not only an Heresy in matters of worship, but also in the Doctrines of Repentance, Faith, etc.

VII. Their Religion is but a confused mixture of Popery, Armineanisme, Socineanisme, Judaisme, etc.

VIII. The People called Quakers (in effect) hold no God, no Christ, no Spirit, no Angel, no Devil, no Resurrection, no Judgment, no Heaven, no Hell, but what is in man.

IX. All that their Religion requires (externall and internall) to make converts and proselites, amounts to no more than what a Reprobate may easily attain unto and perform.

X. The Popes of Rome doe not swell with and exercise a greater Pride than the Quaker spirit hath expresst and doth aspire unto, although many truly humble souls may be captivated amongst them, as may be in other religions.

XI. The Quakers' Religion is more obstructive and destructive to the conversion and Salvation of the Souls of People than most of the religions this day extant in the world.

XII. The sufferings of the Quakers are no true evidence of the Truth of their religion.

XIII. Their many Books and writings are extremely Poor, Lame, Naked, and sweld up with high Titles and words of Boasting and Vapour.

XIV. The Spirit of their Religion tends mainly (1) to reduce Persons from Civility to Barbarisme. (2) To an arbitrary Government and the Dictates and Decrees of that *sudden spirit* that acts them. (3) To a sudden cutting off of People, yea of Kings and Princes opposing them. (4) To as fiery Persecutions for matters of Religion and Conscience as hath been or can be practiced by any Hunters or Persecutors in the world."[1]

The debate naturally attracted great crowds, and was as popular and interesting to the people of that period as a great athletic contest would be now. It seems to have won many new adherents to the Quaker faith—it certainly was felt to be a triumph by those already of the Quaker

[1] *Fox Digged Out of his Burrowes*, pp. 4, 5.

faith, but, looked at calmly and critically from the point of view of our century, it appears a tilting against windmills on both sides. The two books [1] which record the "spiritual battle" are full of antiquarian interest, but they are a melancholy monument to the bitterness of these seventeenth century theological wars, and there is pitifully little in them—and apparently as little in the debate—which raises into permanent view the grace of saintliness, the beauty of holiness, or the persuasive sweetness of the divine Light in men. [2]

Two of these "debaters" were instrumental in carrying Quakerism into many new fields in New England, and in more firmly establishing it where it was already planted—John Burnyeat and William Edmundson. John Burnyeat, a gentle spirit and a powerful preacher, had

---

[1] *George Fox Digged Out of his Burrowes* (Boston, 1676), and *A New England Firebrand Quenched*, by G. F. and John Burnyeat (London, 1678).

[2] William Edmundson's account of the debate gives an interesting though thoroughly prejudiced glimpse of the affair (*Journal*, pp. 65-66):—

"After some Days Travel by Narragansett and those Parts, I came to Rhode Island, where I met with John Burnyeat, John Stubbs, and John Cartwright, where one Roger Williams an old Priest and an Enemy of Truth, had put forth Fourteen Propositions (as he called them) which he would maintain against any of the Quakers that came from Old England, and challenged a Dispute of seven of them at Newport in Rhode Island and the other seven at Providence.

"I join'd with Friends in answering this Challenge, at the Time and Place appointed for the Dispute, which was to be in Friends Meeting-House at Newport ; thither a great Concourse of People of all Sorts gather'd. When those Propositions (as he called them) came to be discoursed of, they were all but Slanders and Accusations against the Quakers ; the bitter old man could make nothing out, but on the contrary they were turn'd back upon himself : he was bafled and the People saw his Weakness, Folly and Envy against the Truth and the Friends.

"There were many prejudic'd Baptists would fain have help'd the Old Priest against Friends ; but they durst not undertake his Charge against us for they saw it was false and weak. So the Testimony of Truth in the Power of God was set over all his false Charges, to the great Satisfaction of the People.

"When this Meeting was ended, which lasted three Days, John Stubbs and I went to Providence, accompanied with many Friends, to hear the other seven Propositions, which lasted one Day. John Burnyeat and John Cartwright going another way in Truth's Service. Now at Providence there was a very great Gathering of People, both Presbyterians, Baptists and Ranters. Roger Williams being there, I stood up and told him in Public, We had spent so many Days at Newport, where he could make nothing out agreeable to his Challenge ; but on the contrary manifested his Clamour, rash and false Accusations, which he could not prove against us, that I was not willing to spend much time in hearing his Clamour and false Accusations, having other service for the Lord, therefore would only spend that Day. So he went on, as he had done at Newport at Rhode Island. We answered to all his Charges against Friends and disprov'd them." As further illustration of the lack of " grace and sweetness " in this debate I quote Roger Williams' estimate of Edmundson : " A flash of wit, a face of Brass, and a Tongue set on fire from the Hell of Lyes and Fury ! "

been brought into the Society of Friends in 1653 through the ministry of George Fox.

"This blessed man, George Fox," Burnyeat writes, "directed me unto the light and appearance of Jesus Christ my Saviour in my heart, so that I came to know Him and the glory of the Father through Him. Notwithstanding all my high professions, from my youth, of an imputed righteousness, by which the guilt of my sin would not be charged upon me, but imputed to Christ and His righteousness imputed to me, I now came to see that there was need of a Saviour to save from sin as well as of the blood of a sacrificed Christ to blot out sin. All my pretence and hopes of justification *through an invented notional faith* were now seen to be but a Babel Tower or an Adam's fig-leaf apron, and as I learned to know Christ's voice and to follow Him, He gave me eternal life and manifested His grace in my heart." [1]

He first visited New England in 1666, where he had extended service, visiting, all the meetings in the Colonies, as far north as " Piscataway," [2] which included the meetings both in New Hampshire and Maine. He covered the same field of service again in 1671, having once more had " blessed service in Piscataway," and having also attended the Yearly Meeting in Newport that year. He was back a third time in 1672, having travelled on horseback with George Fox all the way from Tredhaven Creek in Maryland. Fox says affectionately :—" He travelled with me from Maryland through the wilderness, and through many rivers and desperate bogs, where they said never Englishman nor horse had travelled before ; where we lay out at nights, and sometimes in Indian houses, and many times were very hard put to it for provisions, but the Lord by His Eternal arm did support us and carry us through all dangers." [3] Before the great debate with Roger Williams, Burnyeat had " debates " with " the Elders of the Church " at Scituate, Mass., where " an abundance of people " met in an orchard, and again in Boston, where " several of note "

---

[1] Condensed from Burnyeat's account in his *Journal* (reprint of " Truth Exalted "), pp. 149-158.
[2] *Journal*, pp. 189, 190.
[3] Burnyeat's *Journal*, p. 144.

came to the meeting, and he "had a blessed season to open things to the people."

With two other English Friends, George Pattison and John Cartwright, he went on to "Piscataway," where the Quaker Society was greatly expanded and more solidly established—"all things were settled in sweet unity." On his way back he found an incipient schism in Salem, but "in dread power of the Lord," he powerfully exhorted the meeting to follow the mind of the Spirit and keep in unity. On his return to Rhode Island, Burnyeat broke new ground in Warwick, Rhode Island, "where no Friends had been before," and "several were convinced and did own the truth." Here he "had to do with one Gorton and his company," who, he says, "called themselves Generalists, for they were of the opinion that all should be saved. But they were in reality Ranters." Burnyeat is here somewhat colouring his judgment with prejudice, and he does not do Samuel Gorton justice, though some of the Gortonians may have been, as he says, "filthy, unclean spirits." Gorton was a man of real vision, and, with all his peculiarities, was dedicated to the truth. Dr. Ezra Stiles has recorded the following enthusiastic testimony of Gorton's last disciple, John Angell:

"The Friends had come out of the world in some ways, but still were in darkness or twilight; Gorton was far beyond them, he said, on the highway up to the dispensation of light. The Quakers were in no wise to be compared with him; nor any man else can [be compared with him] since the primitive times of the Church, especially since they came out of Popish darkness. He said Gorton was a holy man; wept day and night for the sins of blindness of the world; his eyes were a fountain of tears, and always full of tears—a man full of thought and study. He had a long walk cut through the trees or woods by his house, where he constantly walked morning and evening, and even in the depths of the night, alone by himself, for contemplation and the enjoyment of the dispensation of light. He was universally beloved by all his neighbours, and the Indians who esteemed him, not only as a friend, but one high in communion with God in heaven." [1]

---

[1] *Collection Rhode Island Historical Society*, ii. 19.

In any case a large number of the Gortonians soon after became Friends and " were very loving." [1] Burnyeat next undertook the task, in which many before him and many after him failed, to plant Quakerism in Hartford and other towns of the Connecticut Colony. [2] There were no prepared groups here with which to make a beginning, and, though John Winthrop of Connecticut was personally very kindly disposed to Friends, and was intimate with William Coddington, the Colony as a whole was impervious to the Quaker message.

William Edmundson arrived in New England on his first missionary visit just in time to lead the great debate with Roger Williams, and he tells us that it proved " a seasonable opportunity to open many things to the people appertaining to the Kingdom of God ·and Way of Eternal Life and Salvation. The meeting [debate in Providence] concluded in prayer to Almighty God, and the people went away satisfied and loving." [3]

He next went on and extended the spiritual conquests in Warwick among Gorton's people, already begun by Burnyeat—" the Lord's power was largely manifested, and the people were very loving, like Friends." He had " refreshing times " in Newport, Narragansett, Scituate, Sandwich, and Boston, and then sailed for Ireland. He came back for a more extended missionary work in 1675, coming from Barbadoes in a yacht, with " a good comfortable passage " of three weeks. It was " the perilous time " of King Philip's War, and " Indians lying hid in bushes shot men down as they travelled." [4] Whether connected with the terrible uprising led by King Philip or not, a fierce Indian war broke out in the north-eastern section of New England, and the years 1675 and

---

[1] Burnyeat, p. 211.

[2] For an account of this undertaking see his *Journal*, pp. 212-216.

[3] Edmundson's *Journal*, p. 67. William Edmundson was born in Westmorland in 1627, and had fought under Cromwell in the Parliamentary army. In 1652 he settled in Ireland for purposes of trade, but on a business trip to England the next year he heard George Fox and James Nayler preach, and was " convinced " and " seized upon by the Lord's power." He became from that time one of the foremost exponents of the new faith in Ireland, and, as we shall see, was one of the leading publishers of Quakerism in Virginia and North Carolina.

[4] *Ibid.* p. 77.

1676 were crowded with tragic events for this region—
the Piscataqua country being one of the centres of
hostility. William Edmundson, at the very height of the
trouble, struck out for the country "eastward, towards
Piscattaway," where "by reason of the war it was dangerous travelling." "However," he says, "I committed my
life to God who gave it, and took my journey"—going
by way of Sandwich, Boston, and Salem. After holding
meetings on the New Hampshire side of the Piscataqua—
which he calls "Piscattaway"—he crossed over by boat
into Maine, where he had "large and precious meetings,"
and "much ground was broken" in the southern end of the
Province of Maine. While he was staying in the home
of "Nicholas Shapley" [Major Shapleigh]—"a man of
note in that country," a pioneer Quaker of the Piscataqua
region—"fourteen lusty Indians, with their heads trimmed
and faces painted," came to the house. William Edmundson
"discoursed with them" and discovered that they "intended
mischief in their hearts, but the Lord calmed them down,
and they went away without doing any harm." [1]

As he came back through the Massachusetts towns,
"travelling with his life in his hands," many were
convinced by his preaching, especially in Marblehead and
Reading. Most of the people, wherever he came in those
parts, were, he tells us, "in Garrisons for fear of the
Indians, except Friends." He held an extraordinary
meeting in a garrison house in Reading, where, he says,
"*my heart being full of the Power and Spirit of the Lord, the
Love of God ran through me to the people!*" His listeners
were broken into tears by the demonstration of the Spirit
which awakened their consciences, and an old man rising
up took the speaker in his arms, and thanked God that
the message had *found* him. The people asked with
naiveté, what the difference was between their ministers
and their visitors. Edmundson's answer, which sounds like
Anne Hutchinson's charge, was: "Your ministers are satisfied with talk about Christ and the Scriptures; we are not
satisfied without the sure, inward experience of God and

[1] *Journal*, p. 79.

Christ, and the enjoyment of the comforts which the Scriptures promise and which believers in primitive times enjoyed." After many successful meetings in Massachusetts, where people were "tender and loving" as he told his message, he sailed from Boston to Newport, and soon followed up John Burnyeat in another unsuccessful attempt to spread Quakerism in Connecticut.[1]

One of the most important events in what I have been calling "the second expansion" of Quakerism in New England, was the planting of it in the island of Nantucket. The first settlers of the island were in close sympathy with Friends and were, *at heart*, in intimate accord with their message, though they had not become actual members of the Society. The real pioneer of the little island-colony was Thomas Macy, who embarked from Salisbury, Mass., in a small boat in 1659, in company with Edward Starbuck, Isaac Coleman, and probably James Coffin, and sailed round the Cape to Nantucket. Macy had been a man of influence in Salisbury. He was a Baptist of the seeker-type and frequently "exhorted" in public. He came into collision with the authorities for preaching without ordination, and again for entertaining Quakers in violation of the law of 1657.[2] The reason assigned for his migration was his desire to follow his conscience, and to get free from "the tyranny of the clergy and those in authority." Tristram Coffin, father of the James mentioned above, soon joined the settlers on the island, and became their first chief magistrate. The settlement was composed of persons of liberal spirit and it grew rapidly. In 1673 Richard Gardiner and his wife, being persecuted in Salem "for attending Quaker meeting," moved to Nantucket. Stephen Hussey, son of Christopher, who was one of the original purchasers of the island, became a "convinced Quaker" during a sojourn in Barbadoes, and John Swain appears also to have been a Quaker before there was a meeting on the island.[3] But

---

[1] See *Journal*, pp. 83-92.
[2] Pike's *The New Puritan* (1879) pp. 35 and 54 *seq.* See also Coffin's *History of Newbury*. Whittier has told Macy's story in his poem " The Exiles."
[3] See Thomas Story's *Journal* (1747), p. 353.

the real creation of the Quaker Society in Nantucket was due to the ministry of three noted men—Thomas Chalkley, John Richardson, and Thomas Story—between the years 1698 and 1704.

Thomas Chalkley,[1] then a young man and on his first visit to America, came by sloop to the " Isle of Nantucket " in 1698. He spent "several days" on the island, where "people did generally acknowledge the truth and were tender-hearted." Two hundred came to hear him, though "it was never known before that so many were together on the island." He made a deep impression on his hearers, and had the satisfaction of seeing Nathaniel Starbuck, an important citizen, "convinced."[2] John Richardson, a native of Yorkshire and a man of very interesting character, soon followed after, and carried the spiritual work, begun by Thomas Chalkley, much farther on. He came by sloop with Peleg Slocum from Newport, and the Nantucket settlers crowded to the shore, "possessed with great fear" that the sloop was French, loaded with arms and men, come to take their island, for war was raging between England and France. They were greatly relieved to hear that their visitors "came in the love of God to hold meetings among them." The visitors went directly, by a kind of homing instinct, to the house of Nathaniel Starbuck, who was "in some degree convinced of the truth." Here they found "Mother Mary Starbuck whom the islanders esteemed as a judge among them, and little of moment was done without her." The "prophet" in Richardson came immediately into play, and he *saw* that here was the pillar for the building of a new Church. "At the sight of her," he writes, "it sprang into my heart, To this woman is the everlasting love of God." It was soon arranged that the proposed meetings should be in her house.[3]

[1] Thomas Chalkley was born in Southwark, London, in 1675. He moved to Philadelphia in 1701, and from that time to the end of his life in 1741 he was closely identified with Philadelphia Yearly Meeting. He was a great traveller, a powerful minister, and his *Journal* is important for this period of American history.

[2] Thomas Chalkley's *Journal* (1751), pp. 19, 20.

[3] She was the wife of Nathaniel Starbuck, sen., her maiden name being Mary Coffin.

The first meeting was held in a "large and bright rubbed room, with suitable seats or chairs, the glass windows being taken out of their frames and many chairs placed without very conveniently." Before the meeting began, John Richardson had been walking up and down in the woods "under a very great load in spirit." When it gathered, "the mighty power of the Lord began to work," and as John Richardson records, "the Lord's heavenly power raised me and set me on my feet as if one had lifted me up"; whereupon he proceeded to "open and deliver things." "For most of an hour," he continues, "the great woman [Mary Starbuck] fought and strove against the message, sometimes looking up into my face with a pale and then a more ruddy complexion; but the strength of the truth increased, and the Lord's mighty power began to shake the people . . . and when she could no longer contain she submitted to the power of truth and lifted up her voice and wept." Not only was "the great woman" won, but "the inhabitants of the island were shaken and most of the people convinced of the truth." And when the meeting came to a close, "they sat weeping universally," and could not disperse. "After some time Mary Starbuck stood up, held out her hand, spoke tremblingly, and said, 'All that ever we have been building, and all that ever we have done, is pulled down this day; and this that we have heard is the everlasting truth.'" "She, and as many as could be seen, were wet with tears, and the floor was as though there had been a shower of rain upon it."[1]

Nobody can read John Richardson's account of his visit on Nantucket without feeling that there was a power attending his speaking of a very novel and unusual sort, and his presence and his words seem to have had an extraordinary transforming effect upon the people. He, however, did not take any steps toward the organization of a "society" out of those who were "convinced." That step was taken by Thomas Story in the summer of 1704. Story was one of the most remarkable publishers of

[1] *An Account of the Life of John Richardson* (1783), pp. 84-94.

Quakerism in the first half of the eighteenth century, a powerful debater, always ready to accept the challenge of any Quaker opponent, a moving minister when the Spirit opened a message within him, and a too voluminous writer, whose style at rare intervals is clear, vivid, and marked with beauty. He visited again and again all the settlements of Friends in the American Colonies, and he took a large part in the eighteenth century expansion of Quakerism. On his extended travels through New England he found his way to Nantucket. He at once saw, as John Richardson had done, the peculiar gifts and graces of Mary Starbuck, and he realised the power for service which lay in her. She was, he says, " A wise, discreet woman, well read in the Scriptures, in great reputation throughout the island for her knowledge in matters of religion, and an oracle among them on that account, insomuch that they would not do anything without her advice and consent." [1]

After holding a number of meetings on the island Thomas Story had a powerful " concern of mind," which took away his sleep, that a permanent meeting ought to be established in Nantucket, and his thoughts turned to Mary Starbuck as " the chief instrument " for maintaining it. She received the suggestion with " great gravity, and it became *her* concern," and the meeting was accordingly started in the home of Mary Starbuck, where the neighbours of the island met, week by week, " to wait on the Lord." [2] The meeting thus begun had a steady growth, and by the opening of the nineteenth century Nantucket was one of the great centres of Quakerism in America. Edmund Peckover, of England, visited Nantucket on his travels through New England in 1743. He found on the island " a brave, weighty, solid people, living pretty much in love and unity together." He reports three hundred families there, and estimates that two hundred and fifty of them are frequenters of the Quaker meeting. He says that the meeting-house holds fifteen hundred

---

[1] *Journal*, p. 350.
[2] Nantucket Monthly Meeting was established the 26th of May 1708.

persons, "and it was very full when we were there."
"They have seven or eight Public Friends."[1] Samuel
Fothergill, who was on Nantucket in 1755, says that
more than fifteen hundred attended the meeting which
he held there—most of them professors of truth. He
adds that "the richest part of the inhabitants [of the
island] embraced the principles of truth from conviction ;
the others thought the expense of maintaining a priest
would be too heavy for them and have turned Quaker to
save money !"[2]

It is not possible, within the space at command, to
speak of the other contributors, of whom there were
many,[3] to the spread of Quakerism in the New England
Colonies in the eighteenth century. Something, however,
must be said, though briefly, of the extraordinary work
and influence of the Fothergills—father and son—and of
two or three other "publishers" of special historical
importance. The two Fothergills, John and Samuel,
were highly endowed, broad in their intellectual outlook,
refined and gentle in breeding, possessed of the best
culture of their time, and withal delicately responsive to
celestial currents, so that through them the New England
Friends and their neighbours became partakers of the
maturest fruits of the spiritual life of that period. John
Fothergill came from his English home three times—in
1706, 1722, and 1737—traversing each time the entire
circle of Quaker communities from Newport to the
Piscataqua region. In 1722 he reports two thousand
persons at the Newport Yearly Meeting at which there
was "a demonstration of the Eternal power of God and
a confirmation of many souls."[4] His final visit occurred
when "the Great Awakening" in New England was in its

[1] Journal of Edmund Peckover, printed in *Journal of Friends' Historical
Society* (London), i. 95-109. He says that the inhabitants of Nantucket cleared
20,000 pounds sterling from their catch of "Sperma Ceeti whales" during
their last fishing season (p. 106).

[2] Fothergill's *Memoirs*, p. 107. H. B. Worth, in his *Quakerism on Nantucket*
(1896), estimates that in 1794 half the population of the island, then amounting to
5600 inhabitants, attended the Friends' meeting.

[3] No less than 576 "public Friends" visited Nantucket meeting for the purpose of ministering, between the years 1701 and 1780.

[4] *Life and Travels of John Fothergill* (1753), p. 151.

first stages. His son Samuel came after the " Awakening " had run its full course, and he was admirably, almost perfectly, fitted by nature and grace to "speak to the condition" of the serious, seeking souls who had been first highly wrought up by the revival, and then left somewhat stranded by the back ebb which succeeded the high tide of religious emotion.

One of the primary ideas which the Leaders of "the Great Awakening," especially Jonathan Edwards, had insisted on was the fact of the immediate contact of the Holy Spirit with the human soul, and the necessity of a *change* wrought thus directly upon the soul by this influence. The soul must be touched by the Holy Spirit, Edwards had urged, or it cannot be saved. The energising will of God must act upon it and move it to a passionate desire for salvation. Under the powerful preaching of Edwards and Whitefield there were many evidences of immediate divine influence, but involved with the move-ment there was such intense emotion, such high-wrought enthusiasm, such vivid appeals to the imagination, that many distressing phenomena, of the sort usually occurring at times of high nervous tension, broke out, and, as intimated above, when the long revival period had run its course, there came a serious spiritual ebb and a positive reaction.[1]

It was at this critical moment that the distinguished English minister, Samuel Fothergill, arrived in Newport, where fifteen years before George Whitefield had begun his wonderful tour of the New England towns. Fother-

[1] While the work of Whitefield was at its height, the Friends of Rhode Island received a most peculiar challenge to *try their religion* with Moses Bartlett, who styled himself "a real Christian." His letter was as follows: "To the Quaker Ministers in this town and Colony: There is a wonderful Reformation in Connecticut Colony among the Presbyterians, where the everlasting gospel is preached; but I have heard some of you blaspheme against it abominably; but I desire you to Dispute me in order to vindicate your Orders, which you call Friends Orders, for they are antiscriptural, and so consequently of the Devil; You shall have the liberty to pick out as many able men as you please, if it be as many as there was Prophets of Baal; only I will have the same measure of time as you; and we will have it all written. It may be you will ask what People I am of? To which I answer, you may call me a Presbyterian if you please, but I call myself a real Christian." Printed in Arnold's *History of Rhode Island*, ii. 138.

gill's coming—the result of ten years of deep travail of
spirit—was a happy event for the religious life of New
England.   He, too, believed with all his profound being,
that the Holy Spirit of God was in immediate relation
with the lives of men.   He believed, no less definitely
than Edwards did, that the important changes in human
lives are due to the work of God within, but he insisted
that the energising will of God worked in all men and
not alone in an elected few, and that the choice which
brings salvation is a human choice.   With him this great
truth that the soul has immediate contact with God had
passed from the stage of intense enthusiasm, which always
goes with its discovery, to a stage of calm and dignified
power due to the penetration of his personality with this
inward light and grace.   He was a glowing exhibition, as
he stood before the great throngs that came to hear him,
and as he moved quietly among men in his daily walk, of
a type of life which demonstrates beyond all arguments
the incoming of the divine into the human.

The divine favour which attended his ministry in
Rhode Island "brought the deepest reverence upon my
soul," he writes, "and tears of joy and comfort" from the
people, and "the Great Name spread itself afresh."[1]   He
visited all the Quaker centres, and broke new ground in
the Province of Maine, going as far as Casco Bay.   He
writes of this eastern visit, "Truth has opened my way
in several places where no Friends lived, and my heart
has been bowed with reverence to observe and feel the
openness and visitation of love and life.   The people
flock into meetings in crowds and behave with great
solidity."   The effect of his preaching and the impression
he made is well shown in his modest account of his great
public meeting in Boston, held almost exactly a hundred
years from the time of the arrival of those first unwelcome
Quakers :

[1] He says that the number of people at New England Yearly Meeting at the
time of his visit was very great, it being in attendance the largest Yearly Meeting
in the world.   *Memoirs*, p. 188.   Edmund Peckover says that the attendance in
1743 was not less than 5000.   "I never was at so large a meeting before—a
most solemn, weighty, awful time.   People from 150 miles to the eastward came
to it."—*Journal Friends Historical Society*, i. 102.

"*2nd of 8th Month.*—I dropped my pen yesterday under a weighty concern to appoint an evening meeting in this place, and upon its being mentioned to the magistrates, they cheerfully offered either one of their own places of worship, or the Town-hall, saying that our own house was too small to accommodate the people who inclined to come in. I found more freedom to accept their offer of the hall, and had a very large meeting in the evening, at which were present about two thousand people, and amongst them nearly all the magistracy of the place, several of their ministers and principal people : it was a time, I believe, never to be forgotten ; the power and the wisdom of Truth was a canopy over the meeting, and I believe the Truth itself gained great ground ; let every part of the gain, glory, and profit be ascribed to that excellent Name in and from which all wisdom and strength proceed. One of their ancient professors said pretty loud, at the close of the meeting, 'I thank God that I have once heard the Gospel of life and peace preached in its purity as it hath been this day.'"

Samuel Fothergill's visit to the meetings of the Friends in the Province of Maine marks an epoch in the development of Quakerism in that section of the country. There had been a few scattered Friends in the Province since the visit of Alice Ambrose and Mary Tomkins to Kittery in 1662, when a meeting was formed in the Eliot section of this township. The town records of Scarboro, Maine, state that Stephen Collins and Sarah Mills were fined in 1665 for refusing to support the minister of the town, and in 1671 Moses Collins and Sarah Mills were whipped for being Quakers [1]—the only instance of whipping a Quaker in the Province of Maine.

A meeting was begun in Falmouth, now Portland, the Casco Bay of Fothergill's account, about 1740. The Rev. Mr. Smith, Congregational minister in the church at Falmouth, records in his diary, 30th July 1740, this memorable fact : "The Church kept a day of fasting and prayer on account of the spread of Quakerism" ; and 22nd July 1745, he records that there are "many strange [*i.e.* foreign] Quakers in town." [2] This group of Friends at Falmouth was visited in 1743 by the English minister,

---

[1] *Collection of Maine Historical Society*, iii. 71 and 154.
[2] *Ibid.*, vii. 221.

Edmund Peckover and his companions. "We went," he writes, "about seventy miles farther [from Dover, New Hampshire] by the seaside to a place called Gascoe Bay [should be Casco Bay] where a few Friends are settled. They have got a meeting both First days and Week-days. I believe there are not fewer than thirty who come pretty constantly to meetings and, I think, have three or four who appear in public testimony."[1]

A third meeting within the Province of Maine owed its origin to a remarkable visit of the Pennsylvania Quaker, John Churchman. He made a tour of New England in 1742, and went as far east as Kittery, where he found a "tender people," probably the group composing the Eliot meeting. As he lay in bed at a Friend's house he felt a "call" to a new field. In his own quaint language he tells the story:

"On third day morning, as I lay in bed, I felt my mind drawn towards the north-west, which was an exercise to me; for I had before thought myself at liberty to return towards Boston. I arose about sun-rise, and asked the friend where I lodged whether any Friends lived at a distance on that quarter, for that I had a draft that way? He answered, No, and asked how far I thought to go. I told him it did not seem to me to be more than ten miles. He said there was a people about eight miles distant, which he supposed was the place to which I felt the draft. I desired him to send a lad with a few lines to some person that he knew, to inform them that a stranger would be glad to have a meeting among them at the eleventh hour of that day, if they were free to grant it; which he did, and with his wife went with me: so that we got to the place near the time proposed, and found a considerable gathering of people, that I wondered how it could be in so short a time, not more than three hours' warning. They were preparing seats, by laying boards on blocks in a pretty large new house, and soon sat down in an orderly manner. I went in great fear and inward weakness; and at the sight of such a gathering of people, and none of our profession among them, except the friend and his wife who accompanied me, and two others who joined us in the way, my spirit was greatly bowed, and my heart filled with secret cries to the Lord, that He would be pleased to magnify His own power;

and, blessed for ever be His holy name ! He heard my cry, and furnished me with wisdom and strength to declare His word to the people, among whom there were some very tender seekers after the true knowledge of God ; and the doctrine of truth flowed freely towards them, the universality of the love of God being set forth, in opposition to the common predestinarian notion of election and reprobation. When the meeting was over I felt an uncommon freedom to leave them, for they began to show their satisfaction with the opportunity in many words. So speaking to the friend that went with me, we withdrew and went to our horses ; and I immediately mounting, beheld the man of the house where the meeting was held running to me, who, taking hold of the bridle, told me I must not go away without dining with them. I looked steadfast on him, and told him that I did believe this was a visitation for their good, but I was fearful that they, by talking too freely and too much, would be in danger of losing the benefit thereof, and miss of the good that the Lord intended for them ; and my going away was in order to example them to go home to their own houses, and turn inward, and retire to that of God in their own hearts, which was the only way to grow in religion. So I left him and returned with my friend Joseph Eastes and his wife." [1]

This was apparently the beginning of Quakerism in the township of Berwick. The fourth group was formed in the town of North Yarmouth (now Harpswell) in 1751, and from this settlement it spread out into new regions north and west. In *Historical Collections of Maine* is preserved this interesting petition to Governor Shirley in 1756, from the citizens of Merryconege Neck, in the Province of Maine : [2]

"The Inhabitants of the Neck, Being desirous of the good Welfare and Increase of this Place, most humbly beg, etc. The Parish is But a New Settlement and there are many Opinionists [a footnote explains that they are Quakers] settled among us which is a Great Damage to ye Parish ; and we have been at very Great charges of late respecting some Public Affairs, and those Opinionists will not in the least Strive for the Promotion of Sd Parish or in ye least Pay Precinct Charges." [3]

---

[1] *Gospel Labours of John Churchman*, p. 73.
[2] The upper part of Merryconege Neck adjoined the township of Brunswick, and the lower part joined North Yarmouth.
[3] *Collection of Maine Historical Society*, xiii. 42.

These new groups were visited in 1757 by William Reckitt, an English travelling friend. He says :

"We went to Barwick and had several meetings there; travelled through the woods to Casco, where we had an opportunity with Friends and such as attend their meetings. We crossed the Bay to Small Point, and in our return had a meeting upon a Neck of land called Meryconeague."[1]

About 1771 most of the Friends who formed the little society in Harpswell moved to the Plantation of Royaltown, which afterwards became the township of Durham, and a Quaker centre of great future promise sprang up here. Another group was formed during the 'sixties of that century in the town of Windham.

The great expansion of Quakerism in Maine was, however, due to the work of David Sands, a minister from the Colony of New York. He was, like most of the missionaries who have figured in this history, a man of rare sensitiveness to inward impressions, loyally obedient to intimations of duty, quick to feel what ought to be done with a given situation, and withal possessed of much of that indefinable influence which we call spiritual power. To him more than to any other one individual we must attribute the spread of Quakerism through the great county of Kennebec, in the south-central part of Maine, where it has since flourished.

He spent two years and six months on his first tour, starting in the spring of 1777. Much of the time he was travelling in wilderness country, carrying his axe to clear his way as he went, going frequently on foot and "enduring great hardships."[2] Like most of these itinerant ministers who were the real creators of New England Quakerism, he went first to the well-organised centres, such as Newport and Nantucket, where he visited not only meetings but every family of Friends. Then he pushed on to the newer, less organised centres at Falmouth and Windham, and finally he struck out on foot into wilderness regions, making for the scattered

[1] Reckitt's *Life and Labours* (London, 1776), p. 113.
[2] See *Journal* of David Sands (1848), p. 11.

settlements which were being formed in the beautiful and fertile Province of Maine. "We had many meetings," he says, "while passing through a wilderness country and found many seeking minds."

"I have spent part of the fall and most of the winter," he writes his wife in 1779, "amongst a people not of our profession, many of whom received me very kindly and also my message, which made them feel near to me, and their hearts and houses are open to receive Friends. I have an untrodden path to tread where no Friends before have travelled in the work of ministry. I have passed through many towns where there are no religious meetings of any sort. The Lord has led me through the wilderness land; He has preserved me through the cold; in sickness and health and through every trial, of which I have had many. In that love which time or distance cannot change I salute thee." [1]

As a result of these patient labours of David Sands and his powerful ministry, often strikingly appropriate to the situation, there was formed a chain of new meetings in the belt of the country fringing the Kennebec River, and the close of the Revolutionary War, that is to say the close of the Colonial Era, thus marks the high-water point of Quaker expansion in New England.

These visiting, itinerant ministers or missionaries have been spoken of as "the real creators of New England Quakerism." So, in a sense, they were. But the statement is only partially true. The true source of its strength and power lay, from the very beginning, in the character of the native material out of which the meetings

[1] *Journal*, p. 25. The following letter from Joseph Wing, a companion to David Sands on a later visit, gives a good idea of their difficulties : "Sometimes traveld from 12 to 17 miles between houses and had the advantage of a foot parth with marked trees to Gide us. Sometimes got but two meals a Day and them were Corse tu ; There were Walks Not very pleasant to the Natural part, but so it is, and it is Not best that we should have Smooth things all the time : we had once to lay in the bottom of a Small bote and coverd us with our Sales, once laid on the beach by the side of a Fier and had our Saddle bags to lay our heads on and our Great Coats and Misketers to Cover us, and once Expected to have laid in the woods without the advantage of Fier or victuals and had Come to a Conclusion in what manner it should take place, but Jest before Daylight left us we saw a lite which proved to be a hous to our great joy and Satisfaction—So the Great Master is pleased at times to try us with the Site of Danger and then from time to time doth preserve us from it : in this Dessolate Wilderness there was many kinds of Wild Varmants which had been known to pray upon people."
—*Bulletin of Friends Historical Society*, Philadelphia, vol i. No. 3, p. 113.

were builded.   Those who were attracted by the message of the itinerant preachers were already prepared in advance for a spiritual type of religion.   They were, as so many of these Journals intimate, already dissatisfied with form and ceremony, out of sympathy with the legal aspect of religion and " seekers " after a life inwardly fed and vitalised.

Mary Starbuck, " the great woman," who seemed to John Richardson and Thomas Story divinely prepared to be the " pillar " of a Quaker Meeting in Nantucket, was no solitary example.   Wherever Quakerism took root and grew there were persons of this prepared type already there, and they formed the nucleus of the local " Society." David Sands found in the Maine woods at Vassalborough a man named Remington Hobby, who was a person of strong native traits and capacities, solid in judgment, inclined to a religion of inward reality, and waiting for a spark to kindle him to the fusing-point.   He, under the personal influence and message of David Sands, became the " live centre" of the new Society in that region. Something like that occurred in each locality where the message became an organising force.   But the one dynamic person, important enough to be named as the " live centre," was only *one among many* of like traits and character.   The reason that these " little societies " in the new world were novel and extraordinary was that they were composed of remarkable persons, prepared by years of experience for a type of religion which called in an unusual degree for individual responsibility and personal initiative, and which dispensed with adventitious helps and brought each member into the apostolic succession. There were no doubt many who were commonplace in endowments and power, and whose religion was in the main perfunctory, but there was at the centre of all the meetings which I have closely studied a group of persons who had a live religion, and who knew how to share their spiritual gains with the group to which they belonged. They, as much as their distinguished visitors, were the creators of New England Quakerism.

CHAPTER VII

A NEW TYPE OF SOCIAL RELIGION

THE Quakers were, as the preceding chapters have shown, a mystical people, holding as a primary article of their faith that the Divine Spirit, or Eternal Christ, is an actual Presence in the human soul, at first appearing as a judging or condemning Principle, and later, through the conformity and obedience of the individual, as an illuminating, inspiring, and guiding inward Spirit. This mystical principle sounded to the ears of their opponents like a dangerous leaven of wild disorder, a seed of Ranterism which, when grown, would topple down the pillars of Church and State. It seemed to mean that individual caprice and subjective whim were to be crowned and mitred, and that moral chaos was to come again. Something very different, however, actually happened— something quite worth study. The most interesting contribution of the Quakers is their success in constructing and maintaining a type of social religion in which the claim of a divine Light, lighting the individual soul from within, was united with a thoroughly ordered and practical group-life quite unique in the history of Christianity.

From the very first the central feature of their religion in the New England Colonies was "the meeting"—the meeting for worship. This was a peculiarly august gathering. The people composing it were plain ordinary men and women, who yoked their own oxen, ploughed their own fields, wove their own cloth, and washed their own dishes. Many of them drove in their wagons several miles to attend it, and through the early period they risked arrest and heavy fines in many parts of the Colony whenever they gathered with their neighbours for this purpose.

In the early stage of the movement the meetings of every sort were held in dwelling-houses, and we have here an interesting repetition of the custom which prevailed in the early apostolic Church.   Recent scholars have shown that wherever Christians went they had "house churches," for which purpose some well-to-do member furnished his house.[1]   So, too, did the early New England Friends, and the gatherings were invariably held in the large living room of some prosperous colonist, for instance in the home of William Coddington in Newport, of John Nowland in Sandwich, of Edward Wanton in Scituate, and of John Chamberlein in Boston.[2]

But, however plain and marked with toil these Friends might be, and however imminent the danger of persecution might be, in "the meeting" on First day morning they felt themselves in heavenly places.   They were moved and animated, quickened and possessed with a common faith that God was with them in their meeting, and that they were admitted behind the veil into the holy of holies. The silence was intense, for it was living and dynamic, and they believed that there in the hush, in their humble group, the great God of the Universe was preparing a mouthpiece for His word, and that when the seal of silence was broken and utterance should come, it would be the *prophetic word of the Lord*.   There were tears of joy and rapture on many faces as they sat in stillness, and a tremulous movement often swept over the company, making the name of "Quaker" not altogether in-appropriate.[3]

[1] Friends appear sometimes to have called their "meetings" Churches.   The following minute is from the Records of Rhode Island Monthly Meeting for 6th July 1688 : "This Meeting thought fit to write to *ye Chirch of Friends in Plymouth*, to remind them to bring in their sufferings to ye next Yearly Meeting."

[2] The Yearly Meeting was held in William Coddington's house until his death, and Quarterly Meeting was held for years in Edward Wanton's house.   Meeting-houses were built in Newport and in Sandwich as early as 1672 and 1673, but they were small structures, and larger meetings were still for some years held in private houses.

[3] I am drawing for my account on the early Journals of Friends.

The speaking, when it came, was somewhat rhythmical and rapturous, loaded with emotion. It was closely interwoven with a tissue of Scripture texts and phrases, bearing mainly on the central idea that God had now come to visit His people, to give them the Day Star experience in their hearts, and to be a present Guest in their midst. Suddenly the voice would drop, the cadence disappear, and the speaker would give, in genuine simplicity, some personal experience which had been granted to him. There might be many such "exercises" from the group, all bearing a common tinge and as though forged in a common experience. If a minister "from abroad" were present, as often was the case in these early days, the "word" would be more likely to come as a discourse of interpretation, instruction, and edification from him, and the listeners, believing implicitly that the visitor was *sent*, would be deeply attentive to what he opened to them and powerfully impressed by it. As some one knelt to pray all hats were removed, for they were generally worn at other times; all stood, and the person on his knees, with trembling frame and tremulous voice, uttered what seemed to him the common need of the meeting as in the stillness it had surged up into his responsive soul. "The meeting" was thus not a place for venting individual whim and personal caprice. It was the time when many individuals were merged and baptized into a living group, with a common consciousness of a divine Presence, and the utterances which were given were expected to be "in the common life," and it was an occasion of profound feeling, of lofty joy, and of real refreshing.

Each locality produced its little school of "prophets," doubtless often of crude and commonplace intelligence, but with some evidence of anointing and able to utter the "word" for the group. It was a bold experiment to dispense utterly and completely with the ordained priest, the professional minister, and to assume that all men were potentially near enough to God to be their own priests, but these Friends actually tried it. It gave those who formed the group an extraordinary sense of spiritual dignity and a no less important consciousness of responsibility. A person was no longer an atom, a mere individual, to be " lost " or " saved " by a system ; he was bound in, vitally and organically, into the life above and the life below—a branch of God's true Vine and a member of a spiritual society of persons, each co-operating for the good of all, and each a possible channel of grace for the rest.

The most important feature of " the meeting " was the powerful sense of *reality* which pervaded it—the peculiar conviction which possessed the members of the group that they had found God. They were no longer hearing about Him and about His covenants and dispensations in past ages ; their own hearts were burning as they partook of the bread which He broke for them and as they drank at what seemed to them the wells of eternal life. It was this assurance of reality, this exalting *experience*, which more than anything else propagated primitive Quakerism. The arguments " about " the Inward Light were much on a level with arguments " about " covenants—both moved in the realm of " conceptions," but the man who had felt his soul fed in such a meeting was " convinced," with a permanent conviction.

Another influence which powerfully tended to foster common ideals, and to unify the group in spirit and aim, was the unbroken stream of itinerant ministry from the mother Society and from the Societies in the other Colonies. The minutes of the meetings show an amazing list of these visitors. When one remembers the difficulties of travel, the expense in time and money, the primitive sort of entertainment which was possible at this period, the element of sacrifice looms very large in this story of travel which must for ever remain unwritten. But the point of importance at the present moment is the formative influence of these unique travellers. They believed, and their listeners believed, that they were " divinely sent messengers." They came into the homes of the native Friends and supplied them with the facts, the news, the personal drama, of the wider Society of which they formed a fragment. By word of mouth those of all sections heard of the progress of events, the issues before the Society, the spread of " Truth " as they called it,[1] and they learned to know, in their isolated spot, the main problems of the whole movement, which they thus in some measure shared. These travellers visited every region, however remote, and they were thus the bearers of ideas and ideals which formed a common stock of thought and aspiration, and without knowing it the native ministers shaped their message and formed their manner of delivering it under the unconscious suggestions supplied by their visitors, so that the Quaker in Dover and the Quaker in Sandwich were almost as alike in inward tissue as they were outwardly in cut of coat !

But the greatest socialising influence, and next to the meeting for worship the most *creative* feature of the Quaker organisation, was " the meeting for business." In the earliest stage " the business meetings " were not clearly differentiated, as they later came to be, into Monthly, Quarterly, and Yearly Meetings. At first, and for some years, all meetings under these various names were primarily enlarged meetings for worship and ministry—a sort of " general meeting " drawing attenders from a wider territory than the local " First day Meeting." The " business " was at first rather meagre, and consisted mainly of accounts of sufferings endured and reports of what was being done to spread the " Truth." [2] The novel feature of all these meetings, from lowest to highest, was the *group-spirit* which prevailed in them. Each individual Quaker believed in divine illumination and spiritual guidance—the Light of Christ within him was the beginning and end of his faith. But it was plain to them all that individuals sometimes erred and missed the

[1] Even the horse which carried the ministers from place to place was called "Truth's horse."

[2] I find a minute of Duxbury Monthly Meeting as late as 1698 to this effect : " We have agreed that the Monthly Meeting which is held at the house of Robert Barker in Duxbury shall be a meeting for business as it is elsewhere among Friends." Evidently before this it had been a general meeting for worship and *extension*. This was later called Pembroke Monthly Meeting.

Guide, or, as an ancient minute says, "ran out of their measure and brought death instead of life!"   It would not do—all the sound Quaker leaders knew this—to call men to follow their inward Light, and then to treat them as atoms and leave them to go their individual way according to the suggestion of inward impulse, which might be from above and might also be from below. They went to work with fine insight and with wise instinct to *mass* their guidance and to make their spiritual wisdom a *corporate* affair.   Every religious meeting they held was supposed to be held in the Light of Christ, and the exercises of it were supposed to move in response to the will of the Spirit, and each member found his own particular part and place by being organic with the whole.   So, too, with the "business" of monthly, quarterly, and yearly meetings.   Each decision was reached by taking the "sense" or "judgment" of the whole meeting, and each such conclusion was supposed to be under divine guidance, and was arrived at only in the *unity* of the body.   From first to last *the group was the unit*, and the individual found his life and his leading in the Life and Light of the formative spiritual group.

Loosely organised local meetings for business were held as early as 1658 in Sandwich and Newport, a little later in Scituate, Duxbury,[1] Salem, and Lynn, with others following soon after, but no meeting records survive for a date earlier than 1673.[2]   The Quarterly

---

[1] There is on record an order of the court held in Duxbury in 1660 : "Whereas there is *a constant monthly meeting of Quakers* from divers places in great number, which is very offensive and may prove very prejudicial to the government, and as the most constant place for such meetings is Duxburrow, they have ordered Constant Southworth and William Paybody to repair to such meetings, together with the marshall or constable of the town, and use their best endeavours by discourse and argument to convince or hinder them."—*Records of Plymouth Colony*, vol. xi. p. 130.

[2] The Records of American meetings were undoubtedly begun at the suggestion of George Fox.   This is the first entry in the Sandwich Book of Records : "At a man's Meeting kept at Will. Allen's house ye 25th day of ye 4th mo. [June, by our modern calendar] 1673.   At wch. Meeting it is concluded yt. for ye future a man's Meeting be kept ye first sixth day of ye week in every month, and for Friends to come together about ye eleventh hour."   The Rhode Island Records begin in 1676.   The following Monthly Meetings were established in New England in the Colonial period :

Meeting, as its name implies, was held four times in the year, and in the earliest period it was a distinctly religious meeting.[1]

It massed together in a definite community the Quaker forces spread over a large area of country, and it was held mainly for the purpose of propagating the Quaker message—"the Truth," as they insisted. There was often a distinguished visitor or visitors present, and those who came were likely to hear the Friends' interpretation of Christianity powerfully presented. It was also the custom to read on these occasions epistles containing a message of Truth from other meetings, or from some prominent Friend who had formerly visited them and had "a concern for their advancement in the Truth." It was, too, quite the custom to hold special meetings for "youth," at which epistles, or passages from Friends' writings were read and advice "in the way of life" given.[2] These Quarterly Meetings gradually developed into meetings for the transaction of business, and matters concerning the wider life of the Church, too weighty to be settled in a local monthly meeting, came up here for consideration. The building of meeting-houses and the raising of money for extensive relief would come before

Sandwich in 1658 : Records begin 1673.
Rhode Island in 1658 : Records begin 1676.
Pembroke before 1660 : Records from 1676.
Salem, date of origin unknown : Records begin 1677.
Dartmouth, 1699.

East Greenwich, 1699.
Hampton (later Amesbury), 1701.
Dover, 1701.
Nantucket, 1708.
Providence and Smithfield, 1718.
Swanzea, 1732.
South Kingstown, 1743.
Yarmouth, Maine, 1761.
Westport, 1766.

[1] After the Quarterly Meeting differentiated into a distinct business meeting, there were three Quarterly Meetings in the colonial period, as follows : (1) Sandwich Quarterly Meeting, which began at least as early as 1680 and originally was composed of Sandwich and Pembroke Monthly Meetings. (2) Rhode Island Quarterly Meeting, which was established in 1699, and was originally composed of Rhode Island, Dartmouth, and Kingstown Monthly Meetings. (3) Salem Quarterly Meeting, which was established in 1705 and was originally composed of Salem, Hampton, and Dover Monthly Meetings.

[2] I find on the Monthly Meeting Records for Newport this minute under date of 12th mo. 14, 1692 : "It is agreed that all our public Meetings be at our Meeting houses as formerly were held. *Our Quarterly Meeting was for the reading of Friends' epistles* ; but there is now a Meeting once in six weeks for that service." The Quarterly Meeting also prepared, "as way opened for it," epistles to be sent to other Quarterly Meetings. I find distinct reference to this service in the minutes.

the Quarterly Meeting.[1]   There is a record of an extraordinary Quarterly Meeting held in Sandwich, "in Wm.
Allen's house," in 1703, with representatives from meetings reaching all the way from Rhode Island to Dover,
New Hampshire.[2]

The reader who has imagination will easily see the
social importance of these gatherings.   Friends from
these widely sundered regions, persons of different social
standing, of all stages of education and spiritual experience,
thus came together, generally for a two days' meeting—
were entertained at the homes in the locality where the
meeting was held, interchanged ideas, and formed, almost
without knowing it, a "group-consciousness" which played
a   powerful   rôle   in   the   life   of   the   Society.   More
important than the "youths' meetings" in their formative
influence over the children were these social visits and
these Quarterly Meeting dinners, when the house was
filled to bursting with Friends from other sections of the
Colony.[3]

Still higher in its scope and more constructive in its
functions was the Yearly Meeting, and this again was still
more significant for its influence in the formation of
"group-consciousness" and of social ideals.   As with
the other meetings, the Yearly Meeting was at first a
large General Meeting for worship and preaching, and for
an impressive massing of the Quaker forces.   The first of

[1] Where the need was extensive the case was brought up to the Yearly Meeting, as will be seen from the following minute of the Yearly Meeting of 1697 : "It
was proposed to this Meeting the necessity of poor Friends to the Eastward [New
Hampshire and Maine, I presume] for some relief : this Meeting did collect ye sum
off ten pounds, and did order ye same by ye hands off Samuel Collings to Matthew
and Richard Estes to be distributed by ym.

"Itt is desired by this Meeting yt ye ffriends appointed to write to ffriends in
England doe also write to ffriends in Long Island, East and West Jersey, and to
Philadelphia, conserning ye necessytie off poor ffriends to ye Eastward, and desire
their assistance to help relieve them."

[2] The following localities sent representatives :

Rhode Island Meeting.	Sandwich Meeting.
Dartmouth ,,	Greenwich ,,
Salem and Lynn ,,	Hampton ,,
Scituate ,,	Dover ,,

[3] As late even as 1784 there were only three Quarterly Meetings for business
established.   They were (1) Rhode Island, which was held in turn at Smithfield,
Dartmouth, Swansea, and Greenwich ; (2) Salem, held at Falmouth in Maine,
Dover, Hampton, Salem ; (3) Sandwich, held at Nantucket, Long Plain, Falmouth
in Massachusetts, and Sandwich.

these Yearly Meetings was held at Newport, Rhode Island, in 1661. It seems to have been called at the suggestion of an English Quaker, named George Rofe, who was at that time on a religious mission to this country. He writes to his friend Richard Hubberthorne in 1661 :

"We came in at Rhode Island, and we appointed a General Meeting for all Friends in those parts, which was a very great meeting and very precious, and continued four days." [1]

This meeting was so large that, according to Bishop, the Boston officials, "made an alarm that the Quakers were gathering to kill the people and fire the town of Boston !" It steadily grew in importance and in numbers, and soon came to be the great event in the Quaker year. From far away Piscataqua at one extreme, and from Long Island at the other, the Friends flocked to Newport, for until 1695 the Quakers on Long Island came to Rhode Island to Yearly Meeting.[2] By 1743 it was attended by five thousand Friends, and the attendance continued very large throughout the century. Similar Yearly Meetings were held for many years in different sections of New England as well as at Newport, so that nearly all communities where Friends abounded had a large annual visitation.[3] But the Newport Yearly Meeting was "the

---

[1] Letter of George Rofe to Richard Hubberthorne, 18th November 1661, in the A.R.B. Collection, No. 62, *Devonshire House Portfolio.*

[2] "It is also agreed yt ye Meeting at Long Island shall be from this time a Yearly Meeting, and yt John Boune and John Rodman shall receive all such as shall come to ye Yearly Meeting in Long Island, and correspond with ffriends appointed in London."—*Minute of New England Yearly Meeting for 1695.*

[3] I find the following Yearly Meetings in existence under date of 1693 :

"Duxberry Yearly Meeting of Worship begins ye furst 6th day in every 8th mo.

"Salem, ye generall Meeting of Worship begins ye first and second days of every 7th month.

"Piscattua (Piscataqua) Yearly Generall Meeting of Worship begins ye 7th ffirst day after Salem Meeting.

"Dartmouth Yearly Generall Meeting of Worship begins the 4th sixth day in every 8th month.

"Warwick Yearly Generall Meeting of worship begins and is appointed ye second ffirst day in every 3d mo[th].

"Providence Yearly Generall Meeting of Worship begins ye last ffirst day of the 5th mo[th].

"4th mo. 14, 1695.—There shall be kept a Meeting at Lin [Lynn], ye third day next after ye Yearly Meeting at Salem is over."

Samuel Bownas says : "They [the Friends of New England] have in almost every place once a year a General Meeting which they call a Yearly Meeting, and by this popular abundance more people come together in expectation of something

child of promise" and soon outstripped and gradually swallowed up the others.[1]

Definite arrangements were made in 1699 for Representatives to the Yearly Meeting from the Quarterly Meetings, and from this time on the legislative and constructive aspect of the Yearly Meeting became more pronounced, and less emphasis was put upon it as an occasion for worship and ministry.[2]

The Monthly Meeting, beginning as we have seen in a very unassuming fashion, soon expanded in importance, and came to have a profoundly formative social influence over the life of the individual members, and it absorbed into the corporate body of the meeting the functions of "cure of souls" and guardian of morals—usually delegated by the Churches to a priest or an ordained clergyman. From the earliest period of the systematic Monthly Meeting it was the custom to read, in a solemn way, a set of "Advices," embodying the religious ideals of the Quaker founders, and setting forth the type of "walk and conversation" which befitted a Friend.[3] To these

extraordinary to be met with."—*Life and Travels of Samuel Bownas* (London, 1761), p. 149.

[1] I find a record of a Yearly Meeting at Sandwich as late as 1756, and this curious minute arranging for the holding of Providence Yearly Meeting :

6th mo. 11, 1761.—" By epistle from Rhode Island Quarterly Meeting, informing us they have Providence Yearly Meeting altered to begin at Warwick the sixth day before the fourth First day of ye 8th month, and at Providence the Seventh day following, and at Smithfield on First day. For divers reasons offerde at this Meeting it is agreed that said Meeting for the future be altered agreeable to their request."

[2] " Itt is agreed by order and consent of this Meeting, yt the second day of the week be for the business and service of the Meeting for the future, according to the antient order of Truth amongst us, and not for public worship, and yt two ffriends from each Quarterly Meeting, and where no Quarterly Meeting two or more from each Monthly Meeting, to attend ye service of ye Yearly Meeting till business is ended, and as many other sober friends as hath freedom."—*Yearly Meeting Minutes for* 1699.

The meeting of the ministers, as a meeting apart, began in 1700 under the following minute :

4th mo. 17, 1700.—" It is agreed upon by this Meeting yt ye sixth day morning of ye Yearly Meeting before ye public Meeting for Worship begins be for ye future for Friends of ye Ministry to meet together, and such other sober Friends as hath freedom."

[3] The following minute of Sandwich Monthly Meeting for Eleventh month, 8th, 1680, indicates that the "Advices" were at this time read four times a year. They are called " The testimonies of Truth's concern." At this Meeting it is ordered " yt the *testimonies of Truth's concern* are to be read four times in a year at our Monthly Men and Women's Meeting."

"Advices" there was added, at least as early as the year 1700, a set of definite "Queries," the reading of which was intended to furnish the members an occasion for inward silent "confessional."[1] The "Queries" called for an examination of the life from at least a dozen moral and spiritual view-points, and tended to present a concrete moral ideal for the daily life at home and in business occupations. When the "Advices" and "Queries" were read the Friends "of light and leading," especially visiting Friends from abroad, used the opportunity for imparting counsel and advice upon practical matters of life among men. There can be no question that all this, presented as it was with religious atmosphere and with all minds in a peculiarly receptive attitude, *worked* with deep suggestive power and tended to produce a common moral type. But the Monthly Meeting did not stop with public "Queries," and with its admirable method of "group suggestion," it brought positive pressure to bear to mould the lives of the individual into the moral fashion which the group approved. For this purpose there were "Overseers," who visited the homes and kept a careful watch over the lives of the members.

There was, as we should expect, a tendency to make conduct conform to rather stiff and rigid standards, for the Friends to a large degree shared the Puritan ideals in regard to "Christian manners in the world." Then, too, in addition to their scrupulous guardianship over morals, they were always as zealous to maintain certain "testimonies" which were the badges of their "peculiarity" as a people of the Lord. They were as keen and watchful for deviations from these "testimonies" as the Puritan elders were over deviations from sound theology, for that larger liberty which leaves the individual entirely with his own conscience—with his personal sense of what is

---

[1] I find this minute in the Records of the Yearly Meeting for 1701 : "Twelve Queries were made at the Quarterly and Monthly Meetings and sent to the Yearly Meeting." Before this time a set of Queries prepared by George Fox had been extensively used. I find this entry in the Sandwich minutes under date of 1673 : "It was ordered that Jedediah Allen pay John Fowler 5 sh. for copying G. ff. Queries." The custom of preparing set answers to the "Queries" began in 1755.

right for him—had not yet come. The "minutes" of all types of meetings, from their origin, indicate a highly developed moral sensitiveness, and, all interwoven with this, there appears an excessive concern over things which were in the class of the *ceremonial, i.e.* things which had a function only as they helped form a "peculiar people."[1]

One of the matters which most profoundly concerned these Friends was the guardianship of the marriage of their members. They refused from the very beginning to allow any member to be married by what they called "a priest," for this seemed to them to be the very essence of sacerdotalism. They adopted a simple ceremony by which the bride and groom pledged themselves in marriage "before the Lord and in the presence of Friends"; and after enduring many hardships they won from the courts the decision that this form of marriage was legal. As the idea developed that Friends were "a peculiar people of the Lord," there naturally went with it a disapproval of the marriage of a Friend with "a person of the world." This soon became a *fixed idea*, and the monthly meeting records contain a host of minutes which report "dealings" with members who have deviated in this all-important matter of marriage.

In regard to the prevailing "vices" of the times Friends appear generally to have taken an advanced position. When lotteries were looked upon by almost all Christian people as at least tolerable institutions, and

---

[1] I give two illustrations of the way meetings "watched up" their members on matters of daily life: "The overseers inform this Meeting that two Friends have allowed fiddling, dancing, and playing at cards in their houses, for which they decline to condemn the offence to Friends' satisfaction. Therefore this Meeting doth appoint Joseph Gifford and Barzellai Tucker to labour with them and make report to the next Monthly Meeting." "This Meeting having considered the answers of the several Quarterly Meetings relating to the extravigant and unnecessary Perry Wiggs, and a concern remaining on the minds of Friends for preventing the same prevailing among us Do conclude, and it is the judgment of this Meeting that all Friends who suppose that they have need of wiggs, ought to take the advice and approbation of the visitors [*i.e.* overseers] of their respective Meetings before they proceed to get one. And it is the tender advice, and brotherly request of this Meeting that all be careful to observe the same, and not in a careless or overly-minded cutt of their hair (which is given for a covering) to putt on a wigg or indecent capp which has been observed of late years to be a growing practice among too many of the young men in several parts, to the troubel of many honest Friends, it plainly appearing (in some) for an imitation and joyning with the spirit and fashion of the world."

were being used by churches and educational institutions as a beneficial provision for raising funds for the work of the Lord, New England Friends, "in the light of Truth," saw that they were pernicious, and refused to allow their members to profit by them. This minute from Dartmouth Meeting shows the prevailing sentiment among Friends as early as 1759.

"Whereas we understand that there has been a practice of late amongst our younger set of people of making lotteries which we think to be of very hurtful consequence, therefore, it is the advice of this Meeting for all under our care to be careful not to be in such practice, and that all Friends belonging to this Meeting endeavour to suppress the same." [1]

At a time when the use of spirituous liquors was an almost universal custom, Friends were nevertheless very *sensitive* on the subject. They began, from the first of their existence as a people, to insist on a clean, temperate life for their members. The Minutes of all the monthly meetings from 1673 down contain many items like this :—

"A Friend of Richmond Meeting hath taken strong liquor to excess, a committee is appointed to labour with him."

"A complaint was brought against a Friend for excessive drinking, this meeting appoints two Friends to discourse with said Friend."

"The overseers inform that a Friend hath suffered too much liberty in his tavern which tends to bring a reproach on Truth, wherefore Joseph Tucker and Abraham Tucker are appointed to labour with him." [2]

---

[1] A little later horse-racing was included in the list of " vices " which could not be tolerated as the following minute shows :
" 2/15/1762.—Whereas we understand that horse-racing is a prevailing practice therefore the Meeting doth conclude to make a minute against all such practices. And if Friends are found guilty of any such practice they are liable to be dealt with as offenders."

[2] I find in the Records of the Yearly Meeting for 1784 a minute on the subject which seems to me a noble paper for the eighteenth century to have produced. " The excessive use of Spirituous liquors of all kinds has for a long time been seen by our Society to be a practice tending to lead from calmness and innocency to the many evils which are the consequences of intemperance, and a concern having arisen for the spreading of this Testimony, not only to the disuse of distilled spirituous liquors amongst us except as a medicine, but that others also may by our example be encouraged to restrain its use within the limits of Truth, we recommend to all Friends everywhere, carefully to look at

Fidelity to one's word of promise was held to be a most sacred obligation, and every Friend was expected to make righteousness in trade and dealing "an affair of honour." Every book of Monthly Meeting Records has many minutes similar in spirit to the following :

"There was a complaint brought up that a Friend refuses to fulfil a promise he made two years ago respecting performing of his proportion of work on the high ways, therefore, in consequence of said complaint we do appoint John Gifford, Benjamin Tripp, and Peleg Huddestone to inspect into said complaint, and if they find the Friend refuse to fulfil his promise agreeable to said complaint, to labour with said Friend to fulfil it, so that Truth and the professors thereof may not suffer on that account any longer."

" There was brought a complaint to this Meeting against a Friend for refusing to come to a settlement in a division of a fence in the line between him and another Friend, therefore we do appoint Nicholas Haviland and James Soule to labour with said Friend to do what they shall think reasonable in the case after they have informed themselves the circumstances thereof."

"The overseers informed that there is a bad report concerning two members salting up beef, and exposing it for sale, which was not merchantable ; and they have made some inquiry, and do not find things clear, therefore this Meeting appoints a committee to make inquiry."

Under no consideration or provocation might a Friend take an oath, either as an " expletive " to relieve his mind, or as a judicial sign that he was about to tell the truth and nothing but the truth, for he was under a sacred obligation to make his ordinary word as true as a bond. In Rhode Island this was an easy matter, as the statutes of that Colony always made provision for an affirmation

the motives of being concerned therewith not only for using, but distilling, importing, trading, or handing out to others, who from habit may have acquired a thirst, and inclination after it, tending to their hurt ; we tenderly advise all such as are concerned therein, *to centre down to the principle*, leading to universal righteousness, and as we apprehend a continuance in such practices, will in this day of light weaken the hands not only of those individuals concerned to further the reformation, but tend greatly to obstruct Society from holding up a standard to this important Testimony, as becometh our holy profession. We entreat. therefore, those who have begun well, and made advances in the way towards their own peace, that as soon as may be, they forbear the said practices that a line may in due time be drawn, and the standard be raised and spread to the nation.

instead of an oath, but this provision was not made in Massachusetts until 1759.

Friends felt that it was even more important to keep the Society absolutely clear of everything that belonged to warfare, or which encouraged fighting with what were known as "carnal weapons," for the Quaker had no objection to any warfare which he could properly call "spiritual"! This "concern" ran up against a deep-seated natural instinct, and it entailed, of course, a harvest of difficulties, particularly in the early days of Indian warfare.

During the French and Indian War of Queen Anne's reign Friends were subjected to very severe sufferings, and stringent measures were taken to force them at this time to do military service.[1]

At the time of the Louisburg Expedition in the campaign of 1758-59 the Quakers in Massachusetts were forced to hire men to go as substitutes ; and when they refused to pay for substitutes, as they generally did, their property was distrained to cover the amount. Moses Farnum of Uxbridge, Massachusetts, in 1759 headed a petition to the Legislature setting forth that the sums assessed against the Quakers were greatly in excess of the actual amounts paid for their substitutes. On investigation this was found to be true, and large sums were returned to the Friends who had suffered.[2] The difficulty of being a "consistent Friend" in the critical period of the Revolutionary War was, of course, even greater, for now the Quaker testimony came into violent collision with the

---

[1] The following minute of the Yearly Meeting for 1712 gives a glimpse of the situation :—

"4/12/1712.—At our Generall Yearly Meeting held at Portsmouth. Peter Varney and John Kenny were imprisoned ye 8th day of 5th month 1711 to go in ye expedition to Canada, and remained under confinment until ye 8th month 1711 being under ye command of Sydrach Walton who suffered them not to be abused during the time of their voyage as per account brought into this meeting.

"John Terry and Moses Tucker were likewise imprisoned to go on ye said expidition to Canada, and being in hopes of getting discharged went to Boston, and after much labour thereabouts were nevertheless sent as prisoners to the castle at Boston, and from thence conveyed by force on board Transport under ye command of Major Roberton, whose hard usage was such that one of ye above Ffriends (John Terry) died within twenty-four hours after their return to Boston, as may be seen by a particular account thereof presented to this Meeting."

[2] See *Provincial Laws of Massachusetts*, xvi. 488 and 521.

fundamental instinct of patriotism.   There was, however, no parley on the part of the Meetings—principle was principle—and no man could remain a Friend if he participated " in the spirit of war."   Even so blue-blooded a Friend as Nathanael Greene of Rhode Island—a patriot of the patriots—had his name expunged from the list of members for the offence of " taking arms."   It was when the colonies were face to face with this war with the mother country in 1775 that New England Friends first organised a meeting distinctly called " The Meeting for Sufferings," composed of delegates from all sections and designed to deal with the difficulties likely to arise from the approaching catastrophe of war.[1]

The work of oversight was not confined to moral and spiritual matters.   It touched the whole of life.   The most important aspect of it from a social point of view was the care bestowed upon those who were in trouble or in financial straits.   It belonged to the sacred " honour of Truth " that no Friend should be allowed to suffer want, or should be compelled to receive support from the township.   The amount of time which some of these capable and practical Friends must have spent in looking after the needs of poor members gives one a very wholesome respect for the sincerity of their Christianity.[2]   In times of general calamity, widespread suffering, or the havoc of war, the Meetings which were less exposed raised large sums of money for the relief of suffering Friends and for others.   This outreaching relief work was carried on throughout the entire period of this history ; but it finds its best illustration in the effort of Friends to relieve the sufferings which resulted from the siege of Boston during

---

[1] This Meeting for Sufferings eventually took on a great variety of functions, and managed the important public affairs of the Society in the interim between Yearly Meetings.

[2] This Minute will illustrate what was happening in every Quaker community : " And whereas there has been a great charge arisen upon a man Friend by reason of his lameness, and Doctor's charges, we think it our duty to see into the affair, and order Abram Tucker, Isaac Smith, and Peleg Russell to see what ye charge is, and what way he is to pay it."

" We cannot find that the man Friend can do anything valuable towards paying the Doctor for curing his leg.   The charge is £15, 14s. lawful money which this Meeting hath concluded to pay."

the Revolutionary War. An appeal was made to Friends in Pennsylvania and New Jersey to join in these extensive relief measures, and the extraordinary sum of nineteen hundred and sixty-eight pounds sterling was expended under the care of a committee of the Meeting for Sufferings. This committee visited General Washington and General Howe, explaining that their mission was visiting the fatherless and widows, feeding the hungry, clothing the naked, *without distinction of sects or parties.* The Generals would not allow the Friends to pass through the lines into the city of Boston, but arrangements were made for them to send in their funds to be distributed by Friends who were shut up in the besieged city. The members of the committee then took up in person the laborious task of relieving the distress—as a kind of eighteenth century Red Cross Society—in the towns about the city, where multitudes of people " were in want of victuals, wood, and clothing." In Salem, for instance, the Friends, in company with the Selectmen of the town, went from house to house and distributed their relief through the very streets along which Quakers had been whipped a hundred years before. There stands on the Records of the town of Salem for 1775, and again in 1776, a "vote of thanks" to the Friends for their generous relief in this time of need.[1] The towns which were visited and relieved in like manner, were Lynn, Marblehead, Charleston, Medfield, Bolton, Lancaster, Marlborough, Sudbury, Weston, Woburn, Reading, Sherborn, Holliston, Northbury, and Waltham, and through these towns—many of them towns through which Quakers had been whipped—working in company with the Selectmen, the Friends, with personal painstaking care, dispensed their gifts of love.[2]

One of the most stubborn fights in the spiritual warfare of the New England Quakers was for freedom to worship God as their own hearts dictated, a privilege now common to all Anglo-Saxon peoples, and also for

[1] See *Annals of Salem*, ii. 399.
[2] The full accounts of this work are given in the Records of " The Meeting for Sufferings."

freedom from supporting any system of worship which their consciences did not approve. The privilege to worship in their own way and in their own gatherings was won at terrific cost, as we have seen, but it was comparatively quickly won. It was discovered by an overwhelming demonstration that the denial of the privilege could be maintained only by the extermination of the sect, and thus there was no rational alternative but to yield. The other privilege, the privilege of exemption from tithes for the support of the established ministry, was won only by a long, hard fight, but when it *was* won it was won for everybody.

From the first Friends refused to pay the Church "tithes," which they called "priests' rates," for they insisted that "spiritual ministry" must be without money and without price. They were imprisoned for their refusal, and they were furthermore subjected to a capricious seizure of goods, roughly estimated by the authorities to equal in value the amount of the tithes. Cows, horses, pigs, farm produce, wearing apparel, household silver, wagons, implements of all sorts were carried away, while the poor family looked helplessly on and saw themselves stripped to pay for a ministry which supported itself by such methods![1] The Meetings, with their splendid group spirit, made these losses a corporate matter and all shared, as far as they could, the sufferings of each. The Meetings rose to the crisis and year after year raised great sums to cover the losses of Friends both at home and in remote sections.[2] But they did not stop with passive resistance to the tithe system. They laboured for three-quarters of a century by every

[1] This minute from Dartmouth Monthly Meeting will illustrate the sort of distraints which were endured :

"4/2/1725.—The accounts of some sufferings of Peleg Slocum, and John Tucker having their creatures taken away off their Islands (called Elizabeth Islands) by distraint by John Mayhew, constable of Chilmark, was presented to the Meeting.

"Taken from Peleg Slocum eighty sheep for the Priests' rate and towards the building of a Presbyterian Meeting house, ye said sheep were sold for £34.

"And taken from John Tucker on ye like occasion one horse sold for £10, 10s. and one heifer sold for £2, 10s., demand was for £7, 15s. 4d."

[2] I give three Minutes from the Yearly Meeting to illustrate this corporate action :

"4/11/1730.—The amount of sufferings brought up from the Quarterly Meet-

method known to their intelligence, or "revealed by the mind of Truth" to get the tyranny abolished by statute.[1]

In the year 1678, four prominent Friends, Edward Wanton, Joseph Coleman, Nathaniel Fitsrandal and William Allen, presented to the General Court of Plymouth, "conscientiously and in all tenderness," their reasons why they could not "give maintenance to the established preachers." "We suppose," they say, "it's well enough known that we have never been backward to contribute our assistance in our estates and persons, where we could act without scruple of conscience, nor in the particular case of the country rate . . . until this late contrivance of mixing your preachers' maintenance therewith," which, in short, they declare they cannot under any circumstances pay. They thereupon undertake at some length to prove from the New Testament that "settled maintenance upon preachers" is contrary to the gospel. Whether their exegesis carried weight with the Court or not, their concluding remark must have occasioned some serious reflection : "We request, for conclusion, you will please to consider whether you may not prejudice yourselves in your public interest with the King (*you yourselves having your liberty but upon sufferance*) if you should compel any to conform in any respect to such a church government or ministry as is repugnant to the Church of England. We leave the whole to your serious

ing are as followeth : For Priests rates taken from Friends in Salem Quarterly Meeting £118, 11s."

"4/11/1731.—Friends Sufferings from Rochester, Massachusetts, for priests rates £23, 17s. Friends suffering from Salem for Priests rates £10, 17s. 6d."

"4/8/1732.—Friends sufferings from Priests rates in Kittery in the County of York and Province of Maine £15, 10s."

[1] The work of petitioning the governing authorities at home and abroad went on year after year with admirable persistence. Here is an interesting minute of the year 1708 : "It being proposed under the consideration of this Meeting the detriament yt may attend Friends by an act past in the Massachusetts Provence in the year 1706 joining the Priests rate to the Province tax [making it extremely difficult for Friends to escape paying it] this Meeting doth desire, or order, Richard Borden and Thomas Cornell Jr. in behalf of said Meeting to inform the Governor thereof by way of writing, requesting his relief therein, *otherwise to signify to him that they shall address the Queen* [Queen Anne] *in that matter* ; and said Cornell to sign the same in behalf of the Meeting, being clerk thereof ; and Joseph Wanton, and Richard Borden are appointed to do said writing to ye Governor and speal [spell] the same."

consideration."[1] The writers of this document evidently remembered the " King's missive."

A half-century later, in 1724, the English King, through his council, did finally declare himself in no uncertain words on this matter of " maintenance of ministers," and this second missive, this time from George I., though not as dramatic as the famous one from Charles II., hastened the end of persecution for refusal to pay church rates. Appeal to the King had been made in 1724 by Thomas Richardson and Richard Partridge on behalf of Joseph Anthony, John Sisson, John Akin and Philip Taber, Quaker assessors of Dartmouth and Tiverton, who had been imprisoned in New Bristol jail for refusing to collect taxes to support the ministry.

Their case was argued before the Privy Council and the following significant decision was rendered at a Court held at St. James', the 2nd day of June, 1724, and attended by the King's Most Excellent Majesty, His Royal Highness the Prince of Wales, the Archbishop of Canterbury, and thirteen other members of the Court. It was as follows : " His Majesty in Council is graciously pleased . . . to remit the additional taxes of £100 and £72, 11s. which were to have been assessed on the towns of Dartmouth and Tiverton [for the maintenance of Presbyterian ministers who are not of their persuasion].[2] And His Majesty is hereby further pleased to order that the said Joseph Anthony, John Sisson, John Akin, and Philip Taber be immediately released from their imprisonment, on account thereof, which the governor, lieutenant-governor, or commander-in-chief for the time being of His Majesty's said province of Massachusetts Bay, and all others whom it may concern are to take notice of, and yield obedience thereunto."[3]

These persistent efforts, made year after year to secure relief from these " rates," finally bore fruit, and the

---

[1] The *Hinckley Papers*, pp. 18-20.
[2] This clause is in the report of the Privy Council which was approved by the king.
[3] The Petition and the decision of the Privy Council, with the King's message are given in full in Gough's *History of the Quakers* (Dublin, 1790), iv. 218-226.

colonial government of Massachusetts passed a law in
1746 giving Friends temporary exemption from all
charges for the maintenance of ministers. The Yearly
Meeting appointed a committee in 1747 to petition the
General Court of Massachusetts to make this law
perpetual. They succeeded for the moment in getting
only another temporary act of exemption, which, however,
very soon became a permanent law ; and from this time
on the subject disappears from the minutes, and the
Quaker enjoyed his own meeting in peace and kept his
cows and his silver spoons for his own use !

The next great contest into which the Friends threw
their energies was a more unselfish cause and one which
was grounded distinctly in humanitarian principles—
I mean the conflict against human slavery. The
Narragansett Bay country was the region where negro
slavery most "flourished" in New England. Ships sailed
from Newport to the coast of Guinea and brought back
live freight which was sold among the prosperous colonial
farmers along the fertile shores of the Bay.[1] There were,
too, slaves in many other parts of the New England
colonies.

There was little or no moral sentiment in the colonies
against slavery in the seventeenth century, and Friends
fell in with the custom, as others did, with few apparent
scruples. They were, however, from the first awake to
the fact that black people were human, and deserved
proper treatment as human beings, though they evidently
did not see, before the middle of the eighteenth century,
that slavery *per se* must go.[2]

[1] See Caroline Hazard's *College Tom* (Boston, 1893) p. 25.

[2] These minutes from Sandwich Monthly Meeting are interesting as illustrating
the way the meeting dealt with inhumanity to slaves :

"3/30/1711.—Whereas a woman Friend hath given over to hardness of heart
to such a degree she hath been not only consenting but encouraging the unmerciful
whipping or beating of her negro man servant, he being stript naked, and hanged
up by the hands, in his master's house, and then beating him, or whipping him
so unmercifully that it is to be feared that it was in some measure the occasion of
his death that followed soon after, the which we do account is not only unchristian
but inhuman for which cause we find ourselves concerned to testify to the world
that we utterly disown all such actions, and perticularly the Friend above
mentioned."

"10/17/1711.—A paper being presented to this Meeting from the Friend who

The enlightened members, even in the first quarter of the eighteenth century, "felt a weighty concern" to have the Society "cleared" of what seemed to them an evil, and their influence was great enough to get the matter well before the Yearly Meeting at Newport, and to get this minute adopted in 1717:

"A weighty concern being on this Meeting concerning the importing and keeping slaves. This Meeting therefore refers it to the consideration of Friends everywhere to waite for ye wisdom of God how to discharge themselves in that weighty affair, and desires it may be brought up from our Monthly and Quarterly Meetings to our next Yearly Meeting, and also yt merchants do write their correspondents in the islands and elsewhere to discourage their sending any more [slaves] in order to be sold by Friends here."

Again in 1727 the Yearly Meeting rose to a more direct and positive position, indicating that the moral tide had risen during the decade. The minute of this date declares:

"It is the sense of this Meeting, that the importation of Negroes from their native country and relations is not a commendable nor allowable practice and that practice is censured by this Meeting."

Thomas Hazard of South Kingstown, Rhode Island, generally called "College Tom," seems to have been one of the first Friends to awake to the evil of slave-holding, though he was brought up in the very atmosphere of it. He was sent, while still in his youth, by his father to Connecticut to buy cattle to stock the farm upon which at his marriage he was to settle. While there he fell in with a friend of his father's, a deacon of the Church, who invited him to his home. The deacon in conversation made the chance remark that " Quakers were not Christian people." The young Quaker, fresh from college, was ready for a hot argument, and was marshalling in his mind the arguments of attack when all his heat was

was disowned for unmercifully beating her Negro, wherein she desires to come into unity with Friends, and ye sense of this Meeting is that she should wait until Friends have a sense that she is still to be accepted, and Eleazer Slocum and William Soule are appointed to give her ye mind of the Meeting."

suddenly dampened by the deacon's reason for his bold statement—"they are not Christians because they hold their fellow-men in slavery!" The Quaker youth had no more to say; but the stray shot took deep effect and the son came back to his father with altered views on the question.

"College Tom's" father was at this time—about 1730 —one of the largest slave-owners in New England, and he vigorously objected to his son's new ideas, threatening to disinherit him if he persisted in the view; but the conscientious son remained unmoved, and cultivated his farm with free labour.[1] He seems also to have quietly propagated his ideas, for we learn that his intimate friend, Jeremiah Austin, soon after this freed his one slave inherited from his father.

Meantime the spirit of opposition to slavery was steadily growing throughout the Quaker groups scattered over the New England colonies, and Yearly Meeting minutes of 1743 and 1744 indicate that the "inner eye" was getting clearer in many a Quaker breast.

"4/9/1743.—It being represented by the Quarterly Meeting of Rhode Island that the practice of keeping slaves is a matter of uneasiness to many concerned Friends, and the minutes formerly made by this Meeting being also considered. It is agreed by this meeting that we request by our Epistles to the Yearly Meeting of Friends in Pennsylvania an account of what they have done in that matter."

"4/7/1744.—By the Epistle we have received from Philadelphia concerning slaves, this Meeting is encouraged to revive, and recommend to Friends the careful observation of the minute of this Meeting made in 1717 concerning that matter, and that they also refrain from buying them when imported, and to make return by the epistles from the several Quarterly Meetings how the same is observed."

---

[1] See *College Tom*, chapter iii. A law was enacted in the Rhode Island colony in 1729 allowing a master to manumit a slave provided said master should give a security of £100 that the manumitted slave should not become a public charge. Bishop Berkeley during his stay in Rhode Island became deeply interested in the negro slaves and urged that they should be baptized, using these enlightened words : "Let me beseech you to consider them not merely as slaves, but as *men* slaves and *women* slaves, who have the same frame and faculties as yourselves, and have souls capable of being made happy, and reason and understanding to receive instruction."—Updike's *History of Narragansett Church*, pp. 176, 177.

In 1747 New England was visited for the first time by that saintly Quaker from Mount Holly, New Jersey, John Woolman, whose sensitive soul was already burning with love for his dark-skinned friends in slavery. He visited "among Friends in the colony of Rhode Island" and probably came into personal relation with Thomas Hazard, as Updike calls the latter John Woolman's friend. One of the earliest documents against slavery in New England, and certainly one of the quaintest ever written, is a letter of Richard Smith of Groton, Connecticut, to South Kingstown Monthly Meeting of which he was a member. He declares that "*the Lord by his free Goodness hath given me a clear sight of the cruelty of making a slave of one that was by nature as free as my own children,*" and to turn his "clear sight" into practice he concluded:

"I hereby declare that now that my Negro garl Jane hath arived to eighteen years of age she shall go out free from bondage as free as if Shee had been free born, and that my Heirs, Executors or Administraters shall have no power over her or her postirity no more than if she had been free born." [1]

To his straightforward, downright Letter Richard Smith added a curious postscript which contains another item of his *experience*:

"Now my Friends to tell you plainly, some years befor this my intent was to have bought Some Negro Slaves for to have Done my work to have Saved my hiring of help. But when I was about buying them I was forbiden by the same Power that now Causes me to set this Garl at Liberty, for the matter was Set befor me in a Clear manner more Clear than what mortal man Could have Done and theirfore I belive it is not write for me to Shrink or hide in a thing of So Greate a Consarnment as to Give my Consent to do to others Contrary to what we our Selves would be willing to be don unto." [2]

---

[1] Records of Greenwich Monthly Meeting.

[2] The Monthly Meeting entered this minute: "This meeting received a paper of Richard Smith as his testimony against keeping slaves and his intention to free his negro girl, which paper he hath a mind to lay before the Quarterly Meeting, all which is referred for further consideration." The matter did not receive much attention at the time, and meeting after meeting passed without definite action, but Richard Smith's "testimony" was good leaven, and soon the whole lump was permeated with it.

Three years after this testimony—in 1760—came the epoch-making second visit of John Woolman, now fully alive to his Divine mission in behalf of the slave. He writes:

"We had five meetings in Narragansett [the section covered by Greenwich Monthly Meeting] and went thence to Newport on Rhode Island. . . . In several families in the country where we lodged, I felt an engagement on my mind to have a conference with them in private concerning their slaves; and through Divine aid I was favored to give up thereto. . . . I do not repine at having so unpleasant a task assigned me, but look with awfulness to Him who appoints to His servants their respective employments." [1]

The crisis of his visit came at the time of his return to Newport for Yearly Meeting, after having completed extensive travels over New England, reaching "eighty miles beyond Boston eastward." His own quaint way of telling the story is most impressive:

"Understanding that a large number of slaves had been imported from Africa into that town, and were then on sale by a member of our Society my appetite failed, and I grew outwardly weak, and had a feeling of the condition of Habakkuk, as thus expressed, 'When I heard, my belly trembled, my lips quivered, I trembled in myself, that I might rest in the day of trouble.' I had many cogitations, and was sorely distressed. I was desirous that Friends might petition the Legislature to use their endeavours to discourage the future importation of slaves, for I saw that this trade was a great evil, and tended to multiply troubles, and to bring distresses on the people for whose welfare my heart was deeply concerned. But I perceived several difficulties in regard to petitioning, and such was the exercise of my mind that I thought of endeavouring to get an opportunity to speak a few words in the House of Assembly, then sitting in town.

"This exercise came upon me in the afternoon on the second day of the Yearly Meeting, and on going to bed I got no sleep till my mind was wholly resigned thereto. In the morning I inquired of a Friend how long the Assembly was likely to continue sitting, who told me it was to be prorogued that day or the next. As I was desirous to attend the business of the meeting, and perceived the Assembly was likely to separate before the business was over, after considerable exercise, humbly seeking to the Lord for instruction, my mind settled to attend on the business of the meeting; on the last day of which I had prepared a short essay of a petition to be presented to the Legislature, if way opened. And being informed that there were some appointed by that Yearly Meeting to speak with those in authority on cases relating to the Society, I opened my mind to several of them, and showed them the essay I had made, and afterwards I opened the case in the meeting for business, in substance as follows :

"'I have been under a concern for some time on account of the great number of slaves which are imported into this colony. I am aware that it is a tender point to speak to, but apprehend I am not clear in the sight of Heaven without doing so. I have prepared an essay of a petition to be presented to the Legislature, if way open ; and what I have to propose to this meeting is that some Friends may be named to withdraw and look over it, and report whether they believe it suitable to be read in the meeting. If they should think well of reading it, it will remain for the meeting to consider whether to take any further notice of it, as a meeting, or not.' After a short conference some Friends went out, and, looking over it, expressed their willingness to have it read, which being done, many expressed their unity with the proposal, and some signified that to have the subjects of the petition enlarged upon, and signed out of meeting by such as were free, would be more suitable than to do it there. Though I expected at first that if it was done it would be in that way, yet such was the exercise of my mind that to move it in the hearing of Friends when assembled appeared to me as a duty, for my heart yearned towards the inhabitants of these parts, believing that by this trade there had been an increase of inquietude amongst them, and way had been made for the spreading of a spirit opposite to that meekness and humility which is a sure resting-place for the soul ; and that the continuance of this trade would not only render their healing more difficult, but would increase their malady. Having proceeded thus far, I felt easy to leave the essay amongst Friends, for them to proceed in it as they believed best.

"The Yearly Meeting being over, there yet remained on my mind a secret though heavy exercise, in regard to some leading active members about Newport, who were in the practice of keeping slaves. This I mentioned to two ancient Friends who came out of the country, and proposed to them, if way opened, to have some conversation with those members. One of them and I, having consulted one of the most noted elders who had slaves, he, in a respectful manner, encouraged me to proceed to clear myself of what lay upon me. Near the beginning of the Yearly Meeting, I had had a private conference with this said elder and his wife, concerning their slaves, so that the way seemed clear to me to advise with him about the manner of proceeding. I told him I was free to have a conference with them altogether in a private house ; or if he thought they would take it unkind to be asked to come together, and to be spoken with in the hearing of one another, I was free to spend some time amongst them, and to visit them all in their own houses. He expressed his liking to the first proposal, not doubting their willingness to come together ; and, as I proposed a visit to only ministers, elders, and overseers, he named some others whom he desired might also be present. A careful messenger being wanted to acquaint them in a proper manner, he offered to go to all their houses, to open the matter to them—and did so. About the eighth hour the next morning we met in the meeting-house chamber, the last mentioned country Friend, my companion, and John Storer being with us. After a short time of retirement, I acquainted them with the steps I had taken in procuring that meeting, and opened the concern I was under, and we then proceeded to a free conference upon the subject. My exercise was heavy, and I was deeply bowed in spirit before the Lord, who was pleased to favour with the seasoning virtue of truth, which wrought a tenderness amongst us ; and the subject was mutually handled in a calm and peaceable spirit. At length, feeling my mind released from the burden which I had been under, I took my leave of them in a good degree of satisfaction ; and by the tenderness they manifested in regard to the practice, and the concern several of them expressed in relation to the manner of disposing of their negroes after their decease, I believed that a good exercise was spreading amongst them ; and I am humbly thankful to God, who supported my mind and preserved me in a good degree of resignation through these trials." [1]

This tender soul, by his gentle spirit and his words which seemed given him from above, moved many Friends to a higher moral level. The advance is very apparent in the minute of the Yearly Meeting adopted this year :

" We fervently warn all in profession with us, that they be careful to avoid being in any way concerned in reaping the unrighteous profits of that iniquitous practice in dealing in

---

[1] *Journal*, pp. 163-165 and 166-168.

negroes.   We can do no less than, with the greatest earnestness, impress it upon Friends everywhere, that they endeavour to keep their hands clear of this unrighteous gain of oppression."

A clause was added to the Queries at this same Yearly Meeting, asking if Friends who hold slaves "treat them with tenderness, impress God's fear in their minds, promote their attending places of religious worship, and give those that are young, at least, so much learning that they may be capable of reading," it being taken for granted that no Friend was to buy any new slaves.   From this date onward the light spread rapidly, and the Society went to work with zeal, doubtless sometimes exhibited in harsh and narrow ways, to clear its skirts not only of traffic in slaves, but of ownership of them as well.

Shortly after John Woolman's visit, Greenwich Monthly Meeting brought its member, Samuel Rodman, "under dealing" "on account of his buying a negro slave," and passed judgment against his act.   The advice of the Quarterly and Yearly Meetings was asked in the matter, and both these meetings confirmed the Monthly Meeting in its "Sence and Judgment," which was "that there ought to go out a publick Testimony and Denial of Samuel Rodman"; he was accordingly disowned.[1]

In 1769 Greenwich Monthly Meeting sent a request to the Yearly Meeting, through the Quarterly Meeting, that the "Query" of 1760 should be so changed as "not to imply that the holding of slaves was allowable."   As is the custom with Friends, such a weighty proposal, affecting the affairs of many members, would receive most careful consideration, and a conclusion would be arrived at only as "the way of Truth" opened.   The first step was to appoint at the Yearly Meeting in 1769 a committee of eleven, made up of the leading men of the Society, to collect information, and to visit all slave-holding

---

[1] I find this minute on the Records of Newport Monthly Meeting for 7/29/1761 : "A Friend appeared in this meeting and condemned his conduct in importing of Negroes, and selling some, and hopes he shall be more careful for the future, and desires Friends to put it by, which is taken for satisfaction." The famous case of continued dealing with Joshua Rathbun, beginning in 1765 and covering eight years, is given at length in Caroline Hazard's *Narragansett Friends' Meetings*, pp. 144-152.

Friends in the territory of the Yearly Meeting to "dissuade them from the practice of keeping slaves." The report of this committee, given in 1771, is a valuable document, and shows pretty clearly the prevailing state of mind. It is as follows :

"We have pretty generally visited the members belonging to the Yearly Meeting who are possessed of negroes as slaves, and have laboured with them respecting setting such at liberty that are suitable for freedom. Our visits mostly seemed to be kindly accepted, some Friends manifested a disposition to set such at liberty as were suitable ; some others not having so clear a sight of such an unreasonable servitude as could be desired, were unwilling to comply with the advice ; a few others, whom we have with sorrow to remark were mostly of the elder sort, manifested a disposition to keep them still in a continued state of bondage."

Two years later, in 1773, the Meeting faced the question of the " Query " in this plain and straightforward fashion :

"In regard to the Query from Rhode Island Quarterly Meeting proposing the freeing of all slaves, it is our sense and judgment that *Truth not only requires the young of capacity and ability, but likewise the aged and impotent, and all in a state of infancy and nonage, among Friends to be discharged and set free from a state of slavery that we do no more claim property in the human race as we do in the brutes that perish*."

Under this decision of the supreme legislative body of New England Friends, the subordinate meetings now went to work everywhere to carry out the spirit and principle of 1773, and the records for the next ten years contain numerous minutes of "dealing" with Quaker slave-owners, showing in every case that the only way for a Friend owning a slave to avoid disownment was to "give the negro a manumission to Friends' satisfaction." The most celebrated case of "dealing" in New England was that of Stephen Hopkins, a member of Smithfield Monthly Meeting. He had been governor of the colony of Rhode Island for nine annual terms. He was easily the foremost citizen of his colony, but he owned one slave woman and would not set her free. This is what the meeting did with the case :

"The matter concerning Stephen Hopkins holding a negro woman as a slave was considered, and as he still refuses to set her at liberty, though often requested, this meeting puts him from under their care, and appoints Moses Farnum and George Comstock to draw up a paper of denial against him, and bring to next Monthly Meeting." [1]

As soon as the machinery was well in motion for the removal of every trace of human slavery from the Quaker group, positive efforts were at once inaugurated to bring influence to bear in shaping legislation in the direction of abolition. In 1774 this minute was adopted at the Yearly Meeting :

"This Meeting, manifesting a concern that the liberty of the Africans might be fully restored, we appoint our Friends Thomas Hazard, Ezekiel Comstock, Thomas Lapham, Jr., Stephen Hoxie, Joseph Congdon, Isaac Lawton, and Moses Farnum, a committee to use their influence at the Generall Assembly of the Colony of Rhode Island, or with the members thereof, that such laws may be made as will tend to the abolition of slavery, and to get such laws repealed as in any way encourages it." [2]

And in 1787 a powerful memorial was sent from the Yearly Meeting to the General Court of Massachusetts, urging that as that commonwealth had been "the first on this continent to constitutionally abolish slavery" in its domain, so it should now formulate legislation to prevent its citizens from engaging in "the unrighteous traffic" in slaves, "manifesting thereby," they say, "your endeavours that the great revolution of this country, founded on a declaration against invasion of civil liberty, may not be tarnished by suffering your subjects to continue a traffic which perpetuates slavery." A boy born in 1807, the descendant of ancestors who had taken part in this slow

[1] "Drawing up a paper of denial" is a euphemism for "disowning," *i.e.* expulsion from membership. As Stephen Hopkins went out of the Quaker Society his friend Moses Brown of Providence came in, and as a preparation to this step freed all his slaves. See Augustine Jones' *Moses Brown : A Sketch.*

[2] Rhode Island Legislature passed an Act that very year, 1774, by which the enslaving of negroes was for ever prohibited. Stephen Hopkins was the author of this famous Bill.

Quaker uprising against the wicked custom of enslaving men, was above all others to sound the trumpet against it in the nineteenth century, and was to stand in the front of the moral battle for freedom—John Greenleaf Whittier.

Friends have always emphasized the importance of education, and wherever Quakerism flourished the school-house followed close after the "meeting-house," while in some notable instances there has been one building for both. The first minute on education which I have found in New England is on the Records of Newport Monthly Meeting under date of twelfth month 24th, 1684:

"Upon request and desire of Christian Loddwick to have the use of the Meeting House in Newport for keeping of a school, Friends, upon consideration and desire to do him good, do grant it and are also willing to give him what encouragement they can."[1]

The course taken by the Newport Friends was a very usual one in any Quaker community. For the first hundred years of their history the New England Friends had only these local schools for the "guarded education" of their children, but in the 'seventies of the eighteenth century there appears to have been a powerful awakening to the need of broader education and for a more adequate educational system. A large committee of broad-minded men was appointed at the Yearly Meeting of 1779, and the Quarterly Meetings were asked to appoint co-operating committees of "solid Friends," who after the usual careful and weighty deliberation, carried on for three years, recommended the establishment of a central school for the entire Yearly Meeting, one of its functions being the

---

[1] There are two further minutes which throw interesting light on the history of this school :—

12/26/1711.—"The Friends appointed to lay out as much land as might be thought suitable for to set a school-house on, made report that they have laid out a certain piece of land adjoining to Sam. Easton's land containing sixty feet fronting upon the lane and eighty feet deep."

6/26/1718.—"The proprietors of the school-house in Newport have freely surrendered and given up their rights in said School-house to the Monthly Meeting to be continued by said Meeting for a school-house, and that said Meeting pay to the several proprietors what they have advanced more than their subscriptions within one year's time with reasonable interest. The money advanced by the several proprietors which is to be paid by this meeting is £56 : 4 : 8."

preparation of teachers for the local communities. It was a difficult matter to fix upon a satisfactory location, but finally Portsmouth, R.I., was selected as the favoured place. The school was accordingly opened there in 1784, being the first Yearly Meeting School established in America. Isaac Lawton was selected to be the "master" of it, and he accepted the position in the "*trust* that he will receive seventy-five pounds per year to keep the school."[1] The price of board was arranged to be four shillings per week for children under fourteen, and "four and six for those above." The hoped-for funds for this important venture did not materialize, and in 1788 the school came to a speedy close of its career.[2]

Friends came into collision at so many points with the Churches of what they call the "Presbyterian system" that there was little opportunity for them in colonial days to co-operate with their Christian neighbours in New England in moral and philanthropic undertakings. The result was that they felt themselves forced to discover their own peculiar moral activities and their own humanitarian efforts. Quite naturally, at first they were specially absorbed in the work of winning their own emancipation from what appeared to them the tyranny of those who made laws for them, but as fast as they won their freedom they took up the fight on behalf of other peoples who were oppressed and hampered, and they proved to be good leaders of what seemed at the time "lost causes" and "forlorn hopes." Their primary concern, as I have already implied, was the formation of a "peculiar people." This aim, to my mind, always hampered them, limited their scope, and narrowed their field of public usefulness, but as I am endeavouring to give a faithful historical picture, I must dwell for a little, in concluding this chapter, upon their zealous labours to construct their own "beloved Zion."

They were the bearers of a religious message which in

---

[1] This extravagant fee was soon dropped to fifty pounds !

[2] Through the persistent efforts of Moses Brown of Providence, one of the main creators of this Portsmouth school, and by the assistance of his generous gift, the school was revived in 1819, located at Providence, and has had a famous history and has rendered great service to the cause of education.

essence and idea contained much that was permanent and universal. They showed a real genius for feeling out the great elemental truths of Christianity and for avoiding the scholastic formulations which were doomed, sooner or later, to have "mene" written on them. While others were still speculating over the "decrees" and "schemes" of a divine Sovereign, they were living in a joyous consciousness of a divine Father who was, and is, and will be the inward Spirit and Life and Light of all who strive and aspire. They no doubt often talked about their conception of God in narrow and somewhat forbidding terminology, but wherever one comes upon their great central idea, adequately expressed, in epistle, sermon, or autobiographical journal, he finds a glimpse, at least, of an ever new yet ever old truth, that God is immanent, self-revealing, and eternally redeeming the race, and working His Life into the lives of men.[1] But the moment one leaves this central doctrine and turns to the efforts which were made to maintain peculiarities, the "genius" appears lacking, and the movement seems to be caught in a back-wash. There was, no doubt, a real call in the middle decades of the seventeenth century for a vigorous and uncompromising campaign against sham and hollowness, and for a protest against fashions and forms of etiquette which were a burden to the life, and which buried the *person* under a rubbish of meaningless mannerisms. The Quaker uttered that protest with a commendable fearlessness, and he had a straightforward way of calling things by their plain names and of bringing the naked truth to the front. That was good service ; and so, too, was his steady insistence on human equality and the potential nobility of every man.

[1] Here are two sample passages from epistles which were read in all their meetings : "Be careful and labor in the peaceable gospel, to settle, stay, and establish peoples' minds in *the holy principle of Life and Light . . . and where there is the least budding or breaking forth of Life let it be nourished and encouraged.*"—*London Epistle of 1672.* "And now, dear friends, who profess and possess that which is above all religions, ways, and worships in the world, our desire is that you may outstrip and exceed the world in virtue, in purity, in chastity, in godliness, and in holiness ; and in modesty, civility, and in righteousness and love, so that your sober life may appear to all and may answer that of God in all."—*Epistle of George Fox to New England Friends in 1684.*

But it is an unmistakable fact that the *principle* soon fell to a subconscious level, and the "testimonies," which probably had their *origin* in vitality, as a graphic method of uttering human principle, became an end in themselves and were finally cherished as the badges of a peculiar people. The use of "thee" and "thou" was initiated from a sincere desire to emphasize the equality of men, for the plural "you" was used only in addressing persons of dignity and standing; but the use of "you" rapidly became universal custom, and whatever principle may have attached to "thou" disappeared, and the New England Quaker of the eighteenth century could give no reason for this peculiar language. The hat "testimony" came to be even more devoid of significance and rationality. There may have been some point once in keeping covered because of a desire not "to give to men an honour which belonged to God," but the custom of wearing the hat before magistrates and in religious assemblies soon became only a "custom." It ceased to have an inner meaning, and it proclaimed no important truth, as one realises at once when he reads the explanations which were given for it. When we remember that almost nothing cost so much in suffering as did this refusal to "uncover" we can only wish the life had been staked on a greater issue.[1]

The refusal to take an oath was in a higher region of principle—the determination that there should be but one standard of truth-telling. But the significance of even this testimony was much blurred by the failure to exhibit its living import and by the tendency to treat it as a "command." It was, again, a great drop when the Quaker passed from his primitive call to simplicity of life and freedom from the yoke of fashion, and took the dangerously easy method of adopting a garb, which soon came to be

---

[1] It is evident that the Quaker converts in New England at once adopted this badge. Humphrey Norton gives us this interesting passage about the case of William Shattuck of Boston, who is here speaking for himself: "After I was convinced by the Light of the Lord in me I was brought to their court, and entering with my hat on, John Endicott looking on me with great disdain said, Art thou come to this?"—*Ensign*, p. 65.

another peculiar badge and a mark of "spirituality."[1]
These things have, no doubt, been often defended, and
they were pursued in unmistakable sincerity ; but they
plainly drew attention away from the real spiritual
message, they quickly became ends-in-themselves, and as
they rose in importance, the propagation of spiritual
religion as a way of living for all men as men declined.
One reads to-day with melancholy and a sense of sadness,
of the vast labour and pains which these good people
bestowed on these " fences," and one wishes that the same
zeal had been bestowed in expanding their central living
truth of an indwelling and Emmanuel God who is un-
weariedly at work making a divine kingdom out of men
like us ! But while we speak with regret of the excessive
activity directed to the cultivation of customs, in their
very nature bound to arrest spiritual development, we can
review with enthusiasm the persistent efforts which these
same people made to emancipate the minds and bodies of
their fellow-men in New England and elsewhere, and one
is profoundly impressed with the conviction, as he goes
through their journals and epistles, that they had discovered the supreme secret—how to find God and enjoy
Him in the pathway of this our earthly life.

[1] The importance of these badges appears in very early documents. An
Epistle of 1697 says : '' Friends everywhere, keep to plainness in speech, habit,
and dealing, and keep to our testimony in calling the months and days by
Scripture names and not by heathen.''

CHAPTER VIII

NEW ENGLAND QUAKERS IN POLITICS

THE first opportunity for a Quaker experiment in government came to the Friends in Rhode Island, where for more than a hundred years, with temporary fluctuations of their influence, they had an important share in the direction of the affairs of the colony.

The Colony of Rhode Island was founded, as we have seen, by a group of men who came into sharp collision with the religious system of the Puritan Colony of Massachusetts. Some of them were compulsory exiles, and some of them were voluntary exiles, from the mother Colony of Massachusetts, because they were highly resolved to be free themselves and to set other men's souls free from all ecclesiastical tyranny.[1] The leading persons in the group—Coddington, Coggeshall, Easton, the Clarkes, Hutchinsons, Dyers, and Bulls—had already arrived at a type of religion in many respects like that of the Quakers, and those who joined themselves to that movement, just beyond the middle of the seventeenth century, adopted the new name with hardly a change of idea, ideal, or practice. Coddington (b. 1601, d. 1678) was the foremost man of the group.[2] He was

[1] The history of this controversy is told in Chapter I.

[2] In the Preface of his *Demonstration of True Love*, written "To the Rulers of the Colony of Massachusetts " in 1672, Coddington says : "I was entrusted in the first settling [of the Massachusetts Bay Colony] and with the chiefest in all public charges [*i.e.* affairs] even before Boston was named or any house therein. I builded the first good house, in which the governor now dwells. I having spent much of my estate and prime of my age in propagating Plantations, and now come to the last period, the seventieth year of my age ; in discharge of my conscience toward God and in tender love and due respect to all, I write, as I have done, to warn you of your general calamity, upon which I parted from you, that persecuting spirit let loose ; and I rest yours in love, W.C."

judge of the Portsmouth Colony until Newport was
founded, and then he was chosen judge of that Colony.
When the two Colonies of Portsmouth and Newport were
united under one government he was successively chosen
Governor from 1640 to 1647. When the four Colonies
of Providence, Newport, Portsmouth, and Warwick were
united in one government under the charter of 1647,
John Coggeshall was chosen first President. William
Coddington was, however, elected to this office in 1648,
but was afterwards suspended from office, apparently
because of his over-zealous efforts to bring the Colony into
the New England Confederacy, which he felt was the
necessary step for the fulfilment of the larger destiny of
the Colony on the Narragansett. Soon after this he went
to England with large designs in his mind. He was
nursing the dream of a great island Colony in Narragansett
Bay, and his two attempts—in 1644 and 1648—to bring
the Colony into the New England Confederacy had been
with the aim to safeguard and strengthen the infant state.
These attempts had failed. He now embarked for
England with a still bolder dream in his mind, to make
the Narragansett islands play the rôle in America which
the British islands had played in the old world ! He
assiduously cultivated the friendship of Sir Harry Vane,
formerly his friend in the days of Vane's governorship,
dining frequently with him ; seeking also the assistance of
his old theological opponent Hugh Peters, now a man of
large influence. Finally, in spite of the opposition of
Edward Winslow of Plymouth, Coddington secured,
through the British Council of State and the Committee
of Admiralty, a patent, signed April 1651 by Lord
President Bradshaw, making him proprietor of the islands
" Aquidnet " [otherwise Rhode Island] and " Quinunagate "
[otherwise Conanicut] and Governor for life.

This act of Coddington's was, to say the least, a rash
act, a profound blunder, and the colonists of Rhode Island
and Providence Plantations denied his authority and sent
John Clarke, a man of great parts, a genuine apostle of
soul liberty and a wise diplomatist, to England to get the

Coddington charter annulled.[1] In 1656 Coddington, in honourable and manly fashion, retreated from his mistaken course. He was never a traitor, as Turner assumes,[2] and wrote a letter engaging to submit "with all his heart" to the lawful authority in the Colony, he having already in 1652 signed a paper surrendering all claim to anything more than his own share of the island of Aquidneck.[3] From this time to his death he was prominent in the affairs of the Colony, and, as we shall see, steadily received the mark of public confidence, and was raised to the highest office in the gift of the people. Weeden, in his valuable volume,[4] declares that Coddington was "a man of substance materially and mentally. Judge Durfee considers that the well-organised judiciary of the island betokens the presence of some man having not only a large legal and legislative capacity, but also a commanding influence. It was probably Coddington. It is more than doubtful whether Rhode Island could have attained a stable government without Coddington's effort."

Nicholas Easton (b. 1592, d. 1675) built the first house in Newport. He was one of the nineteen signers of the Aquidneck Colonial "Contract," and his is the second name on the "Agreement" of the Newport Colony. He and John Clarke were appointed in 1639 to correspond with Sir Harry Vane upon the state of affairs in the new Colony. He was elected "Assistant" from 1640 to 1644. He was President of the Colony in 1650, 1651, and 1654, and he was thus prepared for the larger services to which he was called in his distinctly Quaker period.

Sometime between 1657 and 1660—the evidence seems to point to the former date as the time—Coddington, Nicholas Easton, John Easton, Joshua

---

[1] Roger Williams went with Clarke as representative of the mainland towns.

[2] See article by Henry E. Turner, hostile to Coddington, in *Rhode Island Tracts*, No. 4.

[3] See *Colony Records of Rhode Island*, i. 327. He was that year elected a commissioner to the General Court, which would not have happened if the people of Newport had not believed in his integrity.

[4] Weeden's *Early Rhode Island* (N.Y., 1910), p. 64.

Coggeshall (son of John who had died in office in 1647), Walter Clarke, Caleb Carr, and many other leading citizens of the island-colony, joined the Quaker movement with their families, and at once gave the persecuted people the support of their names and their influence. It is interesting to note that their affiliation with the religious movement, so unpopular everywhere else, had from the first no detrimental effect upon the political career of the men who joined the Quaker meeting at Newport. Nicholas Easton and his son John Easton were both elected commissioners to the General Court of Rhode Island and Providence Plantations in 1660, and Nicholas was chosen Moderator of the Court that year, and John was made Attorney-General, a position to which he was many times elected until 1674, when he was raised to a higher office. The following year, 1661, Caleb Carr was elected Treasurer-General of the Colony, and he likewise continued to hold a prominent place in the affairs of the Colony until he was finally chosen Governor in 1695.

Nicholas Easton was the first Quaker to be raised to the governorship of the Colony, he having been already five times Deputy-Governor, beginning with the year 1666.[1] His term of office as Governor extended from 1672 to 1674. It was his lot, as it was also that of the later Quaker Governors, to come into public prominence at the critical time of war. This period, from 1666 to 1674, when Easton was almost continuously in public office, was disturbed by two wars between England and Holland, and the Colonies which were within easy reach of the Dutch in New Amsterdam were continually harassed with anxiety, even though not actually involved in border warfare. The first Dutch war of Charles II.'s reign began in 1664, and was ended by the Peace of Breda in 1667. The second war began in 1672 and was terminated in 1674, permanently settling New York as English territory. The wars between the mother-country and the continental nations were complicated by alliances

---

[1] The Great Charter of Rhode Island, secured from King Charles the Second, had gone into operation in 1663.

of Indian tribes against the English colonists, and the Rhode Island Quaker officials must many times have had their consciences severely tested in these periods when preparation for war was forced upon them. Left to themselves the Rhode Island colonists could have maintained peace, for their Indian policy was wise, humane, and enlightened, and gained for them the confidence and love of their Indian neighbours.[1] But they were a tiny part of a larger political system. They could not live unto themselves. They received their Charter from the English Government, and they were of necessity involved in the schemes and quarrels of the mother-country as well as in the expanding movements of the Colonies surrounding them, and, try as they might to keep their domain in peace, they found themselves dragged into the grinding millstones of war.

The Quaker officials in the Rhode Island Colony were in every instance devoted to the maintenance of peace. They exerted themselves to the utmost to keep the Colony out of actual war ; but they seem to have settled it as their policy to stay in office, when they were put there by the people, even though they found themselves compelled, by unavoidable conditions and circumstances, to perform public acts of a warlike nature. When they found that the great current of events could not be forced to take the course which in their vision seemed the ideal one, they faced the stubborn conditions that existed and did the best they could with them. They discovered, what all practical workers discover, that the achievement of great ends and high ideals can be won only by slow stages and by graceful bends around obstacles which are for the moment immovable. There has always been in the Society of Friends a group of persons pledged unswervingly to the ideal. To those who form this inner group compromise is under no circumstance allowable.

[1] One of the significant acts of Nicholas Easton's administration as Governor was the order that one-half of the jury which was to try an Indian for murder should be composed of Indians, and that Indian testimony should be received on the same basis as the testimony of Englishmen. See Arnold's *History of Rhode Island*, i. 367.

If there comes a collision between allegiance to the ideal and the holding of public office, then the office must be deserted. If obedience to the soul's vision involves eye or hand, houses or lands or life, they must be immediately surrendered. But there has always been as well another group who have held it to be equally imperative to work out their principles of life in the complex affairs of the community and the State, where to gain an end one must yield something ; where to get on one must submit to existing conditions ; and where to achieve ultimate triumph one must risk his ideals to the tender mercies of a world not yet ripe for them. John Woolman, the consummate flower of American Quakerism in the eighteenth century, is the shining type of the former principle, and the Rhode Island governors are good types of the other course.

Nicholas Easton was the first to face this hard issue of war, and his policy, distinctly at variance with that later pursued by the Pennsylvania Quakers, was followed by all the Quaker governors of Rhode Island.

By act of the General Court the 13th of May 1667, he was appointed chairman of a committee to make a rate for the levying of £150 for the defence of Newport against a common enemy, and for " mounting the great gun," " in order to prevent such mischiefs and miseries as may happen for the want of the same." [1] It appears from the Records that the Quaker Deputy-Governor did not help to " mount the great gun," as it was mounted by the military men of the Colony.[2]

Just before Nicholas Easton was raised to the governorship the Colony was believed to be in imminent danger of aggressive attack, as the following record of the General Court shows :

" *August* 31, 1671.—There being a great necessity to put the Colony in a posture of defence att this time, wherein there are soe apparent grounds to expect some treacherous designes and

---

[1] *Colony Records of Rhode Island*, ii. 197. Daniel Gould, John Gould, and Peter Easton, all Friends, were on this committee.

[2] *Ibid.*

practices from the Indians, itt is therefore ordered, that the Towne Councills and Councills of Warr, of each respective towne on the Island, shall meete at Mr. Geo. Lawton's dwelling-house in the bounds of Portsmouth, on Tuesday, the fifth day of September, now next insueing, at nine of the clock in the forenoon, then and there to consider of some wayes and means for secureing the inhabitants and their estates in these times of imminent danger." [1]

That was surely a difficult time for the infant state, and it was a hard crisis for the beginning of a Quaker administration. The new "administration" was, however, prevailingly Quaker. Nicholas Easton was Governor, John Cranston, Deputy-Governor,[2] John Easton, son of Nicholas, was Attorney-General, and Joshua Coggeshall, John Easton, and Peter Easton were assistants. One of the first acts of the Council under this Quaker administration looked toward preparation for the military defence of the Colony, though here again we have no way of knowing what part, active or passive, the Quaker members actually took. The Act reads:

"Whereas, wee have received speciall order from his Majestie for the Proclamation of Warr against the Dutch, and the puttinge this Collony into a posture of defence, this Councill doe recommend and doe order and empower the Magistrates, together with the Captain, Lieutenant, and Ensigne of the respective townes, or the major part of them, to take care, order, and putt the inhabitants of each towne into the best posture of defence may be, for the maintaininge the King's interest in this Collony; and to that end, to act and order to the best of their discretion, until the Generall Assembly or Councill take further order; and especially to take care for powder, shott, and ammunition, and to inquire after and secure what may be found in the Collony." [3]

At the election of 1673, when the war was at its height, when the Colony was in feverish anxiety, and when the coolest heads were needed in counsel, Easton was again elected Governor, William Coddington was chosen Deputy-Governor, and Walter Clarke, one of the foremost

---

[1] *Colony Records of Rhode Island*, ii. 409.
[2] John Cranston was not a Friend in membership though he attended the Yearly Meeting in 1672. See Fox's *Journal* (edition 1901) ii. 168.
[3] *Colony Records of Rhode Island*, ii. 463.

members of the Newport meeting, was added to the list of assistants.

The Dutch succeeded in recapturing New York on the 30th of July 1673, and this caused much commotion in Newport. A special session of the General Assembly was called to provide for the defence of the Colony, and many military measures were passed. The following Act would certainly put a peace-loving Quaker in a hard dilemma :

"Voted, forasmuch as there seemeth a present danger by reason of the Dutch forces, whoe the 30th of July last tooke New Yorke, and may unhappily assault and fall upon us, as a ready provision and fittings against such said danger :

"It is enacted, that authority is given to the Governor, and in his absence to the Deputy-Governor, and major part of the assistants, for the time beinge (at any time when the Generall Assembly is not sittinge), to nominate, appoint, and constitute such and soe many commanders, and military officers as to them shall seeme requisite for the leadinge, conductinge, and trayninge up the inhabitants of the said Plantation in martiall affaires."

And it was further enacted :

"that the Governor or, in his absence, the Deputy-Governor, [both Quakers] and all the Assistants on this Island, if the Dutch or any other public enemy shall, in open hostility against the King, assault it or fall upon his subjects here ; then all of them, if able and in health, shall in all time of danger be with or as neere as may be convenient to the eldest Captaine in chiefe [John Cranston] to give to him speciall and perticular directions as the danger shall then occasion, for the safety of the whole ; and the Governor, or Deputy-Governor, and all the Assistants on the Island that shall be able, shall with the first information, allarm, or knowledge of the approach or invasion of the said enemy come together and be ready in the most convenient place to consult and agree how for the best safety and best loyalty to answer any summons such said enemy may send to them." [1]

The Assembly thereupon proceeded to draft a pension law for the "reliefe of souldiers that lose their limbs and the reliefe for the relations whose dependency was on

---

[1] *Colony Records of Rhode Island*, ii. 489.

such as are slayne "—one of the earliest American pension laws. In the next Act the hand of the Quakers is plainly seen. They had been unable to stop the *occasion* of the present war, and they were powerless to prevent the war-like preparations for the defence of those who believed in the propriety of war, but they now made full provision for the relief of tender consciences. This Act of exemption from military duties for conscience' sake, passed the 13th of August 1673—the first Act of the sort ever passed in America,—is a very curious and quaint document full of odd Scripture texts and allusions, but it is too long to be given in full.

The Act declares that " the inhabitants of this colony have a conscience " against requiring taking an oath, " how much more," it adds, " ought such men forbear to compel their equal neighbors against their consciences to trayne to fight and to kill."

" Bee it therefore enacted, and hereby it is enacted by his Majesty's authority, that noe person (within this Collony), that is or hereafter shall be persuaded in his conscience that he cannot or ought not to trayne, to learne to fight, nor to war, nor kill any person or persons, shall at any time be compelled against his judgment and conscience to trayne, arm, or fight, to kill any person or persons by reason of or at the command of any officer of this Collony, civil nor military, nor by reason of any by-law here past or formerly enacted ; nor shall suffer any punishment, fine, distraint, pennalty, nor imprisonment, who cannot in conscience traine, fight, nor kill any person nor persons for the aforesaid reasons." [1]

At the next general election William Coddington was chosen Governor, and John Easton Deputy-Governor, while Peter Easton filled both offices of Attorney-General and Colonial Treasurer. Shortly before his election to the governorship Coddington had built himself a great house in Marlborough Street. It was spacious and adapted for the entertainment of many visitors. In the great room of this house the Quaker meeting of Newport was held for many years, and at the time of George Fox's visit the Yearly Meeting was held there, and in this house

---

[1] This Act is in the *Rhode Island Colony Records*, ii. 495-499.

Coddington entertained the Governor of Massachusetts, Richard Bellingham, on his memorable visit to Rhode Island.[1] Soon after the election which freed him from the responsibility of public office, Nicholas Easton passed away full of years and having achieved the highest honours his Colony had to bestow. He had helped form the infant settlement in Newbury, Massachusetts; he had built the first English house in Hampton; he had bravely followed his light in the trying days which parted the Puritan colony into two religious groups, and he had been in the front line of the pioneers of religious freedom on Rhode Island. He had built the first house in Newport, the first windmill on the island; and he had been among the first to throw in his lot with the new-born Quaker Society. He had been the constant companion of George Fox in his two months of labour in New England, and he had finished the course of an eventful life by piloting his Colony through two administrations complicated by the problems of imminent war.

During Easton's period of public service the Colony was swept by a cyclonic disturbance of internal contention. The colonial records describe it as "an uncomfortable difference of which there seemed to be no peaceable composure"; as "dangerous contests, distractions, and divisions among our ancient, loving, and honoured neighbours, the freemen of the town of Providence, by which the town is in an incapacity of transacting its own affairs," making "a breech in the whole."[2] This bitter quarrel had broken out over William Harris' claim of ownership to extensive lands stretching up the Pawtuxet River and other streams. Harris was a strenuous man of affairs, "pertinacious in temperament," and inclined to be a local storm-centre. His opponents, in the pamphleteering manner of the times, called him "a fire-brand," "a salamander always delighting to live in ye fire of con-

---

[1] "Did I not entertain Richard Bellingham and his company nine or ten days in my house on Rhode Island?"—*A Demonstration of True Love*, p. 15. The first Friends' Meeting-House in Newport was already built in 1672, but many of the meetings were still held in Coddington's house. Stephen Gould, who saw this house torn down, has left a very interesting sketch of its history.

[2] *Rhode Island Colony Records*, ii. 289-293.

tention," "a raging sea casting forth mire and dirt!"[1]
He, in turn, called them—the Roger Williams faction
and the Fenner party—"the makers of poysonous
plaisters against our rights in lands and laws." So fierce
was the storm that a special session of the General
Assembly was called, and two Newport Quakers, John
Easton and Joshua Coggeshall, were "chosen and authorised" to call a Providence town meeting in the name of
the General Assembly, superintend the choice of officers,
and bring civil order out of the chaos—a delicate and
difficult task which was in the end successfully carried
through.[2]

As Coddington began his administration news came to
the Colony that peace was established between England
and Holland, and the strain and anxiety of war seemed
happily over. One disturbance disquieted the Colony.
There were visible signs that Rhode Island was to have
difficulty in establishing its rightful claim to the Narragansett country on the west shore of the Bay—a region
for many years in hot dispute. One of the new Governor's
first acts was to proceed with his council to the district in
dispute and to establish there the township of Kingstown
(now called Kingston), which was incorporated by the
General Assembly as the seventh town of Rhode Island.
After one peaceful term of office William Coddington was
re-elected, but the days of peace and calm were over, and
his second term of office was destined to see the fiercest
storm of Indian war which the New England Colonies
ever experienced—the contest known in history as "King
Philip's War."

This war was the natural outcome of the irresistible
collision of two races, two civilisations, incompatible with
each other. The collision came at this particular crisis
because the Indian cause just then happened to be
embodied in a great natural leader of men in the person
of the Indian chief, King Philip, son of Massasoit. Philip

---

[1] *Rhode Island Historical Society Collection*, x. 78.
[2] Lott Strange and Joseph Torrey were added to the committee of two "for
Counsel and Advice," *Records*, ii. 293. Harris himself became a Quaker after
George Fox's visit to the Colony.

believed that he had been greatly wronged by the English, especially those of Plymouth Colony, and he saw no hope of gaining the old time rights, privileges, and conditions of Indian life, except by a master stroke at the life of the English settlers.

It was always the Quaker way to endeavour to prevent war by removing the occasion for it, and the Quakers in authority at this crisis made a vigorous trial of their method. As the sky was darkening with ominous clouds of war, five men, with John Easton, the Deputy-Governor of the Colony of Rhode Island, at their head, rowed up to King Philip's headquarters at Mount Hope—a promontory jutting into Narragansett Bay—to try counsel and persuasion with him in order to bring about, if possible, an arbitration of the difficulties.

The five visitors all came to the council unarmed, and Philip laid aside his weapons for the occasion, though his warriors, about forty in number, were armed ; and Easton, who wrote the only account of this famous conference, says : " We sat veri friendly together. We told him our bisness was to indever that they [the Indians] might not receve or do rong." [1] " We told them," the narrative continues, " that our desire was that the quarrel might be rightly decided in the best way, not as dogs decide their quarrels." The Indians " owned that fighting was the worst way, but they inquired how right might take place without fighting. *We said by arbitration.* They said that by arbitration the English agreed against them, and so by arbitration they had much rong." [2] " We said they might chuse a Indian King and the English might chuse the Governor of New Yorke, that neither had case to say that either wear parties to the difference. They said they had not heard of this way. We were persuaded that if this way had been tendered they would have accepted." [3]

Philip then proceeded to spread before them a long list of Indian grievances. Philip said : " Their King's father [Massasoit], when the English first came, was a

---

[1] Easton's *Narrative* (Hough edition), p. 7. This narrative is a marvellous specimen of seventeenth-century spelling !

[2] *Ibid.* p. 8.   [3] *Ibid.* p. 10.

great man and the English as a littill child. He constrained the other Indians from ronging the English, and
gave them corn and shewed them how to plant it and was
free to do them ani good."   "But their King's brother
[Alexander], when he was King came miserably to dy,
being forced to court, and as they judged poysoned."
"Another Greavance was, if 20 of their onest Indiands
testified that a Englishman had dun them rong it was
nothing, but if one of their worst Indians testified against
any Indian, or their King, when it pleased the English, it
was suficiant."   Finally Philip complained that the
English were " eager to sell the Indians lickers [liquors]
that most Indians spent all in drynknes and then raved
upon the sober Indians ! "[1]

The visitors pleaded all day for arbitration, but there
seemed no practical way of bringing it about, for the five
counsellors were incapable of convincing the Indians that
they could bring the other Colonies to their peaceful view,
and Easton concludes his *Narrative*, written while the
war was in progress, with the sectarian remark :

" I am persuaded of New England Prists [ministers] they are
so blinded by the spirit of Persecution and [so eager] to maintain
their hyer [hire] that they have been the case [cause] that the law
of Nations and the Law of Arems have been violated in this
War [war was begun without any formal declaration]. The war
would not have been if ther had not bine hyerlings."[2]

Upon the very heels of this conference the storm
broke with fury upon the inhabitants who lived along the
shores of the bay.[3] The Quakers of Rhode Island held
the view throughout the conflict that it was an unnecessary
war, and might have been avoided if the other Colonies
had shown Philip fair treatment, but in any case the
innocent were involved with those who were responsible
for the calamity, and the mainland of Rhode Island came

---

[1] Easton's *Narrative* (Hough edition), pp. 12, 13.   [2] *Ibid.* pp. 30, 31.
[3] King Philip's war began 24th June 1675, the Easton Conference occurred
17th June. The Narragansett Indians were most kindly disposed toward the
Friends on the Island. The Indian chief Pessicus told the Newport magistrates
that his heart was affected and sorrowed for the English, but " he could not rule
[*i.e.* overrule] the young Indians nor persuade the other chiefs."

in for a heavy share of the suffering.   It was the Quaker policy ·to make the Island a safe city of refuge, and to bring the outlying inhabitants thither.[1]   Providence and Warwick sent urgent appeals for military assistance, and the General Assembly of 1676 answered them through a committee of six, of which the Quakers, Walter Clarke, Joshua Coggeshall, and Caleb Carr were members, as follows :

" After searious debate and well weighings of your hazardous and present condition, wee declare that wee finde this Collony is not of ability to maintaine sufficient garrisons for the security of our out-Plantations.   Therefore, we thinke and judge it most safe for the inhabitants to repaire to this Island, which is the most secureist.   Newport and Portsmouth inhabitants have taken such care that those of the Collony that come, and cannot procure land to plant for themselves and families, reliefe may be supplied with land by the townes ; and each family soe wantinge a libertye, shall have a cow kept upon the commons ; butt if any of you think yourselves of abillity to keepe your interest of houses and cattell, and will adventure your lives [by staying where you are] we shall not positively oppose you therein ; but this the Assembly declares as their sense and reall beliefe concerninge the premises, that those that soe doth make themselves a prey, and what they have as goods, provisions, ammunition, cattell, etc., will be a reliefe to the enemy at their pleasure, except more than ordinary Providence prevent, therefore we cannot but judge them wisest that take the safest course to secure themselves, and take the occasion from the enemy." [2]

There exists a very odd letter, signed by Walter Clarke, written 28th January 1676, which further indicates the Quaker policy.   It is in answer to an appeal for assistance from Providence.   Clarke endeavours to quiet " the discontent of spirit" which prevailed in Providence toward the Newport authorities, " as if they were not worthy to live," by explaining that " the weal of the Colony " would have been attended to if the weather

[1] Drake's *Old Indian Chronicle* says, "Rhode Island now became the common Zoar, or place of refuge for the distressed," p. 224. A minute of the executive council of New York of this date says that "Great Numbers of the people flockt to Rhode Island from their habitations destroyed, insomuch that the inhabitants [of the island] are very much straitened by their numbers, and will quickly want provisions."

[2] *Colony Records of Rhode Island*, ii. 532-535.

had not "obstructed" the execution of orders for defence. He further offers the explanation, certainly not very satisfactory to the sufferers, that if the " Administration " had furnished soldiers to protect " the out-inhabitants " and their property, the people would have been " damnified by the charge for wages, ammunition, and diet ! " " The island," he says, " has expended eight hundred pounds to provide for the security and provision of those who are there ; and all who cannot be secure where they are " had best be transported hither," " for we are not of ability to keep soldiers under pay." " Sorrows are to increase," he thinks, and to have soldiers to pay and care for would only add to the troubles of the already heavy times. He warns them not to appeal for help to the other Colonies, for they will in the end " make a prey of you "——there was apparently no help left for the suffering " out-inhabitants," but to wait for the salvation of the Lord ! This curious sentence was perhaps meant to be a comfort :

"I have done to the uttermost of my ability for your good and shall do, yet we know the Lord's hand is against New England [evidently Massachusetts and Plymouth] and no weapon formed will prosper till the work be finished, and the wheat [the Rhode Island saints !] must be pulled up with the tears [tares] and the innocent suffer with the guilty ! " [1]

On the 12th of April the same year, Walter Clarke wrote again, in a somewhat more encouraging vein, with less religious comment and with more practical direction :

" Only this for your present encouragement : we well approve your advice and willingness to maintain a garrison, and have agreed to bear the charge of ten men upon the Colony's account, till the succeeding authority take further order,[2] and that you may take four of our men to strengthen you, or if it be wholly by yourselves, we, as abovesaid, will bear the charge of ten of them, and after the election, if those concerned see cause, and the Colony be of ability to do it, I shall not obstruct, if it be continued all the year. Be pleased to dispatch our ketch.[3] I

---

[1] Clarke's letter is printed in Staples' *Annals*, p. 167.
[2] General election was about to occur, at which the writer of the letter, Walter Clarke, was elected Governor.
[3] A " ketch " was a strong two-masted vessel, generally carrying guns.

have no more to you but my kind love and desire of your peace
and safety as my own. WALTER CLARKE.[1]

A carefully planned attack was made on the Indians
by the colonial forces at South Kingston, near Tower Hill,
in the winter of 1675. It was a fierce engagement, 68 of
the English being killed and 150 wounded. The
wounded were brought across to the Island, where they
were kindly cared for. Drake's *Old Indian Chronicle*
says that "Governor William Coddington received the
wounded soldiers kindly, though some churlish Quakers
were not free to entertain them until compelled by the
Governor.[2] Coddington at this time wrote a letter to the
Governor and Council of Massachusetts in a Postscript to
which he contrasts the way the Quakers have treated the
suffering soldiers of Massachusetts with the way the
people of Boston have treated, and are treating, the
Quakers there. The letter itself is very laconic :

"The Governor and Councell of ye Massachusetts and
Committee of ye United Colonies writing to us do give us
thanks for transporting their soldiers and Provisions, and that
sloops transported their wounded, and desired us to lett out
100 or 200 Souldiers, we answered you denying soe to do and
gave you our Grounds."

The Postscript, for which the letter was evidently
written, deals with a contemporary Boston proclamation
for a day of humiliation, in which proclamation was given
a list of Puritan "sins" that had brought this war upon
the nation as a judgment. The curious catalogue of sins
included : neglect to catechise the young, excess in
apparel, wearing of long hair, rudeness in worship, such
as, for example, the practice of leaving the church before
divine service had ended, and *the recent neglect to suppress
the Quakers and their meetings*. To show that the
proclamation was no empty call to repentance, a law was
simultaneously passed imposing a fine of five pounds

---

[1] Staples' *Annals*, p. 167.
[2] *Old Indian Chronicle* (Boston edition, 1867), p. 211. These Quakers
believed the war thoroughly unjust, and desired to withhold from all acts which
might seem like taking part in the war, though in declining to nurse wounded
soldiers they were surely pushing their scruples too far.

upon every person who should attend a Quaker meeting, with imprisonment at hard labour upon bread and water.[1]

Of this proclamation and law Governor Coddington, with grim humour, writes in his Postscript :

"There is come to our Hands certain Lawes or Orders of ye 3rd November 1675 set forth by ye authority of your generall Assembly of ye Massachusetts, your secretaries Hand being to them, *wherein you say you have apostated from the Lord with a great backsliding*: To which I do consent ; so great [as] hardly to be paralleled, all things considered. We were a people prfessing ye Feare of ye Lord in England against Bishops and Ceremonies in tender Love to all that prfessed Godliness, and so departed from the land of our Nativity, declaring the Ground of our Removall into N.E. viz. to seek out a Place for our Brethren where we might enjoy the Liberty of our consciences that ye sons of wickedness might vex us no more.

"How well this hath bin performed by you, let your printed Lawes declare and this amongst the Rest : Our houses are open to receive *your* wounded and all in distress, we have prpared a Hospitall for yours, but you a House of Correction for all that repaire to our Meetings. Your ministers with us have not been molested, ours with you have been persecuted. Is this a time for you to establish Iniquity by a Law—will not the Lord be avenged on such a Nation as this that sets up Ministers that are not made Ministers by ye power of an endless Life, but of ye Letter that kills, and not ye spirit that gives Life, and a Worship that is not in Spirit and Truth set [up] by Christ above 1600 yeares agoe ; we cannot come to you without departing from ye Lord as you have done, therefore desiring your return to ye Power that made you, ye true Light that is in you. This is written by one who above 45 yeares past was one of you and now is one that desires your true Good both Eternall and temporall, as I did when I was with you and am yours in Love.—W. C."[2]

As a result of the great suffering occasioned through-out the Colony of Rhode Island by the progress of the

---

[1] *Colony Records of Massachusetts*, v. 59.

[2] Easton's *Narrative*, Appendix, pp. 132-135. A still more interesting piece of Coddington correspondence is a letter under date of 22nd December 1675, from Governor Andros of New York, charging the Governor of Rhode Island with having seized powder and arms from a ship bound to the port of New York. There is, unfortunately, no answer extant to this letter, which I give herewith : "Hon. Sir,—This is by a sloop bound to yor parts not to omitt noe good oppor-tunity, though there bee nothing new, but that I heare that you stopped a vessel bound to this place, on acc. of some Powder and Armes in her, which (as re-

war—both Warwick and Providence were burned to the ground—the General Assembly, at its meeting in April 1676, roused itself to military preparation in response to the urgent calls of the non-insular inhabitants. It was voted that "there appears absolute necessity for the defence and safety of this Colony," and that "for the orderly mannagings of the millitia this Assembly doe agree to chose a major to be chiefe Captaine of all the Collony forces." John Cranston was chosen to be the major, with commission to use his "utmost endeavor to kill, expulse, expell, take and destroy all and every the enemies of this his majesty's collony," which commission is signed by Governor Coddington.[1] The Assembly thereupon sent John Easton and George Lawton, both Quakers, "with all convenient speed," to Providence with full power "to determine whether a garrison or garrisons shall be kept there at the charge of the Colony and the place or places where they shall be kept and whether at all." They decided on one garrison with seven men and a commander.[2]

At the summer election of 1676, Walter Clarke, in spite of his somewhat halting "Quaker war-policy," was chosen Governor, though major John Cranston was associated with him, as Deputy-Governor, to take charge of military affairs.[3] The Colony was in a sorry plight when the new administration began. The war was

presented) would not only reflect on mee and the magistrates of this government but on his Royall Highnesse and the King himself whose commissions I have. I cannot give creditt to this report, not having heard from yorselfe or colony of it, which I am confident I should, yet being told mee by sufficient men I pray I may, etc.—E. ANDROSS." Easton's *Narrative*, pp. 130-131.

[1] See *Colony Records*, ii. 537-539.

[2] *Colony Records*, ii. 545. The commander was Captain Fenner, and his commission was signed by Walter Clarke, the next Quaker Governor.

[3] William Edmundson, who visited Newport at this time, says : "Great troubles attended Friends by Reason of the war, which lay very heavy on places belonging to that Quarter without the Island, the Indians killing and burning all before them ; and the People who were not Friends were outrageous to fight; but the Governor being a Friend (one Walter Clarke) could not give commissions to kill and destroy men."—Edmundson's *Journal* (ed. 1715), p. 82. At the end of the war the Magistrates of Plymouth wrote to the King their opinion of Quaker Governors in war time : "The truth is the authority of Rhode Island being all the time of the warr in the hands of Quakers, they scarcely showed an English spirit, either assisting us, their distressed neighbors, or relieving their own plantations upon the Mayne."—*New England Papers*, xxxiii. 5.

brought to an end by the mid-summer of 1676, when Philip was hunted to his death in the swamps by Mount Hope near the scene of Easton's arbitration conference, but the non-insular towns of Rhode Island were almost wiped off the map. Every house but one between Providence and Stonington was destroyed, and most of the territory outside the islands was like a desert.[1] The new Governor was fortunately relieved from the actual din of war, but he found himself loaded with many problems which the war had left in its wake. One of the problems was the treatment of the defeated Indians. The other Colonies sold their captives as slaves. To Rhode Island belongs the signal honour of having inaugurated a more enlightened policy. An Act of the Assembly was passed that "no Indian in this colony be a slave." Some of the leaders who were captured were brought to Newport, and tried by court-martial and shot. Three Quakers, the Governor, John Easton, and Joshua Coggeshall, were members of the court, but apparently they did not attend the session, owing to their conscientious scruples against capital punishment.[2]

Governor Clarke took the first opportunity of peace to discharge the garrison at Providence, to which he had consented only because of the overwhelming force of popular demand. It was restored, however, by the succeeding Governor, Benedict Arnold, who was a non-Quaker. About this time a plague of some sort, a very deadly epidemic, broke out and ravaged the Island. William Edmundson, the Quaker traveller, has given us our only account of it. He says :

---

[1] Drake says that there was only one house left standing in Warwick, three in Providence, and none in Pawtuxet (*Old Indian Chronicle*, p. 244). The scholarly editor of Callender's *Historical Discourse* thinks that the sufferings of the Colony and the lack of union in matters of defence "were not owing only to the religious principles of the gentlemen then at the head of our administration." He points out that there are still in existence commissions signed and sealed by the Quaker Governor and the Quaker Deputy-Governor directing Benedict Arnold, jun., "to go in an armed sloop to visit the garrisons at Providence." The Deputy-Governor gave solemn evidence that he was "not against giving commissions that are for the security of the King's interests in this colony."—*Op. cit.* note, p. 134.

[2] See Easton's *Narrative*, pp. 173-190.

"Whilst I staid at Rhode Island, the heat of the Indian war abated, for King Philip, in that war of the Indians, was killed and his party destroyed and subdued. Presently a sickness came which proved mortal and took many away, few families but lost some, in two or three days' sickness. Many Friends died, yet I constantly visited sick families of Friends, although the smell of the sickness was loathsome, and many times I could feel all the parts of my body as it were loaden with it, so that I would say to sick families, *It was much I did not carry their sickness away, I was so loaden therewith.* After sometime it seized upon me with such violence that I was forced to keep my bed at Walter Newberry's in New-Port."[1]

In addition to the problems of restoring the devastated province, now swept also by plague, and the problem of the treatment of the Indians of the Colony, the Governor had to face again the aggressions of Connecticut on the Narragansett territory. Three Rhode Island citizens who were engaged in restoring their desolate homesteads in Narragansett were seized by Connecticut officers and carried prisoners to Hartford. Appeal was made to Governor Clarke, and he and his council wrote immediately, demanding their release, and threatening reprisal if it was refused.[2] This affair, however, went over to the new administration, for at the election of 1677 the Quakers went out of office and the war-party triumphed. One of the first acts of the new Assembly was a Militia Bill which struck at the provision for Quaker exemption. This Bill still insisted that there should be "free liberty of conscience for the reall worship of God," but it declared that

"Some under pretence of conscience hath taken liberty to act contrary, and make voyde the power, strength, and authority of the millitary soe necessary to be upheld and maintained, that the civill power (in which the whole freedome and priviledges of his Majesty's subjects are kept and preserved) cannot without it be executed, and have soe far acted therein, that this his Majesty's Collony at this time is in effect wholly destitute of the millitary forces for the preservation thereof, and inhabitants

---

[1] Edmundson's *Journal*, p. 82.
[2] Arnold's *History of Rhode Island*, i. 425.

therein, and may thereby be made a prey unto the weakest and meanest of his Majesty's enemys." [1]

The Act proceeds to provide for an efficient militia into which all freemen are subject to draft :

"Provided, alwayes, and this Assembly doe hereby declare, that it is their full and unanimous resolution to maintaine a full liberty in religious concernments relateinge to the worship of God, and that noe person in inhabitinge within this jurisdiction shall bee in any wise molested, punished, disquieted, or called in question for any differences of opinion in matters of religion, whoe doe not actually disturbe the civill peace of the Collony." [2]

Benedict Arnold, who had served the Colony twelve times as Governor, and who was generally chosen when the Quakers were not in office, died before his term of office expired, and William Coddington, now an old man, was selected to take the vacant place, but he did not live to finish out the term, being on his deathbed when the Assembly met, 1st October 1678, and dying two days later—"a good man, full of days," as Callender says, "he died promoting the welfare and the prosperity of the little commonwealth which he had in a manner founded." [3]

At the time of his death the Island colony, in which he had been the chief figure, was five times as wealthy as the other plantations in Rhode Island,[4] and was forging ahead with the promise of becoming one of the busiest ports on the American coast, and one of the leading centres of wealth and culture in the new world. The old Governor had done much to make this development possible, and Rhode Island owes him a large debt, even though Judge Durfee's epigram upon him is in some measure true : "He had in him a little too much of the future for Massachusetts, and a little too much of the past for Rhode Island." [5]

At the next election, and for five years running, Walter Clarke was chosen Deputy-Governor, and during

[1] *Colony Records*, ii. 567.   [2] *Ibid.* p. 571.
[3] *Historical Discourse*, p. 52.   [4] Weeden's *Early Rhode Island*, p. 97
[5] Judge Durfee's *Historical Discourse*, p. 16.

this period John Easton, Caleb Carr, Peter Easton, and Henry Bull, all of whom were Quakers, were almost continuously in public service in one office or another. William Coddington, son of the old Governor, filled the governorship from 1683 until just before his death, which occurred in 1685. This period, from the close of King Philip's war to the coming of Andros—soon to be described—was a time of fierce controversy for the integrity of the Colony, as Connecticut, Plymouth, and even New Hampshire were all laying claims to the territory of the mainland of Rhode Island—a controversy too long and complicated for this chapter.

When the junior Coddington found himself too ill to accept office again—in 1685—a fine old Quaker gentleman, one of the original founders of Aquidneck, Henry Bull, was elected Governor.[1] It was plain to everybody during this year that stormy times for the Colony were coming on, and at the next May election Walter Clarke, who had been continuously in office for many years, was elected Governor, and three Quakers, John Easton, Walter Newberry, and Edward Thurston, were chosen assistants. Soon after election the storm broke. The Assembly was informed in June of 1685, by a writ of *quo warranto*[2] "from his gracious majesty King James II., by the hand of Edward Randolph, Esq., secretary for the New England colonies," that the charter of the Colony was "vacated," and that Rhode Island was annexed to Massachusetts, "under his Majesty's laws and government." Randolph's task in the Colonies had been for some years to collect information which would furnish adequate ground to annul the charters and bring the whole of New England under the direct control of the Crown, and upon his so-called "information" the King now began to put into operation his large plans for an extensive royal colony.

---

[1] He was one of the sympathizers with Anne Hutchinson, and was "disarmed" as a signer of "the petition." He married Nicholas Easton's widow Ann. He, too, like Coddington, had a famous house in Newport in which meetings were often held—a house which is still standing.

[2] It was one of the charges in the *quo warranto* that the Governor, Deputy-Governor, assistants, deputies, and other officers were *under no legal oaths.*

The Rhode Island Assembly saw that resistance was in vain, and "voted not to stand suit with his majesty," but they prepared "a humble address," asking that their ancient privileges and liberties might be preserved.[1] This General Assembly, which was the last one to be held until 1690, made provision for the separate towns of the Colony to govern themselves, while the central colonial administration was annuled. Each town was authorized to hold an annual meeting of five days, or longer, and to manage all matters pertaining to the life and prosperity of the local civic community.[2]

In June 1686, Sir Edmund Andros, formerly Governor of New York, was commissioned Governor of the united Royal Colony, and almost upon entering upon his administration, Andros wrote, "in his Majesty's name," demanding the surrender of the charter of Rhode Island, but Walter Clarke did not "feel way open," to *send* the precious document of their liberties, and it remained in his house. He and another prominent Friend, Walter Newberry of Newport, were selected to be members of Governor Andros's Council for New England,[3] and they attended the first meeting of the Council in Boston, 30th December 1686, when they took affirmation, refusing to swear. Governor Andros at this time demanded the delivery of the charter. The Rhode Island members answered that, "'Twas at the Governor's house in Newport, and that it should be forthcoming when sent for, but in

---

[1] *Rhode Island Colony Records*, iii. 190. The Friends sent a special address to the King, in which they "humbly prostrated themselves before him," and begged that their views in regard to oaths and war might be respected. Printed in British State Paper Office (New England), vol. iv. p. 419.

[2] *Rhode Island Colony Records*, iii. 191.

[3] Randolph wrote to the authorities in England, 31st March 1687 : "Our council, consisting of twenty-six persons, has in it but three persons who are of the Church of England. The rest are Quakers, Anabaptists, and either members or followers of the congregational churches. You may from thence make your estimate at what rate his Majestie's interest can be carried on."—*Randolph Correspondence* (Prince Pub.), vi. 218. Walter Clarke was able to be of considerable service on the council to Friends, working particularly for the principle of voluntary contribution for the support of ministry in place of compulsory rates. See *Randolph Papers*, ii. 19. Randolph himself wrote a vigorous letter to Governor Hinckley of Plymouth, calling him to sharp account for the "arbitrary, illegal, and unheard of" methods of compelling Quakers to support the established ministry.—*Randolph Correspondence*, iii. 267.

regard to [*i.e.* on account of] the tediousness of the bad weather it could not be brought ! " [1]

Each request for surrender was put off by temporising methods, until finally Andros appeared in person with his troops, returning from his fruitless charter " hunt " in Connecticut, and demanded the Rhode Island charter then and there. Walter Clarke, its custodian, was ready for him since he had anticipated such a visit. The story is well told in Theodore Foster's unpublished manuscript :

" In the month of November 1687 Sir Edmund Andros came to Newport from Hartford attended by his suite and more than sixty regular troups in order to possess himself of the charter. Governor Clarke, who had it in possession, on hearing of his arrival, sent it to his brother with orders to have it concealed in some place in the knowledge of his secretary, with instructions that the Governor himself should not be informed where it was. Governor Clarke then went to wait on Sir E. Andros and invited him to his house, and so contrived the business that though there was a great parade of searching for it, it could not be found while Sir Edmund remained in Newport. After his departure it was returned to Gov. Clarke, who kept it, until the reorganisation of the government in 1689 when he [Clarke] was again elected to the office of Governor. His usual caution prevented him from accepting the office, and induced him to refuse to deliver up the charter until after the election of Henry Bull, and on order of the sheriff to take him into custody and confine him in prison—on which he sent the charter to Gov. Bull." [2]

The " fall " of Andros came with the success of the English Revolution, closing the Stuart regime and bringing in William and Mary. When the news reached Newport that the government of " usurpation " was at an end, Walter Clarke wrote a letter to the freemen of the Colony, informing them that the Government under which they had been " subservient is now silenced and eclipsed," and calling them to meet at Newport on the day designated in the precious charter for elections, " there to consult and agree on some suitable way in this present juncture." [3]

---

[1] *Proceedings of the American Antiquarian Society*, N.S. xiii. 242.

[2] *Foster Papers* relative to the History of Rhode Island, i. 337, in the Providence Historical Society.

[3] This letter, in Walter Clarke's handwriting, is in vol. iv. of the *Foster Papers*.

In accordance with this "call" the freemen of the colony met at Newport 1st May 1689, and adopted an address indefinitely, "to the present supreme power in England," "being ignorant," they say, "of what titles should be given and also not so rhetorical as becomes such personages." [1]

Andros had reported that the "Quaker Grandees of Rhode Island," who had royally entertained him when he was Governor of New York, "had imbibed nothing of Quakerism except its indifference to forms," and that they cared nothing for the restoration of the old government.[2] But the outburst of joy which was manifested at the fall of Andros disproved his estimate. The Newport Assembly declared their "gratitude to the good Providence of God which had wonderfully supported their predecessors and themselves through more than ordinary difficulties and hardships," and they take it to be their duty "to lay hold of our former gracious privileges, contained in our charter," and then by a unanimous vote the old officers were confirmed. Walter Clarke, with excessive Quaker caution, hesitated to return to the functions of his interrupted office until he knew what the character of the new English government was to be, and what colonial policy it was to adopt.[3]

For ten months there was no central executive government, the meeting of the Assembly called for October by Governor Clarke having been prevented by heavy storms. At the Assembly in February 1690, Clarke still declined to serve as chief magistrate. Christopher Almy was elected and also declined. "It was then," as Bancroft says, "that all eyes turned to one of the old Antinomian exiles, the more than octogenarian, Henry Bull; and the fearless Quaker, true to the light within, employed the last glimmerings of his life to restore the democratic charter of Rhode Island." [4] Governor Bull was succeeded in office at the end of one term by John Easton, son of

---

[1] *Rhode Island Colony Records*, iii. 268.   [2] *Ibid.* iii. 339.
[3] Walter Clarke's course at this time is hard to fathom, though he seems to have had a settled policy and the people appear to have been with him for he was soon again the colonial leader.
[4] *History of United States*, ii. 448.

Governor Bull's old friend, Nicholas Easton. He, too, as his father before him, had had an almost continuous career in public office, and he was trained in all the intricacies of colonial affairs. He had been among the leaders of the colony in the dark days of King Philip's war, and he now came to the highest office in his colony when another serious war was devastating both continents—the French and Indian War of William and Mary's reign. The colonies were harried both on the coast and on their inland borders. It was, oddly enough, during the administration of this Quaker that the first naval victory of Rhode Island was won. A fleet of seven French ships descended on the Narraganset coast and did much damage to the defenceless shore, when suddenly they were met by two sloops manned with Rhode Island freemen under command of Captain Thomas Paine, who furiously attacked the enemy, killed or wounded half their force, and drove them off to sea.

One of the fiercest contentions during Easton's term of office was over the control of the militia. Massachusetts and Plymouth had been united under a royal Governor, Sir William Phipps, whose commission gave him the command also of the militia of Rhode Island. This commission was vigorously challenged by the authorities at Newport on the ground that their precious colonial charter gave them power over their own militia. During the winter of 1693, Sir William came in person to Rhode Island and read his commission to Governor Easton. When the reading was over, the imperturbable Quaker quietly replied that when the Assembly met, if it had anything further to say, he would write. It was not easy to overawe such colonial governors. The question of the control of the militia was fought out at great length, the colonists ably holding their position, until finally Queen Mary "surrendered" and wrote to Governor Phipps withdrawing his control of the Rhode Island militia.[1] At the same time the Queen *asked* Rhode Island to furnish

---

[1] The documents of this controversy are printed in *Rhode Island Colony Records*, iii. 285-300.

forty-eight men to aid in the defence and security of the colony of New York.

The actual demand for these "men" came in a request from the Governor of New York in the administration of Caleb Carr—another Quaker politician of long experience —who succeeded Governor Easton in 1695. Governor Carr, like all the other Quaker Governors, disliked extremely to get drawn into affairs beyond the home field ; and he was, too, conscientiously opposed to adopting any actual war measure.   He urged that there were great difficulties in the way of supplying the desired "men" and asked of the Governor of New York that his colony might furnish "some other reasonable assistance in computation of said forty-eight men."   This request was denied, and the "men" were demanded ; but again new reason was found why they could not be sent just then ! Meantime Governor Carr died in office and the old custodian of the charter, Walter Clarke, came back into the governorship, with his old Quaker companion, Walter Newberry, as an assistant.   The ancient demand for troops for New York came up again with increased urgency. Governor Clarke replied that the colony had no "men" to spare.   "They had themselves," he wrote, "forty miles of sea-coast, with three inlets and no forts, therefore all the soldiers the colony possesses are too few for our defence, and furthermore Massachusetts has 'detained' several of our towns, further incapacitating the colony." [1] The "men" never went to New York !

There is a letter in the British State Paper Office, signed by W. Clarke, dated 17th September 1702, which declares that the charter of Rhode Island "granted by Charles II. of blessed memory placed *the sole power of the militia in us*," and the letter significantly adds : "We conceive it our duty to continue the militia as formerly until we receive further order." [2]

A new trouble now broke out upon the colony of Rhode Island.   There came at this time a radical change in the

---

[1] *Rhode Island Colony Records*, iii. 316.
[2] Record office, C.O. 5. 1302.

plan and method in the Home Office in London of administering the British Colonies, and with the change came also a thorough and searching investigation of the internal affairs and procedure of the colonies. The "investigation" was carried on under the oversight of Edward Randolph, who had already become notorious in the colonies as a collector of "information." The main charges against the colony of Rhode Island were that its officials were not under oath, that the laws of the colony were not published and were badly kept, that the British acts of trade and navigation were disregarded, and that little or no effort was made to suppress piracy—at that time a prevailing evil.[1] It was even charged that Rhode Island had become, through the leniency of the Quaker rule, a nest for "pirates, smugglers, and sea-robbers," and this condition was attributed to "the remissness or connivance of such as have been or are Governors."[2]

Meantime Jahleel Brenton, who had gone to England in the interest of colonial affairs, returned with a commission to administer to Governor Clarke an oath of obedience to the acts of trade, and with a commission also to establish in Rhode Island a court of Admiralty. The Governor, as a Quaker, would not take any oath; and so he refused to take *this* oath, even though demanded by his sovereign. But he went still further in his boldness. He positively refused to allow the court of Admiralty to be established, because he held, in the spirit of the colonists of '76, that it was *an invasion of colonial rights*.[3]

Edward Randolph gives this interesting glimpse into the situation, reporting his visit to Newport. He writes that he found all the colonists planting tobacco, and he continues :

"As the governing power is in the hands of the Quakers and Anabaptists, neither Judges, Jurys nor witnesses are under

---

[1] This was the period of Captain Kidd.

[2] *Rhode Island Colony Records*, iii. 326.

[3] Walter Clarke, planting himself squarely on the rights of the charter and refusing to allow royal interference, is one of the beginners of the movement toward Independence.

any [sworn] obligation, so that all things are managed acc. to their will and interest [!]. An attempt being made by Mr. Brenton to erect a court of Admiralty under the commission from England, Governor Walter Clarke would not allow it, *telling the assembly, then in session, that it would utterly destroy their charter, which empowered the colonists themselves to establish such a court with the proper officers.*" [1]   [The italics are mine.]

On this issue, actuated by the highest motives of loyalty to the rights of the colony, Walter Clarke went out of office, stubbornly refusing to yield an iota from the rights of the charter which he had saved for the colony.

Samuel Cranston, not a Quaker, but a nephew of Walter Clarke, and in hearty sympathy with the Quaker policy, was put in as Governor and served continuously until his death in 1727, Walter Clarke being Deputy-Governor with him continuously from 1700 to his death in 1714.[2] Randolph's "investigations" read very much like the partisan newspaper investigations of the present day ; and one can find here in 1698 partisan charges of "graft" quite similar to those we read to-day. Randolph declares that the Quaker political "machine" has for a long time been growing rich and fat off its connivance in piracy ! Two pirates, he says, were recently captured in Newport and about £1500 in gold and silver taken from them. They were put in prison :

"But about two days after they were admitted to bail, by the Governor (I am informed), one of the Governor's uncles being their security. By which means they have opportunity given to escape, leaving their money to be shared by the Governor and his two uncles, *who have been very great gainers by the pirates* who have frequented Rhode Island. Walter Clarke, the late Governor and his brother [Weston] now the Recorder of the place, have countenanced pirates and have enriched themselves thereby [!]." [3]

---

[1] *Randolph Papers* (Prince Pub.), ii. 152.

[2] Randolph informed the Home Office in 1700 that Cranston is the present Governor but the Quakers have the sole administration of the government. A similar report was made the year before : "Mr. Cranston was one of the demi-Quakers only put in to serve the Quakers." See Palfrey's *History of New England*, iv. 236.

[3] To the Board of Trade, 30th May 1698, *Rhode Island Colony Records*, iii. 339.

He admits, in a postscript, that the two pirates are to have a trial, but he says that he *expects* that they will be acquitted. He adds that he learns that the people are with Walter Clarke in his refusal to take orders sent from England, inconsistent with their charter privileges, and he understands that they are raising money to send Clarke to England to represent the colonial case.[1]

Here, with the close of Walter Clarke's career in 1714, ends the first period of Quaker influence in the colony. Clarke had been four times elected governor, and twenty-three times deputy-governor, dying in the office to which he had been fifteen times *successively* elected. From the beginning of the colonial government under the charter of 1663, Friends were continuously in office, of one sort or another, occupying the governorship nineteen terms and being a potent force in the Assembly. John Easton, Caleb Carr, and Walter Clarke were among the foremost spiritual leaders of the Quaker society during the period of their political activity. Easton and Clarke were ministers of the gospel and frequently went forth on public religious service. They were constantly involved in issues of the most complex and difficult sort, and they seem through all the shifting currents to have kept true to what they believed was the path of duty and at the same time to have kept the confidence of the people. They were perhaps not great statesmen, but they were brave forerunners of the American idea that the colonists should govern themselves, and they deserve to be drawn out of the oblivion into which they have somewhat fallen, if for nothing else, for their devotion to the principle that gave birth to the American nation and on which its political life rests to-day.

The second period of Quaker influence in Rhode Island politics began with the rise of the Wanton family in the early years of the eighteenth century and ended with the disownment of Stephen Hopkins in 1774. It

---

[1] Brigham, in his *Rhode Island*, p. 160, declares that "actual complicity between the colony as a government and the pirates, as so often charged, was never shown by any letter or report submitted to the English authorities."

was throughout most of this period more an individual influence than a group influence. In 1700 half the white population of Newport were Quakers,[1] but as the century progressed other cities in the colony, especially Providence, rapidly grew in population and influence so that the Quakers no longer held their proportion to the whole number of the inhabitants of the colony. They continued, however, to produce men of light and leading ; and they were yet for many years to have a large place in the administration of the colony which they had done much to foster in its formative period.

Edward Wanton was one of the foremost figures of the New England Society of Friends in its early days. He had been an officer of guard in Boston on the occasion of the execution of the first Quaker martyrs, and he was deeply moved by their innocence and heroic bearing. He came home from the execution greatly changed, saying as he unbuckled his sword : " Mother, we have been murdering the Lord's people, and I will never put a sword on again." [2]

He thereupon took every opportunity which offered to inform himself of the Quaker faith, and sometime before 1661 he had openly avowed himself a Friend. He moved to Scituate, in Plymouth colony, in 1661, and started a very important venture in shipbuilding. He was from the first the leading person in the Quaker group of Scituate, and his house was the home of the meeting and headquarters for all visiting Friends, he himself being the foremost minister in that region. He died in 1716, as the historian of his town remarks :

" With faculties unblurred, mind clear, piety fervent, faith unwavering and active as he nearer approached its realisation, from which he could often review his past life and with soul-stirring eloquence and deep sympathy exhort all to stand fast in the faith."

His oldest son, Joseph, moved to Tiverton, Rhode Island, in 1688, and started there a branch of the ship-

---

[1] *Annals of Trinity Church*, p. 10.
[2] Deane's *History of Scituate, Massachusetts*, p. 372.

building business.   He was much like his father in large-
ness of view, in hospitality, and in his deep interest in
the Quaker Society.   Both he and his wife (Sarah
Freeborn) were public ministers, and they entertained in
princely fashion, being also noted far and wide for their
benevolence and charity.

Two other sons, William (born in 1670) and John
(born in 1672), moved to Newport and established there
a branch of the shipbuilding industry about 1704.
They were men of large business capacity and rapidly
acquired great wealth for those times, and soon came to
have a very commanding part in the colonial government.
William was not a Friend during his public career, though
he evidently never lost his love for his father's faith,
to which he swung back toward the end of his life.   He
broke away from the Society of Friends in his youth to
marry Ruth Bryant, whose parents were as much opposed
to Quakerism as William's family was to Presbyterianism,
the creed in which Ruth had been reared.   There is a
tradition that William one day said : "Ruth, let us break
away from this unreasonable bondage.   I will give up my
religion and thou shalt give up thine, and we will go to
the Church of England and to the devil together."[1]

Both the brothers who came to Newport had a military
strain in their blood, and in the period of youth they
performed dashing naval exploits, chasing and capturing
pirates and privateers, and taking an active part in the
famous naval expedition of 1709 against the French in
Canada.[2]   Two of William's vessels were used for the
Canadian expedition, and he was on the committee to
select officers for the Rhode Island ships.   He was almost
continuously in some public office between 1704 and his
death in the governorship in 1733, to which he was twice
elected, having previously been Speaker of the Assembly
for seven years.   A short time before his death he

---

[1] *History of Scituate*, p. 374.

[2] There is a current story that the good Quaker father once said : " It would be
a great grief to my spirit to hear that you had fallen in a military enterprise, but
it would be a greater grief to hear that you were cowards."—*History of Scituate*,
p. 374.

solemnly remarked : " My father's God is my God and I shall die in the faith of the Quakers." [1]   The Wantons were at the height of their financial and social position when the famous philosopher, George Berkeley, came to Newport with large plans for planting a great college in the New World, and they frequently entertained him. " The Quakers with their broad-brimmed hats, came and stood in the aisles " to hear him preach on Sundays,[2] and after the Church service was over the philosopher was accustomed to go home to dine with William Wanton.

John swung back to his father's faith much earlier in life than his elder brother, and from about 1712 he became a pronounced Friend in faith and practice. He early developed a powerful gift in ministry, and devoted much of his time to religious service, preaching both in his home Meeting at Newport and travelling far and wide to deliver his messages when he felt called to go forth. His biographer says :

" He was a powerful and eloquent preacher. No eloquence like his, it is said, had been heard in New England. Multitudes flocked to his preaching wherever it was known he was to be present. He travelled extensively in New England and southerly as far as Pennsylvania in which missionary tours he gathered multitudes to the Society of Friends." [3]

He was considered the wealthiest man in the colony ; his manners were refined, and, though a minister of the Society, he wore " a bright scarlet cloak lined with blue ; " his mind was well cultivated ; his spirit was generous ; he was very popular ; and he had great ability for public service in colonial affairs. His political career began in 1712, the year of his positive affiliation with Friends. He was elected that year a Deputy to the General Assembly and successively until 1721 when he was chosen Deputy-Governor. He was continuously Deputy-Governor from 1729 to 1733 when he was elected Governor to fill the place made vacant by his brother's death. He served

[1] " History of the Wanton Family," by J. R. Bartlett, in *Rhode Island Hist. Tracts*, No. 3, p. 33.
[2] *Annals of Trinity Church*, p. 10.
[3] *Rhode Island Hist. Tracts*, No. 3, p. 49.

the colony as Governor for seven successive terms, finally dying in office as his brother had done.

Like many Quaker Governors before him he was called upon to steer the colony through a serious war—this time the war between Spain and the mother country in which the colonies were deeply involved.[1] An act was passed by Rhode Island in 1740 putting the colony in a state of defence and providing for the enlistment of soldiers to serve in the West Indies. Governor Wanton, now a prominent Quaker minister, was put in a most delicate and difficult situation. He was obliged as Governor to issue military commissions and to perform many duties of a warlike nature which looked like inconsistencies and which brought him under a fire of criticism from the authorities of the Quaker Meeting. He, however, took the course which his predecessors in office had taken, that as a public officer his first and clearest call was the performance of those duties which the colony had laid upon him, and on the performance of which the life and welfare of the colony rested. He met the committee of Friends unmoved, listened to their charge of inconsistency, and replied that he clearly felt it right to fulfil his obligations as the executive of the colony, one of those same obligations being the protection of the inhabitants of the colony. " I have endeavoured," he added, " on all previous occasions, as on this, to do my whole duty to God and to my fellow-men, without doing violence to the law of my conscience, but in all concerns listening to the still small voice of divine emanation and being obedient to it." [2]

The only other Quaker Governor from the Wanton family was Gideon, son of Joseph of Tiverton and grandson of Edward of Scituate. Gideon Wanton was Treasurer of Rhode Island from 1732 to 1744, and he was Governor of the colony at the time of the famous expedition against Cape Breton in the war with France. As Governor he was called upon to furnish troops for the

---

[1] War between Great Britain and Spain was declared in 1739.
[2] *Rhode Island Hist. Tracts*, No. 3, p. 55.

enterprise, and he complied with the call as his uncles had done in similar straits.

Another interesting character, whose colonial services stretched over a period of forty years, and whose influence upon the destiny of the colony was at times greater than that which a Governor could wield, was Richard Partridge, foreign agent of the colony in London. He was the son of William Partridge, who was for several years Governor of New Hampshire, and was born in 1683,[1] probably in the town of Newbury, where his father was a prominent member of the Church. He moved to England in his early manhood, joined the Society of Friends, and was for fifty years an acceptable and edifying minister of the Gospel, counting among his personal friends the leaders in the Quaker Society on both sides of the Atlantic.[2] He was appointed foreign agent for Rhode Island in June 1715, "to transact," as his commission says, "for this colony all its concerns beyond seas, to represent this colony before the king and council or otherwise as the affairs of the colony shall require, and he shall be allowed for his salary £40 per annum."[3] He immediately proved his fitness for the delicate diplomatic tasks entrusted to him, for at the autumn session of 1715 the Assembly voted him its thanks for "powerfully exerting himself and using his utmost efforts for *excepting* the colony of Rhode Island out of the Bill of the House of Commons for regulating the charters of the American colonies."[4] He was always called upon in times of war to arrange the quotas and contributions which Rhode Island was to furnish, and on a number of occasions he was asked to act for other colonies than Rhode Island. His wisdom and far-sighted judgment appear in all his diplomatic undertakings. The way in which he handled the veto question of 1731 is one interesting illustration. The Governor of Rhode Island had vetoed an important Bill and had thus aroused a stormy opposition. His right of

[1] *New England Historical and Genealogical Register*, xiii. 265.
[2] Thomas Story calls him "my long acquainted friend Richard Partridge."— *Journal*, p. 683.
[3] *Rhode Island Colony Records*, iv. 187.   [4] *Ibid.* iv. 200.

veto was challenged, and he decided to ask the officers of the crown to pass upon the rights of veto granted to the colonial governor by the charter. Partridge at once saw that it would be dangerous for the colony to raise this question and to call the attention of the crown to the extensive privileges granted in the Rhode Island charter. " Such a course," he wrote, " will prove of ill consequence to the colony." [1]

Always on the watch for what would affect the rights and privileges of his colony, he anticipated the danger lurking in certain proposed measures regulating trade in the West Indies. He wrote to the Governor of Rhode Island :

" The West India gentlemen are not quiet ; they have begun to work through a Bill for encouraging trade with the sugar colonies which will be disadvantageous to the Northern Colonies." [2]

This refers to the famous " Molasses Act," or " Sugar Act." The neighbouring colonies were notified of the impending danger, and were asked to join Rhode Island in opposing the Act ; and the entire case for the northern colonies that were especially affected was put in Partridge's hands. He presented a vigorous Petition to the Board of Trade, in which he claimed that the proposed Act involved a *violation of the rights of the colonists as Englishmen since it imposed taxes on citizens who were not represented in Parliament*.[3] This is a direct announcement of the principle which was formulated in the Declaration of Independence and which was fought out in the Revolutionary War. The opposition effort was not wholly successful, but an unpublished letter from Partridge says : " By my efforts the Bill has been made vastly different from what it was originally drawn." [4]

[1] Letter in *Foster Papers*, ii. 147. There is also a valuable collection of Partridge Letters in the John Carter Brown Library.

[2] *Ibid.* ii. 149.

[3] I have searched the British Record Office in vain for this Petition which is referred to in Arnold's *History of Rhode Island*, ii. 124, but I have found a letter from the Proprietors of Pennsylvania, undoubtedly transmitted by Partridge, which declares that " the proposed ' Sugar Act ' takes from his Majesty's faithful subjects in North America that liberty and freedom of commerce which is their birthright yet unrestrained ! "—Public Record Office C.O. 5, No. 13.

[4] This Letter is in the Rhode Island State Library.

In 1752 an order of the King was passed which seemed to the Governor of Rhode Island to threaten the liberties of the colony. He wrote to Richard Partridge :

" *Use all your efforts to prevent anything being done to lessen our charter privileges.* You will understand how much uneasiness the very thought of losing our liberties creates in the inhabitants of this colony and how much dependence they must necessarily have on you, who have been so long their agent and whom they look upon by principle as well as interest so much a friend of liberty. You will exert yourself to the uttermost." [1]

One of his difficult diplomatic tasks was that of securing from Great Britain financial compensation for the colony's expenses in connection with the expedition against Cape Breton. He finally succeeded in getting an appropriation of £6332 : 12 : 10, which was precisely the amount which the colony claimed. It was, however, quite another matter to squeeze the actual money out of the Treasury, but, to use his own phrase, he "left no stone unturned." It was in appreciation of such unswerving fidelity and painstaking effort that the colony wrote to him officially in 1756 :

" The long experience the colony hath had of your diligence and faithfulness in their service leaves no room to doubt of your doing all in your power in this affair [the Crown Point Expedition] for their interests, and as you have hitherto been *generally successful in your undertakings* on their acct. so they hope you will bring this business to a happy issue for you and them." [2]

In 1759, Partridge was compelled by age and feebleness to resign his position as agent, and the same year he died.[3]

No other Quaker in American history, with the exception of William Penn, has achieved such a distinguished political career or has contributed so much to the development of our national life as Stephen Hopkins of Rhode

---

[1] *Rhode Island Colony Records*, v. 359.
[2] Letter in *Rhode Island Historical Manuscripts*, vi. 23.
[3] Richard Partridge was also employed by the London Meeting for Sufferings as their parliamentary agent, for which service he received £40 annually and expenses. (See Minutes of the Meeting for Sufferings, vol. xxx. pp. 83, 194, 320 and *passim.*)

Island. He was in a true sense one of the "makers" of the American nation. He was born in Massapauge, now known as South Providence, in March 1707, though his early years were passed in Chapsumscook now Scituate. His mother, Ruth Wilkinson, was a birthright Friend, a woman of large culture and of marked spiritual gifts, daughter of Samuel Wilkinson who was noted for his "erudition in divine and civil law, historical narrative, natural and politic." [1] In 1726 Stephen Hopkins married Sarah Scott, great-granddaughter of Richard and Catherine Scott, the first Quakers of Providence. His bride was of unbroken Quaker ancestry, back to these "first Quakers," but they were not "married in Meeting," as Stephen Hopkins at this time was not a "member of the Society." He, however, "joined Meeting" about 1755, near the time of his second marriage, which occurred in Quaker Meeting and was by Quaker ceremony. [2] The Friends' Meeting was frequently held in Stephen Hopkins' home, [3] and it is the testimony of those who knew him that: "In the simplicity of his demeanour, the hearty frankness and calm dignity of manner which were characteristic of him, he reflected no unworthy credit on the training of his Quaker mother." [4]

Like most of the great leaders in the formation of the nation, Stephen Hopkins had a long apprenticeship in local affairs. He first "found" himself and his political principles in the colonial Town-meeting, being chosen "moderator" (*i.e.* presiding officer) of the Town-meeting when he was twenty-four. He was continuously in township service until he was called to higher colonial and federal spheres of activity. He was still in his youth when he became a citizen of Providence and in this larger Town-

[1] Updike's *Narragansett Church*, i. 54. It has been pointed out that in Ruth Wilkinson's home there was "a circulating library," containing the best literature available at the time, one of the earliest circulating libraries in Rhode Island and probably in the colonies. (See *Rhode Island Hist. Tracts*, No. 19, pp. 46-47.)

[2] See *Historical Collection of the Essex Institute*, ii. 120. The Quaker marriage certificate is in the Roberts Collection at Haverford College.

[3] See Letter of Moses Brown to Robert Waln (1828).

[4] W. E. Foster's "Stephen Hopkins, a Rhode Island Statesman" (in *Rhode Island Hist. Tracts*, No. 19), p. 58.

meeting he was again and again—often in great crises—chosen moderator. He went to the General Assembly when he was twenty-five, and was a member of this body continuously for six years. He had also an important judicial training and a distinguished career on the Bench, rising to the highest judicial place in the gift of the Colony. He was elected Governor in 1755, the year he became a Friend, and between that date and 1768 he served in the governorship nine terms, through one of the stormiest political contests in the history of Rhode Island, and he finally declined to accept further nomination as Governor in order to end the political fight which had lasted with much heat for ten years, since he saw the importance of having the Colony united for the greater conflict which was now coming into sight upon the horizon. During these years of judicial and political activity he had, with his lifelong friend Moses Brown, been contributing his great powers to the commercial and intellectual expansion of the city of Providence, for it was at this period that Providence forged forward to its prominent place among the colonial cities. " He was," as Chief-Justice Durfee has said, " a man of extraordinary capacity, omnivorous of knowledge, which his energetic mind rapidly converted into power ; and wherever we see the colony or any parts of its people moving in ways higher than the average, there we are sure to find Stephen Hopkins prominent in the movement." [1]

He was first chosen for intercolonial service in 1746 during the second Spanish War, when he was selected one of the commissioners from Rhode Island to meet with those from the other Colonies to consult for the defence and safety of the country. Again in 1754—during the " French and Indian War "—he was a delegate to the famous colonial Congress held in Albany, at which Franklin proposed a plan of union, and he was commissioner in the colonial Congresses of 1755, 1757, and 1758. He was one of the first to see clearly the principle of the unconstitutionality of taxation without

[1] *Rhode Island Hist. Tracts*, No. 19, p. 124.

representation. He had reached his insight of this principle at least as early as 1756, as the following passage, taken from a deposition of Job Almy in a lawsuit between Stephen Hopkins and Samuel Ward, plainly indicates :

"I dined," the deposer says, "at Mr. Jonathan Nicholas', Innholder at Newport, March 1756, where were present Stephen Hopkins, Esq., then Governor of this colony and President of the said Court [the Superior Court], Wm. Richmond, Esq., another of the Justices of said Court, and Mr. John Aplin, with some other gentleman. And as in conversation I was blaming Mr. Aplin (who was my attorney) for not insisting on the late Act of Parliament wherein it is expressly declared that no Bills of public credit would be a legal tender for any money debt, the said Stephen Hopkins with some warmth replied: 'What have the King and parliament to do with making a law or laws to govern us any more than the Mohawks have? And if the Mohawks should make a law or laws to govern us we were as much obliged to obey them as any law or laws the King and parliament could make.' At the same time the said Stephen Hopkins further said that as our forefathers came from Leyden [*i.e.* the Pilgrims] and were no charge to England, the States of Holland had as good a right to claim us [tax us?] as England had." [1]

As soon as news reached America that Parliament was considering a proposition to lay taxes on the Colonies, Stephen Hopkins began a remarkable series of articles in the *Providence Gazette*, of which he had been one of the founders, on the Rights of the Colonists. These articles of his went deeper into the foundation principles of self-government and the true safeguards of liberty than any documents which had up to that time appeared in the colonies. The substance of these papers was gathered up in an important pamphlet and laid before the General Assembly of Rhode Island in 1764, a year before the Stamp Act was passed, and this document was put into general circulation, and was very widely read throughout the Colonies, and became one of the creative documents in shaping the course of American history.

[1] The *Law Reporter* for 1859, vol. xxii. p. 338.

Already, in this early paper, Stephen Hopkins taught the colonists to think in terms of *country*.

As soon as news of the actual passage of these Acts of colonial taxation reached Rhode Island, Governor Hopkins called a special session of the General Assembly, and he was the leader in the great Town-meeting of Providence which formulated a draft of instructions to the General Assembly.[1] It even surpassed in boldness the resolutions adopted by the House of Burgesses ·of Virginia under the eloquence of Patrick Henry, and it ended with the downright assertion :

" The inhabitants of this colony are not bound to yield obedience to any law or ordinance designed to impose any internal taxation whatever upon them other than the laws and ordinances of the General Assembly." [2]

Parliament, under the storm of opposition, repealed the Stamp Act, but asserted its *right* to tax the Colonies, and emphasized the right by the imposition of a tax on certain imports. A Town-meeting was called in Providence to propose a plan for avoiding this tax. A committee, of which Stephen Hopkins was a member, drew up a resolution that only home-produced articles should be used while this tax was in force. These resolutions are in the handwriting of Moses Brown.[3] As the storm of hostility against the mistaken course of the mother-country grew in violence, Rhode Island, always a liberty-loving Colony, became one of the most intense storm centres of opposition. It was from the city of Providence that the party of " patriots " headed by John Brown, the brother of Moses Brown, sallied out and burned the King's ship *Gaspée*, stationed in the Bay to enforce the revenue acts ; and as the storm gathered still darker, it was the Town-meeting of Providence, in which Stephen Hopkins was the foremost person, that made the first formal and official proposal for a Continental Congress, and Rhode Island was the first Colony to elect delegates to that congress, Stephen Hopkins being one of

---

[1] Hopkins was chairman of the committee which formulated this document.
[2] Staples' *Annals of Providence*, pp. 210-213.   [3] *Ibid.* p. 217.

the delegates.[1] In 1776, with trembling hand, trembling not from fear but from advancing palsy, he signed the Declaration of Independence, toward which he had been for more than a decade steadily moving and leading the people.[2]

This chapter of Quaker political history is far from a complete account of the part which the Quakers took in the colonial politics of Rhode Island.   It has dealt only with the leaders ; but the unnamed people behind the leaders are always at least as important a factor as the leaders themselves, and there was always a large group of Quakers around each Quaker leader.   This deeper history of the people themselves cannot be written.   This chapter, furthermore, of necessity has treated the Quaker factor quite too much in isolation.   The Quakers were not a class apart—a peculiar order of humanity.   They were simply men like other men, sometimes peculiarly dressed and using somewhat odd speech, but a part of a larger whole and owing much of their political success to the non-Quaker element with which they worked.   They had then, as we have now, narrowness, greed, corruption, and misrepresentation to face.   Conditions were no more angelic then than in the present year of grace, and these adherents of the inward Light were throughout their political career on the " perilous edge."   Every issue had its practical complications, its mean aspects.   No claim is here made that these " heroes " were always wise, or always right, or always great, but they are a fair illustration of our best common people, doing their duties with fearless spirit, uniting religion with practical daily life, exhibiting *loyalty* in the hard field of politics, and never bartering for selfish ends " the priceless jewel of their soul."

[1] When the order came to arrest the "patriots" who burned the *Gaspée* and send them to England for trial Stephen Hopkins, then Chief-Justice of the colony, said : " I will neither apprehend any person by my own order, nor suffer any executive officers in the colony to do it."—Weeden, *Early Rhode Island*, p. 336.
[2] He was, however, at the time of signing the Declaration no longer a member of Meeting for reasons given in the preceding chapter.

BOOK II

QUAKERISM IN THE COLONY OF NEW YORK

CHAPTER I

THE PLANTING OF QUAKERISM IN NEW YORK

"NEW YORK" was a part of the Dutch Colony of New Netherlands when the Quaker "invasion" of the Colonies began. The Dutch had passed through their baptism of fire in one of the most heroic struggles in history, and had, at great cost, won their religious freedom. They had before most peoples gained the tolerant attitude. They had furnished, in their home-land, an asylum to the harried English Separatists; and they had long been accustomed to the "lay-type" of Christianity, embodied in the Mennonite Anabaptists, who had, before George Fox, advanced many of the ideas and peculiarities of the Quakers. The Proprietaries of New Netherlands had expressly directed that all forms of religion should be tolerated in the Colony.[1] It would have been a natural prediction, therefore, that Quakerism would flourish undisturbed in the Dutch Colony, but on the contrary it spread here, as in the Puritan Colonies, only in the face of stern opposition.

Long Island, however, presented a prepared soil for the new religious seed, something like that which we have seen in Rhode Island, Sandwich, and on the island of Nantucket. Though under the Dutch Government, many of the towns on the island were settled by English colonists, a large number of them being persons who had left Massachusetts in order to secure greater religious

---

[1] The settlers of Maspeth (Newtown) on Long Island, to cite a particular instance, were induced to come to the Dutch territory on the promise of civil and religious freedom.—*Ecclesiastical Records of New York*, i. 138.

freedom. We have seen how the religious teaching of Anne Hutchinson prepared the way for the spread of Quakerism on Rhode Island and at other places in New England ; so, too, it was in large measure due to the religious influence and leadership of another woman that the towns of Long Island were prepared for the Quaker message which came to them in 1657. This woman was Lady Deborah Moody.

Her maiden name was Deborah Dunch, and she belonged to a distinguished family, her father, Walter Dunch, having rendered good service to his country in the reign of Elizabeth. She married Sir Henry Moody of Garesden in Wiltshire, but was left a widow in early life. She showed, even in her English period, great independence of mind and a determination to follow fearlessly her own light. This independent spirit soon brought her into collision with the Court of the Star-Chamber ; and being an intimate friend of the Winthrops, she resolved to migrate to Massachusetts to secure the freedom which she despaired of gaining at home. She settled in Lynn about 1640 and purchased an extensive estate called " Swampscot," [1] but was hardly settled there on her beautiful cliff farm before her liberal views brought her into trouble with the Salem Church. The Court proceedings, under date of December 1642, report that " Lady Deborah Moody, Mrs. King, and the wife of John Tillton were presented for houldinge that the baptising of Infants is noe ordinance of God," [2] in other words a group of Anabaptists was forming in Lynn with Lady Moody as its spiritual leader. Winthrop gives an interesting glimpse of her " heresy " :

" The Lady Moodye, a wise and anciently religious woman, being taken with the error of denying baptism to infants was dealt with by many of the elders and others, but persisting still and to avoid further trouble, etc., she removed to the Dutch against the advice of all her friends. Many others, infected

---

[1] Letchford, in 1641, says : " Lady Moody lives at Lynn but is of the Salem Church. She is a good lady but almost undone by buying Master Humphries' farm Swampscot."

[2] Newhall's *History of Lynn* (Boston, 1865), p. 204.

with anabaptism, removed thither also. She was after ex-communicated." [1]

As Winthrop intimates, she refused to accept the offered theological direction, insisted upon her right to live in the faith which seemed to her true, and once more migrated to secure the privilege of freedom. She moved to Long Island and purchased a large estate at Gravesend, and with her migrated also a large number of the Lynn settlers, " infected," as Winthrop says, " with Anabaptism." A Petition to the General Court in 1645 refers to this migration as follows :

" Those fewe able persons which were with and of us it's not unknowne how many of them have deserted us, as my Lady Moody." [2]

Three years before Lady Moody's pilgrimage to Gravesend, forty families from Lynn had planted a Colony on Long Island with large guarantees of freedom and with the design to build up there a Church " gathered and constituted according to the minde of Christ, for," they say, " wee do ffreely lay down our power at the ffeete of Christ," [3] and throughout this decade there were frequent migrations from Lynn to the Long Island towns, so that in Flushing, Gravesend, Jamaica, Hempstead, and Oyster Bay there were many persons who had deserted Lynn to find religious freedom, and who shared with Lady Moody the advanced and liberal ideas which in that generation were gathered up under the name of " Anabaptism." A characteristic entry in the Massachusetts Records for 1643 says :

" Rev. Mr. Walton of Marblehead is for Long Island shortly, there to set down with my lady Moody, *from under civill and church ward*, among ye Dutch."

The ecclesiastical records of New Amsterdam make the fact very plain that many of the English inhabitants of these Long Island towns were not kindly disposed toward the prevailing orthodox Calvinism, but on the

---

[1] Winthrop's *History of New England*, ii. 148.
[2] *History of Lynn*, p. 214. [3] *Ibid.* p. 194.

contrary were either of the *Anabaptist* or of the *Seeker* type. In 1653 the Director-General of the Colony complained that magistrates on Long Island were being selected without regard to their religion, and especially, he says, "the people of Gravesend who elect libertines [free-thinkers] and anabaptists."[1] Three years later William Hallett was banished from the Province of New Netherlands for allowing conventicles and gatherings in his house at Flushing, and William Wickendam, a cobbler by trade, was also banished for having taken the leading part in these house meetings, which seem to have been meetings for worship after the manner of the small dissenting sects.[2] In 1657, the year the Quakers arrived on Long Island, two of the leading Dutch ministers in the Colony, Joannes Megapolensis and Samuel Drisius, both keen in the scent of heresy, wrote to the Classis of Amsterdam a full account of the religious condition in New Amsterdam. They reported the people at Gravesend to be Anabaptists of the Mennonite type. "The majority of them," they say, "reject the baptism of infants, the observance of the Sabbath, the office of preacher, any teachers of God's word. They say that thereby all sorts of contentions have come into the world. Whenever they meet, one or the other reads something to them." "At Flushing," the report says, "many persons have become imbued with divers opinions. They absented themselves from the sermon and would not pay the preacher [Francis Doughty] his salary.[3] Last year a troublesome fellow, a cobbler from Rhode Island came there saying *he had a commission from Christ*" [evidently William Wickendam]. At Middleburg, a part of Newtown, the people are said to be mostly Independents who have an unordained preacher "who does not serve the sacraments." At Hempstead "the people listen attentively to the sermons of Richard Denton, a pious, godly, and

---

[1] *Colonial Documents of New York*, xiv. 235.
[2] *Ecclesiastical Records of New York*, i. 361-362.
[3] The salary of Francis Doughty was to have been six hundred guilders, but it was never paid ; and it was found, when the minister sued for his salary, that Wm. Lawrence's wife had destroyed the contract by "putting it under a pye."

learned man," but when he began to baptize children, "many persons rushed out of the church!"[1] Such, then, was the spiritual condition of the Long Island towns when the first messengers of Quakerism came thither to make convincements. There was already in existence here a type of religion which was independent of ordained ministers, which regarded the sacraments as unnecessary and which welcomed the common man who came with a direct commission. They were by the bent of their minds open to the word of the preachers of the inward Light. In fact, one Quaker seems to have been raised out of their own group even before any messengers came. This was Richard Smith. He had been to England on a visit in 1654, had apparently come under the influence of William Dewsbury,[2] and had returned a convinced Friend, so that he was the first Quaker in the American colonies. When the eight Friends came out from England in 1656 on their missionary journey to New England, they halted either at New Amsterdam or on Long Island and picked up this Richard Smith on their way and took him with them on their bold venture. He was hurried back to Long Island by ship that he might not contaminate or infect any body by a land journey![3]

"The spiritual Argonauts" who came in the ship *Woodhouse*, with Captain Fowler in 1657, were the first Quakers known to have landed in New Amsterdam, now New York city. Five of the eleven, Robert Hodgson,

---

[1] *Ecclesiastical Records of New York*, i. 393-399.
[2] Francis Ellington's Tract, *A True Discovery* (London, 1655).
[3] This was Richard Smith of Southampton, Long Island, and not, as Bowden (vol. i. p. 310) assumes, the famous trader of that name who in 1641 "erected a house of trade and entertainment" in the Narragansett country. This latter Richard Smith never became a Friend. He settled at Maspeth, on Long Island, about 1645 and remained there a few years (see Riker's *Annals of Newtown*), but he was back in Narragansett by 1649. The *Records* of Southampton for October 1656 furnish one piece of information about Richard Smith the Quaker: "It is ordered by the General Court that Richard Smith, for his unreverend carriage toward the magistrates contrary to the order, was adjudged to be banished out of the town, and he is to have a week's liberty to prepare himself to depart; and if at any time he be found after this limited week within the bounds of the town he shall forfeit twenty shillings. It is ordered by the General Court that Richard Smith for his unreverend carriage to the magistrate was judged to pay the sum of 5 pounds to be levied immediately upon the goods and chattels of the said Richard Smith." He is in the same Records called "an emissary of Sathan, a Quaker."

Richard Doudney, Mary Wetherhead, Dorothy Waugh, and Sarah Gibbons, stopped in the Dutch Colony while the rest went on to Rhode Island. Captain Fowler, before the *Woodhouse* left the port of New Amsterdam, with Robert Hodgson, paid a visit to Governor Stuyvesant and found him " moderate both in words and actions." His " moderation " was, however, soon changed. The next day Mary Wetherhead and Dorothy Waugh preached to the people in the streets of New Amsterdam, and the effect of this novel sight upon the Dutch inhabitants was instantaneous and pronounced. They had no desire to see their womenfolk catch this odd custom of preaching in the streets, and they soon had the two women in " a noisome, filthy dungeon "——a more than usually vile jail even for the seventeenth century ; and after eight days they brought them out of the dark hole, and sent them with their hands tied behind them to that " sewer of heretics," Rhode Island, to join their companions.

The two ministers already quoted, Joannes Megapolensis and Samuel Drisius, wrote to the authorities in Amsterdam an interesting account, though considerably coloured, of this invasion :

" On August 6th (or 12th) a ship came from the sea to this place, having no flag flying from the topmast, nor from any other part of the ship. . . . They fired no salute before the fort. When the master of the ship came on shore and appeared before the Director-General, he rendered him no respect, but stood with his hat firm on his head as if a goat (!). . . . At last information was gained that it was a ship with Quakers on board. . . . We suppose they went to Rhode Island for that is the receptacle of all sorts of riff-raff people and is nothing else than the sewer of New England. They left behind two strong young women. As soon as the ship had departed, these [women] began to quake and go into a frenzy, and cry out loudly in the middle of the street that men should repent, for the day of judgment was at hand. Our people not knowing what was the matter ran to and fro while one cried ' fire ' and another some-thing else. The Fiscal seized them both by the head and led them to prison." [1]

---

[1] *Ecclesiastical Records of New York*, i. 399.

The other three members of the party who remained behind made a tour of Long Island, where they found many hearts ready for their message, especially in the towns of Gravesend, Jamaica, and Hempstead. Hodgson concluded to stay in Hempstead for a larger service, while his two companions went on through the island and across to Rhode Island, and upon him fell a baptism of persecution of a peculiarly furious sort. Hodgson had invited the inhabitants of Hempstead to a meeting in an orchard on a certain " First-day," and as he was pacing back and forth in quiet meditation among the trees of the orchard waiting for meeting to begin, he was "violently seized" by a local magistrate named Richard Gildersleeve who took him as a prisoner to his own house. The officer left his prisoner and went to the morning religious service. When he returned he found a company gathered and Hodgson preaching to them ! He was thereupon moved to the house of a magistrate and still the people came " to hear truth." Word was now sent to Governor Stuyvesant, who despatched a sheriff and jailer with a guard of twelve musketeers to bring the prisoner to New Amsterdam. They pinioned Hodgson and left him closely bound for a whole day while they hunted out the persons who had entertained him. Two women were finally arrested on this charge, one of whom had two small children—one a babe still on the breast. They were placed in a cart, to the tail of which Hodgson was tied, and thus they journeyed through an entire night to Brooklyn ferry, and so across to New Amsterdam.[1] The women were soon set free, but Robert Hodgson was sentenced to a fine of a hundred guilders, or hard labour at a wheelbarrow with a negro for two years, " in order to suppress the evil in the beginning." As Friends always did do, he refused to pay the fine. He was brought out and chained to the wheelbarrow, but feeling himself innocent of any violation of law, he refused to work.

---

[1] There is a Dutch account of Hodgson's arrest and punishment preserved in *Ecclesiastical Records of New York*, i. 410. This account gives the distance Hodgson was carried as twenty-one English miles.

He was thereupon beaten almost to death with a tarred rope, then chained to the barrow, and left in the hot sun all day. The next day he was again brought out, chained to the barrow, and ordered by the Governor in person to *work.* Proving unyielding, he was next tied up by the hands with a heavy log of wood hung on his ankles and whipped on his bare back, and then thrust into a dungeon "too bad for swine." As news of his sufferings got abroad, a humane Englishwoman got into the prison to see him, washed his stripes, and told her husband of his desperate condition. The husband offered the officer in charge one of his oxen if he would release the Quaker. Others also came forward and offered to pay the fine. Hodgson declined to accept liberation on this principle, as he was innocent. His sufferings, however, made such a deep impression on the liberty-loving Dutch people that powerful influences were brought to bear on the Governor, who finally set him free without any payment at all, and Hodgson passed on to join his friends in Rhode Island.[1]

This brief and hampered presentation of Quakerism on Long Island was remarkably effective, and resulted in the rapid formation of Quaker groups. The people were in an expectant state, with spirits *prepared* for the new message and the new manner of life, and they accepted the Quaker faith almost by whole communities. If we may trust Gerard Croese, an inaccurate though contemporary Dutch historian, Lady Moody almost at once became a Friend. "There was at Gravesend," he says, "a noble lady, the countess of Mordee who turned Quaker." "She gave the people of this Society," he continues, "the liberty of meeting in her house, but she managed it with such prudence and observance of time and place that she gave no offense to any stranger or person of any other religion than her own, and so she and her people remained free from all molestation and

---

[1] The accounts of this episode are found in Bishop's *New England Judged*, p. 213; Sewel's *History*, i. 398; Bowden's *History*, i. 312; Brodhead's *History of New York*, i. 636.

disturbance." [1] The first convincements were made almost entirely among her friends and sympathisers. The Tiltons, the Townsends, the Farringtons, the Thornes, the Feakes, and a number of other families had probably been her associates in Lynn and had come to Long Island at the time of her migration. As soon as persecution came upon the new movement the first local heroes came out of this prepared group. Governor Stuyvesant was the instrument of this early persecution, but, as nearly all the authorities imply, he was urged and almost pushed to it by influence from Massachusetts. When once he had undertaken the course of suppressing the invading "heresy," he pursued it with the tenacity native to his race and disposition. The first step against the movement was the proclamation of a law imposing a fine of fifty pounds upon any colonist who entertained a Quaker even for one night, and providing for the confiscation of any ship which should import a Quaker into the Colony,[2] and at the same time an old, somewhat dormant law against conventicles was revived.

Henry Townsend of Flushing was the first person to suffer under this new system of extermination which the Governor had inaugurated. He was found guilty of violation of the conventicle law and was heavily fined, but he absolutely refused to pay his fine though he found the prison into which he was thrown extremely "irksome." His wife, however, "moved by the cries of her small children," gave the authorities two young oxen and a horse for her husband's release.[3] The inhabitants of Flushing were profoundly stirred by this invasion of their liberties. They gathered in a public meeting, expressed their disapproval of the acts of persecution, and drew up a remonstrance which was signed by thirty-one men and sent to the Governor, the signers of which included the town clerk Edward Hart, who wrote the document, and

---

[1] Croese, *General History of the Quakers*, translated (London, 1696), ii. 157. Lady Moody was intimate with Governor Stuyvesant, which fact no doubt protected her meetings. She, however, died in 1663 soon after the movement began.
[2] *Laws and Ordinances of New Netherlands*, i. 439.
[3] Bishop, pp. 218-219.

the sheriff, Tobias Feake. The remonstrance declared that the patent, or charter, of their town "grants liberty of conscience without modification," and that the signers intended to stand by their precious rights regardless of what it might cost them in suffering. They say in straightforward fashion :

" Right Honourable, you have been pleased to send up unto us a certain command that wee should not receive or entertaine any of those people called Quakers. . . . For our parte wee cannot condemn them, neither can wee stretch out our hands against them. . . . Wee desire in this case not to judge least wee be judged, neither to condemn least wee be condemned, but rather let every man stand or fall to his own. Maister, wee are bounde by the Law to doe good unto all men, especially to those of the Household of faith ; and though for the present wee seem to be unsensible of the law and the Lawgiver; yet when death and the law assault us, if wee have not our Advocate to seeke, who shall plead for us in this case of conscience betwixt God and our soules ? The powers of this world can neither attack us nor excuse us ! " [1]

A number of these thirty-one signers had come from Lynn to Long Island in pursuit of the precious privilege of religious liberty ; others on the list were English Separatists who, like the Pilgrim Fathers, had lived in Holland to escape oppression and had migrated from there to the New World under promises of freedom.[2] They knew what freedom was worth and they were resolved to have it, even " though death and the law assault " them.

" I do not know," John Fiske says, " whether Flushing has ever raised a fitting monument to their memory. If I could have my way I would have the protest carved on a stately obelisk with the name of Edward Hart, town clerk and the thirty other Dutch and English names appended, and would have it set up where all might read it for the glory of the town which had such men for its founders." [3]

The vengeance of the Governor fell with severity upon

---

[1] The Remonstrance is given in full in *Ecclesiastical Records of New York*, i. 412.   [2] See Thompson's *Long Island*, ii. 69.
[3] *Dutch and Quaker Colonies*, i. 235.

fine, sober people that feared God and were convinced of the blessed Truth. They did receive me and my testimony readily with gladness. Many meetings of the people were settled under the teaching of the Lord Jesus Christ, our free Teacher, at Gravesend, Seatancott,[1] Oyster Bay, Hemsted, and other places, sometimes in the woods and wilderness." [2]

Another island now comes into prominence in the history of Quakerism, " Shelter Island," near the east end of Long Island, between Gardiner's Bay and Peconis Bay. It was originally named " Farret's Island," but was purchased by three citizens of Barbadoes, Thomas Rous, Constant and Nathaniel Sylvester, and an Englishman named Thomas Middleton. They paid sixteen hundred pounds of sugar for the island. The Sylvesters bought out Rous' share in 1662, and by the payment of one hundred and fifty pounds, " one half in beef and the other half in pork," the owners got their island exempted for ever from taxes and military duty.[3] Nathaniel Sylvester, who finally came into possession of the island, was a Quaker, and he proceeded to make his island a real " shelter " for harried Friends. John Taylor landed on this island on his way out from England, and he spent some time on it in 1659. He speaks as though there were already many Friends on the island. Beside those already there, " several Friends," he says, " came from other parts in New England." " We had several brave meetings there together, and the Lord's Power and Presence was with us gloriously." [4]

George Rofe, an Englishman, gives us our next glimpse through Quaker eyes of the Dutch colony. He sailed in 1661 " in a small boat with only two Friends," from Maryland, and came into the port of New Amsterdam. He writes :

---

1 " Seatancott " must mean Setauket, whose inhabitants in 1659 petitioned the General Court of Hartford for jurisdiction, and many of them came later to Matinecock as Quakers, for example, the Underhills, the Cocks, and others.

2 *Memoir of John Taylor* (London, 1710), p. 18.

3 Brodhead, *op. cit.* ii. 106.

4 *Memoir of John Taylor*, p. 22. Lawrence and Cassandra Southwick came to Shelter Island in 1659 to escape their unbearable persecutions in Salem.

the signers of the remonstrance, especially upon those
held official positions, and the town of Flushing
deprived by the Governor of its right to hold To
meetings, but the Governor's course did not crush
spirit of these earnest men who insisted on "the excelle
order and custom of the Fatherland"; it rather hasten
the formation of a Quaker society in the neighbourhood
A contemporary record says that "most of the inhabitan
of Flushing are Quakers, who rove about the countr
from one village to another, corrupting the youth.
Domine Megapolensis and Drisius report in 1658:

"The raving Quakers have not settled down, but continu
to disturb the people of this province. Although our government has issued orders against these fanatics, nevertheless they
do not fail to pour forth their venom. There is but one place
in New England where they are tolerated and that is Rhode
Island which is the sewer of New England. Thence they swarm
to and fro sowing their tares."[2]

Among those who "swarmed" into Long Island in this
early period must be mentioned Thomas Thurston and
Josiah Coale who passed through Long Island on their
foot-journey from Virginia to New England. They were
"much refreshed" to find in the towns of Long Island
"some Friends in the Truth,"[3] and there seems already
in 1658 to have been quite a nucleus of Quakers in
several towns.

The next year, 1659, a quaint and interesting Friend,
named John Taylor, from York, England, made a tour of
the island. He writes:

"It came into my heart to go and visit the people of Long
Island and to seek the lost. And it pleased the Lord so to order
my way, that I found in several towns and villages *a pretty many*

---

[1] John Tilton and his wife Mary, the wife of Joseph Scott, and the wife of
Francis Weeks were among those who had to endure hard persecutions. Nine
Quakers were in the jail in New Amsterdam at one time. "Goody Tilton, wife
of John Tilton, was charged with the crime of having, like a sorceress, gone from
door to door to lure and seduce the people, even young girls, to join the Quakers."
Her husband was charged with having "permitted Quakers to quake at his house
in Gravesend."—Thompson's *Long Island.*

[2] *Ecclesiastical Records of New York,* i. 433.

[3] Letter of Josiah Coale to George Bishop, 1658.—Bowden, i. 18.

"I had good service among both Dutch and English. I was in the chief city of the Dutch, and gave a good sound, but they forced me away; and so we had meetings through the islands in good service."[1]

The little society in Flushing soon found a yeoman leader in one of its own members, John Bowne, "the blameless Bowne," as Bancroft calls him. He had immigrated from Derbyshire, first to Boston and then to Long Island where in 1656 he married Hannah Field, who became attached to the new Society in Flushing, and took the risks of going to the meetings, which at first were held in the woods to escape the notice of those who were hostile. John Bowne out of curiosity went with his wife to a meeting, was impressed with the spiritual reality of the movement, and invited the Friends to hold their meetings in his house—a fine dwelling-house erected in 1661 in the eastern end of the village near two magnificent oak trees. He soon allied himself positively with the new venture and became a member of the Society.

It was quickly reported that the Bowne house had become a "conventicle" for Quakers, and the owner was arrested, fined £25, and threatened with banishment on non-payment. The threat, as usual, made no impression. At the end of three months, during which Bowne had lain in prison, an Order was passed in Council to transport him, "if he continues obstinate and pervicacious," from the province, "for the welfare of the community, and to crush as far as it is possible that abominable sect who treat with contempt both the political magistrates and the ministers of God's holy Word, and endeavour to undermine the police and religion." He did continue "pervicacious," and was transported by the ship *Gilded Fox* to Amsterdam. Upon landing he laid his case before the Directors of the West India Company, and as soon as their liberty-loving spirits were wakened they gave him satisfaction—"they spoke no word tending to the approval of what had been done against Quakers."

---

[1] *A.R.B. Collection* (Devonshire House), No. 62.

They wrote a letter to Stuyvesant, not quite as dramatic in its delivery as the "King's Missive" in Massachusetts, but absolutely effective for its purpose. The substance of the message was :

"It is our opinion that some connivance is useful, and that the consciences of men ought to remain free and unshackled. *Let every one remain free* as long as he is modest, moderate, and his political conduct irreproachable." [1]

Soon after his return as a free man, John Bowne was walking the street of Flushing and met the Governor. The chief magistrate "seemed much abashed for what he had done," but showed his manliness by saying, "I am glad to see you safe home again." The straightforward Quaker acknowledged his greeting and added, "I hope thou wilt never harm any more Friends." [2] And he never did. Bowne's victory had, as moral victories generally do have, far-reaching consequences. He not only won his personal freedom, but he called forth from the Directors of the Colony a proclamation of the principle of complete religious toleration, "The consciences of men ought to remain free and unshackled." But that was not all. When the next year the Colony was conquered by the English, an article establishing "liberty of conscience in divine worship and church discipline" for all Dutch subjects was put in the articles of agreement surrendering the territory. In 1664, the year the Colony passed into English control, the "Duke's law" provided that "no person shall be molested, fined, or imprisoned for differing in judgment in matters of religion," and from that time on the principle was recognised throughout the Colony as a fundamental right, though in *practice* it was still occasionally violated.[3]

[1] *Ecclesiastical Records of New York*, i. 530. Bowden's *History* (i. 324-325) gives the correspondence in full.

[2] Bishop, p. 423.

[3] There were sporadic attempts to harry the Quakers throughout the seventeenth century, always in the interests of the Established Church. I have found this interesting letter from Richard Gildersleeve, constable, to Governor Andros of New York :

"RIGHT HONORABLE—Whereas your honor was pleased to lay some command

The Colony became English territory by the terms of surrender in 1664, and was organised as a British Colony with a Governor from the mother country. It was reconquered by the Dutch in 1673, but with the settlement of peace in 1674 it was restored to the English. The little groups of Friends in the Colony were in this transition period much expanded, and entered upon a new stage of their development, as a result of the visits of important missionary Friends. The first of these constructive visits was that of John Burnyeat, who makes the first mention we have of a permanent organisation of the Friends on Long Island. He writes :

"I arrived at New York the 27th day of Second month [April old style] 1671, and from New York I went to Long Island, and visited Friends on the island and other places thereaway [probably Shelter Island], and was with them at *their half-year's meeting at* Oyster Bay." [1]

Burnyeat was back again for extended work at the end of six months, when he visited all the meetings on the island, and attended again the Half-Year's Meeting at Oyster Bay.[2]

"The Lord's power broke in upon the meeting, and Friends' hearts were broken, and there were great meltings among us. Friends were comforted and the seed and life reigned over all." [3]

---

upon mee for the prevention of Quaker Meettings within our towne of Hemstead, which accordingly I have done to the best of my power by forewarning Captain John Seman. Being sick and not able to go myself, I sent two overseers to forewarn him that he should not entertain any such meeting att his house, yett nott withstanding his answer was that he tooke no notice of the warning, and proceeded to have and had a very great meeting the lastt Lordsday being the 28th of this instant. Hopping these few lines may find your honors favorable acceptance, and render mee excusable, and thatt your Honor will be pleased to take it in to your serious consideration for the ffuter pruention of the like : nott troubleing your Honor any further I remain Your Honors Humble seruantt Richard Gildersleeve, Hemstead, May 26, 1679."—*Ecclesiastical Records of New York*, i. 723.

[1] *Journal of John Burnyeat*, p. 196. This Oyster Bay Half-Year's Meeting was until 1695 a part of New England Yearly Meeting.

[2] He found the Long Island Friends at this time somewhat divided, as a result of the influence of a party in England opposed to George Fox and the system of organisation which was being put into operation. The contention was increased at this time because Burnyeat had brought with him a copy of Fox's *Book of Advice and Discipline*, and the Ranters produced their "Book" in opposition.—See *Journal*, pp. 197-198.

[3] *Journal*. p. 198.

On his way south, Burnyeat held a meeting in New York City, which is the first mention I have found of a Quaker meeting held on Manhattan Island.

At the next gathering of the Oyster Bay Half-Year's Meeting, in April of 1672, the great founder himself, George Fox, was present, having travelled from Maryland by forced marches—"earnestly pressed in spirit "—to get to Long Island in time for it.   Fox writes :

"The Half year's meeting began on First day of the week and lasted four days.   The first and second days we had public meetings for worship, to which people of all sorts came.   On the third day were the men's and women's meetings wherein the affairs of the church were taken care of." [1]

He found, as Burnyeat had the year before, some " contentious spirits " who were making trouble.   He met them face to face to consider their objections and complaints, and " the Lord's power broke forth gloriously, and the Truth of God was exalted and set over all." [2]

On his way back from New England Fox visited Shelter Island.   He had a famous meeting with the Indians on the little island.

" I had a meeting," he writes, " with the Indians, at which were their king, his council, and about a hundred Indians more. They sat down like Friends and listened attentively.   After meeting they appeared very loving, and confessed that what was said to them was Truth.   Next First-day we had a great meeting on the island, to which came many people who had never heard Friends before. . . . They were much taken with the Truth." [3]

After a very stormy passage he got to Oyster Bay, where he had " a very large meeting," and, in company with Christopher Holder and James Lancaster, he went across the Sound, " to the continent," as he calls it, and held a meeting at Rye, at that time in " Winthrop's territory " (*i.e.* in Connecticut) ; then to Flushing, " where we had a very large meeting, many hundreds of people being there, some of whom came about thirty miles to

---

[1] Fox's *Journal*, ii. 167.

[2] *Ibid.* ii. 168.   There are evidences in all the Journals of the period that there were many Ranters to be found in the Colonies as there were also in England.   [3] *Ibid.* ii. 172.

it.   A glorious and heavenly meeting it was," and, finally, " three precious meetings " at Gravesend.[1]

This work was immediately followed up and carried farther by the great colonial missionary of Quakerism, William Edmundson.   His *Journal* for 1672 says :

" I took passage by sea [from Maryland] and about ten days after landed at New York where no Friends lived.   We lodged at a Dutch woman's house who kept an inn.   I was moved of the Lord to get a meeting in that town, for there had not been one there before.[2]   I spoke to the woman of the house to let us have a meeting.   She let us have a large dining-room and furnished it with seats.   We gave notice of it and had a brave, large meeting !   Some of the chief officers, magistrates, and leading men of the Town were at it ; very attentive they were, the Lord's power being over them all.   Several of them appeared very loving after the meeting.   The woman of the house and her daughter, both being widows, both wept when we went away." [3]

Edmundson followed the regular Quaker route through Long Island eastward, finding " many honest, tender Friends " in the towns, and having a memorable visit with the Friends on Shelter Island, from whom he " parted in the sweet love of God " for New England.

On his return journey, having " set all the town [of Hartford] a-talking of religion," he crossed to Long Island.   Here he found an outbreak of Ranterism :

" Friends were much troubled in their meetings with several who had gone from Truth and turned Ranters.   They would come, both men and women, into Friends' meetings, singing and dancing in a rude manner which was a great exercise [annoyance] to Friends.   We staid sometime and had large and precious meetings, at several places.   Many of the Ranters came to the meetings and the Lord's power was over them and chained them down.   Some of them were reached and brought back to the Truth." [4]

[1] Fox's *Journal*, ii. 174.

[2] Edmundson is wrong in this statement, as Burnyeat had held one in the city before this.

[3] Edmundson's *Journal*, p. 64.

[4] *Ibid.* p. 92.   These Ranters apparently did not stay " chained," for Thomas Chalkley, writing in 1698 of his visit to Long Island, says : " I met with some of the people called Ranters who disturbed our meeting.   I may say as the apostle Paul did, that I fought with beasts there ! "—Chalkley's *Journal*, p. 22.

As has already been said, there was, at least in all the northern Colonies, in the seventeenth century a large and dangerous sprinkling of Ranters. They did not originate from the Quakers, as they ante-dated the latter by some years. They were a part of a widespread, though somewhat chaotic movement in England,[1] and there was an out-cropping of the same tendency in America. Among the groups of Anabaptists, Seekers, and so - called "Antinomians," wherever they appeared, there formed a radical wing composed of those who were less stable mentally, less organized morally, and less under the social direction of the groups to which they belonged. The Friends, with their lack of ecclesiastical authority, and with their doctrine of the Light within, were almost certain to suffer from the Ranter propagandism, and the movement did pick off some of the members who were ill-balanced and easy subjects of fanaticism. The Quaker leaders had powerfully proclaimed the possibility of complete salvation from sin, and it was only to be expected that some emotional Quakers, especially such as had a strain of hysteria, would make extravagant claims. One illustration of this Ranter tendency will suffice, taken from the *Annals of Newtown*, Long Island.

"There resided at the English Hills in Newtown several individuals holding the religious opinion of the Quakers. Among them was Thomas Case, who assumed the office of preacher, and at his house the faithful were wont to convene for worship. He set up a new form of Quakerism, and labored with great zeal to promulgate his views, not unfrequently continuing his meetings many days in succession. Inspired with a fancied holiness of his character and office he asserted that he was come to perfection and could sin no more than Christ, and he maintained that when he should die he would rise again the third day."[2]

This "new sort of Quakerism," as this chronicler calls it, ran into a wild fanaticism, and these "half-Quakers" were dealt with vigorously in 1675 by the town authorities.

[1] See my *Studies in Mystical Religion*, the chapter on "Seekers and Ranters."
[2] *Annals of Newtown*, pp. 93-95.

They were also vigorously dealt with by the Quaker meeting itself, as the following minute of Westbury Quarterly Meeting indicates :

"At a Quarterlie Meeting ye 30th day of ye 6th mo. 1675, We ye people of God, being weightily meett in ye feare and dread of ye Lord, being much conserned in our Spirits considering a people that is arisen in this day which calleth themselves by ye name Friends. These people oppose and denye ye truth of our Lord Jesus and speak evill of his way and people, wherefore we ye people of God, being seriously meett together in ye name and feare of ye Lord, feiling ye out-running of those people to be as a weight vpon vs, we, in obedience vnto god and his blessed truth, doe vnanimusly signifye our dislike of yt spirit they are guided by and give forth our testimonies against it.

Whereas those people being risen in ye pretence of ye truth in this western part of Long Island and some upon ye main, who call themselues young Friends or new friends, the leading persons of them being Thomas Case, Garsham Lockwood, Lydia ffoster, Elizabeth Cleave, with many others against whom we bear testimony for their confused practices, and have openly denied their Spirit of delusion by which they are led and guided, yet the presisting in and by ye deluding spirit and dark power wch opperates in them has bretrayed many into ye same snare wherein they become the country's discourse, wherefore we are nessecitated for ye baring of ye precious truth and for ye renouncing asperations yt may arise of us cleare from owning their way or evill practices to be in or by ye Spirit or power of God, and do giue forth our public testimonies to all yt may see ye same, yt we utterly deny them and all yt joyned in those confused practices, and ye spirit and power by wch they are led and guided."[1]

Two official reports of this period throw some light on the place which the Quakers held in the estimation of the Government.   The first extract is from the Report of

---

[1] *Minutes of Westbury Quarterly Meeting.*   The following letter from Edward Taylor to Increase Mather may possibly throw a glimpse of light upon these "new Quakers," though it is more probable that the incident reported is a fiction of the imagination of minds always on the watch for signs of witchcraft and for signs that the Quakers were objects of divine disapproval.   Edward Taylor writes, January 22, 1683 : "At Mattatuck, about 16 miles S.W. from Farmington, about 10 o'clock at night, there was seen by about 6 or 7 men a black streake in the skie like a rainbow. . . . About the same time it was credibly reported with us that the Quakers upon Long Island were on the Lord's day to have a horse race, and the riders mounted for the race were dismounted again by the All Righteous offended Judge striking them with torturering pains whereof they both died."—*Massachusetts Historical Society Collections*, Part iv. vol. viii. p. 630.

Governor Andros on the religious condition of the Province of New York in 1678, and the second extract is from a similar Report made by Governor Donegan in 1687:

"There are here Religions of all sorts, one church of England, several Presbiterians and Independents, Quakers and Anabaptists of several sects, some Jews, but Presbiterians and Independents most numerous and substantial." [1]

"Here bee many of the Church of England; few Roman Catholick; *abundance of Quaker Preachers, men and women; especially Singing Quakers, Ranting Quakers.*" [2]

One of the most memorable and historically important of the many missionary visits to Long Island for the purpose of extending Quakerism was that of Samuel Bownas of England, a young man of twenty-five at the time of his visit in 1702. He appointed a meeting, soon after his arrival, at Hempstead in a great barn and it was attended by a crowd of people. At the instigation of George Keith, formerly a leading exponent of Quakerism, but at this time a bitter opponent of Friends,[3] who had followed Bownas from Philadelphia in order to block his work, a warrant was sworn out, charging Bownas with "speaking lies and reflections against the Church of England" in his sermon at Hempstead. When the High Sheriff, accompanied by a posse of men "armed with guns, swords, pitchforks, clubs and halberts" came to arrest the prisoner, the Half-year's Meeting was in session at Flushing (29th November 1702), and Samuel Bownas was sitting in the ministers' gallery. The Sheriff marched up the aisle, pulled out his warrant, and said "You are my prisoner." After some parley the Sheriff consented to wait till meeting was over, and his men piled up their motley arms at the door and all sat down in the Quaker meeting. The "silence" at first astonished the officers of the law, but as they were beginning to whisper that Bownas

---

[1] Governor Andros' Report on the Province of New York in 1678.—*Doc. Hist. New York*, i. 92.

[2] *Ibid.* i. 186, Governor Donegan's Report on the Province in 1687. The "Singing Quakers" and "Ranting Quakers" naturally made an *impression*, though they were certainly few in number.

[3] For an extended treatment of Keith, see Book V. Chapter II.

was frightened by the show of force, he felt " the Word like a fire and stood up and had a very agreeable service." At the close of the meeting the Sheriff gave him an extension of liberty until the Half-Year's Meeting was concluded, at the last gathering of which " near two thousand people " were present.

At the hearing before the Justices, Bownas was asked to give £2000 bail or be committed to the common jail. His answer was, " If the bail were fixed at three half-pence I would not give it." One of the Justices thereupon took him to his own house for the night, and the next day he was committed to jail for three months, at the end of which time he was brought before the court of Oyer and Terminer, Chief Justice John Bridges presiding. The grand jury refused to bring a true bill against Bownas. The judge was thereupon very angry with them and endeavoured to compel them by threats of imprisonment and fine, but one of the jurors boldly answered : " You may hang us by the heels if you please, but if you do the matter will be carried to Westminster Hall ; for juries, whether grand or petty, are not to be menaced with threats, but are to act freely." [1]   The browbeating continued over to the next day, but the men remained unmoved and stood for the privilege of juries.   Whereupon the judge declared in wrath, " As justice cannot be come at here, I will send the prisoner to London chained to the deck of a man-of-war."

As Samuel Bownas was sitting alone, wondering what the issue of his case would be, an old man named Thomas Hicks, who had been chief-justice of the province, came to see him, took him in his arms, and with tears in his eyes said, " The Lord has used you as an instrument to put a stop to arbitrary proceedings in our courts of justice. There has never been so successful a stand made against it as at this time.   You need not fear ; they can no more send you to England than they can send me."

The prisoner was, however, confined, by order of the

---

[1] The judicial decision in the Bushnell case, which arose out of the trial of Penn and Mead, had settled the law that no jury could be fined for its verdict.

judge, in a small room made of logs, where he was kept until October 1703, and then set free because the jury again refused to find a bill against him. He had supported himself in prison by making shoes ; getting his bread, he says, "with my own hands, as was agreeable with Paul's practice." Having been held a close prisoner almost an entire year, he received "a kind of triumph" on his release, and "visited every corner of the island, and had very large and open meetings." He had an odd dream at Cowneck :

"I dreamed," he says, "that an honest Friend was fishing in a large stone cistern, with a crooked pin for a hook, a small switch stick for rod, and a piece of thread for line ; and George Fox [who died twelve years before] came and told me that there were three fishes in that place, and desired me to take the tackling of the Friend since he lacked the skill to handle the matter. Then, methought, the Friend gave me the rod, and the first time I threw in I caught a fine fish. George Fox then bade me try again, for there were two more in the place. I did and took up another. He bade me cast once more. I did and took the third. Now, said George, there are no more there ! "

The next day at meeting Bownas had forgotten the dream as though it had not been. A Friend rose and spoke for a little on *universal grace*. As soon as he stopped, Bownas, with "his heart full of the matter," took up the same subject and landed his fish : "We had a blessed meeting and the dream came true ! " [1]

Thomas Story's Journal is a valuable source of information on the condition and growth of Quakerism in New York.[2] He visited New York City for the first time in 1699, having "a small meeting" there. He gives us the interesting information that he "fell in opportunely with a Yearly Meeting at Westchester on the main, about twenty miles from New York." [3] He found a good many Ranters still in evidence on Long Island, one of

---

[1] A meeting was soon after established there. The Bownas incidents are told in his *Life and Travels* (London, 1761), pp. 61-95.

[2] *Journal of Thomas Story.*

[3] *Ibid.* p. 177. This was evidently not a Yearly Meeting for church affairs, but a General Meeting for the purpose of "expanding Quakerism."

whom " hooted like an owl and made a ridiculous noise as their manner is ! " [1]   He had " glorious meetings " in most of the Long Island towns ; he speaks of a " Quarterly Meeting " at Westbury and one in New York City, and he held a great meeting by appointment at Westchester, " across the sound," to which " an abundance of people came from as far as Horseneck."   " The people," he says, " were very still and affected with the testimony of Truth." [2]

While they were at Newtown, a part of the present city of Brooklyn, report reached him of the " pestilential fever " which was then raging in Philadelphia.   He and his companion, Roger Gill, were eager to go to their " distressed friends " in Philadelphia, but felt called before leaving to hold a meeting in New York City, where " the people seemed to have good understandings generally." The meeting was appointed at the request of Thomas Story, and was held in the house of Thomas Roberts, " a convinced man in the heart of the city."   " The room was large, and all about the doors and windows were full of people," but Thomas Story got no chance to speak. " I had," he says, " a great weight and exercise on my mind, but Roger Gill stept in between and took up most of the seasonable time, till my spirit almost sunk under the load ; and while it was working up the second time after he sat down, Samuel Jenings stood up and took the rest [of the time] ; and then I totally fell under it, and was greatly oppressed in spirit, though I bore it undiscerned by any ! " [3]   He came back from Philadelphia before the end of the year (1699), and had another meeting in the same house " . . . the concern having remained in secret," i.e. on his mind.   This meeting was large and he delivered himself of his " concern," and was " fully clear and easy." [4] In 1702 he had " a glorious meeting in the new meeting-house " at Westbury.   " Many hundreds of Friends and abundance of other people were there.   The meeting being over, there came over the Plains with us at least

[1] *Journal of Thomas Story*, p. 220.   [2] *Ibid.* p. 221.
[3] *Ibid.* p. 222.   [4] *Ibid.* p. 243.

100 horse to their several habitations." [1] In 1703 he was at a meeting in Westchester, "which was more open than usual in that place." Toward the end of 1704 he went to New York City, having heard that Lord Cornbury, the Governor of the Colony, was going to arrest him if he ever came into that jurisdiction again. " I was," he says, " at the Sheriff's house several times, but the Lord preserved me free to the service of the blessed Truth." [2]

The Journal of James Dickinson gives a good picture of conditions in 1698 :

"We crossed Amboy ferry in two canoes, which the watermen lashed together to carry our horses over. Next day we went to Elizabeth-town [New Jersey], took boat for New York, and were all night upon the water, being exposed to wind and storm : it rained all night and we had no shelter, for the boat was filled with wood and we sat upon it. About break of day we got to New York where we staid a little ; then passed over in a canoe to Long Island, and travelled up and down, laboring in the work of the gospel ; and had good service for the Truth. Several were *convinced*, particularly a captain in the army and a justice of the peace, who were afterwards called before the Governor of New York ; and because they could neither swear nor fight any longer, they laid down their commissions, having received the Truth in the love of it. In New York City many hearts were deeply affected and tendered, both among the Dutch and English, and the Lord's power was over all." [3]

Thomas Chalkley, the great Quaker traveller in the first half of the eighteenth century, was one of the foremost instruments in the expansion of New York Quakerism. He had already visited Long Island near the close of the seventeenth century——" fighting beasts " there,—but his important visit came in 1704. He travelled by horse and canoe from North Carolina, having narrow escapes from rattlesnakes, and

" Lodging like good Jacob on his way to Padan Aram. Very sweet was the love of God to my soul as I waked, and the dew of the everlasting love refreshed me." [4]

---

[1] *Journal of Thomas Story*, p. 256. [2] *Ibid.* p. 370.
[3] *Journal of James Dickinson*, in " Friends' Library," vol. xii. p. 393.
[4] *Journal of Thomas Chalkley*, p. 38.

"So we travelled on to New York and Long Island, where we had divers meetings, as at Flushing, Westbury, Jerusalem, Jerico, Bethpage, Matinicook, and also at West Chester *on the main*." [1]

On his return journey Thomas Chalkley had large and powerful meetings again through Long Island. A still more constructive tour was made by Thomas Chalkley through the New York meetings, especially on Long Island, in 1724. Much new ground was broken, and many "were convinced of the Principle of Truth." He visited Westchester again, and held a meeting at Newtown which was so large that the meeting-house could not contain the people. He held a meeting with "those few Friends at New York—the quietest meeting I ever had there!" [2]

Edmund Peckover visited Long Island in 1743. He, however, gives only one or two concrete pictures of the actual state of things there then. He attended the Yearly Meeting at Flushing that year, and he says that "the Top Sort of people for many miles round about the country were there." He reports but few Friends in New York City, but the yellow fever was raging at the time of Peckover's visit, and he did not see the city in its normal conditions. [3] William Reckitt visited the meetings through this region in 1758, and his report indicates that a decline had set in on Long Island. "Lukewarmness and indifference much prevailed," he says. Again, he makes the comment that "at Oister Bay there had been a large meeting, but now it was much declined." [4]

The last account which I shall give of conditions in the Colony in the eighteenth century shows that crystallisation was settling down upon Quakerism, and that the period of expansion was over. It is from the Journal of John Griffith of England, who visited the New York meetings in 1765 :

"Quarterly Meeting at Flushing (22nd of Fifth Month) was small, and things, as to the life of religion, were felt to be very

---

[1] *Journal of Thomas Chalkley*, p. 39.   [2] *Ibid*. pp. 118-120.
[3] For Peckover's Journal see *Journal of Friends' Historical Society*, vol. i. pp. 95-109.   [4] *William Reckitt's Life*, pp. 120-121.

low, a painful gloominess having spread itself through a want of living concern in many of the members . . . the vital part of religion seemed to be much obstructed." [1]

Griffith's Journal introduces us to a number of new meetings, which had been established by migration and expansion, like a chain of forts, running north from Long Island Sound, parallel to the Hudson, between the river and the Connecticut line, but he sees almost everywhere the marks of deadness :

"We went to New Milford meeting [in the Edge of Connecticut] on Firstday the 3rd of Eighth month. I had nothing to offer in the way of ministry. After meeting we ascended to the Oblong, and a long ascent it was, to the summit of the hill, called Quaker Hill [on the New York side of the line]. We had a very large meeting at a commodious house built by Friends on that hill. They who attended were generally professors of the truth, and mostly 'plain' and becoming in their outward garb; yet, alas! when they came to be viewed in the true light they appeared dry and formal, many, I fear, having clothed corrupted nature with a form of religion, and in a 'plain' dress sit in their religious meetings like dead images.

"We had a large meeting at the Nine Partners [East of Poughkeepsie] and we had a painful afflicting meeting at Oswego. On First day, the 10th of Eighth month, we were at the Oblong meeting again; my travail through the entire meeting was in suffering silence. We had meetings [travelling south] at Peach-Pond, North Castle, Purchase, Mamarineck, and West Chester. On Firstday the 17th we were at two meetings in the city of New York. I had a good deal of satisfaction among Friends in this city, and *I hope there is a growth in best things.*" [2]

Our next chapter will show this Quakerism of New York more from the inside, and we shall see what it was as its own records reveal its activities. The material for the present chapter has been drawn almost entirely from outside sources, especially from Public Records and the Journals of visiting ministers.

We have seen these little societies of Friends spring up and grow in the towns of Long Island, in New York

[1] *Journal of John Griffith* (London, 1779), p. 393.
[2] *Ibid.* pp. 408-411.

City, and northward along the chain of hills back of the
Hudson. We have seen them confronted, first by the
fierce hostility of an established religion ; next by the
more subtle danger of Ranterism, which picked off the
fringe of less stable members ; and, finally, we have seen
these groups facing the subtlest of all enemies to religion,
the tendency to cool off, stagnate, and become the
crystallised reproduction of an ancestral faith. There was,
however, from the beginning to the end of the period a
real spring of vitality which will appear more clearly in
the next chapter. Their own estimate of their condition,
made in 1680, is on the whole sound and true :

"Through patience and quietness," the New York Friends
wrote to London Yearly Meeting, "we have overcome in and
through the Lamb, and we have found of a truth that the Lord
takes care of his people. Our testimonies go forth without any
hindrance and return unto us not wholly empty, but have their
fruitful workings both upon Dutch and English nations. In a
sense of this our hearts rejoice in the Lord for that *His holy light
of life breaketh through the darkness as the dawning of the day.*"

There is nothing better in this world of ours than a
people living in and practising the faith that the holy
light of life is breaking through the darkness as the dawning of the day !

CHAPTER II

NEW YORK QUAKERISM—ITS MEETINGS AND ACTIVITIES

THE external husk of any religious movement is obvious and describable, the inner core is indescribable, and is missed by all except those who are initiated. The garb and language, the external peculiarities, and the odd " testimonies " of the Colonial Quakers struck most observers. The novel experience, the fresh sense of God which had come to them, was what the casual onlooker failed to understand, and yet this was in reality the only thing that mattered—it was the inner core.

The meeting for worship which was held for the very purpose of cultivating this fresh sense of God was thus the heart of the whole Quaker system. All religions which move men profoundly and make them able to endure the world's crucifixions have some method of bringing God and man together in a face to face experience. The Quaker method was extremely simple, but, at its best, powerfully effective. It called for no material apparatus and it made use of no sacred symbols. It consisted alone of the hushing of the noise and din of the outer activities of life. Its supreme and central axiom was the faith that God is Spirit and so as near the human spirit as air is to the breathing lungs or sunlight to the living plant. But as this spiritual relationship is a personal matter it calls for a peculiar attitude of will, or, in the language of an earlier time, a certain condition of *heart*. God, the Quaker assumed, did not need to be brought nearer ; man alone needed to be adjusted and made appreciative. He could no more find God when he was full of himself and of the world, than one can enjoy beautiful music with his mind crowded with the whirr of factory wheels. He must be hushed and attuned. Just this hushing and attuning was the service of the meeting for worship. Those who formed the nucleus of the Quaker group were thoroughly tired of theological arguments and of sermons which began and ended on the level of logic—or "knowledge about.". They wanted a new approach. They were eager for a direct "knowledge of acquaintance"—an experience which made their hearts burn with a sense of the Divine Presence, and they found this in the meeting for worship.

We know to-day much more than they did of the psychology of corporate silence, and there can be no doubt that there is a "borderland" state of consciousness produced by unbroken silence in which the deepest strata of the self come into function in ways not usual to the normal consciousness. If it is true, as I believe, that the Divine and the human are conjunct, then it is further true that the corporate silence is an admirable preparation for spiritual correspondence. But, in any case, it is beyond question that these meetings for worship made those who participated in them *feel* sure that they had been meeting and communing with God, and they were, therefore, very dynamic occasions, and the members believed that they had found, in the hard surroundings of pioneer life, a real "upper room" religion.

In its earliest stage on Long Island, as everywhere else in the colonies, Quakerism was primarily a method of worship. Its organisation was very slight indeed. Those who found *a new life* in the meetings for worship risked reputation, goods, and life to go to them, and, in doing so, they were thereby Quakers. Certain marked habits, which had almost unconsciously formed in the Quaker groups, would naturally be quickly taken up, such as the use of "thou and thee" in speech, the refusal to conform to fashion in dress, the scruple about oaths, and the care to avoid everything that had to do with war. There formed, too, gradually of course, a certain disposition, or mental "atmosphere," which characterised a Quaker of the inner circle as much as his dress or speech did. Its leading feature was a bloom of joy which came into the life with assurance of salvation and confidence in the love of God. There were, no doubt, Quakers of hard faith and stern face, but the tone of character which goes with consciousness of fellowship with God was the usual mark.

Little by little, here as in the other colonies, the organisation took on shape and grew defined. The influence of George Fox upon the formation of the colonial meetings in the early period is everywhere clearly evident, and the earliest Records generally open with an epistle from him. The earliest minute in the New York Records runs:

"At a men's Meet ye 23 day of 3d month 1671. It was agreed yt ye first dayes Meetings be on one day at Oyster bay and another day at Matinacock; and ye weekly Meeting to begin about ye first houre in ye afternoon. It was allso agreed ther shall bee a Meeting keept at the wood edge [Westbury] the 25 of the 4th month and soe every 5th first Day of the week." [1]

This is the earliest extant minute of a Friends' meeting in America and is probably the earliest one written on the continent. John Burnyeat who attended this meeting in 1671 brought with him a minute-book which George Fox had sent to Long Island Friends by his hand. The above minute is followed by a letter of advice from George Fox which begins with his usual salutation, "In the Truth of God which changes not in whom is my love." He then reminds his distant Friends that "there hath been [among them] a stoppage of ye truth and power of God," and that they need to be "searched to ye bottom" and so "come into ye sanctified life" — and for this purpose he calls for a careful examination of the persons who claim to be Friends, and a winnowing of those who walk unworthily

---

[1] This Book of Minutes was discovered in a garret at Flushing in 1868 and is in the vault in the Meeting House at Rutherford Place, New York, John Cox, junior, custodian.

and are in "the rotten principle of ye ranters." He urges further a careful collection of the list of sufferings endured in "the plantation." From this time on, the organisation, *for purposes of order* and *for purposes of relief*, gradually progressed.[1]

There is an interesting link of connection between the Long Island Friends and those in New England to be found in an epistle of Advice from the latter to the former in 1679:

"Dear friends, ye know that the Lord God of heaven hath appeared and manifested His mighty power which hath reached unto thousands and hath redeemed many out of nations, tongues, kindreds, and peoples to be a peculiar people, and hath taught us by His holy Spirit to denie ye customs, fashions and words of ye world. . . . It lieth upon us, ye people of God assembled together at ye Men and Women's Meeting in Road Island, to stir up ye minds in one another that ye principles of ye blessed truth be allwaise stood in and continued for that God over all may be honoured and his people preserved in purity and good order in ye truth that changeth not, that soe they may be preachers of Righteousness unto ye world in their words and actions."

The "Advice" which follows this salutation is an interesting revelation of the things which seemed to the early Friend of greatest moment. No Friend is to "walk disorderly in anything"; nor to live in any way "not according to Truth"; "nor to oppress or defraud any man in his dealings"; no one is to "weare needless attire" and all Friends are to "indever to bring up their children to use plaine language and weare plaine and deasent cloathing and demeane them in all things according to ye truth which we make profession of." [2]

At this earliest stage the records do not sharply mark off one type of meeting from another—"a men's meeting"

---

[1] John Bowne, John Tilton, Samuel Spicer, and Samuel Andrews, who were in the list of Friends addressed in the Epistle, were the leaders in the group of Long Island Quakers. John Feake, Hugh Cowperthwait and Anthonie Wright may also be mentioned among those of largest influence.

[2] "Given forth at a Generall Man and Women's Meeting at William Coddington's at Road Island ye 12th of ye 4th mo. 1679."—First Book of Records of Flushing Monthly Meeting.

may be a "monthly meeting," or a "quarterly meeting," or a "half-years meeting." Little by little, however, two types did differentiate, and there were formed Flushing Monthly Meeting and Westbury Quarterly Meeting which in the spring and autumn sessions was frequently called, though not officially, " Oysterbay Half Years Meeting "— all of which "belonged " to New England Yearly Meeting until 1696, when New York Yearly Meeting was established as an independent body.[1]

The two Monthly Meetings composing Westbury Quarterly Meeting appear to have been established, and regularly held by the year 1682, as the following minutes of the Quarterly Meeting held in 6th month 1682 indicate :

" Ffriends of ye Monthly Meeting of New York and Gravesend [Flushing Monthly Meeting] doe agree yt ye Monthly Meeting is to be keept at Yorke two months following & ye 3d at Gravesend, the first Meeting at Gravesend to be YE FIRST FOURTH day in the 6th mo. & soe sucksesifly."

" Friends at this Meeting hath left unto ye consideration of

---

[1] It was set off from New England Yearly Meeting by the following minute :

" At a Generall Yearly Meeting at ye house of Walter Newberry's in Road Island ye 14th daye of ye 4th mo. 1695. . . . It is Agreed yt [that] ye Meeting at Long Island Shall Bee from this time a Yearly Meeting and yt John Bowne and John Rodman shall take care to Receive such papers as shall come to ye Yearly Meeting in Lông Island and Corespond with Friends Appoynted in London. . . ." The first session was on 3rd month [May] 29, 1696, and it has met every year since in the latter part of the same month.

" At the Yearly Meeting at our Meeting house in fflushing ye 30th ye 3d mo. 1696 Henry Willis and Hen Coperthwaite are by this Meeting desired to get a release for ye title of our Meeting house and Land belonging and bring it to our next Meeting."

This was the first session of what is now called New York Yearly Meeting. It was then generally called the Yearly Meeting held at Flushing.

By the following minutes of the Yearly Meeting it appears that Westbury Quarterly Meeting was held three times in the year and that the Yearly Meeting took its place in the fourth quarter.

" Whereas this Meeting is now Concluded to be a Yearly Meeting and not a Quarterly one it is Thought Proper that the order of the state of Meetings or anything else from the Monthly Meetings of Flushing and Westbury be first carryed into the Quarterly Meeting at Westbury in the Twelfth Month and from thence Recommended unto this Meeting until Friends see cause to order it otherways."

Westbury Quarterly Meeting was composed of two Monthly Meetings : Flushing Monthly Meeting (later called New York), and Westbury Monthly Meeting, established in 1682 and held at Oyster Bay, Matinecock, Hempstead, and Jericho.

Friends at ye Monthly Meeting at Oyster bay ye sattling of ye Meeting of Friends at ye farms & at woodedg whether it be conventient or not for them to be in two settled Meetings or not."

The "farms" was the early name of Jericho and "Wood edge" was Westbury.

The following Minute settles still more definitely the jurisdiction of Flushing Monthly Meeting:

"The 20th day of ye 3d mo. 1684: Then agreed by Friends at this Meeting yt ffriends at Yorke, Gravesend, and Flushing and Westchester, ye Kills, and Newton doe all belong unto one Monthly Meeting to remain at Gravesend at ye 4th mo. Quarterly Meeting and soe to continue by their own appointing wt place they see convenient after."

It was always held at Flushing from 1695 till 8 mo. 6, 1742 then Flushing and Newtown until 6 mo. 1st, 1768 then Flushing, Newtown, and New York until 11 mo. 1, 1780, after which it was not held at Newtown. The name was changed to the Monthly Meeting of Friends of New York 7 mo. 1, 1795.

The plan for the holding of the Quarterly Meeting was marked out as follows in 1686:

"At our Quarterly Meeting at Jericho on Long Island this 27th day of ye 12 mo. 1685-6: By Joynt Consent of said men and women's Meeting for regulating our Quarterly Meeting for most Conveniency it is thought fitt and Vnanimously Agreed for the futur ye said Meetings shall be at such times and places as here Vnder Nominated.

"Vizt: Att Flushing a Quarterly Meeeting the last first day of the third month. Att Oyster Bay the last 7th and 1st day of the Sixth month. Att Flushing the last 7th and 1st day of the ninth month. Att Jericho the last 7th and 1st day of ye 12 mo. Att Westchester a Yearly Meeting for worship the last first day in ye 4 mo. Att ye Kills the last first day of the 5 mo. Att Jameca ye last first day of ye 7 mo." [1]

The important "business" of all these meetings in their primitive period was (1) dealing with persons who got entangled in "the ranting spirit" which swept Long Island in the 'seventies and to the end of the century;

[1] Quarterly Meeting Records.

(2) guarding the high moral standard which the Friends had set themselves to maintain, and (3) preserving the peculiar Quaker "testimonies."

A specimen minute under each of these heads will indicate how these internal problems were met. The first is a minute concerning a certain Thomas Phillips who had developed "a ranting spirit":

"And now, dear friends, this may let you understand yt a few months since there arrived at this island one Thomas Phillips who as he sd was formerly a liver at Oyster Bay, he being a hatter by trade, who when he was here in sum small time sought to thrust himself amongst Friends, he being as we afterwards perceived in need of money. But some of ye Friends wth whome he first came acquainted not liking his discourse, he setting up ye Ranting Spirit and its followers who goe vnder ye name of *new friends*, a Friend now living in this Island (by name John Brown who formerly was banished to some of those parts and had some knowledge of those people) did desire to speak with him believing that he was one of them in their spirit wch. he in five words persaued soe, and warned him to come out of it. But he still frequented our Meetings and growing more subtil and crafty, did frequently in company of some weak Friends, as their manner is, beguile them."

He was finally induced to "give forth a paper," condemning his errors, "but it was much too short in several respects," and so did not satisfy the Monthly Meeting, which proceeded to give its testimony against all "disorderly ways" of life, and a *call* to its members to "walk in the everlasting way of holiness—the King's highway—and to be kept by the Lord alwaise of sound judgment and right understanding in things that are of greatest weight and concernment."[1]

The way Friends followed up the doings of their members and scrutinised their reputations is well illustrated by this Minute sent from Westbury Quarterly Meeting to Friends in the Island of Jamaica:

"ffrom our Quarterly Meeting at Flushing ye 30th day of ye 6th mo. 1678: We having been informed at this Meeting by

---

[1] First Book of Records under date 5th mo. 29, 1680.

our friend Rob. Story yt one John Inyon, a marchant in New York, exclaimed against Friends after this manner : saying the greatest cheats in the world goe under the name of Quakers. His reason being demanded he said he consigned a vessell to one William Shattlewood and to another man in Jemica which he called Quakers, and he saith they will give him no account of his concerns [consignments].   These are to desire Friends to examine ye matter and write to us, if any Friends have received anythings we would have them give an account how disposed of, that we may have something to answer him.   These with our deare love." [1]

Dorothy Farrington's "case" is an illustration of the third type of "business" :

"The 8th of ye 10th mo. 1676: At a men and women Meeting in ye house of Matthew Prior at Killingworth [later called Matinecock] it was agreed on in ye Meeting that such as could find anything upon them shall go vnto Dorety ffarington of fflushing and speake unto her in love and in ye meekness to know whether she will owne judgment for her walking and acting contrary unto ye truth in taking a husband of ye world and not in unity of Friends." [2]

There is a very fine early minute explaining to the Governor of the Colony why Friends cannot help build the fort in New York harbour, and this minute well presents the way in which the Friends put their testimonies before those in authority :

"To ye Gouernor of New Yorke.

"Whereas it was desired of ye country that all who would willingly contribute towards repairing ye fort of New Yorke

---

[1] First Book of Records under date 6th mo. 30, 1678.

[2] First Book of Records.   A bill concerning marriages was passed by the Legislature in 1684 which provided that "nothing in this Act Shall be Construed or intended to prejudice the Custome and manner of marriages amongst the Quakers, but their manner and forme of marriages shall be judged Lawful ; provided they Admitt of none to marry that are restrained by the law of God contained in the five books of Moses."

Here is a humble apology from Daniel Lawrence which is quite of the common type : "To the Monthly Meeting at Flushing ye 3rd 5th mo. 1716. Friends in as much as I have made profession of ye Blessed truth with you which would preserued and kept me out of the many Euils that are in the world but I must say that with sorrow of hart I haue giuen way to An ary Spirit and too much joyning myself in fellowship with men of libertine spirits and alsoe in that insuitable frame of minde made sute upon account of marriage with one that was not a Friend or Friend's child the which actions I doe with censerity condemn and hoop for time to come to be more carefull and sircumspect so I shall subscribe myself your friend who desires to doe well and hue in vnity with friends for time to come.   DANIEL LAWRENCE."

would give in their names and summes ; and we whose names are under written not being found on the list. It was since desired by ye High Sheriff yt we would giue our reasons unto ye Gouernor how willing and ready we have been to pay our customs as County raytes and needful towne charges and how we haue behaued our Selues Peaceibly and quietly Amongst our Neighbours ; and are ready to be seruisable in anything which doth not Infringe upon our tender consciences but being in measure Redeemed of warres and stripes we cannot for conscience' sake be concerned in vpholding things of yt nature as you your-selves well know. It hath not not been our practice in Old England since we were a people ; and this in meekness we declare. In behalfe of ourselves and our ffriends, loue and good will vnto thee and all men.

JOHN TILTON. SAML. ANDREWS.
JOHN BOWNE. MATT. PRYER.
SAML. SPICER. JOHN VNDERHILL.
JOHN RICHARDSON. JOHN FEKE.

" fflushing ye 30th of ye 10th month 1672."

Westbury Quarterly Meeting was the only quarterly meeting in the colony until the year 1745, when Purchase Quarterly Meeting (often called "Oblong Quarterly Meeting" and sometimes "the Quarterly Meeting on the Main") was established. It was the only quarterly meeting "on the main" within the period of this history.[1] It was composed of Purchase Monthly Meeting and Oblong Monthly Meeting. Purchase Monthly Meeting was established June 9, 1725, and was the first monthly meeting "on the main"—the third in the Province—and was in its early period generally called the "Monthly Meeting for Westchester."[2] Oblong

---

[1] Nine Partners Quarterly Meeting was established 11th month, 13th, 1783.

[2] The opening Minute reads as follows :—

"Whereas our last Yearly Meeting at Flushing did consent and appoint a Mounthly Meeting to be held at Westchester for this county of Westchester, accordingly we are met to hold our Mounthly Meeting this 9th day, 4th month, 1725. Being present the most part of Friends of Westchester, of Mamreneck and Rye."

It would seem to have been generally held at the Meeting-house at Westchester till 7th month 12, 1728, then "at the house of Josiah Quinby" at Mamaroneck till 10th month 11, 1739, when the meeting-house was built in Mamaroneck. It was held for the first time at Purchase in 3rd month 1742, and thereafter for some years twice at Mamaroneck and once at Purchase, preceding each Quarterly Meeting, and later was held every other time at Chappaqua till that was set off as a separate Monthly Meeting in 1785.

Monthly Meeting was set off from Purchase Monthly Meeting, and was established in 1744. In 1769 a monthly meeting was set off from Oblong and established as " Nine Partners Monthly Meeting," and in 1778 Saratoga Monthly Meeting (later called Easton) was established, which brings us to the end of the period covered in this volume." [1]

[1] For exhibiting to the reader the localities in which Quakerism took root I add a list of the local, or " Preparative," meetings established up to the year 1780 :—

FLUSHING MEETING dates from 1657, though it was perhaps not a regular congregational meeting until 1662.

WESTBURY MEETING (first called the Meeting at Woodedge) goes back into the 'sixties though the first official mention is 4th month 25, 1671.

MATINECOCK MEETING was probably a regular congregational meeting in the 'sixties, though the first mention on the Records is 1671.

JERICHO MEETING (in the earliest accounts called the " Farms Meeting ") dates also from the 'sixties.

COW NECK MEETING also has a long period without·official Records, but is first officially named in 1702.

NEW YORK CITY MEETING cannot be definitely dated, but is first officially settled in 1681.

NEWTOWN MEETING (sometimes called " the Kills," and sometimes Maspeth) has a long unrecorded period, but is first officially named in 1682.

WESTCHESTER MEETING goes back to 1684, but was officially established as a Preparative Meeting in 1716.

MAMARONECK MEETING established as a meeting for worship 1711, as a Preparative Meeting in 1728.

PURCHASE MEETING, originally part of Westchester Meeting, but made an independent Preparative Meeting in 1742.

OBLONG PREPARATIVE MEETING established 1742.

CHAPPAQUA MEETING was allowed in 1745, and a few years later was made a Preparative Meeting.

NINE PARTNERS MEETING (Meeting for worship first called " Crumelbow " in 1742) established a Preparative Meeting in 1744.

NEW MILFORD MEETING (a meeting for worship probably as early as 1733) established as Preparative Meeting in 1777.

OSWEGO PREPARATIVE MEETING established 1758.

PEACH POND MEETING (a meeting for worship as early as 1760) established a Preparative Meeting in 1779.

POUGHQUAIG (sometimes spelled "Appoughquage" and sometimes "Poquage" was a meeting for worship in 1771) established a Preparative Meeting 1773.

EAST HOOSAC MEETING (in Western Massachusetts) was begun as a meeting for worship in 1774, and became a part of Saratoga Monthly Meeting about 1775. It was established a Monthly Meeting in 1778.

AMAWALK MEETING established a Preparative Meeting to be held once a quarter in 1774—a meeting for worship some years earlier, probably in 1766.

CREEK MEETING established as a Preparative Meeting of NINE PARTNERS Monthly Meeting in 1776—a meeting for worship in the house of Jonathan Hoag in 1771.

SARATOGA MEETING, a meeting for worship in 1774, a Preparative Meeting in 1776.

CORNWALL MEETING, a meeting for worship in 1773—a Preparative Meeting in 1777.

MARLBOROUGH MEETING, a meeting for worship in 1776, a Preparative Meeting in 1783.

The most illuminating glimpse we get into the actual *life* of Quakerism in this Colony in its early period is offered us in an Epistle which these Friends sent to London Yearly Meeting in 1701. There is no " doctrine " in it, and no attempt is made to analyze the religious condition of the Colony but a brief extract will show that there did prevail at this date a fairly *live* type of Christianity in the Quaker group. It reads :

" Dear Friends in our Lord Jesus Christ : In that Love which comes from God and in which we are united, we dearly salute you in true brotherly kindness. We signify unto you the prosperity of Truth amongst us to the Joy of our Souls. The Lord is giving an increase daily to Friends and many are added to the number of the Lord's people, and the people round about where Friends dwell increase in love to Friends and frequently come to Friends meetings—especially when the Lord sends His servants [in the ministry] to visit us. We pray our gracious and merciful God that we may walk worthy of his Love and that the Lord may continue his tender regard to us in sending His servants filled with His power and wisdom. The government is kind to Friends and we enjoy our liberty." [1]

These " servants of God filled with power and wisdom " did continue to come, as the writers of this Epistle prayed, and there is an amazing list of such itinerant ministers on the records of the various meetings. In fact the one weakness which comes out clearly in this Epistle is the indication of the poverty of the native ministry and the dependence for ministry on visitors from abroad. There was no effort whatever made to develop ministry within

BEDFORD MEETING, "allowed" in 1777 by PURCHASE MONTHLY MEETING "for Friends who live remote from Amawalk."

There were also "house" meetings "allowed" at the following places : An "allowed meeting" at Hempstead every five weeks beginning in 1765 ; at Huntington, allowed by WESTBURY MONTHLY MEETING in 1732 ; at Rockaway allowed by WESTBURY MONTHLY MEETING in 1739 : at Setauket allowed by WESTBURY MONTHLY MEETING in 1762.

3/3/1744.—"The Monthly Meeting of the Oblong desired the approbation of this Meeting in settling *a Visitation Meeting* at Salisbury to be kept at Joshua White's twice in a year, one on the 3d day of the week before ye Monthly Meeting at ye Nine Partners in the 3d month, and the other on the 3d day of the week before said Monthly Meeting in the 7th month, which this Meeting having had under consideration doth approve of." (Minutes of Purchase Quarterly Meeting.)

[1] Yearly Meeting Records for 1701.

the body. It was looked upon as something wholly in the inscrutable will of God, who conferred or withheld His *gifts* as He would. This ignoring of the human element was one of the most costly blunders which Friends made, not only in New York but everywhere else, and there is no question that the sporadic character of the ministry was a forbidding aspect to most persons outside the membership. An attempt was made in a feeble way in 1704 to meet this condition of weakness.

It was decided by action of the Westbury Quarterly Meeting, November 25, 1704, that a meeting should be held every three months for "all who minister in public speaking in meetings for worship" and that "faithful Friends out of each meeting be joined with them." This came to be called "the meeting for ministering Friends," and was primarily designed for the "encouragement" of the development of gifts. If some plan had here been matured for the cultivation and development of "spiritual gifts" the story of Quakerism would have been very different. But the policy of timidity prevailed, and the meeting of ministers gradually and somewhat unconsciously became the guardian of "soundness" and the defender of ancient standards, rather than the nursery of vital ministry. It was composed naturally of those who were far past middle life, who had travelled away from the enthusiasm and creative power of youth, and who could not think or act in fresh and constructive ways. The result was that "the meeting of ministering Friends" became a solid force for the *status quo*, and did little or nothing for a genuine development of fresh and vital ministry. Such ministry did arise *occasionally* out of the meetings themselves, as we shall see, and sometimes a powerful *voice* appeared, but the development of a "gift" was not because of the preparation made for its development, but rather notwithstanding the obstacles which existed.[1] There were, it is true, special meetings held for

---

[1] I find considerable evidence that "the meeting of ministering Friends" was occupied largely with checking rather than encouraging. There are many minutes like the following :

"At a Meeting of Ministering ffriends at ye house of Samuel Bowne in

"youth," but they were "youth's meetings" only in name, for all the members attended them, and the point of difference between them and ordinary meetings seems to have been that the youth were urged to " be faithful."

Gifts did, however, appear and develop in spite of the neglect of methods to cultivate them. In 1745 a boy was born at Cow Neck on Long Island and named David Sands. He educated himself, studying often by firelight, and grew up a diligent, eager-minded, spiritually-inclined youth. As he was entering early manhood he attended a Friends' Meeting at which Samuel Nottingham, an English minister, spoke, and the message reached his spirit and powerfully impressed him. He became an attender of the Quaker Meetings on the Island and later in New York City, and found in them what his spirit was seriously seeking—a religion which seemed to him real. He soon moved to the country and joined in membership in the meeting at Nine Partners, where he often broke the silence with simple messages. His words were felt by the little group of Friends with whom he belonged to be full of life, and little by little, as he obeyed his Light, his power to interpret the spiritual meaning of life enlarged. By the time he had reached his thirtieth year he was recorded a minister, and almost immediately began his remarkable travels through New England, expanding the sphere of Quakerism wherever he went. Later he travelled extensively in Great Britain and on the

---

fflushing 28th 9 mo. 1712, ffriends at this meeting, having wayed ye inconvenience of some coming amonge us from other parts without certificates and appearing in publick to preach, hath appointed John Rider and Robert Heald out of fflushing Meeting, and William Willis and Henry Cock out of Westbury Monthly Meeting, to inquire of all such for a certificate as they shall think need may Require."

" At a meeting of Ministering ffriends held at ye house of ye Widdow Willis'es at Jereco, Robert Heald Declared at this meeting that he was sorry and Troubled for his accompanying his sister Charety Willet in going home with her to her new Dwelling She being married the day before out of ye unity of ffriends ; ye said Robert declaring his sense of it was not well, with wch ye Meeting was satisfied."

" ffrom our Meeting of Ministering ffriends and Elders ye 25th of ye 3 mo. 1728 at the Meeting house in fflushing, this Meeting having considered this complaint that hath been made from Westchester County of Richard Rogers appearing in publick preaching in their said Publick Meetings to their Grief. This Meeting hath advised him by this present Instrument to forbear for the time to com so to appeare in Publick until ffriends have unity."

Continent of Europe, speaking under diverse and often difficult circumstances with much penetration and insight, and exhibiting a very simple and genuine life of real religious experience. The few glimpses that are given in his *Memoirs* of his interpretation of inward religion show that he had a sure grasp of the seed-principle of the founders of Quakerism. He says that though we live far separated in time from the miracles of the apostolic period, we lack in no sense a convincing evidence of the divine character of Christianity, since there is an internal testimony to the Gospel of Christ in the heart of every one that receives it—the Spirit of God witnesseth with our Spirits, the changed heart becomes the house of God, revelation proves to be a present and continuous fact, and the soul has its own altar within.[1]

This case of the normal and effective spiritual development of David Sands is by no means an isolated case ; such instances of the blowing of the Spirit as it listed are fairly frequent, but the fact remains that David Sands himself was, throughout his life, hampered by the way in which his human development was neglected, and by the lack of adequate method for the cultivation of what in his case was a very remarkable gift.

If the Friends did not always handle their internal affairs with what seems to us at this far date to have been "wisdom," they had, at any rate, a sure insight when they attacked moral issues. The most massive moral problem, here, as in the other colonies, was slavery, and as soon as the evils of the system impressed the consciousness of Friends they grappled manfully with the issue—first clearing their own skirts and then endeavouring to cleanse the country itself. The awakening to a *consciousness* of the evil did not come until after the middle of the eighteenth century.[2] The "awakening" was almost certainly due to the visit of John Woolman— a "beloved disciple" of liberty whose conscience was as

---

[1] *Memoirs of David Sands (1745-1818)*, London, 1848.
[2] The Half Year's Meeting on Long Island, 14th October 1684, appointed John Bowne and Wm. Richardson to raise money "on cheap terms" to supply to John Adams "part payment for a Negro man that he hath lately bought."

sensitive to social evils as mercury is to temperature. He travelled among the Friends of New York Colony in 1760, and there came a powerful moral uprising against the evil of slave-holding almost directly after that date. The sentiment was at least well developed by the middle of that decade. Flushing Monthly Meeting dealt in 1765 with Samuel Underhill for the "misconduct of being concerned in importing negroes." He made the following apology which was accepted :

"Whereas I have sometime past *contrary to Friends Principles* been concerned in the importation of Negroes from Africa, which has caused some uneasiness in my mind, I think I can now say I am sorry I ever had any concern in that Trade, and hope for the future I shall conduct myself more agreeable to Friends principles in any such matters ; I am your friend, etc.— SAML. UNDERHILL."

A similar apology came from a Friend in New York City two years later, the record of which is as follows :

"At a Monthly Meeting held at Flushing the 7th of ye 5th mo. 1767. A few lines was read in this Meeting from Thomas Burling, son of James Burling deceased, acknowledging he had taken a Negro boy in the West Indies for a bad debt and therein did condemn the practice of trading in negroes and was sorry for the breach of unity made thereby which this Meeting accepts." [1]

The country Friends were travelling rather faster than the Friends who were living in the environment of the city, and the next step in advance was taken by the meetings in Dutchess county. Friends were, by this time, pretty generally agreed that it was wrong to buy or import slaves, but in 1767 Oblong Monthly Meeting raised the question whether it was "consistent with a Christian spirit" to hold a person in slavery at all. This question impressed the members *as being in the life*, and it was carried up to the Quarterly Meeting for maturer judgment. It was thoroughly, or, as Friends say, "weightily" considered at Purchase Quarterly Meeting,

[1] Both these incidents are taken from the Records of Flushing Monthly Meeting.

held in the Oblong, May 2, 1767, and this Minute was adopted :

"In this meeting the practice of trading in Negroes, or other slaves, and its inconsistancy with our religious principles was revived, and the inconsiderable difference between buying slaves or keeping them in slavery we are already possessed of, was briefly hinted at in a short Query from one of our Monthly Meetings, which is recommended to the consideration of Quarterly Meeting, viz. *If it is not consistant with Christianity to buy and sell our fellow-men for Slaves during their lives, and their posterity after them, whether it is consistant with a Christian Spirit to keep these in Slavery that we have already in possession, by purchase, gift, or other ways.*"

This " Query " from the Quarterly Meeting came up for consideration in the Yearly Meeting, May 30th of the same year, and was " left for consideration on the minds of Friends until next Yearly Meeting." At the next Yearly Meeting (May 28, 1768) a committee, consisting of John Burling, Thomas Seaman, John Cock, Isaac Doty, Matthew Franklin, Thomas Franklin, Samuel Bowne, Jr., Thomas Dobson, and Daniel Bowne, was appointed to formulate an answer. These men were not yet quite ready for the speed at which the country Friends were travelling, and they produced a conservative, but at the same time a very clear-sighted, report, which was adopted. It was as follows :

"We are of the mind that it is not convenient (considering the circumstances amongst us) to give an answer to this Querie, at least at this time, as the answering of it in direct terms manifestly tends to cause divisions, and may introduce heart-burnings and strife amongst us which ought to be avoided, and charity exercised, and persuasive methods persued, and that which makes for peace. We are, however, fully of the mind that Negroes as rational creatures are by Nature born free ; and when the way opens liberty ought to be extended to them ; and they not held in bondage for self ends. But to turn them out at large indiscriminately (which seems to be the tendency of the Querie) will, we apprehend, be attended with great inconveniency as some are too young and some too old to procure a livelihood." [1]

---

[1] Minutes of New York Yearly Meeting for 1768.

It was the unvarying custom of Friends in the colonial days not to take any new step which could not be taken *in unity*. That involved fairly slow progress, but it also meant that the corporate body was behind a movement when it was positively launched. In 1771 the Yearly Meeting decided that Friends who owned slaves should not sell them as property, except with the consent of their Monthly Meetings, and a solid committee was appointed to visit all persons in the Society who held slaves, to see if the freedom of these slaves could be secured. This method of investigation was speedily adopted by the subordinate meetings as well, so that by 1776 all the monthly meetings in the colony were investigating the individual cases of slave-holding, and were labouring to eliminate it absolutely. It was decided further at the Yearly Meeting that year (1776) that meetings should not receive services nor accept financial contributions from any Friends holding slaves, and from that time on the Monthly Meetings adopted the practice of disowning from membership those belated Friends who had not yet got their consciences awake to the evil of *owning* persons.

From the outbreak of the Revolution Friends began to concentrate their efforts to secure better conditions for those who had been slaves, and to work first for the limitation and then for the abolition of the slave trade in the country at large. The part which Friends took in the great struggle for emancipation does not concern us here, but it is a fact of historical importance that when the separation of the colonies from the mother country was finally accomplished, Friends themselves were free and clear of slave-holding.[1]

[1] The Meeting for Sufferings of New York sent this following Petition to the Governor, Senate, and Assembly of the State in 1784 :

" The Petition of the Meeting for Sufferings representing the People called Quakers of the same State :

" Respectfully sheweth

" That our minds being impressed with an ardent concern for the general good of our fellow-creatures, and that all may enjoy their natural and unalienable rights without distinction, we believe it to be our duty to address you on behalf of the poor Negroes, who have long been a people under great oppression, many of them originally torn from the land of their nativity ; and brought into this and

Here as everywhere else in the American colonies the
Revolutionary War brought Friends face to face with
issues which profoundly tested their principles of peace
and which necessarily somewhat *sifted* the Society.
The Meeting for Sufferings in this Province was established
in 1758 and this Meeting dealt with many difficult
questions, rising out of the war.   The tendency of the
Society in New York seems to have been one of sympathy
with the old order of things, though every possible effort
was made to keep the meetings from being implicated on
either side.   In 1775 the Committee of Safety for the
Colony of New York requested a complete list of male
Quakers between sixteen and sixty.   Friends "felt
uneasy" to make the list, and the Meeting for Sufferings
refused the request.   The Minute reads :

"We are of the mind that we cannot comply, consistent with
our religious principles.   We hope you will not consider such
refusal as the effect of an obstinate disposition, but as it really
is a truly conscientious scruple."

" In the trying situation of outward affairs," when all
occupations were interrupted, the Meeting for Sufferings
recommended that a "stock for relief" be raised and set
apart for helping Friends who were in distress and straits.
In '76 a requisition was made by the military officers of
the colonial forces that Friends should give a bond of
security to endeavour to keep their cattle from falling into

other parts of America, and sold into slavery.   Numbers of whom, with many of
their offspring, are yet continued in a state of bondage.   And as there is a Law
subsisting which operates to the discouragement of many of the conscientious
and well-disposed inhabitants of this state, against liberating their slaves, and no
Legislative provision yet made for those who have been set at liberty from
Religious motives.   We therefore with submission intreat that ye may afford
them such relief as you in wisdom may see meet, believing the entire abolition
of Slavery a matter worthy of the most serious attenticn of the Legislative Body.
And tho' we think it needless to use arguments to gain the assents of your minds
to this great truth that all mankind without distinction have equally a natural
right to freedom, yet we would take the liberty in this case to call your attention
as fellow believers in Christ, to that excellent rule laid down by him, ' that whatsoever ye would that men should do unto you do ye even so unto them.'
" With due respect we subscribe ourselves
"Your real friends
" Signed by order, and on behalf of said Meeting held in New York 14th 12th
mo. 1784,

"EDMD. PRIOR, clerk."

the hands of the English troops. The advice of the Meeting for Sufferings was "that Friends do not comply with this requisition."

In 1777 Governor Tryon informed the Meeting for Sufferings that some Quakers had incurred the displeasure of the authorities by being "too busy and active in the present commotions," and to offset this activity he proposed that the Society of Friends should raise a sum of money to provide the troops with stockings and other necessities. The answer of the Meeting is calm and dignified but very positive. It is as follows :

"We may inform the Governor that it is with sorrow we may acknowledge the deviation that hath appeared in some under our name, notwithstanding a care which hath been extended in our collective capacity to caution and advise our Members in these respects. But apprehending that the proposed contribution is manifestly contrary to our religious Testimony against war & fightings which as a Religious body we have uniformly maintained ever since we were first distinguished as such. We are therefore under a necessity of declining a compliance therewith, Very sincerely acknowledging our obligation to the Governor for his friendly disposition heretofore manifested toward us we can at the same time assure him that our motives in thus declining his proposal are purely conscientious."

In 1781 certain Friends were appointed by the Yearly Meeting to visit the meetings on Long Island, and were "stopped by military men," at the order of General Washington. A committee was appointed thereupon to visit General Washington in person and explain to him the peaceful nature of the "concern," but he still refused to let them pass. During the hard closing months of the New York campaign, Friends once more issued a document to the membership, "affectionately recommending the members of the Society that they be careful to cherish in themselves and in one another their tender scruples against contributing to or in any wise giving countenance to the spirit of war, and that they preserve a conduct uniformly consistent with our peaceable principles and profession."

When the war was over and the new order established, Friends loyally accepted it, but they were themselves deeply affected by the fires through which they had passed. Those who had believed that it was right to fight in a great emergency had been sifted out of the Society, and those who were left were furnace-tested peace men and pledged henceforth to maintain " consistency to the profession." The Revolution was an epoch period for the Society not only in issues of peace and war, but for the reformation of ideas in all matters of vital policy. The purging of slavery was, no doubt, the beginning of the new moral awakening among Friends. The hard crisis and the stern siftings of the Revolution further touched the moral quick, and from this epoch the leaders of the Society were consecrated with a new zeal to the business of preparing a people of the Lord. The Revolution was followed by a decided expansion of the territory of Quakerism in the state of New York, and by a revival of education within the Society. During the 'eighties there arose a demand for schools from every section, and from this time dates the birth of the Quaker ideal for a carefully educated membership. All local meetings were recommended " to use their exertions in endeavouring to promote schools for the education of the rising generation." The definite plan for a school in New York City was formulated in 1781, and was sent to London in the hope of securing from England a Friend competent to teach the proposed school. The plan is an interesting revelation of educational conditions at that time. It is as follows :

" Our Yearly Meeting for this Province held at Westbury on Long Island taking into consideration the expediency of our Youth being properly instructed in the use of learning under the tuition of a sober discreet Friend recommended the same through the Quarter to the Monthly Meeting. And we being impressed with a like concern, well knowing the importance of a suitable Education to Society as well as to individuals, take the liberty to request the aid & assistance of your Meeting to furnish us as soon as may be convenient with a young man, unmarried, a member of our Society, of exemplary life and conversation, a very good writer, well versed in Arithmetic, and a competent Knowledge of English Grammar. To such a one this Meeting will engage to give annually the sum of £200 currency or £112, 10s. od. sterling, and we will allow him £42 sterling for his passage to this city where he will reside. A school house will be found him at our expense, but his board and all other expenses he must meet himself. We apprehend the board may at present cost him about £100 currency or £58, 5s. od. sterling not more. The number of scholars probably about forty. We would not wish to debar him from keeping an evening school which if he inclines to, the money from thence arising will be a perquesite to himself. But the money arising from the scholars taught in the day time will go toward defraying the above expenses." [1]

Great things not only for Friends but for the education of New York City sprang from these feeble beginnings, for the school thus organised became in time the first public school in New York City, and is now the Friends' Seminary in that City. The period just beyond the Revolution was one of worldly prosperity for Friends, and they were to the front in commercial undertakings in the growing metropolis, but they did not win their success by compromise. At the close of our period there were probably about a thousand Friends in the City,[2] and they were an eminently respectable group of people, with strict requirements of moral behaviour and with lofty ideals of spiritual religion.

[1] From the Minutes of New York Monthly Meeting 7/11/1781. In 1787, the teacher had every alternate seventh day off, but had to furnish the ink and firewood!

[2] There were by actual count 1826 Friends in New York City in 1830.

BOOK III

THE QUAKERS IN THE SOUTHERN COLONIES

CHAPTER I

THE PLANTING OF QUAKERISM IN THE SOUTHERN COLONIES

IN New England the Quaker societies were formed mainly out of persons who were already profoundly religious, but dissatisfied with the rigid theology which prevailed about them ; and the persecution which rained like fire on the apostles and adherents of the inward light came from the men who were consecrated to the task of building in the New World a Puritan City of God, with the Bible for its Magna Charta. In New . York the nucleus of each Quaker group was, as it had been in New England, a company of persons already in revolt from the religious system about them, but earnestly seeking real Bread for their souls. The persecution, here, too, fierce indeed, but not motived to the same extent as in Massachusetts by the conviction that utter extirpation of the heresy was the only hope for the colony, came from the Dutch magistrates and was administered in the interests of civil order rather than for the protection of an established church. In the southern colonies, to a very much greater extent than in the North, Quakerism, especially in the Carolinas, drew its material from the unchurched classes and gathered in persons of no definite religious affiliation. The persecution which was meted out in these colonies was, with a few exceptions in Virginia, comparatively mild and was inflicted in the interests of the established [English] Church.

The first attempt to propagate the Quaker message in the southern colonies, so far as our records and Journals furnish information, was made by Elizabeth Harris of London, who came out on this hazardous mission in 1656, about simultaneously with the arrival of Mary Fisher and Ann Austin in Boston.[1] It has generally been supposed that her religious labours were in Virginia, and that the first persons won to Quakerism in the South were residents of this colony, but it seems practically certain, from the evidence at hand, that Elizabeth Harris' " convincements," at least those of which we have definite information, were made in the colony of Maryland, though she may have performed some labour of which we have no accounts in Virginia as well.

Gerard Roberts, writing to George Fox in July 1657, says :

> " The Friend who went to Virginia [evidently Elizabeth Harris] is returned in a pretty condition. There she was gladly received by many who met together, and the Governor is convinced." [2]

The person here called " the Governor who is convinced " is perhaps Robert Clarkson. Thomas Hart of London, referring to Robert Clarkson in a letter to Thomas Willan and George Taylor in 1658, says, " I suppose this man is the governor of that place," *i.e.* the place visited by E. Harris.[3] Now Robert Clarkson was beyond any question a citizen of Maryland. He was never " governor " of the colony, but he was a member of the General Assembly, or House of Burgesses, from Ann Arundel County,[4] and the correspondents have probably used the word " governor " in a loose and untechnical

---

[1] There occurs an interesting reference to Elizabeth Harris in John Stubbs' letter to George Fox in connection with the Battledore : " Here is [in London] Elizabeth Harris who sometimes goes forth to steeple-houses in sackcloth and she hath much peace in this service ; there was some seemed rather to be against it, which troubled her a little. She spoke to me with many tears about it several weeks ago, and I said I thought I might write to thee about it, and she desired I might. After she had been at Cambridge, it came to her she must go to Manchester the sixth month. And so she would be glad to have a line or two from thee about it before she go, as soon as can be, the time draws near of her passing."—Crosfield MSS. (1660) Devonshire House.

[2] Swarthmore Collection, iii. 127.

[3] Swarthmore Collection, iv. 197.

[4] *Archives of Maryland*, i. 382.

sense. They have also been vague and hazy in their colonial geography, and have probably used the word "Virginia" for this general section of the great, more or less unknown, New World.

The most concrete information which we possess about the success of Elizabeth Harris' labours and the locality reached by her is a Letter written by this "convinced governor," Robert Clarkson. His letter is written from Severn under date of January 14, 1658 [Old Style, Eleventh Mo. 1657], and reads as follows :

"Elizabeth Harris, Dear Heart, I salute thee in the tender love of the Father, which moved thee toward us and I do own thee to have been a minister by the will of God to bear the outward testimony to the inward word of truth in me and others. Of which word of life God hath made my wife a partaker with me and hath established our hearts in His fear, and likewise Ann Dorsey in a more large measure; her husband I hope abides faithful; likewise John Baldwin and Henry Caplin; Charles Balye abides convinced and several in those parts where he dwells.[1] Elizabeth Beasley abides as she was when thou was here [apparently "convinced"]. Thomas Cole and William Cole have both made open confession of the truth; likewise Henry Woolchurch, and many others suffer with us the reproachful name [of Quaker]. William Fuller abides convinced. I know not but William Durand doth the like.[2] Nicholas Wayte abides convinced. Glory be to God who is the living fountain and fills all that abide in Him.

"The two messengers thou spoke of in thy letters have not yet come to this place; we heard of two come to Virginia in the fore part of the winter,[3] but we heard that they were soon put in prison, and not suffered to pass. We heard further that they desired liberty to pass to this place, but it was denied them, whereupon one of them answered, that though they might not be suffered, yet he must come another time. We have heard that they are to be kept in prison till the ship that brought them be ready to depart the country again, and then to be sent out of

---

[1] The Charles Bayly mentioned here helped John Perrot in 1661 to secure release from his confinement in Rome and became one of his extreme followers in the schism which is discussed farther on in this chapter.

[2] William Durand was one of Cromwell's Commissioners for the government of Maryland and was Secretary of the Commission. He may possibly have been the person referred to as "governor."

[3] Probably Thomas Thurston and Josiah Coale.

the country. We have disposed of the most part of the books which were sent, so that all parts where there are Friends are furnished and every one that desires it may have benefit of them ; at Herring Creek, Rhoad River, South River, all about Severn, the Brand Neck, and thereabouts the Seven Mountains and Kent. . . . With my dear love I salute thy husband and the rest of Friends ; and rest with thee *in the Eternal Word which abideth forever.* Farewell, ROBERT CLARKSON." [1]

It is evident that the writer of this letter was not in Virginia. He has heard of the arrival of two Friends in Virginia, but he says, " they have not come to this place," and he adds that " they desired liberty from their prison in Virginia to pass to this place." Robert Clarkson was, as has been shown above, an inhabitant of the colony of Maryland. In 1662 he was arrested and brought before the court of Ann Arundel County for having violated the military act of that colony and was fined five hundred pounds of cask-tobacco.[2] He had thus at that date plainly become a Quaker. William Durand was also a citizen of Maryland. Thomas and William Cole and Henry Woolchurch, mentioned in the above letter, were also Maryland Friends. Severn is a well-known Maryland region, and all the places named where the books were distributed are familiar localities not far remote from the present city of Annapolis. Therefore, in spite of the fact that Bowden and Janney [3] and most other writers on Quaker history have located Elizabeth Harris' " convincements " in Virginia, between the Rappahannock and York Rivers, I am forced to the conclusion that we are here dealing with the origin of Quakerism in the colony of Maryland.[4]

Sometime in 1657, Josiah Coale, of Bristol, and Thomas Thurston, a Quaker preacher, from Gloucestershire, England, already known to us for their labours in the Northern Colonies, landed in Virginia, having come, as one of them

---

[1] The original, which I have somewhat shortened, is in Swarthmore Collection iii. 7.

[2] Besse, ii. 381.

[3] Janney's *History of the Friends*, (1860) i. 431.

[4] For a similar view see M'Illwaine's *The Struggle of Protestant Dissenters for Religious Toleration in Virginia* (Johns Hopkins Studies, vol. xii.), p. 20.

writes, because they "were made sensible of the groaning of the oppressed seed in that place."[1] So far as we know they were the first to plant the Quaker "seed" in this great southern colony. They seem to have spent six months or more in Virginia—some of this period perhaps being *wasted* in prison[2]—and they were evidently very successful in reaching the people, since there are many evidences from this time forward of the widespread prevalence of Quakers in several parts of the colony.

We have seen already that the incipient movement was somewhat interrupted by the arrest and imprisonment of the visitors. We must now examine briefly the methods which were contrived in Virginia for suppressing the tide of new religious thought which was sweeping—as it proved, irresistibly—into this Episcopalian colony. As little as in Massachusetts had there formed in the minds of the Virginia colonists any adequate idea that religious toleration was a virtue. The early laws of Virginia insist with much iteration on *uniformity*. The earliest danger to uniformity in the colony came from the immigration of adventurous Roman Catholics, and the first anti-toleration laws were therefore framed against these. In 1642 it was decreed that "no popish recusants shall at any time hereafter exercise the place or places of secret counsellors, register or comiss : surveyors, sheriffs, or any other publique place, but be utterly *disabled*."[3] The Act further provides that any one holding office and refusing to take "the oath of allegiance and supremacy" shall be dismissed from said office, and fined 1000 pounds of tobacco. The following year it was enacted that "all ministers whatsoever which shall reside in the collony are to be *conformable to the orders and constitutions* of the Church of England, and not otherwise to be permitted to teach or preach publickly or privately. And the Governor and Counsil do take care that all nonconformists, upon notice of them, *shall be compelled to depart* the collony with all convenience."[4]

---

[1] Letter oı Josiah Coale to Margaret Fell.—Bowden, i. 342.
[2] We learn this fact from Robert Clarkson's letter.
[3] Hening's *Statutes at Large of Virginia*, i. 268-269.
[4] Hening, i. 277.

When the Quakers first disturbed the religious uniformity of the colony these laws—grown innocuous with time—were revived and set into operation to meet the novel situation, but they were soon found to be inadequate for the trouble in hand, and the lawmakers grappled anew with the emergency.[1] In the spring of 1660 a definite Act was passed against Quakers as such, and the wording of the Act implies that the objection to Quakers was not primarily based on doctrine, but on the supposition that they were a menace to the stability of social life and civil government. The Act is entitled " An Act for Suppressing Quakers," and reads :

"Whereas there is an unreasonable and turbulent sort of people, commonly called Quakers, who, contrary to the law, do dayly gather together unto them unlawfull Assemblies and congregations of people teaching and publishing lies, *miracles*, false *visions*, *prophecies*, and doctrines, which have influence upon the communities of men, both ecclesiastical and civill, endeavoring and attempting thereby to destroy religion, lawes, communities, and all bonds of civil socitie, leaving it arbitrarie to every vaine and vitious person whether men shall be safe, laws established, offenders punished, and Governors rule, hereby disturbing the publique peace and just interest : to prevent and restraine which mischiefe : *it is enacted* that no master or commander of any shippe or other vessel do bring into this collonie any person or persons called Quakers, under penalty of £100 to be levied upon him and his estate, etc. That all Quakers as have beene questioned or shall hereafter arrive shall be apprehended wheresoever they shall be found, and they be imprisoned without baile or mainprize till they do adjure this country or put in security with all speed to depart the collonie and not to return again. And if any should dare to presume to returne hither after such departure to be proceeded against as contemner of the lawes and magistracy and punished accordingly, and caused again to depart the country. And if they should the third time be so audacious and impudent as to returne hither to be proceeded against as ffelons. That noe person shall entertain any of the Quakers, . . . nor permit in or near his house any Assemblies of Quakers in the like penalty of £100.

---

[1] It should, however, be stated that this earliest attempt to frustrate the work of Quaker missionaries was in the Commonwealth period, when the Puritan influence was strongest.

"And that no person do presume on their peril to dispose or publish their books, pamphlets, or libells, bearing the title of their tenets and opinions." [1]

In 1662, under an Act to prevent the profaning of Sunday, new measures were levelled against them. The Act provides that:

"Quakers who, out of nonconformity to the Church, totally absent themselves, are liable to a fine of £20 for every month's absence from Church. And all Quakers, for assembling in unlawful assemblies and conventicles, shall be fined and pay, each of them, there taken, 200 pounds of tobacco for each time." [2]

In the same year it was decreed that as there are in the colony "many persons who, out of aversenesse to the orthodox established religion, or out of new fangled conceits of their owne heretical inventions, refuse to have their children baptized," they shall be fined 2000 pounds of tobacco for every refusal—half to go to the informer. [3]

These laws, however, though they were vigorously applied, proved utterly ineffectual. Quaker ministers continued to come as though they were wanted, and the people were "convinced" as though it were the popular course. The fact of the increase of Quakerism is proved not from partisan Journals, but from Colonial Records. In March 1662 it is declared that "persons called Quakers do assemble themselves *in greate numbers* in several parts of this colony," and they are charged with "maintayning a secret and strict correspondency among themselves," and of holding "dangerous opinions and tenets." It is thereupon enacted, evidently in imitation of the English Conventicle Act, that for separating from the Established worship, and for assembling to the number of five or more in religious worship not authorised by the laws of Virginia, a fine of 200 pounds of tobacco shall be imposed on each person, with banishment from the colony for the third offence. A fine of 5000 pounds of tobacco was imposed

---

[1] Hening, i. 532-533. [2] Hening, ii. 48.
[3] Hening, ii. 165. This statute implies that there were Anabaptists in the colony as well as Quakers, for the latter not only objected to the baptism of infants, but of adults as well.

"for entertaining Quakers to teach or preach in their houses." All fines were to be remitted if the Quaker would give security that he would "forbeare to meete" in such assemblies in the future.[1]

The most objectionable feature of this anti-Quaker legislation was the provision that a proportion of the fine —in some cases a half of it—should go to the informer, and this mean incentive was offered to induce neighbours to spy on each other, and to report violations of uniformity. The colonial records show that there was considerable suffering under these laws, and Besse has preserved the story of one case of brutal persecution, namely, the imprisonment at Jamestown of George Wilson of England, and his companion, William Cole of Maryland. They were thrown into an intolerable dungeon—"a nasty, stinking prison" where Wilson "laid down his life"—and the story of the sufferings in this prison is so dreadful that it is hardly printable in detail, but the spirit of love and forgiveness and the triumphant note which breathe through their communications are most impressive. "For all their cruelty," writes Wilson, "I can truly say, 'Father, forgive them, they know not what they do,'"[2] and the biographer of William Cole says : "Through his ministry many were established in the truth, and though he was much decayed in his body by his cruel imprisonment, and never recovered from it, he felt the living presence of the Lord with him."[3]

This persecution was imposed and these anti-Quaker laws passed in spite of royal instructions in favour of religious liberty. Charles II. wrote to Governor Berkeley in 1662 :

"Because wee are willing to give all possible encouragement to persons of different persuasion in matters of Religion to transport themselves thither with their stocks ; *you are not to suffer any man to be molested or disquieted in the exercise of his Religion*, so he be content with a quiet and peaceable enjoying it, not giving therein offense or scandall to the Government."[4]

---

[1] Hening, ii. 181-183.
[2] Besse, ii. 381 ; Bishop, p. 351.
[3] *Piety Promoted*, i. 80-81.
[4] Neill's *Virginia Carolorum*, p. 392.

"But notwithstanding enactments against the Quakers," writes Neill, "their travelling preachers persisted in going to out of the way places, without money and asking for none, yet preaching a gospel of peace and good will, as far as they understood the teaching of Christ. Their cheerful endurance of hardship, with their plain teaching, attracted the attention and aroused the consciences of rude frontiersmen, who, hitherto, had no one to care for their souls, and Quaker meetings multiplied." [1]

The first Quaker missionaries in Virginia were, as we have seen, Josiah Coale and Thomas Thurston. They travelled northward, labouring as they went, especially in Maryland, and so on, by an almost unimaginable wilderness journey, to New England, where they took their share of the vials of the Puritan medicine for Quakers. Thurston, however, was soon back in Virginia, where he had another period of imprisonment. On his release he appears to have carried many colonists into the Quaker movement, for Josiah Coale, writing from New England to Margaret Fell, tells her that Thomas Thurston is in Virginia, and says: "The living power of the Lord goes along with him, and there is like to be a great gathering." [2]

Three of the *Woodhouse* voyagers, William Robinson, Christopher Holder, and Robert Hodgson, did missionary work in Virginia in 1658—probably Humphrey Norton was there in 1659—and as happened wherever these enthusiastic souls went, there were marked results of their preaching and personal labour. William Robinson says in an extant Letter: "There are many people convinced, and some in several parts are brought into the sense and feeling of truth." [3] Josiah Coale was back in the colony in 1660, and wrote of his visit to George Fox in these encouraging words: "I left Friends in Virginia generally very well and *fresh in the truth*. I believe I shall be in Virginia again." [4]

George Rofe, an English Quaker who had a long list of imprisonments behind him, contributed in 1661 to the

---

[1] Neill's *Virginia Carolorum*, p. 296.
[2] Letter in Bowden, i. 343.
[3] Letter of William Robinson, 1659, quoted by Bowden, i. 346
[4] Coale's Letter in *A.R.B. Collection*, No. 44.

spread of Quakerism in Virginia. Our only account of his visit is in a letter of his to Stephen Crisp :

" God hath prospered my soul according to my desire and hath blessed His work in my hands ; and hath made me an instrument of good to many through these countries. . . . The truth prevaileth through the most of all these parts [Barbadoes], and many settled meetings there are in Maryland and Virginia and New England . . . through all which places I have travelled in the power of the Spirit and in the great dominion of the truth, having a great and weighty service for the Lord." [1]

There was a large convincement to Quakerism in Lower Norfolk County, and the County records show that the Friends of this region had much to suffer. Under date of June 27, 1663, Governor Berkeley appointed a commission to see that " the abominate seede of ye Quakers spread not," and he urges the gentlemen named on the commission to have " an exact care of this pestilent sect of ye Quakers." [2]

But already before this urging came from the Governor the desire for a share of the fines was pushing the sheriffs to activity. There are many entries like the following :

" June 10, 1661. Whereas Mr. John Hill, high-sheriff, hath given information and presented Benjamin Forby for admitting and suffering Quakers at his house being contrary to ye lawes of this country, ye said Forby is taken into custody to be tried for breaking the lawes against such people." [3]

" December 20, 1662. The High Shreive of the County did take divers persons who were at an unlawful meetinge with those commonly called Quakers—They were fined 200 pounds of tobacco each person, of whom there were twenty." [4]

" May 3, 1663. Twelve persons were arrested at the house of Richard Russell, and Russell was fined £100 for entertaining and permitting the meeting, half of which went to the informer, William Hill, ' High Shreive.' The 12th of November, twenty-two ' persons called Quakers ' were arrested at Richard Russell's house where John Porter, junior, was ' speaking.' The preachers

---

[1] *Crisp Collection* of MSS. No. 102. There were many other labourers in this field of whose work we possess few or no details. Mention should be made of Elizabeth Hooton, Joan Brocksoppe, Joseph Nicholson, John Liddal, and Jane Millard.

[2] *Lower Norfolk County Antiquary*, iii. 78.

[3] *Ibid.* iii. 105. [4] *Ibid.* iii. p. 141.

were fined 500 pounds of tobacco, the 'entertainer' of the meeting 5000 pounds, and each attender 200 pounds." [1]

"November 20, 1663. Nine 'people commonly called Quakers were seized for holding an unlawful assembly aboard ye Shipp *Blissinge*, riding at anchor in the southern branch of the Elizabeth River.' John Porter, junior, was speaking. They were all fined 200 pounds of tobacco." [2]

Some of the prominent Friends of this Elizabeth River region had been the actors in a strange lawsuit a few years before they became Friends. In 1659 Ann Godby —a person often arrested in the 'sixties as a Quaker—was charged with " casting slander and scandall on the good name and creditt of Nicholas Robinson's wife, terming her a witch." Ann was proved guilty of the charge, and her husband was fined 300 pounds of tobacco for the freedom of his wife's tongue. John Porter, junior, was one of the Justices in the suit. Three years later Ann Godby was a staunch Quaker, and John Porter, junior, was the foremost Quaker " minister" in the county. Whether Nicholas Robinson's wife came into the new Society or not I cannot prove, though I find that many Robinson women did. [3]

It seems impossible, in this world of conflicting views, to have any movement for the illumination and spiritual enlargement of men which is not more or less blocked and hampered by the blunders, the littleness, and the selfishness of persons who are one-sided, and who push some one aspect of the " truth" out of balance until it turns out to be misleading " error." Every apostolic undertaking is more or less marred by some misguided Hymenaeus or Philetus "whose *word* eats like a gangrene." [4] John Perrot, originally " a man of great natural parts," and who was inspired in 1660 with the conviction that he was divinely sent to Rome for the conversion of the Pope, became the instrument of confusion and schism in Virginia, and nearly wrecked the work so well begun in the colony. There was evidently a strain of insanity in him, but even

[1] *Lower Norfolk County Antiquary*, iii. pp. 79-110.   [2] *Ibid*. iii. p. 109.
[3] *Ibid*. iii. p. 36.   [4] 2 Tim. ii. 17.

his very unusual psychic traits only made him more captivating and influential with the simple-minded people who were impressed that he exhibited "greater spirituality" than did the other exponents of Quakerism. He pushed the testimony against form and ceremony to the absurd extreme of "nihilism"—there were to be no forms, not even the "form" of holding meetings for worship! Details of his visit in Virginia are lacking, but the correspondence and *Journals* of travelling Friends bear witness to what they call "the leaven of his unclean spirit." "He has done much hurt," write in 1663 Mary Tomkins and Alice Ambrose, two persecution-tried missionaries, who visited Virginia in 1662, "and he has made our travels hard and our labours [in Virginia] sore. What we have borne and suffered concerning him has been more and harder than all we have received from our enemies." [1]

It has been shown that the first "convincement" to Quakerism in the South was in Maryland under the ministry of Elizabeth Harris, who gathered a large group of Friends about Severn and Kent. This beginning was soon followed up by the work of Josiah Coale and Thomas Thurston, who visited many sections of this colony on their travels to New England in 1658. They appear to have found considerable response to their message, and there were many colonists who were ready to hazard everything for what powerfully appealed to them as the truth. [2]

The Records of the Governor and Council of Maryland furnish our main clues to the success of their undertaking, and to the suffering which it involved. [3] The

[1] Letter of Mary Tomkins and Alice Ambrose to George Fox (Swarthmore Collection, iv. 239) What they actually received from their "enemies"—the authorities of Virginia—was the infliction of thirty-two lashes apiece from a nine-corded whip, they being pilloried "in an uncivil manner," with seizure of all their goods and expulsion from the colony.—*New England Judged*, p. 439.

[2] They were entertained in Maryland by Richard Preston and William Berry, both of whom were prominent men in the colony. Berry's home was at Choptank, and he became a leading man and a preacher among the Friends.

[3] The Provincial Assembly of Maryland had adopted an Ordinance of Toleration in 1649. It was, however, not effective in practice. This change of attitude in the matter of toleration was largely due to the influence of the new Governor of the colony, Governor Fendall.

first entry about Quakers in the Colonial Records of Maryland is under date of July 8, 1658. It is in a minute of the proceedings of the Council, or Upper House, held at Patuxent, and it reports the " alarm " felt by " the increase of the Quakers." [1]

Under the same date (July 8, 1658) appears this entry : " Upon information that Thomas Thurston and Josiah Coale had refused to subscribe the engagement by the Articles of 24th March [involving an oath] a warrant was issued to the Sheriffs to bring them to Court." [2]

July 16, 1658 : " Upon information that Thomas Thurston was in prison and Josiah Coale was at Anne Arundel seducing the people and dissuading the people from taking the engagement [on account of the oath] ordered the Sheriff of Anne Arundel to take the body of Josiah Coale and Thomas Thurston." The warrant states that " all who are of their Church or Judgment do refuse to subscribe the engagement." [3]

July 22, 1658 : It is recorded that William Burges and Thomas Meares refused to take the oath as commissioners and justices of the peace, " pretending that it was in no case lawful to swear." [4] As they had both formerly taken the oath without any compunctions, it is evident that they had come under Quaker influence. When the case of these justices came up for action, Michael Brookes of Calvert County joined them in the refusal to swear, and the three were fined. [5] Thomas Meares appears later in the colonial records as a full-fledged Quaker. [6]

July 23, 1658 : The Council took into consideration " the insolent behaviour of some people called Quakers," who " stood covered " in presence of the Court, " refused to subscribe the engagement," and exhibited principles which " tended to the destruction of the government." They were given their choice of subscribing the engagement by the 20th of August, or to " depart the Province on paine due to rebels and traitors." [7]

[1] *Archives of Maryland*, iii. 347.   [2] *Ibid*. iii. 347.   [3] *Ibid*. iii. 348.
[4] *Ibid*. iii. 351.   [5] *Ibid*. iii. 358.   [6] *Ibid*. iii. 394.   [7] *Ibid*. iii. 352.

On his return from New England, Thomas Thurston engaged again in religious work in Maryland, and again came into collision with the authorities. Under date of July 23, 1659, this record appears :

"It is well known in this province that there have bin several vagabonds and persons known by the name of Quakers that have presumed to come into this province, as well dissuading the people from complying with the military discipline in this time of danger [there was at the time an armed contest between the 'Baltimore faction' and the 'Clayborne faction'], as also from giving testimony [under oath] or being [sworn] Jurors or bearing any office in the province."

Such persons are ordered whipped from constable to constable until they reach the bounds of the province.[1] Eleven days later (August 3, 1659), Thurston was "forever banished this province," on pain of being whipped thirty-eight lashes, and then sent out of the province. It was decreed the same date that "any person presuming to receive, harbour, or conceal the said Thomas Thurston" should be fined 500 pounds of tobacco.[2]

Besse furnishes a long list of persons—presumably persons "convinced" of Quaker principles—who suffered under the Maryland government in 1658 for refusing to fight, or to take an oath, or for entertaining Quakers. This list contains thirty names, which probably indicates the number of adult males who had become Friends in the colony in 1658.[3] The fine for entertaining a Quaker missionary was £3, 15s.

This colony was also visited, as Virginia was, by William Robinson, Christopher Holder, and Robert Hodgson in 1659, and as happened everywhere "a large convincement" resulted from their labours. Josiah Coale came through Maryland a second time, for a visit of ten weeks, in 1660, and, under the influence of the Restoration in England, he found "the spirit of persecution chained down for a season." He reports "precious meetings" and "the Lord's precious presence and love

---

[1] *Archives of Maryland*, iii. 362.   [2] *Ibid*. iii. 364.
[3] Besse, ii. 378-380.

amongst us in our assemblies."[1] The "chaining" of the spirit of persecution did not last long, for Coale was apprehended and banished soon after this letter was written, and prosecutions for refusal to swear and fight are frequent.[2] An important letter from Coale, written from Virginia, Feb. 3, 1661, says: "As concerning Friends in the Province of Maryland, I left them generally very well and fresh in the truth, though I found them not so ; for through judging one another and clashing amongst themselves they were even become as dry branches and there was little savour of life amongst them."[3]

George Rofe soon followed on after Josiah Coale, and he reports, under date of 1661, finding "many settled meetings in Maryland," and he says that he "travelled in the power of the Spirit and in great dominion of the truth, having a great and weighty service for the Lord."[4] We have too few data to enable us to present in any impressive way the actual internal life of the new society at this early stage of its career, but it is evident that Friends in this region at this period were in constant jeopardy in body and goods,[5] though there is abundant evidence that they were valiant in spirit, and ready to suffer to any limit for their loyalty to their light. It should, however, be noted that the persecution which came upon them in Maryland at this early stage of their history, was motived, not by intolerance of their religious teachings or sectarian bigotry on the part of the authorities, but by the sincere though mistaken conception that the Quakers were hostile to government, and were inculcating views that were incompatible with a

[1] MS. Letter of Josiah Coale to George Fox, 1660.—*A.R.B. Collection*, No. 53.

[2] There is a curious case of the prosecution of John Everitt who "ran from his colors when prest to goe to the Susquehanna Fort, pleading that he could not bear arms for conscience's sake." He is to be "kept in chaynes and bake his own bread" until the jury is impanelled.—*Archives of Maryland*, iii. 435.

[3] Josiah Coale to Margaret Fell, *Crosfield MSS.* in Devonshire House.

[4] *Crisp Collection of MS.* No. 102.

[5] One case, that of Peter Sharpe, a physician who owned an island in the Choptank River, will suffice. He held a note against Adam Staples for 1700 pounds of tobacco. Because Sharpe refused to take the oath of engagement, Staples petitioned the Court to annul the Note, which the Court did.—Besse, ii. 380.

well-ordered civil régime. They were *supposed* to be disrespectful to magistrates, revolutionary in design, aiming to annul courts and undermine all means of forceful defence.

As soon as the solid people of the colony discovered the real nature of the new religion which was getting a foothold in Maryland, there came to be a general attitude of respect toward it. This change of attitude was largely due to the coming of three great leaders of the movement —the men who were the real "founders" of Quakerism in the Southern colonies—John Burnyeat, George Fox, and William Edmundson. Burnyeat was the first of the three in the field. He arrived in Maryland in April 1665, coming from Barbadoes, the "nursery" of Western Quakerism, and he spent the entire summer in the province of Maryland, travelling and labouring in the ministry, holding "large meetings in the Lord's power"— "Friends were greatly comforted and several were convinced." [1] At the end of the summer he went down into Virginia, where he found much havoc wrought in the little Society by the "bewitchment" of John Perrot, who with his quietistic notions had led Friends to "forsake their meetings" and to become "loose and careless." Burnyeat appears to have turned the tide and saved the day: "Friends were revived and refreshed, and raised up into a service of life through the Lord's goodness and renewed visitation." [2] He was back in Virginia in 1671, with Daniel Gould of Rhode Island for his companion, and he now "found a freshness of life among them. They had grown up to a degree of their former zeal and tenderness. I found a great openness in the country and had several blessed meetings. I advised them to have a men's meeting [for Church business] to settle things in good order and to keep things sweet." [3]

---

[1] Burnyeat's *Journal*, p. 187. The sad episode—"sore exercise," he calls it—of his visit in Maryland was the "fall" and defection of Thomas Thurston, who had been a valiant pioneer in the early planting of Quakerism in all the colonies. He was, in an evil moment, caught and carried away by the spurious "spirituality" of Perrot's teaching, and became "lost to the truth" and "a vagabond as to his spiritual condition."

[2] *Ibid.* pp. 188-189.   [3] *Ibid.* p. 199.

He spent the spring of 1672 in Maryland, doing the same kind of constructive work as he had done so successfully in Virginia. In April he appointed a meeting at West River, Maryland, for all Friends in the province —the birth-date of Baltimore Yearly Meeting, the second to be organised in America—and it was "a very large meeting which continued for several days." Meetings for men and for women were organised for the transaction of business and "for the blessed ordering of the Gospel." [1]

"Through the good Providence of the Lord," George Fox landed in the Patuxent (West) River just in time to attend this General Meeting. He had spent six weeks in the passage from Jamaica to Maryland—a voyage so boisterous and full of hazard that they all "admired the Providence of God who preserved them." Fox notes with much satisfaction that "many people of considerable quality in the world's account" were at the great Maryland Meeting. "There were five or six Justices of the Peace, the Speaker of their parliament or Assembly, one of the Council, and divers others of note." [2] This marks the turning-point, and from that time on Quakerism was considered an eminently respectable religion in Lord Baltimore's province. Fox held another large meeting at the Cliffs—north of the Patuxent.[3] He arrived there soaked with water, his boat having capsized when he was in a great perspiration, having "come very hot out of a meeting before," but "the Lord's power preserved [him] from taking hurt," and "many people came to the meeting and received the truth with reverence." Fox, with a large band of helpers, including John Burnyeat, "went over by boat to the Eastern shore" of the Chesapeake, where they had "a large and heavenly meeting," with "several persons of quality and two Justices of the Peace" at it. He held an extraordinary meeting with the "Indian Emperor, his kings and their cockarooses," telling them that "God was raising up his tabernacle of witness in their wilderness country."

[1] *Journal*, pp. 199-200.
[2] Fox's *Journal*, ii. 161-163.
[3] *Ibid.* p. 165.

On his return journey from New England—a journey crowded with toil and peril and dramatic happenings— Fox arrived in Maryland again toward the end of September 1672 wet and weary, and "dirtied with getting through bogs," and held a large meeting near St. Michael's, where there were already many Friends. Here a judge's wife came to the meeting and declared : " She had rather hear us once than a priest a thousand times ! " In October a great General Meeting " for all Maryland " was held at Tredhaven Creek on the eastern shore. The meeting lasted five days—the first three days being for worship and preaching and then two for church business. " Several magistrates with their wives, many Protestants of divers sorts, and some Papists and persons of chief account in the country," were at the meeting. " It was thought there were a thousand people, and there were so many boats passing on the river that it was almost like the Thames ! One of the Justices said he never saw so many people together in that country before. It was a very heavenly meeting, the presence of the Lord was gloriously manifested, Friends sweetly refreshed, people generally satisfied, and many convinced." [1] For a month following, Fox was pushing on from meeting to meeting, almost living in a boat, often "wet and weary with rowing," but having "good service," "very large meetings," giving "a thundering testimony to the truth," convincing "Justices and other persons of quality," and "seeing the truth reach into the hearts of the people beyond words." [2]

The 5th of November, with Robert Widders, James Lancaster, and George Pattison, he sailed away for Virginia, having won to his cause a very large number of persons of "upper rank," as he calls them. He landed at a "place called Nancemond, about two hundred miles from Maryland." The region of Fox's activity in Virginia

---

[1] Fox's *Journal*, ii. 179.

[2] *Ibid.* pp. 180-183. Among the places now visited by Fox was Severn (now Annapolis) where there was such a crowd that " no building would hold them." Three Friends, William Cole, William Richards, and John Gary, writing in 1674 for the meeting to Friends in Bristol, England, say : "Much people there be in our country that come to hear the truth declared . . . and many by it are convinced."—Bowden, vol. i. 381.

was the strip of country lying between the James River and the North Carolina border. He found isolated Friends scattered through the district. "Officers and magistrates" came to his meetings which were "precious." Men's and women's meetings for business were established. A large meeting, too greatly attended for any house to contain the people, was held at Pagan Creek, and "the sound of truth was spread." He went on south, through a "plashy" country, "full of great bogs and swamps," "wet to the knees, lying abroad at night in the woods." At Somerton he found a woman who "had a sense of God upon her," and who arranged for the little party to sleep on mats before her fire. Proceeding on they struck Bennett's Creek (which he calls "Bonner's") and paddled into the Chowan River (then called the Macocomocock), and down this river by canoe into the regions bordering on Albemarle Sound.

Fox's own account of this journey is quaintly told in the manuscript Journal of the American visit.

"We passed in a canoe downe the creek to Mattocomake River and came to Hugh Smithick's [Smith's] house and people of the world came to see us (for there were no Friends in these parts). Wee went to Nathaniell Batts house; he was formerly Governor of Roanoke and is most commonly known by the name of Captaine Batts; he is a rude, desperate man who has great command over yt countrie, especially over ye Indians."

But as Fox had been preceded in this country by William Edmundson, and as the latter was the real pioneer in the Carolinas, I shall turn aside to describe Edmundson's path-breaking visit. He was with Fox at the Patuxent General Meeting in 1671, and when the latter travelled north, Edmundson turned south, visited Virginia, holding "powerful meetings," "settling men's minds in the truth," establishing "a men's meeting for discipline," and then started off south with two Friends as companions.

"It was," he writes, "all wilderness and no English inhabitants or padways, only some marked trees to guide people; the first day's journey we did pretty well, and lay that night in the woods, as we often used to do in those Parts. The next Day being wet

Weather we were sorely soyled in Swamps and Rivers, and one of the two that were with me for a Guide, was at a stand to know which way the Place lay we were to go unto: I perceiving he was at a Loss, turn'd my Mind to the Lord, and as He led me, I led the Way. So we travel'd in many Difficulties until about Sun-set; then they told me, They could travel no further; for they both fainted, being weak-spirited Men: I bid them stay there, and kindle a Fire, and I would ride a little farther, for I saw a bright Horrizon appear through the Woods which Travellers take as a Mark of some Plantation; so rode on to it, and found it was only tall Timber Trees without Underwood: But I perceived a small Path, which I follow'd till it was very dark, and rain'd violently; then I alighted and set my back to a Tree, till the Rain abated: but it being dark, and the Woods thick, I walked all Night between the Trees: and though very weary, I durst not lie down on the Ground, for my Cloaths were wet to my Skin. I had eaten little or nothing that Day, neither had I anything to refresh me but the Lord. In the morning I return'd to seek my two Companions, and found them lying by a great Fire of Wood: I told them how I had far'd; he that should have been the Guide would have perswaded me that we were gone past the Place where we intended; but my Mind drew to the Path which I had found the Night before: So I led the way, and that Path brought us to the Place where we intended, viz. Henry Phillip's House by Albemarle River.

"He and his wife had been convinc'd of the Truth in New England, and came there to live, who having not seen a Friend for seven Years before, they wept for Joy to see us: yet it being on a First Day Morning when we got there, although I was weary and faint, and my Cloaths all wet, I desired them to send to the People there-away to come to a Meeting about the middle of the Day, and I would lie down upon a Bed, and if I slept too long that they should awake me. Now about the Hour appointed many People came, but they had little or no Religion, for they came and sate down in the Meeting smoking their Pipes; but in a little time the Lord's Testimony arose in the Authority of His Power, and their Hearts being reach'd with it, several of them were tender'd and received the Testimony. After Meeting they desir'd me to stay with them, and let them have more Meetings."[1]

The colonists in this region, with the exception of Henry Phillips and his wife, were not Friends, and apparently, Edmundson says, "had little or no religion," *i.e.*

[1] Edmundson's *Journal*, pp. 58-59.

they had no organised religion, no church, no ministry, though " their hearts were open " and they were eventually gathered in in large numbers into the Society of Friends. A Justice of the Peace named Francis Toms, who lived three miles from Phillips' house, " received the truth with gladness," and, at a meeting in his house, several more " had a sense of the power of God, received the truth and abode in it." [1]

On his return to Virginia—a return journey more full of peril and difficulty than one ordinarily finds even in these biographies of the Quaker pioneers, everywhere crowded with incidents of extraordinary endurance —Edmundson continued his work of organising and strengthening the meetings for discipline throughout the sections of Virginia where there were Friends.   He visited the Governor, Sir William Berkeley, but he found him " pevish and brittle." [2]   He, however, succeeded better with some of the other officials of the colony.   Justice Taverner and " several other persons of note " came to his meetings. Major-General Bennett and Colonel Dewes were " reached by the witness of God."   This major-general, who had " a great estate," desired to contribute to the expenses of the Society, and finally became a member of it—" He was a brave, solid, wise man.   He received the truth and died in it." [3]

When Fox arrived in the Albemarle country of North Carolina in 1672 he found a little Quaker nucleus there as the result of William Edmundson's work.   The little band of Quaker missionaries, led by Fox, found a man on their travels, living on the banks of the Chowan river, who was named Hugh Smith, to whose house " people of other professions " came to see and hear the travellers.   Farther down the river they found a " captain," who was " very loving," and who lent them his boat, as they were very

---

[1] Edmundson's *Journal*, p. 60.

[2] When Edmundson related to Major-General Bennett that the Governor was "brittle and pevish," the General asked, "Did he call you *dog* or *rogue*?" When Edmundson answered that he did not, the General said, "Then you took him in his best humor!"

[3] Edmundson's *Journal*, p. 63.

wet by the water "splashing" into the little canoe. With the captain's boat they started off for the Governor's house at Edenton, but they found the water so shallow that "the boat would not swim." "We were fain to put off our shoes and stockings and wade through the water some distance. The Governor, with his wife, received us lovingly." [1] A doctor at the Governor's house "would needs dispute," and he denied that "the light and Spirit of God" was in every one, declaring that it was not in Indians. "Whereupon," says Fox, "I called an Indian and asked him whether or not when he lied or did wrong to any, there was not something in him that reproved him for it. He said that there *was* such a thing in him that did so reprove him and make him ashamed. So we shamed the doctor before the Governor and people." [2] The Governor kept them all night, and treated them very "courteously." The party from here went by Sound, about thirty miles, to the house of Joseph Scott, who was "a representative of the country." The people in these parts were "tender and much desired meetings." Four miles farther on another meeting was held, to which the Governor's Secretary came, "the chief Secretary of the Province," who was already "convinced." On their way back they visited the house of the Secretary of the colony, had an illustration of "the great power of God who carried them safely twenty-four miles in a rotten boat, the water being rough, and the winds high," and held a precious meeting at Hugh Smith's. They were eighteen days in North Carolina, and Fox felt that they had "made an entrance of truth upon the people" there.[3] They arrived on the nineteenth day of their travel, "exceedingly wet and dirty," at Somerton in Virginia, and lay that night in their clothes by the fire at the home of the woman who "had a sense of God upon her," and on the morrow they had a "good meeting" with the people about Somerton who "had a great desire to hear." [4]

The territory covered by this early missionary activity

---

[1] Fox's *Journal*, ii. 185.   [2] *Ibid*. ii. 185.
[3] *Ibid*. ii. 186.   [4] *Ibid*. ii. 187.

of Edmundson and Fox in North Carolina comprises the three present counties of Chowan, Perquimans, and Pasquotank. The increase from these "beginnings" was evidently rapid, for Governor Henderson Walker, writing to the Bishop of London in 1703, says: "George Fox . . . did infuse the Quaker principles into some small number of the people, which did and hath continued to grow ever since very numerous,"[1] and William Gordon, writing to the secretary of the Society for the Propagation of the Gospel in 1709, says: "There are few or no dissenters in this Government but Quakers. . . . Some of the most ancient inhabitants, after George Fox went over, did turn Quakers."[2] This missionary effort along the Albemarle was the first organised effort of any kind to carry the religion of Christ into North Carolina. No Episcopal minister had yet come to the colony, and no dissenting ministers appeared in this field before Fox and Edmundson. They were, therefore, in more senses than one, "path-breakers," as they pushed through the southern wilderness and answered the "great desire" of the people.[3]

George Fox spent a short time in Virginia, having "many large and precious meetings, to which a great many magistrates, officers, and other high people came." "The people were wonderfully affected," "the power of the Lord was gloriously seen and felt," and "a victory was got over the bad spirit which was in some"—evidently the remaining leaven of the Perrot movement which died hard.[4] Having finished "the service that lay upon him" in Virginia, Fox set sail in "an open sloop" for Maryland. The voyage was unusually tempestuous; they were a good deal of the time "completely wet" and almost frozen with cold, for it was in January. Part of the time Fox himself sat at the helm and steered the sloop, but as soon as they reached the Patuxent the "precious meetings"

---

[1] *Colonial Records of North Carolina*, i. 571.
[2] *Ibid.* pp. 708-710.
[3] For further evidence that the Quakers brought the first message of Christianity to North Carolina see Dr. Weeks's *Religious Development of North Carolina*, Baltimore, 1892.
[4] *Journal*, ii. 187-188.

began again, and the people were "convinced." This
third visit of Fox to Maryland (covering the period from the
3rd of January to the 21st of May 1673) was probably the
most effective and constructive work of his entire American
tour. He was at the very height of his efficiency as a
preacher and organiser. His physical endurance seemed
unlimited. He was almost continuously in a boat when
not holding a meeting, often rowing himself. He held
meetings in barns, in tobacco houses, in Friends' houses,
and in the wigwams of the Indians—the weather being
mostly too cold for out-door meetings. He had as usual
an eye for public officials and "high people," and the
meetings of this period saw the convincement of "a
great many people of account in the world"—justices,
magistrates, majors, captains, and "divers others of
considerable account in the government." Just before
sailing for England he attended another great General
Meeting for the whole of Maryland, at which "many
things were opened for edification and comfort," and the
organisation was put into permanent working condition.
"Parting in great tenderness, in the sense of the heavenly
life," Fox sailed away for Bristol, leaving behind a strong
group of Friends stretching, with some breaks, from the
coast of New Hampshire to Albemarle Sound in the
Carolinas, and having accomplished a piece of colonial
missionary labour which, so far as I know, no visitor to
America in colonial times paralleled.[1] From a letter
written in 1674 by three Virginia Friends to Bristol
Monthly Meeting in England, we learn that George Fox's
labours had borne great fruit. "Our meetings are at this
time more than doubled, and a large convincement is
upon many who as yet stand off" [i.e. do not join in
membership].[2]

In 1676-77 the Southern colonies received another
extensive visit from William Edmundson, whose wilderness
travels on this visit reach about the climax of hardship

---

[1] In the MS. *Journal* of Fox's American journey he estimates that he travelled
16,149 miles.
[2] Bowden, i. 356.

and difficulty. One sample of the sort of thing he went through will perhaps be sufficient :

"It was very cold, foul weather [on the Patuxent river], sleet and snow, and we were all day and most of the night before we got to the place intended. When we got to shore I could neither go nor stand, except as two bore me up, one by each arm, I had such pains and weakness in my back and groins with piercing cold. . . . We were forced to stay three nights on a small island, the weather being foul and stormy. We had no shelter but the open skies, the wet ground to lie on. This augmented my cold and pain, but the Lord bore up my spirit, and enabled me to bear it." [1]

He found the "affairs of truth" a good deal out of order in Virginia—"there were many unruly spirits to deal with, but I had good service and success." It was the period of the Bacon Rebellion, and the "country was in great trouble," but "Friends kept clear."

Then follows in the *Journal* a notable passage that reveals the *spirit* in which these Quaker missionaries did their work :

"Now I was moved of the Lord to go to Carolina, and it was perilous travelling, for the Indians were not yet subdued, but did mischief, and murdered several. The place they haunted much was in that wilderness betwixt Virginia and Carolina ; scarce any durst travel that way unarmed. Friends endeavoured to dissuade me from going, . . . so I delayed some time. In the meantime I appointed a meeting on the north side of the James River, where none had been, and there came several Friends a great way in boats. There came also the widow Holland's eldest son, with whom I walked near two miles the night before the meeting, advising him about some disorders in the family, and so we parted ; . . . but before morning a messenger came to tell me that the young man was dead. Then the word of the Lord came to me, saying : 'All lives are in my hand, and if thou goest not to Carolina, thy life is as this young man's ; but if thou goest, I will give thee thy life for a prey.' . . . The next day I made ready for my journey, but none durst venture with me, save one ancient man, a Friend." [2]

He had "many precious meetings" along the Albemarle, revisited his old Friends who were convinced on the former visit, saw "several turned to the Lord," and found the people generally "tender and loving." "There was no room," he writes, "for priests [*i.e.* paid ministers], for Friends were finely settled, and I left things well amongst them"—and the old soldier in both kinds of warfare turned his face homeward, never again to help "settle truth's affairs" in the colonies where he had laboured so faithfully to plant Quakerism.

There was another period of Quaker suffering in Virginia between 1675 and the accession in 1680 of Lord Culpepper to the Governorship, who was inclined to spare the Quakers. Under date of 15th June 1675, the record states that "The Hon'ble Governor being informed that there are several conventicles [of the Quakers] in Nansemond county, it is ordered by this court that they be proceeded against according to the laws of England and this country," and the Justices of the lower counties of Virginia were instructed to make strict inquiry, and to proceed against any person who meets in a conventicle.

There are, too, definite entries of fines against persons who have refused to have their children baptized, or who have "suffered meetings of Quakers at their houses," or who have been "living as man and wife without legal marriage," *i.e.* who have married according to Friends rules.[1] The Friends in Maryland endeavoured to assist their suffering brethren in Virginia during this period, and under direction of the Meeting at Tredhaven, in December 1690, William Berry and Stephen Keddy undertook the service of relieving the sad state and condition of the Church in Virginia.[2]

For a hundred years after the first planting of Quakerism in Virginia, Maryland, and the Carolinas—that is, from the middle of the seventeenth to the middle of the eighteenth century—it continued to grow and expand with some eddies and backwashes. There was here, as in New England, an almost unbroken succession of itinerant preachers who year after year visited all the Quaker centres in their rounds and often broke new ground and

---

[1] Weeks, *Southern Quakerism and Slavery*, pp. 43-45.
[2] Janney, *History of Friends*, ii. 359.

so formed new centres. Whenever a prominent Friend migrated to a pioneer locality he carried his Quakerism with him as he did his household stuff, and his house was likely to become the centre of a new Quaker church. The itinerant ministers in their travels found their way to the homes of these isolated Friends, and on their arrival a meeting was sure to be appointed for the neighbourhood, and if "convincements" were made, as generally happened, the "circle" would increase and become a "meeting." The *Journals* of these itinerant workers show the steady increase of the Quaker Society during the century, as I have indicated. The most important of these *Journals* for tracing the growth and life of the Society are those of Thomas Story, Thomas Chalkley, Samuel Bownas, John Fothergill, and John Richardson. A few illustrations from Thomas Story's *Journal* will be sufficient to show the type of work done by these travellers at the close of the seventeenth century, the date of the following itinerant service being 1698. Thomas Story and his companion Roger Gill sailed up the York River, Virginia, the 11th of February, and held their first meeting at the house of Edward Thomas—"a Friend who was zealous for Truth"—at Bangor House on Queen Creek : "Several who were not Friends were tendered, and this was the first fruit of our ministry in this country." On the 15th, a meeting was held sixteen miles from Bangor House, at Daniel Akehurst's on Warwick River—"a good meeting."[1] Next day they were at Martin's Hundred at the house of Robert Perkins. On the 21st, a meeting was held at Scimmins [spelled many ways in the *Journals*] in York county, "where no meeting had been before," and "John Bates and his wife were convinced of Truth"—a very important "convincement." The next day Story was back at Bangor House where William Clayborn, captain of the militia, grandson of the famous Colonel Clayborn, was won to the Quaker cause. "At the foot of Queen's Creek," Thomas Cary and Miles Cary and their families "were comforted, having been lately convinced." Across

---

[1] We shall hear of this Daniel Akehurst later as a man of note.

the James River at Chuckatuck, Thomas Story visited the old Massachusetts hero of persecution, " our ancient Friend John Copeland, the first of those who had their ears cut in New England for the testimony of Truth." " At my request," Story says, " he showed us his right ear ! " The Friends of the neighbourhood came in and they had together " a tender season of God's love." Meetings followed at Derasconeck, Western Branch [of James River], " where several confessed Truth "; Southern Branch, " where the Grace of God was plentiful, the people were tendered, and the meeting was in the dominion of Truth " ; and at Barbican, " the last meeting in Virginia toward Carolina." In this town was a " priest [*i.e.* established minister] who, being taken with an infirmity in his tongue and limbs, had not preached much for five years, and the people, being just to their own interest, paid him only as often as he exercised his faculty ! They gave him a hogshead of tobacco for every sermon, but no sermon no tobacco."

From here the travellers (Nathan Newby of Virginia going as companion) passed down into North Carolina, " through a wilderness, there being no house in all that way ; we ate bread and cheese and drank of the brook." At the head of Perquimans Creek they came to the house of Francis Toms, " who was one of the Provincial Council " —evidently William Edmundson's convert. They had a large meeting, " several persons of note " attending, after which they were entertained by the lieutenant-governor of the colony. Prominent Friends mentioned in this region are Thomas Simons, Henry White, Gabriel Newby, Stephen Scott, and Anne Wilson.

On his northward passage through Virginia, Thomas Story had very successful meetings in the old centres and in some new ones, and we get a good glimpse of the wide extent of Quaker influence. " At Pagan Creek," he writes, " we had a large assembly, most of whom were not Friends, and the power of the Lord was gloriously with us." The visitors were in most places " treated with beer and wine," or " had a little cyder " or " punch made of drams, sugar and nutmeg in horn cups," nobody yet having any scruple about such things. The places mentioned where meetings were held are Chuckatuck, Elizabeth River, Elizabeth Town, Southern Branch, Levy Neck, Lion's Creek, Burleigh (where James John was the leading Friend), Curles, Black Creek, Mattapany River, Powmunky Neck (where Captain Clayborn had his plantation, " in a wilderness region every way" and where "several were tendered "). At Hickory Neck, where no meeting had ever been before, a large gathering was held—" some people were tendered though a few persons were airy ! " At York City they held " the first meeting of Friends that had been there " —" the people were rude and senseless of good." At Pocoson, " where there had never been a meeting before," there was a " divine shining of the Light." At Kickatan, " things of great moment were opened," and " the daughter of that unhappy apostate, George Keith " was brought to " gentle tears " and hope was raised " that she might be restored to the Truth." At a great meeting at Remuncock " many persons of note in those parts " attended, among them Major Palmer, Captain Clayborn, and Dr. Walker, " all of whom were sedate and some broken."

His travels in Maryland were not so extensive as in the colonies farther south, since he had the opportunity of attending the Yearly Meeting for Maryland where he met most of the Friends of that Colony.

It was held on the Western Shore, and was " very full " and for two days " peaceable," " the good presence of the Lord in it," but on the third day there occurred a furious discussion with two " priests," and all the issues between the established church and the Quakers were threshed over. Naturally Thomas Story felt that " the invisible Truth came over their lofty and self-confident heads," and he reports with satisfaction that " several Justices who were present expressed their sentiments altogether in our favour." [1] We learn from Story's *Journal* that the " only

[1] A good illustration of the popular interest which was aroused by such discussions appears in Story's account of his next visit to the Western Shore a year later. A '' priest " came to the meeting for a discussion. He was on horseback ; Thomas Story stood on a bench outside the meeting-house, a large company

ministering Friend at that time in all those parts" [the Western Shore of Maryland] was Anne Galloway, who was "an honest, innocent, lively, and honourable Friend in the Truth who was everywhere acceptable in her service."[1]

Samuel Bownas gives one or two interesting glimpses of Southern Quakerism in the eighteenth century, the date of his visit being 1726.

"The Yearly Meeting in Maryland," he says, "is held four days, three for worship and one for business. Many people resort to it and transact a deal of trade one with another, so that it is a kind of market or change, where captains of ships or planters meet and settle their affairs; and this draws abundance of people of the best rank to it!"[2]

He gives a valuable passage for the light it throws on colonial travel:

"I met a Friend from London, his name was Joshua Fielding, who had visited Virginia and South Carolina, and had travelled by land about five hundred miles in three weeks, mostly alone, a difficult and hazardous attempt, but he got through safe though he had no provision but what he carried with him, and met with but about four or five houses or plantations in all the five hundred miles travel [from South Carolina to Virginia] which obliged him to lodge in the woods frequently. Having a small pocket-compass it was his guide, when sun and stars were hid from him."[3]

It was through just such faith and pluck and tireless effort that Quakerism was planted in this long stretch of coast from the Eastern Shore of the Chesapeake to Charleston, South Carolina.

Edmund Peckover, who travelled extensively through the Southern Colonies in 1742, gives many interesting glimpses of life and religious conditions as they were at this time. He is on the whole impressed with tendencies

---

gathered round, when to the discomfiture of the priest a woman shouted: "You refused to baptize my five children, unless I would give a hogshead of tobacco for each one of them. *Now* I don't care one farthing for your baptism." The service "ended in divine peace and consolation."—Story, p. 229.

[1] I have drawn my information from pp. 153-176 of Thomas Story's *Journal*, edition of 1747.

[2] Bownas's *Journal*, p. 140.   [3] *Ibid*. p. 139.

toward decline in spiritual life and power of Quakerism in Maryland. He laments that many worthy Friends in the Choptank region of Maryland have recently died and that " many of their offspring come very far short of them " —few even keep up " the outward appearances " ; but he prophesies that " a good visitation hangs over their head." Spiritual affairs are, he thinks, " at a low ebb " in the other parts of Maryland—the offspring of the " antient worthies " are as " gaudy and fine in their apparel as any who go under our name either at London or Bristol ! " He finds a much more encouraging state of affairs in Virginia—" a good visitation has been extended to the inhabitants of those parts " ; Friends " are growing in the Best Sense and have several ministers among them." [1] He was, too, favourably impressed with North Carolina. He found five meeting-houses in the compass of thirty miles with large meetings and " many solid, weighty, good Friends." " Six or seven hundred persons attend these meetings, and there are nine or ten persons gifted in ministry, with more developing." [2]

During the last half-century of the colonial period— roughly from 1725 to 1775—there occurred a large and very influential migration of Friends from Pennsylvania and colonies farther north, especially from Nantucket in New England, to the Southern Colonies. It is difficult to discover the reasons for this extensive shifting of population in a country not at all thickly settled, but it was probably due in the last analysis to economic reasons. In any case it was this migration of solid Quaker families, building a chain of flourishing meetings across Maryland and Virginia and down into North Carolina, that began a new epoch for Quakerism in these colonies, and prepared the way for the powerful migration of Quakers to the west during the next century.

The movement began with the migration of a group of

[1] The places visited in Virginia by Peckover were Caroline, Cedar Creek, Swamp Meeting, Black Creek, Wain Oak, Surry, Pagan Creek, West Branch, Nansemond, Chuckatuck, Blackwater, Notaway, Burleigh, Warwick, Curles, and Genitee.

[2] *Journal of Friends Historical Society*, i. 96-99.

Friends from Salem, New Jersey, and another group from Nottingham, Pennsylvania, to the country along the Monocacy River, a tributary of the Potomac, in Maryland. Sometime before 1730 a meeting, called " Monoquesy," was formed in this region, near the present village of Buckeystown. This was the first migration of Friends toward the west and away from the navigable waters, a movement which has ever since continued. In 1732 a migration southward was undertaken by Alexander Ross and a company of Pennsylvania and Maryland Friends, who secured from the Governor and Council of Virginia one hundred thousand acres of land for a colony on Opequan Creek, another tributary to the Potomac. This led to the formation of two meetings, Opequan and Providence, which were formed into Hopewell Monthly Meeting in 1735.[1] In 1745 Fairfax Monthly Meeting was established in what was then Fairfax County, but now Loudoun County.[2] From this beginning the movement spread southward, frequently increased by large migration from Pennsylvania, until there were twenty meetings for worship, five monthly meetings, and one quarterly meeting in this section of Virginia. A southward movement continued, and from the middle of the century onward meetings sprang up in the south-central counties of Virginia. One of the most interesting episodes of this Quaker expansion in Virginia during the middle years of the eighteenth century, was the formation of a Quaker centre at Lynchburg, due to the pioneer work of Charles Lynch and his wife (Ann Terrell) of Cedar Creek Meeting. They were married in 1755, and pushed out from home to settle a large tract of unoccupied land in the beautiful region about the present city of Lynchburg. The Indians broke up the little meeting which Lynch and his wife started; but, undaunted, the devoted pioneers took the meeting to their own house, and went bravely and tactfully to work to change the attitude of the

---

[1] This was for some years called Opequan Monthly Meeting.
[2] All the Meetings mentioned above belonged, until 1789, to Chester Quarterly Meeting in Pennsylvania.

Indians from one of hostility to one of peace and fellowship.

The same current of migration pushed farther on, and brought fresh streams of Quakerism into North Carolina. It was this influx of families from the north that builded the Quaker meetings in Alamance, Chatham, Guilford, Randolph, and Surry counties, and gave Quakerism in the south and west future promise and increased spiritual power. One of the most important Quaker settlements which this migration brought about was that at New Garden in Guilford County. It was begun about 1750, and the monthly meeting of that name was established in 1754. Between 1754 and 1770, eighty-six Friends became members of this monthly meeting by migration to this section of North Carolina. Of these, forty-five came from Pennsylvania, thirty-five from Virginia, one from Maryland, and four from north-eastern North Carolina.[1]

The migrations from Nantucket were of later date, and were even more numerous. The first date in the minutes of New Garden Monthly Meeting for the latter is 1771. After that time the records abound in names ever since then familiar in the annals of North Carolina Yearly Meeting, and also in those Yearly Meetings of the West which were largely composed of Friends, who, during the anti-slavery agitation and the distressing period just before the Civil War, emigrated to the free soil beyond the Ohio River. Within a period of five years there were no less than forty-one certificates from Nantucket in New Garden Monthly Meeting alone, and other Friends settled within the limits of Cane Creek Monthly Meeting. Many of these were young unmarried men, who were seeking to improve their fortunes. The island of Nantucket was crowded, two-thirds of its population being Friends—and its hardy sons were ready for adventure and pioneer life. In many instances they secured the latter without a corresponding increase in estate, and moved on into

[1] Weeks's *Southern Quakerism and Slavery*, p. 105. For further details of this migration see Weeks, *op. cit.* pp. 96-108 ; Janney's *History of Friends*, iii. 248-249 ; and *Life and Labours of William Reckitt.*

South Carolina and Georgia to found settlements and meetings which have entirely vanished. The minutes abound in declarations of intentions of marriage, and these Nantucket men were soon united with daughters of Pennsylvania, and from these two sources in the main is the birthright membership of North Carolina Yearly Meeting derived. There was also some admixture of Welsh and German blood. This migration came simultaneously with what is known as the Scotch-Irish migration. Through this channel the strong Presbyterian element which has since existed in Central Carolina was introduced.

These two influences, in many respects diverse, were thus simultaneously established on Southern soil. They continued to exist side by side with little friction until the outbreak of the Civil War. At that time the question of slavery forced an antagonism which the War of the Revolution did not engender. The Scotch-Irish were ready to fight. The Friends maintained their principle of peace, and abstained from participation in politics, contenting themselves with the rigorous insistence upon the rules of discipline, educational and business affairs, leaving the others pretty much in political authority.

There is little definite light available on the early settlement of Quakerism in South Carolina. The first public document referring to the coming of the Quakers to the Southern Colony is a letter written by Lord Shaftesbury, June 9, 1675, to Andrew Percivall on the Ashley River. The letter is as follows:

"There is coming in my Dogger [small ship], Jacob Waite and too or three other familys of those who are called Quakers. These are but Harbengers of a great number that intend to follow. 'Tis their purpose to take up a whole colony for themselves and theire Friends. I have writ to the Governor and Councell about them and directed them to set them out 12,000 acres. I would have you be very kind to them and give them all the assistance you can in a choice of place or anything else that may conduce to theire convenient settlement. For they are people I have great regard to and am obliged to care of. I am your affectionate friend, SHAFTESBURY." [1]

Some letters from John Jennings of Barbadoes to Edward Mayo and Jonathan Fitts of South Carolina, written 1679, have recently come to light, showing that the Barbadoes Quaker had sent five slaves to the Carolina Quakers. He asks his correspondents to return one of the " negromen," and to sell the rest for " Porke or Tobacco or bills of exchange," though he says, " if I had been sensible of what I now am [sensible of] I should not a sent them to that place." [1]

In 1681 George Fox, by epistle, endeavoured to bring the Friends in South Carolina into organic relation with the North Carolina Friends. He wrote :

"If you of Ashley River [S.C.] and you of Albemarle [N.C.] had once a year, or once a half-year, a meeting together somewhere in the middle of the country, it might be well." [2]

But the distance between the two settlements and the difficulties of travel made a union of forces impossible. We get a slight glimpse of these Charleston Friends in 1713 from Thomas Chalkley's *Journal* :

"After a month at sea " [in passage from Philadelphia] he writes, "it pleased God that we arrived at Charleston in South Carolina. We had a meeting there and divers others afterwards. There were but few Friends in this province, yet I had several meetings in the country. The people were generally loving, and received me kindly. . . . The longer I staid the larger our meetings were." [3]

He visited the Governor, who said that he " deserved encouragement " in his mission.

As the country grew in population Friends about Albemarle Sound gradually pushed south, and a chain of meetings was formed down the coast of North Carolina. Core Monthly Meeting was established in 1733 in Carteret County, and Falling Creek Monthly Meeting was set up in what is now Lenoir County in 1748. Weeks says that by the middle of the eighteenth century there were probably Quaker Meetings for worship in

---

[1] *Journal of Friends Historical Society*, vii. 65-66.
[2] Bowden, i. 413.　　　　[3] *Journal*, p. 80.

Hyde, Beaufort, Craven, Carteret, Jones, Bladen, and Lenoir counties,[1] so that the great gap between the Quaker settlements in the two Carolinas was fast closing up. But Quakerism never flourished in the great Southern Colony. Mary Peasley (afterwards Mary Neale) and Catherine Peyton (afterwards Philips) visited Charleston in 1753, and found a group of Friends there "who walk in the sight of their own eyes and the imagination of their own hearts, without being accountable to any for their conduct." [2]

Samuel Fothergill was at Charleston in 1755, and he writes : " I am here amongst a poor handful of professors, and I believe I must visit all their families." [3]

But there was one Quaker in South Carolina who did not "walk in the sight of her own eyes, nor in the light of her own imagination," and she was no mere " professor." This was Sophia Hume, a native of the Province, a granddaughter of Mary Fisher of Boston fame, a person of some refinement and culture, and a woman of very unusual religious experience, who, in 1747, issued *An Exhortation to the Inhabitants of South Carolina.*[4] The book was written under a powerful sense of compulsion—" I would not have you imagine that any consideration less than the Favour of God could have prevailed on me to appear in print "—and she believed unmistakably that she was uttering a divinely-given *word*, and not " the productions of an enthusiastick brain." I shall give her message in a few words to show what the best Friends of this period held to be essential.

" There is one truth," she says, " on which all I have to say to you greatly depends, namely, that *all mankind* have within them a measure and manifestation of the

---

[1] *Southern Quakers and Slavery*, p. 87.

[2] *Memoir of Catherine Philips* (1797), pp. 63-101.

[3] *Memoirs of Samuel Fothergill*, p. 173. Friends were even less successful in spreading their truth in Georgia. Samuel Fothergill went into Georgia, and he remarks that George Whitefield hurried to get there ahead of him to "save the flock," but there was little permanent result from Fothergill's visit. A Quaker settlement was, however, made in the Colony in 1758 near Augusta, and another settlement was made in what is now M'Duffie county in 1770. For details see Weeks's *Southern Quakers and Slavery*, pp. 117-124.

[4] First edition printed in Philadelphia by Benjamin Franklin in 1748.

Light, Spirit, or Grace of God, so that salvation is a matter of personal obedience."[1] Then comes her own testimony: "I myself have through the Grace of God and the obedience of faith witnessed the Peace of God myself, and am greatly concerned for the inhabitants of my native country to have this same Peace."[2] She declares her belief that it is possible by strict obedience to the inward Guest and Guide of the soul to *walk in the light*, and she wisely says that the true test of guidance is the discovery that our actions promote peace, goodwill, charity, and benevolence in the neighbourhood, "for such actions proceed from no other than God."[3] She says "the first day's work of the new creation in my soul was that happy season when God opened my eyes, and appeared in the Beauty of Holiness to my soul."[4] She insists rightly that the reason the heavenly Jerusalem does not come in our age is that Christians are no longer sensible of the presence of God, no longer have the Gospel-Power, do not live in the Eternal Spirit, and substitute words and outward services for Spirit and Life.[5] And she drives home to her "friends and neighbours"—in fact she says that she has come back from England under "the constraint of the Almighty" to tell them—that "Religion is a heart-work, the battle is an inward one, nothing counts but victory over sin, nothing but the inward possession of the Love of God. God visits you, the Voice of the Spirit calls you. Obedience will bring the Light and Truth into your inward parts, and you may be the Redeemed of the Lord."[6]

It is a simple little book, with some chaff, but with some real wheat in it, and it gives a clear idea of the type of preaching which was heard in all the meetings of the South as the itinerant messengers came among them.

---

[1] Substance of pp. 5-7. [2] P. 10. [3] P. 17.
[4] Condensed, pp. 22-23. [5] Pp. 140-141. [6] P. 156 *seq.*

CHAPTER II

THE GROUP LIFE AND WORK OF SOUTHERN FRIENDS

THE little groups of Friends which began to form in Maryland in 1656, in Virginia in 1658, and in North Carolina in 1671, gradually developed here as elsewhere into organised meetings for worship and for "truth's affairs." At first the meeting for worship, where the little local group gathered in the living faith that God was a real presence among them, was almost the whole of Quakerism. Those who were newly "convinced" quietly marked their change by a severer simplicity of outward life, by the unvarying use of "thou" and "thee," instead of "you" for a single person, by refusal to remove the hat as a mark of etiquette or honour, by the absolute omission of every kind of oath, and by attendance of the meeting for worship twice each week at the home of some leading Friend in the Community.

For the first dozen years in Maryland and Virginia the organisation of the Society was a very slender affair.[1] No central meeting was held in either Colony prior to 1672, and the local meetings for business were irregularly held, and dealt with but few matters, such as the sufferings of members subjected to persecution, the marriage of members, the needs of poor families, the times and places of holding meetings, and exercised perhaps some general oversight over the "walk and conversation" of those who constituted the "meeting."

[1] For example, Burnyeat found in 1665 that under the influence of John Perrot Friends in Virginia had "quite forsaken their meetings, and did not meet together once in a year."—Burnyeat's *Journal*, p. 188.

The earliest attempts at organisation of the Society in these colonies were made by Josiah Coale and George Rofe, both of whom were men of the constructive type ; but the work of systematic organisation was finally carried through by John Burnyeat, George Fox, and William Edmundson. Burnyeat began his constructive work in the two colonies in 1665, but he carried it much farther in 1671-72. He travelled through the Virginia towns where there were Friends in the autumn of 1671, and advised them to hold a men's meeting for business affairs. In the following spring he performed the same service in Maryland, and arranged a General Meeting for the Colony at West River to be held in April, which George Fox, opportunely landing from Jamaica, attended. In the summer of 1672 William Edmundson found affairs unsettled and out of order in Virginia, and he appointed " a men's meeting for settling Friends in the Way of Truth's Discipline," and, upon his return from North Carolina a few weeks later, this appointed men's meeting was held for settling the affairs of the Society.

Edmundson writes :

" The Lord's Power was with us in the Men's Meeting, and Friends received Truth's Discipline in the Love of it, as formerly they had received the Doctrine of Truth. Before I left those Parts Friends desired another Men's Meeting ; so we appointed another." [1]

This proved to be a very large meeting, and was occupied with " the affairs of the Church " : " to provide for poor widows and fatherless children : to take care that no disorders were committed in the Society, and to see that all lived orderly according to what they professed." [2]

These accounts show plainly enough that previous to this time the organisation was of the loosest character, business meetings being held only at the call of some travelling Friend with a constructive turn of mind. George Fox continued this organising work, " wonderfully opening " to the people the use and value of meetings for Church affairs ; and when he sailed for England he could

[1] *Journal*, p. 60.   [2] *Ibid.* p. 62.

honestly say that "Friends in those parts are *well established* in the Truth."

The earliest official document from Friends in Maryland is an epistle from the General Meeting for the colony held at West River, June 6, 1674, and addressed "to the Men's Meeting of Friends in Bristol," England. The epistle is largely occupied with homily, but there are a few living passages in it which reveal the condition of these people who have formed themselves into a Society. "We truly desire," they say, "to tread and walk in the blessed truth." "Much people there be in our country," the epistle states, "that comes to hear truth declared, which in its eternal authority is over all and many there be that by it are convicted."[1]

No minutes of any Quaker meeting in Maryland are extant for a date earlier than 1677, the first surviving minute being that of a Men's Meeting held at the house of Wenlock Christison on the Eastern Shore of the Chesapeake, March 24, 1677. Christison is the old hero who had braved the dangers of missionary activity in Massachusetts and had been condemned to die on the Boston gallows, but was finally released and given his life. He settled, not long after his "escape," at Tredhaven in Talbot County, and became one of the leading personalities and one of the foremost influences in the Maryland Society ; but his heroism and his distinction as an apostle who had suffered much did not raise him above the *judgment* of his fellow-members. He had been valiant for the truth in Boston, and had steered his course straight on through all the wiles of the enemy, but evidently he had succumbed to the attraction of some woman "not of the Society." The Men's Meeting in July held at his own house "took him under dealing":

"Att our Mans Meeting at Wenlock Christison's house ye 14th of 5th mo. [July] 1677, Wenlock Christison declared in ye meeting that if ye world or any particular person should speak evilly of ye Truth or reproach Friends concerning his proceedings

---

[1] The original copy is on the Bristol Minutes. It is printed in Bowden, i. 379.

in taking his wife, that then he would give further satisfaction and clear ye Truth and Friends by giving forth a paper to condemn his *hasty and forward* proceedings in ye matter, and he said that were ye thing to do again he would not proceed so hasty, nor without consent of Friends."

For many years the General Meeting for the Colony, consisting both of "a Men's Meeting" and "a Women's Meeting," were held alternately at half-year periods on the Western Shore and the Eastern Shore. Monthly Meetings were also held dating probably from the time of Fox's visit, at the localities where there were large numbers of Friends. The Minutes of the Men's Meeting for 1679 held on the Western Shore received reports from several local meetings of the Monthly type, as follows: Severn, South River, West River, "The Cliffs," Herring Creek, Patuxent, Muddy Creek, Accomack, Anamessicks, Munny, Choptank, Tuckahoe, Betties Cove, Bay Side, and Chester River. Quarterly Meetings began in Maryland, as far as the records indicate, in 1679. One was organised that year for the Western Shore "to be kept at Ann Chew's house at Herring Creek for the easing of the Monthly Meeting and Half Years Meeting, so that they may not be so much concerned with outward matters."[1] Another Quarterly Meeting was established on the Eastern Shore, probably the same year, as the first official reference to it occurs under date of 14th November 1679.

The earliest minutes contain interesting information of the way the meeting funds were raised and expended. All the funds of these meetings in the primitive days were in terms of tobacco. In 1677 the Friends of the Eastern Shore "thought it fitt and meet" to gather a "stock" or general fund, "for the service of Truth," "every Friend being left to his freedom what to give," and for the care of the poor, for which purpose the members contributed 8650 pounds of tobacco. A similar fund was raised for the Western Shore and "kept at John Gary's for the service of Truth." Eighteen hundred

[1] Minutes of Men's Meetings, 4th July 1679.

pounds of tobacco out of this latter fund were used to purchase "a shallop for Friends' service," as a boat furnished the readiest method of travel to and from meetings along the shores of the Chesapeake. All the meetings of every type were held in the homes of members during the first twenty years of the history of the Society. The first meeting-house built in the Colony was at Betties Cove on the Eastern Shore, and by the minutes of a Men's Meeting held at Wenlock Christison's in 1678 it appears that this house was at that time still unfinished, for it was then decided to "loft it," and to "partition it with falling windows hung on hinges," but for a long time even after this Friends continued to hold "house-meetings" in most localities of Maryland.

In Virginia there were no *regular*, settled meetings "for the affairs of Truth" before the visits of Fox and Edmundson. The General Meeting for the entire Colony was begun at the suggestion of George Fox in 1673. Fox's letter to the scattered Friends of the Colony is a brief and lucid expression of the true idea of a Quaker meeting :

"Meet to geather in the power and wisdom of God and keep a mans meeting and see that all who proffeseth the Lord and Glorious Gospel of Christ Jesus *may walk in it and stand by Righteousness and holiness as becomes the house of God, and stand for Gods glory and his name, so that all that doe proffes his Name may nott dishonor it nor cause his name to be blasphemed, nor his gracious truth to be evill spoken off, and see that nothing be lacking amongst ffriends meetings ; and see that you all be as one famyly together in the house of God."* [1]

The earliest monthly meetings in the Colony go back to about the same date as the central General Meeting— 1673, though no official accounts appear from this primitive stage. Chuckatuck Monthly Meeting was certainly in existence in 1683, and Curles (later called Henrico) was established in 1698. White Oak Swamp Monthly Meeting was established in 1700 and Nansemond,

[1] Minutes of Lower Virginia Meeting.

Pagan Creek, Surry, Wain Oak, and Warwick have records dating from 1702.[1]

The first Quarterly Meeting in the Colony was Lower Virginia Quarterly Meeting which was established at least as early as 1696. It was known, as most of these Virginia Meetings were known, under many variant names. Upper Virginia Quarterly Meeting dates from 1700, and in 1706 the Lower Quarterly Meeting was divided, forming a new one occupying the middle section of the Quaker region under the name of Chuckatuck.

North Carolina Yearly Meeting was organised in 1698, as appears from a minute of the Quarterly Meeting held at the house of Henry White the 4th of June 1698 :

"It was unanimous agreed by friends . . . that on the last seventh-day of the 7th month in Every yere to be the yerely meeting for this Cuntree at the house of ffrancis tooms [Toms] the Elder, and the second day of the weke following to be seat apart for business."

The Quarterly Meeting at which this action was taken was Eastern Quarterly Meeting which was established probably in 1681 for Friends in Pasquotank, Perquimans, and Northampton Counties. The earliest monthly meeting record for this Colony is that of one held at the house of Francis Toms in 1680, though according to the usual custom of Friends there were probably meetings "for the affairs of Truth" much earlier than this. By the year

[1] I give as complete a list of Virginia Monthly Meetings as I have been able to make out :

Black Water	Established	1757
Caroline (sometimes called Cedar Creek)	,,	1739
Chuckatuck	Known to be in existence as early as	1683
Curles (later called Henrico)	Established	1698
Denby	,,	1716
Fairfax	,,	1744
Hopewell	,,	1735
Isle of Wight	Records under this name begin	1767
Nansemond	,, ,, ,,	1702
Pagan Creek	,, ,, ,,	1702
South River	Established	1757
Surry	,,	1702
Wainoak	,,	1702
Warwick	,,	1702
White Oak Swamp (probably a variant name for some other Monthly Meeting)	Dates from about	1700

1700 there seem to have been three monthly meetings in this Colony : one at the house of Francis Toms in Perquimans County ; one at the house of Jonathan Phelps, also in Perquimans ; and one in Pasquotank.[1]

The most impressive feature of these various meetings, stretching in a long chain of Quaker settlements from the Chesapeake on the North to Charleston on the South, was their watchful care over the outer and inner life of the membership—what the Friends of that time called " the walk and conversation." The paternalism of this early Quakerism would with difficulty be endured to-day, but it fitted the needs of that period well ; and it produced results in social morality and in individual character which could hardly have been surpassed under any freer methods. The quiet ministry to the necessities of the poor members, as it was managed by the Quaker Meeting, cannot be too highly praised. Every effort was made to assist the needy to help themselves and, where this was manifestly impossible, the administration of charity was handled in a most private and unobtrusive way. "Great care and serious weighing" was bestowed upon the estates, condition, and education of orphans committed to the oversight of Friends. By a minute of Maryland Yearly Meeting for 1678, provision was made that one person in every local meeting should be chosen to see that no orphan is abused, nor his estate wasted, and that proper opportunities for his education are supplied. The Women Friends, always alive to formative influences,

---

[1] I give the following list of the other Colonial Monthly Meetings in the Carolinas, compiled from the appendix of Weeks' *Southern Quakers and Slavery* :

Bush River	Founded 1770
Cane Creek, N.C.	,, 1751
Cane Creek, S.C.	,, 1773
Carver's Creek	,, 1746
Centre	,, 1772
Contentnea	,, 1743
Core Sound	,, 1733
Deep River	,, 1778
Dunn's Creek	,, 1746
Falling Creek	,, 1748
Fredericksburg (later called Waterie) . . .	,, 1750
New Garden	,, 1754
Rich Square	,, 1760
Wells	,, 1764

took up the subject of education at their Half Year's Meeting in Maryland in 1679, and adopted this quaint minute which probably bore some fruit :

" We takeing it into serious Consideration Consurning our Childrens going to Scolle hath thought meett in ye wisdoum of god to giue ocation to all ffriends that those that are scoole masters may be Exhorted to teach their Children in ye practice boath in words, ways and actions wh beComes ye Blessed truth, and that we cannott, neither will, allow them to practice any of ye worlds liberty in any manner of practice wch ye truth alowes not, and alsoe its desired that ffriends be diligent to provide ffriends and scripture Boocks, and if possible to have a ffriend to be scool Master or Mistress.

" This being presented to our brethren of ye Mens Meeting at ye time aforesaid they had Unity with it." [1]

A similar " serious Consideration Consurning Childrens going to Scolle " appeared in all the other Quaker sections, and led to the establishment of a great many small schools for the " guarded " education—within rather severe limits—of the children of the membership.

The meetings followed up their distant members, and exercised a paternal care over those who moved into towns where there was no meeting for them to attend. If a member was going on a journey far from home, he was supplied with an indorsed document from his meeting, which introduced him to Friends in the places to which he was going, and prepared the way for him as he travelled. A few concrete minutes will illustrate the manner in which these matters were handled. The first one is the case of a Friend who had moved from Maryland to Virginia, and had consulted his meeting for advice whether he should stay or return. The Minute reads :

"William Kuton very honestly applies to this Meeting for advice in order to his staying or removing from Rapahanock [Va.] Inasmuch as there is no ffriends meeting there *but himself*, he signifyeth that he finds something stirring in his heart with love of god to the people, and by himself hath not freedom to remove. He desires that if the Meeting do judge

---

[1] Minutes of Women's Half Year's Meeting for 1679.

it meet he should stay, they would take care that he may be visited on all opportunities that present, and that ffriends would acquaint travelling ffriends of that same, that so if possible the desire of his heart may be answered concerning that people. The Meeting approveth of what ye ffriend hath proposed, and doe advise that his request may be answered by ffriends on both shores as opportunity offereth."

The following minute—from the year 1686—is a good illustration of the care taken for journeying members :

"Humphry Emerton laid before this Meeting his intention of a voyage for England *about his outward concerns.* This Meeting desires first to know the willingness of his wife, and in order thereto hath appointed Richard Harrison to discourse with her,"

and forthwith a document suitable to introduce him was prepared.

When a Friend went out on a religious visit "a minute of unity" like the following was given to open the way for his message and service :

"Our well beloved Friend and sister Anne Galloway laid before this Meeting, that she finding some drawings in the love of God to visit Friends in some parts of Pennsylvania, desired some lines by way of certificate of their unity with her. And whereas our beloved Friend Samuel Galloway hath informed this Meeting that he hath an intention of accompanying his wife in her intended journey (if extraordinary occasion prevents not) desires that he may have a few lines by way of certificate of Friends unity with him."

Even as early as 1705, Friends in Maryland began to be disturbed by the excessive use of tobacco and spirituous liquors, and there are frequent minutes about this "concern of Truth." The earliest minute which I have found on the subject, under date of 1705, will indicate the way they dealt with the difficulty :

"This Meeting having a weighty sense upon their minds concerning the immoderate use of Tobacco, does advise that all may forbear the abuse of the same, and that those friends that are appointed to give accompt of the state of the Meeting they belong to may forbear the excess of smoking themselves, and also caution and advise all friends against the immoderate use of the same, and that they give accompt to the Monthly Meeting what progress they have made therein." [1]

The Friends in Maryland were troubled for many years by the sale of liquors in the near neighbourhood of the meeting-house at the time of their Yearly Meeting. The occasion was seized upon by "the world's people" as a good time to "transact trades," and, to the scandal of Friends, the meeting-place was made "a kind of market or change where the captains of ships and the planters met and settled their affairs." The Friends were pleased to have "the abundance of people from the country round about" flock in, but they were also determined to "prevent ye buying of drink at the time of Yearly Meeting," and thereupon they addressed the government of Maryland "for ye prevention and suppressing of the evil practice with the evil consequences attending it." [2] Their appeal was in due time effective, for an Act was passed in 1725, preventing the sale of liquors in booths within one mile of the Quaker meeting-house in Talbot County, or within two miles of the meeting-house near West River in Ann Arundel County. [3]

Virginia Friends took the position, as Friends elsewhere did in the early stage of moral awakening on these matters, that liquor-drinking must be done, if at all, in *moderation*. The Yearly Meeting of 1704 expressed in a minute the advice that members of the Society "do keep out of *unnecessary providing* of strong drink, and do keep in Christian moderation at times of births, burials, or marriages." [4] One of the most amusing minutes

---

[1] Minutes of the Yearly Meeting for 1705.
[2] Minutes of Yearly Meeting for 1711.
[3] Bacon's Laws 1725, chapter 6.
[4] It was not until 1782 that Virginia Yearly Meeting took action prohibiting the distillation of liquor by their members :

"The Meeting being deeply concerned at this time to endeavour to remove from amongst us such things as appear to be an evil tendency, and as the distilling spirits from grain is believed to be wrong, Friends are therefore hereby prohibited using grain of any sort in that manner ; and if any should continue so to do, such ought to be treated with as disregarding the unity of the body. And as trading in spirituous liquors, and frequent, and unnecessary use thereof hath also appeared to have many bad effects ; Friends are therefore advised against these practices."

on the subject of moderation came from North Carolina, where Friends were urged to "use tobacco with great moderation as a medison and not as a delightsome companion!"[1]

There was, however, a strange mingling of the large and the little, the important and the petty, in the paternal care which these meetings exercised. The moral and the merely ceremonial ran blurringly together. Dress, speech, and marriage with a companion "of the world" early came to be questions of first importance. In 1700 the Women's General Meeting for Maryland decided "under waity consideration, in the wisdom of God" to hold three times a year "a private meeting of the solidest women Friends to wait upon the Lord and to inspect into the most waitiest affairs of Truth"—these "waitiest affairs of Truth" being mainly matters of dress and marriage. A minute of this "private meeting," dated 1708, declares :

"It Lies very Waityly uppon us to Desir all friends Profesing truth to be very Carefull to keep out of all Imytations of Fashghons which the world Runs into : Butt to keep to Plainness of Speach and Plainness in Dress in our Selves, and our Children ; Labouring in our Selves and with them to be clothed with ye meak spirit of Jesus as such as are waighting for his coming."

Similar minutes come from every section of Quakerdom throughout the entire colonial period from the time when meetings for business affairs were organised. The following specimen minute from the North Carolina Records has a peculiarly naïve flavour :

"Friends are advised against wearing coats and other garments made after the new and superfluous fashions of the times, and no Friend is to wear a wig, but such as apply to the monthly meeting giving their reasons for so doing."

But the subject of overwhelming importance was that of marriage, for it had early become a *fixed idea* with Friends that there should be no mixed marriages, *i.e.* marriages with persons "not of the Society." We have

---

[1] Quoted from Weeks's *Southern Quakerism*, p. 128.

already seen how the Meeting on the Eastern Shore of the Chesapeake compelled its foremost member, Wenlock Christison, to apologise for his "hasty marriage," and it allowed no one to deviate "from good order" in this matter. As an illustration of the care taken even when both bride and groom were Friends, the following minute is of interest:

"Att a Halfe Years Womens Meeting at the house of John Pitt ye 3rd of ye 5 mt. 1678.

"Obadiah Judkins Lay'd a matter of maradge before us with Obedience Jenner and wee taking itt into Consideration, she Coming lately from England, thought it Requisite that they should stay till a Certificate can be secured, and in ye meantime they should dwell asunder."

There are many such entries as this of the year 1687:

"We are informed of a yong ffriendly woman dwelling at Choptank [Maryland] that is married to one of ye world and after ye manner of ye world; ye care and consurn of which is referred to ye womens meeting on ye Eastern Shore."

The women Friends of Maryland made a most drastic proposal in 1691 to force the children of the meeting to live up "to the testimony of Truth."

"Itts the Sence of this Meeting that when Parents that have Children that Marries against and Contrary to their Parents mind, and shall give them any part of their outward Estates it is encoiragement for others to take the like disobedient Course and it is of bad Consequence, and this Meeting Advice is that all Friends that may be Concerned in like Case *doe Refrain from giving such Rebellious Children any part of their outward Estates that soe such like Spiritts in Friends children may be discouraged and not encouraged.*" [1]

By means of an extensive epistolary correspondence, beginning from the earliest organisation of the Society in America, the Friends, withdrawn from the rest of the "world," kept in constant *rapport* with each other. So long as George Fox lived, he wrote frequently to the

---

[1] This attitude toward "rebellious children" was adopted by the Men's Meeting both in Maryland and in Virginia.

meetings in the colonies, and after his death his wife continued the correspondence.

A minute of the Yearly Womens' Meeting at West River in 1699 reports :

"An Apistle from our Dear friend Margaret fox from the Quarterly Meetting att Lancaster, In Old England was read in our Meeting and ffriends haueing True Unity with ye same and Desireing wee may Eye the great Love of Oure God in this and all things agreeable to his blessed truth to ye end of our Dayes, Doth appoint Eliz. Talbott, and Ann Galloway to Write and answer to the aboue Said Apistle and to send itt by the first opportunity In behalf of Said Meetting."

The Yearly Meetings, both for men and for women, all over the world sent Epistles to each other, and it was quite usual for the lower or subordinate meetings to send similar Epistles if special occasions called for such action, or "if something rose freshly in the minds of any as a living message." One of the most amusing incidents in this widespread intercourse of love and fellowship was the sending of two hogsheads of tobacco from the women Friends of Maryland to the women of London in 1678. The minute of this "concern" says :

"We hauing Reseaved many Episels from our dear friends in London and of late a Prcell of Boocks as a token of true love to our women's Meetting here in Maryland, it is agreed upon at this our generall Meetting to wright a Lett^r. from ye womens Meetting hear in Maryland to ye Womens Meetting in London and to send it with two hhd. of tobacco, and it is agreed upon that Eliz. Larance and Alice Gary doe take Care to prouide one hhd. for ye Western Shore, and Madgdelin Stevens and Sarah Thomas to privd one hhd. for ye Eastern Shore, and if possible they be sent together, and Margarett Berry is desired to wright ye Letter to ye womens Meetting in London."

By the opening of the eighteenth century the Friends were *one* people throughout the world, though there was absolutely no *bond* but love and fellowship. There was no visible head to the Society, no official creed, no ecclesiastical body which held sway and authority. But instead of being an aggregation of separate units the

Society was in an extraordinary measure *a living group*. Friends had suffered together and they were baptized into one spirit.   Wherever any Friend was in trouble the world over, all Friends, however remote, were concerned, and were ready to help share the trouble if it could be shared.   The way in which Friends bore each other's burdens is well illustrated by a passage in an epistle to George Fox from the Half Year's Meeting in Maryland in 1683 :

" There are many Friends in this province who find a concern laid upon them to visit the seed of God in Carolina, for we understand that the spoiler makes havoc of the flock there : so here are many weighty Friends intending to go down there on that service." [1]

Every meeting took care of its own poor, and had a permanent poor-fund always ready.   There is no unifier like love, and nothing creates the group-spirit as does the fellowship-interest.   Nowhere except in the primitive Church has there been a more amazing interchange of fellowship, a more spontaneous itinerancy, than among the Friends.   Harnack says :

" At a time when Christianity was still a homeless religion, the occasional travels of brethren were frequently the means of bringing churches together, which otherwise would have had no common tie." [2]

A living interest in the collective Church of Christ, he points out, throbbed with intensity through each particular Church, and the men of spiritual vision and leadership contributed themselves to the *whole Church*.   So it was, too, in the formative period of Quakerism.   The greatest and the best of the entire Society made their way from meeting to meeting, and from house to house—even into the cabin of the settler on the frontier—and they wove an invisible bond, stronger than the infallible decrees of Councils, which held the whole body together as an integral unit.   Hospitality with the Quaker was not a virtue, it was an unconscious *habit*.   His house was wide

[1] Quoted from Bowden, i. 385.
[2] *The Mission and Expansion of Christianity*, i. 179.

open to every Friend who passed that way, and, especially on great meeting-days, there were practically no limits to the hospitality of board or bed.

"Differences," disputes, and controversies between Friends were not taken into court, but were settled in meeting by the family method. However complex and complicated the affairs at issue might be, the meeting grappled with them, and brought order out of chaos. For example, two Friends in Virginia in 1749 had a financial difference, which the Monthly Meeting considered would, if continued, have "pernishous consequences to the trooth and its prosperity." The meeting took up the case, and induced the contenders to refer their controversy to the judgment of three Friends. It was thus settled satisfactorily, "brotherhood between them was preserved, and scandal was prevented."[1] There are hundreds of similar arbitrations on the various minute books, and generally, if not always, the meetings proved able to settle the affair in dispute, and preserve brotherhood.

The simplicity and artlessness of these colonial Friends appear in almost all their methods as a few samples will show. In 1702 Virginia Friends had "a deep and weighty sense" that the affairs of the Church could be improved, "if but one person should speak at a time," and the Yearly Meeting gave "wholesum counsil" to meetings everywhere to practise this plan of procedure, "which will be," the minute of advice says, "a sweet savour, we doubt not!"[2]

In 1724 Thomas Pleasants asked to be released from the duties of clerk to his monthly meeting, "since it hath pleased the Lord to give him a few words to speak in the assemblies of God's people." A touchingly simple effort to advance "the truth" appears in a letter from two rural Friends in Henrico county, Virginia, in 1701.

"Friends, wee thought to acquaint you that we are willing to have a First-day Meeting at our house, hoping it would be for the glory of the Lord, and the prosperity of his blessed Truth."

---

[1] Minutes of White Oak Swamp Monthly Meeting, 1749.
[2] Minutes of Virginia Yearly Meeting for 1702.

One of the earliest corporate activities of Friends in the Southern colonies was directed toward the achievement of religious freedom, because their very chance of survival as a religious people hung upon the attainment of such freedom. The system of Church *uniformity* weighed most severely in Virginia. Nowhere except in Massachusetts was the pressure so heavy, and, in the form of distraints for tithes, it was continued long after the New England Quakers were living in peace. The kind of persecution to which all Friends in Virginia were subjected in the eighteenth century may be seen in the laconic report of Thomas Jordan to his Monthly Meeting in 1700 on his sufferings :

"Six weeks Imprisonment for being Taken Att A Meeting in my own house and Released by the Kings Proclamation ; again taken at a meeting at Robert Lawrence, and bound ouer to the Court of Nansemond, and, for refusing to swear according to their will and against the Command of Christ, was sent up to Jamestown a Prisoner upwards of ten months. Presently After John Blake tooke away my 3 servants And left my wife in a Distressed Condition with A young Child sucking at her Breasts that to help her selfe the Child did hurt Itt selfe with Crying, wch. servants were kept about nine weeks and then returned again by the Governors order. Taken by Distress by Jno. Blake, hed Sheriff of Nansemond County : Two feather bedes and three feather Boalsters and furniture to them with other goodes wch. did amount to 3967 Pounds of Tobbacco, also a servant man that had 3 years to serve. Taken by distress by Thomas Godwin Sherieff : Ten head of Cattells and delivered to Wm. Stinton of James Towne."

Robert Jordan has left his own account of his sufferings, which will touch the reader with sympathy for this defender of the American idea that religion and religious contributions are matters for the individual conscience to settle :

" Being committed to prison, I was first placed in the debtor's apartment, but in a few days was removed into the common side, where condemned persons are kept, and for some time had not the privilege of seeing anybody, except a negro who once a day brought water to the prisoners ; this place was so dark that I could not see to read even at noon, without creeping to small holes in the door ; being also very noisome, the infectious air brought on me the flux, so that, had not the Lord been pleased to sustain me by his invisible hand, I had there lost my life ; the governor was made acquainted with my condition, and I believe used his endeavors for my liberty ; the commissary visited me more than once under a show of friendship, but with a view to ensnare me, and I was very weary of him.   I wrote again to the governor, to acquaint him with my situation, and so, after a confinement of three weeks, I was discharged, without any acknowledgment of compliance, and this brought me into an acquaintance and ready admittance to the Governor, who said I was a meek man." [1]

" Destraints for priest's wages," as Friends called these forced contributions, lasted in Virginia until the adoption of the Bill of Rights at the opening of the Revolutionary War.

The sixteenth section of this famous Bill, which was drafted by Patrick Henry, embodied this noble principle for which the Quakers had wrought and fought for a hundred years, and for which they suffered imprisonment and annual loss of goods :

" Religion, or the duty which we owe to our Creator, and the manner of discharging it, can be directed only by reason and conviction, not by force and violence, and therefore all men are equally entitled to the free exercise of religion, according to the dictates of conscience ; and it is the mutual duty of all to practice Christian forbearance, love, and charity toward each other." [2]

This principle was put into practical effect in October of the same year by the definite enactment that all laws prescribing punishment " for maintaining any opinions in matters of religion, forbearing to repair to Church, or the exercising of any mode of worship whatever " should be repealed, and a universal exemption is made from all levies, taxes, and impositions for the support of the church or its ministers.[3]

The struggle to secure relief from military exactions was not so soon over, and it was in all the Southern

[1] *Memorials* (Philadelphia, 1787) quoted from Weeks, p. 151.

[2] Hening, ix. 112.

[3] Hening, ix. 164, 312, 387, 496. The Church, however, was not disestablished in Virginia until 1799, though more than two-thirds of the inhabitants of the Colony were dissenters when the Bill of Rights was adopted.

colonies a prolific source of suffering.   In an enactment
of the Virginia legislature in the year 1666 it is noted
that " divers refractory persons refuse to appeare upon the
dayes of exercise [of the militia] and other times when
required to attend upon the publique service," and a fine
of one hundred pounds of tobacco is imposed for such
neglect.[1]

A minute of Henrico Monthly Meeting under date of
5th July 1729 shows what happened when the fine was
not paid, and also what Friends considered was " for the
honour of Truth."

" Our Friend Tarlton Woodson having related to this Meeting
his case of having had a horse wrongfully seazed by the sheriff
for a Melishey fine, for not bearing arms according as the Law
directs, and desires of this Meeting advice whather he may sew
[sue] the sd. auficer for not acting according to Law.   This
Meeting after deliberate concideration think it may redound
more to the honour of Truth to suffer wrong patiently than to
take a remedy at Law."

By an act of 1738 Friends were exempted from
military service, but were required to furnish a substitute,
which, for their conscientious ideas, was no relief at all,
and the records for the next quarter of a century are full
of accounts of distraints for military fines,[2] and the period
of the French and Indian war was a time of very great
suffering on the part of Friends in Virginia as well as
everywhere else.   Under the law of 1756, providing that
every twentieth man should be drafted for the war, seven
young Friends were carried to the frontier.   They appear
to have remained faithful to " the Truth " in their hard
trial, and the Virginia Epistle to London in 1757 reports
that the young men are now released from imprisonment.

---

[1] Hening, ii. 246.

[2] Minutes of this type can be found in every Record Book :

For not bearing arms			Thomas Pleasants	500 lbs. tobacco.		
,,	,,	,,	Ephrim Gartrite	500	,,	,,
,,	,,	,,	John Crew, for	300	,,	,,
			a mare worth . . . £6		0	0
,,	,,	,,	John Lead, a bedd and pair of sheets			
			worth . . . £6		0	0
,,	,,	,,	Thomas Ellyson, for 500 lbs. tobacco			
			a man (i.e. slave) worth . . £9		0	0

A law which furnished some relief was passed in 1766. This exempted Friends from "exercising" at musters, and they were released from the general requirement to provide a set of arms. The militia officer of each county was required to prepare a list of all male Quakers of a military age, and no person was exempted unless he could prove that he was a *bona fide* Quaker. In time of actual war, however, the Quaker was still liable to be drafted, though he could furnish a substitute or pay a fine of ten pounds sterling.[1]

The meeting records show many entries like the following :

"At our monthly meeting held at the Western Branch in Isle of Wight County in Virginia the 27th of the 6 month 1757 :

"The overseers of each meeting are desired to collect the names of each of their members that are liable by a late act of assembly to be enlisted in the militia against our next monthly meeting, that a list may be given to the Colonel or chief commanding officer of each county as by Act of assembly directed ; and have the indulgence granted by the same."[2]

At the beginning of its colonial history North Carolina possessed a very large measure of religious freedom. In the earliest charter granted by King Charles II. to eight of his favourites in 1663, and extended in 1665, toleration of dissenters was provided for, though it was assumed that the Church of England would be *the Church* in the Carolinas. The terms offered to the settlers at Cape Fear in 1665 show an unusual breadth of toleration for that century :

"No person . . . shall be any ways molested, punished, disquieted, or called in question for any differences in opinion or practice in matters of religious concernment, but every person shall have and enjoy his conscience in matters of religion throughout all the province."[3]

---

[1] Hening, viii. 241.

[2] The difficulties on account of military requirements were by no means at an end in 1767. The Friends had much to suffer during the Revolution, and fines for refusal to train in the militia were imposed for many years after the Colony was a state.

[3] *Colony Records of North Carolina*, i. 80-81.

Locke's Fundamental Constitution for the Carolinas provided that any seven persons agreeing in any religion should be constituted " a Church or profession to which they shall give some name to distinguish it from others," and this Fundamental Constitution provided that no person of one faith should disturb or molest the religious assemblies of others, nor persecute them for opinions in religion or for their ways of worship.[1] Everything possible was done by the proprietors to invite dissenters to come to the new colony, and Friends were not slow to take advantage of the open door. The Established Church did absolutely nothing in the colony and had no minister there before 1700. For a quarter of a century Quakerism was the only organised form of Christianity in the colony, and, as Weeks says :

" When the eighteenth century dawned, the Quakers, by their thorough organization and by their earnest preaching, by their simple and devoted lives, by their faithfulness and love, had gathered into their fold many men and women who primarily belonged to other denominations. They became Friends and remained faithful to their new-found form of belief." [2]

During this period of freedom, Quakerism had, as the next chapter will show, a large and influential share in shaping the political development of the Colony, and the story of the struggle for freedom from tithes and from bearing arms during the eighteenth century will be told in that chapter.

Most of the travelling Friends who visited the Southern colonies in the eighteenth century—and even earlier— felt a strong concern against the ownership of slaves, though it was not until 1760 that this subject really gripped the consciences of the Friends who *lived* in these colonies.[3] It seems to us now somewhat amazing that a

[1] This Fundamental Constitution drawn up by John Locke is printed in the *Colony Records of North Carolina*, i. pp. 187-207.

[2] *Religious Development in North Carolina*, p. 32.

[3] A Minute of Maryland Half Year's Meeting of Women Friends for 1678 shows that even at this early period the Quaker women were sensitive in the matter of a true and kindly treatment of the children of the negro race, and that they considered it important to have their own children trained in courtesy toward and reverence for others. The minute is dated June 18, 1678, and reads :

" We are informed of a ffriend's Children that belonged to West River Meetting

man so enlightened and so sensitively conscientious as
Wenlock Christison—a man who was ready to die for his
faith—could have bought and sold slaves, but such is the
fact. He owned a number of white slaves, evidently
immigrants sold for debt, but there is also evidence that
he bought and owned negroes; for a minute of Tredhaven Monthly Meeting, under date of September 27,
1681, informs that "one Diggs" has sued the executors
of Wenlock Christison, concerning some negroes sent by
Wenlock Christison out of Barbadoes to this country,"
and three years later William Dixon, who married
Wenlock Christison's widow, asks the advice of the
Monthly Meeting about "selling a negro his freedom."
This attitude toward the existence of slavery seems to
have gone on pretty much unchanged until the time of
the visit of Samuel Fothergill of England (1754) and
John Woolman's second visit (1757)—both well-beloved
disciples of liberty. Fothergill, who was deeply stirred
on the subject, wrote: " The price of blood is upon that
province [Maryland] — I mean their purchasing and
keeping negroes in slavery." Of North Carolina he
writes, " Friends have been a lively people here, but
Negro-purchasing comes more and more in use among
them." [1] Woolman's first journey through Maryland and
Virginia was in 1746, of which he writes, with his usual
sensitiveness:

"Two things were remarkable to me in this journey: first, in
regard to my entertainment. When I ate, drank, and lodged
free-cost with people who lived in ease on the hard labour of
their slaves I felt uneasy; and as my mind was inward toward
the Lord, I found this uneasiness return upon me, at times,
through the whole visit. Where the masters bore a good share

---

that they are very badly and Corruptly Educated concerning the importance of
strict justice being duly attended to on account of the Affricans and their Posterity
formerly in Slavery, in regard to Christian instruction, Education, and Treatment
towards the Youth of that race, as well as the circumstances of those more
advanced in years, which it is desired may have place amongst us, and the weight
of the subject rests on the mind of friends, now assembled, that when we return to
our several Meetings we may be enabled to impress on the minds of our Brethren
and Sisters a close consideration of what may be called for at our hands in regard
to this People, in consequence of our high profession of Justice and Equity."

[1] *Memoirs*, pp. 282 and 283.

of the burden, and lived frugally, so that their servants were well provided for, and their labour moderate, I felt more easy; but where they lived in a costly way, and laid heavy burdens on their slaves, my exercise was often great, and I frequently had conversation with them in private concerning it.   Secondly, this trade of importing slaves from their native country being much encouraged amongst them, and the white people and their children so generally living without much labour, was frequently the subject of my serious thoughts.   I saw in these southern provinces so many vices and corruptions, increased by this trade and this way of life, that it appeared to me as a dark gloominess hanging over the land; and though now many willingly run into it, yet in future the consequences will be grievous to posterity. I express it as it hath appeared to me, not once, nor twice, but as a matter fixed on my mind."

At the time of his visit in 1757 he found himself constrained by his conscience not to accept *free* entertainment in Friends' homes where there were slaves, and on leaving such homes he put money in the hands of his host, asking him to distribute it among the negroes.   He took great pains to make Friends see the evil effects— spiritually, morally, socially, and economically—from slave labour, prophesying, with clear insight, that if Friends " prefer their outward prospects of gain to all other consideration, and do not act conscientiously toward their fellow-creatures, I believe the burden will grow heavier and heavier.[1]   He urged more care in the education of negroes and greater endeavours to guide them in moral and religious matters, " as souls for whom Christ died," and at Virginia Yearly Meeting he was deeply disturbed in spirit to note that, in adopting the Query of Philadelphia Yearly Meeting, " Are there any concerned in the importation of negroes, or in buying them after they are imported ? " they had changed it to read : " Are any concerned in the importation of negroes or buying them to trade in ? "   He spoke strongly against this change. He wrote a beautiful epistle to the new Meetings in what he calls " the back settlements of North Carolina "—New Garden and Cane Creek—in which he says: " To rational creatures bondage is uneasy, and in tender and most affectionate love I beseech you to keep clear from purchasing any." [1]

From this time on there are frequent minutes dealing with the care of slaves, gradually advising against the purchase of them, and finally making it "a disownable offense" to purchase a slave. Maryland Friends at their Yearly Meeting in 1760 had a weighty consideration " of their duty in the matter of holding slaves," and there was " some uneasiness felt about the propriety of buying negroes." The Meeting for that year limited itself to an advice against "importing." The year following (1761), however, it adopted this minute :

" At a Yearly Meeting held at West River last Spring relating to Negroes a weighty exercise revived in this Meeting, and a solid conference was held thereon, and wholesome exhortation to attend to the mind of Truth, after which this Meeting concludes that Friends should not in any wise encourage their importation by buying or selling those imported, or other slaves, and that those that have them by inheritance or otherwise should be careful to train them up in the principles of the Christian religion." [2]

From the time of this awakening the feeling gradually grew among Friends that it was inherently wrong to hold slaves at all. Maryland Yearly Meeting of 1772 adopted a minute " discouraging the iniquitous practice of holding slaves" and advised that Monthly Meetings do extend their care and assistance to those who remain possessed of these people, in brotherly affection and Christian tenderness, labouring in the ability that may be afforded for their relief."

---

[1] The account of this important visit of Woolman through the South occupies chapter iv. of the *Journal*.

[2] There had been an official care shown in North Carolina as early as 1740, when the Yearly Meeting recommends to those holding slaves " to use them as fellow-creatures and not to make too rigorous an exaction of labour from them." Even as early as 1722, Virginia Yearly Meeting asked the Query : " Are all Friends clear of being concerned in the importation of slaves, or purchasing them for sale? Do they use those well they are possessed of, and do they endeavour to restrain from vice, and to instruct them in the principles of the Christian religion ?"—Weeks, p. 201.

Five years later the Friends of Maryland came to this vigorous conclusion, that :

"should any of the members of our Religious Society remain so regardless of the advices of this Meeting from time to time communicated, as to continue to hold mankind in a state of slavery *the subscription of such for the use of the Society ought not in future to be received*, and in order that Truth's testimony may be clearly maintained against this oppressive practice, our several Quarterly and Monthly Meetings are earnestly enjoined to extend their help and assistance to such in profession with us, as have hitherto neglected to do justice to that oppressed people, and if any should continue so far to justify their conduct as to refuse or reject the tender advice of their brethren, it is the solid sense and judgment of this Meeting that their continuing in this oppressive practice is become so burdensome, that such persons must be discontinued from our Religious Society." [1]

Similar minutes appear in the records of Virginia and North Carolina with a very similar ripening of anti-slavery sentiment. In 1767 Western Branch Monthly Meeting in Virginia took this tentative position :

"It is the Judgment of this meeting that no Friends for the future doe purchase any slaves without first applying and have the consent of the Monthly Meeting, except it be for securing of such debts as cannot otherwise be got."

Sentiment developed so rapidly that the Yearly Meeting of 1768 adopted this conclusion :

"The subject of negroes, being brought before the Meeting, and duly and weightily considered, it appears to be the sense of the Meeting, and accordingly is agreed to, that in order to prevent an increase of them in our Society, *none of our members for the time to come shall be permitted to purchase a negroe, or any other slave, without being guilty of a breach of our Discipline*, and accountable for the same to their Monthly Meeting."

This strenuous action produced considerable opposition, and the subject came up again in the Yearly Meeting of 1772, with much the same result :

"The sense of this Meeting being requested upon the minute of 1768, prohibiting the purchase of Negroes, whether or not

---

[1] Minute of Baltimore Yearly Meeting for 1777.

the Monthly Meetings ought to disown such as do purchase [Negroes] which matter having been duly and weightily considered, it is the unanimous sense of this Meeting, that if any professing themselves members of our Society, shall purchase a Negro, or other slave, *with no other view but their own benefit or convenience*, and knowing it to be contrary to the rules of our Discipline, the Monthly Meeting to which they belong ought to testify their disunion with such persons, until they condemn their conduct to the satisfaction of the Meeting." [1]

One of the most prominent opponents of slave-holding that America produced in the eighteenth century was Warner Mifflin, who was born in Accomack county, Virginia, in 1745. He determined in his youth never to be a slave-holder, but he became possessed of slaves through his wife, Elizabeth Johns, and he also received some from his father. He, however, soon returned to the conviction of his youth, and by the year 1775 he had unconditionally emancipated all the slaves who belonged to him. From that time until his death in 1798 he assiduously laboured to promote emancipation; but as he had in early life moved into Delaware, the story of his splendid efforts toward freedom does not belong to this chapter. [2]

In North Carolina a minute was adopted in 1772 advising Friends not to buy negroes except of Friends, or to prevent the separation of husband and wife, or parent and child, or with the approval of the Monthly Meeting, and in 1776 the Yearly Meeting earnestly and affectionately advised Friends to " cleanse their hands of slaves as soon as they possibly can," and further, " any member of this meeting who may hereafter buy, sell, or clandestinely assign for hire any slave in such manner as may perpetuate or prolong their slavery" was to be disowned. [3]

From the period of the war of the Revolution it was

---

[1] Owing to the fact that it was against the law of the Colony to manumit a slave Friends in Virginia found it difficult to free the slaves they owned, and they endeavoured in vain in 1770 to get this law repealed.

[2] See *Life and Ancestry of Warner Mifflin*, compiled by Hilda Justice (Phila., 1905).

[3] Weeks, p. 208.

clearly settled in all the Southern Colonies that no Friend was to buy a slave, and that as fast as possible those negroes owned by members of the Society should be given their freedom and provided for. From this time, too, a feeling of responsibility for the education of the negroes grew upon Friends, and there are many minutes in the Records of the last quarter of the eighteenth century providing for the enlightenment of the coloured people.

This chapter has dealt only slightly with the *deeper aspect* of the religion of these Quakers in the South—the essence and heart of their religion, their personal experience of life with Christ. They did not, during the period we have been studying, produce many great interpreters of the fundamental Quaker idea, they added very little to the prophetic literature of the movement, and they have, therefore, left scant material for the formation of an estimate of their inward power. The voluminous Records of their meetings and the Journals of their visitors, how- ever, leave the impression with the reader that they formed, in their various localities, live centres of an efficient spiritual religion. There was considerable re- iteration of their central doctrine of the inward Light too often presented, perhaps, in rather dull fashion, with too little psychological insight of its meaning and too little of the warm and tender message of the Light revealed in the concrete Person of Galilee and Jerusalem. There was, it is certain, too much of the scribal concern over dress, speech, and "testimonies" grown sacred with age. But there was, nevertheless, something very real and vital in these Quaker groups. They kept alive a true democracy in which all persons were spiritually equal, they exhibited a congregation governing itself and uttering itself through the members themselves, even the simplest. They showed, too, in their meetings for worship an overwhelming sense of the *real presence*—a hush and awe of spirit before the God of the outer and inner universe.

Almost all the Journals of the itinerant ministers inform us that they found in their travels among the people at large religion at a low ebb, but there was kept alive in these Quaker centres a type of religion which was in some sense quickened with streams from the living Fountain, and which produced real flower and fruit in spiritually ordered lives—what Fothergill calls, "a lively remnant in this land," "purified hearts in which the word of the Lord God grows."[1] They were more sensitive, I think, than their neighbours to the meaning of social evils, and they were more intensely concerned to be in harmony with the will of God. They failed, where so many others have failed, by building little tabernacles over their mounts of vision, by trying to keep for themselves a Light meant for the race, and by failing to grasp, *intelligently*, their principle of religion, which became to them a kind of fetish, untranslatable to the world about them ; but they did bless the world by producing here and there, now and then, specimens of personal lives, penetrated by the Spirit of Christ, radiant with His Light, taking upon themselves the burdens of the world and living in a busy and material world as though they knew that their main business here was to help to bring in the kingdom of peace and love and brotherhood. In so far as they did *that*, they succeeded.

[1] Samuel Fothergill's *Memoirs*, p. 166.

CHAPTER III

SOUTHERN QUAKERS IN PUBLIC LIFE

WHEREVER the Quakers, in the early colonial period, found avenues open for political activity they entered them by a sort of natural instinct. There were in this creative stage of Quakerism, no scruples against a political career. On the contrary, the foremost Friends felt a profound responsibility laid upon them to work out their principles of the Light within, in the fields of political life. Rhode Island and Pennsylvania furnish the most massive illustration of this statement, for these colonies offered the best conditions, but the same *tendency* appears everywhere where the Quakers were numerous—the tendency to put their ideas into actual operation. In fact, John Archdale, Governor-General of the Carolinas, is one of the most interesting figures in the entire list of public Quakers, and for a brief period this great colony of the Restoration seemed likely to have its career and destiny shaped by Quaker statesmen.

Maryland and Virginia presented but slender opportunities for Quaker activity in public life, and the story of political activity in these two colonies is soon told. The early "convincements" in Maryland included a number of public men. William Durand, who was "convinced" by Elizabeth Harris in 1656/7, was a member of Cromwell's commission for the government of Maryland, and was the secretary of that commission.[1] He seems soon after—apparently at the Restoration—to have moved to Carolina and to have settled a plantation

[1] *Archives of Maryland*, i. 339, 355.

on the Roanoke, and the George Durand conspicuous in early Carolina history was apparently his son.[1]

Another of Elizabeth Harris's converts was Robert Clarkson, who served his colony for some time in the House of Burgesses as member from Ann Arundel County.

Thomas Meares and William Burges were two important public servants of the colony who became Quakers. They frequently appear in the Records of the colony as judicial commissioners, justices of the peace, and members of the Assembly, and in 1657 they both refused to take the oath of office, declaring that it was " not lawful in any case to swear," though they had formerly done so without compunction. These two above named members of the Assembly from Ann Arundel County, and Michael Brookes for Calvert County, were fined, October 6, 1657, for refusing the oath.[2] Thomas Meares appears again as a member of the Assembly in 1663, and Michael Brooks also figures in the Records as a member, in spite of the difficulty over the oath, and he was put forward for positions of trust and public service.[3] Dr. Peter Sharpe is another of the early Quakers in Maryland who was prominent in public life and political activity. He, too, was entrusted by the Assembly, of which he was a member, with important colonial matters.[4] Thomas Taylor was " convinced " by George Fox's preaching in 1673. He was at the time Speaker of the Lower House and one of the most influential men in public affairs. He went to hear Fox preach at William Cole's house on the Western Shore and was so impressed that he drove seven miles the next day to attend another meeting at Abraham Birkhead's house. Here at a " blessed meeting " the Speaker was " convinced," and he seems to have stayed " convinced," for a little later a meeting was held in his house.[5] He continued for many years in legislative

---

[1] See Neill's *Virginia Carolorum*, p. 306.

[2] *Archives of Maryland*, iii. 358.

[3] *Ibid.*, i. 359, 362.

[4] *Ibid.*, i. p. 362. Peter Sharpe left in his will, "for perpetual standing a horse for the use of Friends in the ministry!" See Davis's *Day Star*, p. 78.

[5] Fox's *Journal*, ii. 182 and 194.

service. His name occurs seventy-one times in the Records of the Assembly between 1666 and 1676, and he was also a member of the Governor's Council.

William Berry, too, a leader in all the affairs of the new Society, a hospitable entertainer of travelling Friends, a liberal subscriber to the funds of the meeting, was for some years a deputy in the Assembly, beginning his term of service in 1674. He was frequently selected for important committee work, and appears to have enjoyed the trust and confidence of the colonial officials.[1]

The most interesting Quaker in politics in this colony was, however, the old persecution-tried pioneer of Quakerism, Wenlock Christison of Talbot County, who had sat in the shadow of the Boston gallows. He settled in Maryland probably in 1670. In that year Dr. Peter Sharpe transferred a piece of land, containing one hundred and fifty acres—one of the finest sites on the Chesapeake Eastern Shore—to Wenlock Christison "in consideration of true affection and brotherly love," and "also for other divers good causes and considerations." In 1673 another Friend, John Edmondson, also "out of brotherly love," gave him a hundred acres more, adjoining his "Peter Sharpe farm," while a third Friend, Henry Wilcocks, presented him with "a serving-man," named Francis Lloyd.[2] He was thus a well-provided citizen. His house was the place of assembly for the Friends' meetings and he was the foremost Quaker minister in the colony.[3]

His first public service on record was to prepare, with three other Friends, one of them being William Berry, a petition to the Governor, the Council, and the Assembly for the passage of an Act allowing the substitution of an affirmation for an oath. It was an able, straightforward document, and was referred to Lord Baltimore, "who hath formerly had Intentions of Gratifieing the desire of sd

[1] See *Archives of Maryland*, ii. passim.
[2] See Samuel A. Harrison's *Wenlock Christison* (Baltimore 1878), pp. 52-54.
[3] Peter Sharpe, in his will, left forty shilliugs apiece "to Friends in ye ministry, viz. Alice Gary, William Cole, Sarah Mash [Marsh], if then in being ; Winlock Christeson and his wife, John Burnett [probably Burnyeat] and Daniel Gould [Burnyeat's companion]."—Davis's *Day Star*, p. 78.

people called Quakers." It was, however, finally decided that it would be "utterly unsafe to make a Law in this Province to exempt the people thereof from testifying upon oath." [1] Christison and his friend John Edmondson, both of Talbot County, were chosen deputies to the Assembly in 1678. What they did about the oath of office we have no way of knowing, but they were at all events enrolled as members of the Lower House the 21st of October 1678.[2] Christison at once received important appointments to service for the House and was, strangely enough, selected to serve on a Committee of six to prepare an "Act for the Security and Defense of the Province" and for drawing up the "necessary articles of Warre!" [3] There is no way of discovering what this peace-loving Quaker did on the military Committee, though the Records plainly show that he accepted the appointment, and that he received nine hundred pounds of tobacco from the colony for his service as a deputy.[4] In 1681, the Records of the Lower House announce a vacancy in the representation from Talbot County due to the death of Wenlock Christison.[5] His fellow-member, John Edmondson, had a much longer term of service, and was throughout his period of service on important standing committees. September 6, 1681, William Berry and Richard Johns, both apparently at the time members of the Lower House, introduced another petition urging the privilege of affirmation, which they presented so effectively that the House adopted the following Resolution:

"If the Rights and Privileges of a freeborn Englishman, settled on him by Magna Charta and often confirmed by subsequent Parliaments, can be preserved by yea and nay in wills and testaments and other occurients, the Lower House may do well to prepare such a Law." [6]

The Friends followed up this favourable action by

---

[1] *Archives of Maryland*, ii. 355. [2] *Ibid.*, vii. 7.
[3] *Ibid.*, vii. 19. [4] *Ibid.*, vii. 87.
[5] *Ibid.*, vii. 134. The actual "Act of Security and Defense" was not drawn up until after Christison's death. See *Ibid.*, vii. 143.
[6] *Ibid.*, vii. 153.

presenting a paper giving six reasons for a modification of the law on oaths. In their dignified address, taking up the reference to Magna Charta, they said : " We are Englishmen ourselves, and freeborn, although in scorn commonly called Quakers, and therefore so far from desiring the least breach of Magna Charta, or of the least privileges belonging to a freeborn Englishman, we had rather suffer many degrees more than we do (if that were possible) than willingly admit the least violation of those ancient rights and liberties which are our birthright. And had we not been full well assured that our sufferings may be redressed and our request granted without violating Magna Charta in the least degree we would not have desired it ! " If William Berry and John Edmondson and Richard Johns wrote that document they were good men to represent the Society of Friends in Maryland. The Bill passed the Lower House but did not at that time receive Lord Baltimore's approval.[1] He, however, issued a proclamation in 1688 making an oath unnecessary in testamentary cases, for which act the Quarterly Meeting at Herring Creek sent him an address of appreciation, and in 1702 Friends were entirely relieved of the oath.

It was during the session of the Assembly in the autumn of 1681 that Lord Baltimore announced to both Houses that " moved by the frequent clamours of the Quakers," he was resolved henceforth to publish to the people the Proceedings of all the Assemblies [2]—surely a distinct right of the people. In 1682 the Lower House voted that " no member whatsoever be at any time during the sitting of this House, admitted with his hatt on ! "[3] This was presumably directed against the Quaker members, and yet in spite of this vote, two years later, in a speech before the Assembly, Lord Baltimore reproves certain members " for rudely presuming to come before his Lordship with their hats on," which would indicate that there were a number of Quakers still in the House.

---

[1] See Neill's *English Colonies in America*, pp. 305-306.
[2] *Archives of Maryland*, vii. 221.   [3] *Ibid.*, vii. 353.

There were, too, many members of the Society of Friends at this time occupying judicial positions in the colony. In Talbot County in 1685 three out of the ten judges of the county were Quakers—William Sharpe, William Stephens, one of Fox's "convincements," and Ralph Fishbourne, a prominent member of the meeting.

This Quaker activity was not allowed to pass unchallenged. The "practical politicians" of the time circulated a report against the Friends who were in the Assembly, charging that these Quaker members were the cause of "the leavyes [*i.e.* taxes] being raised soe high!" The Monthly Meeting thereupon appointed a committee "to treat with Lowe [the politician who made the charge] for ye clearing of Friends and ye Truth!"[1] "Truth" was, for the time being, "cleared," but the feeling steadily grew in "the Society" that it was *safer* to keep out of politics, and Maryland Friends in the eighteenth century contented themselves with sending *petitions* to the legislature instead of sending *members* to it, a change of policy which was a distinct loss to the colony and a still greater loss to the Society itself.[2]

The opportunities for public service on the part of Friends in Virginia were very meagre. There were, however, a number of men in official station who threw in their lot with the Quakers, and as a result found themselves relegated to private life. John Porter is an interesting instance of this. The story is laconically told in the *Colonial Records* for September 12, 1663:

"Whereas Mr. John Hill, high sheriff of Lower Norfolk, hath represented to the House that Mr. John Porter, one of the burgesses of that county, was loving to the Quakers and stood well affected toward them and had been at their meetings, and was so far an Anabaptist as to be against the baptising of children; upon which representation, the said Porter confessed himself to have been and to be well affected to the Quakers, but he conceived his being at their meetings could not be proved, upon

---

[1] Minute of 14th October 1677.
[2] In this particular Friends were in line with the early Christians. Tertullian says (*Apol.* xxxviii.): "Nothing is more alien to us than politics."

which the oaths of allegiance and supremacy were tendered to him which he refused to take, whereupon it is ordered that the said Porter be dismissed this House." [1]

John Porter, junior (who, oddly, was the brother of the above-mentioned John Porter, senior), was Justice of the County Court of Lower Norfolk, and tried a witch case in 1659, and had been High Sheriff of the county in 1656. He was "convinced" as a Quaker in the early 'sixties, and became the foremost preacher of that section of the colony. He was again and again arrested for preaching, and was once sentenced to be transported from the colony. Quite naturally he ceased to hold public office. John Bond (probably a Quaker) was declared "unfit to be continued a magistrate and incapable henceforth of any publique trust or employment *because of his factious and schismatical demeanour.*" [2]

The most interesting glimpse we get of Quakers in public life at this period comes from a section of the colony which was claimed both by Virginia and Maryland. As soon as the Virginia Assembly passed its Act of 1660 against the Quakers, those who were living on the eastern shore of Virginia petitioned the Governor of Maryland to grant them the privilege of moving up into the limits of his colony. The Governor of Maryland appointed three commissioners, John Elzy, Randall Revell, and Stephen Horsey to arrange for the settlement of such persons as wished to come over into his Province, assigning to them " any parts below the Choptank River," [3] and a large number accepted the opportunity, as we are informed that there were in May 1662 "fifty tithable persons seated at Monokin and Anamessicks " [on the eastern shore south of Nanticoke River [4]].

Colonel Edmund Scarborough, who was one of the original commissioners for the transfer of these settlers, for some reason turned his service over to the Governor of Virginia and became the agent of the latter colony for

---

[1] Hening, *Statutes at Large*, ii. 198.   This was John Porter, senior.
[2] Hening, ii. 39.
[3] *Archives of Maryland*, iii. 469.   [4] *Ibid.*, iii. p. 452.

collecting the rents of the Anamessick settlers on the claim that they still belonged to Virginia. " Wee lye," the settlers write to the authorities in Maryland, " between Sylla and Charibdis, not knowing how to get out of this Labarinth." [1] While this somewhat momentous issue was being settled by the two colonies, Colonel Scarborough, "with forty horsemen for pomp and safty," arrived at Anamessicks on a Sunday morning (October 11, 1663) to force the issue. Here he found, he says, " some contemptuous Quakers and a foole in office" [evidently Stephen Horsey, a Quaker and the Agent of the colony of Maryland.]

Colonel Scarborough well illustrates the usual official attitude toward Quakers in the early period of their history, and his description is coloured both with humour and spleen. He arrested Stephen Horsey because he would not acknowledge the authority of Virginia, and he put the " broad arrow " on his door. He continues:

"Wee went to ye house of Ambrose Dixon, a Quaker, where a boat and two men, belonging to Groome's shipp, and two running Quakers were, also George Johnson and Thomas Price, Quakers." He found there "a certain Hollingsworth, merchant of a northern vessel [William Hollingsworth of Salem, Massachusetts], who presented his request for liberty to trade, which I doubted [i.e. suspected] was some plott of ye Quakers."

"Stephen Horsey," he continues, "ye ignorant yet insolent officer, a cooper by profession, who lived in ye lower parts of Accomack [belonging to Virginia] once elected a burgess by ye common crowd and thrown out by ye Assembly for a fractious and tumultuous person, a man repugnant to all gov'mt, of all sects yet professed by none, constant in nothing, but opposing church government, his children at great ages yet unchristened. He left the lower parts [i.e. Accomack] to head rebellion at Annamessecks. George Johnson, ye proteus of heresy . . . is notorious for shifting, schismatical pranks. Thomas Price, a creeping Quaker, by trade a leather dresser, whose conscience would not serve to dwell amongst the wicked and therefore he retired to Annamessecks where he hears much and says nothing els but that he would not obey government, for which he also stands arrested. Ambrose Dixon, a caulker by profession, that lived long in ye lower parts [*i.e.* in Accomack] was often in question for his quaking profession, removed to Annamessecks where he is a prater of nonsense.   A receiver of many Quakers, his house is ye place of their resort [*i.e.* their meeting-place]. Henry Boston, an unmannerly fellow, stands condemned for slighting and condemning the laws of the county, a rebell to gover'mt and disobedient to authority . . . hath not subscribed [*i.e.* to the oath.] These are all, except two or three loose fellows who follow the Quakers for scrapps, whom a good whip is fittest to reform." [1]

Stephen Horsey—" the ignorant, insolent officer "— became one of the first judges of the new county, organised by the government of Maryland, and he was also the first sheriff of the county, a man of solidity, trustworthiness, and large public service.   Henry Boston—" the un- mannerly fellow "—and George Johnson—" the proteus of heresy "—were both selected as county Judges! George Fox visited the Anamessick region in 1673 and added many new members to the little Society, the nucleus of which had migrated thither from the Accomack strip in Virginia.

A provision was made in 1705 by the Legislature of Virginia which granted the Quakers of that colony the privilege of affirmation, but the time had already then gone by for them to take up political activity and then, too, they still remained in the thought of their Episcopal neighbours a people apart—a peculiar sect. [2]

There was at least one interesting exception to the aloofness of the Virginian Quakers from the responsibilities of public life.   Charles Lynch, the founder of Lynchburg, and the pillar of Quakerism in that region of the colony,

[1] Neill's *Virginia Carolorum*, p. 302.   This region became in 1666 a part of Somerset County, Maryland.

[2] The provision referred to is found in " An Act for establishing the General Court and settling the proceedings therein."   Section 31 reads : " *Provided always*, That the people commonly called Quakers, shall have the same liberty of giving their evidence, by way of solemn affirmation and declaration, as is prescribed by one Act of Parliament, *Septimo et Octavo Gulielmi Tertii Regis*, intituled *An act that the solemn affirmation and declaration of the people called Quakers shall be accepted instead of an oath, in the usual form* ; which said Act of Parliament, for so much thereof as relates to such affirmation and declaration, and for the time of its continuance in force, and not otherwise, shall be, to all intents and purposes, in full force within this dominion."—Hening, iii. 298.

was asked, in the critical period of the early 'sixties in the eighteenth century, to become a member of the Colonial Assembly. At first he declined because he felt that such a public position would be inconsistent with the requirements of his Quaker faith. As the storm increased, however, and the colonial crisis plainly grew imminent, he yielded, and in 1764 went as member from his county to the Virginia House of Burgesses. He was a member when Patrick Henry delivered his famous speech which heralded independence, and he remained a member until the colony became a state. He was, however, eventually disowned by his Meeting for his complicity with warlike activities, though he continued until the end of his life to attend Quaker meetings.

As soon as we turn to North Carolina we are in another type of social and political world. Here the only organised form of religion which existed before the eighteenth century was that of the Society of Friends. King Charles II., in his first Charter to the Proprietaries of the colony, granted in 1663, gives "full and free license and liberty and authority" to tolerate all persons in the colony who, "in their judgment and for conscience sake, cannot conform to the liturgy and ceremonies [of the Church], or take and subscribe the oath."[1] That same year [1663] Sir John Colleton, one of the Proprietors, wrote to the Duke of Albemarle, another Proprietor, informing him the Carolina colony can be "planted and settled" only on a basis of "liberty of conscience," without that privilege, he declares, "settlers will not goe."[2] The result was that the Proprietors issued in August 1663 this "declaration and proposal to all that will plant in Carolina":

"We will grant, in as ample manner as the undertakers shall desire, freedom and liberty of conscience in all religious or spiritual things, and to be kept inviolably with them, we having power in our charter so to do."[3]

---

[1] *Colony Records of North Carolina*, i. 32.
[2] *Ibid.* i. 34-35.
[3] *Ibid.* i. 45.

And the Fundamental Constitution, drafted by John Locke, contained this enlightened article :

"No person whatsoever shall disturb, molest, or prosecute another, for his speculative opinions in religion, or his way of worship." [1]

Here then was an "open door" for the Quaker who desired to make his principles prevail in the affairs of the colony, and here, too, was forming. throughout the last quarter of the seventeenth century a very live and aggressive band of Quakers, who saw themselves for once in a region where their type of Christianity had no rival. The influence of Friends in the colony dates from the visits of Edmundson and Fox in 1672. The Governor [Carteret] and his wife received George Fox "lovingly," and accompanied him through the wilderness, and in the home of Joseph Scott, a deputy in the Assembly, the Quaker missionaries held a "precious meeting." The "chief secretary of the colony" was already a convinced Friend at the time of Fox's visit, having been *reached* apparently by Edmundson.

"For three weeks," writes a North Carolina historian, "Fox lingered among these people of the forest, whom he described as tender and loving and receptive of the truth, holding meetings to which they flocked. The seed fell on good ground. The faith of the zealous evangelist, who appealed so effectively to the consciences of his hearers, took firm root in Albemarle. No other religious meetings were held calling the people into communion, and at once ministering to their human needs, and satisfying their spiritual longings. It was in sympathy with the solitude of their surroundings and the quietude of their daily life." [2]

Francis Toms, Christopher Nicholson, and William Wyatt, three of the leading men of the colony—all three of whom held their land under the Great Deed of the Lord Proprietors—had become Quakers by the year 1673, and had meetings held in their houses.

---

[1] Section 109, *Colony Records*, i. 204.
[2] Ashe, *History of North Carolina* (1908), i. 109.

In 1677 the colony passed through a mild revolution, known in history as "Culpepper's Rebellion," undertaken and carried through with the aim of securing colonial self-government—"a government by our own authority, and according to our own model."[1] One of the foremost leaders of the little revolution was George Durand, who became attorney-general of the colony in 1679. The prevailing opinion among those who have described this Rebellion has been that Durand was a Quaker, but that seems improbable. Fox never mentions him, and there are no contemporary evidences that he was in membership with Friends.[2] Friends did their best during this crisis to keep from being entangled on either side in a movement which involved bloodshed, though Timothy Biggs, the deputy collector of customs—apparently a Quaker—was unduly aggressive in favour of the *status quo*, even suggesting to the Proprietors that a ten-gun vessel would have a marked influence in restoring order ! The official utterances of the Society, however, declared Friends to be "a separated people, standing single from all seditious actions," and in their petition to the Lords Proprietors in 1679 they ask for protection from "the heads of the sedition who now sit in Parliament," *i.e.* in the colonial legislature.[3]

John Archdale first comes into connection with the Carolinas by the purchase of Sir John Berkeley's share in the proprietorship of the colony for his minor son, Thomas Archdale, about 1680. His name is first mentioned in the colonial records on March 26, 1681, when he commissioned Daniel Akehurst—formerly of Virginia—to be his deputy.[4] He had, however, already had a long apprenticeship in colonial affairs, having served from 1664 to about the end of that decade as agent for Sir Ferdinando Gorges, Governor of Maine.[5] He was not at this time a Quaker, but became one soon after his return to England,

---

[1] *Colony Records*, i. 228.   [2] See Weeks, *op. cit.* pp. 33-34.
[3] *Colony Records*, i. 250-253.
[4] *South Carolina Historical Collection*, i. 104.
[5] The *National Dictionary of Biography* makes Archdale brother-in-law to Gorges.

probably in the early 'seventies.[1] He seems to have been reached by Fox himself, for in a letter, written in 1686 to the Quaker founder, he says :

"I desire to be had in remembrance by thee, having faith in the power that was by thee, in this last age of the world, first preached, and [which] convinced me . . . and separated me from my father's house."[2]

Soon after he became a Proprietor, he came over to America, and settled in the colony—at least we find him there in the winter of 1683, for the new appointee for Governor, Seth Sothel, received instructions (dated December 14, 1683) to consult with John Archdale in making his official appointments. The instructions order

"That he doe forwith, with the advice of Mr. Archdale, choose four of the discreatest honest men of the county who were no way concerned in any of the said disturbances to be Justices of the County Court, and also an able man so qualified to be sherrif of the county, that there may bee a Court of impartiall persons for the tryall of all actions that have relation to the late disorders that those injured may have right done them according to Law."[3]

During a part of the years 1685 and 1686 Governor Sothel was out of the colony, and John Archdale temporarily performed the duties of the governorship, evidently to the great satisfaction of the colonists. It was during this period of colonial service that he wrote the letter to George Fox, already referred to. He complains in the letter that opportunities for intercourse between the colony and Great Britain are meagre, though the colony produces many exportable commodities. "The country produces plentifully all things necessary for the life of man, with as little labour as any I have known. It wants only industrious people, fearing God." He gives an interesting account of the way he has dealt with the Indians, and brought them into peaceful conditions—" I

---

[1] Isaac Milles, who was vicar of Chipping Wycombe parish from 1674 to 1681, expresses his regret that John Archdale has turned Quaker, because " he is the chief gentleman of the village."

[2] Letter in Bowden, i. 416.

[3] *Colony Records*, i. 346. There are, too, other orders to consult John Archdale. See especially *Colony Records*, i. 346, 350, and 351.

look upon their outward civilising," he says, " as a good preparation for the Gospel, which God in his season, without doubt, will cause to dawn among them." He is impressed with the spread of the Quaker faith, which, undoubtedly, his presence in the colony had done much to advance, but his reference to it is in these simple, unostentatious words : " The growth of the Divine Seed in these parts is an encouragement to all that witness it." [1]

He apparently returned to England sometime during the year 1686 ; to come back a decade later with greatly enlarged powers. Between the years 1686 and 1695— *i.e.* the period of Archdale's absence in England—the affairs of the colony were in a troublous condition. Sothel became impossible either as Governor or Proprietor, and was forced out of the country, but none of the men who tried to direct affairs was possessed of wisdom or prestige enough to quiet the disturbances, or to settle the issues which were embroiling the different sections of the great colony.[2] The Proprietors were finally aroused to the urgency of the situation by a letter from Governor Smith, who was vainly trying to bring the colony into order, calling upon the Proprietors to send over one of their number.[3] The colonists suggested that Lord Ashley was the " proper person for such a worke," but " his circumstances would not admitt of his absence from England, though his heart and affections were intirely inclined hither." It was then that Archdale was summoned to the task. To quote his own words : " Ye Proprietors were pleased to look upon mee as one that would be impartiall in examining into ye causes [of discontent], and thereby bee ye more capable of judging equally ye parties concerned in ye differences " ; and furthermore

[1] Bowden, i. 415-416.
[2] Carolina was divided into the North and South Colonies about 1688, though still under one proprietorship.
[3] In his opening speech to the Assembly in South Carolina Archdale said : '' The occasion of my coming hither was . . . that there came various letters from Carolina, signifying ye great discontent and division ye people were under, but especially one . . . wherein it was signified that ye heates and animosities amongst you was growne almost irreconcileable, and that, except a proprietor did speedily come over, there was no hopes of any reconciliation amongst you." This address is printed in full in *Historical Collection of South Carolina*, ii. 102.

his appointment had "the encouragement of several Carolinians then in England."[1]

The official appointment of Archdale was made by Lord Craven, Palatine[2] of the Carolinas, and was as follows:

"WILLIAM, EARLE OF CRAVEN, VISCOUNT CRAVEN OF UFFINGTON, BARON CRAVEN OF HAMPSTEAD, MARSHALL PALATINE

"To JOHN ARCHDALE, Esqr.
one of the Landgraves and
Governour of Carolina.

"Whereas it is agreed by ye Lords Proprietors of ye said Province that the Palatine should name ye Governour, I out of the Trust and confidence I have in ye Wisdom, Prudence, Integrity and Loyalty of you John Archdale, Esqr., Doe hereby nominate, Constitute and Appoint you ye sd. John Archdale to be Governour and Commander-in-Chief of Carolina, with full power and authority to doe Act and Execute all such Jurisdictions and Powers as by virtue of ye Rules of Government and Instructions given by myself and ye rest of ye Lords Proprietors of ye sd. Province a Governour is to doe and Exercize. And you are to follow such instructions as are herewith given you or that you shall hereafter from time to time receive from myself and ye rest of ye Lords Proprietors of ye said Province and thus to continue during my Pleasure. Given under my hand and Seale this 28th day of November 1694.

"CRAVEN, Palatine."[3]

This document is, however, only the official certificate of his appointment, for the Proprietors had already, on the 31st of August of the same year, "constituted and appointed" "our trusty and well-beloved John Archdale, Esqr., Governour of our whole province of Carolina, reposing special trust in ye courage, loyalty, and prudence of ye sd. John Archdale." They had given him very large and comprehensive power:

[1] From Archdale's Speech in the South Carolina Assembly.
[2] The Palatine was the highest order of nobility in Locke's Constitution for the Colony.
[3] From the *Archdale Papers* in the Roberts Collection at Haverford College. I find from the British State Paper Office for October 17, 1694, the Governor's salary was £200 *per annum*.

" Wee do hereby further Impower, constitute and apoint you our sd. Governour to be Admirall, Capt. Generall and Commander-in-chief of all ye forces raised or to be raised both by sea and land within our sd. Province and over them to appoint a Lïeutenant General, or Lieutenant Generals, Vice Admirall or Vice Admiralls both of South and North Carolina "

with further extensive power of appointment and with far-reaching authority over internal affairs.[1]

The new governor sailed almost immediately upon his appointment, landed in New England, visited Boston, Plymouth, Rhode Island, and travelled by land to his province, arriving in North Carolina June 25, 1695. His daughter, who was married to Emanuel Lowe, resided in Albemarle, and here, among his own people, organising the troubled affairs of the northern colony and adding new life and power to the Quaker meetings along the Sound, he remained about six weeks. On his arrival he had found Thomas Harvey—probably a Quaker—acting as deputy governor, and when he departed to go to the Southern Colony, he left Harvey in charge of the administration in North Carolina.[2] Archdale arrived in Charleston, South Carolina, early in August, and set himself to work to get at the seat of the colonial troubles. In his own account he says :

" When I arrived I found all matters in great confusion and every faction apply'd themselves to me in hopes of relief. I appeased them with kind and gentle words and as soon as possible called an assembly." [3]

There was much hard feeling and jealousy between dissenters and churchmen, and between moderate church-

[1] These instructions are in the British State Papers Office for North Carolina, and are printed in *Colony Records of North Carolina*, i. 389-390.

[2] When Thomas Story came to North Carolina in 1699 he had letters to Thomas Harvey who received him and entertained him (*Journal*, p. 157), and it appears further that Harvey did not take an oath as Governor, since Governor Nicholson of Virginia refused to recognise his authority to appoint commissioners to settle the boundary between North Carolina and Virginia on the ground that the Governor was not under oath in office (Ashe, i. 150). Daniel Akehurst, a Quaker, was at this time Secretary of the Colony, and Francis Toms was an assistant. See *Colony Records*, i. 413.

[3] Archdale's " Description of Carolina," written in 1707, printed in *Historical Collection of South Carolina*, ii. 85-120.

men and high churchmen, and in forming his Council Archdale endeavoured to "mix" his forces. He gives this quaint account of his plan :

"Although my power was very large, yet I did not wholly exclude the High-Church party out of the essential part of the government, but mixed two moderate church-men to one High Church man in the Council whereby the Balance of Government was preserved peaceable and quiet in my time." [1]

The choice of the Assembly was left with the people, and it met for official business August 17, 1695. The Governor was not required to take an oath, but gave affirmation to the following engagement :

"Att a Councill Held at Charles Towne the 17th day of August Anno Domi. 1698 : And Psent the Rt. Hono[ble]. John Archdale Esqr., Governor.

> PAUL GRIMBALL.
> STEPHEN : BULL.
> Dep[tys]. RICHARD : CONANT.   Esqrs.
> WILLIAM : SMITH.
> WILLIAM HAWETT.

This day the R[t]. Hono[ble]. John Archdale Esqr., Governor, in open Councill Tooke the following oaths or declarations according to the forme of his profession.

You being Governor doe solemnely promise and Ingage that you will govern according to the Lords Proprs. Instructions and Rules of Government and as the Law Directs : you will Distribute equall Justice without delay to the Rich and poore : The Secretts of the Council you will keep, In all things you shall endeavour to discharge the Trust reposed in you on behalfe of the Lords for the good of the people according to your power and the best of your understanding. This you declare according to the forme of your profession.

You shall well and truely to the best of yo[r] Skill, use your utmost endeavour to cause the severall Clauses contained in the Acts of Parliament Called an Act for the Encouraging and Increasing of Shipping & navigation, passed or made in the twelfth yeare of the Reigne of our Late Soveraigne Lord King Charles the Second ; And the Acte of Parliament Called an Act for the Encouradgement of Trade, passed or made in the

---

[1] *Historical Collection of South Carolina,* ii. 113.

fifteenth yeare of our saide Late Soveraigne Lord King Charles the Second.   This you declare according to the forme of your profession.

I doe solemnely promise to beare faith and true allegiance To King William.

> A True Coppy taken from the Records and examined this 17th day of August 1695, P. Jⁿᵒ., Depᵗʸ. Secty." [1]

He, thereupon, addressed the Assembly explaining why he had been " endued with such considerable power of trust," and promising " faithfully and impartially " to " answer their expectations."   " And I appeal," he says, " to that of God in your consciences."   " I shall endeavor to heale all ye differences amongst you, to reconcile all persons."   " I hope you will heartily joine to carry on ye public good," and " by ye good settlement of this hopefull colony, posterity will have cause to blesse God." Finally he urged speedy action toward the reasonable and honorable ordering of all things because of the un-certainty of life—" my own mortality and that of others " —" I hope these considerations will quicken you." [2]

Archdale's expectations were more than fulfilled.   He proved to be, not a crude compromiser, but a genuine *pacifier*, because he possessed, in an extraordinary measure, the genius for putting his finger on cardinal issues, and for penetrating through the husks of controversy to the inner core of righteousness.   When he proposed his solu-tion of an issue, it generally satisfied all parties concerned, because it was seen to be wise and fair.

In their humble address to the governor at his leave-taking, " the commons " expressed their thanks for his " prudent, industrious and indefatigable care and manage-ment."   They declared that he had " worked for the

---

[1] From the *Archdale Papers* in the Roberts Collection.   The following amusing account of Archdale's scruples appears in the Report of William Gordon, repre-sentative in North Carolina " of the Society for the Propagation of the Gospel." " Mr. Archdale uncovered his head to hear a foolish woman make an unaccount-able clamour before meat, at his own table, but when he subscribed the oath [affirmation] to be taken for putting in execution the laws of trade he did it with his hat on, which is an error no Barclay has made an ' apology ' for ! "—*Colony Records*, i. 708.

[2] Address to the Assembly.

peace, welfare, tranquility, plenty, prosperity, and safety of the colony," and they assure him that he has "removed all former doubts, jealousies, and discouragements of us the people." [1]

Archdale had four main problems to solve: (1) To establish harmony and peace among the colonists themselves; (2) To reconcile them to the jurisdiction and authority of the Proprietors; (3) To establish a colonial policy toward the Indians, and to regulate traffic with them; (4) To secure an amicable basis of relationship between the English colonists and the Huguenot refugees who were being discriminated against. In the first two matters, he was, for the time being, entirely successful— "he has removed all former doubts, jealousies, and discouragements."

He was peculiarly qualified to succeed with the Indians, and he is one of the finest embodiments of the Quaker attitude toward these native peoples. He insisted that Indians should be treated as *persons*, and should be protected in their elemental rights. One of the first Bills which he drafted was an Act to prevent debauching Indians. It reads:

"It is enacted that every person which shall give, or any other way dispose of any rum or brandy, or any sorte of spirrits to any Indian or Indians . . . shall forfeit for every time he shall dispose of any such liquors as aforesaid the summe of twenty pounds." [2]

He himself has left a very happy illustration of the effect of a kindly policy toward the natives. He says that during his administration he made a treaty of friendship with a coast tribe of Indians. Not long after, a company of adventurous immigrants from New England were shipwrecked on the same coast, and, finding themselves surrounded by Indians, expected to be murdered. They entrenched themselves as well as they could, and prepared to defend their lives. The Indians tried in every way to declare their attitude of friendship, but the

---

[1] *Historical Collection of South Carolina*, ii. 104.
[2] *Statutes of South Carolina*, ii. 109.

stranded immigrants would not trust them, until they were forced, by the exhaustion of their provisions, to throw themselves on the mercy of the Red men. These received them with great civility, furnished them with provisions, and helped them to send a delegation to Charleston for relief.[1]

His attempts to settle the Huguenot difficulties were less successful, though the solution was in sight before he left the colony. The crux of the difficulty was that the English settlers refused to allow the French—French-English animosity being then very *quick* and keen—to sit in the Assembly or to vote for its members. Archdale found that he could not grant the French these privileges of citizenship without losing the goodwill of the English colonists, and he yielded for the moment. But he urged the English to treat their alien neighbours in the spirit of friendship, and to temper all their dealings with them with "levity and moderation." He carried on a friendly correspondence with the Huguenots, and he prepared the way for their complete naturalisation. A letter from the Proprietors to him says that they are glad to hear that the Assembly is inclined to grant naturalisation to the French;[2] and soon after his return an Act was passed, which provided that "all aliens of what nation soever, which now are inhabitants of South Carolina shall have all rights, privileges, and immunities which any person born of English parents within this province has."[3]

He oversaw the construction of improved public roads. He prepared the first Act on record in South Carolina for the regulation of the liquor traffic,[4] and he also prepared a beneficent measure for the administration of charity, and for the care and relief of the poor.[5] Many complications had arisen over the inadequate methods of "granting" lands and of collecting quit-rents. He brought about a readjustment of methods, which greatly relieved the old settlers, and which encouraged new

---

[1] *Historical Collection of South Carolina*, ii. 108.
[2] In British State Paper Office under date of September 10, 1696.
[3] *Statutes of South Carolina*, ii. 131.
[4] *Ibid.* ii. 113.   [5] *Ibid.* ii. 116.

immigrants to come in. He worked out a plan for protecting the colonists round Cape Fear against kidnappers, and he insisted on kindness toward mariners who were shipwrecked on the coast. He was so far tolerant of other faiths than his own that he took up friendly relations with the Catholic Spaniards of Florida. Four Indians, converts of the Spanish priests, were captured by Carolina Indians and exposed for sale as slaves. Archdale ransomed them and sent them to the Spanish Governor at St. Augustine. " I shall manifest reciprocal kindness," wrote the Spaniard, and he was true to his promise.[1] Settlers from New England were attracted to this " American Canaan," as Archdale calls it, and they recognised that the Southern colony now " stood circumstanced with the honour of a true English government, zealous for the increase of virtue, as well as outward trade and business." [2]

When the Quaker Governor had finished his term of service and was returning to England, the representatives of the freemen of the colony expressed to him their profound appreciation of his great work among them, and declared, " By your wisdom, patience, and labor you have laid a firm foundation for a most glorious superstructure." [3]

One of the most immediate after-fruits of his sojourn was the passage of an Act, March 10, 1697, which granted liberty of conscience to all colonists—"except only papists "—" All Christians which now are or hereafter may be in this province shall enjoy the full liberty of their conscience." [4] Archdale himself did not receive such broad and enlightened treatment. Soon after his return to England he was elected to Parliament as member from the borough of Chipping Wycombe, but being unable, for conscientious reasons, to take the oath, he was refused his seat.

Before sailing from America he revisited North

---

[1] *Historical Collection of South Carolina*, i. 120.
[2] Letter preserved in *Historical Collection of South Carolina*, ii. 105.
[3] *Ibid.* ii. 104.   [4] *Statutes of South Carolina*, ii. 133.

Carolina, and travelled through the province with James Dickinson who was there on a religious visit.[1] He reconfirmed the appointment of Thomas Harvey as governor of the northern colony, and so far won the regard and confidence of the colonists that they wrote officially to the Proprietors of him : " It was his greatest care to make peace and plenty flow amongst us." [2]

This " American Canaan," however, was not long to remain in " peace." In 1700, the first minister of the Church of England arrived in Albemarle, and from that time on, a strong party formed in the colony determined to make life difficult for all who would not " conform." An act was passed in 1701 which practically *established* the Church in the colony. The dissenters—who were mainly Quakers—rallied themselves at the next election, and got control of the Assembly. Governor Walker—who succeeded Harvey—and who was determined to make North Carolina a Church of England colony, wrote to the Bishop of London in October 1703 :

"I beg leave to inform you that we have an Assembly to sit on the 3rd of November next ; above one-half of the Burgesses chosen are Quakers, and have declared their designs of making void the Act for establishing the Church." [3]

The Act was, however, annulled by the Proprietors themselves, but the issue was still very much alive.

In 1704 Rev. John Blair came to the colony as the first representative of the " Society for the Propagation of the Gospel in Foreign Parts." He found the Quakers "the most powerful enemies to Church government," and he found in the colony a large number of persons who would have been Quakers " if the demand for purity of life had not been too great for them." [4]

The report of William Gordon (made in 1709), plainly shows that the Quaker influence in politics at the beginning of the century was very great. He says :

---

[1] *Friends Library*, xii. 396.
[2] John Archdale's will, dated 1713, is preserved in Portfolio 14, Devonshire House.
[3] *Colony Records*, i. 572.　　　　　　　　　　[4] *Ibid*. i. 600

"They [the Quakers] were made councillors and grew powerful, for the council granting commissions, in a short time they had Quaker members in most of their courts; nay in some the *majority* was such. They were very dilligent at the election of members of the Assembly, so that what by themselves, the assistance of several unthinking people and the carelessness of others, they carried it so far that no encouragement could be obtained for ministers [of the Church]." [1]

This Report of William Gordon, though full of prejudice and hostility to the Quakers, gives some light on their numbers in North Carolina. He says:

"As to their number, they are at this time but about the tenth part of the inhabitants; and if they were more, they would be but the greater burden, since they contribute nothing towards its defence." . . . "The Quakers in the precinct of Perquimans are very numerous, extremely ignorant, insufferably proud and ambitious, and consequently ungovernable." . . . "The next precinct is Pasquotank, where as yet there is no Church built; the Quakers are here very numerous; the roads are, I think, the worst; but it is closer settled than the others, and better peopled in proportion to its bigness. In their way of living they have much the advantage of the rest, being more industrious, careful and cleanly." [2]

In 1704 South Carolina passed an act "for the establishment of worship according to the Church of England" and the "Vestry Act" of North Carolina, which was passed soon after, appears to have virtually disfranchised all dissenters in that colony. [3] Edmund Porter, a representative Friend, was sent to England to present the complaints of the dissenters and to secure relief, and the old governor, John Archdale, soon after, wrote his "Description of Carolina" to express his protest against the attempted limitation of religious freedom in the two colonies.

Troubles, however, increased. By an Act of Parliament (1704) all persons holding public office were required to take an oath of allegiance to the new Queen, Anne. The oath was administered by Governor Daniel to the

---

[1] Gordon's *Report, Colony Records*, i. 708-715.
[2] *Colony Records*, pp. 708-715.
[3] Act is described in Gordon's *Report, Colony Records*, i. 708-715.

Quakers in the Council and Assembly of North Carolina, and, on their refusal to take it, they were thrown out of office, and also dismissed from all courts of justice. Porter, the Quaker "ambassador" from the colony, seems to have succeeded in his mission to the extent of securing a change of governors. Thomas Cary, supposed to be in sympathy with dissenters, and himself a son-in-law of Archdale, was selected for the new governor. He proved, however, to be a hollow reed, for he, too, administered the oath, which again cleared the Assembly of Quakers, and a fine was imposed on any person who should act officially without taking the oath. This time, John Porter, a man of great determination and large influence, was sent to England as the agent of the colony to secure relief from these new grievances. Such matters moved slowly in those days, and Porter needed patience, but he finally, in 1707, secured a suspension of the laws imposing oaths, and also an order suspending Cary as governor.[1] John Porter, on his return, with consummate political skill, won over Cary to the dissenters' side, and got him chosen president of the Council, and so *ex-officio* governor. The Quaker party was now a prominent influence in the control of affairs. A strong reaction against the Cary government set in, and in 1710 Edward Hyde was selected by the Proprietors to be governor of North Carolina. He decided to force the Quakers out of the Council and the Assembly, and Cary's government was declared a "usurpation." Cary and John Porter were seized but escaped, and a tiny "rebellion" followed in which one man was killed. The real issue was the principle of religious liberty, but the Quakers were not active in the rebellion, and did not sympathise with the methods adopted by Cary and Porter, however much they were consecrated in spirit to the principle at issue.[2] But, though the Quakers

[1] *Colony Records*, i. 709.

[2] Cary was, as said above, a son-in-law of Archdale, but he was apparently not a "member of meeting," nor probably was John Porter. Emanuel Lowe, however, another son-in-law of Archdale, and an active participant in the "rebellion," *was* a "member." He was "dealt with" by the Yearly Meeting for "having acted divers things contrary to our ways and practices." See *Southern Quakerism and Slavery*, p. 166.

were not directly responsible for the fiasco, it ended unfavourably for them.   It marked the end of their political
influence.   One Quaker, William Borden, was elected a
member of the Assembly from Carteret County in 1747,
and presented himself to take " affirmation," but the
affirmation was denied him, and a new election for his
successor was ordered.[1]   Henceforth, during the colonial
period, Quakerism was a quiet spiritual force, apart from
public affairs, and concerned with the formation of an
inward life and the creation of a peculiar people.

[1] *Colony Records*, iv. 885-887.

BOOK IV

THE EARLY QUAKERS IN NEW JERSEY

By AMELIA M. GUMMERE

CHAPTER I

THE SETTLEMENT OF THE JERSEYS

" My friends, that are gone or are going over to plant and make outward plantations in America, keep your own plantations in your hearts with the spirit and power of God, that your own vines and lilies be not hurt."—GEORGE FOX, *Epistles*.

THE causes of Quaker emigration to the American colonies are not so much to be sought in the desire to escape from persecution, as in the idea which took shape in the mind of William Penn, to show Quakerism at work, freed from hampering conditions. Here, too, may be seen the guiding hand of the founder himself. Ten years before the "Holy Experiment" was tried in Pennsylvania, George Fox and his companions—several of whom were men of the true pioneer spirit—traversed that part of the colonial wilderness destined to be the Quakers' refuge from the increasing storm of persecution which followed the Restoration. The latter was doubtless a contributing cause, but the impulse to emigrate came as much from within the sect itself, as from the outside pressure of circumstances. The idea was not a new one. As a matter of fact, effort in the direction of Quaker settlements in the middle colonies of America was made nearly twenty-five years before William Penn came to Pennsylvania. The coast from Maine to Florida being already apparently in possession of other adherents of the King, the Quakers turned their first attention inland with a proposal which came to naught, but which has escaped the attention of most historians except Bowden.

Josiah Coale, an interesting Gloucestershire Friend,

visited America within a year after the three pioneer women, Elizabeth Harris, Mary Fisher, and Ann Austin, and appears to have penetrated farther west among the Indians of the interior than any one else. His second visit in 1660 was under commission from the English Friends to treat with the Indians of the Susquehanna for the purchase of lands.[1] The absence of an influential arbitrator familiar with savage customs, as well as the violence of the tribal wars then being waged, prevented further steps being taken at that time by Josiah Coale, who returned home without having accomplished his purpose. The liquid syllables of the Susquehanna long had an alluring sound to English ears, for one is reminded of the " Pantisocracy " of a century later, when the same region for a time offered a refuge for bruised literary and democratic hearts after the French Revolution, until that too proved vain, and Wordsworth's sonnet to the " Degenerate Sons " of Pennsylvania expressed his chagrin when his financial speculations fell out.

So early as 1630 the white man was in New Jersey, called, according to Indian tradition, " Scheyichbi." The "New Albion" settlement of Sir Edward Plowden, the Irish nobleman, and the Dutch occupancy of the lower Delaware in 1632, together with the Swedish undertaking at the instance of Gustavus Adolphus carried out in 1637, were followed by several companies of settlers, who, after the complete destruction of more than one village and fort, succeeded in establishing themselves in the neighbourhood of the Dutch and Swedes near New Castle, and on the Jersey side of Delaware Bay. Before 1663 an occasional Puritan, Baptist, or Quaker appears to have drifted over from the New England colonies in search of a less restricted religious atmosphere, and to have found the tolerant Dutchman a congenial companion. In this year a group of New Englanders settled on the Raritan river, and soon there were villages at Piscataway, Woodbridge, and Newark, the latter under the spiritual guidance of

---

[1] Coale's Letter is in the A. R. Barclay Collection, No. 53 (1661).

Abraham Pierson, who with his followers in 1666 had rebelled at the prospect of annexation to Massachusetts, and had left New Haven and the theocratic rule of the "Saints," to found a home in a more democratic community. A few New England names still survive among the descendants of Quakers who, in this early period, came from Massachusetts to New Jersey, where the meeting at Shrewsbury grew to great importance. Before 1675, the enormous tract of intervening country between these settlers and those on the lower Delaware formed a great wilderness, untrodden by white man, except the occasional trader, who followed the Indian trail leading from "Achter Koll" (Back Bay) now Newark Bay, to the Delaware at the Falls. This was the "Upper Road." The "Lower Road" branched off five or six miles from the Raritan river, made a sweep to the east, and struck the Delaware at what is now Burlington. Traces of this trail, known for over a hundred years as the "Burlington Path," could until recently be distinctly seen. There were one or two primitive inns *en route* by 1695, and the province appropriated ten pounds annually for repairs to these "highways," which, so late as 1715, were only passable for horsemen or pedestrians.

It was along the southern branch of this trail that George Fox travelled in 1672, to visit the Quakers of New England, Long Island, and East Jersey. On his way east, Fox tells us that they had difficulty in procuring guides.

"They were hard to get," he says, "and very chargeable. Then had we that wilderness country to pass through, since called West New Jersey, not then inhabited by English, so that we have travelled a whole day together, without seeing man or woman, house, or dwelling-place. Sometimes we lay in the woods by a fire, and sometimes in the Indians' wigwams or houses. We came one night to an Indian town and lay at the king's house, who was a very worthy man. Both he and his wife received us very lovingly, and his attendants (such as they were) were very respectful to us. They laid us mats to lie on, but provision was very short with them, having caught but little that day. At another Indian town, where we stayed, the king came to us and he could speak some English. I spoke to him much, and also to his people, and they were very loving to us." [1]

The Quaker invariably met with similar treatment from the savages, who were always kind when unprovoked. Fox was on his way to the General Meeting in Rhode Island, that memorable occasion when :

" The glorious power of the Lord which was over all, and His blessed truth and life flowing amongst them, had so knit and united them together, that they spent two days in taking leave one of another, and of the Friends of the Island, and then, being mightily filled with the presence and power of the Lord, they went away with joyful hearts to their various habitations." [2]

Returning by way of Flushing and Gravesend, at each place finding Quaker settlers, Fox and his companions, among whom were William Edmundson and Robert Widders, came to Richard Hartshorne's at Middletown, the " twenty-sixth of Sixth month," 1672. He describes the bad bogs and swamps they had to cross before reaching Shrewsbury, where, on the first day, " they had a large and precious " meeting. Men's and women's meetings were held, to which came Friends " out of most parts of New Jersey. They are building a meeting-house in the midst of them, and there is a Monthly and General meeting set up, which will be of great service in those parts." While at Shrewsbury the accident befell John Jay, the Barbadoes planter, who was also in the party. Thrown from his horse with violence, he fell upon his head, and was taken up for dead by his companions. But Fox, with the ready common sense of the experienced traveller, found his neck not broken but dislocated.

"I took his head in both my hands," says Fox in relating the incident, "and setting my knees against a tree, I raised his head and perceived there was nothing out or broken that way. Then I put one hand under his chin and the other behind his head and raised his head two or three times with all my strength and brought it in. I soon perceived his neck began to grow stiff again, and then he began to rattle in the throat and quickly to breathe." [3]

---

[1] *Journal*, ii. 166.　　　[2] *Ibid.*, ii. 169.　　　[3] *Ibid.*, ii. 176.

With returning consciousness he was carried into the house and laid by the fire, when Fox ordered bed and a warm drink to be administered ; "and the next day we passed away (and he with us, pretty well)," riding sixteen miles !

Fox set off from Middletown on the return journey, the " 9 of 7 mo.", travelling forty or fifty miles a day.

"At night, finding an old house which the Indians had forced the people to leave, we made a fire and stayed there at the head of Delaware Bay.   Next day we swam our horses over, about a mile, at twice, first to an island called Upper Dinidock [Matiniconk] and then to the mainland, having hired Indians to help us over in their canoes." [1]

The vacant dwelling which sheltered the party was the house, built in the Swedish fashion, of a Dutchman, Peter Jegou, who had received a tavern licence from Governor Carteret in 1668.   The Indians plundered and drove him away for some offence in 1670; his neighbours apparently in alarm deserted the two other houses of which we have record at that point.   George Fox landed at Bristol, England, in 4th mo. 1673, where his wife and other members of his family joined him.   With them came William Penn and his wife Gulielma.   A short stay with London Friends followed, when there was an interesting house-party at Rickmansworth, where Penn's young wife was hostess, their wedding having occurred a few months before.   As soon as Fox left Penn's hospitable roof, he was followed and taken for his eighth and last imprisonment.   It is not too much to infer that this visit

[1] *Journal*, ii. 177.   "Mattinagcom" or "Matiniconk," now Burlington Island.   The Indian name for island was *Tiniconk* or *Tenacong*.   At the time Fox crossed the Delaware, this island was known as Upper Tineconk, to distinguish it from Lower Tineconk, upon which now stands the city of Burlington, close to the east shore of the river.   It is easy to see how George Fox mistook the unfamiliar Indian name.   Editors of his *Journal* have further confounded the name with the island [or "Tenacong"] of *Tinicum*, named and settled by the Swedes, near Chester, Pennsylvania.   Comparison with early authorities on the subject shows Fox's account to be very accurate, "near the head of the Bay" meaning, undoubtedly, near the head of navigation.   It took him two days' travel over seventy miles of bad roads and a "desperate river" to reach Newcastle, which would not have been the case had he crossed at Tinicum.   [See Benjamin Ferris, *History of the Original Settlements on the Delaware* ; Jasper Dankers and Peter Sluyter, *Journal of a Voyage to New York*, 1679 ; *Record of the Court at Upland*, Pennsylvania, 1676-1681, etc.].

of Fox, with his report fresh from the Friends in America, must have made a great impression upon William Penn, then a young man of eight and twenty.

The peaceful conquest of New Netherland by the English in 1664 gave its royal proprietor, the Duke of York, the great province lying between the "North" or Hudson and the "South" or Delaware rivers. This, for loyal service, was at once granted by the impoverished Duke to two men of influence at Court—John, Lord Berkeley, Baron of Stratton, a brother of Sir William Berkeley, Governor of Virginia, and in 1674 Ambassador to France; and Sir George Carteret, a turbulent and interesting man, companion of Samuel Pepys, who frequently mentions him in his famous diary. The old Norman family of de Carteret of St. Ouen, in the island of Jersey, was prominent for many generations in history. The present representative had gallantly defended Jersey against the Roundheads, and was the last Commander to lower the King's flag. In compliment, therefore, to him, the province received the Latin name for the island, "Nova Caesarea," but the vernacular was from the first preferred by the people, and except on early seals, documents, etc., the new acquisition was known as New Jersey. Sir George was sixty-one years of age at this time, a member of the Privy Council of Charles II., and Vice-Chancellor of the Household. As the representative of the owners, Philip Carteret, a relative of Sir George, was sent out, and in 1668 the first Assembly convened at Elizabethtown. Such, however, were the dissensions as to the veto power of the Governor, the adjustment of quit-rents, and the taxation of the colonists, that it was seven years before another Assembly could be called which was other than illegal. A slight period of Dutch rule was followed in 1674 by permanent English possession, the right to legislate independently having meantime been demanded by the people. The Treaty of Westminster[1] necessitated the bestowal anew of the

---

[1] Signed 9th February 1674, when the Prince of Orange made over the Dutch possessions to King Charles II.

province by the King upon the Duke of York, by whom were disregarded the claims alike of those who held title under him, and under Berkeley and Carteret. Amid the technicalities that followed, Sir George Carteret demanded and obtained from the Duke a separate grant of East Jersey, with a division line loosely drawn from Barnegat Bay on the coast, to just below Rancocas Creek on the Delaware; both the Jerseys remained under the administration of Sir Edmund Andros, Governor of New York until 1680, when Carteret discomfited Andros at a special Court of Assize, thus securing the independency of both the Jerseys. In 1674 Lord Berkeley had become a very old man, and his finances, as one result of the quit-rent quarrel, had materially shrunk. Disheartened by the situation, he determined to sell, preferably to the Quakers, and this became their opportunity. In March of that year he conveyed the whole of the vast estate to two Quakers—John Fenwick, a Buckinghamshire yeoman, and Edward Byllynge, a merchant of London, for the sum of one thousand pounds !

This moment marks the entrance of the Quaker into the affairs of government in the middle colonies, following the example of Rhode Island, where the Quakers had long been the administrators of the law and of the King. It was by no accident that this purchase took place within a short time after the return of George Fox to England from America, and Bowden is doubtless right when he says that the property was acquired for the benefit of the Society at large. Fenwick was a litigious old Cromwellian soldier recently converted to Quakerism, and the details of a dispute between him and his partner cannot here be recited. The actual facts at this distance of time are hazy, and are only vaguely referred to in two or three letters [1] from William Penn, written while the latter was acting as arbitrator. The quarrel resulted in a division of the property, one-tenth being awarded to Fenwick, while complications in business soon forced Byllynge to

---

[1] Three of these are quoted by Bowden, *History of Friends in America*, i. 391, from the Harleian MSS. in the British Museum.

assign his nine-tenths in trust for his creditors to William Penn, Gawen Lawrie, and Nicholas Lucas, all of them Quakers. Subsequently, Fenwick's tenth also came under their control.

The idea of emigration to England's western possessions had been rapidly maturing in the minds of the leading Quakers, led doubtless by William Penn. Penn had been associated with John Locke, the philosopher, in drawing up a theory of government for Carolina, and Berkeley and Carteret were both already proprietors of the southern colony when they became owners also of the Jerseys. The part taken by William Penn in the settlement of New Jersey has never yet received due recognition from any historian. No sudden inspiration led him to ask of Charles the grant for Pennsylvania in liquidation of the debt of the crown to his father. George Fox made his report to him in 1673, and when, in the following year, his friend and neighbour John Fenwick, near Rickmansworth, besought his aid as arbitrator, he was obliged to give attention to conditions in the new country. His trusteeship for Byllynge immediately after, necessitated further acquaintance with the situation. It is not too much to assert that these services as arbitrator and trustee were the immediate causes leading to his East Jersey proprietorship, and ultimately to the settlement of Pennsylvania.

The "Concessions," etc., signed by Berkeley and Carteret were drawn up by a group of men, not one of whom was familiar with the country or its inhabitants for whom they legislated. The terms were liberal, and the laws tolerant, but the whole was based upon theory. The second "Concessions and Agreements of the Proprietors, Freeholders, and Inhabitants of West Jersey, in America" gave to the spirit of liberty a wider range than had heretofore been the case in any record of Anglo-Saxon organic law. These Concessions are dated 3rd March 1676 (O.S.), after the return from America of Coale, Burnyeat, Fox, and Edmundson—all men of intelligence and experience, who, we know from their journals, reported the character of the country and the situation of the settlers then beginning to come in, to William Penn and his advisers.   Lucas and Lawrie were business men, little versed in statecraft, and Penn himself was at this time but thirty-two.   The making of constitutions was a fashionable amusement.   It had occupied Penn's friends, Locke and Algernon Sidney, chiefly as a means of illustrating their theories of freedom and philanthropy. But the Quakers had known persecution, and it had taught them and their leaders the value of personal freedom, and of liberty of conscience.   The Concessions were placed for signature by the subscribers, (who did not all sign at once) in London, and were probably later taken to Yorkshire, as the grouping of signatures would lead one to fancy, for the same purpose.   Then, as though with a sigh of relief, Penn and his partners wrote to the most prominent Quaker in the Jerseys, Richard Hartshorne at Middletown, from London, 26th June 1676:

"We have made concessions by ourselves, being such as Friends here and there (we question not) will approve of. . . . There we lay a foundation for after ages to understand their liberty as men and Christians, that they may not be brought in bondage but by their own consent, for we put the power in the people."

There breathes in the great charter for New Jersey, whose anonymous author is beyond doubt William Penn, a spirit of religious and political freedom that is even more marked than when, seven years later, he came to draw up the famous "Frame of Government" for his own Pennsylvania.

It will be noticed that East Jersey remained the property of Sir George Carteret alone, while West Jersey thus became a Quaker colony.   The Quakers at once set about publishing and distributing literature inviting their people to emigrate to the new country, some of these pamphlets being so enthusiastic in character that the conscientious Penn issued a caution lest the unprepared find the expected paradise too great a wilderness.   He and his partners in the trust, in their cautionary address, after stating the facts of the purchase, continue :

"'The ninety parts remaining are exposed for sale on behalf of the creditors of Edward Byllynge. And forasmuch as several Friends are concerned as creditors as well as others, and the disposal of so great a part of this country being in our hands, we did in real tenderness and regard to Friends and especially the poor and necessitous, make Friends the first offer, that if any of them, though particularly those that, being low in the world, and under trials about a comfortable livelihood for themselves and families, should be desirous of dealing for any part or parcel thereof, that they might have the refusal. This was the real and honest intent of our hearts, and not to prompt or allure any out of their places, either by the credit our names might have with our people throughout the nation, or by representing the thing otherwise than it is in itself."

It was, therefore, with a pretty clear idea of the real facts, and with full understanding of difficulties ahead of them, that the first Quaker emigration to West Jersey began, when, in 1675, John Fenwick sailed with a number of Quakers in the ship *Griffin*, from London, landing at a spot, which, from the " delightsomenesse of the land," he called Salem. Nearly all were Quakers, and they at once began holding meetings, a monthly meeting being set up the next year after their coming. Meantime, Penn and his associates were rapidly selling off portions of the Byllynge estate, and a number of Quakers who were the latter's creditors accepted lands in liquidation of the debt. Thus were acquired the properties held in such familiar names in modern times as Hutchinson, Pearson, Stacy, and many others.

The next year, 1677, was made the second important effort at colonisation, when the ship *Kent*, from London made the Delaware safely in October of that year, landing her passengers, numbering two hundred and thirty, at Raccoon Creek. The departure of so large a group of Quakers at one time attracted public attention in England, and was observed with interest by the King, who took his yacht in the Thames to see the unusual sight. Greeted by his loyal subjects, he asked if they were all Quakers, and gave them his blessing. Upon landing, the settlers, acting under the instructions of Penn and his colleagues, proceeded at once to the site of what is now Burlington, which, it will be remembered, was the spot where Fox had swum his horse across five years before, and which, with the keen eye of the experienced and observant explorer, he had recorded in his journal. Here a town was laid out, and the company being equally divided between London and Yorkshire Friends, it fell to the latter to give it a name, and Bridlington or Burlington was chosen, from the town of that name whence many came. The home-sick longing for familiar English names accounts for the disappearance of most of the beautiful Indian local names throughout the middle colonies. Interesting details of the settlement and apportionment of land are given by Smith.[1] The Quakers " treated with the Indians about lands," and purchases were made from the natives, but as the settlers had not goods sufficient for all they had bought, the land was not occupied until it was fully paid for. Herein they followed precedent, for to the Dutchman is due the credit of giving the Indians full value for what lands they occupied or claimed. It was not money that was lacking. The supply of trinkets, jews' harps, and brass buttons gave out. An example of one purchase will suffice for the rest.

" 30 matchcoats, 20 guns, 30 kettles, and one great one, 30 pair hose, 20 fathom of duffields, 30 petticoats, 30 narrow hoes, 30 bars of lead, 15 small barrels of powder, 70 knives, 30 Indian axes, 70 combs, 60 pair tobacco tongs, 60 scissors, 69 tinshaw looking-glasses, 120 awl-blades, 120 fish-hooks, 2 grasps of red paint, 120 needles, 60 tobacco boxes, 120 pipes, 200 bells, 100 Jews' harps, 6 anchors rum."

Soon after the settlement made at Burlington, another ship from London brought within the year seventy more passengers, who divided between Burlington and Salem, and another from Hull brought one hundred and fourteen more. Next year, in 1678, in the *Shield* from Hull, came over a hundred more settlers, followed closely by a

[1] Samuel Smith, *History of New Jersey*, p. 98, 2nd edition.

London craft whose name is not known. Fully eight hundred Quakers joined and settled in the new colony within the first eighteen months, many of them persons of large property and wide influence ; while up to the year 1681, at which time William Penn was negotiating for the purchase of Pennsylvania, upwards of fourteen hundred had found their way to the new province.

Sir George Carteret's death in 1679 necessitated the sale of East Jersey by his widow to pay his debts. The opportunity was again seized by the watchful Penn and his associates, who, pleased with the success of their first effort at colonisation, after a slight delay, purchased the eastern province. In February 1681 it was conveyed to William Penn and eleven other Friends. These immediately joined with them twelve others as owners, among whom were Robert Barclay, the Earl of Perth, Lord Drummond, and several other prominent Scotchmen, not Quakers. These twenty-four proprietors formed a " Council of Proprietors," that for East Jersey being appointed in 1684, and that for West Jersey in 1687. These together were established as the original *Council of Proprietors*, which, upon the accession of Queen Anne, in 1702, unconditionally surrendered the right of government for the united province of New Jersey into the royal hands, the acceptance of which surrender was one of the first official acts of that eventful reign. This unique body retained, however, its proprietary rights, and exists to-day, with quaint ceremonies of proclamation on the street corners of Burlington and Gloucester, to effect an occasional sale or transfer of the few unclaimed lands on the New Jersey coasts of which they are still the rightful owners. The organisation is the oldest existing proprietary body in America.

The choice of Governor for the newly purchased Quaker territory fell upon Robert Barclay of Ury, author of the " Apology," who accepted the trust, but never came out, and Thomas Rudyard was made his deputy. Upon the latter's death soon after, Gawen Lawrie took his place. The attention of the Scotch, who were then and shortly after suffering in the Cameronian wars, was directed to the lands in East Jersey by their countrymen of power and influence, who followed the example of the Quaker owners of the western division in the distribution of much literature setting forth the advantages of emigration. They were very far from coming to similar conditions to those in West Jersey, there being at this date nearly five thousand inhabitants already settled in the eastern division. A large number of Scotch and Quakers came into Monmouth county in the next few years, the former being of the " Auld Kirk "—Covenanters and Presbyterians.

Among the Scottish Quakers was George Keith, whose presence in the Jerseys was soon to become a matter of no slight importance in the history of Quakerism. Born in 1638, of the Keiths of Keith Hall, Aberdeenshire, he took his M.A. at the University of Aberdeen in 1662, about which time, in the heat and fire of his youth, he left the rigid form of Presbyterianism in which he had been brought up, to embrace the doctrines of Quakerism. He was a surveyor and mathematician, but seems to have given up most of his time to preaching, which, together with his share in the famous discussion of Quakerism in 1675 at the University of Aberdeen, in company with Alexander Jaffray and Robert Barclay, occasioned one of several imprisonments. Various theories have been advanced as to the object of his emigration to America ; the chief reasons given are his choice by Barclay to run the " Province Line," and his selection as master for William Penn's new school in Philadelphia. It is no more necessary to seek for an ulterior motive in the case of Keith than in that of any of the other Friends who went to America to improve their fortunes and to live in peace.

Keith's intimate acquaintance with the Barclays was doubtless a large factor in his determination to emigrate. The provincial records show that in 1684 he arrived with his wife Anna, his daughters Anna and Eliza, an apprentice named Richard Hodkins, and two maid-servants, Mary Smith and Christian Ghaine. Robert Bridgman, a merchant, came with him and "imported himself." Keith was shortly after made Surveyor-General of East Jersey, and joined Andrew Robeson, who held a similar office for the Western division, in 1686 in running the famous " Province Line," which, after two centuries of dispute, was in 1886 finally confirmed by a special board of commissioners. The tracts of land taken up by Keith in Monmouth county, near Freehold, where he first settled, were gradually disposed of in lots to various purchasers, and he removed in 1689 to Philadelphia, to take up once more his calling of school-master, which he had been pursuing in Edmonton, England, at the time of his determination to emigrate. Between this date and that of his expulsion from the Society for schism by the Yearly Meeting at Burlington in 1692, his history belongs to that of Pennsylvania Quakerism. His next appearance upon the soil of New Jersey is as the accredited agent for the newly created Society for the Propagation of the Gospel in Foreign Parts, in which capacity he laid the foundation stone of St. Mary's Episcopal church in Burlington, in 1703, and was instrumental in establishing Episcopalianism upon a sure basis in the Jerseys, at the cost of many converts from Quakerism.

Connected with the Keith controversy were the two printers, Daniel Leeds of West Jersey, and William Bradford of Philadelphia. The latter removed to New York early in the history of the schism, but it is supposed that for a short time, his press was set up at Burlington. Leeds's " Allmanack " was suppressed by the meeting, and he himself forced to make an acknowledgment for his statements, which, the Friends said, " evinced a froward spirit." He became on intimate terms with the " Mystics " in Germantown, approved and published their astrological predictions, and finally joined the " Christian Quakers," as the Keithian separatists preferred to call themselves.

Thus came the Quaker settlers into the fertile lands of the Jerseys. Many hardships had to be endured, but, thanks to an abundant and bountiful return for their first efforts in the field, they were spared nearly all the suffering and sorrows which, in a more unfriendly climate, fell to the lot of the Pilgrims in Massachusetts. Many enthusiastic letters home, from which it is a temptation to quote, still exist in praise of the new country. "I like the place well," said one, "it's like to be a healthful place, and very pleasant to live in." "It is a country," writes another, "that produceth all things for the support and sustenance of man." "Whatever envy or evil spies may speak of it, I could wish you. all here," declared a third.[1] Not lightly did they speak. Many of the little company had lain in loathsome English gaols, and many of their sufferings may be found described by Besse.[2] They had proved their faithfulness; had borne their persecutions patiently; they had declared, as had Penn for them, that they were not fleeing to escape trials that they were called upon longer to endure. Justified by their years of hardship, now they longed for the wider outlook which provided a secure home for their children in the future. "I wish," wrote one of the number [3] years after, "I wish that they that come after may remember these things." "The settlement of this country," says another witness, "was directed by an impulse on the spirit of God's people, not for their own ease and tranquillity, but rather for the posterity which should be after them."[4] It was not commercialism which established them so firmly in the new country. The trading spirit, strangely enough, has never yet sufficed for effectual colonisation. Men of good estate, their English homes were not left without a sigh.

"O remember us," they write, "for we cannot forget you. Many waters cannot quench our love, nor distance wipe out the deep remembrance. . . . Though the Lord hath been pleased to remove us far away from you, as to the ends of the earth, yet are you present with us. Your exercises are ours, our hearts are dissolved in the remembrance of you."

---

[1] S. Smith. *History of Nova Caesarea, or New Jersey*, where various letters are given more at length.

[2] J. Besse, *Sufferings of the Quakers*, 2 vols. folio.

[3] Mary Murfin Smith, who came as a child with her parents. Drowned in 1739.

[4] Thomas Sharp, *Newtown Monthly Meeting Records*.

CHAPTER II

MEETINGS AND SOCIAL LIFE

THE Friends' first care was to settle meetings. These, both at Salem and Burlington, like the services of the first comers to Virginia, were held in tents made of the sails of their ships. They next met in their own dwellings, and the early minutes of most of the meetings of the Jerseys begin in a private house, before any record can be found of a meeting-house. Very soon, however, there was an effort to build suitable accommodation for the increasing numbers. The original meeting for the middle colonies appears to have been at Shrewsbury, where one was settled as early as 1670, and where George Fox mentions the building of a meeting-house going on at the time of his visit in 1672. These Quakers were from New England, the first child born in the settlement in 1667, according to an old authority, having been Elizabeth, daughter of Eliakim Wardell, who, with his wife Lydia, in 1665 had been cruelly and publicly scourged for the appearance of the latter almost unclothed as a "sign" before the Puritan congregation in the meeting-house at their New England home in Hampton. They would seem to have taken refuge in East Jersey, where Bowden [1] refers to their residence two years later. Doubtless meetings had existed in the Jerseys a few years before. The meeting began at Salem in 1675, and the next year the monthly meeting was set up, being held for some time in the dwelling house of hewn logs belonging to Samuel Nicholson. Bowden calls

[1] Bowden, *History of Friends in America*, i. 405.

attention to the fact, which is impressive, that several of the American meetings were organised in the interval between the first proposal of monthly meetings by Fox at Durham, 1653, and their regular establishment in England thirteen years later.

Seven months after the landing at Raccoon Creek, a Monthly Meeting was set up at Burlington.   The minutes begin with the following preamble :

"Since by the good Providence of God, many Friends with their families have transported themselves into this Province of West New Jersey, the said Friends in these upper parts have found it needfull, according to our practice in the place wee came from, to settle Monthly Meetings for the well ordering the affairs of ye Church it was agreed that accordingly it should be done, and accordingly it was done the 15th of ye 5th mo^th. 1678."

Many small meetings were held in scattered plantations not many miles removed from each other, since the "going," according to early minutes, was too bad in inclement weather to allow Friends to journey far.   Very willingly the different settlements aided each other in clearing roads, and the old colonial highway, still known as the "Salem Road," was laid out by ten men from Salem and ten from Burlington, at the people's expense.

The first meetings in Burlington were held at the house of Thomas Gardiner.   From here the Monthly Meeting, under date "7th of ye 12th mo. 1680," sent what Bowden asserts to have been the earliest recorded epistle addressed to London Yearly Meeting by *any* meeting in America.   Care for the spiritual welfare of their savage neighbours and provision for their poorer members are evident from the early minutes ; but the necessity for proper certificates as to the character of the new-comers who so soon appeared, made the presentation of proper credentials, particularly in cases of marriage, of paramount importance.   No less than thirteen couples in the first three years presented themselves with that object before the meeting in Burlington.   Hence the following document was sent to London.

"To our Dear Friends and Brethren at the Yearly Meeting at London.

"DEAR FRIENDS AND BRETHREN—Whom God hath honoured with his heavenly presence and dominion, as some of us have been eye witnesses (and in our measures partakers with you) in those solemn annual assemblies ; in the remembrance of which our souls are consolated, and do bow before the Lord with reverent acknowledgment to him, to whom it belongs forever.

"And, dear friends, being fully satisfied of your love and care and zeal for the Lord and His truth, and your travail and desire for the promotion of it, hath given us encouragement to address ourselves to you, to request your assistance in these following particulars, being sensible of the need of it, and believing it will conduce to the honour of God and the benefit of His people ; for the Lord having, by an overruling Providence, cast our lots in these remote parts of the world, our care and desire is that He may be honoured in us and through us, and His dear truth which we may profess may be had in good repute and esteem by those that are yet strangers to it.

"Dear Friends, our first request unto you is, that in your several counties and meetings out of which any may transport themselves in this place, that you will be pleased to take care that we may have certificates concerning them; for here are several honest and innocent people that brought no certificate with them from their respective Monthly Meetings, not foreseeing the service of them, and so never desired any, which for the future, in cases of which defect, we do entreat you who are sensible of the need for certificates, to put them in mind of them ; for in some cases where certificates are required (and they have none), it occasions a great and tedious delay before they can be had from England, besides the hazard of letters miscarrying, which is very uneasy to the parties immediately concerned, and no ways grateful or desirable to us ; yet in some cases necessity urgeth it, or we must act very unsafely, and particularly in cases of marriage in which we are often concerned.

"So if the parties are single and marriageable at their coming away, we desire to be satisfied of their clearness or unclearness from other parties, and what else you think meet for our knowledge. And if they have parents, whether they will commit them to the care of Friends in general in that matter, or appoint any particular person in whom they can trust. And if any do incline to come that do profess truth yet walk disorderly, and so become dishonourable to truth and the profession they have made of it, we desire to be certified of them and it by some other hand (as there are frequent opportunities from London of doing it) for we are sensible that here are several that left no good savour in their native land from whence they came, and it may be probable that more of that kind may come, thinking to be absconded in this obscure place; but, blessed be the Lord, He hath a people here whom He hath provoked to a zealous affection for the glory of His name, and are desirous that the hidden things of Esau may be brought to light, and in it be condemned; for which cause we thus request your assistance as an advantage and furtherance to that work; for though some have not thought it necessary either to bring certificates themselves or require it of others, we are not of that mind, and do leave it to the wise in heart to judge whence it doth proceed; for though we desire this as an additional help to us, yet not as some have surmised, that we wholly build upon it, without exercising our own mediate sense as God shall guide us. Some, we know, that have been otherwise deserving, have been unadvisedly denied their impartial right of a certificate and very hardly could obtain it, merely through the dislike of some of their undertaking in their coming hither, which we believe to be an injury; and though we would not have any should reject any sound advice or counsel in that matter; yet we do believe that all the faithful ought to be left to God's direction in that matter; most certainly knowing by the surest evidence that God hath had a hand in the removal of some to this place, which we desire that all who are inclined to come hither, who know God, may be careful to know before they attempt it, lest their trials become insupportable to them, but if this they know, they need not fear, for the Lord is known by sea and land the shield and strength of them that fear him.

"And dear Friends, one thing more we think needful to intimate to you, to warn and advise all that come professing of truth, that they be careful and circumspect in their passage.

"So, dear Friends, this, with what further you may apprehend to tend to truth's promotion in this place, we desire your assistance in, which will be very kindly and gladly received by us, who are desirous of an amicable correspondence with you, and do claim a part with you in the holy body and eternal union, which the bond of life is the strength of, in which God preserve you and us, who are your friends and brothers."

Here follow signatures of thirty-seven Friends.

"From our Men's Monthly Meeting, in Burlington, in West New Jersey, the 7th of the Twelfth Month, 1680."[1]

---

[1] Bowden, *History of Friends in America*, i. 402, *et seq.*

At the monthly meeting held in 3 mo. 1681, it was determined to establish a Yearly Meeting, to begin in the 6 mo. following. Notice to this effect was widely circulated, and the transactions of the meeting, to which came Friends from New England, Long Island, and as far south as Maryland, occupied four days. Few particulars of their business remain. Here the Yearly Meeting continued to be held until the meeting-house was finished which was ordered to be built in 1682. Thomas Gardiner died in 1694. The establishment of a Quarterly Meeting was a part of its action, as the first minute of that meeting shows :

"Whereas, the Yearly Meeting saw it necessary yt there should be Quarterly meetings kept in several places in this Province of West New Jersey, and yt this Quarterly Meeting of Friends for Burlington and ye Falls should be held at ye house of William Beedle [Biddle] in Mansfield (being pretty near ye middle of Friends belonging to it) at ye times hereafter mentioned, viz., upon ye last second-day of the 9 mo. ; last second-day of ye 12 mo. ; last second-day of ye 3 mo. ; and ye last second-day of ye 6 mo. ; and to begin at ye 10th hour, which said conclusion of ye Yearly Meeting ye Friends of this meeting are satisfied with.

"29 of 9 mo. 1681."

The second yearly meeting for the Jerseys met in 7 mo. (September) 1682. In the interval a large ship had come to the Delaware shore, and landed three hundred and sixty more settlers, thus greatly augmenting their numbers. But most important was the information they brought that William Penn and a large company of Friends were about to sail for the same neighbourhood. Penn landed from the *Welcome* at Newcastle in October 1682, and attended the Yearly Meeting at Burlington in 1683. At this meeting it was proposed to hold a Yearly Meeting for all the North American colonies, but the proposition fell through. In it may be clearly seen the guiding hand of William Penn.[1]

The first meeting-house in Burlington was ordered to be built in 1682, but was delayed for several years. It

[1] Monthly Meetings were established at Shrewsbury, 1670 ; at Salem, 1676 ; at Burlington, 1678 ; at Newtown, 1681.

was a curious little octagonal building, with no means of heating, and seems to have been copied in architecture by Penn's colony in their first house soon after. Several examples of this octagonal style of building for places of worship and for schools used by the Dutch and the Quakers still exist in northern New Jersey and in Delaware County, Pennsylvania. The great increase in the size of the Yearly Meeting, to which belonged the Friends from Long Island to Maryland, including the rapidly growing town of Philadelphia twenty miles below, in 1696 necessitated for this early house at Burlington a brick addition, capable of being warmed in winter by huge fire-places. Here were held the town-meetings, the school, and the Court, and on the doors were nailed up all public notices, whether a royal proclamation, the required banns for a marriage, or the cattle brand assigned to each planter.[1]

Sometimes a great Indian conference drew the savages to the town. The Yearly Meeting of 1685 especially considered the Indians, and in 1686 the meeting minutes desire the Indian interpreters to be notified to attend the meeting up the river proposed to be held for the Indians by Thomas Budd and Robert Stacey.

The close of the seventeenth century saw a marvellous growth of Quakerism in New Jersey, attracting much attention in England. The economic and social life of the two divisions of the province differed as much as did their natural features. The influence of Puritan New England was as marked in East Jersey as was the more benign and peaceful, not to say indifferent, attitude of the English Quakers in West Jersey. In the former, trade on a smaller scale flourished, as was to be expected of a Puritan, Dutch, and Quaker alliance. The intense ardour of the Calvinist produced a note of individualism, whose outcome was democracy, expressed in the town-meetings held in Quaker meeting-houses, its religious aspect laying the foundations of Presbyterianism in New Jersey. The

---

[1] An interesting census for 1699 shows the number of West Jersey Freeholders who were Quakers to be 266 in a total of 832. The report (*New Jersey Archives*, ii. 305) quotes the 566 others as "Christians," in distinction !

Quaker of West Jersey, naturally a Conservative, clung closely to his English and sectarian institutions, and, joining acre to acre, observing the custom of primogeniture, and insisting rigidly on the ecclesiastical law which compelled his young people to marry within the pale of their membership, he built up gradually a great land-owning class which brought many thousand acres into comparatively few hands. Puritan influence is shown in the difference in the administration of law, thirteen classes of crime being punishable by death in the eastern division, and none in West Jersey, which did not permit capital punishment. Differences of manners, nomenclature, traditions of commerce, and legal custom are traceable even to-day, and Dutch and Scotch imprints remain in Bergen (now Hudson) and Monmouth counties, as evident as the old English inheritances in West Jersey, where farmers' leases to this hour expire on Lady Day, 25th March, and where eggs may still be bought by the score, as in old Yorkshire. In East Jersey, the town-meeting was the political factor to be reckoned with and the town the unit of activity. In West Jersey, the county was the unit, and the resemblance between the western province and Virginia is as clear as that between East Jersey and the Puritan home whence came its people. William Penn's personal influence was much more felt in West than in East Jersey. Many a time Governor Penn, in the brief period of eighteen months which rounded out his residence at his " palace " at Pennsbury, stopped at Burlington in his barge on his way up and down the Delaware. Sometimes he came to the fairs, which were an important social feature of the day, so important that when Monthly Meeting fell on fair day, in Burlington or Salem, it was adjourned until the fair was over, as on " ye 4th of ye 8 mo. 1697, Ordered at this meeting that our next Monthly Meeting be deferred one week longer than the usual Day, because the fair falling on that day ye Meeting should be." Semi-annual fairs were held in spring and autumn, and these market days were kept up until the Revolution. In 1729 they became an abuse, and the Monthly Meeting at Burlington petitioned the Assembly to remedy their evil effects.

William Penn was in England during the culmination of the Keith controversy, but his advice was sought regarding the disturbances of Keith's followers, who were organising separate meetings at the time of his second visit. Their doctrines had been promulgated by Daniel Leeds and William Bradford, the printers, and several prominent men had joined Thomas Budd in secession. Another element occasionally felt was the " mystic " society at Germantown and on the Wissahickon, whose apostles occasionally came into meetings, and after one invasion at Burlington, ascended the Court House steps, and from there harangued the people.

The social life of the Quakers in the Jerseys was unique. The prominent Friends in both colonies, although chiefly in the western, were Governors, Councillors, and members of Assembly. They were great planters, and merchants on a large scale, sending their vessels, built on the Delaware, to China and the West Indies. Perth Amboy in East Jersey, and Cohansey (Bridgeton) and Burlington in West Jersey, were the ports of entry. Great activity began before the end of the century in the exchange of ministers between London and the American colonies. All of these were obliged to cross New Jersey on their travels between New England and the south. The Wardells and Richard Hartshorne, at Shrewsbury and Middletown respectively, were the earliest resident Quaker ministers of whom we have record. Samuel Jenings, John Skein,[1] Thomas Olive, all of them Governors ; William Peachy,[2] Thomas Gardiner, William Cooper, George Deacon, Edward Barton, Elizabeth Day, Jane Seaton,

---

[1] John Skein, born in Scotland, at Aberdeen. Imprisoned 1676, and suffered distraint for fines imposed because he refused to give bond not to attend meetings (Besse, ii. 516). Emigrated to West Jersey 1678, where he was Governor for two years. He died in 1687, a useful and much respected man. A minister with an " edifying testimony."—Smith, *History of New Jersey*, 1765.

[2] William Peachy, who, says Proud (*History of Pennsylvania*, i. 158), with Thomas Olive, was the " first among Friends in West Jersey who had a public ministry." He was from London, but had been imprisoned with his young wife in Bristol, where she died. He arrived in West Jersey in 1677 on the *Kent*, was elected to the Assembly in 1682, and died in 1689 at Burlington.

Mary Smith (widow of Daniel), Peter Andrews, and Abraham Farrington were all early preachers of Quakerism in West Jersey, the last two dying in England on religious visits abroad.

It is not surprising that several of the most distinguished Quakers, whose influence told greatly in both Church and State, emigrated to America just before or immediately after William Penn, and were all from the neighbourhood of Rickmansworth. Thomas Ellwood appears to have been untouched by the spirit of emigration; but his friends, John Archdale and Samuel Jenings, of High Wycombe and Aylesbury respectively, left an indelible impress upon the affairs of two great provinces.

The minute from their home meeting of Coleshill for Samuel Jenings and Ann, his wife, and their children, is dated " 26th day of ye 3d. mo. 1680," and states that they " have lived in these parts many years; have walked Conscientiously and honestly Amongst us Agreeable to ye profession and testimony of Truth." It is signed by sixteen men, among whom are the names of Thomas Olive, Thomas Ellwood, and John Archdale. Samuel Jenings came out in the official capacity of Deputy-Governor for Edward Byllynge, who at first declined to relinquish the prerogative of government along with territorial rights to purchasers. Governor Jenings reached the Delaware in the late summer of 1680, and six weeks after sent a letter addressed to William Penn, Edward Byllynge, or Gawen Lawrie, to apprise them of his safe arrival, and to convey the welcome information that the duties exacted illegally by the Governor of New York had been removed. He wrote:[1]

" DEAR FRIENDS,—This may give you an account of mine and my families safe arrival in New Jersey, with all the rest that came with us. I might say something concerning our passage at sea, but I waive it for want of time, and in fine may observe all was well; for which I bless God; and the Lord keep us all sensible of it, with the rest of his mercies for ever.

"Dear friends, about six weeks since, we arrived in the Delaware

---

[1] Smith's *New Jersey*, p. 124.

river, where I expected to have met with a combat in the denial of customs. In our passage at sea I had communicated to all that had any considerable cargo on board the opinion of council concerning any illegal demand thereof, with what else I thought might be for their information; which thus far prevailed that most if not all concerned, seemed resolved to deny the paying of custom here; having paid all the King's duties in England. In good time we came to anchor in Delaware, where one, Peter Alrick, came aboard, and brought a handsome present to our commander, and sent for me into the round-house, where they both were, and Peter told me he had nothing to say to us relating to customs; he had no commission for it, nor did he know of anybody that had; so we had all our goods safely landed after this unexpected easy manner.

"In pursuance of the trust committed to me after my arrival, I acquainted those nominated in the commission with me of it; but in a short time after I received your letters, giving an account of a new grant obtained, wherein the customs are taken off, a free port confirmed and the government settled on Edward Byllynge; which, I doubt not, will be very acceptable to every honest man; but as yet I have not had time to let the people in general know it. And now, seeing the ports are made legally free, and the government settled, I would not have anything remain as a discouragement to planters. Here are several good and convenient settlements already, and here is land enough and good enough for many more." SAMUEL JENINGS.

"New Jersey, the 17th October 1680."

Samuel Jenings took up land and settled at Burlington. The following year he called together the first West Jersey Assembly, and agreed with them upon certain fundamental points of government. The Assembly dissolved on the 28th of ninth month, having passed in addition thirty-six laws, many of which were later on repealed. The tact of Governor Jenings, who was thoroughly acceptable to the settlers, avoided open rupture, and quieted the prevalent discontent. To silence the protests of all parties, whose resentment was increasing against Byllynge, Jenings was chosen, and duly elected Governor by the representatives of the people in the Assembly of 1683. He was thus empowered to act independently of Byllynge's appointment. He and the council elected at the same time—all of them Quakers, with one exception—gave their solemn promise in lieu of an oath of office.[1] The Governor's salary was the right to take up six hundred acres of land above the Falls of the Delaware.

When the provinces were united under one Royal Governor, in the person of Lord Cornbury, the Queen's cousin, who arrived in 1703, Samuel Jenings was elected Speaker of the Assembly. In this position he was called upon to silence the voice of controversy, the Assembly supporting him loyally in his valiant opposition to the unjust demands of the brutal and licentious governor. This culminated in the famous *remonstrance* of the Assembly of April 5, 1707. Repeatedly stopped in his reading of the paper by Lord Cornbury's ejaculations of " Stop ! " " What's that ? " etc., he quietly paused and then resumed, with dignity repeating what he had previously read, laying greater emphasis than before upon the points which he desired to bring out, and quite undaunted by the evident anger of Her Majesty's representative :

" We cannot but be uneasy," he deliberately read, " when we find by the new methods of government our liberties and properties so much shaken that no man can say he is master of either, but holds them as tenant by courtesy and at will, and may be stript of them at pleasure. Liberty is too valuable a thing to be easily parted with."

Upon the departure of the House, Lord Cornbury, with emotion, turned to those about him, and exclaimed, " Jenings has impudence enough to face the Devil ! " [2] The reply of the Assembly to the Governor's answer— which concluded with the words, " I was going to give you some wholesome advice, but I consider it will be but labour lost, and therefore shall reserve it for persons who, I hope, will make a right use of it ! "—showed their adherence to the Quaker customs by the insertion of the following note, frequently appended to other official documents :

" Divers of the members of this Assembly being of the people

---

[1] Smith, *History of New Jersey*, p. 164.   [2] *Ibid.*, p. 295.

called Quakers do assent to the matter and substance, but make some exception to the stile."

When the people of New York added their voice in remonstrance to the evil proceedings of Cornbury, the Queen ordered his withdrawal.

In the affairs of the meeting Samuel Jenings appears in innumerable capacities as a church-officer. During the height of the Keith controversy he took an active part, exhorting to wisdom in individual cases; assisting the Friends in Philadelphia on behalf of William Stockdale and Thomas Fitzwater, the particular objects of George Keith's attacks; publishing a fair setting forth in defence of the Quakers in his pamphlet, known as "The State of the Case Considered," etc.; and finally in the latter part of 1693 sailing for England on behalf of Friends in America, where at London, together with Thomas Duckett and William Walker,[1] he laid the true facts before London Yearly Meeting. The result was the disownment of Keith by the Yearly Meeting of London in 1695, following the action taken at Burlington in 1692. In 1702, after George Keith returned to America as an officer of the Society for the Propagation of the Gospel in Foreign Parts, he appeared at Burlington and endeavoured to draw the Quakers into controversy, and succeeded in attaching a number of the less loyal to the Church of England. The new arrivals challenged the Quakers to meet them, and reply to their charges at a public meeting in the town-house at Burlington, which the Friends quietly declined. Soon after, the clerical gentlemen went so far as to invade the Quaker meeting, this being one of the offences so often attributed to the Quakers themselves. A letter from the rector of the recently founded church in that place to George Keith, dated New York, October 20, 1705, says :

"Mr. Sharpe was very jealous to bring ye Quakers to stand a tryal; he carried one of ye 'Bombs' (an attack published at this time) into their meeting, and read a new challenge I had

---

[1] The latter died while in England.—Bowden, *History of Friends in America,* p. 52.

sent them to answer what they had printed ; but all in vain. Samuel Jenings stood up and said, ' Friends, let's call upon God.' Then they went to prayer, and so their meeting broke up."

Samuel Jenings held office as Speaker of the Assembly until the year before his death, which occurred . in 1709 at his home, " Greenhill," in Burlington, and he was interred in the Friends' graveyard in that place. A fine tribute to his character is paid by the historian Smith, whose father knew Governor Jenings well.

" He was early an approved minister among (the Quakers)," says Smith, " and so continued to his death. Common opinion, apt to limit this sphere of action, will, however, allow general rules to have their exceptions, as instances now and then, though perhaps but rarely, occur, where variety of talents have united in the same individual, and yet not interfered. Such, the account of those times (strip'd of the local uncertainties of faction and party), tell us, was the circumstance with regard to Jenings. His authority, founded on experienc'd candour, probity, and abilities, enlarged opportunities, rendered him not in one capacity or in one society only, generally useful. . . . With a mind form'd to benevolence and acts of humanity, he was a friend to the widow, the fatherless, and the unhappy. Tender, disinterested, and with great opportunities, [he] left but a small estate. Abhorring oppression in every shape, his whole conduct discovered a will to relieve and befriend mankind, far above the littleness of party or sinister views. His sentiments of right and liberty were formed on the revolution establishment, a plan successfully adapted to the improvement of a new country, or any country. He was, notwithstanding all this, sometimes thought stiff and impracticable, but chiefly on account of his political attachments. Yet there were instances where better knowledge of his principles, and the sincerity with which he acted, totally effaced those impressions, and left him friends where none were expected. Much of his time . . . was long devoted to the publick with a will to be useful. West Jersey, Pennsylvania, and New Jersey, after the surrender, for near twenty-eight years successively, were repeated witnesses of his conduct in various capacities. He studied peace and the welfare of mankind. . . . He just lived long enough to see (the country) emerging from an unpromising state of litigation and controversy to more quiet than had been known for many years."

He remembered his old friend and neighbour, Thomas

Ellwood, in England, by leaving a bequest to him of twenty pounds to buy "my long-acquainted, worthy, and endeared friend a gelding or otherwise as he shall think fit."

Thomas Olive (or Olliffe) of Wellingborough in Northamptonshire, was a convert to Quakerism by the preaching of William Dewsbury in 1655. He was imprisoned in 1665 under the Conventicle Act, and in 1666 had sixty pounds of cloth seized and taken from him.[1] He came out to the Jerseys as a London Commissioner in the ship *Kent* in 1677, and was the first Speaker of the Colonial Assembly, holding office several years. In 1684 he became Governor. While Justice of the Peace for the district of Burlington he gained the love and esteem of all his countrymen.

"He had," says Smith the historian, "a ready method of business, often doing it to good effect in the seat of judgment on the stumps in his meadows; he contrived to postpone sudden complaints until cool deliberation had shown them to be justly founded, and then seldom failed for accommodating matters without much expense to the parties."

Thomas Olive died in 1692.[2]

Too much emphasis cannot be laid upon the important part taken in the political affairs of New Jersey by the Quakers of the earlier period. Their staunch integrity and courageous defence of their actions in everything that involved a sense of duty to the public, is beyond praise, and undoubtedly was an important factor in forming the government of the state upon present lines. Three Quaker governors have been named. In May 1696 the legislature selected as King's Attorney (Prosecutor of the Pleas) George Deacon, a Quaker arrival on the *Willing Mind*, who came to the Delaware in the winter of 1677, and who held office in various capacities. In 1696 Benjamin Wheat[3] served in the

---

[1] Besse, *Sufferings of the Quakers*, i. 534-536.
[2] Thomas Olive's salary as Governor was £20 per year !
[3] Benjamin Wheat with another Friend furnished the handsomely designed pine table, upon which the meeting at Burlington transacted its business, and which is still in use.

same position, and was followed, two years later, by Thomas Gardiner, son of the Thomas Gardiner at whose house the early meetings were held. There were no regularly admitted lawyers at the New Jersey Bar before 1702, and the "Rules of the Supreme Court" show that from 1704 to the date of the Declaration of Independence, only two chief-justices, out of eight that held the office, were licensed attorneys of the province.[1] Of twenty-two associate justices, only three were regularly admitted, and of the three, two, only on the day they were elevated to the bench! English standards, of course, governed the practice of law, and the Supreme Court was modelled on the Court of Queen's Bench, and set up in 1704. Less concerned with the technicalities of the courts than with the administration of substantial justice, the old Quaker idea of righteousness in dealing with rights of property owners and with offenders may well have laid the foundations of a system which to-day makes " Jersey Justice " proverbial in the United States.

There were many Quaker Justices of the Peace ; lenient and fair-minded as a class, these occasionally meted out severe punishments, as when in 1682 Governor Jenings and Justices Cripps and Stacey ordered a runaway pair who added lies to their crime, at "the tenth hour in the morning," to be " whip'd on their naked bodies," the man thirty stripes and the woman thirty-five," he " paying the ffees."

In East Jersey, marriages had been regulated according to the practice of the Scotch Kirk, requiring the publication of banns three times, the Governor's licence, and consent of parents. Equally stringent in West Jersey were the marriage customs, where the House made no legislative regulations, but where the Quaker meetings saw to it that no laxness crept in, or if it did, that it met with proper punishment. When disagreements occurred, reconciliation was recommended, as when, some time before 1694, a quarrelling pair were summoned before the Quaker justices at Burlington and asked if they would live

[1] F. B. Lee, *New Jersey as Colony and State*, i. 312.

peaceably together. Mary agreed and so did Thomas, he stipulating that Mary " will acknowledge that shee hath scandalized him wrongfully." To this the woman consented, adding an expression eternally feminine, " but saith shee will not own that shee hath told lies of him to her knowledge ! " At this point the negotiations naturally come to a standstill. " But after some good admonitions from ye Bench," says the record, " they both p'mise they will forgett and never mention what unkind speeches or Actions have formerly past betweene them Concerninge each other." [1]

After the Crown took over the government in 1702, the granting of marriage licences was placed in the hands of the Governor, and the Church of England was established. The nonconforming members of the Assembly, however, for a long time opposed the passage of England's ecclesiastical regulations of marriage.

A Women's Yearly Meeting was held in 1681. From this time on, there was an increasing number of English Friends in the ministry who crossed the ocean to visit the American Colonies. James Dickinson paid three visits to the Jerseys—in 1691, 1696, and 1714, when, he says, " some of the meetings were the largest I had ever been at. People flocked so to them that several hundreds were forced to stand without doors, the meeting-house being not large enough to contain them." At Burlington Yearly Meeting " the Lord owned us with His living presence, and we had a glorious season together. The meeting held five days and there was such a concourse of people that we held two meetings at once, one in the Court House and the other at the meeting-house." [2] The annual meeting of ministers, which was held at the house of Samuel Jenings in Burlington, was in 1698 attended by William Ellis, of England, who is a rare instance of an intelligent visitor who took notes on the spot—a custom which we may well wish had been followed by others. Upon this deeply interesting occasion,

---

[1] F. B. Lee, *New Jersey, etc.* i. 324.
[2] *Journal of J. Dickinson.*

which lasted from the 17th to the 23rd of 7 mo. (O.S.), much time was taken up in the careful perusal of papers presented for publication for which the judgment of the meeting was sought, and without whose authority their dissemination was impossible. Pamphlet wars were then the fashion upon every topic of public interest, and everybody rushed into print at the smallest provocation. At this time the meeting set its approval upon Caleb Pusey's answer to Daniel Leeds's " News of a Trumpet Sounding in the Wilderness," a late heretical pamphlet with the usual allegorical title, which sympathised with George Keith. The Yearly Meeting which immediately followed at the same place stated, in its epistle to London :

" We may in truth say through the large mercy and the wonderful goodness of our God, we have had very blessed and heavenly meetings. The presence of the great God overshadowing us, many living and powerful testimonies were delivered."

All the letters of visiting Friends at this time give evidence of great growth in the meetings. Thomas Chalkley, who came over just before, mentions a very large meeting which he held under the trees at Crosswicks, West Jersey, where the convincement took place of Edward Andrews, who, he says, was " mightily reached," and who built up the Society in the neighbourhood of Little Egg Harbour.

The Salem Friends at the end of the seventeenth century formed a flourishing settlement, with a large and growing meeting. Into this more southern community of the Jerseys there arrived in the year 1700 from England, a young girl of only eighteen, who came out to occupy a plantation on land taken up some years previously by her father, a London Quaker merchant, who had invested in the scheme with his friend, William Penn. After going so far as to send out mechanics to build him a dwelling, he had, for reasons now unknown, altered his mind and remained at home. His daughter, upon hearing her father's proposal to sell his New Jersey property, felt a drawing towards America, and that it was her duty to settle there herself. This feeling was sympathised with and shared in when, with much emotion, she made it known in family conclave, and the result was that John Haddon made over to his daughter Elizabeth the lands which he had taken up. Under the care of a widowed friend and two faithful menservants, this Quaker daughter of wealth came to the unbroken wilderness, followed by the blessings and prayers of her God-fearing family. The instance is unique in Quaker records. In the pleasant town of Haddonfield to-day, pilgrimages are made to Haddon Hall, where, after a most picturesque courtship, Elizabeth married John Estaugh, and where forty years of married life were spent. John Estaugh died on a preaching tour in the Island of Tortola, where his brick tomb may still be seen. Of Haddon Hall, only the old brew-house now remains, with its latch-string still out, as when Elizabeth there made her many simples and remedies for the sick of the entire settlement, who all came under her care. The present house stands where the original stood, burned to the ground years since in a disastrous fire. But the old yews which she planted still flourish in a green old age in the garden which she laid out so long ago.

At the close of the century, in 1699, Philadelphia had an awful visitation of yellow fever, which broke out in June, just before the time of Yearly Meeting, and in eight weeks had carried off several hundred people. The Friends in the Jerseys were consulted as to the propriety of postponing the meeting, or holding it elsewhere, and the subject engaged the attention of the meeting of ministers and elders, which preceded the regular meeting. Thomas Story and his companion Roger Gill were present, and the former tells us : [1] " The testimony of Truth went generally against the adjournment or suspension, and the Lord's presence was greatly with us to the end. Friends were generally much comforted in the divine truth and the fear of the contagion was much taken away." It was at this Yearly Meeting that Roger Gill

[1] *Life of Thomas Story.*

prayed that "if the Lord would accept his life as a sacrifice, he freely offered it up for the people." He went immediately after to Burlington, and was taken upon his return with the dread disease from which he died shortly after, and the journals of the time note that the ravages of the fever almost immediately ceased.

Although still in the midst of political disturbance—which, however, was lessening somewhat, only to break out on the coming of Lord Cornbury—there was a remarkable degree of prosperity in the conduct of the Quaker meetings. They appropriately noted in the meeting at Burlington in 1698, in a minute which fittingly closes the century :

"Whereas, it was the way of the world to forget God, yet the Lord had gathered us, His people, to Himself, that we could not forget Him ; for though we came poor and empty together, yet the Lord in His wisdom, and goodness, and love, met us with a full hand, to comfort and strengthen us, that we might not faint in our minds, but be renewed in our strength."

CHAPTER III

JOHN WOOLMAN : THE NEGROES

THE Friends of Pennsylvania began to hold annual meetings immediately after their arrival with William Penn, but as a Yearly Meeting was already well organised by the Friends of the Jerseys, and the two settlements of Philadelphia and Burlington were but twenty miles apart, it was agreed in 1684 that for the future, the meetings should be held alternately at the two places—an arrangement which continued for seventy-five years. There was an agitation in 1711 toward changing the Yearly Meeting permanently to Philadelphia, but the time had not come, and the minute speaks for itself:

"At our Monthly Meeting ye 7th of ye 11th mo. 1711. The minute of the Yearly Meeting was read at this meeting in Relation to Removing of ye Yearly Meeting to Philadelphia, which this meeting are all in general against, but would have it kept in its common course as it hath been used & in ye same place and ye same time both as to worship & Business & with the same authority as formerly."

But Philadelphia was rapidly growing, and settlements in Pennsylvania and Delaware (then the "Three Lower Counties") drew the centre of the Quaker population to the south. Agitation was revived in the middle of the century, and in 9 mo. 1760 the Yearly Meeting removed permanently to Philadelphia. The change from the sixth to the ninth month was made in 1755 ; from this to the fourth month, which is the present time, in 1798.

In 1701, John Richardson came to America, and upon his second visit in 1731, he records his satisfaction at the enormous growth of the meetings in the interval. John Fothergill's three visits were made in 1706, 1721, and 1736, the last continuing for three years, during a period of great sensitiveness to spiritual teaching throughout the country. In 1703 Samuel Bownas, although but twenty-seven years of age, made a remarkable impression upon the American meetings. Appearing at the time when George Keith was preaching in the Jerseys as a missionary clergyman of the Church of England, he earnestly attacked the latter's attempts to lead away the Quakers, often with marked success. Both were men of great ability. They became pronounced rivals, and did not hesitate to denounce each other. For a severe snub administered to him while in Maryland, Keith contrived to have Bownas seized and imprisoned as he crossed the Jerseys, and for nearly a year detained upon the accusation that he " spoke against the Church of England " —then the established church in the Jerseys and New York. Upon the release of Bownas, he visited nearly all the New Jersey meetings, where he "found the Truth growing."

In 1704 all " public meeting-houses " were ordered recorded in the archives of New Jersey, and it is unfortunate that the list of deceased Friends since the settlement of Burlington sent up to the Yearly Meeting from subordinate meetings should not now appear to exist. In this year the meeting at Burlington issued a certificate for one hundred and twenty-two of its members, pursuant of the " Act of Assembly for Settling the Militia of the Province," declaring these male members to be of " Ye Society of ye people called Quakers," and willing to " receive ye benefit of ye favour expressed to ye said People " who, for conscience' sake, could not bear arms and were, therefore, exempted from service. Rumours of war were numerous. Some Spanish and Indian runaways from a vessel in the Delaware roused a widespread report that the French were at Cohacksink. Four young men, in making their acknowledgment to the meeting at Burlington naïvely gave their reasons for taking up arms in defence :

That it seemed best for those that had guns to take them, not with a design to hurt, much less to kill, man, woman, or child ; but we thought that if we could meet these runaways, the sight of the guns might fear them ! " No less a person than James Logan, William Penn's secretary, had shortly before made an acknowledgment which was read at the Quarterly Meeting at William Biddle's house in 1 mo. 1702, for going with the Sheriff and an armed posse to the " Reed Islands of the Delaware."

All through the French and Indian wars there were sufferings and distraints for the New Jersey Quakers who were one with their Philadelphia Friends of the Yearly Meeting in the action taken on the subject of war. The results of disturbances on the frontier of Pennsylvania came closely home to them as officials of the Yearly Meeting, and met with sympathy upon their part. The proportion of New Jersey Quakers in the Yearly Meeting may be gathered from the fact that in 1730 and for years after, as many as thirty or thirty-five representatives were annually sent from Burlington Quarterly Meeting to attend the Yearly Meeting.

"It equally concerns men in every age," wrote John Woolman, in speaking of the war tax of 1755, "to take heed to their own spirit. . . . It requires great self-denial and resignation of ourselves to God to attain that state wherein we can freely cease from fighting when wrongfully invaded, if, by fighting, there were a probability of overcoming the invaders. Whoever rightly attains to it does in some degree feel that spirit in which our Redeemer gave his life for us."

In 1757 (August) orders came by night to the officers of Burlington County, directing them to draft the militia for the relief of the English at Fort William Henry, New York. A general review was held, and soon after, three times as many were called for, to be in readiness at any moment for marching orders. A considerable number of the young men who were Friends were thus drafted into the army. John Woolman reflects upon the circumstance, and sees in it "a fresh opportunity to see and consider the advantage of living in the real substance of religion, where practice doth harmonise with principle." Some of the young Quakers left home and remained away until the trouble was over. Others agreed to go as soldiers. Still others expressed a "tender scruple" against all war, and after holding council with John Woolman, who encouraged them in it, informed the captain that they could not bear arms for conscience' sake, nor could they hire any to go in their place, being "resigned as to the event." They finally obtained permission to return home, with the warning to be ready when called upon to march. They were not obliged to serve, the fort being taken and destroyed by the French. In April 1758 John Woolman was the reluctant host of a soldier who was quartered upon him for lodging. He refused the payment to which he was entitled, "having admitted him," Woolman told the officer, "into my house upon a passive obedience to authority. I was on horseback when he spake to me, and as I turned from him he said he was obliged to me, to which I said nothing; but thinking on the expression, I grew uneasy, and afterwards, being near where he lived, I went and told him on what grounds I refused taking pay for keeping the soldier."

No history of Quakerism in New Jersey can be complete without due regard to one who is not only the most conspicuous of his own community, but is as well the best known American-born Quaker of colonial times.

When Charles Lamb recommended his readers to "get the writings of John Woolman by heart, and so learn to love the Quakers," he voiced the feelings of other cultured and sympathetic minds whose experience of life nevertheless differed widely from anything Quaker. Men like Henry Crabbe Robinson and William Ellery Channing —to name but one on each side of the ocean—submitted to the spell which yet lingers about the pages of one of the most pure and gentle souls that ever committed its tender thoughts to paper. The fifty-two years which formed the life of Woolman—he was born at Mount Holly, New Jersey, in August 1720, and died in York, England, 7th October 1772—were an important period in the world's history, as well as that of the Quaker Church. The philosopher may trace in Woolman the culmination of that intense sensitiveness to the breathings of the Divine spirit which marked the best element of Quakerism at a time when it was seeking diligently, even if ineffectually, to perform an impossible task—to live a life of perfect service, while withdrawn from contact with all external influences.

Bred most simply in a social atmosphere which was, perhaps, the most exclusively conservative of any within the Quaker pale, the simple and unlettered youth had opportunity in his country life and ample leisure to allow a reflective spirit and an intelligent mind to follow their own bent. The life of Woolman, whose love of mankind has only been equalled at rare intervals in the world's history, produced two very important results. One of these was due to his personal labours, the other, with less visible immediate effect, is only to-day reaching the wider world. The first was his successful effort in rousing an anti-slavery sentiment and promoting the abolition movement ; the second, the wonderful influence exerted in the world of letters and religion by his very remarkable *Journal* and ethical essays.

The number of slaves held in the province of New Jersey in the middle of the eighteenth century was large. In one Quarterly Meeting alone there were eleven hundred owned by Friends. The evil had increased with the growth of the settlements and the need for more servants. Early Quaker movements towards abolition instituted by Fox in Barbadoes, by Edmundson in Maryland and Virginia, by the Mennonites, or "German Quakers," at Germantown, and by various isolated bodies of Friends in the more enlightened subordinate meetings of Pennsylvania and New England, had all been without important results upon the main body of comfortable and prosperous Friends who were slave-holders. It was not that they were knowingly cultivating a revolting and indefensible practice. The laws of Great Britain and of the colonies countenanced the trade, and most people were persuaded that to treat a slave well, and to teach him the doctrines of Christianity, even while holding him in bondage, was the kindest method possible with a member of the inferior race. The Quakers would seem to have been the first people able to see through the mists of social prejudice, and, in the light of absolute justice, to discern the dangers to society at large, which lay at the root of a prevalent and corrupt social custom.

The necessity for preparing a bill of sale for a negress, during Woolman's apprenticeship, in the year 1742, first brought home with a shock to the young man's mind the true meaning of the situation. From that moment to his dying day, his life had but one object—to free the slave. He at once set out, like a wise reformer, to discover the true facts, and in tears and sorrow were they revealed to him. In 1756 he made his first journey to the South. This was followed by various other and similar journeys and the Indians were also included in his solicitude. The Indian conferences at Burlington and Easton were held in the summer of 1758, at a time when Woolman was under a special exercise on the subject of negro bondage. His many and often successful private efforts to ameliorate the condition of the negroes had attracted general attention among the Friends to the subject. London Yearly Meeting in that year in its epistle condemned the unrighteous traffic; and New England Yearly Meeting placed upon its discipline the Query against slavery:

"Are Friends clear of importing negroes, or buying them when imported, and do they use those well, where they are possessed by inheritance or otherwise, endeavouring to train them up in principles of religion?"

The culmination of all of Woolman's earlier efforts came in the Yearly Meeting which met at Philadelphia in 1758. In that meeting for a long time John Woolman sat, bowed in silence, unmindful of other important matters which claimed the attention of Friends. When, finally, the subject of slavery was introduced, and advice was given to "wait"; that eventually a "way would be opened " ; and procrastination and delay were the order of the hour, it almost seemed to the agonized servant of the Lord that the meeting was engaged in a justification of slavery. He rose, and these were his solemn words : [1]

" My mind is led to consider the purity of the Divine Being, and the justice of His judgments, and herein my soul is covered with awfulness. I cannot forbear to hint of some cases where people have not been treated with the purity of justice, and the event has been most lamentable. Many slaves on this continent are oppressed, and their cries have entered into the ears of the Most High. Such are the purity and certainty of His judgments, that he cannot be partial in our favour. In infinite love and goodness he hath opened our understandings from one time to another, concerning our duty towards these people, *and it is not a time for delay.* Should we now be sensible of what he requires of us, and through respect to the private interests of some persons, or through a regard to some friendships which do not stand upon an immutable foundation, neglect to do our duty in firmness and constancy, still waiting for some extraordinary means to bring about their deliverance, God may by terrible things in righteousness answer us in this matter."

This appeal moved the hearts of the large assembly to a sense of their neglected duty. Sympathetic discussion followed, and finally the Truth triumphed over all opposition, and the first committee then appointed began its actual aggressive work. More than any other one man, Woolman aided the English-speaking nations to throw off the disgrace of slavery ; and although so late as 1800, there were still 12,442 slaves held in New Jersey, of these, thanks to the labours of John Woolman, almost none were held by Friends. Instead, a few might be found in each of the colonies who were received into membership with the Society, notably the famous sea-captain, Paul Cuffee, of Massachusetts.

John Woolman's personal influence had far-reaching social and moral effects. The humility and self-abasement of the author of the journal are, however, so great, that the reader unfamiliar with contemporary history

---

[1] Woolman's *Journal*, Whittier's Edition, 1871, p. 18.

might well fail to understand the importance of the movements there recorded. Fear of exceeding the standard of extreme humility which he had set for himself has lost to us from his *Journal* any reference to great events in which he was an actor. Unfortunately, no mention of himself occurs with any adequate description of his part in affairs. The world to-day is swamped with strenuous literature in which the personal element is conspicuous. Possibly, however, had this quality appeared in his works, we might not have been able, with Henry Crabbe Robinson, to call the *Journal* "a perfect gem." Its flavour of purity and grace might be altogether absent, had he given us more of himself. As it is, a soul singularly full of "sweetness and light" transfers to the printed page those exquisite moral qualities which breathe forth like the perfume of a flower. All other passions to which ordinary mortals are prone are in Woolman swallowed up in the passion of love to mankind.

Woolman's ethical essays make an appeal even more appropriate to our own day than to his own. Their scope may be imagined from the subjects he treats: "On Pure Wisdom and Human Policy," "On Labour," "On Schools," "On the Right Use of Outward Gifts," "On the True Harmony of Mankind," "On the Example of Christ," "On Merchandizing," "On Divine Admonitions," "On Loving Our Neighbours as Ourselves," "On a Sailor's Life," "A Word of Remembrance and Caution to the Rich." Do not these seem timely topics for discussion in a Christian spirit to-day? "To labour," says Woolman, "for an establishment in Divine love, where the mind is disentangled from the power of darkness, is the great business of man's life."

The *Journal* nowhere betrays any selfish solicitude for his own well-being, either spiritually or physically, and his close searchings of soul are only as he feels himself to be one with all mankind. In the essays may be clearly discerned a singular detachment of spirit from everything sordid or worldly. He wrote as one who "had seen in the Light of the Lord that . . . he that is omnipotent is rising up to judgment, and will plead the cause of the oppressed," and he adds, " *he commanded me to open the Vision.*" The mystic finds expression in such passages as these, and the following :

" I have frequently found a necessity to stand up, when the spring of the ministry was low, and to speak from the necessity in that which subjects the will of the creature, and herein I was united with the suffering seed, and found inward sweetness in these mortifying labours."

A desire had for some time been upon Woolman's mind to visit Friends in England, and in 1772 he landed at London, and straightway made haste to the meeting of ministers and elders, which had then been sitting for less than an hour. It was the 8th of June, and the only thing he tells us of his soul-trying experience at this first appearance among his English brethren is that " his mind was humbly contrite." A New Jersey Friend, however, was the medium through whom Whittier obtained the actual facts, which the former had from an English Friend who could verify them. The vessel reached London on the fifth day of the week. Coming in hastily and unannounced, the stranger Friend, just out of the vessel's steerage quarters, with a correspondingly dishevelled toilet, which was in itself peculiar in its undyed homespun and grey-white beaver hat, naturally created some apprehension. Even the certificate which he presented as a credential from Friends in America did not suffice to quiet the alarm ; and a Friend suggested that possibly Woolman's submission to this apprehended service might be accepted, and the stranger now feel at liberty to return to his home. Greatly affected by this reception, John Woolman sat silently in tears, awaiting further guidance. After a time he rose and respectfully stated that he could not feel himself released from his prospect of ministry, yet the unity of Friends was necessary, and this being withheld, he preferred to support himself. He stated his familiarity with his trade, and desired employment in his own business.

The " wise simplicity " of the stranger touched Friends

greatly, and when, in the silence that followed, Woolman again rose with a Divine message upon his lips, all hearts were moved, and he was owned and confessed by his brethren, and passed forth to his brief labours. Four months later, at York, on the 7th of October 1772, John Woolman died of smallpox. Friends everywhere paid the highest tribute to his character and labours, his saintly life and example. His *Journal* is a classic, not alone for Quakers, but for all the world. These modern days, with the search for Truth in the abstract, should be even more sympathetic than his own to the teachings of Woolman. Students of religion, of philosophy, and of social science may alike find in him inspiration and aid.

> " For since those miraculous days
>   When marvellous wonders were rife ;
> When the blind gaz'd with joy, and the dumb sang with praise,
>   And the dead were restored unto life—
> I know not of one whom my heart could allow
> More worthy the name of Apostle than thou."
>   BERNARD BARTON,
>   on JOHN WOOLMAN.

CHAPTER IV

JOHN WOOLMAN : THE INDIANS

HISTORY shows an honourable course pursued by the settlers in the difficult problem of how to handle the Indian. Peaceable under friendly rule, he became a fiend when aroused by real or fancied ill-treatment. Strict justice demanded and received at the hands of the Quakers full remuneration for the lands obtained from the Indian tribes of New Jersey, and efforts were made to Christianise these red brethren very soon after the Quaker settlements began. William Penn at one time held a theory that the Indians belonged to the Ten Lost Tribes of Israel. Samuel Smith, the historian, thought the idea a delightful solution of a difficult problem ; and Elias Boudinot's *Star of the West* elaborates it further. However that may be, the Indian in the seventeenth century was a very present menace to safety, and the Quakers adopted the wise course.

The tribe of the Delaware or Lenni-Lenape Indians who were scattered throughout the Jerseys, although at no time very numerous, were frequently called into council by the Quakers. Confused by the dissensions among other Christian bodies and unable to comprehend an altruistic faith, the Indians had yet a crude system of justice among themselves, and it is quite possible that the absence of complicated machinery, combined with the evident spirit of justice conspicuous among the Quakers, obtained for the latter a better hold on the savage nature than was the case with other religious denominations. In any case, the control was not very permanent, and the missionary efforts of the Quakers were only a degree less unorganised than had been those of the Dutch and Swedes before them. The quarter-century from the Dutch cession to the English until the surrender of the government of the united provinces to the Crown in 1702, covers the period when the intercourse between the whites and red men was most marked. This was chiefly for purposes of trade. New Jersey enjoyed greater freedom from Indian disturbances and outbreaks of war than other colonies. In the purchase of lands, all titles had to be cleared of Indian ownership in both the Jerseys. Thus the Indian claims had been nearly or quite extinguished by the period of the Revolution. At no time was the Indian on a political equality with the white man, although West Jersey Quaker equity permitted a mixed jury of Indians and English when the interests of the former were involved. The Indian, despite certain benevolent enactments of the Legislature, remained in a position of servitude, cut off from any industrial privileges or rights. Severe penalties were laid upon any persons outside of the province of East Jersey who traded with an Indian ;[1] while in West Jersey, a policy of indifference left the helpless savage largely to himself. The Quakers, however, continued throughout the colonial period to hold meetings for the Indians, and set aside certain portions of their meeting-houses for Indians and negroes, both of whom were held as slaves. The wilder nature of the American Indian, however, prevented satisfactory domestic service. The interesting Indian conference at Burlington in the late summer of 1758 was followed shortly after by a very large and important Indian conference of the Six Nations at Easton, Pennsylvania, on the upper Delaware. The Governors of both the provinces, together with the well-known Indian interpreter, Conrad Wieser, and others were present. At this time deeds were obtained by which the Indians, for the sum of one thousand pounds, surrendered all claims on lands in New Jersey with the exception of a small reservation. This—a matter both of charity and pro-

[1] F. B. Lee, *New Jersey as Colony and State*, i. 69.

tection, the first Indian reservation ever established in the United States — was located at " Edgepelick " or Brotherton (now Indian Mills), among the pine barrens of Burlington County.   Here the Indians of New Jersey were settled on three thousand acres which maintained them and their descendants until 1802, when they were transported, first to New York State, then to Green Bay, Wisconsin, and finally, in 1832, to Indian Territory.   At this time the New Jersey legislature, for the sum of two thousand dollars, purchased the remnant of land, and thus, with a measure of justice, obtained clear title to the entire province.

Just before this reservation was established, Samuel Smith, for years Treasurer of the province and a leading Quaker, had drawn up a Constitution (1757) for the " New Jersey Association for Helping the Indians "—an organisation exclusively Quaker.   It aided the Brotherton Indians substantially, and did effective service in a field in which Quaker philanthropy has always been prominent.   A good example of the cordial relations between English and Indian in a Quaker community is described in the account of the death of King Ockanickon, at Burlington in 1681.[1]   The old chief, on his death-bed, sent for his nephew, Iahkursoe, and addressing him as " Brother's Son," told him of his selection as King in succession.   " This day," said the dying man, " I deliver my heart into your bosom.   I would have you love what is good, and keep good company.   Be plain and fair with all, Indians and Christians."   Thomas Budd, one of the proprietors, was present, and listened to the exhortation of the old man with emotion.   After he had continued for some time until too exhausted to speak further, Thomas Budd took the opportunity to remark that there was a great God, who created all things ; that He gave man understanding of what was good and bad, and after this life rewarded the good with blessings, and the bad according to their doings.   Ockanickon replied, " It is very true, it is so.   There are two ways, a broad and a

[1] Smith, *History of New Jersey*, pp. 148-150.

straight way ; there are two paths, a broad and a straight path. The worst and the greatest go in the broad, the best and fewest in the straight path." The old chief died shortly after, and was attended to his grave in the Friends' graveyard in Burlington with great solemnity by a large gathering of silent Indians, and by the English settlers to whom he had always been a true friend.

A long journey to the Susquehanna to visit the Indians at Wehaloosing was undertaken by John Woolman with one companion in 1763. To go was to take his life in his hands. He set out in May of that year, and the quaint narrative gives us glimpses of the dangers by the way. From the outset Woolman underwent much spiritual travail. He even disregarded the friendly warning of a deputation of Philadelphia Friends who arrived at Mount Holly late on the night before the journey. An express rider had reached Philadelphia, with word of an uprising at Pittsburg, where the Indians were on the warpath, and had slain some of the English. Certain elderly Friends in Philadelphia thought it right to give Woolman a word of warning, and sent an able-bodied deputation post-haste. Every one in the town was abed and asleep when they arrived, and Woolman had already taken leave of his neighbours. They rode to the tavern, and despatched a messenger to call Woolman from his bed. He appeared at once, received the message, and returned to bed without telling his wife until next morning, when, he writes, she was greatly distressed at the news, and they had " an humbling time." Nevertheless, so great was his assurance of protection, that he departed in the fear of the Lord. Israel and John Pemberton set him on his way to his friend Samuel Foulke's in Bucks County, Pennsylvania, where he joined four Indians—a man and three women—who were returning to the Wyoming Valley, after a business trip East, and who had agreed to act as guides.

At this point, Woolman met another test. He writes :

" Here my friend Benjamin Parvin met me, and proposed joining me as a companion—we had before exchanged some letters on the subject,—and now I had a sharp trial on his account.   As the journey appeared perilous, I thought if he went chiefly to bear me company, and we should be taken captive, my having been the means of drawing him into these difficulties would add to my own afflictions.   So I told him my mind freely, and let him know I was resigned to go alone.   But after all, if he really believed it his duty to go on, I believed his company would be very comfortable to me.   It was indeed a time of deep exercise, and Benjamin appeared to be so fastened to the visit that he could not be easy to leave me.   So we went on."

They soon struck into the wilderness, and their camp the first night was pitched upon the banks of the Lehigh, in the Blue Ridge Mountains.   Walking about at sunset, Woolman reflected upon the horrors of war, whether among these children of the woods or civilised nations. Upon the sides of the great forest trees, peeled for the purpose, were drawn in red and black paint rude representations of Indians on the warpath, going and returning from battle, with others suffering horrid deaths.   They were on a familiar Indian trail, often used by the savage warriors, and as Woolman studied these fierce Indian histories, his soul was moved to reflect on the afflictions which " a fierce, proud spirit produceth in the world."   He meditated on their fatigues in hard mountain travel ; on their misery and distress when wounded far from home ; on their unnecessary bruises and weariness in thus chasing one another over rock and stream ; on the restless, unquiet mind of all those who live in the spirit of war and hatred ; and on the inheritance transmitted to their children,—and he yearned to tell the whole human race the message of peace and love which he so fully believed was his.   The next rainy day, as he sat in his tent, he was led to reflect upon the nature of the exercises which attended him.

" Love was the first motion, and thence arose a concern to spend some time with the Indians, that I might feel and understand their life and the spirit they live in, if haply I might receive some instruction from them, or they might be in any degree helped forward by my following the leadings of Truth among them."

The dangers of the way increased. One Indian with whom Woolman talked, produced a tomahawk which he had kept concealed under his coat. He made no use of it, however, and sat down to a friendly pipe, when conversation became general. The hatchet, Woolman said, had a very " disagreeable appearance," but it was only intended for readiness in case of attack. On June 17 they reached their destination, and as the afternoon shadows stretched over the mountains, the first person whom they saw was a modest old Indian woman, with a Bible in her hand, who addressed the guide, and then the strangers, telling them she had heard of their coming. This rejoiced their hearts, and they sat on a log while the conch-shell was blown to call the people together. Going into a house near the town, they found some sixty persons awaiting them in silence. Woolman addressed them, and a few interpreted for others, and he greeted them from their white brethren, naïvely showing these dark savages his certificate from the Monthly Meeting, which he endeavoured to explain. The difficulties of the Delaware tongue increased his labours, and as the days went on, and the spirit of good-will was evident, he frequently dispensed altogether with an interpreter. Once, feeling his mind covered with the spirit of prayer, he assured the interpreters that if he prayed aright, God would hear him without their aid, and the " meeting ended with a degree of divine love." An old Indian named Papunehang—a " tender man," says Woolman—appreciated the spirit and atmosphere of the meeting, even if he did not comprehend the words, telling the interpreter afterwards, " I love to feel where words come from."

The little town of forty houses, the largest thirty feet long and eighteen feet wide, standing compactly together for protection, received the care and solicitude of John Woolman for the remainder of his stay. On the 20th of June he felt at liberty to return home, which he reached by the end of the month. Thankfulness at having accomplished his task and finding his family well caused him to check his joy, lest the feeling might seem selfish in being "glad overmuch"!   A minute stands on the books of his meeting :

"1st of 8 mo. 1763.   Our friend John Woolman being returned from his visit to some religiously disposed Indians up Susquehannah, informed the last meeting that he was treated kindly, and had satisfaction in his visit."

Burlington, headquarters of Quakerism in New Jersey, was but five years old when the Assembly of 1682 passed an act "to encourage learning for the better education of youth."

This act set aside a valuable tract of land in the Delaware opposite Burlington known as Matiniconk Island, to "remain to and for the use of the town of Burlington . . . for the maintaining of a school for the education of youth."

The revenues from a part of this land, cared for by a committee known as the "Island Managers," are still devoted to the original purpose.   This is probably the oldest trust fund of an educational character now existing in the United States.

Thomas Budd, one of the most prominent Quakers of the time, and author of an interesting pamphlet, *Good Order Established in Pennsylvania and West New Jersey*, in a comprehensive plan of education which was largely adopted, urged compulsory education at the "publick Schools" for a period of seven years.   "Schools should be set up in all towns and cities with persons of known honesty, skill, and understanding, chosen by the Governor and Assembly, to teach in them."   He would have the children taught "true English and Latin . . . and fair writing, arithmetic, and book-keeping."

The first mention in the meeting minutes of a school for Friends occurs in a minute of the Monthly Meeting of Burlington for "7th of 11th mo. 1705."

"It is the request of some Friends of Burlington to this meeting that they may have the privilege of allowing a school to be kept in this meeting-house in Burlington, which request is answered by this meeting."

Schools were speedily set up in the country neighbour-hoods of the adjoining Quaker counties, being often held in the meeting-houses, and while no high degree of learning was reached, a fair average for the day was maintained, with the exception of certain isolated settlements, where both educational and religious interests suffered greatly. That a high standard of intellectual attainment was reached by the more cultivated Quakers may at once be perceived when we recall the evidences of wide reading and liberal views shown in the correspondence and literary work of the leading Quakers of the early eighteenth century. Closely in touch with the activities of the Society in religious matters, they maintained with England a lively corre-spondence, both with the leading Friends and some of the literary men of the day in London. Among these were the Morrises, Smiths, Kinseys, Coxes, and Dillwyns, of Burlington, which always maintained its position as the chief town and centre of culture in the Jerseys. The Yearly Meeting had been transferred to Philadelphia when the Quaker *revival of learning* came at the end of the eighteenth century. The War of the Revolution startled the Friends into an appreciation of their pre-carious position. Shutting themselves up within their defensive walls of discipline in the effort to strengthen themselves, they disowned all offenders against the sentiment of conservatism urged by the newly created " Meeting for Sufferings," and began to teach a " guarded education."

In 1720 we find the meetings in correspondence with all the meetings at home and abroad, and still growing in numbers, although more slowly. Some of the Friends of the second generation had begun that movement to the lands in the West which later became so great ; and when, in 1742, Edmund Peckover attended Burlington Yearly Meeting, he noted that while not many who had started West had been of " much note," when arrived there they developed greatly in a spiritual sense, as they were thrown more upon their own resources, and promised to build up good and lively meetings. The list is a long one of those who came to refresh their American brethren from the old home, but there were already growing up within the circle of the meetings certain ultra-conservative tendencies which were detrimental to the best spiritual growth.

The following very interesting remarks stand appended to a minute of the Meeting of Ministers and Elders, of which John Woolman was Clerk, for Burlington and Chesterfield Monthly Meetings, under date five years before his death. In the absence of statistics for that period, the list he gives is valuable, and is our only record of these officers of the meeting. The writer's comment was not intended for public perusal, but was a simple expression of his feelings on making the list.

LIST OF MINISTERS AND ELDERS OF BURLINGTON QUARTERLY
MEETING, DATED 2 MO. 22nd, 1767.

1. John Sykes	21. Katherine Kalender	41. Sarah English
2. Joannah Sykes	22. Ebenezer Mot	42. Amos Middleton
3. Josiah Foster	23. William Lowrie	43. Samuel Worth
4. John Butkher	24. Benjamin Field	44. Joseph Horner
5. Mary Bunting	25. Edward Whitcraft	45. Samuel Gaunt
6. Samuel Sattertwaite	26. *Anthony Benezet*	46. Meribeth Fowler
7. Thomas Buzby	27. *Joyce Benezet*	47. Anthony Sykes
8. William Morris	28. Sarah Newbold	48. Peter Harvey
9. Daniel Smith	29. Hannah Bickerdike	49. Mary Harvey
10. Joseph Burr	30. Elizabeth Shinn	50. Mary Buzby
11. Jane Burr	31. John Smith	51. John Sleeper
12. Jacob Andrews	32. Peter Worral	52. Caleb Carr
13. Josiah White	33. Susannah Worral	53. Katherine Wetheril
14. Daniel Doughty	34. Benjamin Jones	54. Asher Woolman
15. Edith Doughty	35. Elizabeth Jones	55. Esther Atkinson
16. Joseph Noble	36. Thomas Middleton	56. Elizabeth Hatkinson
17. Edward Cathrel	37. Patience Middleton	57. Sarah Woolman
18. Rachel Cathrel	38. Elizabeth Smith	58. Abner Woolman
19. Elizabeth Woolman	39. Mary Brown	59. John Woolman
20. Elizabeth Bordon	40. Jane Smith	60. William Jones

"The 22, 2 mo. 1767 this list was entered in This Book and the persons above named are, I believe, now living. As, looking over the minutes made by persons who have put off this Body, hath sometimes revived in me a thought how ages pass away; so this list may possibly revive a like thought in some when I and the rest of the persons above named are entered in another state of Being. The Lord who was the guide of my Youth hath in Tender mercies helped me hitherto. He hath healed me of

wounds ! He hath helped me out of grievous entanglements !
He remains to be the strength of my life, to whom I desire to
devote myself in Time and Eternity.   JOHN WOOLMAN."

The period when John Woolman was most engaged
in the ministry is a striking one in the history of the
Church. Social and religious conditions on both sides of
the Atlantic were undergoing great changes. As a rule,
the Quakers, although perhaps unconsciously, felt the
influences pervading all classes of society ; and the fresh
breath of what has since been known as the " *Great
Awakening*" swept even into the quiet atmosphere of the
Quaker meeting. One of the great leaders among the
English Friends was Samuel Fothergill, who followed a
few years later directly in the footsteps of Whitefield.
The latter, in 1739, passed like a ghostly whirlwind over
the Jerseys, holding meetings in the open air, and on the
steps of the Court House in Burlington. Not once, but
many times, did the strange preacher vehemently exhort
his hearers to a holier life, and many were his converts.
His ministrations could not have been without a certain
influence upon the Society of Friends, and indeed, through
his indefatigable efforts, there were many converts to
Methodism, albeit Whitefield was no longer a follower
of Wesley.

John Woolman was a youth of eighteen at the time of
Whitefield's first visit, and the religious excitement in the
very air must have told upon him. Be that as it may, he
very soon became the most striking figure among the
Quakers of New Jersey, or, indeed, of America. Just at
the time when, with his highly ethical and spiritual views
of the conduct of life, he was seeking to arouse Friends
from the religious indifference into which over-attention
to the letter of the law had led them, Samuel Fothergill
arrived from England. He was the son of that John
Fothergill who had made three visits to America, the last
extending from 1736 to 1739. His preaching was
forceful, and it is worthy of note that at this period near
the middle of the century, Whitefield, Woolman, and the
Fothergills, father and son, were all labouring in their

respective fields with great effect. Whitefield and Woolman died within three years of each other.

Samuel Fothergill landed in 1754. He was a man of remarkable influence and ability, with a gift for organisation and a breadth of view singularly calculated to advise wisely in the perplexed time when he visited the colonies. Remarkable results followed his two years in America. The Indian frontier wars were at their height, and he encouraged Friends to withdraw from activity in the legislative bodies of the provinces, rather than compromise their distinguishing testimonies. To him the Society owes much of the movement which revived and enforced the discipline in London in 1760, with an immediate effect upon all the American meetings.

The mutterings of the Revolutionary War were now beginning to be heard. English Friends continued to visit America, often in the endeavour to strengthen the hands of the brethren, although few of them, except Dr. Fothergill, brother of Samuel, and one or two others who gave careful study to the situation and kept in correspondence with the colonial Quakers, could understand the very difficult position in which the latter found themselves. Among the last to come over was Elizabeth Robinson, from Yorkshire, who, in a visit to the family in Philadelphia where young Thomas Scattergood of Burlington was serving his apprenticeship, was the means of awakening him to a sense of his spiritual needs, and he became a well-known minister. Between 1775 and 1785 no English Friend crossed the Atlantic for service as a preacher, the difficulties being too great. The meeting at Burlington in 1775 notes the reading of the caution issued by the Meeting for Sufferings, advising "close adherence to the principles of Quakerism in these times of commotion." The Quarterly Meeting minutes for 11 mo. 24, 1777, state that twenty-six Representatives from the preceding Quarterly Meeting of Ministers and Elders had been prevented from attending Yearly Meeting because "hindered from crossing the River (Delaware) by military men stopping the boats on this side, on account of the British Troops being in possession of the city of Philadelphia." Germantown also was occupied by General Howe, who had taken possession of the town in September. The Friends at Trenton, New Jersey, were obliged to meet in private houses, their meeting-house being occupied by soldiers ; and when, one day, the Burlington Friends came in to the town to Monthly Meeting, they discovered that the militia had occupied the house for quarters during the night.

The Friends suffered much throughout the war, certain neighbourhoods in New Jersey feeling particularly the sorrows of the time. Both armies moved through New Jersey, General Howe's army causing much damage in the " Quaker " counties of the state. Distraints on the part of the Americans were heavy, one Friend with a wife and child near Mount Holly being obliged to flee, when their home was plundered ; another with eleven children was stripped of all his property by both contending armies. Through the Meeting for Sufferings, English Friends contributed generously to the aid of their persecuted brethren, one of the Friends referred to receiving fifty and the other seventy-five pounds in this way.

Private journals and correspondence of the time show how the subject of national independence was moving Friends in New Jersey. Their position was trying, and speedily became most grave. Many young men yielded to the impulse, which also drew away some of the older ones, to enlist in the cause of the Americans Sympathising epistles came from London, and during the struggle which followed, despite trials consequent upon a position of neutrality among people alive with the spirit of warfare, they steadily maintained their principles and profession, although at the expense, in many cases, of the confiscation of goods and property. To all inquirers they replied, as one meeting stated in a special minute :

"We, the people called Quakers, ever since we were distinguished as a Society, have declared to the world our belief in the peaceable tendency of the Gospel of Christ, and that consistent therewith we could not bear arms, nor be concerned in warlike preparations."

When the hostilities were over, came sufferings in the effort of readjustment,—the price paid for neutrality. Prosperity in material things smiled at last upon the Friends ; but never again were they to see and experience the power and freshness so marked in the earlier days. They had received with almost the last breath of George Fox his thought and blessing in one of his dying expressions—the charge to his companions, " Mind poor Friends in America."

BOOK V

THE QUAKERS IN PENNSYLVANIA

By ISAAC SHARPLESS

CHAPTER I

THE SETTLEMENT

THE persecution of the Friends in England had varying results, depending on the character and circumstances of the victims. To the man of nerve and conscience it taught a more close and fearless adherence to his station and its duties. When the Conventicle Act of 1664 was passed, an Act intended to break up all forms of worship except those of the established church, George Fox wrote to his followers:

"Now is the time for you to stand, you that have been public men (ministers) and formerly did travel abroad; mind and keep up your testimony, go into your meeting-houses as at other times."

He himself went to London "where the storm was about to begin." When he heard that there were stocks prepared for him at Evesham he went there and had "a glorious meeting." Such was usually the conduct of the leaders. They never flinched or fled—almost at times they seemed to court persecution, and enjoy it. William Dewsbury said: "I never played the coward but as joyfully entered prisons as palaces, and in the prison-house, I sang praises to my God and esteemed the bolts and locks upon me as jewels." They fought it out on this line and in the end conquered, but many times the issue seemed doubtful, the conflict interminable, and the reward hardly worth the suffering. To many it seemed that they could do more good by attempting to establish a godly commonwealth in America than by undertaking the seemingly impossible task of reforming the intolerant institutions of England. So when William Penn opened the way, many thousands were immediately ready to take advantage of the offer.

It was not, however, a new idea with Penn in 1681. Twenty years before, George Fox had commissioned Josiah Coale to seek such a home in the new world, and during the intervening time many longing eyes had turned in that direction. William Penn tells us :

"This I can say that I had an opening of joy as to these parts [the American Colonies] in the year 1661 at Oxford twenty years since."

This was when he was a student of seventeen. Whether he referred to this as a dream of youth to found an ideal state, a reflection from his studies or the temper of his associates, or, as the word "opening" was commonly used by the Friends of the time, a divine revelation, we shall not know. But when the opportunity came in the Jerseys to make this dream something of a reality, he quickly embraced it, and wove into the fabric of the government there his advanced ideas of civil and religious liberty and equality.

There was, however, not a clear field. The real Quaker preserve had not been found. At the best it would be a mixed experiment, but it gave him a foretaste and a clear conception of better things which might follow.

The opportunity came in 1681. No other than William Penn could have embraced it. Two considerations came to his aid. One was his great influence at court, an influence gained in spite of his religious peculiarities, and his open opposition to the libertinism of the Stuarts, gained as the result of his father's high station and services, his own most gracious but not obsequious manners, the quickness of his intelligence, and the respect felt for his ability and character. The Duke of York, afterwards James II. was his own and his father's friend, and a long list of titled associates loyally aided his plans.

The other consideration was a claim he had upon the crown for £16,000 due his father's estate for a loan and interest. This he proposed to relinquish in return for a lordly province in America, and Pennsylvania came into his hands. To this the Duke of York added what is now Delaware. The boy's dream was to be realised and the Quaker hopes brought to fruition.

The royal ignorance of geography made trouble in years to come. The King meant to give Penn three degrees of latitude and five of longitude, but the former was impossible between Maryland and New York, and the southern boundary was a source of contest with Lord Baltimore for many years, and kept Penn in England when he wanted to be among his settlers.

He sent over his cousin William Markham to receive the fealty of the few settlers along the western bank of the Delaware—Swedes and Dutch and a few Quakers who had straggled over from New Jersey and settled opposite Burlington, at Tacony and on the Schuylkill, and at Upland (now Chester).[1] Markham was also to arrange for the purchase of land from the Indians, to select the site of Philadelphia, and to lay out the town.

William Penn was Governor of the new state, and had

[1] Dankers and Sluyter, two Dutchmen, travelled through these Delaware Settlements in 1679-80. With no friendly hand they depict the character of these first Quakers along the Delaware. On 19th November 1679, at Burlington, "We went into the meeting of the Quakers who went to work very unceremoniously and loosely. What they uttered was mostly in one tone and the same thing, and so it continued until we were tired out and went away." They describe them as "most worldly of men," as an evidence of which they found a copy of Virgil on the table of one, and also a book of van Helmont's. "Most of them are miserably self-minded in physical and religious knowledge."

When they got down to Tinicum, an island in the Delaware River below Philadelphia, "In the evening there arrived three Quakers, of whom one was their great prophetess, who travels through the whole country in order to quake. She lives in Maryland and forsakes husband and children, plantation and all, and goes off for this purpose. She had been to Boston and had been arrested by the authorities on account of her quakery, . . . They sat by the fire and drank a dram of rum with each other and in a short time after began to shake and groan so that we did not know what had happened and supposed they were going to preach but nothing came of it."

They found at Upland two widows who were at variance and whom the "prophetess" was trying to reconcile. "One of these widows named Anna Salters lived at Tokany and was one of those who, when a certain person gave himself out as the Lord Jesus and allowed himself to be carried around on an ass, shouted Hosanna as he rode over her garments, for which conduct he was arrested, his tongue bored through with a hot iron and his forehead branded with a B for

power to form its constitution and laws subject to the consent of the settlers. He was also owner of the land, and could sell it to whom and on what terms he chose. But he made it cheap, as there was plenty of it, and he must have settlers.

He himself landed at New Castle, Delaware, on the 27th of October 1682 in the *Welcome*. There had been a wearisome voyage of nine weeks, and of the hundred who sailed thirty died of small-pox on the ocean. By easy stages he went to Upland (which he now called Chester), to the hospitable home of Robert Wade, and then to Philadelphia, where he landed at the foot of Dock-Creek. Tradition says that the Indians met him there, and that he gained their confidence by joining them in their feast of roasted acorns and excelling them in jumping. He called together the assembly at Chester, which in a three days' session adopted a constitution and a body of laws.

Friends came rapidly into the province. It need not be assumed that it was release from penalties alone which brought these godly people to Pennsylvania. Before Penn left England he had published *Some Account of the Province of Pennsylvania*. It was an advertisement for settlers, an analysis of the social and political conditions of England, and how these conditions would be bettered for the colonists by emigration. He told of the noble river which fronted the province, the many square miles of good land, the great forests, the wild animals, the furs, the possible productions of the country, in tempting terms.

Then he explained how the government would be free and democratic, without religious or political disabilities. He further urged that there would be place there for

---

blasphemer. She was not only one of these but she anointed his head and feet and wiped them with her hair." This refers to the Bristol [England] episode of James Nayler a score of years before.

Our travellers speak highly of Robert Wade and his wife, the pioneer Friends of Pennsylvania who had come from Salem to Upland in 1675. They were "the best Quakers we have seen" and "could not endure" Anna Salters.

These early days of venture and suffering brought out the crudity as well as the heroism of some of the Friends.

mechanics and tradesmen of all sorts, younger brothers without means, and "men of universal spirits" who wanted to work out the problems of good government.

Many of all sorts came—solid Friends who had endured the horrors of English prisons with a kindly spirit to all the world, men of education and means seeking larger estates, renters who wished to be land owners, millers, handicraftsmen of many kinds, adventurers for gain, some fairly good and some criminal. But at first the better elements were in large preponderance and in absolute control. They entered into the spirit of the enterprise, did their best to support the institutions which their governor and proprietor placed before them, and were melted together in their simple but solemn religious meetings.

For the most of them it was a happy exchange from the social and political rigours of England. Here was a country at their hands, to be owned for a trifling yearly rental, a government in which they were partners, no disabilities to trouble them, no classes to shame them. Some of them had their heads turned by the sudden access of power, and they became, as William Penn expressed it, "too governmentish," too democratic, too inclined to find little grievances, too inappreciative of what they had gained.

The work began promptly :

"At a monthly meeting of the 8th of 9th month (November) 1682 ; at this time Governor William Penn arrived here and erected a city called Philadelphia, about half a mile from Shackamaxon where . . . meetings were established." [1]

At the same time farmers were pressing into the country from Chester, Philadelphia and Bristol, taking up the plots they had purchased in England from rough maps. The work of surveying went on rapidly, but there must have been much neighbourly consideration to allow all to locate so peacefully.

Only two boat loads of immigrants came to Pennsyl-

[1] Watson, *Annals of Philadelphia*, i. 140.

vania in 1681—one from London and one from Bristol. But in 1682 the stream fairly began. Many reached the country before Penn. Twenty-three vessels sailed up the Delaware during the year, and these probably brought 2000 passengers. We hear nothing of any men of prominence in these early days except Friends. The first legislature was made up of Friends and of Swedes and Dutch who were already in the country.

The Pennsylvania Friends represented nearly all parts of the British Isles. Many came from Yorkshire and the midland counties of England. London and Bristol and their neighbourhoods sent their contingents, and Wales a small army. Later many came from the north of Ireland, converted from Presbyterianism by William Edmundson and his friends. The eastern counties, where Puritanism was the strongest, contained fewer Friends. Their restless spirits had gone to New England. Penn's acquaintance along the Rhine brought in the Mennonites and kindred sects, and the province in these early days grew rapidly, and with harmonious elements. But we must study something of the character of the great leader before we can understand the state that he founded and the religious body for whom and with whom he worked.

CHAPTER II

WILLIAM PENN IN PENNSYLVANIA

WITH William Penn as a founder of a state, this history has to do only indirectly. There is little doubt that the democratic character of the ideas which he at the first advocated so enthusiastically produced its effect upon the development of Philadelphia Yearly Meeting. After the partisan struggles of the first thirty years of colonial history, when he was assailed with harsh and bitter criticism, had passed away, a more just appreciation of his services gradually found place. This grew, after his death, into a profound and loyal respect. Friends vied with each other in quoting his religious and political tenets, as authorities which they held in ever increasing veneration.

He wrote easily and he wrote voluminously. He pondered deeply upon many phases of theological and governmental theory, and presented his thoughts in printed form. He wrote too easily and under too varied impulses, and, like such writers, it is often hard to reconcile his statements with each other. The general trend both of his theological and political views is, however, so evident and so abundantly and happily expressed that they became in time the basis of the government of Pennsylvania and the expressions of the doctrine and policy of Philadelphia Yearly Meeting. They were followed too literally and had the odour of too great sanctity. For what with him were only means and expedients, became, under his less broad-minded followers, ends and fixed principles.

To appreciate subsequent history, a critical estimate of this remarkable man, whose qualities shine more highly with each succeeding investigation, becomes a necessity. His biographers have copied from each other, and perhaps too carelessly accepted tradition as to particular events which have not stood the test of closer examination ; but enough of well authenticated facts, letters of himself and of judicious friends, epistles on religion and government, and the undisputed actions of his public and private career, exist from which to frame an estimate of his strength and weakness.

Hepworth Dixon and others seem to have effectually answered Macaulay's charges to his discredit. It is unfortunate, however, that they are embalmed in that historian's brilliant style and perennially interesting volumes. Where a score read the attack but one knows of the defence, and so the misstatements will for ever be renewed and believed.

There are, however, certain weaknesses of Penn's character, not seriously discreditable to him, but which detract something from the universal praise often accorded him. He was a poor judge of character. His Deputy-Governors were often most unfortunate selections. Blackwell, an old Cromwellian soldier, honest and moral, had no appreciation of the Quaker character with which and over which he was to govern. He was, as he admitted, "unequally yoked" and "unfeignedly gave thanks to God" when he was recalled. Evans, a young libertine, swollen with a puerile self-conceit, offended in every way his best friends and made endless troubles for Penn. Gookin, severe and unyielding, with a stubbornness lapsing into insanity, was an unquestioned misfit. The better judgment of Penn's widow saved the day for the family after this succession of failures.

It is true the problem was a hard one. A Friend would not perform the duties which involved certain military declarations and offices ; these they were quite willing that others should undertake, but against them their own consciences rebelled. The Deputy-Governor must,

therefore, not be a Friend. He must, however, be acceptable to them, appreciating their spirit and respecting their
scruples, for by virtue both of numbers and character
they controlled the situation. They were to be his
partners, not his subordinates, and with the extravagant
idea of their rights and privileges which some of them had,
they were no easy partners to work with. The ideal
Governor must not only be self-respecting, but tactful ;
not only a strict moralist, but tolerant of differing
standards ; not only faithful to Penn's interests, but
appreciative of the people's liberties. Not one of Penn's
choices, with the possible exception of Thomas Lloyd,
possessed all these qualities, and bitterly the proprietor
paid the price of his poor judgment in thirty years of
governmental confusion and financial loss.

The account of Penn's relations to his knavish steward
is not pleasant reading for his friends. Ford was a
Friend and a business man of ability. Penn placed all
his affairs in Ford's hands and dismissed his care of them.
Full of great schemes of philanthropy, his influence
eagerly sought for suffering Friends and suitors of all
kinds, this is not a matter of wonder. But when the
fraudulent nature of his doings was known to Penn, or
might easily have been known, he still allowed matters to
proceed, heaping up claim upon claim till the province
became mortgaged and his friends had infinite difficulty
in untangling the complicated fraud. At first it was
misplaced confidence, which any busy man might have
fallen into. Then lest the plight which had happened to
him should injure the Holy Experiment, he allowed it to
proceed and kept it quiet, thus piling up untold suffering
and trouble and a term in the debtor's prison for himself,
and much vexation and expense for his friends, which an
earlier, vigorous exposure might have avoided. There
was nothing dishonest or illiberal in his course, only a
suggestion of a lack of downright positiveness in
extricating himself honourably from an unfortunate
position.

The question of military resistance was the great

difficulty in a Quaker state, which finally wrought the downfall of the body which opposed it. Prior to the downfall, the Friends had, in many cases, held their places by pursuing what seems like a doubtful course, going further than strict consistency would approve. Penn himself was not quite clear of some equivocation in the matter. As we have seen, he appointed non-Quaker deputies to perform acts which he and no other Friend would consider consistent with their profession ; to " be stiff with our neighbours upon occasion" as he once said.

This may be defensible, for liberty of the individual conscience was their great claim. But when Penn recovered his right to govern his province in 1693, it was the result of a promise that he would faithfully transmit to the Assembly all kingly commands for military aid, which " he doubted not " that body would honour. It did not honour the first communication he made in compliance with this implied contract, and Penn must have known that it would not and that he would not urge it to.

Fortunately the trouble was only ephemeral, and no one called for a literal enforcement of the condition, but this hardly acquits Penn of something like hedging in his dealings with the Crown, a stroke of diplomacy very venial in that day, but not quite consistent with an open and perfectly transparent character.

These, then, seem to be the weak spots in Penn's record, an inability to judge men and a certain timidity in dealing with difficult situations, when his larger plans would be thereby endangered. More than this can hardly be fairly charged against him. These were the causes of the most of his troubles. Good deputies and bold strokes to rid himself of the webs of chicanery his personal and political enemies had woven around him would have kept the temper of the colonists sweet and loyal and his own actions free to carry out his plans. When he went to jail for a matter of conscience, every one of his friends must have felt a thrill of pride as he declared : " My prison shall be my grave before I will budge a jot, for I owe obedience of the conscience to no mortal man." But when he sent out his frantic appeals to Logan to gather in his dues, and allowed his friends to raise a subscription to pay off the indebtedness he had unwittingly contracted, when he lay months in Fleet prison waiting for his creditors to come to terms, there must have been a loss of respect among those who looked to him for leadership, even though these were recognised as under the circumstances right and necessary things to do, and to be the result of no moral obliquity on his part.

The other side of Penn's character is more pleasing to contemplate, and is so much more impressive that the flaws seem insignificant. He was profoundly and sincerely religious, and his personal life was far above the ordinary vices of his age. This was questioned probably but once. When a persecuting Judge suggested that the early career of the prisoner had been guilty of some of the sins against which he was declaiming, Penn indignantly denied it and challenged any one to prove that by word or deed he had, even in his more thoughtless youth, ever offended against the standards of a strict morality. The Judge was rebuked by a fellow judge, who admitted the truth of Penn's denial and told his associate that he had gone too far. The truth of the declaration may well be admitted. Only purity of life, or arch hypocrisy, could be the basis of such beautiful precepts of morality and piety as we find in his writings, and the latter alternative will hardly be claimed by any one.

The wisdom of many of his *Fruits of Solitude*, the fervent appeal to the reader at the beginning of *No Cross, No Crown*, the fitting and eloquent eulogy on George Fox, and many others which will occur to any readers of his works, could hardly be the product of a character which had ever suffered a moral relapse. Nor is there evidence that the validity of his inspired ministry or the profound respect and influence accorded to his preaching was questioned by his rather exacting collaborators in the Gospel among Friends. It is no proof of this that crowds flocked to hear him [1] in England when he was expected to be present at a meeting, for this is the meed of every preacher who has for the time being the popular ear.

A better evidence is the judgment of friends expressed in private correspondence. Isaac Norris writes in 1701, just as Penn was leaving the province the second time :

"The unhappy misunderstandings in some and unwarrantable oppositions in others have been a block to our plenary comforts in him, and his own quiet; but these things are externals only. Our communion in the church sweetens all, and our inward waitings and worships together have often been a general comfort and consolation ; and in this I take a degree of satisfaction, after all, that we part in love ; and some of his last words in meeting yesterday, were 'that he looked over all infirmities and outwards, and had an eye to the regions of spirits, wherein is our surest tie'; and in true love, there he took his leave of us." [2]

Again in 1707, when the proprietor was in the darkest days of his difficulties with the Fords, Isaac Norris writes :

"The more he is pressed, the more he rises. He seems of a spirit fit to bear and to rub through difficulties, and after all, as thou observes, 'his foundation remains.'" [3]

William Penn was one of those choice beings whose soul was attuned to Divine harmonies, and whose power could be felt by kindred spirits in the life of Christ. When he was coming to Pennsylvania in 1699, he received three certificates from his Friends in England, one from "the Second-day's Meeting of Ministering Friends," in London, one from the Friends in Bristol, where he had resided for a considerable time, and one from the Monthly Meeting of Horsham. They are all most appreciative. The last tells of—

"Our unity and communion with him. . . . He had been a holy and blessed instrument in the hands of the Lord, both in

---

[1] Thomas Story writes in 1697 of meetings in Dublin : "Great was the resort of people of all ranks and professions to our meetings, chiefly on account of our friend William Penn, who was ever furnished by the truth with matter fully to answer their expectations. Many of the clergy were there and the people with one voice spoke well of what they heard."

[2] *Penn and Logan Correspondence.*   [3] *Ibid.*

his ministry and conversation [conduct] and hath always sought the prosperity of the blessed truth and peace and concord in the Church of Christ; and both walked among us in all humility, good sincerity and true brotherly love to our great refreshment and comfort."

There was some adverse sentiment. In Pennsylvania, this had, to a large extent, a political basis, and was led by David Lloyd and Griffith Jones, both probably estimable men, but whose extreme demands created a partisan feeling that extended into the meeting.[1] These men were correspondents and in sympathetic relations with William Mead and Thomas Lower, who are spoken of in the letters of the day[2] as representing the opposition party. George Whitehead is often associated with them.

This opposition from within was largely due to Penn's supposed aristocratic tendencies and possible departure from a proper simplicity in his relations with the courtly influences among which he moved, and also to the Ford question and the doings of Evans as deputy-governor. It was later swallowed up by the prevailing and warmly expressed regard, as these matters were seen to be perfectly consistent with his profession and exalted character. After 1710, both the personal and political antagonism ceased in Pennsylvania, and those who had been considered as opponents lost their influence. The

[1] " Our meetings for business are now so much injured by some young forward novices and a few partisans of D. Lloyd, still a close member, that the more sound and ancient Friends do not venture upon anything there that concerns the government, expecting a separation upon it whenever it is taken in hand. According to present appearances of things, a separation will in time be unavoidable, and that after Friends (in England) have taken notice of proceedings here, nothing less than a general purge will ensue. J. Logan, 4 mo. 28, 1707."

[2] " There is a short communication held between thy opposites among Friends there and that corrupted generation here. G. Whitehead has wrote a most affectionate letter to Griffith Jones. He expresses himself as thy friend, but we know how he is linked with the Mead and Lower Party. I believe George is mistaken in Griffith, and knows not that he is not received in unity with Friends."
James Logan to William Penn, 6 mo. 10, 1706.
" They address such on this side the water (England) who are judged by them to be not in the best understanding with him."
Isaac Norris to Joseph Pike, 1 mo. (March) 18, 1707.
" Write a close letter to Friends concerning D. Lloyd insisting on that remonstrance and his directing letters to thy enemies."
James Logan to William Penn, 12 mo, (February) 1709.
See *Penn and Logan Correspondence*.

English opposition, always less well defined and based on more shadowy grounds, seems also to have disappeared about the same time. So that, cleared of his financial troubles, his colony loyal, and his enemies evanescent, he spent the last two years of his vigorous life in a serene atmosphere of success and triumph. The stroke that then deprived him of his mental power, but left his spiritual faculties unimpaired, brought him universal sympathy and appreciation.

Mentally, Penn was one of the great men of his times. It was a day of young men. The great preachers were nearly all under thirty, but this might be consistent with ordinary intelligence. Penn was more than a great popular preacher. He was a man of great thoughts and far-seeing plans and definite and courageous convictions based on learning and experience and study. He was ready for Oxford at fifteen. He was but twenty-three when the germ of the principle of universal toleration seems to have taken possession of him, apparently evolved from within, which in time became the great enthusiasm of his life. At the same age he began to preach. The first of his religious works came a few years later, and *No Cross, No Crown* immediately followed. The erudition displayed by one so young was a surprise to friends and enemies alike. Thus, at the age when the average American youth is finishing college, Penn had collected a wonderful store of knowledge, could command an effective English style, and was a master of theological argument of a most serviceable quality.

His development was continuous. His work on constitutions prior to his American experiment betrays the thoughtful student of the best that had been written in the past. He always had great conceptions and projects. In 1693 he published his scheme for "An European Dyet, Parliament or Estates," to which disputes between nations should be referred. All the great Powers were to be represented. The advantages of such a court, and the means to make its decisions acceptable, in order to avoid wars, were presented with great wealth of argument and illustration. The Hague tribunal was there in embryo.

Three years later, he published a plan for the union of the American Colonies. Two representatives of each province were to meet in New York to arrange matters of common interest. They were to settle questions concerning commerce, the return of criminals, and "consider ways and means to support the union and safety of these provinces against the public enemies." This was probably the first suggestion of the movement which culminated about a century later in the Federal Constitution and Union.

But the greatest, and at the same time, most practical conception was the foundation of Pennsylvania itself. That there were errors in detail, none can doubt. An absentee landlord, even though liberal, can hardly avoid criticism and opposition, and such was William Penn to his Colony. His forceful presence would undoubtedly have composed faction and removed difficulties, and it was his full purpose to have lived permanently in Pennsylvania. The idea of a Commonwealth devoted to liberty and peace drew out the best powers of a comprehensive and enthusiastic intellect. There was no room in Europe, but in the great unoccupied expanse of the New World he would carry out his ideals with a selected community in sympathy with them, of a serious and honest sort, to whom he would transfer the governmental power and realty rights he had purchased of the Crown, reserving only such moderate share of each as security for the future and family interests would justify. It was a glorious conception and a no less glorious opportunity, and we find him continually tempering his natural ardour by considerations of duty to God and man, as the seriousness of the task and the risks of failure pressed themselves upon him.

There was, too, in his composition a good share of fighting spirit. He was to have difficulties, but he never quailed. The temper which declared that he would never yield a jot, even though he died in prison, served him in good stead in other contests. "Can my wicked enemies yet bow? They *shall*, or break, or be broken in pieces before a year from this time comes about, and my true friends rejoice," he declared in a crisis with Lord Baltimore. "If *lenitives* will not do, *coercives* must be tried," he announced in another emergency. It was only this determined vigour which carried him through the vast heap of difficulties among which he struggled.

The whole of Penn's life indicates the power of his personality. Where he was present, events shaped themselves towards his purposes. At the court of Charles II., of James II., and of Anne, he had surprising influence. This is all the more remarkable because his Quaker scruples in certain respects must have removed him far from the ordinary courtier. We may assume that his dress, while simple, was comely ; that his speech, while observing the limitations of his sect, was well chosen, pleasing and appreciative of the point of view of his associates ; that his manners, while devoid of the flattering postures and phrases of the day, were never offensive. It is only thus that we can explain what seems his general friendliness with royalty and nobility. "I know of no religion," he says, "that destroys courtesy, civility and kindness," and these qualities, together with a conversation full of interesting matter and a ready wit, seem to have made him generally acceptable. So it was that he interceded successfully at court, not only for hundreds of persecuted Friends, but for Anglican bishops, political refugees, and suffering scholars, as well as crowds of needy suitors of humbler rank.

It was for these purposes, and to counteract the influence of Lord Baltimore in the matter of the boundary line, efforts which never failed of success, that he felt impelled to remain so much in England. Again and again he hoped to come to Pennsylvania, but the demands of Friends and the exactions of Ford kept him at home. Only two visits of less than two years each, all too short for the work to be done, was he able to make to his province.

His personal influence was no less marked among his colonists. When present, faction was stilled, the Indians were pacified, desirable legislation was effected, and under his ministry the meetings settled down into quietness and harmony. Could he have longer remained, another history would have been written. Perhaps it was well that in the tutelage of the colony it should have been left to its own responsibility, and have found its way through confusion to liberty. For had the compelling influence of its founder been continually present, a heroic figure among his friends, certain aristocratic features and social customs might have been engrafted on the government less favourable to liberty than such as were worked out through the stress of partisan conflict. Whether we sympathise with David Lloyd or William Penn in the struggle between them, we may accord to each of them a potent influence in shaping the free government which grew out of the troubled early years of the experiment.

There are many traditions of his life in America : how he outjumped the Indians, and gained their lasting regard ; the great treaty immortalised by Clarkson in history, by West on the canvas, and by Voltaire in happy phrase ; the open house at Pennsbury, where in feudal style he generously entertained red man and white, politician and minister alike ; his " walks " with the Indians and the regard he showed for their prejudices and customs ; how on his way to Haverford Meeting he took upon his horse little Rebecca Wood, and carried her with him to the Meeting, her bare feet dangling on either side ; how at Merion a little boy, curious to see the great Governor, peeped through a hole in the door of his chamber, and saw him on his knees returning thanks that he had been provided for in the wilderness. There is probably more or less truth in all of these. They show that in a little time something of a halo gathered around his name, and his little acts became significant, a sure evidence of influence.

We may make such surmises as we will concerning the

extent of the influence of William Penn upon Pennsylvania Quakerism, based on his character and standing. The Meeting minutes make but limited reference to him. In 1683 a plan, doubtless originating in William Penn's comprehensive mind, was presented to the meeting :

"It being desired to hold a general Meeting of Friends from New England to Carolina, the Meeting appoints : William Penn, Christopher Taylor, Samuel Jenings, James Harrison, Thomas Olive, Mahlon Stacy, to make arrangements by writing to Friends or speaking, and inform London Yearly Meeting."

What difficulties prevented the realisation of this project for nationalising the Society of Friends, we do not know. They were probably material, rather than political. What different development would have resulted is also a matter of conjecture. Something of the same idea occurred to certain Yearly Meetings about two hundred years later.

In 1700, on the occasion of Penn's second visit, we have a record of certificates concerning him being received from Bristol, London, and Horsham. In the same year, "Governor Penn" was appointed on a committee to draw up the epistle to London Yearly Meeting. The next year the following minute was adopted :

"Our Governor, William Penn, having said before this Meeting that he entends for England, and desires that they would appoint ten or twelve Friends to meet him this evening upon some weighty occasion, in order thereunto, Samuel Jenings [and fifteen others] and such public Friends as have freedom, are desired to meet the Governor accordingly about six this evening."

This meeting is probably referred to in the letter of Isaac Norris, already quoted. No other references to him appear on the Yearly Meeting minutes. We may safely assume, however, that he was an important figure in any meeting which he attended.

In the minutes of Philadelphia Monthly Meeting, there are evidences of his interest in the details of society work and his name appears occasionally. On Eleventh-month 1st, 1683 (January 1684):

"A letter of advice from the Governor was read to Friends counselling them to be careful in their behaviour for Truth's sake, that so the Lord might not be dishonoured and the Truth evilly spoken of amongst wicked men."

Again on Sixth-month (August) 5th, 1684 :

"The Governor being present, and his departure for England drawing nigh, he moved the Meeting to give him a certificate as touching his demeanour amongst the people of his province, which was taken into consideration by the Meeting."

And later in the same Meeting :

"A certificate was drawn up in the Meeting according to the motion of the Governor, and subscribed by Thomas Lloyd [and fifteen others] in the name of the Meeting."

During his second visit, he expressed to the Meeting a "concern" that religious work should be done among the negroes and Indians. Acting on this the Friends appointed a Monthly Meeting for negroes to which their masters were to send them, and "be present with them at said meetings as frequent as may be." It was also agreed that when Indians are in town they be invited to a meeting "when our Governor is willing to speak to them."

He worked on ordinary committees, as in the case of the widow of Thomas Lloyd, who thought that the executors of his will had not treated her fairly. The Governor being present on another occasion, "readily condescended" to give the materials of the meeting-house, erected where the City Hall now is, to another in a more accessible part of the city.

When he left in 1701, never to return, though he and they hoped otherwise, another cordial and loving certificate drawn up by Thomas Story, Samuel Carpenter, and Griffith Owen, was given him.

The personality of William Penn may well be assumed to be the most potent influence in the early history of Philadelphia Yearly Meeting. His advantages of birth, fortune, and education, his superior intellectual and moral powers, his position as originator of the conception which had given to all its members their worldly and religious opportunities, his authority as Governor and proprietor, would in any community have endowed him with a towering ascendency. But when to these are added a humility in religious affairs, which asked and would allow no precedence, a record of faithful adherence to principle, through losses and imprisonments, and an endowment of a prophetic gift of remarkable fervour and power, there is no need to doubt that whenever his gracious presence could be felt, nothing could ever compare with it. Even in his absence, his words and memory and spirit hovered over his province in its religious life, and became, long after his death, its inspiration and guide.

CHAPTER III

EARLY DAYS—THE KEITH CONTROVERSY

PHILADELPHIA Yearly Meeting had its origin in the Monthly Meeting of Burlington, New Jersey. On the second of the 3rd month "it was unanimously agreed that a general meeting be yearly held in Burlington, the first of which to be the 28th of Sixth month 1681." This was the first session of Philadelphia Yearly Meeting. It decreed that women's meetings should be held monthly at the same time as the men's.

The next year, 1682, a large number of Friends having come to Philadelphia, an organisation was there effected. These "Friends of God" agreed to meet monthly and make every third meeting a Quarterly Meeting. General Meetings were also held both at Burlington and Philadelphia. The latter in 1684 was attended by representatives from Rhode Island and from Maryland in accordance with William Penn's comprehensive plan already mentioned. Epistles were sent to London and to Carolina, Virginia, Maryland, and New England :

"That it may be presented to them if possible from these remote provinces they may send two or three for each province to our Yearly Meeting here being as a center or middle part that so communion and blessed union may be preserved among all."

This duplication of General Meetings in the case of Friends so closely associated as those in New Jersey and Pennsylvania seemed undesirable, and in 1685 it was concluded to hold them in the future alternately in

Burlington and Philadelphia, beginning at Burlington in 1686. This arrangement continued till 1760, when it was decided that all the Yearly Meetings should be held in Philadelphia.

The territory embraced in the Yearly Meeting in early times included the settled portions of New Jersey and Pennsylvania and the northern parts of Delaware and Maryland and also some meetings in Virginia. Later the whole eastern shore of the Chesapeake was given to Philadelphia, and the Virginia meetings and others on the west side of the Susquehanna both in Maryland and Pennsylvania were transferred to Baltimore.

While in local matters the American meetings were supreme each within its limits, they all paid great respect to the letters of George Fox and the official epistles of London Yearly Meeting. These were both doctrinal and practical, stating the theory of the meeting for worship, setting up the church machinery, giving directions as to the treatment of delinquents and of the poor, advice as to business, dress, and language, and a multitude of other details. One can find practically the whole of formal Quakerism as it existed for two centuries in these early epistles. They are a wonderful tribute to the genius of the Founder, whose followers in after years were almost too faithful in their allegiance. Occasionally there was a ripple of discontent, as John Burnyeat found in Long Island in 1671.[1] But such rebellion became in a little time evidence of " a wrong spirit " wherever it cropped out. The volume of these advices became in time so large that in 1703 a committee of the Yearly Meeting was appointed to codify them, and thus was established the Discipline which became obligatory upon all the meetings. The earliest draft of a discipline, adversely called Canons and Institutions, was the work of Fox and others, and was issued in London in 1668. In a little time these foreign regulations and advices were replaced by others of similar import adopted in the Yearly Meeting to meet the various conditions as they developed.

[1] See p. 229.

In 1685 the Yearly Meeting agreed that " Friends in the Ministry" should meet at seven o'clock in the morning prior to the Yearly or General Meeting. Elders had not yet been created, but this was probably the origin of "the meeting of ministers and elders" which has been carried through all the subsequent history.

The first business meeting held in Philadelphia was opened by this minute :

"The Friends of God belonging in Philadelphia in the province of Pennsylvania being met in the fear and power of the Lord at the present meeting-house in the said city the Ninth Day of the Eleventh Month being the third day of the week in the year 1682 [1]—They did take into their serious consideration the settlement of meetings therein for the affairs and services of the Truth according to that goodly and comely practise and example which they had received and enjoyed with true satisfaction among their friends and brethren in the land of their nativity and did then and there agree that the first Third Day in the week in every month shall hereafter be the monthly meeting day for men's and women's meeting for the affairs and service of the Truth in this city and county and every third meeting shall be Quarterly Meeting of the same."

They agreed to build a meeting-house, and to buy the necessary books ; they advised that all Friends bring certificates ; they arranged for a record of deaths, the care of the poor, and the sanction of marriages, which were very numerous.

Succeeding meetings decreed that ministering Friends should gain the sanction of their Monthly Meetings ; that these bodies should severely look after those who spread false reports ; that Friends should not go to law with each other until an attempt had been made by the meeting to settle the dispute ; and that wrongdoing of various sorts should be closely attended to.

The first Friend who came to Pennsylvania to reside was probably Robert Wade. He had emigrated in 1675 from England to Salem, New Jersey, and within a year crossed the Delaware River and occupied the Essex House, the residence of the old Swedish governors, in

---

[1] 9th January 1683. The year began 1st March.

Upland, now Chester. At this house, on Eleventh Month
10th, 1681, the first session of Chester Monthly Meeting
was held. The Friends of Burlington seem to have exercised some supervisory care over this meeting. William
Penn occupied the same house when he landed in 1682,
and here also met the first assembly of Pennsylvania.
Also prior to the arrival of Penn a number of New
Jersey Friends had crossed the river at Burlington and
settled the Falls Meeting in Bucks County.

When the province was divided into the three counties,
Philadelphia, Chester, and Bucks, three Quarterly Meetings,
coterminous with the counties, were established, while
Monthly Meetings were pushed out into the woods to
meet the rapidly growing needs of the immigrant population.

The early minutes of the meetings betray a great
anxiety to live up to the standard of Fox and his
friends in England. Within a few years after 1682 such
subjects as the following, selected almost at random, were
considered.

A member was disciplined for passing money " not
current " ; again and again were the evils of giving rum
to the Indians pointed out, and Friends urged against it ;
they were urged to attend to the wants of the poor outside
their borders ; not to buy " hog-bells " of the Indians, who
had probably stolen them ; they arranged their meetings
so as not to interfere with " the court," for the same
Friends were influential in both ; they set up schools, at
first in the meeting-houses, afterwards near by, both for
girls and boys ; they laboured with a man who wanted a
certificate for marriage " for the extravagant powdering of
his periwig," and made him promise to be more moderate.
Every matter connected with morals or conduct was a
proper matter for inquiry and church legislation. " To
clear Truth " was given as the object of any disavowal of
loose living, but reformation rather than rejection was
persistently sought for the offender.

The large majority of the settlers were Englishmen,
mostly yeomen. They had bought their lands of Penn
from rough maps before leaving England, at the very

moderate price which he asked of £100 for 5000 acres or smaller tracts in proportion, with a quit-rent annually of one shilling for each hundred acres. This enabled many a poor English renter to become a landowner in Pennsylvania, and, as a matter of fact, these farmers greatly prospered, though Penn had difficulty in collecting his quit-rents. The meeting-houses a few miles apart through the settled country were the first concern after the necessities of living were provided for, and the machinery of the church was easily constructed after the George Fox model. While a number of Friends of education and means found homes in Philadelphia, the Yearly Meeting was essentially rural in its characteristics. This fact and the absence of any provision for higher education created a steady, conservative community, perpetuating its type from one generation to another.

Two other elements of the population must be considered. On the 26th of the Fifth Month (July) 1683, having narrowly escaped capture by a Turkish pirate, landed Francis Daniel Pastorius and Thomas Lloyd, representatives and leaders of little bands of Germans and Welsh respectively. They were both well educated, but Latin was the only language they had in common.

Pastorius, the Pennsylvania Pilgrim of Whittier, had been a Mennonite. But he and his friends, after settling in Germantown, were identified with Friends. We find him appointed on committees of the Yearly Meeting, and his Monthly Meeting was recognised as a definite branch. In 1688 this Monthly Meeting sent up a celebrated protest against slavery :

"There is a liberty of conscience here which is right and reasonable, and there ought to be likewise liberty of the body, except for evil-doers, which is another case. But to bring men hither, or to rob and sell them against their will, we stand against."

The Yearly Meeting deferred action, but the seed was sown.

The Mennonites and other German sects, as well as the little Quaker community of Criesheim, were drawn to Pennsylvania by similarity of doctrine and practice with the Friends, They knew of Friends through the visits of William Penn and George Fox to the Rhine Valley, and the contemporaneous spread of Reformation principles in Germany and England. While but few of them followed the example of Pastorius in joining in membership, they were always sympathetic and doctrinally and politically closely associated with Friends. Their great leader, Christopher Sauer, became a powerful ally of Quakerism in all good works. The later immigration of German Reformed and Lutheran, driven from the Palatinate by the ravages of war, had less in common with the Friends, but up to the Revolutionary War were quite willing to permit the civil ascendency of the Friends to remain unchallenged.

The friends of Thomas Lloyd were more definitely in the fold. He himself became the great leader of Pennsylvania Friends, in the absence of William Penn, in all affairs of Church and State, until his lamented death at the age of forty-five in 1694.

Quakerism had started in Wales when John ap John in 1653 was sent as a " tryer " to hear George Fox preach. It suited him, and he became its great apostle. Joined with him were Richard Davies, and also Charles and Thomas Lloyd, university men of high social position. Nowhere was persecution more severe. The old Briton blood, which boasted that it had never been conquered by Roman or Norman, did not quail. They stood it all heroically, and when William Penn offered them a haven of rest they found an honourable way of escaping the trials which seemed practically endless. But they loved their old country, its language and customs, and a committee of them obtained from William Penn the offer of a " Barony," where they could have a new Wales, and, as they hoped, a government of their own, unmixed with alien influences. They came in great numbers. Their Barony of 40,000 acres, now a beautiful suburb of Philadelphia, was assigned them, and the old names along the Pennsylvania Railroad keep alive its traditions.

It was impossible to give them a complete government and complete possession of the soil. Saxon ideas would creep in, and Saxon men would marry their daughters, and while their countrymen at home retained the Welsh customs, in a generation or two they were lost in Pennsylvania. A political governor ran a county line through their tract, and divided their state interests. The Chester County Friends tried to divert all on their side of the line from Philadelphia Quarterly Meeting, but in this they failed. They did, however, succeed in stopping the growth of new meetings which would not be under their supervision in the Chester territory. Thus the powers, both civil and ecclesiastical, conspired to break their unity. But their vigour and industry made the Welsh tract the garden spot of the province, and many a family, illustrious in colony and state, started here.

They were not all Friends when they arrived. A group of sober people settled in " North Wales," outside the Barony. They heard of their compatriots in Haverford and Merion, and sent a delegation to investigate. The report was reassuring, and John Richardson, who visited their meeting in 1702, says they were "a fine tender people, but few understanding English." They were not then in membership with Friends, but recognition soon followed.

The first settlers sent back good reports to their friends in England, Wales, and Germany. They told of the fertile lands to be purchased cheaply, of the kindly natives, of the easy government, and, more than all, of the possibility of worship as they felt to be right without hindrance from the state, or supercilious disregard on the part of an established church. Multitudes flocked in during these early days, mostly Friends, and the meetings grew rapidly in size and number.

In 1683, within five months of Penn's landing, a group of Friends could write to their brethren at home :

" In Pennsylvania there is one [meeting] at Falls, one at the Governor's House, one at Colchester River, all in the county of Bucks; one at Tawcony, one at Philadelphia, both in that county;

one at Darby at John Blunston's, one at Chester, one at Ridley at J. Simcock's, and one at Wm. Ruse's at Chichester, in Cheshire. . . . And for our outward conditions as men, blessed be God, we are satisfied ; the countries are good, the land, the water, the air—room enough for many thousands to live plentifully. . . .

" Dear Friends and Brethren, we have no cause to murmur, our lot is fallen every way in a goodly place, and the love of God is, and growing, among us, and we are a family at peace within ourselves, and truly great is our joy therefor."

There are many testimonies to this delightful peace and harmony of the early days. In 1684 they write to their friends in London :

" At the two aforementioned General Meetings [in Burlington and Philadelphia] we had such a blessed harmony together that we may say we know not that there was a jarring string amongst us. A great multitude came of many hundreds, and the gospel bell made a most blessed sound. There was the men's and women's meeting in both places in their precious services to inspect into Truth's matters in what related to them ; and God gave them wisdom to do it, and all was unanimous."

They expected still more in the future :

" The majesty of Truth is great here, and does prevail and grow. . . . Yea it will increase more and more to the ends of America. The day of its great visitation is come, and his great power and holy authority is rolling hither like the inundation and breaking and overflowing of waters."

One could hardly suppose it to be otherwise. The men who had through deep conviction joined a persecuted and despised sect, who had endured the discipline of English jails, and who had expatriated themselves for the sake of conscience, were not bitter, suspicious men. Their Divine communion was very real, their human communion was very sweet. When they met together in these early days, full of thanks for the blessings of peace and liberty, needing no words to draw their hearts together in silent worship of their ever near Master, their feelings were too deep and sincere for anything but love and unity.

But the second generation had had no such discipline. Some of them caught the spirit of their fathers and some did not.   They were no longer *all* melted together in spiritual sympathy, and a place was found for division whenever the occasion arose.   This occasion came in the person of George Keith.

He was born in Scotland about 1638 and educated as a Presbyterian.   He studied at the University of Aberdeen, and received the degree of Master of Arts from that institution.   Bishop Burnet says that he " was the most learned man ever in the Quaker sect, well versed both in Oriental tongues and in philosophy and mathematics."   About 1663 or 1664 he joined Friends, and for twenty-seven years was in favour, sharing with the other leaders of the Society the full measure of writing, public discussion, and persecution.   He had the true spirit of the early Friends.   He said in 1665 :

" It lay upon me from the Lord to depart from these teachers who could not point me to the living knowledge of God where I could find it ; and I came and heard men and women who were taught of God who pointed me to the true principle ; and though some of them could not read a letter yet I found them wiser than all the teachers I ever formerly had been under." [1]

Many other of his testimonies are eloquent of the great peace and rapturous joy that came into his heart as the result of the Quaker teaching of God's direct communion with men and his own experience of it.   He found " the gates of the heavenly paradise " opened in himself and came to have a great love for all mankind.   It is unnecessary for our purpose to go over the details of his early life.   His books and sufferings both betray the unflinching spirit of the early Quaker apostle.   He had his full share of imprisonments and beatings, which he bore with humility.   He was especially effective in public discussions, and vigorously espoused his new convictions before hostile audiences of Presbyterian divines.   In 1670 he published his *Benefit, Advantage and Glory of Silent Meetings*, a most sympathetic treatment of the subject written in Aberdeen prison.   " There are immediate revelations now-a-days " is the emphatic point.   In 1675

[1] *Immediate Revelation*, by George Keith, p. 84.

he debated in company with Robert Barclay the principles of his sect before the students of the University of Aberdeen. He joined with George Fox, William Penn, and Robert Barclay in a visit to Germany, and worked in great unity with them. In 1684 he came to New Jersey, where as surveyor he laid out the division line between East and West Jersey. In 1689, at the opening of the Friends' Public School, he was made headmaster, but gave it up in a year, finding that his abilities needed freer scope than in a school of young boys. Up to this time no serious ripple of discontent with Friends or of Friends with him seems to have appeared.

There now began to come out in his sermons and discourses certain doctrinal views, which were looked upon with suspicion by many Friends and received with enthusiasm by others. He charged that Friends had in their preaching of the inward Christ neglected the outward. He asserted that ministers declared that they could be saved by the Christ within them " without anything else," and hence that they undervalued the historic Christ and the Scriptures. When he himself was asked whether ignorant men and infants who had not heard the New Testament could not be saved, it appeared that he had adopted the principles of van Helmont of the transmigration of souls, and that these uninformed people would have another chance in the next cycle. He probably did not press this latter doctrine, but his followers found in it an acceptable refuge. He made, too, a sharp distinction between the human and divine natures in Christ, and the question was debated with great acrimony, whether or not it was the body which was born of Mary that ascended into Heaven.

These doctrinal questions were mingled with others of a more practical nature. He charged a general slackness in the administration of the Discipline. The magistrates were often ministers, and in their civil functions would arrest offenders by force but without loss of life or limb. This Keith declared to be inconsistent with the profession of non-resistance of evil.

In these early days the civil and ecclesiastical powers were so closely united in practice, if not in theory, that it was difficult to distinguish them, and disputes in one court were easily transferred to another.

There were doubtless, owing to the emphasis Friends placed on inspiration as the sole endowment for the ministry, a number of crude and narrow preachers among them. The doctrine of direct divine leading unto all truth was so simple and had such sanction from the leaders of the Society that it is not surprising that it constituted for many the one staple subject of discourse. A scholar like George Keith, whether in general harmony with them or not, could not fail to see the lack of perspective and breadth of such men. That there was no ground for his doctrinal charges would be difficult to maintain. That Friends denied the offices and failed to recognise the divinity of the Christ of Judea was in answer to his challenge emphatically contradicted by official assertions both in Pennsylvania and London. The Friends across the water sent a special message urging a full acceptance of the biblical account of Christ, while not weakening in the least in their belief that the light of Christ reached all men whether they had this account or not. The leading Philadelphians issued another paper defining their position in full in the same strain. It was urged upon Keith that the doctrinal shortcomings of individuals should not be used against the Society. It was also urged that for a score of years while the same conditions existed he had been a strong defender of its teachings.

As late as 1688, he had published a catechism teaching the doctrine he now attacked, that the inward operation of the spirit of Christ was essential and that belief in these outward matters was non-essential but greatly helpful. In the same year he engaged in public discussions with New England Independents to the same purport, in which his fierce and uncontrolled temper seemed so evident that some Friends became suspicious of him.

It was quite as much the spirit as the doctrine of George Keith to which the Friends objected. He loved controversy, and in the days when he was in favour used the severe language of his time against the opponents of Quakerism. His open arguments with Cotton Mather and other New England divines left but little to choose between them as to the courtesies of debate. But to call the leaders of the Yearly Meeting by opprobrious names, to get excited and angry in discussion, and to make statements which he had to retract, were evidences of " brittleness " of temper, according to his opponents, which were inconsistent with a claim to spiritual guidance. He was evidently hot-tempered and pugnacious. He called Thomas Lloyd, then Deputy-Governor, and a man of amiable disposition and excellent abilities and education, " an impudent man and a pitiful governor," challenged Lloyd to send him to jail, and said that " his back had long itched to be whipped." A magistrate he called " an impudent rascal," and a meeting of ministers he said were " come together to cloak heresies and deceit, and that there were more damnable heresies and doctrines of devils among the Quakers than among any profession of Protestants." [1]

It was an age of rough controversy. His opponents

[1] Both in America and in England it was the temper and spirit of Keith that were objected to rather than his doctrines. In *A Quaker Postbag*, p. 57, we find a letter dated 2 mo. 27, 1694, from Henry Gouldney, a prominent English Friend :

" I have little to give thee account of ; the most considerable is G. K.'s being here—He is not a man governed wth. that meekness that becomes his Doctrine who puts a great value upon the outward comeing of our Blessed Lord ; wch. I hope all honnest ffrds. finds it their duty to doe ; yet himselfe far from makeing him a lively example in meekness and humility—ffrds. have had many private meetings wth. him, and by them all, I don't finde great hopes of his comeing more near us in spirit. His doctrines, in the generall, are I think owned by all sound ffriends, but he seems to lay downe abt. 7 points wch. he calls fundimentalls, in any of whome, if we disagree in, we cannot hold ffellow-ship, tho upon the whole, was not his spirit wrong, that would easily be accomodated—He takes commonly large time in meetings, but mostly fflat ; he has a tone sometimes, especially wn. on one of his pticular points that he huggs more than ordinery, that he carrys off more lively—My accnt. is in groese, tis to large and beyond my memmorey to pticularize—I hope it will have one good effect, viz. the more uniteing W. P. and G. W. who chieffly manages him—the other ffrds. that came from Pensilvania appear far the better spirited. Men come in unity of ffrds there, and is so recd. here ; yet some caution upon them that G. K. might not take occation to accot. ffriends partiall—He speaks of appealing to the yearly meeting and will submitt to their judgment so far as it agrees wth. his, and not otherwise—"

did not spare him. Possibly they better controlled their temper in debate, but in the title-page to one of their works written in cold blood a little later the author speaks of

" . . . the apostate convicted . . . in which his apostasy from the Truth and enmity against it is manifested, his Deceit Hypocricie and manifold prevarications are discovered, his false Quotations Lyes and Forgeries out of the Quakers Books are detected, etc."

and even the courteous Thomas Story calls him "that contentious apostate from the Truth of God once made known to him."

Matters could not abide in this state. Keith had complained to the Ministers' Meeting against William Stockdale charging him with saying that Keith had preached two Christs. Stockdale denied the charge, and in reply said that Keith had called him "an ignorant heathen." The meeting blamed them both and tried to make peace. But it was too late. Thomas Lloyd and twenty-seven other ministers issued a temperate epistle representing the troubles they had with Keith, earnestly appealing to him to be reconciled and to lay down the separate meeting which he was then engaged in setting up, and repudiating him as an authorised minister among Friends.

Keith had a considerable following among the Philadelphia Friends, including a few who held high station. He organised his own body, *The Christian Quakers*, with a discipline of its own. This contained some admirable provisions. There are a few copies in existence of a printed Confession of Faith and of manu-script "Queries"[1] which his followers were probably expected to sign. These ask whether in view of the fact that many not really Friends have become nominal members, there should not be some mark of distinction between faithful friends of Truth and such formal pro-fessors ; whether it is not desirable to have a personal public Confession of Belief, the sincerity of which should

---

[1] One of the original copies is in possession of George Vaux of Philadelphia.

be discerned by faithful Friends before recognition of membership ; whether those whose lives do not evidence their inward rectitude and spirituality should be admitted into the fold of the faithful ; whether such a purged body would not increase in discernment so that true judgment could be reached by the aid of the Spirit of Truth ; whether it is not desirable that all new members should make an open Confession of Faith, by answering yea or nay to the necessary principles of doctrine as propounded to them ; whether such a confession and a holy life are not worth more than the plain language and coming to meeting ; whether all Friends' children should not in the same way make confession and be judged by the spiritually-minded before admission to membership ; whether marriage to be sanctioned should not be between faithful Friends only ; whether the discipline should not be impartially enforced against all, great or small, who are out of the unity with Friends ; whether all faithful Friends should not constitute the meetings for business of the church and not the elders only ; whether a record should not be kept of all faithful Friends in suitable books ; whether in such meetings of faithful Friends only there would not be an infallible spirit which would enable them to judge of the ministry, so as to require " sound knowledge, experience, and spiritual ability " before giving liberty to preach or pray in open assemblies.

Some of these, the recording of members and of ministers, the wider attendance of business meetings, the greater rigidity of the discipline against loose livers, and of late the partial abolition of birthright membership have become accepted facts. The uniformity of belief through an open individual endorsement of a set proposition has never been demanded. The queries of Keith were an evidence of an intention to have the body made up of living spiritual members only, united in faith, purpose and spirit, under Divine guidance and influence, a church rather than a society.

The ministry and the magistracy were so associated that Keith in one of his pamphlets laid himself open to the charge of sedition and disturbance of the peace by reviling Samuel Jenings, who was as an ecclesiastic strongly opposed to Keith, and as a judge and magistrate the author of certain acts against privateers which Keith bitterly attacked. The Grand Jury brought in a true bill, and Keith and a friend were fined five pounds each, which fine was never collected. The Justices imposing this fine were all Friends and among Keith's strongest antagonists. They said in an explanation to the public that they would endure all personal reflections and attacks upon their religious body in quiet, but the pamphlets tended to revile State officials and incited to oppose the administration of Justice.

William Bradford, the printer of the seditious pamphlets, was also indicted, and refusing to give bail was committed to jail. The jailer, however, allowed him liberty, and wishing to make an appeal to the court dated from prison, he was disappointed to find the jailer absent with the key. As he could not get in he signed the paper from the entry outside. So fraternally were all things conducted in those primitive days.

The trial of Bradford which followed, and which resulted in a divided jury, is memorable as being the earliest recognition of the principle that the jury is to determine the seditious character of a paper as well as the fact of issuance by the defendant. This principle is the basis of the liberty of the press in all civilised countries. It was laid down first by five Quaker judges in a case where feeling ran high, and in which if they had any prejudices which would warp their judgment, they would be on the other side.[1]

These trials bring out the prominence of ministering Friends in civil positions, a prominence to which Keith and his friends with some justice objected, but which naturally resulted from the Friendly conception of the absence of any definite line of distinction between the preachers as a class, and the other spiritual members of the body.

[1] See Pennypacker's *Colonial Cases.*

"The Meeting of Ministering Friends" and in Seventh Month (September) 1692 the Yearly Meeting itself were the ecclesiastical courts into whose hands George Keith now fell. The latter body after a careful investigation declared :

"We find it our duty to join with our brethren in their testimony against that spirit of reviling, railing, lying, slandering, and falsely accusing which hath risen and acted notoriously in George Keith and his adherents which hath led them into a mischievous and hurtful separation."

This paper is signed by over 200 Friends beginning with Thomas Lloyd, including Pastorius and nearly all those prominent in Church and State.[1]

Keith now became an avowed leader of a new sect, gathered out of the large body of Friends. He set up meetings in Philadelphia, Burlington, and Bucks County. His eloquence, learning, and previous high standing brought many to his ranks. The denial of the outward Christ was his main subject of attack. In these days he had among other public controversies one with James Dickinson, an English minister, in which, according to the account of Dickinson's companion, he was vanquished "and went away in great wrath." Such discussions and voluminous writings fanned the separating spirit.

It was said many times that Keith's doctrinal attacks upon the main body of Friends could be all answered by his own earlier writings, and after examining these one is inclined to think the statement true. He had often pleaded the sufficiency of the Divine Light to lead into doctrinal truth, into correct living, into right public preaching and praying ; and it is impossible to note any difference between his views and those of his friend and fellow-worker and sufferer, Robert Barclay. The charges he now made against the Philadelphia Friends seemed to indicate a change in himself. The main one, that Friends

---

[1] One of the acts which show the turbulent spirit of the times was the erection of a gallery opposite the minister's gallery in Bank meeting by the friends of Keith, for his own use. Two of the trustees of the meeting told them to tear it down, whereupon they tore down the old gallery. The account states that "Keith, who was present, laughed and expressed his satisfaction."

considered the Light within sufficient " without something else," was one to which his own early statements made him quite as fairly liable to attack as his opponents. But they both asserted in positive terms the ordinary orthodox position as to the outer Christ and the Scriptures. It seems impossible to reconcile the Keith of 1670 with the Keith of 1691 and later. Of course he had a perfect right to change his position as to these matters, but he never fairly admitted the change.

In a public discussion Thomas Lloyd had said that one might be saved without the outer revelation of Christ if he had had no opportunity to know of it. But Keith said that this was impossible, and that if such were Lloyd's views " he could not own him as a Christian brother, though he might be a devout heathen." This is hardly compatible with his earlier statement. " God himself . . . is objectively manifest so that he can be heard, seen, tasted, and felt if all Scripture words were out of our present remembrance," [1] or with many other similar statements. In 1670 he had defended Friends against Robert Gordon, who made against them the same charges he was now preferring against the Philadelphians.

Early in 1693, in company with his chief supporter, Thomas Budd, he transferred the controversy to England. He had not secured the control of any of the American meetings, but his party, though considerable in the aggregate, had been disowned by all the regular organisations in America, and now Samuel Jenings, his most active opponent, and Thomas Duckett went to London to represent their meetings before the English Friends. The case was heard before the Yearly Meeting, and unfortunately for Keith he appears again to have lost his temper. There were conventions lasting several days during which the controversy was carried on. The meeting censured Keith for his publications and the magistrates for proceeding against him at law, but the final decision on the main charge was distinctly a disavowal of his spirit and methods:

[1] *Immediate Revelation*, by George Keith, p. 20.

"It is the sense and judgment of this meeting that the said George Keith is gone from the blessed unity of the peaceable spirit of our Lord Jesus Christ, and hath thereby separated himself from the holy fellowship of the Church of Christ."

He appears to have had a very small following in England. William Penn[1] says in a private letter dated 26th of 10th mo. 1696 to Robert Turner, who had been one of Penn's most trusted friends, but had joined the Keith party, "not five people in the unity before he came over here, adhere to him."[2] The matter could go no further, and he established himself in Turner's Hall, London, where he preached to large companies eloquent sermons which were largely directed against the teachings and practices of Friends. He finally joined the Established Church and ably argued its position as to rites and sacraments. He was taken into full standing and ordained by the Bishop of London.

When his followers in Pennsylvania found that he had deserted them, their disintegration began. A few returned to Friends. More became Baptists and quite a number Episcopalians, following the example of their leader. They constituted an opposition element in Church and State for a few years. The "Keithians" are heard of in the journals of Friends and the political records of the province as active allies in any movement attacking the proprietor and his friends, but they were soon ignored. In 1698 Thomas Chalkley could say "there are many large meetings of Friends, and the Lord prospers them spiritually and temporally."

George Keith himself was sent over in 1702 by the Society for Propagating the Gospel in Foreign Parts to gather as many as possible into the Established Church. He was received with much favour by the remnants of the Keithians, and claimed that he had brought 500 of them into the true faith. He immediately began his

[1] Penn at first was inclined to side with Keith. At least this was the report which reached Pennsylvania. He probably remembered his fraternal relations of earlier days, but when he heard of Keith's changed spirit, he repudiated him and became the object of virulent attack. See letter of Hugh Roberts in *Pennsylvania Magazine*, xviii. 205.

[2] *Pennsylvania Magazine*, October 1909.

series of public polemics of which he was so fond, challenging to debates. His old opponents, the Puritans, he now largely left to their own ways, but invaded the meetings of Friends, engaging in dispute wherever he could find an antagonist. His challenges were usually accepted, and the victory seemed to lie upon the side whose account we read. In July 8th and 9th 1702, he met in Lynn, Massachusetts, John Richardson in debate. Both Keith and Richardson give their impressions in their journals. Keith says he read the "vile errors" of Edward Burrough, a prominent English Friend, to the people, and heard the Quaker preachers' "utter abundance of falsehoods and impertinences and gross perversions of the Scripture." Richardson says that he told Keith that "he offered violence to the sense and understanding God had given him." "I spoke in the Lord's dreadful power, and George trembled so much as I seldom ever saw any man do."

George Keith spent about two years travelling back and forth from New Hampshire to Carolina, omitting no opportunity to attend the meetings of Friends, where he usually precipitated an unpleasant controversy. His staple charge would be that they asserted that the Light of Christ within men was sufficient for salvation "without anything else." The answer would usually be that they believed all that the Scriptures said about Christ, but that the inner experience was the essential thing. He also completely reversed himself on the subject of water baptism and the communion, arguing for them with great urgency. He had a collection of sentences from George Fox, Edward Burrough, and Richard Claridge, which he claimed sustained his charges of heterodoxy, and this collection was continually being increased by the statements of present preachers, some of which were doubtless crude enough.

He and his friend William Bradford, the late authorised printer of Philadelphia, who had been tried for sedition, appear to have secured the confinement in jail of Samuel Bownas on a similar charge. Bradford declared that

Bownas had uttered on Long Island in a sermon certain malicious statements concerning the doctrines and practice of Episcopalianism, then the established religion of New York. After great trouble they secured some kind of a verdict, and Samuel Bownas spent nearly a year in jail. Afterwards Keith and Bownas, by accident or design, were frequently at the same place holding meetings and engaging in the public discussions which characterised the times.

George Keith performed at least one valuable service. He gives us in his *Journal*[1] interesting historical statements as to the methods by which Friends in those days maintained and increased their numbers. Their excellent organisation of meetings in which large amounts of money were collected, he says, was the basis of their work. This money was used to help the poor, and hence to proselytise them, and also to pay the travelling expenses of ministers, many of whom from England as well as the Colonies were always in the field. George Fox's *Orders and Canons* were read in those meetings, but never the Bible.[2] Books were circulated exciting their youth to prejudice against the Church of England. "Divers large and fair structures for their meeting-houses, especially in Philadelphia, Burlington and Rhode Island" were being built, and great hospitality was extended to all Friends who attended their meetings. They would set up new meetings without any resident ministers, and men "pretending to extraordinary gifts of the Spirit" would soon be exercising these gifts. If the ministers were poor, they would be especially aided in procuring lucrative work so that they became rich. They dealt with each other in business, married each other, made careful records of births and deaths, and kept out of the militia, and other dangerous employments, on the plea of conscience. They held the allegiance of their people by telling all the unfortunate things which happened

---

[1] Collections of the Protestant Episcopal Historical Society, 1851.

[2] That the Bible was read in the meetings of Friends of early times is certain, though not regularly. Samuel Bownas says, "It came to my mind to stand up and take out my Bible, which I did."

to their enemies, and the happy deaths of their good friends.

The whole is a portraiture, made by no friendly hand, of the customs of Friends in those early days, which, read between the lines, shows a beautiful fraternity and an earnest missionary spirit.

It shows also, perhaps more clearly than any other document, the dawn of those customs which soon crystallized into the conservatism of the succeeding decades. The lack of educated leadership fed directly the tendencies to imitation of the virtues of the past. The fear of innovations and devotion to the orthodox literature of the first generation received a new impulse from the Keith separation and the partisan spirit engendered, and the Society settled down into a century or more of doctrinal ease and quiet.

The influence of the separation also probably brought Friends into a more careful consideration of their doctrinal positions. The necessity to controvert the charge of the Keithians that they disregarded the offices of Jesus Christ and the authority of the Bible gave a new life to these teachings. Otherwise they might have easily drifted into a position that such outward helps to spirituality were not important. They never wavered in their assertion of the efficacy of the Divine Light to lead into all truth necessary to their salvation, but they were equally emphatic in the statement that the Scriptures were from the same source and constituted the test of orthodoxy, and were of inestimable value to the Christian. The Keith controversy steadied them in this position. Had he been better balanced himself, his power would have been greater. As it was, for a century after, their committal to orthodoxy kept Friends somewhat in line with the other Christians of the time, free from the danger which the exclusive exaltation of the inner light might have developed.

The writings of George Keith, both before and after his repudiation of Quakerism, are marked by an excellent style, an earnest spirit, much clearness in thought, and moderation of temper. Perhaps no better presentation of Friendly tendencies, even in the works of Barclay, Penn, Penington, or the other voluminous writers of the times, is to be found than in the books of George Keith in the years of his Friendly communion. They contain not only well-considered defences of Christian positions, but soul-satisfying appeals to live the life most in harmony with the word of Christ. Had he died in 1690, they would have ranked high as Quaker classics.

Perhaps also there are few more able presentations of the positions held at that time by the Established Church of England than are in Keith's writings and sermons after 1697. He was intellectually a great man. His changes from Presbyterianism to Quakerism, from this, after nearly thirty years' advocacy, to Independency, and from this again to Episcopalianism, necessarily made many enemies and required many explanations. His biographies have been mainly written by his opponents who emphasise his faults and his apostasy. He died in 1716, in the performance of his duties as minister of the Established Church.

There is a story, which seems to be well authenticated, that he said before he died "that if God had taken him out of the world when he was a Quaker, it would have been well with him." But the printer of the will of George Keith says that he "never altered his mind to the last."

CHAPTER IV

GOVERNMENT

THE Friends of Pennsylvania, whether they wished it or not, had the responsibilities of government thrown upon them. The first settlers were practically all Friends, and for almost 200 years the rural districts of the south-eastern corner of Pennsylvania had almost exclusively Quaker owners of the soil. In a short time, perhaps in three decades, the influx of others made them a minority in the province. But by the aid of German voters and their own inherent fitness for the task, they retained an easy supremacy in the Colonial legislature till their voluntary abnegation in 1756. It becomes an interesting question to consider whence they derived their principles of government and what those principles were.

On these general principles there seemed great harmony. Their leader found willing followers. The disputes among themselves, which at this distance seem trivial, relate to matters of detail and application. Many of them doubtless had no settled theories, and followed their Church leaders in State affairs with unthinking fidelity. But William Penn always found intelligent and loyal men to carry out his liberal ideas or to oppose them by ideas still more liberal.

The attitude of the early Friends towards active politics in England was largely one of neutrality. Being dissenters, and dissenters of an especially unpopular type, they could not expect to hold office, and there is no reason to assume that they desired to. They were rigidly obedient to law whenever the law did not touch their consciences, and with equal rigidity refused obedience whenever it did. They would go to jail and stay there indefinitely rather than remove their hats in court or take an oath, but having been placed there by lawful powers, no temptation in the shape of open doors and intimations from the jailers could induce them to escape.

The times of the Commonwealth and the later Stuarts were times of vast numbers of plots and counter-plots, but against all of these the Friends were ever ready to testify. They would have nothing to do with them on one side or the other. It became in time a favourite doctrine that they had no responsibility for the creation of any government, and that their only duty was to be entirely obedient to the one that then existed.

They were never revolutionists, but they transferred their allegiance without demur from Cromwell to Charles and from James to William and Mary as soon as the successful revolution was accomplished.

While the responsibilities placed upon them in America caused in various ways a change of attitude towards government, when the American Revolution broke out this old testimony against plotting was made to do duty in the attitude of neutrality which all of their Meetings adopted. Some of the wise Friends protested against this position, while definitely opposing war. They urged such encouragement to the American cause as Friends could conscientiously give. Thus Dr. Fothergill writes:

"If America relaxes, both you and we are all undone. Submission to the prevailing power must be your duty. The prevailing power is the general voice of America."

This very mild advice was considered too strong by many of the Friends, and the impression was given that they were actively hostile to the American cause. We shall have occasion to say more on this subject in the future. Suffice it at present to note that the American Friends had received from their English ancestors such a strong bias in opposition to any change of government, such a firm belief in the necessity of obedience to every

existing law which did not encroach upon their consciences,
that tradition made many of them faithful to British
allegiance who would otherwise have warmly welcomed
American independence. "The setting up and putting
down of governments is God's peculiar prerogative,"
declared their Yearly Meeting.

The testimony against war is perfectly intelligible, but
the testimony against all revolution by any means except
passive resistance is much less so, and probably would not
now be considered an essential part of Quaker polity.
But if, under ordinary circumstances, the Friends were
thus passively obedient to existing powers (relying upon
the frequently expressed advice of George Fox and his
friends to keep clear of all worldly commotions), they
were profoundly disobedient to other demands of the
Government. Obedience to conscience, or what they
assumed to be the Divine command to them as
individuals, in every smallest item was always to be
superior to any obligation of obedience to a human
power. They lived up to this principle with unfaltering
courage. One can see now that the wearing of the hat
and the use of the singular pronoun were testimonies to
human equality which it is fortunate that some one has
borne. But this argument was used by the Friends but
seldom. Their main reliance was a consciousness of
rectitude which was not always voiced in arguments, and
while some of them entered hotly into the theological
controversies of the times, and made many laboured
defences of their positions, many of the reasons which
seemed to them good and effective would appeal very
slightly or not at all to their successors.

The great principles which had been established by
their faithfulness are usually admitted to be the basis of
civil and religious liberty in England, but they did not
feel much responsibility for the conduct of the government. Their responsibility was to themselves as subjects
of the government.

With the exception of William Penn, who publicly
advocated the election of the republican Algernon Sydney

to Parliament, and in other ways made himself active in public affairs, there was very little participation in politics, and even Penn, with the responsibilities of Pennsylvania resting upon him, could write to his children in 1699:

"Meddle not with government; never speak of it, let others say or do as they please; . . . I have said little to you about distributing justice, or being just in power or government, for I should desire you should never be concerned therein."

If, therefore, we are to judge of the public attitude of Friends by reference to early days in England, we have little on which to base an opinion which will be of much service to us in later times. When they came to America, conditions were different. Wherever a group of Friends got together, political instincts came to the surface. In Rhode Island, for several years, they had the important offices in their hands and were the active political workers of the colony. The same was true in North Carolina for a little time under John Archdale. In New Jersey, while there was an effort to deprive them of public influence, it was found that the government could not be conducted without them. In Pennsylvania, they took up the problem with their eyes open and a full comprehension of the responsibilities involved. In this Colony we can best study the application of Quakerism to politics and the problems of the State. The issues were partly determined by the general principles of the Society of Friends, and partly by the broad-minded and forceful personality of William Penn.

The passivity with which Friends suffered in certain circumstances when their convictions were attacked hardly seems to have been their attitude when in active politics. Abuses were checked with a strong hand. Morality of a high order was demanded and secured. Standards were maintained and wrong-doing vigorously and effectively punished. Sometimes we find evidence that their faith that an Almighty Power would rectify abuses gave them confidence in ultimate triumph, even under dark conditions, but it did not seem to cause them to abate their own efforts.

Acquiescence in evil when the means were at hand to strike it down morally never was a part of their principles or practice. It has been left for mercenary and time-serving men of later ages to preach a timid and nerveless policy and then to shelter themselves behind a supposed Quaker example of non-resistance. Quakers were not non-resistants. They resisted most courageously, and at their best most successfully, many forms of political ills. Their resistance only ceased when they were asked to use immoral means. Here they drew the line, and a careful student of Quaker political ethics will find them advocating not supine submission to wrong, but a resistance limited in its methods by the moral law alone. To do evil to correct evil was never a part of their theory of government or public action, and this hesitation sometimes has made them seem less vigorous than others.

On the other hand, the same conscientiousness has kept them true to resistance under circumstances when hope seemed to have disappeared, and other advocates of the good fight have given it up, or postponed it to a more propitious period.

The influence of Friendly ideas upon American institutions, and especially the experiment of William Penn, has been great. It is quite possible that these institutions have drawn more from the principles brought over in the *Welcome* than from the intellectual freightage of any other ship ; that of all the colonial founders William Penn saw more truly than any other the line on which the future would develop ; that himself and his collaborators builded more wisely than any others when they reared a state devoted to democracy, liberty and peace.

It was with them no denominational question. " I would found a free colony for all mankind that shall come hither," Penn declared, and while the early settlers, both British and German, were men of kindred spirit and impulses, the very basis of their union, peace and justice with all and equal rights without regard to religious affiliation, inevitably drew vast numbers of all sorts. So that the Quaker majority soon disappeared, and before the Revolution the province might more truthfully be said to have been German or Scotch-Irish Presbyterian in its prevailing tendencies than Quaker.

Yet through it all, the basis laid down by Penn stood, and when in 1780 to 1790 this band of scattered states was gathering itself into a nation, and painfully picking up the threads of principle, political and social, with which it would weave its permanent fabric, it found them not in the dogmatism of Massachusetts, or the aristocracy of Virginia, but in the civil and religious liberty of Pennsylvania.

When later the nation recovered from its debauch of Indian atrocities and encroachment upon weaker nations, it saw the way in the success of the policy of justice practised for three score years in the eastern end of this province, making it a little oasis in the dreary history of blood and aggression which told the story in New England, New York and the South, and accompanied the frontiers as they were pushed forward to the Mississippi and beyond.

If the signs of the times as represented by the Hague Congresses and the universal demand for peaceful methods of arbitration coming up from the Boards of Trade and the Labour organisations of all countries mean anything, they indicate that the Friendly settlers had a glimpse of a principle in which they had sufficient faith to abide, for a long time deemed Utopian, but now within sight of adoption.

All these were worked out in England by Penn and his many unknown advisers, and were brought to shore at Chester when he called together his first legislative body in the early winter of 1682.

He could not extinguish denominational rancour. Men looked on religious doctrine and belief more seriously than now. It was critical and all compelling. Government was a brand of religion, the Bible was the standard, and each man's interpretation of the Bible was sacred.

So said the zealous religionists of the day. So said some of the Friends themselves. Did we not come over here to create a Quaker preserve whence all error should be excluded and a truly righteous Commonwealth established? Why should we on equal terms admit all others to citizenship with ourselves who have won a little corner of the wilderness where we can work out our destiny in our own way?

The argument was plausible, and other colonies had not been able to resist it. But Penn said, "We should look selfish, and do that which we have cried out against others for, namely, letting nobody touch government, but those of their own way," and the narrow sectarianism disappeared.

But while the doctrine of equal rights in government could not be shaken, when it came to methods men would divide on denominational lines. Quakers and Presbyterians, in the later colonial days, were names not only of religious affiliation but of political policy. "To govern is absolutely repugnant to the avowed principles of Quakerism" declared the Presbyterians in the hot pamphlet warfare of 1764 which followed the invasion of the ".Paxton boys." "To be governed," was the reply, perhaps about equally truthful, "is absolutely repugnant to the avowed principles of Presbyterianism."

A little earlier than this, the Episcopal minister of Chester wrote to his English brethren:

"The flock committed to my charge is indeed small; but God be thanked, generally sound, which is as much as can be expected considering the religion of the bulk of the people among whom they live. I need not tell you that Quakerism is generally preferred in Pennsylvania, and in no county of the province does the haughty tribe appear more rampant than where I reside, there being by a modest comparison twenty Quakers, besides dissenters, to one true churchman."

But these harmless polemics were but the counterparts to actual persecution and disabilities elsewhere. In New England, as Longfellow makes the Puritan minister to say, "There is no room in Christ's triumphant army for tolerationists." So they drove out the Baptists and Episcopalians and hanged the persistent Quakers on Boston Common. In New York after Dutch times, in Maryland when the Catholics lost control, and in all the South, the Established Church held the offices, the jury-box, and the franchise, and the actual liberty and property of dissenters were hardly maintained.

In the State of Rhode Island alone was there equality of political right and freedom of conscience. The experiment among the little handful of people there was not conclusive, and it required no little faith and courage for Penn to embark his whole fortune, his reputation just budding under the favouring friendship of the Stuart kings and paternal influences, the standing and prosperity of his religious society, dearer than fortune or reputation, in an enterprise so largely based on an untried and seemingly impossible principle.

The problems of the relation of Church to State are not yet all worked out. How to give the children of the country the religious education they should have without violating the conscience of any ; how to secure the Biblical knowledge in our country necessary to appreciate our standard literature and maintain our institutions, permeated, often insensibly, by Christian ideas and standards ; how, in short, to prevent a break with the past which will destroy the fruits of our old endeavours and the continuity of history,—this is still our problem.

But no sane man thinks it lies in a State religion or sectarian test. When Penn sailed up the Delaware, the beginning of the end of ecclesiasticism in politics began, and when he pledged himself and his heirs to maintain "inviolably forever" the foremost clause of his charter granting religious liberty to all, it was the legislative enactment which, a century later, had ceased to be an experiment, and was imperishably chiselled into the national constitution.

Liberty always means conservatism. It is the abso-lute monarchy which has to fear revolution. The free government moves quietly forward to the accomplishment of its ends, for progress is the normal condition of humanity, and the strain to prevent it, to keep things fixed, is the danger of every stationary system. The free government feels the gusts of public opinion, bends before them, and rises superior to them, holding fast to the good that is nearly always in them, but quietly detecting and refusing the evanescent or injurious.

One finds in the early government of Pennsylvania a certain sanity which was the logical concomitant of liberty. Her paper money before the Revolution never depreciated, and this, I believe, could be said of no other Colony. She had no witchcraft crazes. The one trial held before William Penn himself in 1683, in Chester, when the usual charges of injuring children and bewitching cattle were brought against an unfortunate woman, simply resulted in a verdict of guilty of the common fame of being a witch, but not guilty as indicted. Her friends took charge of her, and no new cases developed. It was in the next decade that witches were being slaughtered with horrid cruelties in Massachusetts.

Free institutions brought free thought, and free thought is the only atmosphere in which science can flourish. It is no accident that about Revolutionary times a company of scientists, unrivalled elsewhere in America, and perhaps in Europe, sprang up in Philadelphia. The botanists Bartram and Marshall, the astronomer Rittenhouse, the ornithologists Audubon and Wilson, a host of distinguished physicians, and above all, the versatile Franklin, found a congenial home in the uncramped atmosphere of a liberal democracy.

Freedom and peace brought also unequalled material prosperity. The natives of the ravaged Rhine Valley, the battle-ground of Europe, the hardly used tenants of Ulster whose Presbyterianism was attacked, heard of a land where war was unknown and religion was secure, and came in unprecedented numbers.

Though the last to be founded, Pennsylvania grew the most rapidly, and at the time of the Revolution shared with

Massachusetts and Virginia the leading place in prosperity and wealth. Its chief city was the largest, best governed, and most progressive in the colonies. This, Andrew Hamilton, the great lawyer of the province, said in 1737, they owed not primarily to their fertile lands, or great rivers extending into the country, or any other material thing, but to " the constitution of Mr. Penn."

The great hope and lesson is this (and Penn foresaw it, perhaps dimly) : give the people freedom and education, and tendencies dangerous to political or social or material conditions may have their little day, but do not last. Russia has the same physical advantages as the United States, but she has no freedom, no room to develop, and hence is sunk in poverty, immorality, and intellectual stagnation, without security for the future.

The other principle which Penn tried to engraft on his experimental commonwealth was peace. We now see that there were at that time unsurmountable difficulties in the way of a permanent adoption of peace by any one nation, and yet perhaps it did not seem to Penn more impossible than liberty. A necessary element to success must inevitably be justice. It could not be expected that natives or neighbours would be peaceful if aggression were made on their rights, real or supposed. So Penn did more than buy the Indian lands. He bought them of all claimants. He paid what was in their minds a liberal price. He did not cheat them with false maps or deceptive compass bearings, or weights and measures that lied. He kept, as much as he could, fire-water from them. When they got home, and thought the matter over, they had only friendly feelings, and till new forces came into power, and new methods were used, there were no wars.

He meant also to deal justly with foreign powers ; but England *would* fight and her colonies had no control, and demands for troops against Canada made endless trouble, and the policy ultimately broke down through the operation of forces outside the reach of the province. All that the Colony could do was to adopt the advice of Paul :

" If it be possible, as much as lieth in you, live peaceably with all men," which is no slight guarantee of peace. Few men will attack an inoffensive man, and few nations will attack a nation which is known never to do an unjust deed or give any cause of offence.

The argument of Penn and his friends was something like this :

We will act justly, even generously, with all, red men and white men alike. We will never be an aggressor. If attacked, therefore, we will always be in the right. We will not yield one iota of our rights willingly, but will defend them by all means which in themselves are right. We can not fight, for we believe that fighting itself is immoral, and we will not do wrong even for a righteous cause. If there is no other alternative, we can suffer as we have shown our capacity to suffer in England, and conquer by suffering.

It was, as will be seen, a doubtful experiment whose success was dependent on conditions not likely to arise, and yet it pointed the way to the future. It gave the most potential lesson in the world's history of the possibilities of applied Christianity as shown in a policy of justice and moral resistance.

The argument was that the moral law was transcendent to all decrees of king and legislatures, and to all supposed exigencies of circumstances. No conditions permitted its annulment. No necessities were so great as to justify its abrogation. It was the all-wise Creator's law upon which all right human conduct must be based. It could not always be accurately determined, but when known, it was imperative, and so to fight evil with evil was, in the long run, only to postpone the victory of truth and to pile up trouble for the future. Fight, fight continuously and without flinching, but do not play into the hands of iniquity by substituting one form for another—this was the influence and example of William Penn. This is far from non-resistance. The teaching of Penn was not the teaching of Tolstoy. Resist all you can with vigour and practical efficacy but do it morally, said one. Do not do anything, says the other, except your own quiet work ; the truth will triumph of itself if you do not obstruct. There was a vast gap between the two positions.

Liberty and peace : these were the two main elements of the Holy Experiment. There was not room in Europe, for system there was set, and prejudice would not yield. But with all the enthusiasm of his nature, Penn saw the ideal commonwealth growing up in his woods. He was to have bitter disappointments ; his colonies were to be ungrateful, unappreciative of their great opportunities, haggling over little matters of property, led by demagogues into unreasonable demands ; he himself was to lose his splendid patrimony in the enterprise and go to a debtor's jail ; disease was to wreck his great intellect ; the wife of his youth, to whom he was romantically attached, was to be taken from him ; his children were to be bitter disappointments ; but he could not foresee these blows of fortune, and none can blame him if, on the bright October day as he landed at Chester, he felt all the exultation of his seemingly unlimited opportunities.

Proprietor and legislator by the Charter of the Crown, he would use his great powers, not for aggrandisement or personal glory, or a hereditary pre-eminence, but, he says, " I will put the power in the people," and he saw, perhaps, with his far-seeing vision, a commonwealth where idealism should become a reality. His enthusiasm did not see the slow growth and the many set-backs.

The material prosperity has been, doubtless, beyond his wildest dreams. To him, this would have been valuable only as making happy homes and beneficent institutions. The material never would have dominated the spiritual. Righteousness, piety, beneficence : these were the fruits for which the growth of riches was worth while, and without which liberty itself would be no blessing. It is still true, as the old Grecian declared, that " virtue does not come from wealth, but wealth and every other good thing we have comes from virtue."

" William Penn is offered great things," writes James Claypoole, " £6000 for a monopoly in trade, which he refused. I truly believe he does aim more at justice and righteousness and spreading of truth than at his own particular gain."

These were the words of one who wanted to form a trust to secure the Indian trade, but was surprised to learn that the founder cared somewhat, though then in great need of money, for the kind of men who would be let loose upon the frontier to annul his policy of fairness to the Red-men. " I did refuse a great temptation last Second-day," Penn quietly remarked, " but I would not defile what came to me clean."

Plato wrote his *Republic*, Thomas More his *Utopia*, and John Locke his *Fundamental Constitution*, building up in theory ideal commonwealths. The last one was tried in practice and proved a failure. William Penn had the opportunity and the wisdom, a combination which comes to scarcely one man in a millennium, to rear in his study a theory of government on the broadest principles of right and justice, and to set it to work in a vast territory with friendly neighbours and a sympathetic population. These principles, by their inherent vitality, went far beyond the bounds of his commonwealth, and a great nation found in them the best expression of its aspirations and needs, and is living on them to-day.

In the matter of oaths, the Friends had another difficult experiment. They were firmly convinced of their prohibition in the New Testament and of their general inutility. Hence, for themselves, they could do nothing but refuse to take or administer them. But the laws of England demanded them. At first, in Pennsylvania, they attempted to get along without them. But certain Crown officers, not responsible to the Colonial Government, and not Friends, were required by English law to be sworn and to swear others, and concessions to such had to be made. There was much trouble for a number of years, both as to the oath and the form of affirmation, which contained the words " in the presence of Almighty God." This was assumed to be something of the nature of an oath, also to occasion the irreverent use of a sacred name.

In 1718 a settlement of the matter was attempted, making an affirmation valid in evidence and as a qualification for office, and affixing the same penalties for lying and perjury, which Act was confirmed by the English Crown. A few years later, the name of God was stricken from the form of affirmation. Friends could now be freed from any disqualifications, except that they could not hold offices, the duties of which included administering oaths, and the Meetings insisted on their resigning such positions. They were not troubled, however, as witnesses or jurymen, or as members of the legislature, or as other officials, except as above mentioned, and matters still stand practically as arranged in 1725.

The threat of an imposition of an oath in order to drive Friends from power was frequently made both in Pennsylvania and England by those politically hostile. In 1756 it is probable that this threat would have been made good by Parliament, had not Friends resigned from the Assembly.

The "Great Law" of 1682, which William Penn brought with him from England, made capital punishment applicable to the crimes of murder and treason only. So far as is known there was only one case of capital punishment before 1700, and that was for murder. It was charged by the opposition that this leniency encouraged crime and, along with the absence of oaths, it was an indictment of the efficiency of the colonial government. There does not seem to be much truth in the charge, but the Friends were willing to compromise in the matter. The Act of 1718, which made affirmations valid, contained additional clauses accepting the laws of England in their provisions for the penalties for crime, and some dozen of offences were added to the capital list. This Act was drawn up by a Quaker lawyer, and passed by a Quaker Assembly, without protest from the Meetings. There appears to have been no testimony against capital punishment *per se*. The law stood all through the colonial days, but when, in the Revolution, the Quaker control was finally ended, the opposing party readopted the laws of the early times. Penn and his mild penal code died in the same year, and its restoration came about when his denominational successors were driven from power.

The Act of 1718 was apparently a political bargain which extended capital punishment in exchange for a relief from oath-taking. It has been said that Penn's "Holy Experiment" ended with his death. This is true in the one feature of penalties for crime, but hardly otherwise. The absence of any positive testimony against taking human life weakened the position of the Friends on the subject of war, though they were able to point to a valid distinction between police and martial measures. Had they abolished capital punishment, or even kept it down to the limitations of the founder, so far in advance of anything else ever tried, charges of inconsistency, which troubled them considerably in their political arguments, and threw certain forces to the side of their opponents, would have been avoided. But they had not reached this position.

The political principles of Friends seem to have been a logical deduction from their theology. The doctrines of direct Divine messages given to men, created a spiritual democracy. It was this message, rather than any other merits of the messenger, which was to be honoured. It came to the poor and ignorant as well as to the wealthy and learned. The humblest member of a great congregation might break forth in heavenly accents of praise or exhortation. No human ordination and no scholastic requirements were necessarily precedent. All was equality. Closely connected with this root doctrine were the refusal to remove the hat (then a mark of inferiority), the consistent use of the singular pronoun, and the plain spokenness and persistency with which sin was rebuked and illegal authority disowned.

Religious liberty, which is much more than toleration, and civil equality could not fail to be essential parts of a system of government conducted by such men. Freedom of conscience would be its very choicest possession. They would get into the spirit, which, as George Fox said, "took away the occasion of all wars," and love and peace would characterise their intercourse among each other and to all men. However far from this standard were the lives of many of them after persecution ceased, there were always some who were up to it ; and the extreme veneration felt for the holy men of the first generation, kept the others in outward conformity. They buttressed their position by Biblical arguments, and always were willing in their discussions, to abide by the verdict of the book. But among themselves, their own experience of truth and godliness was its own convincing evidence.

CHAPTER V

THE FRIENDS AS POLITICIANS

UNLIKE other colonies, Pennsylvania came under the political control of Friends at the first. When Penn landed at what is now Chester on the Delaware River in the fall of 1682, he called together a Legislative Assembly. This consisted of representatives of the Swedes and Dutch who had previously settled there, and of the newly arrived English Friends. The lines were immediately drawn on the election of the Speaker. At a time when two of the old residents were absent, the Friends carried the day by a majority of one. This was the nearest to losing control of the popular Assembly which they experienced for seventy-four years. Often every member was a Friend. Always they constituted a large and controlling majority.

This division in the first Legislative Assembly seemed to create no permanent feeling, and it proceeded to ratify the laws which Penn had drawn up in England, with some modifications satisfactory to him, with great unanimity.

These first colonists were mostly men who had lost much property, and had felt the rigours of English and Welsh jails for months and years. They were not likely to make trouble in government. They were profoundly thankful for their escape from persecution, for their beautiful country, and for the liberties which their founder granted them. He was among them in the vigour and enthusiasm of mature manhood, meeting every reasonable demand, adjusting difficulties in a statesmanlike and liberal spirit, and enjoying with them the reality of their Divine Communion in the religious meetings. Everything was sweet and harmonious, and the government started under the best of conditions.

" Two general assemblies," Penn writes in August 1683, "have been held, and with such concord and dispatch that they sat but three weeks, and at least seventy laws were passed without one dissent in any material thing."

This first specimen of Quaker legislation embraced provisions for the absence of any religious test, except belief in a God, for extended suffrage, for freedom of conscience, for legal protection of individual rights, for the mildest penal code ever enacted up to that time, for forbidding the sale of liquor to the Indians, for abolishing primogenitures, against swearing, duelling, cock-fighting, stage-plays, lotteries, and drunkenness. The Friends were puritan in the matter of popular amusements, not so rigid as the New Englanders, but still with the idea that it was necessary to maintain a moral and godly common-wealth.

The Charter which Penn gave his colonies was modified several times in the first score of years. In 1701, when he sailed for England, he included in the final form the features which experience had suggested. It became in time a revered instrument, lasting till the revolutionary spirit of 1776 overthrew it in common with every other vestige of subordination to England. But even then it disappeared with the sincere regret of many friends of independence.

The first article grants liberty of conscience to all, but restricts the right to hold office to those who profess to believe in Jesus Christ. The second requires an assembly of one house to be chosen annually, which has power to judge of the qualifications of its members, to make all laws, subject to the Governor's veto, to vote all supplies for the Government, and to adjourn when it pleased. It was too near Stuart times to take any risk of a denial of the rights of the people by arbitrary power. Other articles relate to the election of local officers, the rights of criminals, and the power of Courts to decide all property cases, and pledges the proprietor and his heirs never to invade the consciences of his people.

To what extent did these settlers mean that Pennsylvania should be a Quaker Colony? In so far as this would signify that Quaker rights and privileges should be secure, and that they should be in no danger from a renewal of English persecution, they undoubtedly intended that the then dominant sect should have the rights of ordinary freemen. William Penn expresses this distinctly in a semi-private letter.

"I went thither to lay the foundation of a free colony for all mankind, more especially those of my own profession; not that I would lessen the civil liberties of others because of their persuasion, but screen and defend our own from any infringement on that account."

When the Friends had time to steady themselves in the face of these new principles we find no attempt to grasp at power for sectarian ends or by sectarian machinery. The liberties they claimed for themselves they granted to all others, save in the reservation already noted of the privileges of office-holding to Protestant Christians, and this was probably forced upon them. Their demand for liberty of conscience included a freedom to perform all the civil functions of government without taking or administering oaths, and without being engaged in any martial operations or appropriations. Had all been Friends there would have been no difficulty in these matters, except from outside. But others with equal consistency considered oaths essential, and fighting justifiable or meritorious. How were these views to be reconciled? Practically it came about that the Friends allowed the oaths and the militia, but refused to have any part in them. To take an affirmation instead of an oath was a simple matter of choice; but there might be judicial or magisterial positions, involving administering oaths when they were sanctioned by law, and there the option could not be permitted. Hence Friends refused to allow themselves to accept such positions.

The war question was less easy of solution. William

Penn accepted a Charter from the Crown, which permitted him—

" To levy, muster, and train all sorts of men . . . and to make war and pursue the enemies and robbers as well by sea as by land . . . and by God's assistance to vanquish and take them to put them to death by the law of war, or save them, etc."

This was ample authority for a Quaker Governor, and not infrequently there was a call made for him to exercise these powers. Usually he evaded this by the appointment of a deputy who was not a Friend, who went through the harmless military motions of the times with a clear conscience.

Then there were frequent calls upon the Quaker legislature for appropriations for aid against the French or Indians. Some of these were refused, some evaded, and this finally wrought the downfall of Friendly domination in the province. Up to 1756 it was possible to make the necessary adjustments, but when the issue became clear and definite the Friends resigned or declined re-election.

These two illustrations serve to show their position as to government. They were committed to it, and meant to make it succeed. They voted, and were elected to office. In all ordinary political affairs they were active, even adroit, politicians. But they made their stand on a violation of personal conscience. No ulterior good, however plausible or comprehensive, or even seemingly necessary, could induce them to take an oath or join a military company, because they deemed that these were wrong in themselves, and hence justified by no necessity.

Penn and his heirs held the governorship by virtue of the King's Charter. As during much of the time they could not be present it was necessary to appoint deputies, limited in their powers by instructions. These deputies were usually not Friends, and after the death of Penn and his widow they surrounded themselves with Councils, in which Friends had little place. The Executive management of the Colony was therefore largely out of Friendly control. But the

Friends had no serious opposition in the popularly elected legislative assembly so long as they chose to seek places there. In the local offices of the three south-eastern counties they, by inherent fitness and the popular choice, held everything to which their scruples presented no bar.

These conditions made Pennsylvania for about seventy years a Quaker province. There was enough opposition and enough diversity to make interesting problems, and to test the idea that the political principles and methods, which naturally result from their theological and moral ideals, were adapted to practical conditions. There never has been before or since any other opportunity where they had even an approximate chance to sway the destinies of a State for any considerable length of time.

We will now take up more consecutively the affairs of the State so far as they were determined by the activities of Friends.

After the first burst of good feeling, resulting from the new opportunities and the presence and leadership of Penn, had exhausted itself, the difficulties and bickerings began. A little body of English churchmen were evidently intent on grasping something of the pre-eminence they held in England, and sent home reports discrediting the management. The Friends themselves, unused to political control, seemed to have exaggerated ideas of their personal rights, and to have become unduly suspicious of all authority.

After the founder's short stay in the province Thomas Lloyd was the leader, both in Church and State, of the Friendly forces. Penn made him, either alone or as chairman of a Board, his deputy, as long as he would accept the place. Under his administration matters went smoothly. The same men led both in meeting and politics, and so we find them adjusting their appointments by changing the hour of meeting to suit the " Court " and otherwise. The most of the State leaders were ministers, and they seem to have drawn no definite line which would indicate that one side of their work was more religious or more secular than the other.

In 1688 Thomas Lloyd became tired of the responsibility of government. Penn appointed John Blackwell, a Cromwellian soldier, whom he describes as "not a Friend, but a grave, sober, wise man." The first two adjectives may be true, but the hot fight he immediately found on his hands from Quaker opposition makes us doubt the applicability of the third. The transformation from the submissive martyr of England to the noisy defendant of popular rights in Pennsylvania is also instructive. Here is one of several turbulent scenes in the Council.

"The Governor [Blackwell] declared ye Council to be adjourned till ye next council day, . . . and rose up out of his place to depart accordingly; upon which several members of ye Council departed. But divers remayned, and a great deal of confused noise and clamour was expressed at, and without the doore of the Governor's roome where ye Council had sat, which occasioned persons (passing by in the street) to stand still to heare, which the Governor observing, desired the said Thomas Lloyd would forbear such loud talking, telling him he must not suffer such doings, but would take a course to suppress it, etc., etc."

The Governor could not manage the situation, and was removed by the proprietor, and again Lloyd came into power.

In 1689 there occurred the first of many difficulties due to Quaker scruples on the subject of warfare. Blackwell had asked aid of the Council, then partly Friendly, in providing defence against an apprehended war with France. John Simcock, a minister, could see "no danger but from bears and wolves." Samuel Carpenter, then laying the foundation for his great business career, took the position that he would have nothing to do with it. "I would rather be ruined than violate my conscience." But he would not tie the hands of the Governor if he felt that something should be done. To this his Quaker associates assented, and this seemed generally the position of the Friends. If others wanted to defend themselves they would interpose no barrier, but they would not join in it themselves, for it would violate their consciences. They would not use arms themselves or vote supplies for others.

The recall of Blackwell came in opportunely, and the French danger also disappeared, so that this test was not brought to an issue.

Of the ecclesiastical results of the schism created by George Keith, we have already spoken. His teachings added one more to the political distractions which were discrediting the province. His attacks upon the Quaker leaders were vigorous and eloquent. Thomas Lloyd was especially an object, and it was impossible in those days to separate religious from political prejudices. The Keithian and Foxian Quakers became convenient terms for parties in the state. Keith's claim that no Friends could consistently use any force in affairs of government created a new issue ; and his demand, resulting logically from it, that all members should resign their magistracies and other executive positions would have broken up the Quaker experiment. His party in politics lived for a decade, and then slowly disappeared ; but his friends formed a group opposed to the proprietor, and ready for years to come to unite with any opposition which should form itself.

These unhappy disturbances, magnified in England, and Penn's unfortunate friendship for the exiled King James brought about in 1692 the confiscation by the Crown for two years of Penn's control of the government, The governorship was placed in the hands of Benjamin Fletcher, then also Governor of New York. He was supported by the churchmen and Keithians, while the Friends, as under Blackwell, made a troublesome and vigorous opposition. They still controlled the Legislature, and the two parties managed to block each others' hands till Penn regained his hold on the province and to a large extent his influence in London. Politics moved quietly along till in 1699 he found it again possible to visit his province.

He found a colony which politically seemed unwholesomely full of bickerings. The people were tyros in government. The Friends had been divided among themselves. A little later he wrote, advising his secretary to send some of the chief men of the colony to England, so that they might find how insignificant they were. They were trying to carry points and create parties entirely out of proportion to the importance of the issues involved, and this condition was to continue for another decade.

Penn himself was in deep financial trouble though, as a partial excuse for his colonists' baffling policy, they did not know it.

His steward had fraudulently involved him in debt far out of his ability to manage unless his Pennsylvania property could be made productive. Indeed when he came over his whole interest in the colony had been conveyed to Philip Ford, and leased from him again so that he could collect his quit-rents and encourage immigration. This explains his almost frantic appeals for the money which was his due, and which his political opponents were using to harass him and drive additional bargains, not only for political but also for commercial privileges.

The contrast between the high hopes in his first visit and the mean and mercenary troubles of the second would have broken the enthusiasm of an ordinary man. Yet it does not seem to have done so with him. "The more he is pressed the more he rises," said his best Pennsylvania friend, Isaac Norris. "Friends," Penn said to the Legislature, "if there is anything in the Charter that jars, alter it . . . I desire to see mine, no other than in the people's prosperity."

And the people's prosperity was justifying him. The political troubles were on the surface. Friends and others were flocking in. They were building their houses and clearing the lands. They were establishing Meetings and were coming together semi-weekly in the fear of God. To an outside observer who could fairly judge, the solidity of the state was established under Penn's benign institutions, and the quarrels which make up history were only the froth. Two busy years of Penn's forceful personality cleared away many difficulties. He gave the province, the city, and the school new charters. He bought additional land of the Indians, and cemented their bonds with the whites. He preached in the Meetings and straightened out the church affairs ; and he went through an immense amount of detail, as to property lines, local offices, and public bridges and roads. Could he have remained, much of the subsequent unedifying politics would never have had to be recorded.

When Penn left the province in 1701 three political parties sprang into existence. With the churchmen we need have little to do. They demanded military defence and oaths, but were more of an obstacle to the Pennsylvanians by their reports sent to London than by their direct influence. They were led by certain Crown officials not under provincial authority, whose following was limited in numbers, but just at present was reinforced by the remnants of the Keithians.

The Friends were strong enough to divide. They were now but little if any more than a majority of the inhabitants, but in character, influence, and historic claims constituted the potent social and political forces of the State.

One of the parties was made up of friends of the proprietor, the best educated, most wealthy, and most responsible citizens. Their strength was largely in Philadelphia, but they had their representatives through the Counties. Their agent, and in time their leader, was James Logan, the secretary of William Penn.

He had come with his " master " on the same boat in 1699, a young Friend of twenty-six years. For a half-century he was a most potent factor in provincial affairs. Perfectly faithful to the Penn family, scholarly and genial among his friends, but harsh and unfair in his judgment of his enemies, he was for the coming years the centre of the volcanic disturbances which afflicted the colony. His standing among Friends was not very secure. He believed in defensive war, and was intolerant of their narrow distinctions. He managed the Indian affairs with great skill and quite in the spirit of the founder. Later he became more placable and settled down at

Stenton into an honoured age, devoted to literature and science.

The leader of the opposition was David Lloyd, a Welsh-man of remarkable ability. His standing as a Friend was better than Logan's. He was fully devoted to their extreme views concerning war and oaths. He was an intense democrat, a stout champion of popular rights, a shrewd politician, a man who, if any, deserves the name of the first Pennsylvania " boss." He marshalled the country Friends against the aristocratic tendencies of the pro-prietary party, and opposed with vigour and success any increase of its prerogatives.

Some of his methods seem at this distance unjustifi-able. His attacks upon Penn were, at least, ungenerous, and probably grossly exaggerated the grievances. His enemies gave him ample material for attack, of which he made skilful and generally legitimate use.

Penn had made a young man named John Evans his Deputy-Governor. As usual with Penn's appointees, this was an unfortunate selection. Evans was capable but indiscreet and something of a libertine. He imprisoned a critical member of the Assembly. He tried to discredit the Friends by bringing a false alarm of a French invasion so that they would disown their principles. He collected " powder money " by a tax on commerce, alike burdensome and illegal. In many ways he showed his inability to succeed in a province of Friends. Penn's supporters hung their heads and Lloyd triumphed.

These conditions existed until 1710, when a complete revulsion of feeling in favour of Penn came about. Evans had now been superseded, and the province had, or hoped to have, a sober and acceptable Deputy-Governor. Every member, without an exception, of Lloyd's assembly was defeated, and a loyal and responsible house gave the people a taste of sane progress.

They had had for the time, at least, enough of petty quarrelling. They had found that their founder had been considering the sale of his possessions to the Crown, and had only held back because he could not sufficiently protect their rights. While they had been complaining of little evils and treating him most shamefully he had been sacrificing his own interests to protect theirs ; and when after the election he sent them a letter full of kindly advice, a pathetic plea for friendliness and sympathy, it was everywhere read, and the heart of the people went out as one man to their generous and statesmanlike leader.

It did not come any too soon. William Penn had two years of normal life in which to enjoy the loyalty and respect of his people. His troubles with his steward were also over, and his American property was beginning to yield a comfortable income. His acceptance among his English Friends of all classes was also much more cordial, and the tongue of calumny was silenced. He was about to complete his arrangements for the sale of his privileges in Pennsylvania to the Crown, with the rights and scruples of his colonists fairly protected, when a stroke of paralysis prostrated him, and the transaction was never completed. He lingered for almost six years, his mind weakened but his sense of the Divine presence unimpaired. During this time, and until his death, his Pennsylvania affairs were managed by his wife, Hannah Callowhill Penn.

We now enter upon the happy period of Friendly control of government. For thirty years following 1710 we have a state, satisfied, at peace, enjoying popular liberty and security for its continuance. It was prosperous, too, beyond precedent. The ravaged and outraged dwellers in the Rhine Valley, the battle-ground of Europe, the vigorous Presbyterians of Ulster who were threatened with the invasions of Episcopacy, heard of a land where wars were unknown, where taxes were light, where land was plentiful and cheap, and where every man worshipped as he pleased. The streams from both lands, little rivulets at first, but strengthening with each decade, settled the province at an unprecedentedly rapid rate. The government was simple and inexpensive, making very light demands upon the people. Fortunately England made no calls on her colonies for warlike aid. Oaths were settled so that the question made no trouble. The wise arrangements of Logan kept peace and amity with the Indians. A scheme of paper money supplied the medium to pay for the importations of a growing colony, yet was so cautiously issued, that Pennsylvania probably alone among the provinces always maintained it at par. The parties of the early days were forgotten. Lloyd and Logan preserved, if not friendship, at least decorous intercourse. The Friends carried everything their own way in the state, the Governors selected by Hannah Penn being wisely responsive to prevailing desires and their councils made up of judicious and clear-headed men. The popular assembly was easily theirs by its quiet, scrupulous management of affairs and the aid of the German vote. The days that Penn had dreamed of had been as nearly realised as one has a right to expect of dreams. They were days of which the annals are so uninteresting as to take but little space in history, and yet in which the ends of government were better subserved than in times of internal strife and external warfare.

All that Penn had striven for had not been perfectly secured. His gentle penal code had gone a sacrifice to political expediency. Oaths were given and taken, though not by Friends. Catholics were allowed to worship as nowhere else among the Colonies, but they could not hold office or corporate title to property. There were malefactors, ungodly and immoral people who were hardly restrained. It was not ideal, but as near to it as a reasonable person would expect.

Andrew Hamilton, the great lawyer of the province, when he resigned the speakership of the Assembly in 1739, thus sums up the conditions :

"It is not to the fertility of our soil, and the commodiousness of our rivers, that we ought chiefly to attribute the great progress this province has made within so small a compass of years, in improvements, wealth, trade, and navigation ; and the extraordinary increase of people who have been drawn here from almost every country in Europe ;—a progress which more ancient settlements on the main of America cannot, at the present, boast of. No. It is principally and almost wholly owing to the excellency of our constitution, under which we enjoy a greater share both of civil and religious liberty than any of our neighbors.

" It is our great happiness that instead of triennial assemblies, a privilege which several other colonies have long endeavored to obtain but in vain, ours are annual, and for that reason as well as others less liable to be practised upon or corrupted either with money or presents. We sit upon our own adjournments when we please and as long as we think necessary and are not to be sent a-packing in the middle of a debate, and disabled from representing our just grievances to our gracious sovereign.

" We have no officers but what are necessary, none but what earn their salaries, and those generally are either elected by the people or appointed by their representatives.

" Our foreign trade and shipping are free from all imposts except those small duties payable to his majesty by the statute of the law of Great Britain. The taxes which we pay for carrying on the public service are inconsiderable, for the sole power of raising and disposing of the public money for the public service is lodged in the assembly who appoint their own treasurer, and to them alone he is accountable. Other incidental taxes are assessed, collected, and applied by persons annually chosen by the people themselves. Such is our happy state as to civil rights. Nor are we less happy in the employment of a perfect freedom as to religion. By many years' experience, we find that an equality among religious societies, without distinguishing any one sect with greater privileges than another, is the most effectual method to discourage hypocrisy, promote the practice of the moral virtues, and prevent the plagues and mischiefs that always attend religious squabbling.

" This is our constitution, and this constitution was framed by the wisdom of Mr. Penn, the first proprietary and founder of this province, whose charter of privilege to the inhabitants of Pennsylvania will ever remain a monument of his benevolence to mankind, and reflect more lasting honor on his descendants than the largest possessions in the framing of this government. He reserved no powers to himself or his heirs to oppress the people, no authority but what is necessary for our protection, and to hinder us from falling into anarchy, and, therefore (supposing we could persuade ourselves that all our obligations to our great lawgiver, and his honorable descendants, were entirely cancelled), yet our own interests should oblige us carefully to support the government on its present foundation, as the only means to secure to ourselves a prosperity, the enjoyments of those privileges, and the blessings flowing from such a constitution, under which we cannot fail of being happy if the fault be not our own."

Hamilton was succeeded as Speaker by John Kinsey, the Clerk of the Yearly Meeting. He also became in a few years the Chief-Justice in the province, and held the three offices combining leadership in Church and State till his death.

Times were coming when the political policy of the Friends needed wisest direction. Though they did not know it, their days of easy supremacy were about over. The experience and the entrenched power gained by the thirty years of peace and prosperity carried them along through fifteen years more of troubled politics, and then came the end of official control.

The troubles centred partly around the Quaker attitude toward war. To appreciate this we will retrace our history and mention a few instances.

Governor Fletcher in 1693 wanted money for a French war. He promised that the appropriation should be used for other purposes and not "dipt in blood." Though this was really an evasion the vote was given. In 1701 the Assembly assured the King that they would acquiesce in his requests for money "so far as our religious persuasions shall permit," and voted nothing. Governor Evans made frequent requests for a militia, but the Assembly went no further than to suggest to him that he had authority as Deputy-Governor to form a voluntary organisation, which, however, did not prosper.

In 1709 Governor Gookin asked for 150 soldiers from Pennsylvania to join the quotas of the other states, or in lieu of them £4000 of money. This was a serious proposition, for war was an actual fact. The Friends in Council and Assembly met and debated the question. The former, the Logan party, were of the opinion that though they could not vote war supplies, they must support the general government by a present to the Queen. To this the Assembly agreed, with the promise that it should be placed in safe hands till they were satisfied that it would not be used for war. This was David Lloyd's amendment to the Logan proposition, and when the Governor refused to accept it with the condition, the house abruptly adjourned without his consent.

When the Logan party came into power in 1711 they voted £2000 "for the Queen's use" in response to a demand for a military expedition, though as a matter of fact it was not used for that purpose. Isaac Norris says: "We did not see it to be inconsistent with our principles to give the Queen money notwithstanding any use she might put it to, that not being our part, but hers."

This seems to have been the attitude of the Friends' Assembly in the days to come. The grasping and unfair policy of the sons of William Penn embittered the Indians. The wars between England and France were reproduced among the Indian tribes, and French intrigue took advantage of their excited state to inflame them against the English colonists. Military defence or the abandonment of the frontiersmen to Indian cruelty seemed the only alternatives. The legislators would assert their peaceable principles and their conscience against personal participation, and would then vote money "for the King's use." The Governor would use it to build forts, or to feed the militia, or buy munitions of war. It is true that the causes of the wars were entirely out of their control, and not only so, but, in so far as they could, they had opposed them. The wars were the result of measures which had had their earnest but ineffectual resistance. When William Penn or James Logan bought Indian lands, the Indians were fully satisfied, and went home without the least feeling of hostility. But when Thomas Penn devised his infamous "Walking Purchase" to cheat the Minisinks out of their ancestral homes against their consent, by methods which they well knew were fraudulent, he absolved them from their loyalty to the white settlers, and they bided their time for revenge.

This did not come for a few years. In the meantime other troubles arose. In 1739 England and Spain declared war. Governor Thomas asked for an appropriation to protect the province against a probable attack. This opened a paper discussion between the Governor and the Assembly led by John Kinsey, in which the possibility of conducting a province without war was discussed with some bitterness and considerable ability by both sides. In the first reply of the Assembly they remind the Governor that most of them were "of the people called Quakers, and principled against bearing arms in any case whatsoever." As to other people they said that it would not be fair to throw burdens upon them from which the Friends were relieved, and they suggest that the Governor make the service voluntary. They intimate that rather than show any complicity they would trust the defence of the province to that power which "not only calms the raging waves of the sea, but sets limits beyond which they cannot pass."

The Governor replied that this did not relieve them of the necessity for defence—that sailors must furl their sails in a storm even though they trusted in a Divine Protector. He suggested that they did not hesitate to put a burglar to death, and that there was no logical difference between this act and more extended resistance to an army which would attack their persons and property.

To this last point they objected that the burglar was doing a conscious wrong while the men in the army were probably innocent of any criminal intent.

It is unnecessary to go through the discussion. It wound up with a statement from the Governor that Quaker principles were inconsistent with government, and he followed this by a recommendation to England that the Friends should be made ineligible to office.

James Logan advised the Yearly Meeting to the same effect, suggesting that all Friends who held such scruples should voluntarily resign, but that body refused to permit the paper to be read.

The total result was a Quaker triumph. They refused the appropriation. They strengthened their hold on the legislature, and brought the Governor to terms by a refusal to vote him a salary, and they probably had the better of the argument. The pious reflections and adroit political argument of John Kinsey had carried the day.

The excitement lasted through several years, and culminated in a street fight in 1742, when a number of sailors tried to raid the polls in the interest of the Governor's party, and a bunch of hard-fisted Germans stood by the Assembly. In both the street fight and the elections the Quakers triumphed.

The Spanish war was soon over, but one with France immediately followed. In 1745 the Assembly, again declaring their peaceable principles, but recognising their duty " to give tribute to Cæsar," voted £4000 for " bread, beef, pork, flour, wheat, and other grains" in lieu of military supplies. The Governor is said to have construed the " other grain " to mean gunpowder. French wars were now almost continuous, and again and again money was voted " for the King's use," always, however, receiving for it some addition to their political liberties and powers.

John Kinsey died in 1750. He had no successor capable of coping with conditions within and without the Society of Friends, and the affairs of the " Quaker Party " fell largely into the hands of Benjamin Franklin, who had no sympathy with their anti-martial views. He writes of the Friends in 1747 as " that wealthy and powerful body of people who have governed our elections and filled almost every seat in the Assembly."

Hitherto the wars had been outside the province, but when Braddock's army went down to defeat before Fort Du Quesne in 1755 the exasperated Indians were let loose on the frontiers. During this time of anxiety and real suffering the annual election for the Assembly came, and again Friends had an overwhelming majority.

Philadelphia Quarterly Meeting, writing to the London Meeting for Sufferings in explanation of the situation, says that many of their members had declined executive and some legislative positions, and more would do so if there were others on whose probity and principles they could rely to take their places. Though they were now a small minority of the population, yet such was the confidence reposed in them that even in the back districts where but few Friends resided, these were generally chosen by the votes of others. They add:

"It is remarkable that for 16 years successively, more than half of which was a time of war, a set of men conscientiously principled against warlike measures have been chosen by those of whom the majority were not in that particular of the same principle."

Thus being honourably the recipients of the confidence and support of the Colony, they could not properly evade a manifest duty.

Many of the more spiritual Friends did not, however, take this position. The votes for warlike defence, imposing a tax which some of their members could not conscientiously pay, were too much like temporising to suit the Quaker regard for plain dealing. They urged their brethren to withdraw from a government which involved such inconsistency.

This tendency was strengthened by the English Friends. Dr. Fothergill and David Barclay came into possession of information which led them to believe that the Ministry were about to introduce a bill requiring an oath of all Colonial officials. The real object of this was to drive Friends from public life. By their explanations they secured a stay of this purpose by the promise that they would use their influence to have the Pennsylvania legislators who were Friends withdraw from the house. A delegation from London Yearly Meeting was sent over to enforce by urgent representation this course of action.

It found matters ripe for the purpose. The Governor and his council, the Quaker member, William Logan, alone dissenting, had declared war against the Delaware and

Shawnee Indians, and for the first time in its history the province was actually at war. Certain Friends immediately resigned their places in the Assembly, and when the Englishmen arrived a number of others declined re-election.

Thus ended in 1756 the Quaker régime. They could not carry on a state at war. Had they had executive control they would have pacified the Indians as they did privately a few years later. But all they could do was to vote supplies for a war not of their creation, or be held responsible for cruel massacres of innocent people on the frontier. Their Yearly Meeting gave no uncertain sound. It fully endorsed the action of London Friends and asked all its members to keep out of compromising offices. Committees of Monthly Meetings laboured incessantly to bring this about. Some officials were defiant, many reluctant, but notwithstanding the evident wishes of the people who again and again would have sent up Friends, they managed to keep them down to a minority of the Assembly, though Isaac Norris second, George Ashbridge, and others continued their useful careers in public life till their deaths.

The "Quaker Party," however, did not die. Under new leaders, and supported by the same voters, it controlled the province till the Revolution in 1776 threw down all the old lines. It was always the liberty party of the province, whether led by Lloyd and Kinsey or by Franklin. It wrested from proprietary and Crown one accession of privilege after another, and Pennsylvania never knew tyranny. The spirit of William Penn never deserted it. His name and principles grew in power with every decade. While Friends did not hold the offices their opponents said that they still controlled the government through "Quakerised" Episcopalians and Presbyterians.

In the early days of the province the opposition came from the Episcopalians with such transient aid as they could receive from the Keithians and other malcontents. But by the end of the thirty years' peace a new element, even more inimical to Quakerism, was making itself felt in the province and constituted a rapidly growing power.

The Presbyterians from the north of Ireland, "Scotch Irishmen" as they were called, during the decades just prior to the Revolution were coming in, in thousands. They pressed for the frontiers and bore the brunt of Indian attack. Except on the principle that the Indians should be killed or crowded out, a worse contact could not have been devised. The Germans who constituted the central belt generally were peaceable and just. But "why should these heathens have lands which Christians want?" demanded the militant, vigorous descendants of the Covenanters. In habit of thought and life, in doctrine and testimony, they were the direct opposite of the Friends, whom they considered to be altogether nerveless and despicable. They had some just grounds for opposition. When the new counties came in they were not accorded proportionate representation, and this aided in maintaining Friendly ascendancy in the Assembly. But their other claims for rewards for Indian scalps and a vigorous policy of Indian extinction probably made the Friends feel that they were justified in not admitting such antagonistic elements to a large share of the government. Until the Revolution the Quakers and the Presbyterians constituted the rival political forces of the province. The Episcopalians tended towards the Friends, and the Germans were also usually sympathetic.

These forces maintained the ascendancy till 1776, but the Revolution was three parts out of four a Scotch-Irish movement in Pennsylvania.

CHAPTER VI

FRIENDS AND THE INDIANS

THE importance of the attitude of William Penn towards the Indian natives of Pennsylvania has not been over-estimated, though probably the emphasis has been wrongly placed. It was a just as well as a politic thing to do, to buy their lands, and the great Shackamaxon Treaty, in itself only a symbol of decent treatment, has been interpreted as covering the whole transaction. As some-times understood, this meant that Penn and a few trusted friends brought together the Indian chiefs, and at one great negotiation, with much eloquence and many ex-pressions of fraternity, received the right to occupy the soil of the whole province. It was not at all the first time that Indian rights to the land had been bought. The Dutch and Swedes on both sides of the Delaware river had done it long before Penn had any claims there, and were careful not to settle on unpurchased soil. It had been done in New England, New York, and Mary-land at their early settlements. The neglect to do it had led to massacres and the extermination of several colonies in the south. By 1682 it had been recognised by colonists generally as wise policy. Moreover, Penn did not buy all Pennsylvania at one transaction, or any con-siderable part of it. He had at first no use for any but a little strip along the Delaware, and this was bought of various tribes at different times by separate treaties. This south-eastern part of the state is divided into strips by several " creeks " running down from the upland country to the river. Penn would buy from one creek to another, and the unit of measure up the creek was a day's walk, in his time about twenty miles, though vastly extended later. The Shackamaxon Treaty is only one of several which between 1681 and 1686 conveyed to Penn the south-eastern corner of the state, extending perhaps forty miles inland and running up the river above the site of the present Trenton. These treaties were not only negotiations for sale of land, but also leagues of friendship where, amid much circumlocution in Indian fashion, eternal amity and mutual good-will were promised, and the promises sealed with wampum belts.

But this sort of thing was not new in 1682. It had been done many times before. We must go farther to seek the significance of the Quaker relation to the Indians.

In some colonies the Indians were made drunk, and in this state signed away valuable claims. In others false maps were shown them, or false weights deceived them in selling their furs. The land unpurchased was not always excluded from settlement. They were killed, and no penalty was meted out to the white murderer. Their food was taken, in their eyes unjustly, often by irresponsible whites, but the acts were not disowned by the authorities. They were treated as inferior, and their pride was hurt. The land bought of one tribe was not bought of another which possibly had, or thought it had, superior claims. Rumours of Indian invasions were excuses for bloody attacks.

From all these things the Pennsylvania Indians were preserved. Every effort was made to keep rum from them. Again and again in the minutes of the meetings we find this urged. William Penn refused the right to trade to men likely to abuse the privilege. Every transaction was fairly explained, and in case of conflicting claims all were satisfied. His first "Great Law" enacted that juries which sat on Indian cases should be half white and half red. This was an impracticable scheme, but when given up other fair methods were substituted. The price paid was in their eyes ample and the "walks" were moderately construed. In 1688 it was reported from two sources apparently independent that 500 warriors were about to attack the settlement, and had already commenced depredations. Caleb Pusey, a member of the Council, and one of the prominent Friends of the Colony, offered to investigate the rumour in person, if five others were appointed by the Council to go with him unarmed. They went through the woods to the alleged rendezvous, found the king lying quietly on his bed, with only women and children about him. He had some small claims for money not yet paid for land, but was not troubled about it, and added that the authors of the report "ought to be burned to death."

It was this fair and frank treatment which created the fraternity which held good for about sixty years. No Quaker family in this time suffered from the Indians, except in matters of petty pilfering, which were rectified where possible. Thus the Haverford settlers sent to the Council a charge against the Indians "for the rapine and destruction of their hogs." But the Council sent for the "Kings," and we hear no more of it. The red men were welcome guests in the homes, and hospitably entertained the whites in their wigwams. They supplied them with wild food abundantly, and were paid a satisfactory sum. "As our worthy proprietor treated the Indians with extraordinary humanity they became very civil and loving to us and brought us in abundance of venison," said Richard Townsend. They looked after white children when their parents went away to meeting, and were good neighbours in times of need. They were lazy, improvident, weak-willed, but faithful to their agreements. General W. H. Harrison says :

"A long and intimate knowledge of them in peace and war, as enemies and friends, has left upon my mind the most favorable impression of their character for bravery, generosity and fidelity to their engagements."

The Moravian missionary Heckewelder relates a ceremony which he had often seen, when the old men spread out on a blanket or piece of bark the various wampum belts which commemorated the treaties of William Penn, and explained to the young braves the significance of each and the sacred obligations attaching to it. This custom was kept up for 100 years, and the contract was passed on from father to son.

The Friends, beginning with George Fox and William Penn, made many attempts to convert the Indians to Christianity. At first they had large hopes of success. Their favourite teaching of the universal divine light seemed in consonance with Indian ideas. When spoken to in this way they said that the Good Spirit in their hearts confirmed the words. But this was about as far towards Quakerism as they ever got. Indian converts were practically non-existent. The Moravians, with a definite teaching of ordinances, which appealed to the pictorial sense of the woodmen, were more successful, and some hundreds of them, as the result of the work and influence of devoted missionaries, joined the peaceful sect, only to suffer later the horrible massacre of Gnadenhütten. The Indians respected Quaker teaching and example, but did not adopt them. Had it been possible to have kept from them the physical and moral diseases of the whites and gradually to have influenced them towards civilisation, the results might have been more happy. But the slow development of the Seneca Indians in western New York under Quaker tutelage for a century shows in them an incapacity to accept quickly the moral and religious ideals of their teachers.

William Penn had more influence over them than any other. They attended his conferences, and drank his spirits, which he handed out to them moderately, with great enthusiasm. They were delighted when he joined them in athletic sports, and when he spoke their language. He was evidently a man after their liking, an elder brother, and they listened with becoming gravity to his religious exhortations. Thomas Turner, Thomas Story, John Richardson, and Thomas Chalkley had devotional meetings with them. They listened sympathetically and approvingly but went their own way afterwards.

The corporate "concern" of the Yearly Meeting is expressed in the following minutes :

"1685. This Meeting doth unanimously agree and give as their Judgment, that it is not consistent with the Honour of Truth, for any that makes Profession thereof, to sell Rum or other strong Liquors to the Indians, because they use them not to moderation, but to Excess and Drunkeness.

"1687. We give forth this as our Sense, that the practice of selling Rum or other strong Liquors to the Indians directly or indirectly, or exchanging Rum, or other strong Liquors, for any Goods or merchandize with them, considering the abuses they make of it, is a thing contrary to the mind of the Lord, and great Grief and Burthen to his people, and a great Reflection and Dishonor to the Truth, so far as any professing it are concerned ; and for the more effectually preventing this evil practice as aforesaid, We advise that this our Testimony may be entered in every Monthly Meeting Book, and every friend belonging to the said meeting to subscribe the same.

"1719. Advised, that such be dealt with as sell, barter, or exchange directly or indirectly, to the Indians, Rum, Brandy, or any other strong Liquors, it being contrary to the Care Friends always had, since the settlement of these Countries, that they might not contribute to the Abuse and Hurt those poor people received by drinking thereof, being generally incapable of using Moderation therein ; and to avoid giving them Occasion of Discontent, it is desired, that Friends do not buy or sell Indian Slaves.

"1722. When way was made for our worthy Friends, the Proprietors and Owners of Lands in these provinces to make their first Settlements, it pleased Almighty God by his over-ruling Providence to influence the native Indians so as to make them very helpful and serviceable to those early Settlers, before they could raise Stocks, or Provisions to sustain themselves and families : and it being soon observed, that those people when they got Rum, or other strong Liquors, set no Bounds to themselves, but were apt to be abusive, and sometimes destroyed one another, there came a religious Care and Concern upon Friends, both in their Meetings and Legislature, to prevent those Abuses. Nevertheless, some people prefering their filthy lucre before the common Good, continued in this evil Practice, so that our Yearly Meeting held in Philadelphia in the year 1687, testified, 'That the practice of selling Rum, or other strong Liquors to the Indians directly or indirectly, or exchanging the same for any Goods or Merchandize with them (considering the abuse they make of it) is a thing displeasing to the Lord, a Dishonour to Truth, and a Grief to all good people.' And altho' this Testimony hath been since renewed by several Yearly Meetings, it is yet too notorious, that the same hath not been observed by some persons; and therefore it is become the weighty Concern of this Meeting earnestly to recommend the said Testimony to the strict Observance of all Friends; and where any under our profession shall act contrary thereunto, let them be speedily dealt with, and censured for such their evil Practices.

"1759. The Empires and Kingdoms of the Earth are subject to the Almighty power, he is the God of the Spirits of all Flesh, and deals with his people, agreeable to that Wisdom, the Depth whereof is to us unsearchable; we in these provinces may say, He hath, as a gracious and tender parent, dealt bountifully with us, even from the Days of our Fathers; it was he who strengthened them to labour thro' the Difficulties attending the Improvement of a Wilderness, and made way for them in the Hearts of the Natives, so that by them they were comforted in times of Want and Distress.

"It was by the gracious influences of his holy Spirit, that they were disposed to work Righteousness and walk uprightly one towards another and towards the Natives, and in Life and Conversation to manifest the Excellency of the principles and Doctrines of the Christian Religion, and thereby they retained their Esteem and Friendship: Whilst they were laboring for the Necessaries of Life, many of them were fervently engaged to promote piety and virtue in the Earth, and educate their Children in the fear of the Lord.

"1761. It being observed by the last Epistle from the Meeting for Sufferings in London, that they express their approbation of the proceedings of those Friends here, who have been concerned in using their Endeavours for the Establishment of Peace with the Indians, by pacific Measures, and warmly recommend that a Christian Regard and Notice may be extended towards these people, for cultivating a good Understanding with them, and the Confirmation of peace on the principles of Justice and Equity. Several suitable Observations were now made thereupon, to excite friends individually to a religious Concern and Care in this matter; now especially, as of late, some good Effects of a remarkable Visitation of divine Grace has appeared among some of those people. . ."

The Assembly, in early days under the influence of the

same men that led the meetings, followed the meetings a few years later with its prohibitions against selling liquor, its votes of supplies to maintain Indian friendship and to purchase land, its hospitable treatment of visiting chieftains and its formal expression of eternal brotherhood. James Logan was in charge of the relations with the red men for about fifty years after Penn's second visit of 1701. With skill and kindly hospitality and accurate knowledge of Indian character, he led the colony along the paths of peace. He could not, or did not, however, avert the alienation of the Delaware tribe caused by a series of outrages upon their rights, the most noted of which was the Walking purchase of 1737. Friends were not even remotely responsible for this inequity, but as they had to aid in overcoming its unfortunate results, it is proper to refer to it here.

There was an old agreement, of doubtful authenticity, made in 1686, which conveyed to William Penn certain land in Bucks County and extending northwards as far as a man could walk in a day and a half. With the understanding of the time, this would mean about thirty miles, and would carry the purchase to the junction of the Delaware and Lehigh Rivers where Easton stands. But the land farther to the north between the rivers was greatly desired by Thomas Penn, the son and heir of the founder, and then potent in the management of the executive branch of the government. There were settlers who would buy of him, and some had already gone there and occupied their tracts. The Minisink tribe of the Delaware Indians, whose ancestral home was there, refused to sell, and asked to have it secured from invasion. No one questioned their right, and so artifice had to be resorted to to give an appearance of legality to the claim. The "Walk" would be taken. Two athletes were found and trained. The underbrush was cleared, horses provided to carry the impedimenta, and boats to cross the streams. The runners covered sixty miles, and at the end of the line the surveyors slanted the upper boundary, which was to reach the Delaware River, far to the north so as to enclose all the desired territory. The Indians were told that their land had been sold and were ordered to leave. But, conscious of the fraud, they were sullen and disobedient, and the Quaker legislature would appropriate nothing to enforce the demand. Thus matters remained till 1742, when another power was introduced.

The Delaware Indians were at this time subject to the over-lordship of the Iroquois of New York, "women," in the language of the forest. A great convention was held in Philadelphia, attended by all parties interested. After a due allowance of liquor and many seductive words of friendship, the Iroquois judicially examined the old deeds and the records of the walk and pronounced judgment against the Minisinks, telling them that they had no right to make treaties and that they must immediately remove to the Susquehanna. The alliance was too strong to resist, and they, with bitter hearts, left their old home to the whites.

It may be significant that while many of the Indian treaties and negotiations were held in the Meeting-Houses of Friends, this one was at the house of the Proprietor. The Minisinks went westward and bided their time.

This process of encroachment on what seemed to the Indians their rights now went on. They were drugged with liquor and cheated ; their lands were appropriated in advance of purchase. Their crowning grievance came in 1754, when at Albany the proprietors purchased of the Iroquois, many of the Pennsylvania tribes being un-represented, nearly the whole of western Pennsylvania. To have all their ground sold over their heads and the proceeds go to their feudal lords was bad enough, but those that were present came away with a belief that they had been defrauded. They did not understand, they said, the compass courses and did not know the extent of the sale ; they were told that it was only to clear away some titles which Connecticut claimed ; they believed that some chiefs were privately bought.

The French ingeniously fanned the flames, and when

Braddock went down to defeat before Fort Du Quesne the next year, the long smouldering wrath of the Pennsylvania Indians found vent, and for the first time the frontiers were wet with blood. The Governor and Council declared war, bounties were offered for scalps of the male and female Indians, and the Quaker legislators resigned.

Here was work cut out for the Friends. They formed "The Friendly Association for gaining and preserving Peace with the Indians by pacific measures." They had been charged with parsimony in their objections to war appropriations and the payment of war taxes, and now agreed to give "a much larger part of our estates than the heaviest taxes of a war can be expected to require." They were used to the peaceable method of settling Indian affairs, and knew that it cost money. In times of perfect peace the records seem to indicate that some £500 a year had been expended for Indian presents by the Assembly. Whether this gratuitous aid was good for the Indians may be doubted. The best thing for them would have been never to have seen a paleface. But it was cheaper and better both for white and red men than fighting. Now that war was on, and rewards for scalps substituted for public presents, private liberality was to make the attempt to win back the Indians to peace. They began with the northern Delawares under their great chief Tedyuscung, a diplomatist of no mean order when sober, and a reliable friend of the Quakers. The first conference was at Easton in 1756. Israel Pemberton, the leader of the movement, and a large number of other Friends were present, though evidently not desired by the Governor. The Indian was very plain. "This very ground that is under me (striking it with his foot) was my land and inheritance and is taken from me by fraud." He could not forget the "Walking Purchase" and the enforced emigration. All sorts of compromising suggestions were thrown in his way, but with the aid of Friends he kept a clear course. Then appeared the confidence won by seventy years of fair intercourse. Israel Pemberton said :

"The name of a Quaker of the same spirit as William Penn still is in the highest estimation among their old men, and there is a considerable number of us here united in a resolution to endeavor by the like conduct to fix the same good impression of all of us in the minds of the rising generation."

The next year another conference was held at Easton, which Tedyuscung refused to attend unless the Friends were there. Then, probably at their instigation, he made the demand for a private clerk to note the proceedings. This he also made an ultimatum, and unwillingly the Governor yielded. He chose Charles Thomson,[1] then a young man, master of the Friends public school, afterwards secretary of the Continental Congress and author of a Translation of the Bible.

It took weeks to do the talking, and then they adjourned till 1758, when a still larger number of Indians was brought in. Tedyuscung still was master of the situation, and the eloquence flowed on. He finally got some kind of a recognition that the "walk" was unfair, was given compensation for his stolen lands, and a peace was declared, cemented by the Friendly presents.

The Western Indians were also brought into peaceful lines. The Assembly was short of money, and though now not made up of Friends was thoroughly sympathetic. When the Association offered to lend them money, the House accepted the loan with thanks "for their friendly and generous offer." They sent some £2000 of goods to Pittsburgh for the Indians, and acted as agent of the British government in forwarding another consignment for the same purpose. Peace for a little time through their efforts settled down over Pennsylvania. It was a great work well done, costing the Association about £5000.

Few deductions of historic significance are more evident than that the Quaker method of Indian management if continued through all the years after the death of William Penn, would have saved the Colony from all

---

[1] The best account of all these proceedings is in a book written by Charles Thomson, *The Alienation of the Delaware and Shawnese Indians.*

these wars. As Charles Thomson, who was not a Friend and not opposed to all war, and who had a first-hand knowledge of the whole series of transaction, has conclusively shown, the Delawares and Shawnese were thrown into the arms of the French by indefensible treatment. Had their friendliness been retained they would have been an effectual buffer against western attack, and the frontiers might have remained in security. The Friendly policy of the early settlers is abundantly justified on the score of justice, peace and economy. Had Thomas Penn had the spirit of his father, the Holy Experiment might have been continued as a more potent "example to the nations," and to the advantage of his finances. Incidentally also the active Friendly participation in Pennsylvania politics, and the attitude of the Society to public life, might have been continued at least to the Revolutionary War. That there was in the Indian mind some sense of justice which prevented outrages on regularly purchased land is evidenced by several statements, as for instance one by William Reckitt, an English travelling minister of 1756, who says, "Friends hitherto had not been hurt, yet several had left their plantations and fled back again over the Blue Mountains, where the lands had been rightly purchased of the Indians."

Scarcely had the province settled down into peace, through the efforts of the "Friendly Association" and the final defeat of the French and the surrender of Canada to England, when another cause of disturbance arose which shook the Yearly Meeting to its centre. This time the opposition was not the Proprietors and Governor, but the Presbyterian frontiersmen on the Susquehanna River, the "Paxton Boys," as the records of the time usually call them.

In the fall of 1763 John Penn, the grandson of the Founder, came as Governor. Among the delegations which welcomed him was one from the Conestoga Indians of Lancaster County. Their tribe had made treaties with William Penn, had been permitted to live on one of his manors, had been visited by Thomas Chalkley and other

Friends, and were generally regarded as a harmless company of makers of baskets and brooms, which they sold to the settlers. But white diseases and vices had carried them off, and now only about twenty remained, mostly women and children.

The settlers about them and to the west were mostly Scotch-Irishmen, a militant vigorous people, who based their morality upon the Old Testament, and felt themselves commissioned like Joshua to destroy the people of the land. They were just now irritated by sporadic border outrages, and incensed against the Quakers for befriending the Indians and opposing military expenses. They had adopted the Indian theory that in a time of war all of the opposing colour might properly be killed. They suspected, with how much justice it is difficult to determine, that these Conestoga Indians gave information to their more warlike western brethren, and resolved to annihilate the tribe. This they did, some in their homes, and the rest in the Lancaster jail where the Indians had been placed for safety. This first Pennsylvania lynching created great indignation in the east, but so secure were the " Boys " in the support of their neighbours that they never could be brought to justice.

Encouraged by this immunity, they announced their intention of meting out a like fate to a band of Moravian Indians that had been removed for safety to Philadelphia, and intimated that the Quakers who stood in their way, especially Israel Pemberton, might be treated similarly. A band of several hundred marched in rude array from the Susquehanna, and encamped at Germantown. The town rose to arms to defend the Indians. Many young Friends joined, and it being a cold winter day the meeting-house served as barracks, and the guns were stacked in the gallery.

This show of force was all that was necessary. The raiders were met by Benjamin Franklin at the head of a delegation, which asked their grievances and promised a careful consideration. There was some justice to their claim for increased representation if this were to be based on numbers, but as a matter of fact the only demand which was granted them by Governor John Penn and his council was a reward for Indian scalps, which was intended to stimulate the industry of the frontiersmen in this direction.

The meeting, however, had the problem on its hands of dealing with its members whose conduct had helped to frustrate the intentions of the attacking party. The proceedings in Philadelphia Monthly Meeting were carried over several years. Those who acknowledged an offence were very few. The others justified themselves. No one was disowned. There must have been a secret sympathy with the young men which prevented anything more decided than "labour" to induce them to see the logic of the Friendly position against war. Many of these offenders became a dozen years later active participants in American defence, and lost their rights among Friends as a consequence. Others changed their views, and were strong advocates of the Yearly Meeting's position, and suffered for it. James Logan favoured defensive war during his older years, and the Quakers, of whom Benjamin Franklin in his autobiography writes as actively sympathetic with military measures, were of this same period. But they never represented the official attitude of the Yearly Meeting. The Pontiac Wars immediately followed this episode, and gave the Friendly Association plenty to do, though it probably disbanded soon after.

In 1768 the treaty of Fort Stanwix quieted the Indian Question for colonial days.

An active and virulent pamphlet warfare followed the Paxton Invasion, the combatants being Presbyterians on one side and the defenders of Friends on the other. It is said that none of the publications, except a paper issued by the Meeting for Sufferings, was the work of Friends themselves. The controversy was not mild. The line of attack was that non-military advocacy was an impossible element in a government with outside enemies ; that the best and most practical Friends did not believe in it ; and that the others had no business in state affairs, and were beginning to come to this conclusion themselves. To this it was replied that for seventy years the policy had succeeded until muddled by alien elements, out of line with it, and which could not be controlled ; that it was the encroachments and excesses of the Scotch-Irishmen, rather than the lack of military defence, which were the initial cause of the troubles, and that treaties and presents and friendship rather than killing and fighting were still the means by which peace could best be regained.

With many unjustifiable reflections on either side, which may here be omitted, this question of the adaptability of Quakerism to government was ably debated, and when a temperate official document came out restating the ancient arguments against war, and giving a short résumé of the history of Friends connected with government in the past, the controversy closed, not, however, without leaving many bitter personal and partisan feelings.

CHAPTER VII

FRIENDS AND SLAVERY

THAT Friends have been in point of time leaders in many moral reforms can not well be gainsaid. *Why* they have been so is more difficult to tell. They have not been superior in intelligence or education to many other Christian bodies. They probably have not had more of devotion to goodness, or a greater desire to do right than many others. They have not been in positions where they could see in advance the trend of human thought or impulse better than others. Is there any reason more probable than the one the early Friends themselves would have given, that when they got together in their quiet assemblies, each one seeking to know God's will, with hearts prepared to follow it, and minds emptied so far as possible of misleading prepossessions and prejudices, they received the instruction for which they waited? They rather felt than reasoned that some things were right and others were wrong, and that it was their duty to follow the right in the face of apparent difficulties and danger. It was not a question of results. They were not opportunists, nor did they parley with their fears. The simple revelation came to them that they should follow a certain course in the definite issue before them, and in time it became evident that this was the course the future would sanction. This did not preclude the exercise of reason and common sense. It simply permitted this sense of right to turn the scale in the midst of conflicting arguments on both sides.

There were in colonial times in Pennsylvania several

moral questions affecting politics which have been already considered, as oaths, penalties for crime, the amount of force to be used in supporting law, the treatment of Indians, and war. On these subjects it will generally be admitted that Friends, earlier than other religious bodies, were on the right side. But the impulse which placed them there did not have its origin in politics, but in the church meetings. We find the minute of the Yearly Meeting used as the preamble to a statute a few years later. Such a relation could not fail to exist so long as the same men were prominent in both sets of activities. The lessons learned in the meeting would inevitably crop out in the Assembly.

In no other instance is this growth of sentiment for a moral cause more conspicuous than in the question of slavery. It began as a meeting problem—a problem of individual and church duty. Following this by a few years it came into political life, and as the meeting cleared the air the legislature acted. Very soon after the Yearly Meeting had abolished slavery among its members, the state of Pennsylvania enacted an abolition law.

We will trace the growth of the movement by means of the meeting records of the colonial days. George Fox in a public discourse in 1671 on the island of Barbadoes thus advises the slave holders :[1]

"Let me tell you it will doubtless be very acceptable to the Lord, if so be that masters of families here would deal so with their servants, the negroes and blacks whom they have bought with their money (as) to let them go free after they have served faithfully a considerable term of years, be it thirty years after, more or less, and when they go and are made free, let them not go away empty handed."

William Penn owned a few slaves in Pennsylvania. When he left in 1701 he wrote a will which says, " I give to my blacks their freedom as is under my hand already."

[1] For the most of the quotations in this chapter the author is indebted to a pamphlet published by Philadelphia Yearly Meeting in 1843 entitled "A Brief Statement of the Rise and Progress of the Testimony of the Religious Society of Friends against Slavery and the Slave Trade."

He appears to have intended immediate emancipation, but his wishes in this respect seem not to have been immediately carried out after he left the province. He was, as already stated, deeply interested in a proper education and religion for the blacks.

The first protest after the German memorial of 1688, and it was a radical one, came from the Keithians. Their body in 1693 declared that slavery was opposed to the Golden Rule, and that buying negroes was buying stolen goods; that "to buy souls and bodies of men for money, to enslave them and their posterity to the end of the world, we judge is a great hindrance to the spreading of the Gospel." They advise that no negroes be bought, except to free them, and none be held in slavery after reasonably working out any charges which the masters had incurred for them.

The first official statement of the Yearly Meeting on the subject, after the non-action on the German suggestion of 1688, was in 1696 when the Yearly Meeting advised:

"Whereas, several papers have been read relating to the keeping and bringing in of negroes; which being duly considered, it is the advice of this meeting that Friends be careful not to encourage the bringing in of any more negroes; and that such that have negroes be careful of them, bring them to meetings, have meetings with them in their families, and restrain them from loose and lewd living as much as in them lies, and from rambling abroad on First-days or other times."

This was as far as the meeting would go. Slave Trade was an evil and must be discouraged, and such blacks as were here must be protected and trained as men.

The legislature followed slowly. In 1700, though almost unanimously Friendly, they rejected a bill proposed by William Penn "for regulating negroes in their morals and manners." Five years later they made certain crimes capital for blacks which were not for whites, but the same year they taxed the owners of imported negroes forty shillings per head.

The radical leaders of the reform seem to have resided about Chester. This meeting in 1711 sent up a minute to the Yearly Meeting expressing its dissatisfaction with the encouragement the slave trade received by the purchase of slaves after importation. This brought out the moderate advice that—

". . . after a due consideration of the matter, the meeting considering that Friends in many other places are concerned in it as much as we are, advises that Friends may be careful, according to a former minute of this Yearly Meeting (1696), not to encourage the bringing in of any more ; and that all merchants and factors write to their correspondents to discourage them from sending any more."

In 1712 William Southeby, a Friend, prayed the legislature to abolish *slavery* in Pennsylvania. He was a pioneer. The House would not do this, but levied a prohibitory duty of £20 on every slave imported, which law was repealed by the English Queen.

The Yearly Meeting in the same year addressed their Friends in London, as the central body with which all the others corresponded, asking for some general advice concerning the slave trade in all the American Colonies :

"And now dear Friends we impart unto you a concern that hath rested on our minds for many years, touching the importing and having negro slaves, and detaining them and their posterity as such, without any limitation or time of redemption from that condition. This matter was laid before this meeting many years ago, and the thing in some degree discouraged, as may appear by a minute of our Yearly Meeting (1696), desiring all merchants and traders professing Truth among us, to write to their correspondents, that they send no more negroes to be disposed of as above ; yet notwithstanding, as our settlements increased so other traders flocked in amongst us, over whom we had no gospel authority, and such have increased and multiplied negroes amongst us, to the grief of divers Friends, whom we are willing to ease, if the way might open clear to the satisfaction of the general ; and it being last Yearly Meeting again moved, and Friends being more concerned with negroes in divers other provinces and places than in these, we thought it too weighty to come to a full conclusion therein ; this meeting therefore desires your assistance by way of counsel and advice therein, and that you would be pleased to take the matter into your weighty consideration, after having advised with Friends in the other American provinces, and give us your sense or advice therein."

The suggestion in reply to this was very cautious and unsatisfactory, and in 1714, rather brusquely for a Friendly Yearly Meeting, Philadelphia writes :—

"We also kindly received your advice about negro slaves, and we are one with you that the multiplying of them may be of dangerous consequence, and therefore a law was made in Pennsylvania, laying a duty of twenty pounds upon every one imported there, which law the Queen was pleased to disannul. We could heartily wish that a way might be found to stop the bringing in more here; or at least, that Friends may be less concerned in buying or selling of any that may be brought in ; and hope for your assistance with the government, if any further law should be made, discouraging the importation. We know not of any Friend amongst us that has any hand or concern in bringing any out of their own country ; and we are of the same mind with you, that the practice is not commendable nor allowable amongst Friends; and we take the freedom to acquaint you, that our request unto you was, that you would be pleased to consult or advise with Friends in other plantations, where they are more numerous than with us; because they hold a correspondence with you but not with us, and your meeting may better prevail with them, and your advice prove more effectual."

The next year Chester Friends again stir up the matter. They send a very urgent request to legislate that " Friends be not concerned in the importing and bringing of negro slaves in the future." A little was gained, for the Yearly Meeting decrees :

"If any Friends are concerned in the importation of negroes, let them be dealt with and advised to avoid that practice, according to the sense of former meetings in that behalf; and that all Friends who have or keep negroes, do use and treat them with humanity and with a Christian spirit; and that all do forbear judging or reflecting on one another, either in public or private, concerning the detaining or keeping them servants."

But Chester was not satisfied, and again petitioned the Yearly Meeting in 1716 against " buying any that shall be imported hereafter." They received a discouraging reply which indicated that no forward movement was to be expected at that time :—

"As to the proposal from Chester meeting about negroes, there being no more in it than was proposed to the last Yearly Meeting, this meeting cannot see any better conclusion, than what was the judgment of the last meeting, and therefore do confirm the same; and yet in condescension to such Friends as are straitened in their minds against the holding them, it is desired, that Friends generally do, as much as may be, avoid buying such negroes as shall hereafter be brought in, rather than offend any Friends who are against it; yet this is only caution and not censure."

Three years later they advise:

"That none among us be concerned in the fetching or importing negro slaves from their own country or elsewhere; and that all Friends who have any of them do treat them with humanity and in a Christian manner, and as much as in them lies make them acquainted with the principles of Friends, and inculcate morality in them."

And the same year they adopt this minute showing that Indians as well as negroes were held in slavery by some Friends:

"To avoid giving them [the Indians] occasion of discontent it is advised that Friends do not buy or sell Indian slaves."

Friends had done all they could directly against the slave trade from Africa. They had withdrawn their members from participation, and had secured laws from the legislature which would have stopped others had not the Crown disallowed them. There came a lull till 1729, when Chester again appears on the scene, renewing its old request, which evidently struck at the root of the trade, that all purchases of such as were to be imported should be disallowed. There was evidently a growth in public sentiment in the intervening ten years. The minute of 1730 which followed means more than appears on the surface. The reference to the Monthly Meetings makes such a purchase a disownable offence:

"The Friends of this meeting resuming the consideration of the proposition of Chester meeting, relating to the purchasing of such negroes as may hereafter be imported; and having reviewed and considered the former minutes relating thereto, and having maturely deliberated thereon, are now of opinion, that Friends ought to be very cautious of making any such purchases for the future, it being disagreeable to the sense of this meeting. And this meeting recommends it to the care of the several Monthly Meetings, to see that such who may be, or are likely to be found in that practice, may be admonished and cautioned how they offend herein."

Reports were now sent up yearly as to the faithfulness with which the instructions were carried out.   In 1738 the Yearly Meeting says :

"Divers Friends in this meeting expressed their satisfaction in finding by the reports of the quarterly meetings, that there is so little occasion of offence given by Friends concerning the encouraging the importing of negroes ; and this meeting desires the care of Friends in their quarterly and monthly meetings, in this particular, may be continued."

This advice was crystallized in 1743 into the following query to be answered annually by all meetings : "Do Friends observe the former advice of our Yearly Meeting not to encourage the importation of negroes nor to buy them after imported ? "   In 1755 this was enlarged to :

"Are Friends clear of importing or buying negroes ; and do they use those well which they are possessed of by inheritance or otherwise ; endeavoring to train them up in the principles of the Christian religion ? "

In such an agitation the question of the wrongfulness of slavery itself could not fail to be considered.   Men were asking whether the importation was the only evil.   John Woolman and Anthony Benezet were beginning to write and speak for the blacks.   The former in 1754 published his, *Considerations on the Keeping of Negroes*, which was widely read.

The same year the Yearly Meeting issued a paper written presumably by Anthony Benezet. It attacked slavery as the cause of the slave trade with its attendant horrors, and argued that if any held their slaves for any other reason than the good of the slaves themselves, it indicated that the love of God did not rule their lives.

Slaves seem to have increased in number among Friends, and probably some of them were concerned in the trade, for in 1755 the Yearly Meeting adopted these directions to the Monthly Meetings :

"The consideration of the inconsistency of the practice of being concerned in importing or buying slaves, with our Christian principles, being weightily revived and impressed, by very suitable advices and cautions given on the occasion, it is the sense and judgment of this meeting, that where any transgress this rule of our discipline, the overseers ought speedily to inform the monthly meeting of such transgressors, in order that the meeting may proceed to treat further with them, as they may be directed in the wisdom of Truth."

The year 1758 was the great year in the history of the movement. All this time the sentiment against slavery itself had been gaining ground. The Friends, doubtless, had treated their slaves with great humanity, and some of them argued with truth that they were undoubtedly better off than with irresponsible freedom. But the Quaker conscience could not be lulled with this argument. *Slavery was wrong*, and against this position there could be no effective attack. Ralph Sandiford, John Woolman, Anthony Benezet, and even the eccentric and troublesome Benjamin Lay were preaching it to an ever-increasing circle of sympathetic hearers. It was not wrong *only* because it encouraged the trade—that would now be admitted by all Friends ; it was wrong in itself. No man had a right to hold another man in bondage except temporarily for his own good.

But this struck at many personal and property interests, and these joined together to have the usual minute, so often previously adopted, condemning the African importations and encouraging the good treatment of such as already were here, again sent down to the meetings. These interested advocates of a deeply rooted custom for a time swayed the Meeting. But the fire burned in the heart of John Woolman. He felt rather than saw the sophistries of their arguments. He could no longer be silent. It had been urged that if slavery was wrong God Himself would open a way to abolish it, and that unity and deference were Christian duties. Then he spoke :

"My mind is led to consider the purity of the Divine Being and the justice of His judgment, and herein my soul is covered with awfulness. I cannot forbear to hint of some cases where people have not been treated with the purity of justice and the event has been most lamentable. Many slaves on this continent are oppressed and their cries have entered into the ears of the Most High. Such are the purity and certainty of His judgments that He cannot be partial in our favour. In infinite love and goodness He hath opened our understandings from one time to another concerning our duty towards this people ; and it is not a time for delay. Should we now be sensible of what He requires of us, and through a respect to the private interests of some persons, or through a regard to some friendships which do not stand upon an immutable foundation, neglect to do our duty in firmness and constancy, still waiting for some extraordinary means to bring about their deliverance, God may by terrible things in righteousness answer us in this matter."

To this feeling appeal of John Woolman the Meeting responded. There was an authority in it which quieted opposition, and without spoken dissent the following minute was adopted :

"After weighty consideration of the circumstances of Friends within the compass of this meeting, who have any negro or other slaves, the accounts and proposals now sent up from several quarters, and the rules of our discipline relative thereto ; much time having been spent, and the sentiments of many Friends expressed, there appears an unanimous concern prevailing to put a stop to the increase of the practice of importing, buying, selling, or keeping slaves for term of life ; or purchasing them for such a number of years, as manifests that such purchasers do only in terms, and not in fact, avoid the imputation of being keepers of slaves. This meeting very earnestly and affectionately intreats Friends, individually, to consider seriously the present circumstances of these and the adjacent provinces, which, by the permission of Divine Providence, have been visited with the desolating calamities of war and bloodshed, so that many of our fellow-subjects are now suffering in captivity ; and fervently desires, that, excluding temporal considerations or views of self-interest, we may manifest an humbling sense of these judgments, and in thankfulness for the peculiar favour extended and continued to our Friends and brethren in profession, none of whom have, as we have yet heard, been slain nor carried into captivity, would steadily observe the injunction of our Lord and Master, 'To do unto others as we would they should do unto us'; which it now appears to this meeting, would induce such Friends who have any slaves to set them at liberty,—making a Christian provision for them according to their ages, etc. And in order that Friends may be generally excited to the practice of this advice, some Friends here now signified to the meeting their being so fully devoted to endeavor to render it effectual, that they are willing to visit and treat with all such Friends who have any slaves; the meeting therefore approves of John Woolman, John Scarborough, John Sykes and Daniel Stanton undertaking that service; and desires some elders or other faithful Friends in each quarter to accompany and assist them therein; and that they may proceed in the wisdom of Truth, and thereby be qualified to administer such advice as may be suitable to the circumstances of those they visit, and most effectual towards obtaining that purity which it is evidently our duty to press after. And if after the sense and judgment of this meeting, now given against every branch of this practice, any professing with us should persist to vindicate it, and be concerned in importing, selling, or purchasing slaves, the respective monthly meetings to which they belong should manifest their disunion with such persons, by refusing to permit them to sit in meetings for discipline, or to be employed in the affairs of Truth, or to receive from them any contribution towards the relief of the poor, or other services of the meeting. But if any cases of executors, guardians, trustees, or any others should happen, which may subject any such Friends to the necessity of being concerned with such slaves, and they are nevertheless willing to proceed according to the advice of the monthly meetings they belong to, wherever such cases happen, the monthly meetings are left to judge of the same in the wisdom of Truth, and, if necessary, to take the advice of the quarterly meeting therein."

This meeting of 1758 was a memorable one. Two years before, partly in response to a request of the London Meeting for Sufferings, the majority of the Friendly members of the legislature had given up their places rather than vote supplies to the war against the Delaware and Shawnee Indians which the Governor had declared.

Now the Yearly Meeting sent out definite advices to the Monthly Meetings not to permit any of their members to hold any civil offices which involved any departure from Friendly principles. This would, for a time at least, keep them out of the Assembly, as well as all judicial positions which involved administering oaths. With this withdrawal from public life came the increased zeal for moral causes. The transition was in progress. Friends were no longer to be in the public eye in matters of government, but they were resolved to clear themselves of moral taints and give their energies to the machinery of moral reforms. The transformation was just beginning and the Revolutionary War twenty years later completed it.

The purport of the minute was that slavery as an institution was to be testified against, and all the persuasive influence of the strong men of the Meeting was to be used with slave-holders to induce them to free their slaves. The crusade had begun. The Yearly Meeting was committed and all loyal members were expected to respect its judgment. John Woolman and his associates travelled industriously, and laboured in the meetings and at the homes assiduously. There is but little record of the number of slaves manumitted in the succeeding decade, but there were many.

In 1760, after only two years' service, the Meeting minuted :

" As the growing concern which hath appeared amongst us for some years past to discourage the practice of making slaves of our fellow-creatures hath been visibly blessed with success, we earnestly exhort that Friends do not abate their diligence in this weighty matter, but continue in the love which beareth long and is kind to labor with such as having membership with us do in any manner by buying, selling, or keeping them countenance the trade, to inform their understandings and convince their judgments, and some of us are firmly persuaded, that if this case is diligently and honestly pursued the Society will in time come up more universally in fulfilling the evangelical law of righteousness in this respect."

Again and again the central body repeats the advice,

and after 1767 encouraging statements, not numerical, of the progress of the effort were sent up.

So matters went on till 1774. By this time all willing members had freed their slaves. It remained to be decided what to do with the unwilling ones. The Quarterly and Monthly Meetings were now urged to make one more effort to convince the recalcitrants, and, this failing, they were to be dealt with as offenders against the discipline. This was strengthened two years later, and the directions were added to see that all manumissions were recorded to protect the blacks in the future.

Committees of each Quarterly Meeting were now appointed to visit the homes of the remaining slave-holders. By urgent entreaty, through these dark days of the Revolutionary war, one after another yielded to the kindly solicitations, and a few who persistently refused were disowned.[1] Thus did the Yearly Meeting extinguish the iniquity. By 1780 no slaves were held by members except in peculiar cases where legal difficulties prevented manumission, as where husband or wife was not a member and would not consent.

But the duty was not yet quite accomplished. The minute of 1758 urged besides freedom, "making a Christian provision for them according to their ages." This also was a part of the labour of the committees. Where the blacks had worked long and faithfully they were not to be turned away empty-handed, and many a Quaker ex-slave-holder paid a debt not demanded by the law for the past unrequited services of his slaves.

The interests promoted by slavery were greatly reduced in Pennsylvania by the freeing of the Quaker slaves and its consequent effect upon public opinion. So that of all the states it was the first to pass an abolition law.

All this time efforts were being made to appeal to the negroes religiously. A few joined Friends. Many

---

[1] A manuscript copy of James Moon's Journal describing those efforts in Bucks County is in existence, which shows the long and kindly and successful efforts of one of these committees. See *Quakerism and Politics* by Isaac Sharpless.

attended the meetings appointed for them. Joseph Oxley in 1771 speaks of the "Meetings for Negroes in Philadelphia. Few there but negroes. They generally sat soberly." These meetings were held quarterly at this time, and frequently all through the Colonial period. But the quiet of a Friends' meeting was not the religious atmosphere which the race would appreciate.

CHAPTER VIII

GENERAL CONDITIONS, 1700-1775

It is difficult to estimate the number of Friends in the province of Pennsylvania during Colonial days. The immigration was very active at the start, and the early immigrants were largely Friends. But others, attracted by opportunities for trade, also came. The country settlers were largely, in some districts exclusively, Friends. James Logan in 1702 estimated that the population of the city and of the country were equal, and that one-third of the former and two-thirds of the latter were Friends. This would make them one-half the population at this date, and as, later, non-Friends came in greater numbers, the proportion probably never reached this figure again. In 1698 Gabriel Thomas, who had lived fifteen years in the province, said that there were 2000 houses in Philadelphia, some of them accommodating several families, and gives the total population of the city as 20,000. Putting together the statements of James Logan and Gabriel Thomas, we would infer that about 1700 there were 20,000 Friends in Pennsylvania, which is doubtless too large a figure. Thomas Lloyd writes as early as 1684 that as many as 800 people attend the Friends' meeting in Philadelphia, not all Friends, however. The meetings were very large, surprising the English visitors. They had not been used to such grouping—a whole district of several miles square, containing hardly a family outside the membership. A few quotations from Journals will give an idea of the numbers in attendance.

James Dickinson in 1691 held meetings through Pennsylvania in the winter out of doors, sometimes in deep snow, the meeting-houses not being large enough to contain the people.

Thomas Chalkley, writing in 1701, says:

"Since my settling in the province which is now about a year, some hundreds of people are come here to reside and many meeting houses are built."

In 1726 he visited meetings in the Welsh Tract and found "a religious, industrious, and increasing people."

In 1715 the Yearly Meeting wrote to London:

"Our meeting hath been very large, the people and youth increasing much. . . . Friends generally solaced therein for we may truly say in humility and fear the Lord is still with his people."

Two years later they say:

"There is some convincement in many places and a great increase of young people, so there seems to be occasion for increasing and enlarging our meeting houses."

Samuel Bownas speaks in 1727 of the size of the meetings through Chester County, amounting in several cases to 1500 each.   In Philadelphia the meetings were "exceedingly large," "more like Yearly Meetings than common First Day Meetings."   Between his two visits, twenty years apart, meeting-houses had been enlarged two, three, and four times, and in Pennsylvania thirteen new ones had been built.   Ten places needed new ones (1728) and many old ones should be enlarged.

In 1754 Samuel Fothergill says that the meetings in and around Philadelphia are "exceedingly large and all sorts and ranks of people flock to them."

John Griffith tells us in 1765 that 1500 people attended a meeting in Philadelphia.

Joseph Oxley says in 1770 of Philadelphia Yearly Meeting:

"The meetings were very large, more so than I have ever seen in England, both for worship and discipline."

He says of Wilmington, Del.:

"Attended a very large meeting. The chief part of the inhabitants of this town, which is a very improving one, are under our denomination."

Many other testimonies as to the increasing size of the Pennsylvania meetings might be found. It was, though unofficially, the State religion of Pennsylvania. Its ministers were the most active and aggressive, its discipline the most effective, and its gatherings the most imposing for numbers and solemnity of any religious exercises of the colony. The Episcopal minister of Chester writes in 1712 with evident misgiving:

"I need not tell you that Quakerism is generally preferred in Pennsylvania, and in no county of the province does the haughty tribe appear more rampant than where I reside, there being by a modest computation 20 Quakers besides dissenters to one true Churchman." [1]

This continuous increase brought the number of Friends in the province at the outbreak of the Revolution probably up to 25,000, and adding to this the Friends of New Jersey, Delaware, Maryland, and Virginia, membership of the Yearly Meeting may have reached 30,000. Franklin in 1766 gave the population of Pennsylvania as 160,000, of which he said that Quakers constituted one-third. They probably did for political purposes, and this was what Franklin had in mind, but the number is too large for the actual membership. About the same time another estimate gives the population as 200,000, and of these one-eighth were said to be Friends. The exact figures will never be known, for no census was taken.

The average of spiritual life did not grow with the numbers. This was inevitable with birthright membership. For while the best of Friends kept up the standards a large and increasing minority were Friendly only in name and custom. John Smith of Marlborough, whose

----

[1] *Papers relating to the Church in Pennsylvania*, page 69.

memory extended back to about 1700, said, sixty years
later, that in these early days

"Friends were a plain lowly-minded people, and that there
was much tenderness and contrition in their meetings. That at
20 years from that date, the Society increasing in wealth and in
some degree conforming to the fashions of the world, true
humility was less apparent, and their meetings in general were
not so lively and edifying. That at the end of 40 years many
of them were grown very rich ; and many made a specious
appearance in the world, that marks of outward wealth and
greatness appeared on some in our meetings of ministers and
elders, and as such things became more prevalent so the
powerful overshadowings of the Holy Ghost were less manifest
in the Society. That there had been a continual increase of
such ways of life even until the present time, and that the weakness that had now overspread the Society and the barrenness
manifest among us is matter of much sorrow."

Making all allowance for the divine enthusiasm of
youth, this is a striking statement and represents an
undoubted tendency. John Smith may have been mistaken in associating wealth and show with spiritual
barrenness strictly as cause and effect. They were
probably contemporary results of the same causes.

Samuel Bownas's testimony is something the same.
Comparing conditions of 1727 with those of twenty years
earlier, he says :

"Many of the rising youth come in form more than in the
power and life that their predecessors were in."

Yet he admits that "there is a fine living people
amongst them."

All through these years there were marked periods
of spiritual interest and effectiveness. Jane Hoskens,
writing about 1712, says, "The Lord was pleased to
renew a merciful visitation unto the Friends and inhabitants of North Wales and Plymouth. Many of the
youth were reached, and several were called to the
ministry." And John Griffith writes :

"About this time [1734] a fine spring of ministry was opened
within the compass of our Yearly Meeting. About 100 opened
their mouths in public in a little more than a year."

This meant far more than a simple testimony to Christian conversion. It meant the beginning of a life of ministry, though he admits that "some of them withered away like unripe fruit."

On the whole during these early days of the century the outlook was cheering.

"The Truth prevails and prospers and great openness in many places, and many flocking to hear the testimonies of it, and some are convinced, and some that are young coming forth in testimony; and good discipline increases among the churches,"

the Yearly Meeting reported in 1705. This was the general tone of such statements for a number of years.

But the coming years, as John Smith intimates, saw changes not all for the better.

Not only was there in many members a spiritual decline during the century, but there was also very considerable moral laxity. The offences for which Friends were disowned in large numbers, mentioned in the minutes with great plainness, show this clearly. Life in a new country, when unaccompanied by the refining influences of religion or education, brought out crude and coarse manners and morals. Standards in the body were high and open offenders were disowned, but certain departures from Christian conduct were not reached by disciplinary processes.

The various assemblies of the country people at fairs, vendues, shooting matches, games of "hustlecap" (a species of pitching pennies), gave rise to much drinking, carousing, and fighting.

It was not, however, only these concomitants that were objected to. The Puritan objection to amusements was applied to the games themselves, and many a sport-loving young Quaker had to apologise to the Meeting for acts which would now be part of our settled habits.

A Friend who afterwards became a prominent minister admitted that he was "frisky" in his early years, and in 1714 "acknowledged himself to blame for running at a Horse Race at Chester Faire, and is heartily sorry for it and hopes never to do the like again."

A few quotations will show the nature of delinquencies noticed by travelling Friends :

" Many showed themselves very disorderly in going frequently out of meeting during the time of worship."

" A large meeting, a dry lifeless state in too many and inconsistent conduct in others, especially in excessive drinking."

" I was concerned to exhort Friends to purge the Society of those under our profession who live in open profaneness and are riotous in conversation. The Governor also issued a proclamation against similar evils. But some young people still disturbed our religious meetings and were obnoxious to government."

" There are many earthly-minded and some loose libertine people."

" There is a low vulgar education among the possessors of Quakerism here that if they do not feel and live to what they profess they are very low indeed in behaviour and conduct, which by a spirit of obstinacy which prevails among them is very degrading to the Truth and to Society, and especially in the European opinion who are brought up otherwise. But where Truth prevails it polishes and makes all beautiful and lively."

This last quotation refers to the condition of Friends educationally. The study of this condition will explain a number of failures of Quakerism of the Colonial and following days, and is worth understanding in some detail.

Within a year after Penn's landing, Enoch Flower was commissioned by the Council to open a school for elementary work. About the same time another council meeting, William Penn presiding, proposed that a higher school " of Arts and Sciences " be established. We know nothing of the subsequent history of either of these efforts, but these or other schools were held in the meeting - houses during the next half - dozen years. Gabriel Thomas tells us in 1698 " there were several good schools of learning " in the city. In 1689 William Penn instructed Thomas Lloyd to set up a " Public Grammar School." It was immediately started and George Keith made master. This was the origin of the educational movement which later became the William Penn Charter School, still in flourishing existence. It was intended as a school for the people, whether Friends or not, and the poor were admitted free. There was a charter granted it by Deputy-Governor Markham in 1697, and again by Penn in 1701, 1708, and 1711. Up to 1708 the school was a source of much expenditure of time and trouble to the Monthly Meeting of Philadelphia, under whose control it was carried on. In the charter of this year it was given over fully to the Corporation, all of whom must be Friends. The last charter removed this restriction, but as the body was self-perpetuating none but Friends have ever been appointed to it. The school under this arrangement continued its beneficent work through the Colonial days. It was generally patronised by Friends except such as could afford private instruction. Mathematical, classical, and elementary branch schools were established for boys and girls in the city, and graded prices were intended to accommodate families of varied means.

Other schools were started in other parts of the colony, usually under the control of a meeting. Benjamin Clift was allowed £12 a year for a school at Darby, and Christopher Taylor, a University man and prominent in the official life of the colony, had a private school on the Island of Tinicum. In 1697 the Yearly Meeting minuted:

"Meetings [schools?] for the education of youth are settled in most counties except Bucks, Shrewsbury, and Salem."

These small elementary schools, encouraged by Meeting support, soon became rather general. But by 1746, there appearing some reasons to make the movement more general or more effective, the Yearly Meeting advised:

"We desire you, in your several Monthly Meetings, to encourage and assist each other in the settlement and support of schools for the instruction of your children, at least to read and write, and some further useful learning, to such whose circumstances will permit it. And that you observe, as much as possible, to employ such masters and mistresses as are concerned, not only to instruct your children in their learning, but are likewise careful in the wisdom of God and a spirit of meekness, gradually to bring them to a knowledge of their duty to God and one another ; and we doubt not such endeavors will be blessed with success."

The advice was renewed a few years later, and by the Revolution was acted on to such an extent that the elements of education were within the reach of all Friends except those on the frontiers, and not infrequently by the conjunction of an ambitious boy and an inspiring teacher, excellent scholars were produced. There are several accounts of travellers being surprised to encounter a farmer who read his Hebrew and Greek Testaments or spent his leisure times in the solution of mathematical problems of difficulty, while John Bartram and some of his friends were botanists of the highest order.

John Smith of Philadelphia and Burlington wrote a most illuminating journal[1] which gives us an insight into the private life of the more wealthy and cultured Friends of Philadelphia about the middle of the century. There must have been much book culture among them as well as indefinite sociability of the better sort. John Smith himself read the current books of the day— Pope's Poems, Addison's Essays, and (strange to say), Steele's Comedies and Fielding's novels. As he was an elder and clerk of the Yearly Meeting, besides holding many responsible places in business and public affairs, it is evident that this miscellaneous reading and active life did not unfit him, as would later have been the case, for the confidence and recognition of his associates. Interspersed with it we find references to the approved writings of Friends which show that he had also drunk deeply of the literature and spirit of Quakerism. His own writings and public appointments as companion to many ministers would also show this. The Logans, Pembertons, Norrises, Morrises, Kinseys, and others with whom he was connected by family and social ties seem

---

[1] *Hannah Logan's Courtship*, edited by Albert Cook Myers.

to have been a most delightful combination of denominational zeal and consecration and simple piety with
cultivated minds and manners.

Their formal education was probably received in part
in the "public school," in part by private tuition, but it
was mostly gained as the result of an interest in good
things which impelled them to educate themselves and
each other. The effect of the reading of the journal,
never intended for other eyes than his own, is to impress
one with the feeling of a community in which wealth,
public spirit, free and simple social intercourse and
recreation, considerable mental culture and real religious
feeling were happily blended. At the other extreme the
Meeting minutes display a large proportion of city vices
and ignorance. The gap between the extremes was much
wider than a century and a half later. This contrast is
often indicated. Thomas Chalkley tells us in 1726:

"The Lord was angry with the people of Philadelphia and
Pennsylvania for the wickedness committed by the inhabitants
in the public-houses—with the magistrates for not enforcing
laws against profaneness and immorality—with the representatives
of the people because they do not suppress vice and immorality
—and with the better sort of people because they love the world
more than heaven."

The offenders may not have been Friends, but the
magistrates probably, and the representatives and "better
sort" almost certainly were. But side by side with this
he speaks of the Yearly Meeting

"Wherein divers young men and women appeared who had
lately come forth in the ministry—a large gathering of some
thousands of people."

The liquor problem, as always, was with these Colonial
Friends. At first it was rum supplied to Indians which
caused the trouble, and the Yearly Meeting went so far
as to order a written pledge signed by individual members
through the meetings agreeing not to sell or give away
any strong drink which would be likely to reach the
Indians. Then their own state officials were the objects

of concern, and the legislature passed a law that drunkenness should disqualify a man for holding office. The Deputy-Governor, however, would not, he said, penalise a man for "taking a cup too much."

A practice had arisen of making a burial the occasion of feasting and drinking. The vigour and frequency with which the meetings combated this inexcusable custom shows its hold upon the times. Such opportunities were occasions of vast crowds of people gathering, some of whom came from a distance, and hospitality demanded their entertainment. But this easily grew to excess and caused anything but solemnity.

"When wine or other strong liquors are served (which many sober-minded people think needless) that it be but once"

the Yearly Meeting recommended in 1729.

They strove also in meeting and legislature to abate the evils of public-houses, which were centres of drunkenness and crime. The remedy was to place the business in the hands of men who would wish to control the excesses. It was then respectable to patronise and own such taverns, for they were needed to accommodate the travel of the times.

But the drink habit could not be kept in moderation in many instances. Ministers succumbed as well as the humble people. In the trial of Bradford in 1692 it was intimated that the prominent Friends and ministers of the day were put to bed drunk.[1] This may be a false charge, but many other cases, hardly less conspicuous, might be cited. There were, however, most earnest efforts used by all in authority to remedy the evil of drunkenness, and those guilty of it could not be employed in church services. There was with the years a growing stringency as to the use of spirituous liquors which, however, in Colonial days never reached the position of total abstinence.

But what of the great body of Friends who were neither great saints nor great sinners, neither highly educated nor grossly ignorant? These constituted the

[1] Pennypacker's *Colonial Cases.*

typical Quakers of Colonial days. When they got together in meetings, it was their voice which prevailed, their thoughts and feelings which set the policy of the society. The Yearly Meeting was not a reflex of the educated leaders of the city, nor of the more coarse element among the country people. Its standards were determined very largely by the strong democracy of the farmers. A farming community is apt to be conservative, to be economical, and hence slow to take risks, or make advances without great deliberation, but it is also apt to be clear-headed, honest, direct, and moral. If we form our judgment from the offenders whose cases we read in the minutes of the Monthly Meetings, which occupy so large a proportion of the space, we should infer that the Friends were an outrageously demoralised community. But the very fact that these delinquents are dealt with so plainly and without any condoning of their faults, or relaxation of the standards, shows that there was everywhere a prevailing majority, of whom we read nothing directly, who stood with unyielding sincerity for righteousness.

The journals of travelling Friends are most unsatisfactory exponents of actual conditions. They are full of subjective expressions, telling how the minister felt very "low," or that the meeting was "lively," which judgments might have resulted from the writer's physical or spiritual condition at the time, or might have been a reflex of the external attitude of the Friends. It is impossible to doubt that the former often dictated the expressions in the journal. Thus to John Griffith, who travelled about 1765 through the Yearly Meeting, things were "mournfully low," "few seemed alive," "great weakness and want of living concern," "religion at a low ebb," and many other such disconsolate expressions. While to Joseph Oxley, who journeyed over the same territory about the same time—

"The affairs of the church were carried on in much brotherly love and condescension, a very great deal of becoming plainness and honest simplicity being coupled together in the fear of God.

"The meetings for the most part have been large, comfortable, and to edification, many mothers with their infants attending, the zeal of the mothers I thought sufficiently compensating for the cries of the babes.

"The meeting held fresh and green mostly for six hours."

It is impossible to reconcile the saddening experiences of the one with the hopeful expressions of the other, except by the differing temperaments of the writers.

The whole tenor of the teaching was inward. The best Friends have always been mystics, and mysticism is seldom so pure and exalted as to free itself from an admixture of the elements which come from mental buoyancy or good digestion on the one hand, or the reverse conditions on the other. Hence our Quaker journals must be read between the lines.

It can hardly be doubted, however, that there was a steady increase in the proportion of unspiritual Friends as the century advanced. The journalistic testimony in its entirety would point to this conclusion. Prosperity, leadership in public affairs, birthright membership, absence of the means of education, opened increasing temptations to a non-religious life. The sweetness and light and enthusiasm of the first fifty years were passing away. While many maintained the spirit and standards of the older days, a number, large in the aggregate, were indifferent, substituting formalism for piety. Some were openly rebellious, in spite of, or perhaps in consequence of, the increasing stringency of disciplinary requirements.

The matters with which the Yearly Meeting concerned itself in its endeavour to keep to simple standards were very detailed. In 1694 it testified against challenging to run races, wrestling, pitching "barrs," "drinking to one another," "riding from house to house to drink rum and other strong liquors to excess," "to jest or talk idly," "for children to answer parents forwardly or crossly," "the immoderate and indecent smoking of tobacco," "to ride or go in the streets with pipes in their mouths," and so on. This list is interesting as showing the customs of the age as well as the care of the Yearly Meeting. A little later it testifies against drunkenness, "a prevailing evil," against such as "hold Truth for worldly ends," "publishing books to raise contention," importing slaves, "marrying out," "using unscriptural language,"—thus mingling together serious moral evils and the breaking of the special testimonies of Friends.

In 1695 the meeting advised that all Friends keep to plainness in apparel, and specified as innovations to be avoided "long-lapped sleeves or coats gathered at the sides or superfluous buttons or broad ribbons about their hats or long-curled periwigs," and that women should not dress "their heads immoderately," or "wear long scarves," or buy "striped or flowered stuffs," and that Friendly tailors, who presumably would not sell these gaudy innovations, be dealt with exclusively. They also urge that excesses in building and furniture be avoided, that business be kept down to moderate dimensions, and that debts be promptly paid. The reason they give in 1701 for these advices is worth reading:

"Earth was made for the service of man, not man for the service of the earth. . . . How ignoble and debasing a thing it is for a man to divert that noble, gracious, primitive institution in which he was advanced to a divine dominion, and yield himself a slave to that over which he once was and still should be lord."

In nearly all the meetings, acting on many "advices," beginning with Burlington in 1681, the Monthly Meetings appointed two Friends each to settle differences amicably, to prevent defamation of character by untrue or libellous reports, to administer the discipline as to attendance at and proper behaviour in meeting, and to look after the habits of Friends as to plainness of living and sobriety of conduct. These officials were probably not called Overseers before 1700, but soon after the name seems to have been pretty general. About the same time Preparative Meetings were set up, to attend to the more personal work required to bring the business in good shape to the Monthly Meetings. The overseers were originally the appointees of these Preparative Meetings, which consisted of the more experienced and reliable

Friends only.   In case of an offender these overseers and the Preparative Meetings were expected quietly to reform him, and long-continued efforts were made to this end. If they succeeded, no record was made of the case. Should he prove not amenable to such influences, the Monthly Meeting was informed, and more formal proceedings instituted, resulting either in his acknowledgment of culpability and reinstatement in good standing or disownment.   While therefore the records of the Monthly Meetings, which have been preserved, seem to indicate rather abrupt and arbitrary proceedings, they give us no indication of the private labours which preceded them, of which we have no official accounts.

The creation of Preparative Meetings was made optional with Quarterly Meetings in 1698, and we find John Churchman, as late as 1758, advising their establishment in places where they were unknown.

There is no doubt that the " Queries " had a large effect in maintaining the discipline and standards of the Quaker community.   As we have seen, there was an attempt made in 1703 to codify and arrange the advices and instructions of the Yearly Meeting into a formal " Discipline."   Manuscript copies of this were made, and were added to as new conclusions were reached.   This Book of Discipline was read quarterly in the meetings for worship.   To it was often appended an epistle of doctrinal advice and earnest exhortation to spiritual and holy living.   In 1707 it was concluded to call the Quarterly Meetings by name, and each one was to answer as to the conduct of its members.   Two years later these reports were to be in " wrighting."

The varied questions which the Friends of those days had under consideration, and which the Preparative Meetings and the overseers were expected to attend to, may be seen in a minute of Chester Quarterly Meeting of 1711.   They were instructed to look into the following offences :—

" That against inviting servants to marriages, except near relations.   That against going to the marriages of any that profess Truth, but marry not among Friends. That of keeping company in order for marriage with any one's servant without leave of master or mistress. That about being clear of one before being concerned with another. That of being too hasty in marriage after the death of husband or wife, and against marriage by priests. That against giving occasion of public scandal, and that against all disorderly walkers in general. That about Friends putting their children to apprentices, or otherwise to be brought up by those who are not Friends. That about parents causing their children often to read the Holy Scriptures, and to let them know some degree of writing; and that they be bred up in some useful employment. That against drinking to excess, swearing, cursing, lying, etc. That against superfluity of apparel and furniture in all its branches. That against calling the days and months contrary to Scripture, and against calling them by the names of the idol gods of the heathen. That about speaking the plain Scripture language of *thee* and *thou*. That against buying and trading beyond abilities, and of not keeping to our words and promises. That about attending Weekly Meetings, and against disorderly going in and out; and against sleeping in meetings. That against smoking tobacco in streets, roads, and public-houses, except privately. That against talking and tale-bearing. That against giving any just occasion of trouble to the government, and against our refusing to pay its tributes or assessments. That against selling rum to the Indians, and against buying Indian slaves. That against brother going to law with brother, as explained or amended by the last Yearly Meeting held at Burlington. That against challenging to fight, etc. That against keeping vain or loose company, in fairs, markets, drinking-houses, or any other places, etc. That against vain and frothy discourses, drinking to excess, and against a vain custom of drinking healths, as it is called, and against drinking one to another."

Reports on these subjects were to be made to the Quarterly Meetings usually at first by word of mouth of the representatives. Gradually to induce uniformity, definite subjects were proposed for report, and about 1725 these crystallised into "Queries." They were adopted as a matter of convenience, and were not uniform through the Yearly Meeting. That body in 1743 systematised the plan by the following minute, which is interesting alike as a means of discipline and as an expression of standards :

"This meeting directs that the following queries may be read in the several Monthly and Preparative Meetings within the verge of this meeting, at least once in each quarter of the year; to the end that the overseers, or other weighty Friends, may make such answers to them as they may be able to do, and their respective circumstances may require.   The members of such meetings may, by this means, be from time to time reminded of their duty.

"I. Are Friends careful to attend their meetings for worship, both on first-days and other days of the week appointed for that service? and are they careful to meet at the hour appointed? Do they refrain from sleeping in meetings? or do any accustom themselves to snuffing or chewing tobacco in meetings?

"II. Do Friends keep clear of excess, either in drinking drams or other strong drink?

"III. Are there any who keep company, in order for marriage, with those who are not of us, or with any others without the consent of parents or guardians?

"IV. Do Friends keep clear from tattling, tale-bearing, whispering, backbiting, and meddling in matters wherein they are not concerned?

"V. Are there any Friends that frequent music houses, or go to dancing or gaming?

"VI. Are Friends careful to train up their children in the nurture and fear of the Lord, and to restrain them from vice and evil company, and to keep them to plainness of speech and apparel?

"VII. Are the poor taken care of and are their children put to school and apprenticed out (after sufficient learning) to Friends? and do Friends put their own children out to Friends, as much as may be?

"VIII. Are there any who launch into business beyond what they are able to manage, and so break their promises, in not paying their just debts in due time?   And where differences happen, are endeavors used to have them speedily ended?

"IX. Are there any belonging to this meeting that are removed without certificates? or are there any from other parts appearing as Friends, and have not produced a certificate?

"X. Are Friends clear of depriving the King of his duties?

"XI. Do Friends observe the former advices of the Yearly Meeting, not to encourage the importation of negroes, nor to buy them after imported?

"XII. Are Friends careful to settle their affairs and make their wills in time of health?"

These queries were not at first formally answered.

They seem to have been for the purpose of reminding members of their duties and of testing the work of the overseers. The list was modified from time to time, and in 1755 a definite answer to each query was demanded, which answers were co-ordinated through the various grades, and finally reaching the Yearly Meeting were intended fairly to represent the state of the Society. The formal queries induced, however, formal answers, and it is doubtful if the information was as illuminating as when a freer expression was permitted, as in the earlier days.

The practice of the ministers or "public Friends" meeting together apart from others originated in Philadelphia, in 1685, and soon became general over the Yearly Meeting. At first no regular authorisation of a minister was necessary. Any one who spoke acceptably in the meetings for worship was a minister. But in a little time objectionable speakers would make trouble, and it was decided that all ministers in order to attend these meetings must bring a certificate of acceptability from their Monthly Meetings. These bodies, therefore, became the appointing power.

In 1714, in response to numerous suggestions from Monthly Meetings that a few other Friends be authorised to sit with the ministers, the Yearly Meeting sent down this minute :—

"This meeting agrees that each monthly meeting (where meetings of ministers are or may be held) shall appoint two or more Friends to sit with the ministers in their meetings ; taking care that the Friends chosen for that service be prudent solid Friends and that they do carefully discharge their trust in such matters, and in such manner as the monthly meeting shall from time to time see occasion to appoint them."

This meant *elders*, whose duties at first were scantily defined. In a little time they were expected to assist and encourage acceptable ministers either by spiritual or temporal counsel, and to discourage ill-advised utterances. In time they became a great power, and their repressive influence was sometimes exerted out of proportion to its value.

In 1740 the Yearly Meeting defined its previous minute to include women Friends, and the meeting for ministers and elders, or Select Meeting, became a constituent part of the church machinery, usually assembling just in advance of the Yearly, Quarterly or Monthly Meetings respectively.

The large meetings which we find mentioned in all the journals were drawn together by mixed motives. In many sections there were no other places of worship than the Friends' meeting-houses. The means of travel were limited, being practically reduced to walking and horseback. Where there were other religious services the sentiment against attending them was too strong to be resisted.

The overseers were active in giving official encouragement to regular attendance, and persistent absence was a cause of disownment. The social opportunity was valued by young and old, and the traditions of the earlier generations, reinforced by Yearly Meeting advices and the sermons of many itinerant ministers, created a strong feeling that a meeting was a fixed engagement to which all else must bend. Did a farmer have hay cut in his field to be injured by a storm appearing over the horizon? The hay might suffer, but the mid-week meeting must not be neglected. Did a storekeeper expect a valued customer at meeting hour? The store must be closed, and he and all his clerks must attend the religious service. Nothing but physical disability was a valid excuse for an omission of the prime duty.

It is true that the overworked farmer might sleep through the meeting, or the city clerk interest himself in the contemplation of a young lady across the aisle, but anyhow he must attend. It is even possible that the serious-faced men and women facing the meeting were not so continuously and exclusively engaged in personal worship as their attitudes would seem to indicate to an observant youth. But that many solid and sincere Christians, who above all things permanently desired to do God's will, were produced by this system of home life and communal worship is beyond dispute. And that such honest souls were continuously in control of the tendencies of the Society seems also pretty certain.

John Churchman in 1748 divided the Friends he visited into three classes—those who were glad to hear him and invited him home, though " without much sweetness of truth about their houses," and would tell him he had hit the nail on the head exactly in his sermons ; those who dealt out his exhortations censoriously to others, but did not with any penitence take them to themselves ; and those, " a few in each meeting," who humbly acknowledged their own weakness and the weakness of the church. It was this last class upon whom, as he deemed, the hope of the Society must rest.

There can be no doubt that the peripatetic ministers, both English and American, had a great influence in strengthening and preserving Quakerism among the colonists. They were the most spiritual and often the best educated men and women of the Society. They were listened to, especially those from England, with the greatest respect. Their journals nearly always speak of the great crowds which attended their ministry. George Keith, after his separation, said that it was these " travelling preachers that kept the Quakers so strong in countenance," and in some colonies, in order to stop the increase of Quakerism, the early New England plan of prohibiting their journeying was in the eighteenth century seriously proposed. Besides the numerous American " public Friends," of whom there were nearly always one or more in the field, the following ministers from abroad were engaged in religious visits in Philadelphia Yearly Meeting :—

1684	James Martin	.	.	.	London.
1687	Roger Longworth	.	.	.	Lancashire.
1691	Thomas Wilson ⎰[1] James Dickinson ⎱	.	.	Ireland.
1694	Thomas Musgrove	.	.	.	,,
	Robert Barrow	.	.	.	Westmorland.
	Ralph Wardell	.	.	.	Sunderland.
1695	Jonathan Tyler	.	.	.	Wiltshire.

[1] Brackets indicate that the ministers travelled together the whole or part of the time.

1696	Jacob Fallowfield . . .	Hertford
	Henry Payton ⎱ . . .	London.
	Sarah Clark ⎰	
1698	William Ellis ⎱ . . .	Yorkshire.
	Aaron Atkinson ⎰	
	Thomas Chalkley ⎱ . .	England.
	Thomas Turner ⎰	
	Elizabeth Webb ⎱ . . .	,,
	Mary Rogers ⎰	
	Thomas Story ⎱ . . .	,,
	Roger Gill ⎰	
	Elizabeth Gamble . . .	Barbadoes.
1699	Sarah Clemens . . .	London.
1700	John Salkeld . . .	Westmorland.
	Thomas Thompson ⎱ . .	Essex.
	Josiah Langdale ⎰ . .	Yorkshire.
	John Richardson . .	,,
	John Estaugh . . .	Essex.
1703	Samuel Bownas . . .	Westmorland.
1704	Thomas Turner . . .	Essex.
	Joseph Glaister . . .	Cumberland.
	Mary Banister . . .	London.
	Mary Ellerton . . .	York.
1706	John Fothergill ⎱ . .	Yorkshire.
	William Armistead ⎰	
1707	Patrick Henderson ⎱ . .	North of Ireland.
	Samuel Wilkinson ⎰	
1709	William Baldwin . .	Lancashire.
1713	Thomas Wilson ⎱ . .	Ireland.
	James Dickinson ⎰	
1715	Thomas Thompson ⎱ . .	Essex.
	Josiah Langdale ⎰ . .	Yorkshire.
	Benjamin Holme . .	York.
1717	William Armstrong ⎱ . .	Cumberland.
	James Graham ⎰	
1718	John Danton ⎱ . . .	Swarthmore.
	Isaac Hadwin ⎰	
	Elizabeth Rawlinson ⎱ . .	Lancaster.
	Lydia Lancaster ⎰ . .	Westmorland.
1719	Rebecca Turner ⎱ . .	England.
	Elizabeth Whartnaby ⎰	
1720	John Appleton . . .	Lincolnshire.
1721	Margaret Langdale . .	England.
	Margaret Payne . . .	,,
	John Fothergill ⎱ . .	Yorkshire.
	Laurence King ⎰	
1722	Benjamin Kidd . . .	Banbury.
1725	Abigail Bowles . . .	Ireland.

1726	William Piggott ⎱ Joshua Fielding ⎰ . . .	London.
	Samuel Bownas . . .	England.
1728	Rowland Wilson ⎱ Joseph Taylor ⎰ . . .	,,
1731	Henry Frankland . . .	Yorkshire.
	John Richardson . . .	,,
1732	Mungo Bewley ⎫ Paul Johnson ⎬ . .	Ireland.
	Samuel Stephens ⎭	
	Alice Alderson ⎱ Hannah Dent ⎰ .	Yorkshire.
	Margaret Copeland . .	Westmorland.
1734	John Burton . . .	Yorkshire.
	William Backhouse .	Lancashire.
	Joseph Gill . . .	Ireland.
1736	John Fothergill . .	Yorkshire.
	John Tylee . . .	Bristol.
	Ruth Courtney ⎱ Susanna Hudson ⎰ .	Ireland.
1738	John Hunt . . .	London.
1739	Thomas Gawthrop . .	Westmorland.
1741	Samuel Hopwood . .	Cornwall.
1742	Edmund Peckover . .	Norfolk.
	John Haslam . .	Yorkshire.
1744(?)	Christopher Wilson .	Cumberland.
	Eliezar Sheldon . .	Ireland.
1747	Samuel Nottingham .	England.
1750	Josiah Thompson . . .	,,
	James Thornton . . .	,,
	Mary Weston . . .	,,
1753	Mary Peisley . .	Ireland.
	Catherine Payton . . .	,,
1754	Samuel Fothergill . .	Warrington.
	Joshua Dixon . .	Durham.
1757	William Reckitt . .	Lincolnshire.
	Samuel Spavold . .	Hertfordshire.
	Mary Kirby . . .	Norfolk.
1760	John Storer . . .	Nottingham.
	Jane Crosfield . .	Westmorland.
	George Mason . .	Yorkshire.
	Susannah Hutton . .	England.
1761	Robert Proud . . .	,,
	John Stephenson . . .	,,
	Hannah Harris . . .	,,
	Elizabeth Wilkinson . .	,,
	Alice Hall	,,
1765	John Griffith . . .	Essex.

1765	Abigail Pike .	.	.	. England.
1768	Rachel Wilson	.	.	. Kendal.
1770	Joseph Oxley	.	.	. Norwich.
	Samuel Neale	.	.	. Ireland.
1773	Robert Walker	.	.	. Yorkshire.
	Elizabeth Robinson	.	.	,,
	Mary Leaver	.	.	. Nottingham.

During the ninety-three years which intervened between the founding of the Colony and the Revolutionary War over one hundred Friends from outside America engaged in this travelling ministry.   Many of them would spend years in the country.   The meetings of Friends in and around Philadelphia would therefore frequently be visited. And not the meetings only.   Many of the ministers would visit families, speaking to the conditions of the individual members.   After a little time of silence, with all the assurance of Hebrew prophets they would lay bare internal conditions and address themselves to personal weaknesses.   It seemed to many a member of the quiet assembly that an unerring insight brought their secret thoughts and hidden actions to judgment or gave them the special spiritual message which their souls craved. The frequent recurrence of such public and private opportunities made an indelible impress on many a young Friend.   A young woman writes about 1712 :

"Infinite goodness . . . was pleased to send his servants, both male, and female, filled with life and power who sounded forth the gospel in Divine authority."

This was the spirit in which such messages were received.   The effect of these family visits by home and foreign ministers in the aggregate was very large.   The authority of the word was hardly doubted even when not received, and not a few transformations of life were wrought, where an open heart existed.   Such visits were repeatedly advised by the meetings, and were a very large part of the practice and policy of the Friends.

The attitude of the Friends to other denominations was not marked by any large tolerance.   The Colony beyond all others taught freedom of worship and equal civil rights of all, but the Friends had testimonies to bear which prevented any approach to religious unity. In 1711 they were urged not to go to the " worship houses " of other bodies, or even to listen to their sermons at funerals. This was not so much for fear of doctrinal influence upon themselves as because they wished to bear their testimony against a " paid and stated ministry," a ministry exercised not under the immediate conscious propelling power of the Holy Spirit.

All the needed expenses of the travelling ministers were met with a liberal hand, collections being sometimes taken at the times of meetings for worship, but a distinct line was drawn between payments for necessary expenses and payments for preaching. Many references were made in the journals to silence, because the minister felt that the worshippers were becoming too dependent upon words. " The people seemed full of expectation from one come so far," said the Englishman John Griffith, " but I was shut up." This perfect freedom of ministry was the choicest possession of the early Friends. For this they would not recognise the pre-arranged services of other religious bodies even by attendance. For this they sacrificed all special theological education, and tried to judge a message by its spirit rather than its form. Yet the unbounded hospitality of a new country, the profound reverence felt for those who gave forth the Word of God, insured against suffering all who needed financial aid. If a man could by business operations sustain himself against the day of travel, he felt it a privilege to be free of the help of his friends, and his message derived a greater power and freedom from this knowledge that no thoughts of pleasing the people intruded themselves into it.

Next to the personal influence of the spiritual Friends was the literature of the Society. Books published in England or Philadelphia were subscribed to by the Monthly Meetings, and circulated among the members. Thus endorsed they became almost as authoritative as the Bible, and were read with undoubted confidence. We have from an unfriendly source the effect of the teaching of Barclay's *Apology*. An Episcopal minister writes in 1740 about a man who had brought a wife and nine children to baptism :

"His misfortune was as to this particular that his wife was a Quaker, and her Quaker relations plied him with heretical books especially Robert Barclay's *Apology*, the glory and Alcoran of Friends. 'Tis a pity it escapes so long a clear and full confutation and I beg leave to say that some of our acutest have been worse employed than in taking that hurtful work to pieces. Smith's Preservative was of use to me in gaining the family I spoke of and if that gentleman is alive I hereby tender him my thanks for his endeavours to pull down this stronghold of Satan, Barclay's Works."[1]

In addition to the works of Fox and Barclay, Sewel's *History of Quakers* was thus distributed, also the works of William Dell (who was not a Friend), Moses West's book against mixed marriages, Daniel Pastorius' "Primmer" and others. The meeting agreed in 1705 to have at least one copy of every suitable Friends' book printed in England sent over for inspection.

In 1690 all books approved by the meeting of "Public Friends" were to be taken by the Yearly Meeting to the extent of two hundred copies each and given to the Monthly Meetings. The same meeting opened a subscription to pay for an authorised printer, who was at first William Bradford. His usefulness ended a couple of years later when he imprudently espoused the cause of George Keith. He had, however, a line of successors. In 1703 the management of the press was turned over to the Monthly Meeting of Philadelphia, and Isaac Norris went to England to find a printer, "a Friend if possible." A few years later absolute power was given to any five of a committee of eight appointed by that meeting to issue official documents. Later still the Yearly Meeting resumed its care of publications, acting through the "Overseers of the Press," till 1771, when the matter went to the "Meeting for Sufferings."

[1] Papers relating to the Church in Pennsylvania.

All through these years Friends seemed impressed with the fact that they were making history, and that Pennsylvania was a test of Quaker principles applied to government. They were urged to live worthy of their origin, and not to allow the work to go down in their hands. The Yearly Meeting early began the task of collecting valuable material, and the minutes show through whose hands the collection passed. Cabel Pusey, the zealous and trusted friend of Penn, whose many places in State and Church show the esteem in which he was held, was the custodian till his death in 1725. Following him were David Lloyd, Isaac Norris, James Logan, and John Kinsey, each of whom added something, and probably each of whom had some indefinite intentions of writing the history. After the death of John Kinsey in 1750, Samuel Smith received the papers and compiled a manuscript. This was not published in its original form till 1830 in Hazard's *Register*. Between 1776 and 1780 Robert Proud, the master of Friends' School, compiled a *History of Pennsylvania* which is still the highest authority on all things colonial. He had all the collections of the previous decades as well as Smith's manuscript in his hands and added his personal knowledge. Thus the care of the Yearly Meeting produced its result.

There does not seem to have been any name uniformly adopted by the Society in these early days. It was never called a church, that name being understood as meaning a congregation of vitalized members only. George Fox probably felt that he was preaching a spirit which would draw all men to it ultimately, and for some years did not wish to think that he was forming a distinct organization. Any one who could meet in reverent dependence upon God to worship and receive gifts for work was of his denomination. By the time of the settlement of Pennsylvania this loose aggregation of kindred spirits had been outgrown, and a system was developed which was reproduced in America. But he had not given it a name. The first Monthly Meeting in Philadelphia began its minutes, " The Friends of God . . . being met in the fear and power of the Lord." In future minutes they call themselves " The people of God," " The people of the Lord," " The people called Quakers." The latter was the title most frequently used in documents which were to go outside the ranks. They called each other Friends, but the term Society of Friends seems not to have been adopted as a corporate title during colonial times.

The Monthly Meetings had a source of perennial labour in the matter of marriages. The concern began in the early stages. " Keeping company" with unsuitable persons (non-Friends) was looked into, and parents who did not manage it properly were themselves objects of meeting action. The parties most interested were expected to gain parental consent, and in some cases the approval of the meeting, before they made or accepted final proposals. This being satisfactorily arranged, they stood up in meeting and each one separately announced his or her intention. This was done twice, in some cases thrice, at intervals of a month. Committees of men and women Friends respectively were appointed to inquire into the " clearness from similar engagements" of their member, and the consent of parents was publicly given. After this preliminary the meeting allowed the marriage to proceed, and appointed a committee to see that it was accomplished according to order, and that the entertainment at the house was simple and free from excessive drinking and frivolity.

The parties, flanked by the parents, then stood up in meeting and took each other as man and wife. No priest or minister intervened or dictated the words. No ring symbolised the union. No organ broke the quiet of the occasion. But in the hush and silence of a house full of worshippers they took each other by the hand. In the words of a minute of 1684, John Pemberton did openly declare as follows :

" ' Friends, you are here witness, in the presence of God and this assembly of His people, I take this maid, Margaret Matthews, to be my loving and lawful wife, promising to be a true and faithful husband unto her till death shall us part.' And then and there in the same assembly she, the said Margaret Matthews, did in like manner declare : ' Friends, before God and you His people, I take John Pemberton to be my husband, promising to be a loving and faithful wife until death shall us part.' "

After this open declaration to the world a certificate was produced, which the contracting parties signed, and also many of the spectators as witnesses.

Such contracts, gone into with caution and the advice of Friends, and ofttimes with a sincere desire to know and do God's will, were seldom broken. The need of greater care and publicity was felt because the Quaker form of marriage was specially allowed by English law and must be above suspicion. The form and method, though with slight variation in the words, have always been used in marriages of Friends. It was a binding and religious contract, in which a testimony was borne against the need of any priestly intervention, but in which, in the presence of God with men as witnesses, the man and maiden took their irrevocable vow.

The care of the Meeting extended itself to the bride's house. Simplicity was expected in the entertainment of the guests, and very small details were attended to. Thus in 1773 everything was reported to the Meeting as satisfactory at one of the weddings except that the groom " had assistance in taking off his gloves." In others the hats were not worn in the meeting-house, and many superfluities of apparel were commented on unfavourably.

While the duty of meeting attendance was urgently pressed, it was also recognised that it must be adjusted to other duties to the state and to society. The " Court," an organisation of " Peacemakers " to adjust civil differences by equity, was in early days composed of the same men who guided ecclesiastical affairs, and religious appointments were often changed to avoid conflicts of date. In 1687 the Monthly Meetings which constituted Bucks Quarterly Meeting deferred the meeting because " next Quarterly Meeting and the Philadelphia Fair fall both on the same day." And a few years later a Monthly Meeting in Chester County adjourned because " the greater part of the members of this meeting are called away upon a business relating to government."

William Penn had placed upon Friends the duty of working out the adaptability of Quaker principles to government. In these early days the responsibility was upon them. It was a sacred obligation just as much so as worship. The line between the secular and the religious was not closely drawn, but all duty was compelling, and Friends were used to approach a political problem with the same regard for inward promptings towards righteousness as in their religious meetings. The difference was rather one of the degree of attention to be paid to these promptings. In meeting they would not speak at all without them. In public affairs, if they were absent they did the best they could ; but in all cases Whittier's characterisation is not far wide of the mark :

> "The presence of the wrong or right
> They rather felt than saw."

The Friendly Legislatures of early days began their sessions with a period of devotional silence after their manner of worship, and all activities were carried on in the same spirit.

This identification of varied duties seemed, however, to grow less pronounced as time advanced. Secular interests were made to yield to religious. The demand to drop everything else at the regular time of meeting became more imperious, and the decisions of the church as to a man's outward activities more binding.

The public meetings themselves from a miscellaneous assemblage became better organised. A minute of 1699 contains these explicit directions :

"The meeting having under consideration the indecent sitting and settling of our meetings, doth order, that public Friends do sit in the galleries, and the elder Friends with them, or before the galleries ; and that our women Friends take one side of the house, and the men the other ; and that all sit with their faces towards the galleries ; and that the meeting be kept below, and a fire made above, for such as are weak through sickness, or age, or otherwise, to warm at, and come down again modestly; and keep the meeting soberly, without going out any more than necessity requires." [1]

This arrangement dictated a special style of architecture, and the type is readily recognised down to the present day. The description, except as to the fire, will apply to the internal arrangements of the houses for two centuries following.

The subordination of the Quarterly to the Yearly, of the Monthly to the Quarterly, and of the Preparative to the Monthly Meeting was fully recognised by a minute of 1719, and the machinery was rapidly developed. But the old spirit of personal worship was diligently cherished. In all churchly affairs even relating to ordinary business the same reverent introversive attitude was the standard of the Meeting. " Advised that Friends keep all your meetings in the wisdom of God and unity of His blessed Spirit wherein they were created and settled. . . . Keep all contentions, reflections, and smitings out of your meetings ; and keep down and out all heats and passions and doubtful disputations . . . that they may be managed in the peaceable tender spirit and wisdom of Jesus Christ with decency, forbearance, care and charity towards each other," said they in 1721.

Out of this attitude grew naturally the Friendly method of reaching decisions. When Friends were "gathered inward to the divine principle to know from what spring and motive you act," [2] if this divine principle working in responsive hearts were a reality, it would be a most potent factor in producing unanimity. Hence voting and parliamentary law would be out of place. A quiet religious discussion and much feeling after the truth and the right would bring discordant views into harmony. When this result was reached the clerk, who was supposed to have spiritual discernment as well as clerical skill, would make a minute expressing the decision holding it open till the Meeting decided upon its fairness

[1] Middletown Monthly Meeting.
[2] Yearly Meeting Minutes of 1765.

and validity. It was often a slow proceeding, and probably worked in the interests of conservatism within the body, though, as we have seen in matters of moral reform, Friends were not conservative. But it worked for two centuries, and even now Philadelphia Yearly Meeting has no disposition to change it. Such decisions are not infallible. Prejudice and unreason and narrow conceptions are not so easily expelled. With bitter partisan feeling and selfish ends and unscrupulous methods the system would break down. But the advantage of it was that these ignoble impulses would go to the rear, along with noisy oratory and political appeal. The eloquence which would prevail in a Meeting would be a quiet feeling statement of truths and principles. It is doubtful whether a more wise and just series of decisions extending over so long a time have been reached otherwise.

The decisions of the Meetings with regard to general policy were usually initiated in some progressive Monthly Meeting. This went as a request for advice or direction up through the Quarterly to the Yearly Meeting, which legislated upon it, and sent down the result through the same channel, for definite action. The Monthly Meetings for practical purposes thus became the originating and executive bodies. They came in contact with the individuals, and had power to receive and disown members as well as insist on certain standards of living. These functions were usually performed with great forbearance and caution. There was no effort to induce men and women to join till they were sure that their real church sympathies would be satisfied by the beliefs and customs of the body, and till the Meeting was satisfied that their convincement was genuine. Numbers never counted as such. The disownments, not only for moral weakness, but for disregard of advice as to plain living, to meeting attendance, to the form of marriage, were rigidly administered in all cases where repentance was not forthcoming.

It became customary, in the case of any offender who wished to remain in membership, to require a written acknowledgment of error, and a recognition of the wisdom of the regulations which he had violated. This was read, not only in the Monthly Meeting, but, to make it absolutely public, in the First-day morning meeting, and in early times also before the " Court " (a secular body), after which it was posted on the door of the meeting-house for days. As cases of serious moral delinquency both of men and women were dealt with in this public way, many preferred to take the milder penalty of dis-ownment, which cut them off from church membership, and such losses were counted by the hundreds or thousands. That standards must be maintained, however individuals suffered, was the unflinching rule.

Did two Friends have a difference developing into contention for rights ? They were forbidden to go to law until everything else failed; but the overseers or a special committee of the Monthly Meeting would hear the case and make the award, and the whole power of the Society was behind its acceptance. Was it reported that a man was taking risks in business which would imperil his creditors if everything did not go smoothly? He was warned and almost ordered to protect the innocent before extending his operations. Was a young person evidently attracted by the charms of some non-Friend of the opposite sex ? Both the parents and the possible offender were early advised of the danger and warned to desist. Was a Friendly official in a place which required the administration of an oath or a recognition of some military act ? He was urgently advised to resign rather than compromise the principle. The good name of the Society, the honour of Truth, the bright record of the early days of suffering were appealed to, to preserve at least a remnant true to the purest conceptions of right and duty.

We may have differing opinions as to whether the rigid discipline and final disownment of offenders were wise or not, but we can hardly withhold our approval of the kindly and effective treatment of their own poor, extending into careful scrutiny and intelligent detail.

A man in the country through sickness is reduced to want; the Monthly Meeting gives or lends him a cow. Another is unable to harvest his crops; his neighbours do it for him, or failing this, the Monthly Meeting hires the necessary labour. Another needs clothing; the Monthly Meeting specifies the garments to be procured, and pays the bill. The doctor's charges for another are paid. Another needs a house; the Monthly Meeting orders it to be built and assumes the debt. Another is old and unable to care for himself; the Monthly Meeting finds him a boarding-place and pays the board.

These are all real cases taken from the minutes, and typical of hundreds of others. No Friend in want was allowed to suffer or seek help elsewhere than from the Meeting. The sense of fraternity was very strong.

Nor was the aid confined to their own members. In 1697 a general subscription was taken up for "Friends and others" who were suffering from Indian raids in New England, which was repeated in the early days of the Revolution before the war had migrated to the South. In 1710 there was a general subscription to build a meeting-house in Boston. A century later there was a failure of crops in England and Ireland, and a sum of about £6000 went from Philadelphia to relieve the situation. In 1725 another subscription went to New England to aid Friends carried away·by the Indians. In 1741 a letter of the Governor of South Carolina to the Pennsylvania proprietor was read in the meetings asking aid to recover from a fire at Charleston, which met with a response. During the days of the Indian raids upon the Pennsylvania frontiers following 1755, large subscriptions were made in the meetings for the white sufferers and to buy Indian peace.

A function which had absorbed much of the thought and labour of English Friends had been the collection and tabulation of statistics concerning the suffering of Friends for conscience' sake by fines and imprisonment. From this duty, for a long time, the Pennsylvania Friends were relieved. For freedom of conscience, and especially of the Quaker conscience, was a cherished principle of Penn's province. There were some distraints for tithes in neighbouring provinces where members of Philadelphia Yearly Meeting lived, and these were regularly reported by the Quarterly Meetings. But a "Meeting for Sufferings" seemed to have little place.

When, however, in 1755 the Indian Wars broke out, and there seemed a likelihood of privations for the Friends who lived on the frontiers, the Yearly Meeting directed a subscription of £1000 to be raised to meet the foreseen contingency. To distribute this it was proposed to appoint a committee consisting of twelve Friends of Philadelphia and four of each of the other Quarterly Meetings, appointed by them respectively, who should investigate all cases of suffering and administer relief. This temporary need was the origin of the Philadelphia Meeting for Sufferings, a body of great import in the subsequent history of Friends. Following the example of the English counterpart, it was to have larger powers than its name would indicate. It was

". . . to represent this meeting and appear in all cases where the reputation of Truth and our religious Society are concerned; provided that they do not meddle with matters of faith or discipline not already determined in this meeting; and that at least twelve should concur on all occasions; and that in matters of great importance, notice be given or sent to all members of the Committee."

Subsequent minutes directed them to have their minutes read in the Yearly Meeting; committed to them the proper administration of all legacies and trusts belonging to the Yearly Meeting; still later the work of the Overseers of the Press was also given them. In short they were made the Executive Committee of the Yearly Meeting with large jurisdiction. At first they were appointed from year to year, but in 1768 they were made a permanent body.

This meeting in time, by virtue of the strength of the men composing it, and their long continuance in office, became a most influential body—the inner circle of leaders.

Its ascendency was exerted in all times of stress, and being free from control between the sessions, and having large influence during them, it was able for the succeeding century largely to govern the destinies of the Yearly Meeting, strengthening at all times the tendencies towards conservatism.

CHAPTER IX

THE FRIENDS IN THE REVOLUTION

THE Friends approached the Revolutionary War shorn of some of their political power, but still a strong factor in public affairs. The rift between the ecclesiastical Quakers and the political Quakers which showed itself first about 1755 had been widening since. There were, in Philadelphia especially, a large number of Friends who had adopted the principles of James Logan, that offensive war was never to be considered, but that a war of defence was Christian and therefore justifiable. When that veteran, after nearly fifty years of conspicuous service in the State, proposed this doctrine to the Yearly Meeting, and intimated that any one who did not believe in it was hardly fitted to serve in the Legislature, he seemed to have no following. The one Friend who stood up to support his cause was plucked down by the coat-tail with the remark, " Sit thee down, Robert, thou art single [alone] in the matter." His paper was not even read. But James Logan, while deservedly honoured as a scholar and as a statesman, was never an authority in the affairs of his church. He gave his money to establish lotteries in the public interests. He supported Franklin in his aid to military expeditions. He was a member of the Council and a confidential adviser of Thomas Penn when the alienation of the Delaware Indians was caused by ill-treatment ; and though himself not responsible for this, there was evidently no great sympathy between him and the Friends who later formed the Friendly Association.

But while not influential in the Yearly Meeting, he evidently had a large following among the young Friends of the more prominent families of the city. It was these that constituted the members of the fire company who proposed to buy a great gun for the protection of the city under the name of a fire-engine,[1] who absented themselves when the question of military defence was to be voted on, because, while they approved of it, they did not wish to bring themselves under the censure of their Meetings. It was these also who rushed to arms on the stormy February days of 1764, when the " Paxton Boys" were encamped in Germantown, and who were the objects, in most cases the unsuccessful objects, of the labours of the Monthly Meeting for years to come. It was these who, against the urgent and oft-repeated advice of the Meeting for Sufferings and the Yearly Meeting, maintained the interest in politics that kept, not Quakers, but, as their enemies said, " Quakerized" members of other bodies, in the prominent places in the government, a policy which, while not bringing upon themselves direct censure, was a cause of much concern to the worthy leaders of the Yearly Meeting. It was these also who, after the death of John Kinsey in 1750, ranged themselves under the banner of Isaac Norris 2nd, a Friend of the Logan type, and Benjamin Franklin, and fought at the polls and in the Legislature the battles of freedom against proprietor and crown, yet so conservatively and skilfully that Pennsylvania never drew upon herself the penalties which the greater audacity of Boston had to suffer.

There is no reason to believe that, prior to the Revolution, more than a few of the Friends felt that their political days were for ever ended. The wars of 1756 made it impossible for them to support the policy of the executive. The threat of an enforced oath sent over from England, for ever excluding the Friends of all the colonies from participation in government, they avoided by an agreement to decline places in the Assembly.

[1] Franklin's *Autobiography*.

But they felt that this sacrifice was but temporary, and that the days to come might be a duplicate of those prior to 1750 when they managed the most prosperous, the most peaceful, the most progressive province along the Atlantic coast-line. The people were still with them. More than once the Yearly Meeting had to sound a note of alarm lest Friends should regain their ascendency in the Legislature. James Pemberton of the straitest sect apologised for allowing himself to be elected because by this he could keep a worse man out. The political Quaker was dying hard, and was never beyond the hope of resurrection. When John Adams came down to the first Continental Congress he found the Quaker influence in politics and at the dinner-table almost too strong to be resisted.

The country Friends probably did not draw the lines so clearly. They had complete control over the local offices, and these were not affected by war and oaths. They were not in touch, as were their city brethren, with the greater problems of the day, and were more inclined to accept the traditional unwarlike policy of the early Friends. Hence, when the war actually broke out, we find that among those who definitely espoused the American side in the city were such representative names as Biddle, Marshall, Matlack, Mifflin, Morris, Wetherill, and Wharton, while those dealt with as offenders in the country were often such as had little vital relationship to the Meetings.

The Friends approached the Revolution as a whole with a very meagre education. There was none of the illiteracy of many of the Germans and Scotch Irishmen of the middle and western belts, but there was very little of the possession of the belief in real scholarship. Yet they had a nucleus of it in the isolated self-educated country Friends and the circle of moderate wealth and culture in the city, which read widely and with discrimination the literature of the ancients and of England. Unfortunately for the Society much of this circle, following Logan in his scholarly interests, was also of the group that followed him in their attitude to military defence. Their Quaker impulses kept them true to the cause of liberty. Their knowledge of affairs made them see the strength of the American policy of resistance. Their past leadership and broad training gave them a prominent place in the excitements that preceded the outbreak of war. It was perfectly natural that their mental grasp of problems should have drawn them by insensible degrees not only into participation in, but also into logical leadership of the movement, which, unknown to them for a long time, was carrying the united colonies into the support of Boston and into war and independence.

The attitude of Friends cannot be well understood without a reference to John Dickinson. He was probably not a member, though why he was not it is difficult to explain. His ancestors were Friends for several generations. His wife and children were Friends, and he himself in later life was identified with Friends, used their language and customs, and was so considered by his acquaintances. But he was not married by Friends regulations, and he was for a time a soldier in the Revolutionary army. There seems no record of his disownment, which is explained by some historians by the statement that he was too important a man for such peremptory proceedings, an explanation which any one who knows the temper of the Quakerism of the times will recognise as inadmissible.

There is much in his conservative attitude to point to his Friendly habit of thought. Up to the memorable Fourth of July he was a leader of leaders. His *Farmer's Letters* of 1768 gave the legal and historic basis for American claims. He was better known across the water during these pre-Revolutionary days than any other American. He wrote nearly every important state paper— the appeals to the King and English people, the Declaration of Rights, Articles of Confederation, both the argument to convince and the passionate oratory and poetry to inflame the American mind—up to the date of the Declaration of Independence. Here he halted, and the movement swept by him. He would not sign the

Declaration, not that he did not desire independence, but that he thought the occasion to be premature. He would have preferred longer to try the continuance of protest and appeal to a sense of justice in the English people and the world. He would have waited to take advantage of a change of English ministry, of the hundred ways of solving a problem and securing honourable claims, of a resistance stopping short of arms, instead of the plunge into a war which if unsuccessful would have left America at the mercy of English aggression, and liberty only a name on either side of the Atlantic. Who will now say that if the American statesmen of his day had been all of his mind all that we secured by war could not have been secured by diplomacy and the bitter memories which lasted a century have been avoided? His life was typical of Quaker influence—potent to the very outbreak of war, suddenly and strikingly impotent after it becomes a fact.

The more consistent Friends, who ruled the deliberations of the Meeting, saw the storm coming and began to put up the defences. Many of them had been the leading merchants of Philadelphia, and the Navigation Acts had struck them heavily. For they were not only limited in their trade to English ships and English countries, but the stringent query which every Monthly Meeting had to answer " Are Friends careful not to defraud the King of his dues ? " must be answered in the negative, and so the favourite resort of the multitude, smuggling, was denied them. These merchants joined heartily in all the preliminary measures of resistance. Some fifty of them, including the Pembertons and Whartons, signed the non-importation agreement to defeat the Stamp Act of 1765, and wrote to London Friends explaining and defending their position. This passive resistance suited their principles, but they would not join in the forcible ejectment of the King's officers. In that year James Pemberton was elected to the Assembly on the basis of the temperate measures the Friends proposed, defeating the more radical candidate.

The Stamp Act was repealed. Among the exuberant

expressions of triumph, the bonfires, and burning of effigies by which the repeal was celebrated in Boston and New York, Philadelphia through Quaker influence sent a dignified declaration of appreciation to the King. Franklin lent his aid in these moderate endeavours.

So matters went on till 1773, when the attempt to force tea upon the colonies precipitated the historic act in Boston harbour.

The consignees of the tea in Philadelphia were two Quaker firms, T. & I. Wharton and James & Drinker. A meeting of citizens had decreed that the tea should not be landed. The Whartons were quite willing to join with this movement, and James & Drinker seem to have been forced into it by public sentiment. The results were satisfactory, for the vessel was not allowed to unload any of its cargo, but was sent back, the consignees loaning the captain enough money to see him through.

The next step in the drama was the visit of Paul Revere to secure the sympathy of Philadelphia for the suffering Patriots of Boston. The allies with whom he worked were closely associated with Friends. First of all must be secured John Dickinson, then trusted by everybody. Charles Thomson, not a Friend, but late master of the Friends' School and the faithful clerk of Tedyuscung, was a most efficient aid, as also was Thomas Mifflin, a well-to-do Quaker merchant of Philadelphia, with a distinguished career as General in the army and Governor of the State ahead of him. These three men, representing the more militant Friendly influence of the city carried the day and sent a sympathetic message to Boston, which gave the harassed citizens there great encouragement and opened the way for the first Continental Congress in 1774.

These three men represented not only the more ardent members of the Quaker fold, but at first that larger class who since 1756 had governed the Colony through the Legislature, not Friends but in all but non-resistance perfectly sympathetic with Quaker policy—a conservative, liberty-loving, progressive people who would have gone to any length save independence and war to secure American freedom of trade and taxation and local self-government. Had the movement been left with Thomson, the shrewdest of the three, it is not improbable that he would have brought these moderates into line, and made the course of revolution in Pennsylvania easy and possibly pacific. But the fiery Presbyterians could not be restrained, and much of this non-Quaker conservatism went over to " loyalty," and for a time the issue was doubtful. In the meantime the real Friendly forces were getting into line. War was in the foreground if not actually here. Independence was being uttered, as yet but under the breath. The beneficent charter of Penn of 1701, working for just seventy-five years, was cast incontinently aside, against the advice of Dickinson, Thomson, and Mifflin, and with the aid of Franklin, who had now joined the Radicals, in 1776 a new revolutionary government was effected.

The Friends had a testimony not only against war, but, which is harder to explain logically, against revolution. It probably grew up in this way.

In the troubled days of England in the seventeenth century, there was a continued series of plots and counter plots, some for worthy and some for unworthy purposes. All movements were suspected as covering some traitorous design, and Friends did not escape these suspicions. As a matter of fact they were living in the serene atmosphere of spiritual experiences which forbade all participation in such underhand and questionable designs. Their leaders were continually urging them to keep clear of all com- motions and intrigues of the time, and there grew up in the consciousness of English Quakerism a belief that obedience to the powers that were, whenever that obedience did not trench on conscience, was a fundamental duty of the citizen. This consciousness, doubtless much weakened by the decades of successful government of Pennsylvania, now responded to the new conditions. When the Friends saw the plotting of the leaders tending to weaken the hold of the crown of England upon the colonies, the eager following of a class of people, always their political opponents, who had embroiled them in Indian wars, and

who were associated in their minds with the narrow policy
of early New England, they brought to light again the
advice of George Fox of 1685 :

"Whatever bustlings or troubles or tumults or outrages should
rise in the world keep out of them; but keep in the Lords
power and in the peaceable truth that is over all, in which power
you seek the peace and good of all men, and live in the love
which God has shed abroad in your hearts through Jesus Christ,
in which love nothing is able to separate you from God and
Christ."

They urged their members who were in official position,
positively to oppose measures tending towards revolution,
and finally declared that, quoting an old Friends' document
of 1696 :

"The setting up and putting down Kings and governments
is God's peculiar prerogative, for causes best known to himself."

Hereafter there was a concurrent testimony to be
borne against war and against revolution, which placed
Friends in quiet opposition to the American cause.   Not
only must they keep out of martial operations but they
must keep out of all participation in the new government
set up for the purpose of independence.   They would not
actively oppose it.   Their place was to be in quiet
attendance upon their private and religious duties till the
storm was overpast.   Many of them sympathised with
the American cause.   Many, including the leading
Philadelphians, were in their hearts Loyalists, though
guiltless of overt acts.   All who remained true to their
church allegiance, and they constituted the vast majority
everywhere, were united in a policy of neutrality for
conscience' sake.

In an address to the people of America, dated First
Month 20th, 1776, they strongly define their position,
and reiterate their loyalty to the King of England, but
this was in the early days when even the military associations led by Anthony Wayne vigorously declared that
the idea that they were working for independence could
only originate " among the worst of men for the worst of

purposes." A rapid change of front of many a Patriot took place in the first six months of 1776.

Dr. Fothergill, fully sympathising with the opposition of the Friends to war, and urging them to maintain it firmly and quietly, yet evidently would have them yield to the voice of America and not oppose the general movement. The cause of liberty in England, as in America, was bound up, he said, with its success. It would have saved them much trouble and some indefensible positions had they heeded his advice. For their testimony against the new government made them feel that they must hold no office under it, or pay taxes to it, must not affirm allegiance to it, or even handle its paper money. It is difficult to separate in a time of war the support due to the usual demands and needs of the State from those directly and obviously for war purposes, but had they attempted to make the distinction, as Dr. Fothergill urged, it would have set them right not only with their contemporaries but also with many historians, in whose eyes a Quaker and a Tory were synonymous names. It would have obviated the necessity of meting out the penalties of the discipline to any but those who had trangressed its peace provisions. It is probable that actual disownment was reserved for these only, but others were made to feel that they were out of unity with the body.

There was plenty for the overseers to do in these early days of the war, and there was none of the deliberation and leniency shown in 1764 to the would-be defenders of the Indians. The integrity of Quaker testimony against war was at stake, and gathering up all their reserve of strength, and shutting their hearts against the pleadings of mercy for their brothers and sons who had joined the "associators" or paid war taxes, or placed guns for defence upon their vessels, or paid fines in lieu of military service, or paid fines for refusing to collect military taxes, or in any way aided the war on either side, they cleared the Society of all open complicity with it. The offence was reported to one Monthly Meeting, and at the next the testimony of disownment would go out.

One of the first to go was Thomas Mifflin, and several hundreds of others soon followed. It was in these early days of the Revolution, 1775 and 1776, that the process was most vigorously carried on, and it seemed to halt the tendency to warlike participation. Not half-a-dozen Friends, perhaps, joined the British Army, while those who asserted themselves in an objectionable way in the American cause numbered probably four or five hundred.

This was a small proportion of the 30,000 Friends of the Yearly Meeting, but contained some valuable elements whose loss weakened the prestige of Quakerism for years to come. But it need not be inferred that they were all of this class. As usual the demoralised elements of Society eagerly or weakly would go into the army, and the disownments drove from Friends much that was simply out of touch with all religious or moral principle as well as those whose patriotism asserted itself in divergent views.

The Friends did not officially evade the issue. The new government founded on the ruins of Penn's charter could hardly afford to ignore such a declaration as that of the Meeting for Sufferings of Twelfth Month 20th, 1776:

"Thus we may with Christian firmness withstand and refuse to submit to the arbitrary injunctions and ordinances of men who assume to themselves the power of compelling others, either in person or by assistance, to join in carrying on war, and of prescribing modes of determining concerning our religious principles, by imposing tests not warranted by the precepts of Christ or the laws of the happy constitution under which we and others long enjoyed tranquility and peace."

In 1777 the war came into Pennsylvania. By this time the Friends were generally united as to policy. They would assist neither army. They would allow their goods to be taken by foragers without resistance, and would take no pay for them. Their meeting-houses might be used for barracks or hospitals, and they would at the usual time meet elsewhere. Their pleasant farm-houses and well-filled barns were at the mercy of any needy

trooper. Their vacated city houses could be used for the
sick and wounded, or the winter quarters of soldiery.
They would in the meantime quietly attend to their
business or religious duties so far as circumstances would
permit :

"On the 29th day of the 9th month, 1777," says a minute
of Philadelphia Monthly Meeting, "being the day in course for
holding our monthly meeting a number of Friends met when the
present situation of things being considered, and it appearing
that the King's army are near entering the city, at which time
it may be proper the inhabitants should generally be at their
habitations, in order to preserve as much as possible peace and
good order on this solemn occasion, it is therefore proposed to
adjourn the monthly meeting."

Thus was the British army welcomed by Friends to
Philadelphia. "The people," an old account says,
"appeared sad and serious." If there were any tendency
at the start to look upon these soldiers of the King as
liberators, their actions through that melancholy winter
disabused Friends' minds of it. Not only was their fair
city, the best built and best kept in America, made
a prey to the dirt and devastation of a rude soldiery, but
the revels, and gambling, and lax morality of the officers,
in which many of the well-to-do citizens joined, made it
difficult to maintain their old standards among their
young men. That war was an evil was indelibly
impressed upon them.

But they suffered also from the other side. As the
army of Sir William Howe approached the city from the
Chesapeake, the Continental Congress advised the Council
of the State of Pennsylvania to arrest and seize the
papers of such citizens of Philadelphia as were notoriously
British in their sympathies. It was specified that "a
number of persons of considerable wealth who profess themselves to belong to the Society of people called Quakers
. . . are with much rancour and bitterness disaffected
to the American cause" and should be seized, and their
private papers and minutes of their meetings searched for
evidences of their having furnished valuable information

to the British. The Council thus advised arbitrarily made the arrest of about forty people, many of whom were Friends. They were offered their liberty if they would give their word that they would not leave their houses. This the Friends and a few others refused, and about twenty of them were placed in confinement. They protested against the arrest as an outrage and would make no promises. The list included the Pembertons, the Fishers, Thomas Wharton, Henry Drinker, and others, all prominent in the Meeting. They were sent to Winchester, Virginia, and kept in nominal confinement through the winter. Two of them, John Hunt and Thomas Gilpin, died during their stay, and Israel Pemberton shortly after their return. Nothing in the way of communication with the British was ever proved against them; nor, as we well know now, was there anything except exhortations to faithfulness and explanations of the conduct of Friends found in the minutes of their meetings, which were soon returned to them. Nothing was gained for the American cause by the banishment, except possibly the quieting of some Tories, and this is doubtful. That these Friends desired the success of the British is probable; that they so far stultified their constant advice to keep out of the contest completely, as to give information of either army to the other, is at this distance incredible. Meetings everywhere rallied around the exiles, and the incident undoubtedly drew Friends together. They were finally returned home, with something of an apology and a recognition of their good motives.[1]

The retreat of the British army in the spring of 1778 gave the city again into the hands of the Americans. The condition of Friends was not much improved, for a mob of extreme Revolutionists obtained control, who would have vengeance on all Tory sympathisers. The real Tories were out of their reach in New York, but they hanged Roberts and Carlisle, both Friends, on the

[1] Thomas Gilpin, descendant of one of the sufferers, has written a careful account of the whole affair under the title *Exiles in Virginia*.

charge of treason, on very slight ground. Moderate men like Robert Morris and James Wilson, and even such an ardent supporter of the American cause as Thomas Mifflin, were besieged in their houses and hardly escaped. The windows of Friends' houses were broken with stones and they hooted in the streets. They would neither weep nor rejoice at the command of the State, and even when the crowning victory of Yorktown was announced, " the occasion of a victory of one of the parties of war over the other," as they characterised it in their effort for stern neutrality, they refused to illuminate their houses, and passed a night of danger and damage.

Whatever other effects were produced upon their minds there is no doubt that they appreciated that a time of warfare is an unpleasant time for non-combatants. It was a favourite preamble to their resolutions in the days when they controlled the Assembly :

"While we do not as the world is now circumstanced condemn the use of arms in others, we are principled against bearing arms ourselves."

That is, do as you please, only do not ask us to help you —do not allow any conscience to be strained. They would probably hardly subscribe to this doctrine now, for they would recognise that a neutral could not be let alone, however much he might desire it. They had, doubtless, come to the same conclusion as General Sherman regarding war, and for the same reason, because they had seen it ; though their characterisation was not so trenchant and effective.

The aggregate of Quaker suffering was very great. The Meetings kept actual records and detailed estimates of the losses by fines and distraints and foraging parties. These losses continued for some time after the war was over, probably till about 1787. In general they would not pay the fines, for this would recognise a government based on war and revolution. Distraint would follow, always a costly expedient. Possibly the total direct loss of property to members would not fall short of £50,000.

Personal unpopularity was even harder to stand, and cases of imprisonment were not rare. Six Friends were kept in Lancaster jail for months, because they would not take a test of allegiance to the new government, and when they might have been released they refused to pay the jailer's fees, on the logical ground that they did not choose the imprisonment for themselves, and should not pay for it. School teachers were required to take the test. There were then a number of Friends' schools and teachers. Some closed the schools, and some took the consequences. As is always the case with this class they had no money, and so jailing was the only satisfaction the State got. Friends were elected to offices, as tax collectors, which it was known that they would not fill, then fined for non-compliance. Friends were advised by the Meetings not to furnish supplies, grind grain, or make weapons for the army for money, or allow their goods to be transported in armed vessels.

Moses Roberts and his friends of Catawissa, then a frontier town, who had always been safe among the Indians, were arrested on the way to meeting, sent to Lancaster jail in a canoe, and kept there for months without trial. Their families were driven from their homes without any means of support, and their property seized. Other frontier Friends suffered greatly on the charge that they gave information to hostile Indians.

The Meeting for Sufferings did not cease to protest against these persecutions. The change from the day when they ruled the Quaker Commonwealth by the suffrages of all kinds of citizens to the time when, without change of principle, they were hooted and persecuted, was a bitter change indeed ; and with whatever influence they had left they pleaded their rights to the liberty of conscience which they had always granted to others. As they were a religious, not a political, body, they urged that they could not have any corporate political opinions, and were simply governed by the moral law as they understood it. They asked the government to accept their obedience to all laws which they could obey as a substitute for military aid to either party. They emphasised the thought that they sought to encourage such a temper that they could forgive all injuries, and be friends to all men. But such appeals count for little in a time of war.

The Friends who were disowned generally took the action quietly. Some had lost all interest in Friends, and cared but little for membership. Some were thankful for the opportunity to pose as martyrs when they might have been brought up for moral obliquities or non-attendance at any religious exercises. A few, like Owen Biddle, one of the strongest men of the Yearly Meeting, repented and were reinstated. Besides these, however, there were those whose attachment to the general principles was sincere. The passage from one denomination to another was not so easy as now. They did not care to be unchurched, and they wanted the simple unclerical worship of Friends. But they were sure that their war record was right, and that Friends made a mistake when they did not follow James Logan into the position of military resistance to aggression. These formed a society, the Free Quakers. The discipline was simple. No one was to be disowned. All were to be encouraged in the performance of their civil and military duties. The meetings for worship and business and the habits of living were to be according to the old Quaker customs.

They immediately entered into a controversy with the main body for the use of the graveyards and other property of the Society, and carried the case to the Legislature. They got plenty of sympathy, but their disownments were so regular, and the risks of interfering with the internal affairs of a religious body so great, that they could obtain no legislative relief. They then raised money and built the house now standing at Arch and 5th Street. Washington and Franklin subscribed. The numbers, never large, gradually dwindled, though worship was maintained in the house till 1836, Betsy Ross, the flag maker, being about the last of the original members.

We must now take up some of the effects of the

Revolutionary War upon the main body of Friends who stood by their principles. They entered the war something of a divided body. They came out of it united by the separation of the alien elements and the harmony induced by suffering. There was no longer a minority supporting war. If there was a minority supporting active participation in politics farther than voting and holding local offices, it was very quiet. Penn and Thomas Lloyd, Logan and David Lloyd, Isaac Norris and John Kinsey had no counterparts. The work of Friends by common consent was to be philanthropic only, so far as it touched the outside world, but mainly it was to be given to strengthen the body in its own principles and testimonies, following the teachings of the Holy Spirit. Their ideals of saintliness were expressed by Isaac Penington and John Woolman.

Through these trying war days it was engaged in clearing its own skirts. The disasters which were falling upon it were judged to be due to its own unfaithfulness, and, like Israel of old, it was being urged by its trusted leaders to give up strange gods, and return to its ancient worship in its purity.

In 1777 the Yearly Meeting resolved upon what it called "a reformation." The organisation was set to work in all its ramifications. The Quarterly Meeting appointed Committees, and these, reinforced by local Friends, visited Meetings and families, pressing the reforms.

As an illustration of the way the advice of the Yearly Meeting worked itself out we will follow its course in Chester Quarterly Meeting, perhaps the largest and most influential of the country Meetings. At the first session after the Yearly Meeting the following minutes were adopted :

"The Extracts from the Minutes of our last Yearly Meeting were read over. And that meeting, having had under their weighty consideration the sorrowful complaints of deficiencies in the religious care and Education of the Youth, both with respect to their Pious Education in Friends' families, and also their Schooling, and under the calming influence and Seasoning virtue of Truth, Unanimously Agreed to recommend this weighty subject to the deep attention and speedy care of Quarterly Meetings. That they may appoint suitable Friends in each of them as Committees to visit the Monthly, Preparative, and Particular Meetings or Families of Friends as Truth may point out the way for reformation with respect to the due and wakeful attendance of our religious Meetings, plainness of Speech, Behaviour, Apparrel, and Household furniture, with other deficiencies, mentioned in the Answers to the Queries, which were the cause of deep Concern and Exercise; and in order to strengthen the hands of Friends in the Quarterly Meetings Appointed a Committee of fourteen Friends to take the matter relating to the Youth and their religious Education and Schooling particularly under their care, and give such advice and assistance therein and respecting other deficiencies as they in the wisdom of Truth may see expedient. Divers of which Committee from other Quarters attended here to our satisfaction, and the subject-matter coming solidly under ye Consideration of this Meeting, and some awful remarks made touching the necessity of a real and speedy reformation in ye Church now in this alarming season, Thomas Massey, Caleb Seal, Nathan Yarnal, Jr., Joseph Talbot, Jr., John Perry, Robert Valentine, William Fell, and John Humphries are appointed to the said service, and are Particularly enjoyned by this Meeting to be careful to excite Friends (in the Schooling of their Children) to put them under the care of Virtuous Tutors.

"The care of Friends respecting Grave Stones is desired to be continued untill they are all removed.

"As the Reports from the Monthly Meetings are mostly silent respecting slaves this meeting is desirous that there may still be a fervent concern among Friends to labour with such members who retain any of our fellowmen in Bondage Agreeable to the repeated Advice of the Yearly Meeting, and render an account to our next Meeting."

"Sundry of the Weighty Advices contained in the Extracts being again read, and solidly considered and spoken to, particularly those respecting the Distiling and Use of Spirituous Liquors, and the polluting practice of keeping of Taverns, Beer-Houses, etc., this Meeting, desirous that the good End intended may be answered, appoints Thomas Metier, John Eyre, Robert Johnson, Isaac Massey, Thomas Swayne, Isaac Sharples, and William Lightfoot to labour for a reformation among Friends in this Quarter in those Respects as they may be directed in best Wisdom agreeable to the Advice of the Yearly Meeting, and Report their care and the

Circumstance of Friends in regard to those things to a future meeting."

We have here certain subjects of " reformation " which were to be attended to.   They ultimately arranged themselves under these heads :

1. Plainness in personal habits, including the abolition of gravestones.
2. Schools and literature of definitely Friendly sort.
3. Definite advances in the matter of Temperance and the sale of Intoxicants.
4. The extinction of slavery among themselves.
5. The erection of barriers against alien influences being introduced into the Society.

1. They made a serious attempt to return to primitive simplicity in their dress, habits, and furniture.   The committee of Chester Quarterly Meeting went vigorously to work.   They first visited their own houses and the houses of the overseers of the several Meetings, insisting on the abolition of matters simply ornamental, or unnecessarily complex, and striving to stir the officials of the Meetings to a sense of the importance of their example and religious labour for their fellow members. It was a difficult service, yet they reported that on the whole their visits were well received and effective.   Meetings were held in which Friends were exhorted to return to " primitive zeal and purity," or as elsewhere expressed to " primitive zeal, plainness, and circumspect walking amongst the professors of Truth."   The committee continued its work through about four years, and then relegated it to committees appointed in the several Monthly Meetings.   How much of the services related to outward matters, and how much to the weightier matters of spiritual growth, does not appear in the minutes.   It is expressed in one minute as—

". . . a revival of ancient simplicity in plainness of apparel, household furniture, the education of youth, and a due and wakeful attendance of our religious meetings."

It was deemed a favourable time under the impulse

gained by common suffering to recover lost ground in both these respects. As one meeting expresses it:

" Under the prevailing trials and difficulties we have a prospect that some are so loosened from outward things as to promote a more steady care to keep to true moderation and temperance."[1]

2. They revived and developed the idea of schools where the elements of education could be obtained under religious influences. While one committee was working for a circumspect and zealous life among the members, another was equally interested in promoting a guarded religious school education. A committee of the Yearly Meeting under date of 28th of 3rd month 1778 sent down a stirring piece of advice to all subordinate meetings which afforded a groundwork of labour. They state that " corruption " exists among Friends as the result of their children mixing in schools with children of a different sort. They recall the efforts of the earlier Friends, both in England and America, to extend Christian care to the schools, and now " while reformation is loudly called for," they ask that godly and consistent teachers shall be employed. The letter was signed by Anthony Benezet, Isaac Zane, Nicholas Waln, Warner Mifflin, and George Churchman. The committee visited all the Meetings in the interest of this concern. It is difficult to judge from its reports how successful it was, for they usually state in a general way that the work was progressing in certain quarters. This may mean that some new schools were established, or that a more careful selection of teachers was made. The object, of course, was to influence the youth towards Friendly customs and a Friendly spirit, and so train them for later service in the church.

We have a more definite contribution to the educational conditions of these revolutionary times in the minutes of the Northern District Monthly Meeting of Philadelphia of 7th month, 1779.

That Meeting had appointed a committee to inquire

[1] Northern District Monthly Meeting, Philadelphia, 7th mo. 1779.

into the cause of "the evident degeneracy and corruption in the manner of deportment of many of the youth among us." They conferred with the "Overseers of the Public Schools." There had been an experiment made, they say, in mixing the children of Friends with others in these schools which had produced an unfavourable result.

Attempts would now be made to separate them. The "Overseers" expressed a desire to co-operate with the Monthly Meetings so far as the purposes and history of the schools would permit. They state that the central school was started in 1689 at the cost of the Monthly Meeting. As the result of the increase in value of the property owned by the trustees, and the donations since made by Friends, they had been able to school the children of poor Friends, and some not Friends, freely. They desired to employ masters who would enforce the stringent rules made for them, but these do not always meet with co-operation at the homes. They admit the seriousness of the situation, and ask that Friends should bestir themselves. The committee propounded to the Overseers a series of questions as to what steps the Monthly Meetings should take to remedy the evils, whether the Friends' children may be separated from others, how far parents will go in the restraint of children from running in the streets with unsuitable companions, and whether parents are not evidently lacking in such care, whether poor Friends have ample facilities, whether any new regulations should be added, what number of schools are in existence, and what is the financial condition of the trust.

The Overseers in their answers place the blame for the unfavourable situation mainly upon parents who do not guard their children's morals on the street, and the lack of a pious education when not under the care of the schools. They give a list of nine schools under their care. One of these is primarily for the Latin and Greek languages taught to boys of various denominations. Two are exclusively for Friends' boys. Two schools, one under Anthony Benezet, are for girls, some of whom are to be admitted free. Three are mixed schools both as to denomination and sex, for primary children. The numbers in all of them are not given, but so far as can be judged they average about fifty. Up to the war the funds had permitted them to admit many poor Friends and others into the schools, but now, owing doubtless to the depreciation resulting from the troublous times, there was little money available for charity, indeed they were in debt to some of the teachers.

This narration throws much light on the question of education among the Friends of Philadelphia. The original school of William Penn now had these nine branches presumably educating some four hundred children. They were supplying education at cost to the most of these children, and the income of money invested enabled them to grant it freely to some others. Presumably the children of Friends had first claims, and others were aided with the superfluity. Except among the little children there was no co-education. One school, probably for those in better circumstances, was a classical school, but there was "occasionally taught writing and arithmetic and some branches of mathematics." In the other schools there were taught reading, writing, and arithmetic, and apparently these branches only. It was the era when children were to be made good by the observance of many restrictions laid down for them by wise committees, before student responsibility for government was much recognised. The Overseers disclaim the suggestion that the badness of certain youth was the fault of the schools, and place it, probably justly, on the parents who were not careful to discourage street associations, and for this they had no remedy except advice.

Under other management schools for negro children were established about 1773, but how extensive this movement was during the war it is difficult to determine.

3. They abolished tavern-keeping and the sale of spirituous liquors by their members, and made a determined attempt to limit their use. Coincidently with

the others a third committee was working in Chester Quarterly Meeting on this subject. It reported some deficiency and then the matter was referred to the Monthly Meetings :

"At the Meeting in the Eleventh month was also appointed a committee to labour for a Reformation in Respect to ye Distiling and Use of Spirituous Liquors amongst Friends and the Polluting Practice of keeping Taverns, Beerhouses, etc. Agreeable to the advice of the Yearly Meeting. Which Committee now reported That they attended to the services " And visited friends in their Particular Meetings and taken other opportunity's with some Friends who keep Publick houses of entertainment and such as keep Stills, etc., and find that there are some Friends in each Meeting who are concerned to have the advice of the Yearly Meeting put in Practice, a number of Friends having Used Spirituous Liquors very Sparingly in ye time of our late Harvest and others have with great satisfaction used none at all. Yet think the care of monthly meetings should be continued in these Respects as there are among Friends who are not sensible enough of the necessity of discouraging a Practice that has tended much to Corrupt the inhabitants of this Land. Which Rep^t was read and approved, and the monthly meetings desired to have these matters closely under care accordingly and Report their Several Circumstances and how far Friends do keep to the advice of the Yearly Meeting therein to next meeting."

It was reported in 5 mo. 1779 that "very few Friends are now concerned in keeping taverns in our Quarter," and again "we observe a growing care among Friends to avoid the unnecessary use of spirituous liquors." Three months later

". . . very satisfactory progress has been made in each meeting in dissuading Friends from keeping houses of public entertainment, beer houses, etc., insomuch that very few are now concerned therein."

In 8 mo. 1780 they say :

"There are one or two Friends who continue in the practice of keeping taverns within the verge of this quarter."

A year later

". . . it does not appear that any Friends are concerned in

keeping public houses except some women whose husbands do not belong to Friends,"

and this list the next year was reduced to one woman.

4. They finished up the process of freeing their slaves. When the war ended none were left except in cases where husband or wife was not a member, and where complete manumission could not be secured—or where they were held in trust tied down by old deeds or wills. The long struggle, beginning when Pastorius and his friends of Germantown memorialized their meeting in 1688, was won about a century later. Before the close of the war the Friends had also the satisfaction of seeing a manumission measure passed ⸀by the state of Pennsylvania, the first in the country, though as one of the opposite party expressed it :

"Our bill astonishes and pleases the Quakers. They looked for no such benevolent issue of our new government exercised by Presbyterians."

The Friends were doubtless pleased. Their previous work had cut the ground from under the institution, and though the triumph had come, under the exigencies of the times, when they were out of government, the moral advance was no less gratifying to them.

Henceforward their attention was to be turned to the development of the freed negroes by education and employment, and the advance of the cause of abolition in the country at large.

5. They drew the line more closely about their own membership in opposing participation with others in any religious work, even to the extent of attendance on other religious services, on the ground that their testimony against preaching for pay and without conscious inspiration, could not be maintained in its integrity. In the country districts especially they had been much by themselves out of touch with other denominations. Political lines were drawn on the basis of church affiliation, and an element of suspicion was thus introduced. Their testimonies therefore reinforced their traditional and political

opposition to mingling with others, and in school and society and church services they constituted themselves a body apart from others, a tendency which the war greatly strengthened.

These "reformations" were decreed and carried out in the midst of the war. The heated air of strife was around them. Matters were going any way but theirs in the State and in moral standards. They simply drew together as the world turned against them, more certain of their ground, more determined to maintain it at any cost of suffering and unpopularity. If all around had conspired, as it seemed, to annul Penn's Holy Experiment they would renew it, not externally, that appeared hopeless, but in the hearts of a devoted band. Let others do as they would, they would serve the Lord according to the preaching and example of George Fox and the other heroes of the seventeenth century.

Nor were they without encouragement. A great revival of religious interest followed the labours of the Committees. Many young men, prominent afterwards, consecrated themselves to the work. A real zeal and spiritual enthusiasm followed the indifference of the days just before the war. New and acceptable preachers sprang up. The Query then standing " What remarkable convincements since last report ? " was nearly always answered, " A number of solid Friends have joined the Society." The years to come were to show the greatest growth of numbers of any score since the settlement, so that by the end of the century there were probably 40,000 Friends in the Yearly Meeting.

The Revolutionary War left Philadelphia Yearly Meeting more moral internally, more devoted to moral reforms, more conservative of ancient tradition, custom, and doctrine, more separate from the world, more introversive in spirit, than it found it. In fact the Quakerism of the youth of some of us, in important particulars had its origin here, and would have been greatly different had the Society not gone through this ordeal. Had the active public-spirited Friends, who went off with the revolutionary movement, remained to mould their generation, a type more outward, more progressive, more intellectual would have resulted. Had the Society drifted along as it was drifting prior to the conflict a moral stringency, since characteristic of Quakerism, could hardly have been maintained. As a result of the narrowing and uniting processes combined Friends are what they are. What they would have been with a wider outlook upon life and a looser standard of conduct, we can only conjecture. But he who understands Philadelphia Quakerism of a century past must read it in the light of the Revolution—a revolution not less in Quaker development than in American history.

INDEX

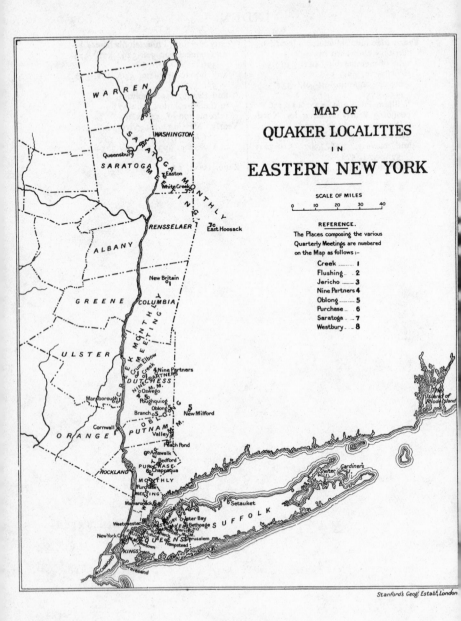

MAP OF
QUAKER LOCALITIES
IN
EASTERN NEW YORK

SCALE OF MILES

0   10   20   30   40

REFERENCE.
The Places composing the various
Quarterly Meetings are numbered
on the Map as follows:—

Creek 1
Flushing ... 2
Jaricho 3
Nine Partners 4
Oblong 5
Purchase .. 6
Saratoga ... 7
Westbury .. 8

Stanford's Geogᵗ Estabᵗ London

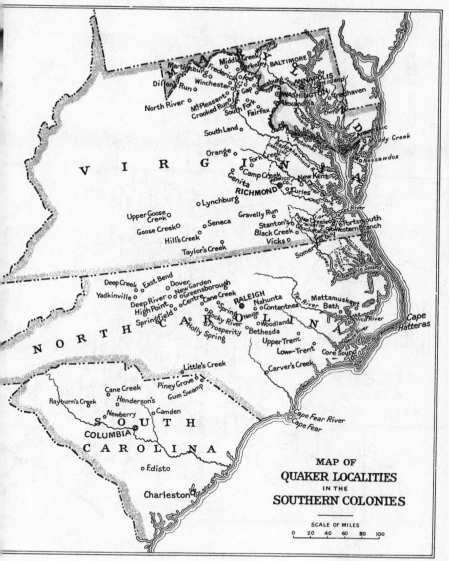

MAP OF
QUAKER LOCALITIES
IN THE
SOUTHERN COLONIES

SCALE OF MILES

0   20   40   60   80   100

Stanford's Geog.! Estab.! London

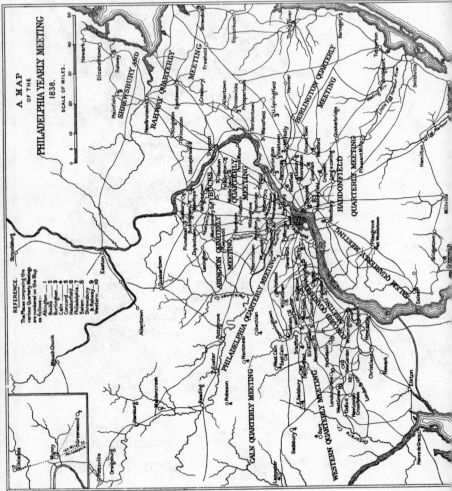